NEGRO EMPLOYMENT IN SOUTHERN INDUSTRY

A Study of Racial Policies in Five Industries

INDUSTRIAL RESEARCH UNIT
WHARTON SCHOOL OF FINANCE AND COMMERCE
UNIVERSITY OF PENNSYLVANIA

Founded in 1921 as a separate Wharton Department, the Industrial Research Unit has a long record of publication and research in the labor market, productivity, union relations, and business report fields. Major Industrial Research Unit studies are published as research projects are completed. Advanced research reports are issued as appropriate in a general or special series.

Recent Industrial Research Unit Studies

(Available from the University of Pennsylvania Press or the
Industrial Research Unit)

No. 40 Gladys L. Palmer, et al., *The Reluctant Job Changer.*   1962. $7.50

No. 41 George M. Parks, *The Economics of Carpeting and Resilient Flooring: An Evaluation and Comparison.*   1966. $5.00

No. 42 Michael H. Moskow, *Teachers and Unions: The Applicability of Bargaining to Public Education.*   1966. $8.50

No. 43 F. Marion Fletcher, *Market Restraints in the Retail Drug Industry.*   1967. $10.00

No. 44 Herbert R. Northrup and Gordon R. Storholm, *Restrictive Labor Practices in the Supermarket Industry.*   1967. $7.50

No. 45 William N. Chernish, *Coalition Bargaining: A Study of Union Tactics and Public Policy.*   1969. $7.95

No. 46 Herbert R. Northrup, Richard L. Rowan, et al., *Negro Employment in Basic Industry: A Study of Racial Policies in Six Industries.* (Studies of Negro Employment, Vol. I.)   1970. $15.00

No. 47 Armand J. Thieblot, Jr., and Linda P. Fletcher, *Negro Employment in Finance: A Study of Racial Policies in Banking and Insurance.* (Studies of Negro Employment, Vol. II.)   1970. $9.50

No. 48 Bernard E. Anderson, *Negro Employment in Public Utilities: A Study of Racial Policies in the Electric Power, Gas, and Telephone Industries.* (Studies of Negro Employment, Vol. III.)   1970. $8.50

No. 49 Herbert R. Northrup, Richard L. Rowan, et al., *Negro Employment in Southern Industry: A Study of Racial Policies in Five Industries.* (Studies of Negro Employment, Vol. IV.)   1970. $13.50

Nos. 1-39 Order from Kraus Reprint Co., 16 East 46th St.,
New York, N.Y. 10017.

NEGRO EMPLOYMENT IN SOUTHERN INDUSTRY

A Study of Racial Policies in Five Industries

(Volume IV—Studies of Negro Employment)

by

HERBERT R. NORTHRUP

*Professor of Industry and Director,
Industrial Research Unit*

RICHARD L. ROWAN

*Associate Professor of Industry and
Associate Director, Industrial Research Unit*

DAROLD T. BARNUM *and* JOHN C. HOWARD

Research Associates

INDUSTRIAL RESEARCH UNIT
Wharton School of Finance and Commerce
University of Pennsylvania

Foreword

In September 1966, the Ford Foundation began a series of major grants to the Industrial Research Unit of the Wharton School of Finance and Commerce to fund a series of studies of the Racial Policies of American Industry. The purpose has been to determine why some industries are more hospitable to the employment of Negroes than are others and why some companies within the same industry have vastly different racial employment policies.

Studies have proceeded on an industry-by-industry basis under the direction of the undersigned. As of October 1970, some eighteen industry studies have been published with twelve more in press or being readied for publication.

This volume is the fourth in our series of books combining industry studies and analyzing the reasons for different racial policies and Negro employment patterns among various industries. The present volume includes studies previously published as Report No. 8 (paper), Report No. 13 (tobacco), Report No. 14 (coal mining), Report No. 19 (lumber), and Report No. 20 (textiles), plus a final section analyzing and contrasting the Negro employment situation in these five as well as in other southern industries.

Volume I, *Negro Employment in Basic Industry*, published early in 1970, contains an introductory section which sets forth the purpose and hypotheses of the overall project and a brief overview of the position of the Negro in American industry. Volume II, *Negro Employment in Finance*, on the banking and insurance industries, and Volume III, *Negro Employment in Public Utilities*, have recently been published. Volumes on land and air transportation and on retail trade are scheduled for 1971 publication; those dealing with maritime industries, selected manufacturing industries, and building construction are in the planning stage. These nine volumes and the various industry reports should contain the most thorough analysis of Negro employment available in the United States.

Negro Employment in Southern Industry is the work of several persons. In addition to the foreword, the undersigned jointly wrote the concluding analysis in Part Six. Part One, on the paper

v

industry, is by Professor Herbert R. Northrup. The paper industry has become a major employer in the South, particularly in areas where large numbers of Negroes reside. Professor Northrup examines the current racial policies of paper mills and converting plants after describing the structure of the industry and the extent of Negro employment prior to 1960. He explains how the racial-occupational employment pattern in southern mills kept Negroes out of the better paying mill jobs until massive government intervention altered the status quo in the mid-1960's. The record of gradual improvement in employment opportunities for blacks is discussed against a background of discrimination and highly institutionalized progression systems that once denied Negroes access to skilled jobs. Professor Northrup points out that the converting plants use largely unskilled labor and racial employment patterns therein are strongly determined by the labor market population mix.

Part Two (lumber) is by Mr. John C. Howard. The lumber industry is the largest industrial employer of Negroes in the South. Even though the industry is not growing rapidly and is unlikely to furnish additional employment to Negroes in the future, it is an important one to study since it portrays the factors which influence the industrial acceptance of Negro labor. Low wages, lack of entrance requirements, and low skill and education level requirements for employment make the lumber industry ideally suited for utilization of a disadvantaged minority group. Mr. Howard analyzes the gradual changes that are taking place in the industry as Negroes, who have always been employed in large numbers, are beginning to move into skilled jobs.

Part Three (tobacco) is also by Professor Northrup. The tobacco industry, employing Negroes since colonial times, has the longest continuous record of factory employment of Negroes in the United States and is today concentrated in the three southern states of Kentucky, North Carolina, and Virginia. An analysis of the racial policies of the tobacco industry affords an opportunity to analyze the impact, over a long period of time, of such factors as southern location, introduction of new products and technologies, mechanization and automation, union attitudes and policies, and government restraints. Professor Northrup shows that, given declining sales and continuing automation, the racial-occupational segregation pattern of the industry was breached too late to open many job opportunities to Negroes.

Part Four (coal mining) is by Mr. Darold T. Barnum. The bituminous coal mining industry was a major employer of Negroes in the past, particularly in four southern states and one border state—Alabama, Kentucky, Tennessee, Virginia, and West Virginia. Since World War II, however, as employment declined rapidly in the industry, Negro employment decreased even more precipitously, accelerating a trend that became apparent in the 1930's. Mr. Barnum analyzes Negro employment in the Southern Appalachian region and explains why "if the present trends continue, the black man will vanish from the coal mines during the next three decades."

Part Five (textiles) is by Professor Richard L. Rowan. In the mid-1920's, the South emerged as the major textile producing region of the country. Today, almost one million people are employed in the textile industry with the majority located in southern states. Negroes were excluded from the industry, almost as a matter of policy, from 1880 until 1960. The 1960 decade, however, witnessed a virtual revolution in employment in southern textile plants, with blacks being used in nearly every aspect of manufacturing. Professor Rowan attempts to facilitate an understanding of the past practices of employers in dealing with the question of black labor and the present process of accommodation where equal employment policies are being designed.

Mr. Barnum is currently a Ph.D. candidate at the University of Pennsylvania and Mr. Howard, a former M.B.A. student who also did statistical work on the paper study in addition to his own project, is now in industry. Several able graduate students participated in the studies. Mr. Robert I. Ash, who assisted Professor Northrup with Part Three, and Mr. Robert C. Gulledge, who assisted Professor Rowan with the statistical work for Part Five, deserve special mention. Both of these young men are now working in private industry.

Major editorial and research assistance was provided by Mrs. Marjorie C. Denison, Mrs. Marie Keeney, and Miss Elsa Klemp. These are the unsung heroines without whom no book is prepared for publication. Mrs. Margaret E. Doyle, our administrative assistant and office manager, handled the administrative details in her usual efficient manner. The manuscripts were typed by Mrs. Rose Elkin, Mrs. Veronica Kent, Miss Mary McCutcheon, and Mrs. Marie Spence.

Many others have contributed to this volume. The fine cooperation of numerous industry and government personnel made it possible to obtain material and data not otherwise available. Their request for anonymity precludes our recording individually the great debt which we obviously owe. Dr. John R. Coleman, President of Haverford College, made the initial grants possible as a staff member of the Ford Foundation, and later Mitchell Sviridoff, Vice-President, and Basil T. Whiting, Project Officer, assured continued Foundation support and interest. Numerous students added their help, questions, or discussions to improve our own understanding.

As in most previous reports, the data cited as "in the author's possession," have been carefully authenticated and are on file in our Industrial Research Unit library.

HERBERT R. NORTHRUP, *Director*
RICHARD L. ROWAN, *Associate Director*
Industrial Research Unit
Wharton School of Finance and Commerce
University of Pennsylvania

Philadelphia

December 1970

CONTENTS

PART ONE

PART ONE

THE NEGRO
IN THE PAPER INDUSTRY

by

HERBERT R. NORTHRUP

TABLE OF CONTENTS

LIST OF TABLES

LIST OF FIGURES

CHAPTER I

Introduction

To paraphrase the one-time slogan of a nonpapermaking company, in America "paper is our most important product." The continued and all-pervasive use of paper in the personal, educational, and business lives of Americans is the basis for this giant industry's great growth and prosperity. Today nearly 700,000 persons are employed in the making of pulp and paper and in converting the basic paper products to various packaging or other consumer uses.

Of special significance for a study in the Racial Policies of American Industry series is the fact that the South, where a majority of Negroes still dwell, is now the most important area for the basic production of pulp and paper while paper converting plants tend to be concentrated in industrial areas, including the major cities which are the centers of the growing urban Negro population. Plant location is, however, only one aspect of the determinants of the paper industry's racial policies. Initial company hiring and promotion procedures have been institutionalized by union contracts, altered by labor market, civil rights, and government pressures, by the changing requirements of ever more automated and otherwise improved equipment, and by market development needs.

This study will examine the industry's current racial policies after describing the structure of the industry and the extent of Negro participation as an employee prior to 1960. The basic data utilized were collected between 1967 and 1969, and supplemented by visits to sixteen pulp and paper mills in the South, Middle West, and East, in addition to numerous converting operations of all types throughout the country.

CHAPTER II

The Pulp and Paper Industry

The art of papermaking originated in China about 100 A.D. and was brought to America in 1690 by William Rittenhouse, who learned the art in Germany and built a mill near Philadelphia.[1] The modern mass production of paper dates from the nineteenth century, with first, "the invention of machinery for making an endless sheet of paper at a high rate of speed; and second, the discovery of methods for converting wood into paper pulp."[2]

Today most paper is made on machines utilizing a moving screen belt (called Fourdrinier) on which wet paper stock is passed through squeeze rolls and driers. Wood is converted to pulp by various chemical or mechanical processes or combinations thereof. The process from tree growth to paper has become more and more mechanized, and the industry one of tremendous capital investment.

Once the paper is made it is "converted" into a variety of products for home, office, educational, business, printing, packaging, or other uses. Plants which perform such work are known as "converting" plants; those which make the pulp and paper are basic production units, or more commonly "mills." Both mills and converters are in turn divided into various types depending upon the product which is being manufactured. Likewise the product determines the type of raw material used—that is, the character or species of wood, wastepaper, chemicals, etc.

THE PRODUCTION PROCESSES

Since paper is made almost entirely from wood, the raw material is procured in forests. Large companies own and harvest wood from their land, from leased lands, or from independent owners and contractors. The wood is cut usually into four foot lengths and trucked or shipped to the mills by rail. Water transportation or running is still occasionally used in the North, but rarely in the South, except

---

1. Kenneth W. Britt (ed.), *Handbook of Pulp and Paper Technology* (New York: Reinhold Publishing Corporation, 1964), pp. 1-2.
2. *Ibid.*, p. 4.

for some barging. The woods operations, once the forte of the lumber-jack, are now heavily mechanized. Bulldozers, cranes, huge machine log cutters and trimmers, and large and specialized trucks and rail cars have supplemented the chain saw and greatly increased the need for trained and carefully competent but fewer personnel. In addition, woods operations are now usually managed by highly trained profes-sional forestry school graduates, whose function is to maximize re-turns and reforest for future pulp sources.

The original paper mills were built by lumber operators anxious to use smaller and inferior trees that were unfit for consumption as wood. Their woods operations were crude and depended on essentially unskilled labor—Negroes in the South. Modern technology in forest operations continues to require less labor and more skill. This pattern, of course, is typical of industry generally; and has in the past resulted in heavy displacement of Negroes.

The cut wood, as noted, is generally brought by truck or train to the mill site, which usually occupies a large tract, where it is segregated by type or purpose and stored in enormous piles. Prior to 1950, unloading and moving wood involved much hand labor, done in the South by Negroes, but now cranes and other mechanized equipment do most of the job. In addition, some mills utilize much of this wood in chip form, purchasing chips from lumber mills, and/or cutting logs into chips at various way stations prior to mill delivery, or in the mill yard after delivery. Chip handling is entirely done by heavy machines and blowers.

At the mill, the logs are debarked in huge drums after being automatically conveyed there by chutes or flumes, either directly from the truck or rail cars, or from the pile. The logs are then cut and chipped. Chips so cut, or previously cut or purchased, are then screened to eliminate foreign matter and too large pieces before being sent to a high pressure cooking operation where they are mixed with chemicals, washed, and thus made into pulp. (This description thus far does no justice to conveying the vast size of the equipment, its automatic character, speed, and complexity, and the area required to handle the bulk product—nor will that which follows.)[3]

The pulping process varies according to the type of wood used and product desired. Essentially, however, it is a form of cooking, in

3. See *ibid.* for detailed descriptions of all phases of papermaking. To understand it, however, visits to various mills are essential.

which huge evaporators and digesters are utilized in order to bring the lime, chemicals, liquors, and chips into a proper relationship. The pulp is washed again at the end of the process and the liquors sent to recovery units to be reprocessed for use again.

Pulp mill work, especially in warm climates, was once most unpleasant with the intense heat of the cooking operation added to the unpleasant chemical odors. In recent years, the working conditions have improved materially. Not only have the pulp mills been greatly enlarged, but instrumentation has replaced valve and control adjusting. Instead of cooking by batches and requiring numerous operators (cooks), assistants, and helpers, modern mills now use a continuous digester—a huge apparatus, six to ten stories high, which is run by a complex instrument panel, closed television circuits, and two or three operators per shift. Unskilled labor has been virtually eliminated from the modern pulp mill—a factor as we shall point out in the declining ratio of Negroes in the industry between 1950 and 1960.

If the mill is producing bleached paper, that, or other special treatments, are performed prior to the basic papermaking stage, together with any other necessary pulp stock preparation. The pulp then flows to the paper machine, where it is made into paper by squeezing out the water between huge, continuous rollers over a Fourdrinier screen. Again the enormous size of some of the machines is difficult to describe. They run three to five stories high, several city blocks long, and produce several hundred tons of paper per day in rolls up to 381 inches long and 10 feet high—with paper machines capable of larger production in the offing. A huge paper machine is operated by no more than seven or occasionally eight men per shift. A new and unique system found in the recently constructed mill of St. Regis Paper Company in Monticello, Mississippi, has the chief paper machine crew man, known as the "machine tender," in an enclosed air-conditioned balcony instead of on the floor by the machine. In this case, the machine tender handles his job by tending a 25-foot long instrument panel and watching several closed television circuit pictures of the machine in operation.

Most machine tenders operate on the floor. Their job is usually the highest paid and most prestigious of the hourly employees, and is achieved only after starting at the bottom—utility or No. 7 operator—and working up the ladder over a long period, or changing mills in order to accelerate the process. Until the current civil rights pressures, it is probable that no Negroes were found in the paper machine line of progression North or South except in very small mills using waste-paper as their basic raw material.

After the paper is made, it is rewound and cut to various stock sizes for shipment or warehousing. A relatively large number of lesser skilled jobs are found in this work, and Negroes have not been excluded from them. Mechanical substitutes for hand cutting, tying, packaging, marking, and intraplant material movement are continuing to reduce the need for such labor.

Additional auxiliary operations are found in most large mills. Requiring tremendous power and located often in isolated spots, mills frequently generate their own power. Mill power plants burn bark and used chemical liquors, as well as coal, natural gas, or oil. The power plants are now largely automatic, and the coal shovelers, firemen, or laborers, often Negroes in the past, have been largely eliminated.

The recovery operation is devoted to reprocessing chemical liquors for further use in the pulping process. It is a typical chemical plant-like operation, with few employees, often closely allied with, or operated from, the power plant. Lime kilns, water preparation, and water purification are also significant operations. Pulp mills must have a large water supply. The water must be purified to meet the chemical standards required by the type of paper product made. The rising need for pollution control has necessitated that paper companies spend millions to control their effluent before it is dumped back into rivers. Similarly, the unrestricted releasing of fumes into the air is more and more subject to control. In general, however, water and air pollution controls require expensive equipment and a few technical and professional employees, but do not add significantly to plant personnel.

The complicated and expensive equipment of paper mills necessitates large maintenance forces composed of a great variety of crafts. In addition, the major companies maintain sizable research laboratories, and at the mill sites, quality control and testing facilities. In these crafts, technical and professional jobs, Negroes were historically not recruited. Only recently has there been some change in this policy.

Converting Operations

Converting operations are found in smaller, simpler, and less machine-dominated plants than are the mill operations, although expensive machinery is certainly an integral requirement of converting. Converted products, for example, often have extensive printing or lithography, the capacity for which requires costly presses and other such equipment.

Corrugated shipping containers, made from paper and paperboard, are the largest product. The corrugating material is laminated between sheets of paperboard on large corrugating machines, and then cut and shaped on other machines. There remains much material handling in such plants, with heavy laboring work common. Such plants are found in all industrial areas, and Negroes have been a significant part of their labor force since, and even prior to, World War II.

Multiwall bags used for such items as cement, fertilizer, and chemicals, also are made on machines and must be moved in bundles. The work is, however, lighter, and once featured much sewn work and female labor. Pasted operations have now replaced much of the sewn operations, and reduced the personnel needs, but printing requirements have become more complicated and extensive. Grocery bags and sacks of various types also involve lighter work than corrugating operations. Perhaps for the reason that bag plants have historically employed many women, they have had fewer Negroes than corrugating plants.

Folding boxes and cartons are often made from wastepaper. Such plants, unlike basic mills using wood pulp, are located in urban centers where wastepaper can be easily accumulated.

Fine papers and bleached papers require much material handling and packaging. Female labor is often used in such operations, with Negroes utilized historically sparingly.

There are many other uses for which paper is converted—newsprint, books and magazines, tissues, fibre cans, building materials, etc. Each subunit of the industry has its unique technology and different labor force requirements.

INDUSTRIAL CHARACTERISTICS

Table 1 shows employment, payrolls, capital expenditures, and other industrial data for the paper and allied products industry, and the important subdivisions thereof, for 1967 by the federal government's standard industrial classification (SIC) system of data collection. The divisions in the three-digit breakdown are somewhat

TABLE 1. *Paper and Allied Products Industry*
Employment, Payroll, Capital Expenditures, and other Data
by Standard Industrial Classification, 1967

	Total (SIC 26)	Pulp Mills (SIC 261)	Paper Mills Except Building Paper Mills (SIC 262)	Paperboard Mills (SIC 263)	Converted Paper and Paperboard Products Except Containers and Boxes (SIC 264)	Paperboard Containers and Boxes (SIC 265)	Building Paper and Building Board Mills (SIC 266)
			Thousands of Employees				
All Employees	643	15	138	64	190	224	12
			Millions of Dollars				
Payroll	4,440	129	1,102	513	1,197	1,416	83
Value added by manufacture	9,676	370	2,316	1,438	2,814	2,554	184
Cost of materials	11,298	408	2,504	1,371	3,397	3,458	160
Value of shipments	20,927	770	4,815	2,807	6,176	6,013	346
Capital expenditures, new	1,426	106	507	405	170	218	20

Source: U. S. Bureau of the Census, *1967 Census of Manufactures*, Series MC 67(P)-1, Summary Series, Preliminary Report, April 1969.

arbitrary. Many mills manufacture both paper and paperboard, and most pulp mills are integrated divisions of pulp and paper complexes. Nevertheless, the data in Table 1 do provide a picture of some of the economic variables of the industry, and the differences between basic mill economics and those of converting operations.

The data in Table 1 show that employment was larger in the converting operations than in the mills, but capital expenditures in the latter far exceeded those in the former. As a matter of fact, it can cost well over $100 million to build an integrated pulp and paper mill, but only a small fraction thereof to set up a converting unit. Moreover, the mill requires forest lands to insure it a supply of raw materials. The result is a tremendous investment in buildings, equipment, and timber reserves, relatively low capital turnover rates, and a consequent high ratio of fixed costs to total costs.

It follows from these economic facts that pulp and paper mills must emphasize maximum utilization of equipment. They thus operate seven days per week, twenty-four hours per day with four shifts, usually rotating. Interruptions of work are extremely expensive in view of their high fixed cost ratio to total costs. Moreover, start-up and stopping costs are in themselves expensive. The entire process is geared to continuous production much like a chemical plant or petroleum refinery. Thus mill management is always anxious to avoid labor strife and to work out accommodations to prevent such strife. The threat of strikes over civil rights issues, for example, has been viewed most seriously by the industry in recent years, and undoubtedly contributed both to its reluctance to change basic hiring and employment policies, and to legal and industrial relations maneuvering to insure government support and approval when change could not be avoided.

In the converting plants, investment is considerably less and round-the-clock operations not prevalent. Two shifts, five days per week is usual practice, although a third shift is run in many corrugating plants. Emphasis in converting operations is more attuned to meeting customer requirements than to maintaining a continuous flow of production. The labor force in converting plants is thus likely to be increased or decreased as sales and production dictate; in the mills there is relatively little turnover given the stable production function, and as we shall point out, high wages.

Industrial Structure

Modern paper companies arrived at their present status from a variety of beginnings. Some began as lumber concerns and entered into paper production in order to utilize their forest holdings more efficiently. Others were original bag, carton, or container manufacturers and entered the paper business as paper replaced textile, wood, tin, or glass as the basic raw material for their product.

Within the paper industry, some gravitated from converted product to basic paper producer in order to insure a supply of their basic raw material; others, originally mill owners, acquired or built converting units in order to gain permanent customers for their basic product. It is not unusual for two companies to join in building a mill to supply each with paper. Mead and Inland Container, for example, jointly own Georgia Kraft, which operates basic mills in Macon and Rome, Georgia, and near Phoenix City, Alabama. The parent companies use all of Georgia Kraft's production. There are many other similar arrangements.

Table 2 sets forth statistics for the twenty-three largest forest products companies in 1968. Some—Weyerhaeuser, Georgia-Pacific, and Boise-Cascade—are more lumber concerns than paper ones. Absent from the list are several companies which are extremely significant in the industry. Thus Continental Can Company, 50 percent of whose business is accounted for by metal cans, is the nation's second largest producer of paperboard, the manager or owner of more than 1.4 million acres of woodlands, and a leading manufacturer of many converted paper products.[4] American Can Company, Olin Mathieson Chemical Company, and Owens-Illinois are among the other major corporations with large paper manufacturing and converting divisions.

Within the paper industry, the largest, by far, is International Paper Company, in 1968, the fifty-fourth largest American industrial corporation. With eleven major mills in the South, and large holdings in the North, Canada, and the Far West, International Paper is a dominant influence, accounting for about 10 percent of the industry's production and sales, and land holdings which make it the largest landowner in the United States except for the federal government

---

4. *New York Times,* January 19, 1969.

TABLE 2. *The Twenty-Three Largest Forest Products Companies, 1968*

Company and 1968 Rank among Industrial Corporations	Headquarters	Sales	Assets	Net Income	Invested Capital	Number of Employees	Net Income as Percent of	
		Thousands of Dollars					Sales	Invested Capital
International Paper (54)	New York	1,561,777	1,713,588	99,870	1,082,458	53,657	6.4	9.2
U.S. Plywood-Champion Papers (70)	New York	1,283,444	1,123,123	54,678	545,301	38,686	4.3	10.0
Weyerhaeuser (98)	Tacoma, Wash.	1,032,753	1,064,661	105,022	713,855	37,620	10.2	14.7
Boise-Cascade (100)	Boise, Idaho	1,026,457	1,027,793	45,390	360,876	29,930	4.4	12.6
Georgia-Pacific (101)	Portland, Ore.	1,023,930	1,268,890	76,620	555,890	35,300	7.5	13.8
Mead (108)	Dayton, Ohio	897,591	719,929	31,572	418,802	23,208	3.5	7.5
Crown Zellerbach (112)	San Francisco	868,351	937,542	65,312	542,983	27,124	7.5	12.0
St. Regis (127)	New York	786,180	891,976	34,022	486,609	31,000	4.3	7.0
Kimberly-Clark (136)	Neenah, Wis.	720,449	787,530	40,240	467,401	26,586	5.6	8.6
Scott Paper (146)	Philadelphia	677,408	750,682	53,267	494,125	20,000	7.9	10.8
Diamond International (210)	New York	466,815	327,634	32,417	229,058	18,196	6.9	14.2
Container Corporation of America[a] (186 in 1967)	Chicago	463,135	397,358	33,971	241,105	19,290	7.3	14.1

West Virginia Pulp and Paper	(239)	New York	391,617	419,410	20,725	247,967	15,370	5.3	8.4
Union Camp	(240)	New York	383,360	479,690	26,408	242,478	14,175	6.9	10.9
Potlatch Forests	(280)	San Francisco	318,115	318,555	16,400	185,017	12,198	5.2	8.9
Bemis	(292)	Minneapolis	300,009	186,069	8,808	103,013	12,987	2.9	8.6
Hammermill Paper	(318)	Erie, Pa.	262,192	202,707	8,615	102,236	8,365	3.3	8.4
Brown	(394)	New York	197,526	186,693	(23,436)b	61,702	9,500	—	—
Fibreboard	(432)	San Francisco	171,077	151,568	7,318	35,041	5,600	4.3	20.9
Inland Container	(434)	Indianapolis	170,179	134,717	9,818	106,186	4,500	5.8	9.2
Hoerner-Waldorfc	(451)	St. Paul, Minn.	160,432	206,444	10,376	88,939	5,595	6.5	11.7
Great Northern Paper	(466)	New York	154,557	265,385	14,976	129,429	3,957	9.7	11.6
Riegel Paper	(485)	New York	149,908	143,306	4,247	91,276	5,521	2.8	4.7

Source: *Fortune*, Vol. LXXIX (May 15, 1969), pp. 168-184.

a Merged with Montgomery Ward & Co. in 1968, data are for year 1967.

b Loss

c Acquired Albemarle Paper Company from Ethyl Corp., 1968.

itself.[5] Other large operations in the South include nearly all the twenty-three concerns listed in Table 2, plus the paper divisions of the major diversified concerns not on the list.

The industry's heavy ratio of assets and invested capital is again emphasized in Table 2. The relatively small number of employees in relation to this aggregation of capital even with converting operations included, as of course they are in Table 2, emphasize the capital intensive nature of the industry.

Many smaller companies are found in the industry, particularly in converting. It is the largest companies, however, which determine the labor and civil rights policies of the industry, and therefore it is their policies upon which this study will focus.

Industrial Growth

The paper industry has grown with the economy since its inception in America. Table 3 shows the trend in production for paper and paperboard, and the various subdivisions thereof since 1920. For the industry as a whole, and for all major segments, growth has continually trended upward.

Of course, for individual companies, the growth has not always been smooth. New mills have been built in times of prosperity and contributed to production gluts during recessions. The results have been serious price declines and overproduction until demand caught up to supply. The 1957-1961 period saw the industry in such a situation, but still usually less affected than many more volatile industries.

Overproduction relative to demand has, however, generally caused only moderate mill employment cutbacks because the cost of shutting down a huge facility is too great. Companies do curtail production, but only as a last resort. In the late 1950's, for example, the larger mills purchased or built many converting plants in order to find markets for their products. There were in this period a significant number of mergers as independent producers found it difficult to generate the funds necessary to maintain equipment and forests in order to keep competitive.

The pressures on costs generated by the competition in the industry directly affected Negro employment. As we shall detail in the following

---

5. Eleanore Carruth, "International Paper Sees the Forest through the Trees," *Fortune*, Vol. LXXIX (March 1969), pp. 105-106.

TABLE 3. *Paper and Allied Products Industry*
Paper and Paperboard Production
United States, 1920-1968

Production (Thousands of short tons)

Year	Total	Paper				Paperboard				
		Total	Printing[a]	Coarse[b]	Other[c]	Total	Container board[d]	Box board[e]	Other[f]	Construction Paper and Board
1920	7,185	4,497	2,581	1,044	872	2,313	n.a.	n.a.	n.a.	375
1925	9,002	5,133	2,915	1,292	926	3,236	1,777	n.a.	n.a.	633
1930	10,169	5,722	2,930	1,580	1,212	3,855	1,915	1,666	274	592
1935	10,479	5,415	2,498	1,632	1,285	4,544	2,358	1,744	441	521
1940	14,484	7,422	3,262	2,501	1,659	6,200	3,435	2,315	450	862
1945	17,371	7,574	2,863	2,403	2,308	8,008	4,131	2,991	886	1,789
1950	24,375	10,639	4,318	3,297	3,023	11,090	5,830	4,007	1,252	2,646
1955	30,178	12,905	5,397	3,687	3,821	14,045	7,551	4,983	1,511	3,228
1960	34,444	15,399	6,704	3,957	4,738	15,851	8,637	5,173	2,042	3,194
1965	44,080	19,187	8,155	4,614	6,419	20,978	12,331	6,035	2,612	3,915
1966	47,199	20,675	8,924	4,731	7,020	22,716	13,661	6,367	2,689	3,808
1967	45,994	20,341	8,651	4,753	6,937	21,975	13,120	6,190	2,665	3,678
1968	49,478	22,156	9,531	4,992	7,633	22,821	n.a.	n.a.	n.a.	4,501

Source: American Paper Institute: *The Statistics of Paper, 1968 Supplement* (New York: The Institute, 1968), pp. 24-41 and *Monthly Statistical Summary*, June 1969.

[a] Newsprint and other printing paper including book and groundwood.
[b] Coarse paper for sacks, bags, wrapping, Kraft, and grease-proof paper.
[c] Tissue, fine papers, etc.
[d] Container board includes linerboard and corrugating medium.
[e] Boxboard includes folding boxboard, set-up boxboard, and foodboard.
[f] Wet machine board, etc.
Note: Years may not add to total due to rounding.

chapter, the laboring jobs were the easiest to mechanize. Because Negroes were concentrated in such jobs, they were disproportionately affected. Especially new mills employed a much smaller proportion of blacks than did older ones as the "Negro jobs" became mechanized.

Employment in converting plants fluctuates more directly with product demand. New uses of paper have brought many new such plants into existence. But the significance of corrugating and other packaging paper in product movement inevitably makes such products highly cyclical—they rise and fall with industrial demand. As in the case of mill employment, however, since industry growth has ever trended upward, employment, as set forth in a later section, has increased despite increased substitution of machines for men.

Customer Orientation

The paper industry, by and large, does not sell products for direct consumer use. The tissue sector of the industry is an exception. Scott's products are sold under the company's name, as are those of some smaller concerns like Hudson's. But although Kimberly-Clark's "Kleenex" has become a generic term for the paper handkerchief, few consumers probably know the manufacturer's name.

Most paper products reach the consumer as packages, wrappings, or as materials used in a final product, rather than a consumer product in itself. Like the steel industry, the paper industry is oriented toward sales to other industries rather than to the consumer. As we shall note throughout this study, this lack of consumer orientation has made much of the industry somewhat remote to social problems and caused it considerable difficulty when faced for the first time with outside pressure in regard to civil rights.

In recent years, the expanding federal government has become a major paper industry customer, not only for writing, duplicating, and other "fine" papers, but also for containers and boxes. This has made the industry very susceptible to government pressure in civil rights matters, and as will also be discussed below, has been a major factor in opening up opportunities for Negroes.

Industrial Location

The South is today by far the leading producer of pulp, paper, and paperboard, accounting in 1966 for nearly one-half the total production in the industry, and three times the total of the middlewestern or far western states. (Table 4) The South's leadership in paper production dates from the refinements of the sulphate process for making kraft paper which occurred in the late 1920's and early 1930's, and the availability, adaptability, and low cost of southern pine as the basic raw material for this process. Improvement in methods of bleaching kraft paper further aided the South in the 1930's. Today its mills not only produce 80 percent of all kraft paper and board, but also newsprint, fine papers, tissues, and other products, using not only pine but other species of wood as well.[6]

TABLE 4. *Wood Pulp, Paper, and Paperboard Production By Region, 1966*

REGION	Wood Pulp Production	Paper and Paperboard Production[a]
	(Thousands of short tons)	
United States	36,640	47,189
South	22,376	20,708
New England	2,250	4,236
Middle Atlantic	1,159	5,586
North Central (Middle West)	3,517	9,921
West (Far West)	7,339[b]	6,739

Source: American Paper Institute, *The Statistics of Paper, 1968 Supplement* (New York: The Institute, 1968), p. 9.

[a] Includes construction paper and paperboard.

[b] Alaska and Hawaii included here, omitted in all other tables.

New England: Connecticut, Maine, Massachusetts, New Hampshire, Rhode Island, Vermont.

Middle Atlantic: New Jersey, New York, Pennsylvania.

North Central: (Middle West) Illinois, Indiana, Iowa, Kansas, Michigan, Minnesota, Missouri, Nebraska, North Dakota, Ohio, South Dakota, Wisconsin.

West: (Far West)[b] Alaska, Arizona, California, Colorado, Hawaii, Idaho, Montana, Nevada, New Mexico, Oregon, Utah, Washington, Wyoming.

South: Alabama, Arkansas, Delaware, Florida, Georgia, Kentucky, Louisiana, Maryland, Mississippi, North Carolina, Oklahoma, South Carolina, Tennessee, Texas, Virginia, West Virginia.

6. See Britt, *op. cit.,* Chapter 7. Paper mills located in the South prior to 1930 were established primarily by lumber mills to utilize stumpage and other waste products. For the story of one of the first mills to be built *qua* paper mill and to produce kraft paper, see Alonzo Thomas Dill, *Chesapeake Pioneer Papermaker* (Charlottesville: University of Virginia Press, 1968).

Other areas produce many paper products, but also specialize. Canada remains the major producer of newsprint, with such American companies as International Paper and Crown Zellerbach having large holdings there. New England's mills produce newsprint, book paper, and fine and specialty papers; those in the Middle West are heavily oriented toward paperboard, and those in the Far West to products made from sulphite pulp and to supplying the general paper needs of the area. Each area's wood supply and species determine to a large extent the character of paper produced.

Except for wastepaper mills, most pulp and paper operations are located in relatively isolated spots. A few older ones are found in industrial centers, but most of those import pulp, an expensive, high cost method of operation, and make only paper at the plant location. Besides needing tremendous acreage and a steady source of water, pulp mills emit noxious odors which ill befit them for urban locations.

Pulp and paper mills located in northern and western regions are generally found in areas in which few Negroes dwell—Maine, Wisconsin, Minnesota, northern California, Oregon, and Washington. Until the industry developed in the South, a Negro in a paper mill town was a rarity except in a few locations, such as Chester, Pennsylvania; or except in plants using rags or wastepaper as their key raw material.

The perfecting of the sulphate kraft process and the rise of the industry in the South changed this. Not only did the South become the first region in the industry, but the industry, by its very nature and needs, located in the nonplantation rural South where in the 1930's a large portion of the Negro population dwelled, and where race relations since Civil War reconstruction days were the harshest and most rigid.[7] The industry, as we shall note, employed a sizable force of Negroes, but rigidly segregated them in accordance with local customs.

Originally, many large companies established major converting operations at mills in order to keep handling and transportation costs at a minimum. Now the trend is definitely the other way, with mill-site converting operations being reduced. The disparity between mill and converting wages and the desire not to have the latter raised by

---

7. For a scholarly study of how segregation patterns evolved after the Civil War, see Vernon Lane Wharton, *The Negro in Mississippi, 1865-1890*, Harper Torchbook edition (New York: Harper & Row, 1965).

the former, the threat of labor difficulties in one operation spreading to another, and probably most significant, the need to locate near the customer to give service, have mostly overcome the initial advantages of mill-site location. Converting plants, particularly corrugated box operations, now often serve only one industrial area, with large companies having small plants in many locations. The dispersal of converting operations has probably aided Negro employment. It has meant reduced operations within the historically segregated and discriminatory practice areas of the southern mills and a greater number of jobs in northern and midwestern cities where such practices have not been as common or as rigid. As we shall point out later in this chapter, jobs in the converting portions of the business in general do not require the skills nor receive the remuneration of those in the mills.

The employment impact of the varying industrial location of mills and converting plants is illustrated by Table 5. Although the South is the leading pulp and paper producing region, it ranks second in total employment to the Middle West which is dotted with converting plants, in addition to the important mill producing areas of its northern tier. The Middle Atlantic states closely follow the South in total employment, again because converting plants are located to serve customers and are therefore concentrated in industrial areas. For the same reasons, paper employment in New England exceeds that in Far West states despite the much greater significance of the latter as a paper producing area.

MANPOWER

Employment in the paper industry has risen steadily during the last thirty years as the data in Table 6 show. The expansion of production, new uses for paper, and the substitution of paper for other products have overcome such negative factors as the replacement of men by machines and the competition of other products, particularly new plastics. In 1968, an average of almost 700,000 persons were employed in the paper and allied products industry as defined in the government standard industrial classification system.

In perspective, of course, the paper industry ranks substantially below aerospace and automobiles, and approximately equal to basic steel as an employer. If steel fabricating plants were included with

TABLE 5. *Paper and Allied Products Industry
Employment by Region, 1966*

Region	All Employees		Production Workers	
	Number	Percent	Number	Percent
United States	632,316	100.0	503,912	100.0
South	161,879	25.6	130,960	26.0
New England	70,786	11.2	55,896	11.1
Middle Atlantic	136,125	21.5	108,030	21.4
North Central (Middle West)	198,687	31.4	156,628	31.1
West (Far West)	64,839	10.3	52,398	10.4

Source: U. S. Bureau of the Census, *Annual Survey of Manufactures, 1966,*
No. 7.1-7.9.
Note: For definition of regions, see Table 4 p. 15; U. S. total by addition.

basic steel—which would be an appropriate comparison in view of
our inclusion of the paper converting plants—paper's employment
would be equal to about one-half of what is known as the primary
metals group.

Nevertheless, the paper industry does employ a significant number
of persons in all areas of the United States; it is a growing industry;
and it affords considerable opportunities to Negroes seeking jobs,
thus making it a key industry for study in our series.

Occupational Distribution

Table 6 shows that production workers still predominate in the
paper industry. It is overwhelmingly blue collar, not white collar,
in sharp contrast to such industries as aerospace, where salaried
workers approximate the number of hourly workers. Rather the
paper industry's production worker ratio is quite similar to that of
the automobile and rubber tire industries—in each about three-
quarters of the work force being production workers[8] despite some
increase in the percentage of nonproduction employees in recent years.
In terms of Negro employment, this does mean that the disadvantaged
status of Negroes, in so far as educational attainments are concerned,
is not as significant as in a highly technical industry like aerospace.

8. See studies of these various industries in the Racial Policies of American Industry series for a comparison of employment data and occupational characteristics.

TABLE 6. *Paper and Allied Products Industry*
Total and Production Worker Employment, 1939-1968

Year	All Employees	Production Workers	Percent Production Workers
	(in Thousands)		
1939	320	266	83.1
1940	333	278	83.5
1941	372	318	85.5
1942	376	326	86.7
1943	389	346	88.9
1944	388	345	88.9
1945	391	345	88.2
1946	447	393	87.9
1947	465	406	87.3
1948	473	408	86.3
1949	455	390	85.7
1950	485	416	85.8
1951	511	435	85.1
1952	504	422	83.7
1953	530	443	83.6
1954	531	441	83.1
1955	550	454	82.5
1956	568	464	81.7
1957	571	463	81.1
1958	564	454	80.5
1959	587	472	80.4
1960	601	480	79.9
1961	601	478	79.5
1962	614	486	79.2
1963	618	486	78.6
1964	626	489	78.1
1965	639	498	77.9
1966	667	518	77.7
1967	681	528	77.5
1968	698	541	77.5

Source: U. S. Bureau of Labor Statistics, *Employment and Earnings Statistics for the United States, 1909-1968* (Washington: Government Printing Office, 1968), pp. 598-600; and *Employment and Earnings,* March 1969, Table B-2.

On the other hand, our study of the rubber tire industry emphasized that, even though production workers still dominate the manpower needs of an industry, standards may be set in high wage industries that work to the disadvantage of Negroes but still provide the industry with all the manpower which it requires.

Table 7 shows the distribution by occupational groups for a large number of mills and converting units. In both branches of the industry, the blue collar ratio is approximately 80 percent. Operatives

TABLE 7. *Paper and Allied Products Industry, Employment by Occupational Group, Mills and Converting Plants, 1968*

Occupational Group	Pulp, Paper and Paperboard Mills[a] Employees		Converting Plants[a] Employees	
	Number	Percent	Number	Percent
Officials and managers	12,777	7.1	6,385	7.6
Professionals	5,939	3.3	1,466	1.7
Technicians	3,831	2.1	1,010	1.2
Sales workers	1,014	0.6	2,453	2.9
Office and clerical	11,828	6.5	7,175	8.5
Total white collar	35,389	19.6	18,489	21.9
Craftsmen	42,255	23.3	15,377	18.2
Operatives	70,870	39.1	30,497	36.1
Laborers	29,309	16.2	19,023	22.5
Service workers	3,270	1.8	1,149	1.3
Total blue collar	145,704	80.4	66,046	78.1
Total	181,093	100.0	84,535	100.0

Source: Data in author's possession.

[a] Mills: 47 companies, 259 establishments; Converting Plants: 34 companies, 340 establishments.

form the largest single occupational group in both mills and converting plants. The operatives group includes a wide range of skills—some actually highly skilled, others requiring little training. Of interest is the fact that the percentage of those classified as operatives in the paper industry is considerably less than in the automobile or rubber tire industries, but the paper industry has a substantially higher percentage of laborers. The reasons could be nomenclature or greater union pressure in some industries than others to eliminate the use of the term "laborer." More than likely, however, the number of employees performing pure laborer jobs in converting plants, mill yards, and forest operations is the basic reason for the large percentage of those classified as laborers in the paper industry.

Table 7 also shows that there are significant differences in the occupational distribution between mills and converting operations. In the mills, the complicated, expensive equipment requires a much larger crew of mechanics than does the less complicated converting equipment. On the other hand, the percentage of unskilled work in the converting plants is substantially larger. The higher percentage of Negroes in converting plants than in mills is related to these occupational differences.

On the white collar side, the percentage of managers is slightly higher in converters because small plants require a higher supervisory ratio than larger ones. Most of the industry's professional and technical employees are found in the mills, but a higher ratio of sales and of clerical employees are found in converting units. The mills have many "captive" sales outlets; their sales tend to be in large amounts to few customers; and they use jobbers and independent sales representatives as well as their own sales personnel. All of this reduces both sales and clerical forces. On the other hand, converters often sell to many customers in small lots, and use mainly their own sales forces; thus their ratio of sales force and clerical help is higher.

Female Employment

The paper industry uses a substantial proportion of female labor, but it is highly concentrated in noncorrugated converting plants. Thus Table 8 shows that 21.5 percent of employees in the total paper and allied products group are female, but in mills that percentage is only 11.2 for paper and pulp and 8.2 for paperboard. In container plants, the percentage is 24.4, but in the miscellaneous converting group, it reaches 35.7 percent. This last group includes the sewing operations in bag plants and the sorting jobs in various converting plants where small lots are made, handled, and ordered.

TABLE 8. *Paper and Allied Products Industry, Total and Female Employees by Major Standard Industrial Classification, 1968*

Industry Subgroup and SIC Number	All Employees	Female Employees	Percent Female
Paper and allied products — 26	698,100	150,400	21.5
Paper and pulp mills—261, 2, 6	220,500	24,700	11.2
Paperboard mills — 263	73,200	6,000	8.2
Miscellaneous converted paper products—264	183,600	65,600	35.7
Paperboard containers and boxes — 265	220,900	54,000	24.4

Source: U. S. Bureau of Labor Statistics, *Employment and Earnings*, March 1969, Table B-2.

In the mills, most females work in offices and in auxiliary converting jobs, particularly packaging and handling fine papers. The yards, paper and pulp mills, the powerhouses, and the digester operations are all generally exclusively manned by males. As we shall note in a later chapter, however, women were used in some of these jobs during World War II. In the mills, Negro women employees are a recent phenomenon; in converting plants, their use began during World War II.

Earnings and Hours

The paper industry ranks quite high in terms of wages and earnings. Average weekly and hourly earnings exceed those in manufacturing industry generally, and by a wide margin, those in the nondurable segment of industry. The mills pay far higher wages than do converting plants, their skill content and percentage of craftsmen, as already noted, being much higher. Moreover, the continuous process operation of mills generally assures substantial overtime work during the year. Table 9 which compares these earnings for the year 1968 also reveals that a longer workweek prevailed in the mills than in converting plants, or in industry generally. High overtime earnings are typical for the well-paid paper mill employees.

TABLE 9.   *Average Earnings and Hours Worked, Production (Nonsupervisory) Workers Paper and all Manufacturing Industries, 1968*

	Average Weekly Earnings	Average Hourly Earnings	Average Weekly Hours
All manufacturing	$122.51	$3.01	40.7
Durable goods	132.07	3.19	41.4
Nondurable goods	109.05	2.74	39.8
Paper and allied products	130.85	3.05	42.9
Paper and pulp mills	149.08	3.35	44.5
Paperboard mills	152.32	3.37	45.2
Miscellaneous converted paper products	113.99	2.76	41.3
Paperboard containers and boxes	117.88	2.82	41.8

Source: *Employment and Earnings,* March 1969, Table C-2.

The lower-compensated, and on average lower-skilled, converting plant employees not only receive lower wages, but are, as already noted, recruited in labor markets where higher-paying plants are common. As a result converting plants in recent years have utilized large numbers of marginal employees, including many Negroes from inner city areas. In contrast, mills are usually located in a one company town or in areas where few other industries exist; typically they are the highest-paying plants in their areas.

TABLE 10. *Average Hourly Earnings of Production Workers, Paper and Allied Products Industry United States and Region, 1963*

Region	Total (SIC 26)	Pulp Mills (SIC 261)	Paper Mills Except Building Paper Mills (SIC 262)	Paperboard Mills (SIC 263)	Converted Paper and Paperboard Products Except Containers and Boxes (SIC 264)	Paperboard Containers and Boxes (SIC 265)	Building Paper and Building Board Mills (SIC 266)
				(Dollars)			
United States	2.73	3.22	2.93	2.89	2.57	2.34	2.66
Northeast	2.63	2.60	2.77	2.68	2.35	2.28	2.80
North Central (Middle West)	2.77	2.73	2.92	2.82	2.46	2.45	2.61
South	2.74	3.19	3.16	2.94	2.19	2.06	2.60
West (Far West)	3.15	3.47	3.18	3.20	2.62	2.72	2.74

Source: *U. S. Census of Manufactures*, 1963, Vol. II, *Industry Statistics*, Part 1.
Note: For definition of regions, see Table 4, p. 15.

Regional wage data are presented in Table 10, but unfortunately 1963 is the latest year for which they are available. The highest rates paid in the mills at that time were in the Far West; the next in the South. These rates are dependent, in part, on machine size and productivity. Significant expansion has since occurred in the South which may now be paying the highest average rates. As we shall emphasize in the following chapter, low wages, unlike the situation in many other industries, were not a factor in the move of the industry to the South.

In converting, the South follows a more typical regional wage pattern, paying the lowest wages of any area. Again the Far West is the wage leader—also a typical regional wage pattern—except in building paper and board mills, where rates in 1963 were higher in the Northeast. In each area of course, mill wages exceed those in converting plants. The lower wages in the Northeast and Midwest mills reflect the smaller size of the mills there. Wage rates of mills and converters in these areas provide for a much smaller differential than those in the Far West and South where very high rates are paid in the newer and larger mills.

Turnover

The high wages paid in the mills and the few opportunities for alternative employment in most instances insure that labor turnover in the mills remains low. When new mills are being built, job changing increases as personnel move in order to obtain promotions faster— a No. 3 paper machine hand in an older mill may secure a job as back tender or machine tender in a newly constructed one. Even then, however, movement is not great.

In contrast, the converting operations traditionally have a high turnover. In times of prosperity, as one executive noted, "it is a virtual swinging door"[9] in corrugating plants. Marginal labor employed in hot, heavy-work jobs is not likely to have a low quit rate.

Table 11 sets forth the rates for various measurements of turnover in the paper and allied products industry by Standard Industrial Classification for 1958, a recession year with high unemployment, and 1968, a period of prosperity and full employment. By all measurements, as would be expected, turnover rates in 1968 are higher; and

---

9. Interview, January 1968.

TABLE 11. *Turnover in Paper and Allied Products Industry, 1958 and 1968*

Per 100 Employees	Year	Total Industry (SIC 26)	Paper and Pulp Mills (SIC 261, 2, 6)	Paperboard Mills (SIC 263)	Miscellaneous Converted Paper Products (SIC 264)	Paperboard Containers and Boxes (SIC 265)
Accessions	1958	2.4	1.7	1.6	3.1	3.0
	1968	4.1	2.4	2.7	4.7	5.7
New Hires	1958	1.5	1.0	1.0	1.8	2.0
	1968	3.5	1.9	2.3	4.0	5.0
Separations	1958	2.5	1.7	1.8	3.3	3.3
	1968	3.9	2.4	2.6	4.5	5.4
Quits	1958	0.9	0.6	0.7	1.1	1.3
	1968	2.5	1.4	1.7	2.9	3.5
Layoffs	1958	1.3	0.9	0.7	1.7	1.5
	1968	0.5	0.4	0.3	0.7	0.7

Source: U. S. Bureau of Labor Statistics, *Employment and Earnings Statistics for the United States*, Bulletin No. 1312-6, pp. 601-615 and *Employment and Earnings*, April 1969, Table D-2.

converting rates, and especially, those for containers and boxes, always exceed those in the mills.

Unionization

The paper industry is a heavily unionized one with employees in nearly all mills and most converting plants represented by a variety of unions. Dominant among these unions are two: the United Paper- makers and Paperworkers, a union formed by the merger in 1957 of the International Brotherhood of Paper Makers, a former affiliate of the American Federation of Labor which originated in Massachusetts in the 1880's, with the United Paperworkers of America, a much smaller union chartered by the Congress of Industrial Organizations as a result of its organizing paper workers in the late 1930's and early 1940's; and the largest union in the field, the International Brotherhood of Pulp, Sulphite and Paper Mill Workers, which originated after a schism in the International Brotherhood of Paper Makers in 1906, and has since organized concurrently with the Paper Makers and its merged successor. In addition, the International Union of District 50 (formerly the "catchall" of the United Mine Workers), the Teamsters, and the International Printing Pressmen and Assistants' Union of North America all have sizable memberships in converting plants, and a large number of craft locals, particularly those of the International Brotherhood of Electrical Workers and the International Associ- ation of Machinists, are found in the mills. Both the nature of union organization and the character of the industrial relations system which has developed are significant for an understanding of Negro employ- ment problems.

The first successful union in the industry, the International Brother- hood of Paper Makers, was, as its name indicates, organized by "paper makers"—that is, those working on the paper machine. Then, as now, these were the elite of the hourly employees, conscious of their skills. Their outlook was, and often still is, highly craft conscious. Initially they declined to accept into membership the less skilled woodyard and pulp mill workers; later they admitted these employees under restrictive rules which, for example, provided that only "a qualified paper maker could be elected president of IBPM."[10] Un-

---

10. Quoted by Irving Brotslaw, *Trade Unionism in the Pulp and Paper Industry,* Ph.D. dissertation, University of Wisconsin, 1964 (Ann Arbor: University Microfilms, Inc., 1964), p. 87. Much of this history is based upon Dr. Brotslaw's study.

happy with such second-class membership, the pulp and yard employees withdrew in 1906 and found the International Brotherhood of Pulp, Sulphite and Paper Mill Workers. After a few years of fighting each other as energetically as they contested with employers, the two unions in 1909 agreed on the Pulp Workers' admission to the AFL and on jurisdictional lines which provided that:

> . . . the IBPM was to organize the skilled workers, including members of the paper machine crew, beater engineers and certain finishing room workers [in general those working in, or directly associated with, the paper mill except janitors and sweepers], while the Pulp Workers were ceded jurisdictional rights to the less skilled—the men who worked in the wood room and in the wood yard, on the digesters and in other phases of the pulp making process and in converting operations.[11]

As a result of this agreement, the general practice of the two paper unions has been to organize mills concurrently and to bargain as a coalition.[12] If an employee transfers from one union's jurisdiction to another, he is usually accepted and bargained for by the second union without initiation fee or other encumbrance.[13] Regional conferences of local unions are regularly held with representatives of both internationals participating.

The jurisdictional lines drawn between these two unions in effect left the maintenance, mechanical, and power house employees to the craft unions. The result is strong craft union representation in the mills in most areas. Representatives of craft unions sometimes bargain separately, and sometimes bargain on a coalition basis with the paper unions.

Like most of the older AFL affiliated unions, the Paper Makers and the Pulp, Sulphite Workers existed on the fringes of the industry, with some periods of greater success, until the early 1930's. Then they were among the few unions to achieve voluntary employer recognition during the early New Deal period—that is, prior to the enactment of the National Labor Relations (Wagner) Act in 1935 or the ruling on its constitutionality by the United States Supreme Court in 1937. From that time hence, few mills have remained unorganized. For example, the author knows of only one major

---

11. *Ibid.*, p. 96.
12. On this subject, see William N. Chernish, *Coalition Bargaining*, Industrial Research Unit Study No. 45 (Philadelphia: University of Pennsylvania Press, 1969), p. 12 and in general.
13. In a few plants, this is not true and rigid separation between the groups is the rule. This is, however, rare.

southern mill which is not unionized, and which has been in existence
for at least two years.[14] In 1968 the Pulp, Sulphite and Paper Mill
Workers claimed a membership of 180,000; the United Paperworkers,
150,000.

Today the dominant union relations pattern finds both paper unions
and two to four craft organizations holding bargaining rights in the
typical mill. On the West Coast, the craft unions are not found in
most mills because the employers sought successfully to exclude them
when they voluntarily recognized the paper unions in the mid-1930's.[15]
In some mills in the South, East, and Midwest, one of the paper
unions has exclusive bargaining rights. Recently, after one of a
succession of merger talks between the two unions collapsed, their
joint organizing no longer became firm policy, but it still occurs.

Before its merger with the International Brotherhood of Paper
Makers, the United Paperworkers organized mills of only one major
company. District 50 has also been successful in only a few cases in
attempts to organize mills, and so far as can be determined, the Teamsters have yet to win bargaining rights in a major mill facility. On the
West Coast, however, the dominant union is now the independent
Association of Western Pulp and Paper Workers, which was formed
in 1964 after a schism in the two AFL-CIO paper unions, and which
soon thereafter won bargaining rights for the bulk of the mills there.[16]

The converting plants find the Pulp, Sulphite union as the dominant
organization, but all unions are represented, including the Teamsters
and District 50. Originally jurisdiction for converting plants was given
to the Pulp, Sulphite union, but many such plants are now organized
by the United Papermakers. Craft unions are not nearly as prevalent
in converting plants which, of course, have far fewer craftsmen than
do the mills. Because of the significance of printing in converted
paper products, the Printing Pressmen and Assistants' Union has
organized a sizable number of converting plants, in some cases having
a craft local of printing machine operators, in others having bargaining rights for the entire plant.

The structure of union organization has proved of considerable
importance to Negro workers. The division of jurisdiction between

---

14. Brotslaw, *op. cit.*, contains a good history of the union movement in the
    industry, and also a thorough bibliography thereon.
15. See Harold M. Levinson, *Determining Forces in Collective Wage Bargaining*
    (New York: John Wiley & Sons, Inc., 1966), p. 89-90.
16. *Ibid.*, pp. 90-92. The western independent has a membership of 23,000.

Paper Makers and the Pulp, Sulphite union in effect gave the most skilled production workers to the former and the largest number of employees to the latter. Employer hiring policies traditionally excluded Negroes from paper mill jobs; union jurisdictional lines and union-management seniority arrangements institutionalized that exclusion. In the South, the Negro employees prior to 1960 were found entirely in the Pulp, Sulphite union except where the Paper Makers had exclusive bargaining rights for an entire pulp and paper facility. In addition, as we shall note in the next chapter, Negroes were segregated in particular departments and in separate local unions. The exclusion from the paper mill was thus reinforced and institutionalized by union barriers.

Likewise, the unionization by crafts of mechanical, maintenance, and powerhouse employees involves additional barriers to Negroes. Except for the trowel trades (bricklaying, plastering, and cement finishing) in which Negroes have worked in the South since slavery days, the skilled trades have been closed to Negroes. The craft unions have been ardent exclusionists, finding race a convenient method by which they can exercise their work scarcity consciousness and monopolize the market for their skill.[17] In pulp and paper mills, as in industry generally, these unions have erected formidable bars to any advancement of Negroes. Another characteristic of the two principal paper unions which has had a bearing on the industry's racial policies has been their internal governmental structure. Until quite recently, both the Paper Makers and the Pulp, Sulphite Workers have had relatively weak international leadership, aggravated by the fact that their presidents tended to remain in power well beyond a normal retirement age. This, in turn, strengthened the independence of local and regional groups and widened the gap between the national officials and the local or regional leaders. Attempts of national leaders to assert strong leadership in such an environment proved costly to their unions by causing the secession of the West Coast locals to an independent union.[18]

From the point of view of union racial policies, weak national leadership has precluded any firm stand (until recently when the

17. See Herbert R. Northrup, *Organized Labor and the Negro* (New York: Harper & Bros., 1944), Chapters I and II, for background and analysis of craft union racial policies.
18. See Levinson, *op. cit.*, pp. 88-92.

leadership changed) against segregation and discrimination. Locals, dominated by white membership anxious to preserve the *status quo,* have traditionally not found serious national leadership opposition by national officials who have been either anxious to maintain their tenure, or sympathetic with the existing practices, or simply lacking in effective authority.

Union racial policies take on added significance when one considers the economic characteristics of the industry and their impact on industrial relations. A strike is extremely costly for a mill. The huge investment required in buildings, equipment, and timber reserves, the relatively low capital turnover rates, and the consequent high ratio of fixed costs to total costs put tremendous pressures on companies to achieve maximum utilization of capital. Given these factors, and the consequent relative low ratio of mill wage costs to total costs, "high wages and union recognition seem a small price to pay for the privilege of operating the costly equipment seven days a week, twenty-four hours a day without interruption."[19]

Union recognition is also difficult for the companies to avoid because mills are located in inaccessible areas to which key skilled employees, invariably union members, must be imported. As we shall see in later sections of this report, most companies in the industry were quite willing to recognize unions and pay high wages without serious opposition in return for guarantees of peaceful and continuous operation and of the right of management to automate, to improve methods, and to operate efficiently without union opposition.

With the acceptance of unions, however, came the institutionalizing of practices of the period in which the union organization commenced. In the South, this was the late 1930's and early 1940's and meant that segregation and discrimination became part of the industrial relations system and therefore difficult to change. Our study of the racial policies of this industry therefore will, by necessity, involve considerable comment on unionization and industrial relations practices.

---

19. Herbert R. Northrup and Harvey A. Young, "The Causes of Industrial Peace Revisited," *Industrial and Labor Relations Review,* Vol. XXII (October 1968), pp. 45-46.

CHAPTER III

Negro Pulp and Paper Employment to 1960

Prior to 1930, few Negroes were found in the pulp and paper industry. The development of the mills in the South had barely commenced, and virtually no Negroes resided in the areas of the North, Midwest, or Far West where the primary industry was concentrated. The use of paper for a host of converting applications was considerably less advanced than it is today, and white employees were readily available for employment in such converting plants as did exist. The large-scale movement of the paper industry into the South beginning in the 1930's, and the shortage of labor created by World War II in the 1940's altered the racial composition of the industry's work force.

Table 12, based upon United States Census data, shows the number and percentage of Negroes in the "paper and allied products industries," 1920-1960. Just slightly more than 3 percent were colored in 1920 and 1930, and only 4 percent in 1940. Undoubtedly in 1920 and 1930, most Negroes in the industries were employed as janitors and laborers in converting plants and in wastepaper using mills located in southern and northeastern cities, and in the few mills already extant in the South.

Impact of Southern Mill Development

It is difficult to underestimate the contribution of the paper industry to the economy of the South during the 1930's. In the midst of depression and dislocation, this industry came South, built mills, and gave employment at good wages for the period in areas where often no other industry existed and where the farm economy was rapidly disintegrating. The leading company in the South, as in the nation, was International Paper, which, by 1939, had eight southern mills in operation.

International Paper's Southern Kraft Division at an early date decided to utilize Negroes in its work force, and other companies did

TABLE 12. Paper and Allied Products Industry
Total Employed Persons by Race and Sex, United States, 1920-1960

Year	All Employees			Male			Female		
	Total	Negro	Percent Negro	Total	Negro	Percent Negro	Total	Negro	Percent Negro
1920a	130,768	4,183	3.2	100,585	3,513	3.5	30,183	670	2.2
1930b	243,389	8,344	3.4	191,980	7,339	3.8	51,409	1,005	2.0
1940c	328,241	13,006	4.0	256,519	12,287	4.8	71,722	719	1.0
1950c	466,378	31,366	6.7	356,880	27,159	7.6	109,498	4,207	3.8
1960c	579,844	35,975	6.2	456,232	31,077	6.8	123,612	4,898	4.0

Sources: *U. S. Census of Population:*
   1920: Vol. IV, *Occupations,* Chap. IV, Tables 6, 10.
   1930: Vol. V, *Occupations—General Report,* Chap. VII, Table 1.
   1940: Vol. III, *The Labor Force,* Part 1, Table 76.
   1950: Vol. II, *Characteristics of the Population,* Part I, Table 213.
   1960: PC(1) 1D, *U. S. Summary, Detailed Characteristics,* Table 213.

a Laborers and operatives only (10 years and older).
b Gainful workers (10 years and older).
c Employed persons (14 years and older).

likewise. The industry generally singled out certain jobs for Negroes and confined them to these occupations, but it did employ Negroes, in contrast to the pattern set many years earlier by the textile industry, and it paid higher wages and gave steadier employment than most southern Negroes, particularly in rural areas, had ever heretofore experienced, even though racial-occupational wage differentials were common.

The impact of this southern development is clearly demonstrated by the regional census data set forth in Table 13. The South by 1940 had already become a major factor in employment in the industry, and Negroes comprised 19 percent of the total in that region. Indeed, in 1940, the South had 9,788 Negro paper employees as compared with 13,006 nationally (Table 12), or 75 percent of all Negroes in the industry.

Segregation governed all policies in the southern paper industry at this time. Companies employed Negroes for some jobs, and whites for others, and gradually over time, it became customary for Negroes to be used only in particular positions. There has been, of course, considerable variation from one mill to another, but in general, the racial-occupational pattern followed these lines.

Negroes were employed in the mill woodyards to handle, load, and unload wood, and later to operate smaller equipment. They also gradually fell heir to a few jobs in the pulp mill, in some cases as a cook's helper, but usually as tube lancers—the hot, dirty, difficult job of cleaning slag out of boilers by "lancing" them with heavy pokers. They were usually assigned the "brokeman," or "broke beater" job in the paper mill—the job of gathering up wastepaper and broke beater for reprocessing, again a tough, unpleasant task, but in some mills the actual beaterman and his helper were white with Negroes confined to gathering up and depositing the waste, or "broke." In the older power-houses, Negroes did the coal shoveling and other firemen's jobs which preceded the introduction of automatic equipment. And of course, Negroes performed as customary, the general laborer, janitorial, and yard service work. The paper machines, heavy equipment, pulp mill digester, powerhouse engineer, and all skilled maintenance remained white men's preserves.

TABLE 13. Paper and Allied Products Industry
Total Employed Persons by Race, Sex, and Region, 1940-1960

Year	All Employees			Male			Female		
	Total	Negro	Percent Negro	Total	Negro	Percent Negro	Total	Negro	Percent Negro
					South				
1940	51,389	9,788	19.0	44,170	9,504	21.5	7,219	284	3.9
1950	94,678	19,726	20.8	78,799	18,684	23.7	15,879	1,042	6.6
1960	144,459	20,061	13.9	121,424	18,907	15.6	23,035	1,154	5.0
					Northeast				
1940	149,811	1,599	1.1	113,011	1,442	1.3	36,800	157	0.4
1950	187,563	6,176	3.3	138,836	4,601	3.3	48,727	1,575	3.2
1960	203,953	9,847	4.8	155,412	7,511	4.8	48,541	2,336	4.8
					Middle West				
1940	105,455	1,465	1.4	81,123	1,188	1.5	24,332	277	1.1
1950	149,521	4,800	3.2	111,737	3,339	3.0	37,784	1,461	3.9
1960	176,199	5,214	3.0	135,002	3,944	2.9	41,197	1,270	3.1
					West				
1940	21,586	154	0.7	18,215	153	0.8	3,371	1	*
1950	34,616	664	1.9	27,508	535	1.9	7,108	129	1.8
1960	55,233	853	1.5	44,394	715	1.6	10,839	138	1.3

Sources: U.S. Census of Population:
1940: Vol. III, The Labor Force, Part 1, Table 77.
1950: Vol. II, Characteristics of the Population, Part 1, Table 161.
1960: PC(1) 1D, U.S. Summary, Table 260.

Note: For definition of regions, see Table 4, p. 15.
*Less than 0.05 percent.

Unionization and Seniority Development

When the major paper companies first built southern mills, they had had little prior experience with Negro labor. As already noted, and as the data in Table 13 emphasize, the industry outside of the South as late as 1940 had only about a 1 percent Negro employee complement. Most Negroes in the North or West, who entered the industry prior to 1940, worked in wastepaper mills or corrugating plants. Faced with the race problem, usually for the first time, the tendency for mill management was to override opposition of some southern whites against employing any Negroes, but to accommodate to southern custom by segregating their white and black employees and confining the latter mostly to the menial jobs. In addition, all cafeterias, locker rooms, recreation, and other facilities were maintained on a strictly segregated basis.

In reaching these decisions, the paper companies found that they conformed in general with the labor supply capability. The industry heavily imported, as well as trained, its skilled work force. As one mill manager in the Deep South recalled:

> When I came to Mississippi in 1935, it was a rural argicultural area. There were a few textile mills and some lumber operations, but no other industry. A large percentage of the population in the area was uneducated, and a much larger percentage of the Negro population was uneducated. Indeed for reasons for which my company cannot be held responsible, the Negroes were nearly all laborers and agricultural workers and lacked the education or background to be much else. They did not have automobiles or tools and were historically given no opportunity to work with them. They were ill-qualified for machine training. Negroes who escaped from this lowly status also escaped from our community and sought a better life elsewhere, usually to the North. Those that we employed, mostly in our woodyard, had little education.[20]

Early Union Racial Policies in the Mills

When unions began their organization attempts after the election of Franklin D. Roosevelt as President of the United States in 1932, the leading paper company, International Paper, did not, like employers in many industries, actively oppose unionization. On the other hand, International at first recognized unions only for the settlement

---

20. Interview, July 1968. For a graphic account of the disadvantaged situation of Negro youth in the South during the 1930's, now available in paperback, see Charles S. Johnson, *Growing up in the Black Belt: Negro Youth in the Rural South* (New York: Schocken Books, 1967), especially Chapter IV, "Youth and the Schools."

of grievances, but declined to sign written agreements. Other southern
paper companies actively opposed unionization in this period. On
the West Coast, however, employers, led by Crown Zellerbach, the
dominant firm there, signed agreements with the two AFL paper
unions in 1934.

After the Wagner Act was declared constitutional in 1937,
unionization spread rapidly in the South. A major victory for the
unions was a master agreement with the Southern Kraft Division of
International Paper, first concluded in 1939 after voluntary recognition of unions by the company.[21] Today southern paper mill employees, as those in other sections of the country, are almost all
unionized.

Unions in the pulp and paper industry, like employers, had little
experience with Negro workers prior to the development of the
southern industry. When unionization developed at some southern
mills, Negroes were placed in locals of the International Hod Carriers
and Common Laborers Union (now the Laborers International Union). This seemed logical to the craft-minded paper unions which
readily recognized the jurisdictional claims of the electrical workers,
machinists, and other craft unions to organize maintenance employees
in the mills.[22]

Fortunately, however, this organizational structure endured in only
one mill.[23] Instead the Pulp, Sulphite Workers asserted jurisdiction
over woodyards. The union structure which developed usually saw
the Paper Makers issuing a local charter for employees in the paper
mill and related stock rooms, finishing, and shipping departments; the
Pulp, Sulphite Workers issuing two charters, one for white employees
in the pulp mill, recovery operation, yard, and related work, and
another for Negro employees throughout the plant; and various craft
unions issuing charters for mechanical, electrical, and sometimes
powerhouse employees. Where woods employees were covered, the

---

21. See Irving Brotslaw, *Trade Unionism in the Pulp and Paper Industry* (Ann Ar-
    bor: University Microfilms, Inc., 1964), pp. 138-141. The author also has in his
    possession a detailed unpublished historical memorandum of southern paper
    unionism, from the files of the National Labor Relations Board, Region 15,
    New Orleans, written in 1939 as background information for a representative
    case involving the Mobile plant of International Paper Company.
22. Initial organization at Mobile placed Negroes in a separate Hod Carriers' local,
    but not at other International Paper plants. Later the Mobile local became a
    segregated local of the Pulp, Sulphite Workers. (NLRB memorandum, *loc. cit.*)
23. This is the Fernandina, Florida, plant of Container Corporation of America.
    The separate Hod Carriers' local existed there until 1968 when the employees
    decertified it and joined the Pulp, Sulphite Workers.

Pulp, Sulphite union usually had jurisdiction, again establishing separate white and colored locals.

Of course, the typical pattern has had many variations. Sometimes the Paper Makers had segregated Negro locals also. Generally, however, Negro employees were found in segregated locals of the Pulp, Sulphite union. Thus they were in a position to demand integration at a later date which would have been more difficult if they had been not only segregated, but also segregated into an entirely different, and essentially nonpaper industry union like the Hod Carriers and Common Laborers. As it was, the interests of the Negro pulp and paper workers were certainly little enough protected.

Race and Collective Bargaining

The segregated locals of the paper unions were not auxiliary unions such as those established by many old-line American Federation of Labor and railroad unions in this period. Auxiliary unions typically permitted their Negro members no voice in national union affairs and made them subservient to the white locals in all matters.[24] The segregated paper union locals theoretically gave their members the same rights as those conferred upon members of white locals. In fact, as in all "separate but equal" arrangements, Negroes found little equality. The whites held full control of the bargaining arrangements. Thus Dr. Brotslaw reported:

The degree of autonomy enjoyed by the Negro locals is questionable. During contract negotiations, whatever settlement is reached by the white locals is ordinarily accepted by the colored locals. In terms of representation from the international unions, Negro members generally must rely upon white officers and representatives. It is unlikely, therefore, that "separate but equal" accurately describes the status enjoyed by Negro members or their segregated local unions in the southern pulp and paper industry.[25]

In the same vein is the comment of Professor Marshall:

The Unions in the pulp and paper industry . . . have maintained segregated locals throughout the South, though there also were some integrated locals. . . . There is also some evidence that although these organizations might not in theory have been auxiliaries, they in fact tended to have many of the same features as auxiliary locals.[26]

---

24. See Herbert R. Northrup, *Organized Labor and the Negro* (New York: Harper & Bros., 1944), Chapters I-III and X, for specifics on auxiliary Jim Crow local unions.
25. Brotslaw, *op. cit.*, p. 142.
26. F. Ray Marshall, *The Negro and Organized Labor* (New York: John Wiley & Sons, Inc., 1965), p. 183.

These observations are not difficult to corroborate. When the southern mills were first started, they paid higher wages to skilled employees than did northern mills, partially because the equipment was newer, larger, and more productive in the South than in the North, but largely to attract skilled workers from the North. As a result the " . . . wage rates for skilled workers in 1939 were considerably higher in some of the southern States than in Maine or New Hampshire. Common labor, on the other hand, was paid a uniformly lower rate in the South."[27] Not till 1946 was the southern common labor rate equalized with that of the smaller northern mills.[28]

The reason for this disparity was the existence of an ample common labor supply in the South, and a policy of paying less to Negroes than whites for the same work. "In 1938, Negro laborers received 4 cents an hour below the base rate for whites. On application of the company and union, the National War Labor Board in 1943, removed the differential, which had increased to 4½ cents an hour."[29]

Not only did racial differentials exist until World War II, but even then Negro rights largely depended on the employer's recognition of fair play rather than any strong union support. Thus a vice-president of a major company reported his introduction to southern paper bargaining:

Soon after World War II, we purchased the ——————————— company with two mills in the deep South. I met with the unions and spent three days negotiating. It was my first southern experience. All during the negotiations three Negroes sat in the back of the room and said nothing. At the end of the third day, the regional director of one of the unions, acting as spokesman for the group, grasped my hand and said: "That wraps it up."

I was about to agree when I noticed that one of the Negroes seemed trying to get my attention. I said: "What about those fellows?" "Oh, yes," the regional director said, "the niggers do want something."

27. William Rupert Maclaurin, "Wages and Profits in the Paper Industry, 1929-39," *Quarterly Journal of Economics,* Vol. LVIII (February 1944), p. 217.
28. U. S. Bureau of Labor Statistics, *Wage Chronology, International Paper Company, Southern Kraft Division, 1937-67,* Bulletin No. 1534 (Washington: Government Printing Office, 1967), p. 5.
29. *Ibid.* International Paper's policies have been typical of, and indeed, a bellwether of the industry. The cheapness of Negro labor in this early period is illustrated by the experience of the Chesapeake Pulp and Paper Company, West Point, Virginia, which initially found it cheaper to allow an expensive barking drum to be idle for four years and have Negroes using Dutch hoes do the debarking. See Alonzo Thomas Dill, *Chesapeake Pioneer Papermaker* (Charlottesville: University of Virginia Press, 1968), pp. 42-43.

I insisted that they be heard. All they wanted was a new job title so that their children would aspire to be something but laborers. I agreed before the regional director could say anything. After that, I made sure that I heard from the colored local at all negotiations.[30]

When such concern on the part of the employer was absent, the dominant white unions not only used their power to institutionalize the system of segregation and discrimination, but sometimes even ignored fair treatment. Thus a company officer told the author:

When we purchased this [deep South] mill from its original owners, we were here almost one year before we discovered that the company store was charging Negroes higher rates on some things than whites. I called the home office and got quick orders: Abolish the practice today; abolish the company store within one month. Later the president of the Negro local told me that he had complained about this practice several times both to the previous management and to the regional union officials, but neither would do anything about it.[31]

On the other hand, there were many cases in which the union leadership did attempt to represent Negroes fairly, within the segregated system. Moreover, the segregated locals gave Negroes an opportunity to attend regional meetings, to develop their own leadership, and to become acquainted with methods and procedures for representing their own interests. And, of course, the general wage increases, negotiated by the companies and unions, steadily raised the rates of pay of southern Negro, as well as white, pulp and paper mill employees.

The Seniority System in the South

Speaking of the early days of unionization, a former pulp and paper mill manager stated:

We had a labor agreement [in 1940], but there were no formal lines of progression. Nevertheless, lines of progression existed, and of course pre-dated union recognition. Everyone knew and understood, for example, that an employee started on the bottom job on a paper machine and learned his way up to the top job. The same understanding prevailed in the woodyard, the pulp mill and so on. . . .

One of the things that the union demanded from the beginning was a meaningful seniority system at our plant. The employees wanted to have contractual rights to advancement and job security based upon seniority. They wanted us to formalize, in effect, what had been our practice. So lines of progression were put into the contract setting forth how a man progressed from one job to the next higher one.[32]

---

30. Interview, June 1967.
31. Interview, March 1968.
32. Interview, November 1966.

Essentially what happened in the paper industry was that on-the-job training programs by which men progressed up the occupational hierarchy were incorporated into union agreements, modified and institutionalized. This was typical of industry generally. Because of the nature of the industry, the seniority lines in pulp and paper mills tend to be "long and narrow"—that is, employees work up one functional line without acquiring skill or seniority rights in another. Thus a person who is employed on the bottom job of a paper machine, for example, No. 7 hand, or utility man, works up over the years toward the top position of machine tender, but he acquires no knowledge of, or seniority rights to, jobs in the pulp mill, or elsewhere in the facility.

If an employee in the pulp mill under this system desires to transfer to the paper mill, he must start at the lowest job on the paper mill seniority list, and his seniority for promotion or layoff commences when he starts there. Moreover, in most union contracts in the industry, such a transferee gives up his pulp mill seniority. Thus few such transfers occur.

Given the expensive equipment and its intricacies, such a seniority system is well-suited to the needs of the industry. Moreover, there is nothing about it which is discriminatory *per se*. Unfortunately, combined with employer hiring practices and with modifications which were obviously dictated by race, the seniority system became an invidiously discriminatory instrument. The following series of diagrams depicting a typical pre-1960 seniority progression in a southern pulp and paper plant illustrate this fact.

Figure 1 shows the typical seniority progression system of a southern paper mill and associated work departments of the type that prevailed in the period up to the mid-1960's. The progressions of the paper machine crews and of the finishing crews exhibit no break. The reason is that only whites are employed in these jobs. (Janitors are not in the progression but this is not necessarily racially motivated nor unusual.)

On the other hand, the shipping crew and beater room progressions have "breaks." Thus in the shipping crew list, the lift truck operator and car loader should be worked in either in the production weigher or shipping clerk progression in a nondiscriminatory system, and the laborer would progress to utility man in the beater room; the broke-man, who is Negro, has no rights to progress to first helper and then

FIGURE 1

Pre-1960 Typical Southern Paper Mill Seniority Progression

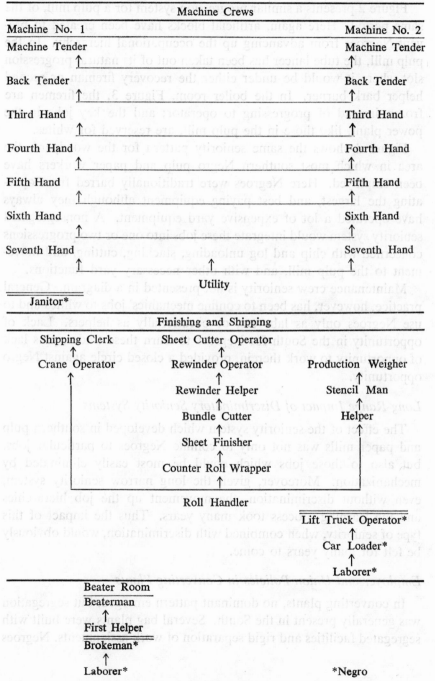

Machine Crews

Machine No. 1   Machine No. 2

Machine Tender   Machine Tender
↑   ↑

Back Tender   Back Tender
↑   ↑

Third Hand   Third Hand
↑   ↑

Fourth Hand   Fourth Hand
↑   ↑

Fifth Hand   Fifth Hand
↑   ↑

Sixth Hand   Sixth Hand
↑   ↑

Seventh Hand   Seventh Hand
↑   ↑   ↑

Utility

Janitor*

Finishing and Shipping

Shipping Clerk   Sheet Cutter Operator
↑   ↑
Crane Operator   Rewinder Operator   Production Weigher
↑   ↑   ↑
       Rewinder Helper   Stencil Man
       ↑   ↑
       Bundle Cutter   Helper
       ↑   ↑
       Sheet Finisher
       ↑
       Counter Roll Wrapper
       ↑

Roll Handler

Lift Truck Operator*
↑
Car Loader*
↑
Laborer*

Beater Room

Beaterman
↑
First Helper
↑
Brokeman*
↑
Laborer*   *Negro

to beaterman, although these would be the logical steps in a non-discriminatory system.

Figure 2 presents a similar progression system for a pulp mill, of the same period. Here again, artificial blocks have been created to prevent Negroes from advancing up the occupational hierarchy. In the pulp mill, the tube lancer has been taken out of its natural progression slot where it would be under either the recovery fireman or second helper bark burner. In the boiler room, Figure 3, the firemen are frozen instead of progressing to operator; and the key jobs in the power plant, like those in the pulp mill, are reserved for whites.

Figure 4 shows the same seniority pattern for the woodyard, the area in which most southern Negro pulp and paper workers have been employed. Here Negroes were traditionally barred from operating the largest, and best paying equipment although they always have operated a lot of expensive yard equipment. A nonsegregated seniority system would integrate these jobs into one or two progressions concerned with chip and log unloading, stacking, cutting, and movement to the pulp mill, and with other necessary yard functions.

Maintenance crew seniority is not presented in a diagram. General practice, however, has been to confine mechanics' jobs to whites and to use Negroes only as laborers, or occasionally as helpers. Lack of opportunity in the South for Negroes to learn these trades, plus lack of opportunity to work therein, provided a closed circle against Negro opportunity.

Long-Range Impact of Discriminatory Seniority Systems

The effect of the seniority system which developed in southern pulp and paper mills was not only to confine Negroes to particular jobs, but also to those jobs which could be most easily eliminated by mechanization. Moreover, given the long narrow seniority system, even without discrimination, the movement up the job hierarchies and the learning process took many years. Thus the impact of this type of seniority, when combined with discrimination, would obviously be felt for many years to come.

Employer and Union Policies in Converting Plants

In converting plants, no dominant pattern emerged, but segregation was generally present in the South. Several bag plants were built with segregated facilities and rigid separation of work assignments. Negroes

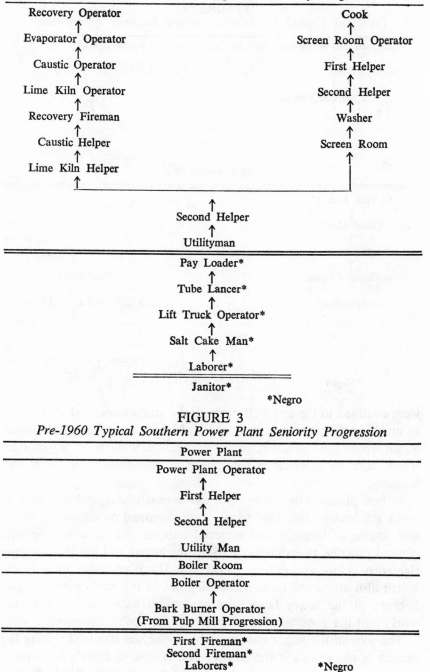

FIGURE 2
Pre-1960 Typical Southern Pulp Mill Seniority Progression

Recovery Operator   Cook
↑   ↑
Evaporator Operator   Screen Room Operator
↑   ↑
Caustic Operator   First Helper
↑   ↑
Lime Kiln Operator   Second Helper
↑   ↑
Recovery Fireman   Washer
↑   ↑
Caustic Helper   Screen Room
↑
Lime Kiln Helper
↑

Second Helper
↑
Utilityman

Pay Loader*
↑
Tube Lancer*
↑
Lift Truck Operator*
↑
Salt Cake Man*
↑
Laborer*

Janitor*

*Negro

FIGURE 3
Pre-1960 Typical Southern Power Plant Seniority Progression

Power Plant

Power Plant Operator
↑
First Helper
↑
Second Helper
↑
Utility Man

Boiler Room

Boiler Operator
↑
Bark Burner Operator
(From Pulp Mill Progression)

First Fireman*
Second Fireman*
Laborers*   *Negro

FIGURE 4

Pre-1960 Typical Southern Woodyard Seniority Progression

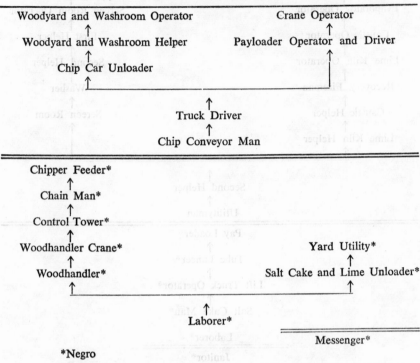

*Negro

were confined to the less well-paying jobs and whites used exclusively as machine operators and mechanics. Many converting plants in the South which utilized an extensive number of females employed only white labor in accordance with the practice initiated by the textile industry.

In box plants, where there still exists much heavy labor and generally unpleasant, unskilled work, Negroes found employment, North and South, as laborers and material handlers. This would become general practice as economic activity quickened and the labor supply tightened before and during World War II. Wastepaper mills in the North also employed quite a few Negroes in this early period, again because of the heavy labor, the unpleasant nature of some of the work, and the generally low wages paid for such employment.

The jobs in the paper industry which Negroes obtained during the decade of the 1940's in the North were, of course, largely in converting plants located in the cities to which they migrated. World War II and the prosperity which it induced and which followed tremendously stimulated the use of paper packaging and the expansion of the industry. Converting plants in the North more and more depended upon southern mills to supply the raw materials. Converting companies built or purchased southern mills in order to insure a supply of raw materials; mill concerns built or purchased converting plants to insure a steady outlet for their basic products. Mill expansion in the South meant more jobs for Negroes, as well as for whites.

The war years in the South, however, saw no permanent change in the racial-occupational employment pattern. If anything, by 1950, segregation of job and facilities had become more rigid.

In a few plants in the North and Midwest, segregated facilities (locker rooms, drinking fountains, etc.) were actually established for Negroes, but these were rare and soon abolished. Customs did evolve which were discriminatory and which may still be found. Thus the heavy "take-off" jobs on the end of corrugating, printing, and lithographic machines were assigned to Negroes, but in some cases the take-off man was not placed in the line of progression to machine operator. Where these practices did occur, North or South, they did not prove as ironclad or as universal as in the mills. Rapid expansion and the need for labor, generated by World War II and the prosperity that followed, insured a large increase in the Negro paper converting plant labor force and an expansion of job opportunities within these plants.

FROM WORLD WAR II TO 1960

Between 1940 and 1950, the number and proportion of Negroes in the paper and allied industries increased both absolutely and proportionately, climbing from 4.0 percent to 6.7 percent of the total (Table 12, p. 32). In the South, Negroes added 10,000 jobs in the industry, and raised their percentage of jobs slightly, increasing from 19 percent to 20.8 percent (Table 13, p. 34). Larger percentage increases, but less numerical increases occurred in the Northeast and Middle West. Whereas in 1940, 75 percent of all Negro paper and allied workers were found in the South, that proportion by 1950 had declined to 63 percent.

Despite the increases in the number of southern Negro pulp and paper workers during World War II, no permanent change in the racial-occupational pattern of employment occurred. During the war, it is likely that Negroes did perform some jobs heretofore reserved for whites. Negro women were also brought into the mills to work. In South Carolina, for example (see Table 14), Negro male employment in the paper and allied industries rose from 31 percent in 1942 to 50.5 percent in 1945, and then commenced a downtrend that reached 29.1 percent in 1950. Negro female employment in South Carolina's paper industry was only 2 percent in 1943, 30.9 percent in 1945, and back to 2.2 percent in 1946![33]

South Carolina is the only state that regularly publishes such racial data. Personnel executives in the industry, questioned about these wartime racial employment changes, affirm that Negroes were brought into mills during the war, and then displaced thereafter, sometimes pursuant to verbal union-management understandings.[34] Negro women who were utilized for manual labor during the war were replaced with men after the war. Since no Negro women were utilized in offices either before or after the war, the sharp increase and decline in their utilization in South Carolina represents their temporary wartime employment. Undoubtedly the South Carolina data are in fact representative of the situation which generally prevailed in the South during and after World War II.

In the North, Negroes became a permanent part of the converting paper plant labor force. Where plants were located became the key factor in the extent of Negro employment. If the facility was in a city with a sizable Negro population, it was likely to have a sizable Negro work force. On the other hand, plants located in suburban areas, or sections of the country where few Negroes lived, were likely to have few Negro workers. This situation prevails today, and is discussed in greater detail in the following chapter.

In northern mills located near urban centers, Negroes were hired in larger numbers during World War II, and tended to retain these jobs. In the northern areas of New England, or the Midwest, or in the Far West, few if any Negroes had entered the industry by 1950.

---

33. The South Carolina data, summarized in Table 14 (p. 61) and Figure 5 (p. 62), are unique among all fifty state labor market reports. For a picture of Negro women being utilized as log cutters see Dill, *op. cit.*, illustration between pages 172 and 173.

34. Based upon a composite of discussions with company personnel officials throughout the southern segment of the industry, 1966-1969.

Automation and Displacement in Southern Mills, 1950-1960

The World War II and postwar years saw a steady increase in wages and benefits in the pulp and paper industry. Demand for paper rose steadily till 1958 and the industry expanded rapidly especially in the South. To take advantage of new markets and to offset rising wages, the industry steadily improved its methods and equipment and rapidly replaced men with machines.

For example, paper machines were dramatically increased in size, then controls made considerably more automatic, and their productivity greatly enhanced. One such modern type machine, with a crew of seven men per shift, can produce much more paper per shift than several of the older, smaller ones each having a five- or six-man shift crew. Since no Negroes were employed on paper machines before the 1960's, this involved no immediate lessening of opportunities for Negroes (or for whites, given the capacity of these machines to offset higher costs, and to facilitate expansion in the industry).

In other departments of the southern mills, however, mechanization disproportionately impacted on Negroes. They were concentrated in the laboring jobs—always the easiest to mechanize. They continued to be barred from the better jobs; and as the wage rates in the lower job spectrum were increased, whites competed for such jobs with the advantages of superior educational backgrounds, and preference on the part of employers for employees who could, without racial restrictions, advance up the occupational hierarchy.

In the forest, large numbers of Negroes were displaced by bigger mechanical saws, heavy moving equipment, and larger log transports. In the mill woodyards, gangs of Negroes (bull gangs) were employed to unload logs from boxcars. "One Negro, one box car" per shift, was the rule of thumb of mill managements who were assured by natives that a white man could not stand the summer heat in a boxcar. The railroads developed special pulp-log freight carriers and a crane unloaded them. Bulldozers, cranes, and other mechanical equipment took over the bull gang's work.

In the pulp mills, continuous digesters replaced batch cooking. Where Negro helpers once existed, they were displaced. Improved boilers first reduced the number of tube lancers from four to one per shift, then eliminated them altogether. Negroes thus lost what was often their highest-rated pulp mill jobs. In the power plants and boiler rooms, automatic equipment eliminated Negro firemen's jobs.

In many of these situations, few Negroes had the educational background to handle the automatic equipment if they had been given an opportunity. Except in the forests and in the mill yards where Negroes were permitted to operate mechanical equipment in varying degrees depending upon local decisions of management, they were given little or no opportunity to work on the more sophisticated machines, regardless of their qualifications.

Not only were Negroes displaced in older mills, but perhaps more important, they were not employed in newer ones in anything like the proportion that had been the case in the decade of the 1940's. As new mills were started, managements found that they were deluged with applicants, many of whom were highly qualified and anxious to move up the occupational ladder by changing jobs. As late as 1962, for example, a mill opened in South Carolina which had 3,000 applicants for 400 jobs. It selected them strictly on its management's criteria of competence. During its first two years of operation, its labor force contained (part of the time) one Negro—a porter.[35]

The results of these developments are clearly seen in Table 12 (p. 32) and Table 13 (p. 34). For the country as a whole, the number of Negroes in the paper and allied industries increased by 4,600, but the proportion of Negroes declined slightly. In the South, however, although Negro employment rose by a few hundred, the proportion of Negroes in the industry fell substantially, declining from 20.8 percent to 13.9 percent. Only in the Northeast of our four regions did the proportion of Negroes increase slightly; yet the percentage of Negroes in the industry who worked in the South continued its decline, falling to 56 percent in 1960, as compared with 75 percent in 1940 and 63 percent in 1950.

The decline in the Negro's share of work in southern pulp and paper plants is graphically illustrated by Table 14 and Figure 5 which reproduce and plot the South Carolina data for nonsalaried employees in the paper industry. The already noted World War II expansion in Negro employment is clearly set forth, followed by an immediate and sharp decline which did not level off until 1964!

Seniority Impact

Despite the evidence from the Census, and the South Carolina data, and from the author's field investigations, a leading industry industrial

_____
35. Personal investigation, 1966.

TABLE 14.   *Paper and Allied Products Industry*
Nonsalaried Workers by Race and Sex
South Carolina, 1940-1968

	All Employees			Male			Female		
Year	Total	Negro	Percent Negro	Total	Negro	Percent Negro	Total	Negro	Percent Negro
1940	1,521	377	24.8	1,521	377	24.8	—	—	—
1941	1,585	459	29.0	1,585	459	29.0	—	—	—
1942	2,512	780	31.1	2,512	780	31.1	—	—	—
1943	2,675	931	34.8	2,525	928	36.8	150	3	2.0
1944	3,225	1,392	43.2	2,821	1,341	47.5	404	51	12.6
1945	3,222	1,548	48.0	2,814	1,422	50.5	408	126	30.9
1946	3,105	1,192	38.4	2,780	1,185	42.6	325	7	2.2
1947	3,371	1,141	33.8	3,063	1,133	37.0	308	8	2.6
1948	3,815	1,220	32.0	3,367	1,211	36.0	448	9	2.0
1949	3,583	1,050	29.3	3,203	1,044	32.6	380	6	1.6
1950	3,270	857	26.2	2,931	852	29.1	339	5	1.5
1951	3,811	949	24.9	3,366	944	28.0	445	5	1.1
1952	3,886	981	25.2	3,466	977	28.2	420	4	1.0
1953	3,774	918	24.3	3,319	915	27.6	455	3	0.7
1954	4,060	1,017	25.0	3,632	1,014	27.9	428	3	0.7
1955	4,011	981	24.5	3,618	978	27.0	393	3	0.8
1956	4,225	1,005	23.8	3,748	1,002	26.7	477	3	0.6
1957	4,859	1,058	21.8	4,273	1,055	24.7	586	3	0.5
1958	4,693	995	21.2	4,065	993	24.4	628	2	0.3
1959	4,931	1,058	21.5	4,304	1,056	24.5	627	2	0.3
1960	5,389	942	17.5	4,720	940	19.9	669	2	0.3
1961	6,607	1,070	16.2	5,784	1,067	18.4	823	3	0.4
1962	6,323	1,045	16.5	5,542	1,042	18.8	781	3	0.4
1963	6,707	1,022	15.2	5,924	1,018	17.2	783	4	0.5
1964	7,060	1,045	14.8	6,285	1,041	16.6	775	4	0.5
1965	7,334	1,053	14.4	6,511	1,047	16.1	823	6	0.7
1966	7,462	1,065	14.3	6,595	1,054	16.0	867	11	1.3
1967	7,467	1,180	15.8	6,481	1,110	17.1	986	70	7.1
1968	7,152	1,150	16.1	6,274	1,077	17.2	878	73	8.3

Source: *Annual Reports,* Department of Labor of the State of South Carolina, 1940-1968.

relations practitioner took emphatic exception to the view that the seniority system adversely affected Negro employment in this period. To some extent, he is correct. First, the decline in the proportion of Negroes employed in the South was primarily a function of newly

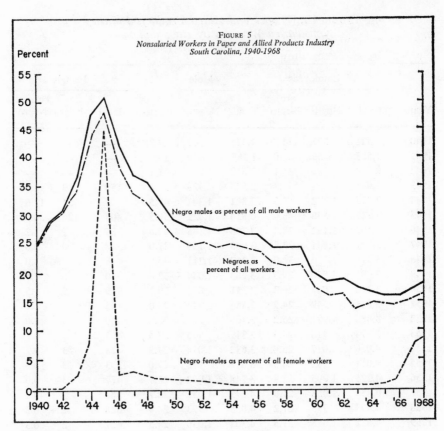

Figure 5
*Nonsalaried Workers in Paper and Allied Products Industry
South Carolina, 1940-1968*

Negro males as percent of all male workers

Negroes as
percent of all workers

Negro females as percent of all female workers

Source: Table 13

built mills employing a far smaller proportion of Negroes than had older mills, rather than of layoffs from the older mills.

Second, it was pointed out that although occupational seniority prevails in general, layoffs from entry or base-rate jobs are governed by mill seniority. Hence in reducing forces employees bump down the lines of progression until they reach the base-rate jobs and from there layoffs are handled on the basis of the newest plant employee being the first furloughed. Since many Negroes had considerable seniority, they have been retained while white employees who had higher-rated jobs but less mill seniority were laid off.

The second point is correct but does not give a complete analysis of the impact of the seniority system *when combined with discriminating hiring policies.* To be sure white employees could not displace

Negroes with greater mill seniority at base-rate jobs. Since, however, Negroes were before 1960 almost universally denied entry into many lines of progression, they did not have the opportunity to exercise seniority nearly as broadly as did whites. Thus, a white worker with much less mill seniority than a Negro could be working while the Negro was unemployed because the white employee had had an opportunity to move up a progression and there to exercise occupational seniority. Moreover, long-service whites could also exercise mill seniority at the base-rate jobs. Thus whites had two bites at the seniority apple on a proportionally much larger basis than did Negroes. And this undoubtedly contributed also to the declining Negro proportion in the South which the data so clearly reveal.

Tests, Qualifications, and Promotions

Another development during the 1950's was the testing of white applicants for jobs. As the machinery and equipment became more complicated and sophisticated, mill managements grew conscious of the need for better prepared and educated personnel. Accordingly testing programs were initiated by an increasing number of mills as an aid to weeding out applicants who would be less likely to qualify for the higher-rated jobs.

Given the seniority system in the industry, this was a quite understandable move. So were two other employee qualification procedures. The first, closely akin to testing, was a requirement for a high school education as a prerequisite for employment. Increased shop mathematics and communication skill needs were an obvious concomitant of the more complicated and sophisticated equipment being used in the mills. The high wages paid in the mills and their frequent domination of local labor markets enabled them to institute tests and educational qualifications without adversely affecting labor supply.

Within the job progressions, employers placed heavy emphasis on displacement of those who could not, or would not, progress. For example, if a No. 4 hand on a paper machine did not advance to No. 3 when an opening occurred, the No. 5 hand might have to jump from his position to No. 3. He would be without experience in No. 4, which includes training for No. 3 by filling in during absences, vacations, etc. This could be a very serious training problem if all four (one for each shift) No. 4 hands were not able or willing to move to

No. 3. Managements therefore tended to insist that those who started at the bottom of a seniority line must be presumed qualified to handle the top job in that line after training. If anyone proved unqualified, or declined a promotion, he could be demoted or in some cases reassigned or even released.

For Negroes, however, a different standard was applied. Since they were confined to particular jobs, which usually demanded a strong back as the principal employment criterion, they were not tested nor held to educational requirements. As a result, many Negroes were employed who would not have been eligible under the standards imposed on whites, but on the other hand the Negro labor force in the industry was therefore less well qualified and less ready for a period when racial restrictions on upgrading were to be lifted.

The Decade, 1950-1960, in Retrospect

The adverse impact on Negroes of developments during the 1950's did not move either management or unions to make any substantial changes in their policies. Basic employment and promotion patterns remained unaltered, and restlessness among Negro employees or local union officials was either ignored or not permitted "to get out of hand." The fact that one of the paper unions was headed by an octogenarian and the other by the former southern representative who helped establish the invidiously discriminatory system undoubtedly helped to make the unions oblivious to change. Proposals to make change advocated by some management personnel were overruled by those who feared costly losses of production if "the boat was rocked."

Yet change was in the offing, spurred by demands of Negroes for fair treatment and an ever more responsive government and public. Like President Truman before him, President Eisenhower had established by Executive Order an agency to enhance equal employment opportunity among government contractors. Known as the President's Committee on Government Contracts, (or "Nixon Committee" because its chairman was the then Vice-President), this committee developed the survey and investigation procedures later used more extensively by successor government civil rights organizations. A number of industries and plants in the South were examined by this committee. In particular, its extensive surveys of the petroleum industry, where a similar pattern of discrimination and segregation existed, had a substantial impact on the policies of the industry and of the Oil, Atomic and Chemical Workers Union.[36]

Records available to the author find no such investigations in the southern pulp and paper industry, but in any case change would have been more difficult. Although similar segregation patterns existed, the national unions in the paper industry were not then nearly as sympathetic to improving the job opportunities of Negroes as were those of the oil workers' union. Moreover, the petroleum industry has long been conscious of its consumer and government relations whereas the paper industry has been much more concerned traditionally with "not rocking the boat" and with maintaining a smooth union relationship.

The Nixon Committee did conduct an investigation in 1958 of two plants of Crown Zellerbach on the West Coast—a large mill at Camas, near Portland, Oregon, and a converting plant at San Leandro, in the San Francisco area. Although neither plant had any Negroes employed, the investigator characterized the company "as one that appears to be susceptible to progress."[37] Progress there, as in the South, however, would await until the next decade when stronger protests, stronger laws and rules, and tighter labor markets insured that change would indeed occur. The Nixon Committee was correct in their analysis of the Crown Zellerbach attitude. In the early 1960's Crown employed a Negro supervisor at Camus and subsequently added approximately 100 Negro employees.

---

36. See Marshall, *op. cit.,* pp. 145-152; and Carl B. King and Howard W. Risher, Jr., *The Negro in the Petroleum Industry,* The Racial Policies of American Industry, Report No. 5 (Philadelphia: Industrial Research Unit, Wharton School of Finance and Commerce, University of Pennsylvania, 1969), especially pp. 35-41.
37. Unpublished report on investigations of the President's Committee on Government Contracts (Nixon Committee) in author's files.

CHAPTER IV

The Impact of Civil Rights and Full Employment, 1960-1969

The 1960's saw the beginnings of change in the racial occupational employment pattern in the southern pulp and paper industry. This change has been pushed by governmental civil rights agencies, but has moved slowly because of the institutional factors involved.

In other parts of the country, a few Negroes have been employed in northern and western paper mills, and thousands in converting plants. Expansion of Negro employment in the latter will be seen as largely a labor market phenomenon, although civil rights pressures and "affirmative action" have played a role.

THE EARLY 1960's

We have already noted that President Eisenhower's Committee on Government Contracts, under the leadership of the then Vice-President Richard M. Nixon, concentrated much of its equal opportunity efforts on the southern petroleum industry where it initiated desegregation and the opening up of opportunities for Negroes, but that its work and success in the southern paper industry were not significant.[38] When, however, President Kennedy organized his President's Committee on Equal Employment Opportunity as a successor to the Nixon Committee, the complaints from Negroes in the southern pulp and paper industry came to its attention almost immediately.

At this time both union relations and civil rights issues in the industry were ripe for upheaval. The labor issues would result in the displacement of the traditional AFL-CIO unions on the West Coast, the first major strike in International Paper's southern plants, and internal upheavals within both unions. The civil rights problems were closely related because they involved fundamental challenges to em-

---

38. F. Ray Marshall, *The Negro and Organized Labor* (New York: John Wiley & Sons, Inc., 1965), pp. 145-152; Carl B. King and Howard W. Risher, Jr., *The Negro in the Petroleum Industry,* The Racial Policies of American Industry, Report No. 5 (Philadelphia: Industrial Research Unit, Wharton School of Finance and Commerce, University of Pennsylvania, 1969), pp. 35-41.

ployment, upgrading, and seniority policies that, especially in the South, had become thoroughly institutionalized.

Aggravating both labor relations and civil rights issues was the industry's drive for increased efficiency which was spurred not only by union wage gains during the 1950's, but also by the recessions of 1958 and 1961. Many mills had difficulty obtaining sufficient orders to operate full time during this period, and the competition for sales spurred improved methods and technology, with resultant manpower reductions in a number of mills. Negro jobs and Negro employment were especially hard hit in the South, but this first heavy taste of job insecurity since World War II tended to harden the opposition of white workers to improved job opportunities for Negroes, while at the same time strengthening the demands of Negroes for a change in the racial-occupational pattern.

Stirring of Change in the South

The President's Committee on Equal Employment Opportunity created in 1961 by Executive Order 10925 was given a larger staff and greater authority than its predecessors to police equal job opportunity, to eliminate segregation and discrimination among government contractors, to insist on improvement or "affirmative action," and to bar companies from government contracts which were found in noncompliance. The opportunities offered by the promise of this Committee were grasped in behalf of Negro pulp and paper workers by two groups: the civil rights organizations and the leadership of the segregated Negro local unions.

Civil rights activities were stirring on all fronts in the early 1960's—consumer boycotts, sit-ins, registration campaigns, marches, etc. Along with demand for equal political and customer rights in the South came those for equal job rights. The National Association for the Advancement of Colored People (NAACP) and the Congress of Racial Equality (CORE) brought cases of discrimination in the paper industry to the attention of PCEEO.

More significant, however, were the efforts of the leaders of a number of segregated paper unions. Sitting in, often silently in negotiations, attending regional and national union conventions, and handling their own meetings, they had gained considerable leadership experience. As the proportion of Negroes in the southern mills continued to decline, these Negro union leaders began to speak out against the system which left them and their constituents "nonpromotable."

Within their unions, their protest evoked two responses. The first was annoyance and resentment. As Professor Marshall commented:

> In spite of the segregated local unions in the South, the paper union leaders argue that they have greatly improved the economic conditions of Negro workers and therefore resent charges of discrimination. These leaders apparently are unable to understand that in an earlier more paternalistic stage in union race relations, Negroes were more willing to have whites represent them and were not as inclined to protest segregated seniority rosters. Now, however, the ferment in the Negro community has produced demands for full equality.[39]

Union officials also responded with what seemed to be both a logical approach and compliance with federal demands for integrating local unions: they ordered the white and Negro locals to merge. This, however, did not always please the Negro groups who felt that they were being swallowed up, their leadership and representative positions destroyed, and at the same time, not really given equal rights on the job. The activities of white paper union local officials in Ku Klux Klan and White Citizens Council groups, their open support of measures to prevent integration in general, and their firm opposition to upgrading of Negroes,[40] all tended to support the proposition that local union integration without safeguards for Negro rights would not be a solution acceptable to the Negro unionists; nor would it necessarily promote equality.

That there has been opposition to a change in the status of the Negro pulp and paper workers on the part of the white workers and unionists in small southern communities should not be surprising. What has been at stake is not only a challenge to industrial practices but to the social structure as well. The highly paid white paper workers in these towns have become a sort of social elite. To some of them, having Negroes on the same jobs challenges their social position and in addition means more competition for work opportunities. Ingrained with what they believe is their "natural superiority" over blacks, these white mill employees see in integration a conspiracy

---

39. Marshall, *op. cit.,* p. 183.
40. For evidence of activities of white local union officials and members in Ku Klux Klan and Citizens Council groups, see Marshall, *op. cit.,* p. 184; *Wall Street Journal,* March 7, 1967, and *New York Times,* November 15, 1968. Further evidence will be set forth below in our accounts of the developments in Bogalusa and other towns.

not only to undermine their job rights, but also to alter the entire community structure as well.

In many cases, job integration in the mill towns is, in fact, just one aspect of altering the general *status quo*. It frequently involves not only job, but political consciousness, and in many of these communities if Negroes band together and vote, they can exercise much more influence. Moreover, as Negroes move into the better jobs, their increased purchasing power permits them to buy better housing and automobiles, to educate their children, and otherwise to put their income to work moving them and their families toward equality. Thus what has been at stake is indeed not only a better share of job opportunities, but of social and political life also.

Company responses to PCEEO requirements for the end of discriminatory practices were slow, but marked the first steps toward the reform of the discriminatory employment and upgrading system. Jobs formerly closed to Negroes were opened to them, but very few qualified. First, they were now required to pass the tests which heretofore had not been given them. Given their disproportionately poor education, training, and backgrounds and the real possibility of cultural disabilities in testing, Negroes found great difficulty in meeting test qualifications.

Moreover, in some companies the tests were applied to whites and Negroes on a differentiated basis. Thus in one Arkansas mill, tests were instituted in 1962 following the opening of all seniority lines to Negroes as well as to whites. This mill then required Negroes in the woodyard lines of progression who desired to enter the pulp mill to pass the two tests that all new hires must pass to qualify for employment. On the other hand, whites hired before 1962 who were in the pulp mill lines had not been tested nor were they required to be tested to progress to higher jobs.[41]

This application of testing was fairly common. It was defended on the grounds that even before testing was instituted, whites were selected for employment on more rigorous standards than were Negroes. Moreover, employers argued that equipment was becoming more complicated, and therefore limited employees should not be added to ones already on the force. It is difficult, however, to see how differential treatment on the basis of race was not in fact being continued, although the treatment was more sophisticated.

---

41. From the author's field notes, January 1967.

A second factor limiting the movement of Negroes during the early 1960's into jobs previously barred to them was the nature of the seniority system. For a man to transfer from one line of progression to another, he would usually be required, as already noted, to start at the bottom of the second line and to give up his seniority in the first. This meant not only loss of job security, but in many cases, an immediate wage reduction in order to qualify oneself for opportunities of higher wages later. The risks and immediate sacrifices involved were usually too great to expect any but a very few to attempt to qualify.

In addition to these institutional obstacles, the early 1960's saw relatively few jobs opening up in southern mills. The large expansion which occurred in the mid-1960's had not begun, and continued automation was offsetting such expansion as occurred.

Nevertheless, some Negroes did move into jobs previously reserved for whites, and won permanent spots at the bottom of seniority lines from which they had previously been barred. From this position they began the slow process of working up the occupational hierarchies that were once white men's preserves. In this they have been assisted by fundamental reversals of previous policies on the part of such companies as St. Regis Paper, Scott Paper, Mead, International, and Continental Can, and by the events which led to the "seniority credit" system developed in litigation by Crown Zellerbach and under government pressure, in bargaining by International Paper Company and others. Before examining these concepts, however, an analysis of the basic data of the 1960's is appropriate.

THE OVERALL PICTURE, 1964-1968

In 1960, the United States Census reported that 6.2 percent of the 579,844 paper and allied employees were Negroes (Table 12, p. 32). Table 15 indicates that there had been little change in the overall picture by the middle of the decade. The Equal Emloyment Opportunity Commission data show that 6.4 percent of 517,250 were Negroes. Of course, data collected by the census and the Equal Employment Opportunity Commission are not strictly comparable. The former are based on responses by people to census interrogators, the latter on reports filed by employers. Yet the great similarity of the findings lends credence to the belief that changes in the Negro ratio were not significant by 1966.

Table 15 also demonstrates that the first half of the 1960's saw little change in the racial occupational pattern of employment within

TABLE 15. *Paper and Allied Products Industry
Employment by Race, Sex, and Occupational Group
2,049 Establishments
Total United States, 1966*

Occupational Group	All Employees			Male			Female		
	Total	Negro	Percent Negro	Total	Negro	Percent Negro	Total	Negro	Percent Negro
Officials and managers	37,953	108	0.3	37,296	102	0.3	657	6	0.9
Professionals	15,133	27	0.2	14,536	24	0.2	597	3	0.5
Technicians	10,031	88	0.9	8,661	68	0.8	1,370	20	1.5
Sales workers	14,363	30	0.2	13,669	27	0.2	694	3	0.4
Office and clerical	47,667	556	1.2	15,877	238	1.5	31,790	318	1.0
Total white collar	125,147	809	0.6	90,039	459	0.5	35,108	350	1.0
Craftsmen	94,349	2,672	2.8	91,416	2,554	2.8	2,933	118	4.0
Operatives	188,508	14,345	7.6	150,324	12,143	8.1	38,184	2,202	5.8
Laborers	100,713	13,294	13.2	78,624	11,857	15.1	22,089	1,437	6.5
Service workers	8,533	2,024	23.7	7,675	1,820	23.7	858	204	23.8
Total blue collar	392,103	32,335	8.2	328,039	28,374	8.6	64,064	3,961	6.2
Total	517,250	33,144	6.4	418,078	28,833	6.9	99,172	4,311	4.3

Source: U. S. Equal Employment Opportunity Commission, *Job Patterns for Minorities and Women in Private Industry, 1966. Report No. 1* (Washington: The Commission, 1968), Part II.

the industry. Negro white collar employment remained at a minimum
—0.6 percent—only 809 Negroes of a total of 125,147 salaried employees, and about two-thirds of the 809 were in the lowest white
collar category, the office and clerical group. In contrast about 98
percent of all Negroes in the industry in 1966 were in blue collar
classifications. Negro blue collar workers, in turn, were decidedly underrepresented in the craftsmen's group—their share here (2.8 percent)
was typical of industry generally—and overrepresented in the service
and laborer occupational groups. About 43 percent of all Negroes
in the industry were classified as operatives, but their representation in
this category was only 7.6 percent.

THE 1964-1968 FIELD SAMPLE

The data published by the Equal Employment Opportunity Commission are also broken down by state and by major Standard Metropolitan Statistical Areas (cities and contiguous labor market areas).[42]
For our analysis, they are, however, deficient in two respects: They
are based on the period immediately after the effective date of Title
VII of the Civil Rights Act of 1964, which became effective in July
1965, and therefore do not reflect significant later developments; and
they do not distinguish mills from converters whereas, as has been
stressed, the jobs and the nature of Negro employment problems in
the two branches of the industry are significantly different.

Accordingly, data were gathered for this study for three years:
1964, 1966, and 1968. Although our sample is not as complete as
that of the EEOC, it is broadly representative. Our data involve,
with few exceptions, the same companies and plants in 1966 and
1968, and sufficient of these in 1964 to support the belief that all
three years are comparable. We are able, moreover, to utilize the
1966 EEOC data as a control to indicate any biases in our sample,
and thus avoid any distortions resulting from sampling procedure.
These will be noted where pertinent. The data gathered for this study
are thus able to give an excellent picture of developments over a span
of time in which both civil rights activity and legislation and economic
prosperity were at all-time high levels.

---

42. See U. S. Equal Employment Opportunity Commission, *Job Patterns for
    Minorities and Women in Private Industry, 1966*, Report No. 1 (Washington:
    The Commission, 1968), Parts I, II, and III.

The basic data resulting from our field study are set forth in the Appendix. Tables A-1—A-3 provide the figures for the three years for the entire industry, nationwide; Tables A-4—A-6, for mills; and Tables A-7—A-9 for converting plants. For convenience of analysis, the percentage of Negroes in the total industry, in the mills, and in converting plants, by occupational groups, for the years, 1964, 1966, and 1968, based upon the nine Tables, A-1—A-9, is set forth in Table 16. The 6.6 percent Negro complement for the total industry in 1966, shown in Table 16 is almost identical with that in Table 15, indicating that the data collected for this study are representative for the country as a whole.

A comparison of the three years shows very little change for the industry as a whole or for mills between 1964 and 1966. By 1966, however, the percentage of Negroes in converting plants began to increase, whereas in the mills that increase did not occur till after 1966. The reasons are not difficult to enumerate.

Converting plants, particularly corrugated box facilities, are highly susceptible to business fluctuations. As business expanded in the early 1960's, these plants expanded and added employees. With tight labor markets, and relatively low wages, converting plants also tend to lose workers to other businesses in such periods. The employees which are attracted are likely to be marginal, and often include large numbers of Negroes. This is particularly true, as we shall document below, for those plants located in center city areas. Although civil rights consciousness undoubtedly played a role in the improved Negro representation in converting plants, labor market conditions were most likely paramount, especially in the period prior to 1966.

In the mills, where turnover is small, a large expansion occurred, especially in the South, but new mills did not commence production in most cases till late 1966 at the earliest, and usually one or two years later. Moreover, as we shall note in our regional analyses below, relatively few changes in the racial employment pattern of the southern mills occurred prior to 1967. The analysis of the occupational representation of Negroes below confirms this slow reaction to civil rights pressures.

Officials and Managers

In 1964 and 1966, only 0.2 percent of the officials and managers in the industry were Negro, and in 1968, the percentage was 0.3 or

TABLE 16.　Paper and Allied Products Industry
Percent Negro Employment by Occupational Group
Total Industry, Mills, and Converting Plants
United States, 1964-1968

Occupational Group	Total Industry			Pulp, Paper, and Paperboard Mills			Converting Plants		
	1964	1966	1968	1964	1966	1968	1964	1966	1968
Officials and managers	0.2	0.2	0.3	0.1	0.1	0.3	0.3	0.3	0.4
Professionals	0.1	0.1	0.3	0.1	0.1	0.4	—	—	0.1
Technicians	0.5	0.6	1.2	0.5	0.5	1.3	0.7	1.4	0.8
Sales workers	0.2	0.2	0.3	0.3	0.1	0.2	0.1	0.2	0.4
Office and clerical	0.9	1.5	1.8	1.1	1.5	2.0	0.6	1.4	1.4
Total white collar	0.5	0.7	0.9	0.5	0.7	1.0	0.4	0.8	0.8
Craftsmen	1.5	1.9	2.2	1.0	1.3	1.5	2.7	4.1	4.2
Operatives	6.9	7.5	9.3	6.2	6.2	8.1	8.2	10.5	12.0
Laborers	15.3	15.3	15.2	18.6	15.8	15.6	11.2	14.6	14.7
Service workers	24.8	25.1	21.9	22.6	23.4	23.4	29.6	30.2	*
Total blue collar	7.8	8.1	9.0	7.6	7.0	8.0	8.3	10.6	11.0
Total	6.1	6.6	7.3	5.9	5.8	6.7	6.5	8.4	8.8

Source: Tables A-1 — A-9

*Because of a sampling error, no meaningful figure available. (See Table A-9.) There is no reason to suppose that the percentage of Negroes in service jobs varied significantly between 1966 and 1968.

63 Negroes of a total of 19,162 (Table A-3). The percentages for mills and converters were not significantly different. Moreover, nearly all Negroes in these classifications were minor supervisors, and in turn, the bulk of these supervised only members of their own race, particularly in the mill yards or woods. The few exceptions are usually in personnel departments where they have been employed by a few companies in order to aid in improving the recruitment of black personnel. A few of these personnel appointments have been in the mills, but most in central offices.

In today's market, the paper industry has relatively little attraction for the Negro with managerial potential. The industry, with the exception of a few companies, did not commence recruiting them until after many other industries had deservedly earned a reputation for much greater effort in civil rights matters. Moreover, few Negroes who are educated and aspire to high jobs in industry desire to live in mill towns. In the North, Midwest, and Far West, such areas are almost devoid of Negro families; in the South, the mill towns often feature a history of rigid discrimination and today promise little in the way of educational, cultural, or social opportunities for the successful Negro and his family and often few opportunities for acceptable housing.

Except for staff jobs, management in the paper industry is likely to be heavily engineering oriented. Few Negroes are as yet engineering graduates, and those that are find much more glamorous and hospitable industries bidding for their services, while relatively few of the paper companies are working vigorously to improve their representation of Negro managers. In converting plants, where location is not adverse to educated Negro employees, as is often the case with the mills, management is largely developed in the companies from sales or engineering, in neither of which fields have Negroes been represented. One may, therefore, expect slow progress at best.

Professional and Technical

The shortage of Negro engineers and chemists has been noted many times. The paper industry has been able to attract a few of these persons, an occasional accountant, but by 1968 had a Negro complement of only 0.3 percent in the professional group and 1.2 percent in the technical classification. Few professional or technical personnel are found in converting plants. Most large mills maintain a laboratory and sometimes a company's main research center is found in a mill complex, although most large concerns have research centers that are located away from all manufacturing facilities.

Professional and technical employment in the industry is, however, a minor factor, being less than 5 percent of the industry's total employment. Some of the most exciting development work for the industry is performed by vendors to it—the manufacturers of equipment, coatings, and chemicals. It is not likely that many qualified Negro professionals or technicians, who now have a wide range of opportunities to exercise their talents, will look to the paper industry for employment. Although jobs once closed to Negroes are now open to them, comparatively few paper companies affirmatively attempt to employ Negroes in these higher categories to the same degree as do concerns in many other industries. St. Regis, Scott, and International Paper have done such recruiting and have been able to employ a few. In general, however, we can expect very slow progress in these occupational groups.

Sales

Sales personnel comprise little more than 1 percent of the total employment in the industry. Mills generally sell a large portion of their output to captive markets, and the use of independent sales agents is common. Converting plants often sell to jobbers or wholesalers who have a large sales staff; in many instances the key function of the converting plant manager is to handle the accounts of its few major customers.

Of course, both mills and converting plants do employ sales personnel. Such selling jobs are generally held by those who understand how to exploit contacts and remain in the good graces of purchasing agents, for essentially the product is not differentiated. Selling becomes under these conditions a highly social relationship.

Paper is graded as are most converted paper products. There are some proprietary items made in the industry. For the most part, however, companies sell products which meet industry or government specifications and which are basically no different than those of its competitors. Said one manufacturer of corrugated boxes:

It is like selling postage stamps. My competitors make the same product, and can give the same service and quality. We are doing very well—for one and only one reason. That reason is M——— [the plant manager]. He has convinced seven companies, who account for 80 percent of our output, that they should buy from us. His contacts, personality, and performance have them sewed up. I employ six salesmen who account for the other 20 percent of the business. I don't need them except as an investment in the future. Right now, I concentrate only on keeping M—— happy so that he holds on to the seven customers—and this job![43]

It is very difficult for Negroes to break into this circle. Country clubs and the social whirl are more often than not closed to them; their newness in industry—particularly in salaried jobs—means few business contacts have been made prior to employment. And they always face the possibility of social and business rebuffs by purchasing agents.

Nevertheless, a few companies, such as St. Regis, Crown Zellerbach, Mead, Scott, and International have successfully employed outside salesmen. Such salesmen have found that, particularly, in the metropolitan areas of New York and Chicago, they can be accepted on their merits. In several cases, however, they have left paper companies to join concerns in other industries, sometimes for salary increases, but in other cases because they found a more encouraging environment elsewhere. Our sample found only twelve sales personnel in 1968—and some of these are inside order takers or handlers. Progress, again, is likely to be slow with so many factors against success and an industry that in general hesitates to alter its practices.

Office and Clerical

One occupational group in which Negroes have made considerable progress during the last several years has been that of office and clerical work. Civil rights pressure combined with increased office and paper work and labor shortages have eased the path for increased equal opportunity in this field of endeavor.

The progress in the paper industry has not been great. Converting plants employ very small office forces; by 1968 only 1.4 percent of these were Negro. Mills have done a little better, reaching the 2 percent mark by this date. In the mills, progress has been slowed by the slight turnover. Mill offices provide the best female jobs in small towns and women tend to hold on to them even after childbirth. Even granting the difficulties, it does seem clear that the paper industry has not made the effort that has achieved results for many industries, such as aerospace.

---

43. Interview, January 1969.

Craftsmen

Craftsmen are a key group in the mills. They not only comprise
23.3 per cent of the total mill force (Table 7, p. 20), but they maintain the huge and ever more complex and expensive machinery, instruments, and controls. Second only to the top personnel on the
paper machines, the maintenance men are an elite group. And like
the paper machine crews they have usually been all white.

The underrepresentation of Negroes in the crafts and trades is not
unique to the paper industry. Although much of the trades work in the
pre-Civil War South was performed by slaves, most trades have been
closed to them since. A vicious circle of inadequate training, job
discrimination, and active trade union exclusion has depressed Negro
representation in nearly all trades in the South since the Civil War,
while never permitting them more than a slight foothold elsewhere.[44]
Even in industries such as automobiles and aerospace, where Negroes
have made substantial progress,[45] they remain underrepresented in
the crafts.

The problem starts before entrance into industry has occurred. Paper
companies, as others, select carefully for the skilled crafts and the
apprentice and training groups leading to these jobs. But Negroes
often have had inferior education in segregated or center city schools.
As a report of the National Association for the Advancement of
Colored People pointed out in 1960:

> Available evidence indicates that Negro youth are deleteriously placed with
> respect to the pre-training factor. Nationally, fewer Negroes attend secondary
> school than whites. They also evidence a lower rate of completion. Because
> of a lack of motivation, derived in part from acknowledged parental frustra-
> tions in the field of employment, portions of Negro youth completing high
> school are not commensurate with its importance in later years . . . Negro
> youths do not emerge from high schools in desirable numbers, nor, if they
> do, is their training on par with that of white youth. . . .[46]

---

44. See Herbert R. Northrup, *Organized Labor and the Negro* (New York: Harper
    & Bros., 1944), Chapter II.
45. See Herbert R. Northrup, *The Negro in the Automobile Industry*. The Racial
    Policies of American Industry, Report No. 1 (Philadelphia: Industrial Research
    Unit, Wharton School of Finance and Commerce, University of Pennsylvania,
    1968), pp. 37-41; *ibid.*, *The Negro in the Aerospace Industry*. The Racial
    Policies of American Industry, Report No. 2 (Philadelphia: Industrial Research
    Unit, Wharton School of Finance and Commerce, University of Pennsylvania,
    1968), pp. 45-50.
46. National Association for the Advancement of Colored People, *The Negro Wage-
    Earner and Apprenticeship Training* (New York: The Association, 1960), p. 15.

The paper mills, until recently, did not employ Negro craftsmen, except in a few instances. These exceptions were likely to be in the bricklaying or masonry trades in the South, in which Negroes have been heavily represented since slavery days.[47] The bulk of the paper mill craftsmen, however, are not found in these trades, but in the electrical and mechanical ones, in which Negroes, North and South, have been traditionally and systematically excluded. Moreover, these are the trades that require the most mathematical and communication skills and the most education generally. Typically, those who perform best in such skills have mechanical backgrounds, often having tinkered with automobiles and motors, and worked with mechanically inclined and/or employed parents. Disabilities in education and background are especially strong among Negroes and harmful in competing for training and jobs.

Located as they usually are in isolated areas and paying high wages, mills attract a high caliber mechanic and apprentice. With paper machine work, these are the best jobs in the mill, and usually in the area. Now that mill hiring policies have changed as a result of civil rights pressures, the mill managements are finding that the supply of qualified labor is very limited. This is true, not only for the reasons summarized in the already quoted NAACP report. In addition, Negroes with qualifications to handle apprentice training, like many of their white counterparts, are more likely to choose to enter college than to accept apprenticeship training. Finally, of course, given alternative opportunities, Negroes are often not convinced that the paper industry will provide the potential that industries which historically accepted civil rights programs more quickly and with more visible results have accomplished.

Craft work requires intimate teamwork and coordination of personnel who are frequently only lightly supervised. Discrimination and ill treatment under these circumstances are easily perpetuated and difficult to control. Given the historic relationships in the mills, in North as well as South, it is not likely that there will be a marked improvement in the number of Negro craftsmen in the mills. The author's

---

47. The large amount of brick and cement work done by maintenance crews in steel mills accounts in part for the relatively high percentage of Negro craftsmen in this industry. See Richard L. Rowan, *The Negro in the Steel Industry*. The Racial Policies of American Industry, Report No. 3 (Philadelphia: Industrial Research Unit, Wharton School of Finance and Commerce, University of Pennsylvania, 1968), pp. 67-68.

field visits found few Negro apprentices in the mechanical trades and virtually none in the electrical ones. A number of companies, however, are now giving this aspect of recruiting their special attention with the result that a sprinkling of Negro apprentices is likely to be found in some of the larger company plants. Of the Negro mechanics who were on the job, most had worked into their positions after serving as helpers and "picking up" the trade. This seems to be the most likely route by which Negroes may find their way into craft jobs. Yet even then, their numbers neither have been, nor are likely to be large.

The situation in converting plants is rather different. Located more in large cities than in country towns, and often hard pressed to find employees, converting plants have turned to large-scale use of Negro labor, not only in unskilled jobs, but in craft work as well. Unfortunately, craftsmen's jobs in converting plants are neither as skilled, as well paid, nor proportionately as numerous as in the mills.

Nevertheless, the percentage gains for Negro workers in converting plants have been substantial. Between 1964 and 1968, the proportion of Negro craftsmen rose from 2.7 percent to 4.2 percent. The author's field work in early 1969 indicates that the improvement in the percentage of Negro craftsmen has continued. Here again, labor market forces and civil rights pressures have worked together to effectuate significant change.

Operatives

As in most industries, the term "operative" in the paper industry covers a wide range of skills. It includes some basically entry jobs, and others which require months, or even years of training. In the paper industry, those Negroes classified as operatives are most likely to be found in the lower brackets of the general category. They were, until recently, either not hired for, or not permitted to advance into the better jobs.

In the mill yards, Negroes have tended to take over many, although not all, of the equipment operator positions where equipment replaced hand labor. On the other hand, some displacement of Negro hand laborers by white equipment operators has occurred. Moreover, mills built since 1950, as already noted, often used white machine and equipment operators in contrast to older mills, which gave Negroes some opportunities to man machines when mechanization occurred.

The tendency to use whites on yard equipment and the total exclusion till recently of Negroes from jobs on the paper machine and from most pulp mill operative positions, accounts for the poor representation of Negroes as operatives in the industry. In 1966, for example, only 6.2 percent of those in mills were Negroes. In contrast, the percentage in the automobile industry was 20.2, and that in steel 17.8.[48] Even in aerospace, with its great emphasis on skill, 11.9 percent of the operatives were Negro in 1966.[49] On the other hand, the percentage of operatives in the petroleum industry, which has had a similar history to paper mills, and once featured a similar racial occupational employment pattern, was 6.8 in 1966[50]—almost identical to that of the paper mills. (We shall note below that the existence of a large laborer group may be a factor in reducing the percentage of Negro operatives in paper mills.)

In the converting plants, Negroes have fared better. Again, the work is less skilled and the increasing needs of the industry to utilize Negroes as a source of employees tend to insure that the available Negro labor force will be utilized.

On the other hand, discrimination is not always absent. The author noticed a tendency in some northern corrugating plants to assign Negroes to the heavy loading in machine take-off jobs; and in some southern plants to remove jobs from the logical progressions when such jobs were occupied by Negroes. Nevertheless, it appears evident that civil rights and labor market pressures will continue to effect an increase in the percentage of Negro operatives in converting, who in 1968 had 12 percent of the jobs in this occupational category as compared with 8.2 percent in 1964.

Laborers and Service Workers

The classification "laborer" has been substantially eliminated from many industries by a combination of automation which has substituted equipment for brawn and by worker and union pressure which has resulted in the reclassification of some work from the laborer to the operative occupational group. In the paper mills, however, laborers, in 1968, comprised 16.2 percent of the labor force and in con-

---

48. See Northrup, *The Negro in the Automobile Industry, op. cit.,* p. 36; Rowan, *op. cit.,* p. 59.
49. Northrup, *The Negro in the Aerospace Industry, op. cit.,* p. 37.
50. King and Risher, *op. cit.,* p. 47.

verting plants, 22.5 percent. (Table 7, p. 20.) In contrast, laborers made up only 3.4 percent of the employees of the Big Three automobile companies in 1966.[51]

There are several reasons for the existence of the large laborer group in the paper industry. There are, first of all, many laborer jobs in the woods, yards, and generally around the mills, although the number has been greatly reduced. Second, in the South, particularly, the existence of the racial employment pattern tended to reduce union interest in upgrading the classification and/or changing its nomenclature. These were primarily Negro jobs although some white laborers have always been employed, and laborer was deemed a fit name for the work—which in truth was originally descriptive of the job. Even as jobs were expanded, enlarged, or made more difficult, the laborer designation has sometimes remained.

In converting plants, laborer work remains common. The industry has made surprisingly little progress with mechanizing its material handling, so that nearly one-fourth of the converting labor force is classified as laborers—a situation found in few other manufacturing enterprises today. Both in mills and in converting plants, Negroes have a disproportionate share of the laboring and service worker categories—certainly not an uncommon situation.

Female Employment

As noted in Chapter II, females in the paper industry are employed in three basic areas: offices, converting plants other than corrugated box factories, and in packing and shipping departments of fine paper and other mills in which small lots are assembled and sold. Since the paper industry, with a few significant company exceptions, has not taken a leading role in the integration of minorities in white collar jobs, it is not surprising that Negro women have not achieved a high proportion of the office and clerical jobs in the industry—1 percent in 1968. (Table A-3.)

For reasons already noted, few Negro women have obtained jobs in mill offices, and no great progress can be predicted, given the job competition in mill towns, the disadvantaged educational backgrounds of Negroes in the small southern towns and rural areas, and the fact that the best educated and most aggressive Negroes are likely to leave

---

51. Northrup, *The Negro in the Automobile Industry, op. cit.,* p. 5.

these areas. In the North, those few mills which are located in areas where Negroes dwell have, like industry generally, begun to employ Negro clerks, secretaries, and other female salaried personnel, but the number and proportion as our data in Appendix Tables A-5 and A-6 show, is not very substantial.

In the converting plant offices, Negro women have not fared much better although many of these plant offices are located in areas easily accessible to Negro urban dwellers. Many of these offices are small, and the tendency is for managers to hire "their own kind." Now that some companies are looking for Negro clerical employees, they find them in short supply and more anxious to work in larger, better appointed city center offices than in plants which are in factory areas and often without pleasant surroundings.

Negro women are beginning to be accepted in fine paper and other small lot paper mill packaging and shipping, in tissue plants, and in other light mill jobs traditionally considered female work. This is now true in the South as elsewhere. In a few plants of this type located in northern city areas, they comprise a substantial proportion of the total force, but for the most part, their proportion is not high. With the normal turnover that occurs in such work and the desire of such companies as Scott, Union Camp, and Kimberly-Clark to increase their proportion of Negro employees, one can expect a gradual increase in Negro female representation in jobs of this character.

On the other hand, there is no immediate likelihood of an increase in female employment, white or black, in the basic mill work. As the South Carolina Department of Labor data demonstrate (Table 13, p. 34), Negro women performed some of the mill jobs during World War II, but were quickly replaced when the war ended. Given the plentiful supply of white and black male labor now available in most mill towns, one cannot expect any increase in female mill employment in the near future.

In converting plants, a high female ratio is found in all but corrugated box facilities where heavy lifting and handling greatly reduces the demand for women. Many of the converting operations other than those in corrugated box plants require sorting, small lot packaging, or other light work in which females are traditionally used. We shall demonstrate below that the extent of Negro employment in converting plants today is essentially governed by the locational factor. If the plant is located near a center of Negro population, it will have a substantially larger Negro work force than if it is located in a suburban or other largely white populated area. Negro female representation in such plants follows the same general rule.

Actually, Negro female employment in converting plants today is no longer seriously controversial. It commenced during World War II as a matter of company labor market requirements, and has proceeded generally as a function of labor needs and black labor availability. For example, during the Korean War, a company in the upper South, desirous of opening a multiwall bag plant, found that no satisfactory white female labor was available. It recruited Negro women and has had a black production work force ever since. Seventy miles away, in a more rural but heavily Negro populated area, a large new multiwall plant was built by another company which walled off one section where Negro sewing operators worked. The latter comprised a small minority of the plant and were organized in a separate local union. In other southern bag plants, only whites were employed except as janitors and laborers.[52]

In recent years, labor shortages have again contributed to increased Negro female employment in converting plants, especially as noted, where they are found in locations of Negro labor availability. These increases have been reduced by the replacement of many sewn operations with pasted ones, the failure of the multiwall bag business to grow as a result of increasing bulk shipments of cement, fertilizer, and chemicals, and automation and improvements in equipment. Nevertheless, general expansion in other converting paper businesses and continued labor shortages indicate further increases in Negro female employment are likely to occur in converting plants.

LOCATIONAL FACTORS

Where a plant is located—both within an area in relation to the centers of Negro population and in what region——has an effect on employment opportunities for Negroes. This section discusses the impact of plant location within areas generally. Regional differences and impacts are discussed in the next chapter.

Pulp and paper mills, except for wastepaper mills, are not particularly well suited for urban areas. To be sure, they are found in some

52. From the author's field notes.

heavily populated areas, but most of those are older mills. The mill layout requires tremendous areas for wood storage, water pollution control, water intake treatment, as well as for the actual mill buildings. Water and air discharges and odors tend to make neighbors unhappy. Another primary reason, of course, is the fact that the forests which supply raw material are not found in urban areas.

The typical mill, therefore, is located today in rural areas. Only in the South do Negroes dwell in such areas. Thus only in the South is intraregion location favorable to Negro employment insofar as the mills are concerned.

Mills manufacturing box board or other products from waste or reclaimed paper are the exception to this rule. Urban areas generate wastepaper in huge quantities, and these mills are generally found in cities for that reason. Although separate data for such plants are not available, field visits and discussions with company personnel tended to confirm the impression that wastepaper mills employ a proportion of Negroes that is above average for the industry, particularly in northern and western cities. One factor is the location in urban areas and the availability of Negro labor there. Another is the relative unpleasantness of the work. It involves much heavy lifting and not too pleasant "broke" operations. Since wastepaper machines are comparatively small and less productive than those in the bigger rural mills, the wages tend to be lower and often not competitive with others in the community. Whites therefore tend to compete for these jobs much less avidly than for other mill work, giving Negroes a greater opportunity.

For converting plants, urban location is a prime factor in Negro employment. Table 17 compares the number and percentage of Negro employees in converting plants generally with those located in large cities, for three regions. Within each region, the percentage of Negroes is substantially larger in the urban areas where not only a substantial proportion of our nation's Negroes dwell, but in addition where other opportunities are available to whites on a proportionately greater basis than in suburban or rural areas.

The concentration of Negroes in urban converting plants is heavily related to the corrugated box branch of the industry. These plants serve other industries and locate near them to be of service and to reduce freight charges. Throughout the country, however, industry is tending to move out of the cities to rural areas or to suburban in-

74   *The Negro in the Paper Industry*

TABLE 17. *Paper and Allied Products Industry
Employment by Race, Selected Regions and Urban Areas
Converting Plants, 1968*

	Region			Urban Area*		
	Total Employees	Negro	Percent Negro	Total Employees	Negro	Percent Negro
Midwest	34,628	2,129	6.1	7,335	1,000	13.6
Far West	10,078	507	5.0	2,100	167	8.0
South	19,843	3,387	17.1	4,352	1,100	25.3

Source: Data in author's possession and Appendix Tables A-36, A-45, and A-54.
Separate data for New England and Middle Atlantic cities not available in sufficient quantity for analysis.

Note: For regional definitions, see Table 4, p. 15.

*Plants in the following cities are included in these data:

Midwest: Chicago, Cincinnati, Cleveland, Detroit, Indianapolis, Milwaukee, Minneapolis, and St. Louis.

Far West: Los Angeles, Portland, and Seattle.

South: Atlanta, Dallas, Houston, and New Orleans.

dustrial parks and other locations. Inevitably the corrugated box plants will do likewise. Thus despite their strong position in the industry, Negroes could see their jobs reduced unless they can and will move with them.

Multiwall bag, grocery bag, and sack plants generally serve customers in a wider radius and thus are not likely to be so concentrated in urban areas. They are more likely to be located to serve a region, and many are already located in outlying areas from cities. On the other hand, folding box plants tend to be closely related locationally to customers and are heavily urban centered, with resultant high Negro employment.

RACIAL RESTRICTIONS AND INTRAPLANT MOVEMENT

Racial restrictions on the intraplant movement of Negroes are, of course, mostly a southern phenomenon. What many ignore, however, is that such restrictions are not found elsewhere perhaps not primarily because of an absence of prejudice. As Professor Marshall has pointed out, "the race problem in the paper industry is restricted mainly to the South because there are relatively few Negroes in this industry outside the South."[53] This statement, of course, applies to mills, not converting plants where the seniority systems are far less complicated because the same training needs, job qualifications, or intricate machinery and processes are lacking, and where Negroes comprise a substantial portion of the work force in all regions.

Of course, discrimination is not absent from converting plants. A Negro student of the author, working one summer in the employment office of a Philadelphia container plant, found that Negro applicants were regularly assigned to heaviest material handling work, while whites were given less onerous jobs. In the South the author encountered seniority arrangements which kept Negro "take-off" employees out of the progression of lithograph and printing presses.

Nevertheless, seniority in a converting plant is relatively broad and movement comparatively rapid. Turnover is much higher than in the mills and the demand for labor such that today, opportunities for Negroes are fairly good. However discriminatory a system might have been, it does not tend to perpetuate limits on the intraplant movement of Negroes in the converting plants because of the breadth of seniority, the turnover, and general expansion which has occurred.

In the mills, all this is different. Here because of the relative absence of Negroes in northern mills, the problem is essentially a southern one. When the industry entered the South in force, it had never had any real experience with Negro labor, and like industry generally, followed local custom. As already noted, its view then accorded with the more liberal southern approaches. It did not exclude Negroes like its neighboring industry, textiles. Having much heavy laboring work and few women, it adopted a policy consistent with its needs by hiring Negroes essentially into labor pools and whites into operating departments. Again according to Professor Marshall:

The main difference between Northern and Southern paper mills was that workers in the labor pool (Negroes) did a lot of the work in the South that was done elsewhere by the operators and their helpers. In the paper industry, as in others, the separate seniority rosters were not invented solely to segregate jobs racially, but also were based on the training needs of the companies involved. The fact that Negroes were hired only for menial, dead-end jobs meant that they usually were not as qualified as whites to move into many higher-paying skilled jobs which could not be filled on the basis of seniority alone.[54]

53. Marshall, *op. cit.*, p. 183.
54. *Ibid.*

The Seniority System Rationale

This statement requires considerable elaboration and refinement. In both this and in previous chapters, the seniority system in the mills has been examined, with special note of its perversion by racial restrictions which have adversely affected the intraplant movement of Negroes. Again it should be emphasized that the seniority system, if not altered for racial factors, *per se,* is not discriminatory, but rather has developed from the natural progression of jobs and in-plant training requirements in the industry.

Since work in a pulp mill or yard does not in fact qualify one for work in a paper mill, there is no reason why seniority in one sector of such work should be exercisable in another. Indeed, quite the contrary is true. Not only is a pulp mill employee, for example, unqualified to exercise seniority in a paper mill, except at a beginning job, but in addition, it would be both destructive and dangerous to attempt any interchange of such work: destructive because of the probability that inexperience would result in the ruin of expensive fourdrinier wire, rollers, instruments, or machinery; dangerous because of the ease of injury to an inexperienced person, or to others which could easily result.

Moreover, employers that insist that employees who leave one seniority line to enter another give up their seniority in their former occupation are not being capricious. Back and forth movement implied by dual line seniority requires extra training, upsetting bumpings, and is costly both directly and because of its impact on efficient production. Similarly, employers understandably insist that a person entering a progression line should be qualified to achieve eventually the top rating in that line. Otherwise, a line can be "blocked" at the middle—occupied by those incapable of upward movement. Blocked personnel prevent those below them from being properly trained on the job for positions above them. In addition, they frequently become less effective on the job, especially if equipment becomes more complicated, as seems always to occur.

Mill seniority rules, in their pure, nonracial form, therefore, like seniority rules in other industries, were developed to meet the needs of the industry. They are logical devices for on-the-job training and intraplant movement. Their use as a racially restrictive device required two characteristics: union-management perversion of the natural seniority rules to create nonpromotable jobs and to break off some natural progression lines; and management policy of employing Negroes and whites on a racially segregated basis with Negroes confined to lower-rated and less pleasant jobs.

Impact of Racial Restrictions

The effect of perverting the natural seniority system undoubtedly initially led to the employment of Negroes who otherwise might not have been hired. Given the status of Negro training and education during the 1930's and 1940's in the South, and especially in the rural South, it is unlikely that many Negroes could have competed for jobs in paper plants if they had been required to possess the same qualifications as whites. Yet some undoubtedly could have done so. Moreover, it must be noted, that southern whites, although much better educated and trained than Negroes at this time, more often than not were not high school graduates or well-versed in industrial processes before they were employed by paper mills. Indeed, as already noted, the companies for a number of years imported key personnel from the North when a mill was built.

Thus although the racially restricted seniority rules designed for Negroes as nonpromotable employees permitted employment of low-qualified and even illiterate persons, they also blocked those who might have advanced and gave opportunities to whites but denied them to Negroes of equal qualification or potential. Moreover, these rules insured that Negroes would be the disproportionate victims of technological unemployment. Unskilled jobs are always the easiest to replace, and the most susceptible to elimination by equipment substitutes or improvements. Wood handling, pulp mill, and powerhouse laboring jobs were largely eliminated in the 1950's, and Negro employment fell substantially.

Of course, a jim crow system is designed to make the employment of Negroes more costly. It is an historic fact that jim crow laws were a product of the era following the Civil War Reconstruction when there occurred the rise to power in the South of the poor white working and farmer classes. Their objective in "putting the Negro in his place" was, among other things, to curb the competition of Negro labor. By confining Negroes to segregated living areas, they were removed from job information and factory locations; by jim crow transportation, Negroes found it more difficult and unpleasant to get to work; by jim crow schools and training, Negroes were made less qualified to compete for work; and by requiring employers to segregate Negroes as employees and to provide duplicate eating, sanitary, and locker-room facilities, these laws made it more expensive to employ Negroes.

Jim crowism thus made Negro labor an adversely differentiated product. Jim crow seniority rules confined that product to particular jobs and departments. If no Negroes were used in the paper mill, no segregated facilities there were essential. As the paper industry grew in the South, the custom of assigning a few Negro laborers to each mill department ceased. Segregated facilities then were required only in the yard, or if a few tube lancers remained, in the pulp mill unless they were required to use yard facilities too. The mill seniority rules, the separate local unions, and discriminatory hiring policies were thus the natural outgrowth of the jim crow system and its successful efforts to make Negro labor most costly and thus less competitive to white labor.

The Legacy of the Discriminatory Seniority

The long, narrow functional seniority progression lines in the mills tend to reduce intraplant movement. Progress up the job hierarchy is confined to one ladder. As the employees near the top, they become very reluctant to leave their jobs since comparable work and pay in the area are generally lacking. Moreover, a transfer would ordinarily result in loss of seniority and the start of the cycle all over again from the bottom job.

The exception to this rule is when new mills open. Generally such mills are flooded with applications of persons who see the opportunity to jump, for example, from fourth hand on a paper machine to back tender, the No. 2 spot. New mills often have a pick of experienced personnel—another reason for the tendency after 1950 for these mills to have fewer Negroes than older ones. Mechanization and automation in the older mills, however, has offset the impact of job changing to a great extent so that turnover remains low and movement up the occupational hierarchies continues to be slow.

Under these circumstances, Negroes who have been excluded from key lines of progression have not only been denied entrance into certain job classifications for the period of the exclusion, but in fact for the better jobs, for many years after the lines of progression are opened up to them. Ending exclusion and tying together seniority lines in a rational, nondiscriminatory manner only opens the door. After Negroes are admitted to the bottom jobs, they must progress up the ladder. It can take five, ten, or even twenty years to reach a top job in a mill progression. For the Negro who was hired twenty years ago, the opportunity to reach a top mill job may have passed if normal progression is followed once exclusion is eliminated.

Thus discrimination tends to perpetuate itself. Merely ending a discriminatory practice does not make whole those who have suffered discrimination nor does it alter for many years the pattern of employment which was created by years of discrimination. For these reasons, courts and government equal employment agencies have become interested in devising methods which attempt to make employees whole by giving them an opportunity to achieve their "rightful place" in the job hierarchy. The impact of the "rightful place" doctrine can be best understood after our discussion of the regional employment situation in more detail, which follows in the next chapter.

CHAPTER V

The Impact of Region, Unions, and Government

The key to Negro employment opportunity in pulp and paper mills has always been in the South. Here is the new center of the industry and here is where expansion has been concentrated in the post-World War II era. And here is where Negro employment has always been both the greatest and the most circumscribed.

In the South, too, union policies have been the most concerned with Negro employees. Discriminatory seniority systems and jim crow local unions are southern union issues. Likewise, it is in the South that the government has moved most vigorously to alter union-management racial practices. It is, therefore, most fitting to examine in detail the racial policies in the southern mills. Before doing so, however, a brief look at other regions will serve to emphasize in what respects southern practices are unique.

REGIONAL PATTERNS, NORTH AND WEST

For purpose of analysis, the non-South areas have been divided into four areas—New England, Middle Atlantic, Midwest, and Far West (regional definitions are found in Table 4, p. 15). In New England, of course, the mills are located primarily in the Maine woods where Negroes simply do not dwell. Table 18 reports the data compiled by the Equal Employment Opportunity Commission for New England paper establishments in 1966. There just 1.1 percent of the industry work force in this region was Negro.

Table 19 summarizes the New England data from our field sample for the years 1964, 1966, and 1968, which are detailed in Appendix Tables A-10—A-18. Table 19, which when compared with Table 18, indicates that our sample is very accurate, shows what one would expect: most Negroes in the New England paper industry are found in converting plants. The slight increase in the proportion of Negroes over the four years is probably primarily the result of labor market

TABLE 18. *Paper and Allied Products Industry Employment By Race, Sex, and Occupational Group 167 Establishments New England Region, 1966*

Occupational Group	All Employees			Male			Female		
	Total	Negro	Percent Negro	Total	Negro	Percent Negro	Total	Negro	Percent Negro
Officials and managers	3,507	4	0.1	3,434	4	0.1	73	—	—
Professionals	1,303	1	0.1	1,266	1	0.1	37	—	—
Technicians	1,211	2	0.2	1,028	2	0.2	183	—	—
Sales workers	941	1	0.1	835	1	0.1	106	—	—
Office and clerical	4,700	10	0.2	1,376	5	0.4	3,324	5	0.2
Total white collar	11,662	18	0.2	7,939	13	0.2	3,723	5	0.1
Craftsmen	10,770	56	0.5	10,335	55	0.5	435	1	0.2
Operatives	17,753	241	1.4	13,750	187	1.4	4,003	54	1.3
Laborers	9,271	252	2.7	7,600	182	2.4	1,671	70	4.2
Service workers	830	7	0.8	759	7	0.9	71	—	—
Total blue collar	38,624	556	1.4	32,444	431	1.3	6,180	125	2.0
Total	50,286	574	1.1	40,383	444	1.1	9,903	130	1.3

Source: U. S. Equal Employment Opportunity Commission, *Job Patterns for Minorities and Women in Private Industry, 1966.* Report No. 1 (Washington: The Commission, 1968), Part II.

Note: For regional definitions, see Table 4, p. 15.

TABLE 19. Paper and Allied Products Industry
Percent of Negro Employment by Occupational Group
Total Industry, Mills, and Converting Plants
New England Region, 1964-1968

Occupational Group	Total Industry			Pulp, Paper, and Paperboard Mills			Converting Plants		
	1964	1966	1968	1964	1966	1968	1964	1966	1968
Officials	—	0.1	0.1	—	—	—	—	0.4	0.3
Professionals	—	—	0.2	—	—	0.2	—	—	—
Technicians	—	0.4	0.2	—	—	0.2	—	2.6	—
Sales workers	—	0.3	—	—	—	—	—	0.5	—
Office and clerical	0.1	0.2	0.3	—	—	0.1	0.2	0.5	0.9
Total white collar	*	0.2	0.2	—	—	0.1	0.1	0.5	0.5
Craftsmen	0.5	0.5	0.7	0.1	0.1	0.2	1.2	1.8	2.9
Operatives	1.5	1.6	2.1	0.7	0.2	0.7	2.4	4.9	5.2
Laborers	0.9	2.7	2.4	0.2	0.4	0.6	1.9	7.4	4.8
Service workers	1.0	1.7	1.3	0.7	1.0	1.0	1.7	3.4	2.0
Total blue collar	1.1	1.5	1.6	0.4	0.2	0.5	2.0	4.8	4.5
Total	0.9	1.2	1.3	0.3	0.2	0.4	1.6	3.9	3.7

Source: Tables A-10—A-18
*Less than 0.05 percent.

conditions in southern New England cities. Although some improvement was made in Negro white collar representation, it was very small.

The Middle Atlantic region showed a much higher Negro employee complement in 1966—7.1 percent. One would expect this, given the concentrations of Negroes in key cities there. Moreover, as Table 20 shows, Negroes, although very unrepresented in salaried positions, were much better represented in the Middle Atlantic establishments than in those farther north. The 4.6 percent Negro craftsmen ratio is also quite high.

This relatively high Negro representation in key jobs is the result not only of labor market factors in converting plants. There are a large number of wastepaper mills in this region and some larger facilities, such as the Scott Paper complex in Chester, Pennsylvania. Both labor market and civil rights pressures have combined to further Negro employment in all occupational groups.

Table 21, which summarizes Appendix Tables A-19—A-27, shows the trend of Negro employment, 1964-1968, for the industry in the

TABLE 20. *Paper and Allied Products Industry*
Employment by Race, Sex, and Occupational Group
399 Establishments
Middle Atlantic Region, 1966

Occupational Group	All Employees			Male			Female		
	Total	Negro	Percent Negro	Total	Negro	Percent Negro	Total	Negro	Percent Negro
Officials and managers	7,413	45	0.6	7,197	43	0.6	216	2	0.9
Professionals	3,122	12	0.4	2,884	11	0.4	238	1	0.4
Technicians	2,138	53	2.5	1,820	42	2.3	318	11	3.5
Sales workers	4,038	18	0.4	3,899	16	0.4	139	2	1.4
Office and clerical	10,313	189	1.8	3,370	46	1.4	6,943	143	2.1
Total white collar	27,024	317	1.2	19,170	158	0.8	7,854	159	2.0
Craftsmen	14,676	679	4.6	14,104	650	4.6	572	29	5.1
Operatives	33,242	3,269	9.8	25,915	2,529	9.8	7,327	740	10.1
Laborers	18,422	2,275	12.3	13,878	1,780	12.8	4,544	495	10.9
Service workers	1,521	225	14.8	1,334	193	14.5	187	32	17.1
Total blue collar	67,861	6,448	9.5	55,231	5,152	9.3	12,630	1,296	10.3
Total	94,885	6,765	7.1	74,401	5,310	7.1	20,484	1,455	7.1

Source: U.S. Equal Employment Opportunity Commission, *Job Patterns for Minorities and Women in Private Industry, 1966. Report No. 1* (Washington: The Commission, 1968), Part II.
Note: For regional definitions, see Table 4, p. 15.

The Negro in the Paper Industry

TABLE 21. Paper and Allied Products Industry
Percent Negro Employment by Occupational Group
Total Industry, Mills, and Converting Plants
Middle Atlantic Region, 1964-1968

	Total Industry			Pulp, Paper, and Paperboard Mills			Converting Plants		
Occupational Group	1964	1966	1968	1964	1966	1968	1964	1966	1968
Officials and managers	0.6	0.9	1.4	0.4	0.9	1.6	0.9	1.0	1.0
Professionals	0.2	—	0.2	0.3	—	0.4	—	—	—
Technicians	1.4	1.2	1.8	1.5	1.4	2.9	0.8	—	0.3
Sales workers	0.5	0.8	0.5	0.8	0.5	0.5	0.2	1.0	0.6
Office and clerical	1.2	0.8	1.5	1.7	1.1	1.6	0.2	0.4	1.5
Total white collar	0.8	0.8	1.3	1.0	0.8	1.6	0.4	0.6	1.0
Craftsmen	2.0	2.7	3.1	1.3	1.8	2.3	4.1	5.2	4.1
Operatives	6.2	7.8	9.3	4.9	6.0	7.7	7.9	11.6	11.8
Laborers	6.2	9.5	11.9	2.4	5.4	9.0	11.6	15.6	14.6
Service workers	16.4	16.4	14.5	18.0	15.5	18.2	9.8	21.0	7.1
Total blue collar	5.4	7.1	8.6	3.7	5.0	7.0	8.2	11.5	10.7
Total	4.0	5.8	7.0	2.9	4.2	6.0	6.1	9.1	8.4

Source: Tables A-19 — A-27.

Middle Atlantic region. Comparing the 1966 data in Table 21 with those in Table 20 indicates that our field sample somewhat underestimates Negro employment. The trend is upward, however.

Again Negroes have a higher representation in converting plants, but mills in this region employ a higher percentage of Negro salaried employees. It is likely that the mill data include the central office and research centers of large companies. These have been under great pressure from the government to increase Negro representation.

The data for the Midwest region in 1966, as set forth in Table 22, show a much smaller Negro representation than is found in the Middle Atlantic area. One reason is that the large paper mills in this region are found in the northern areas of Michigan, Wisconsin, and Minnesota, which like Maine, have virtually no Negro population. There are some paper mills in heavily Negro populated areas—Detroit, Chicago, and northern Ohio—but converting plants are

TABLE 22. *Paper and Allied Products Industry*
Employment by Race, Sex, and Occupational Group
689 Establishments
Midwest Region, 1966

Occupational Group	All Employees			Male			Female		
	Total	Negro	Percent Negro	Total	Negro	Percent Negro	Total	Negro	Percent Negro
Officials and managers	12,390	27	0.2	12,208	24	0.2	182	3	1.6
Professionals	4,239	8	0.2	4,053	6	0.1	186	2	1.1
Technicians	2,982	16	0.5	2,707	9	0.3	275	7	2.5
Sales workers	5,470	4	0.1	5,191	3	0.1	279	1	0.4
Office and clerical	16,372	142	0.9	5,475	44	0.8	10,897	98	0.9
Total white collar	41,453	197	0.5	29,634	86	0.3	11,819	111	0.9
Craftsmen	25,926	745	2.9	24,967	674	2.7	959	71	7.4
Operatives	59,934	2,513	4.2	47,343	1,798	3.8	12,591	715	5.7
Laborers	36,672	2,687	7.3	27,436	2,111	7.7	9,236	576	6.2
Service workers	2,827	355	12.6	2,495	318	12.7	332	37	11.1
Total blue collar	125,359	6,300	5.0	102,241	4,901	4.8	23,118	1,399	6.1
Total	166,812	6,497	3.9	131,875	4,987	3.8	34,937	1,510	4.3

Source: U.S. Equal Employment Opportunity Commission, *Job Patterns for Minorities and Women in Private Industry, 1966.* Report No. 1 (Washington: The Commission, 1968), Part II.

Note: For regional definitions, see Table 4, p. 15.

found not only in such areas, but also in cities in states such as the Dakotas, Wisconsin, and Minnesota—again where few Negroes dwell. Turning to Table 23, which summarizes Appendix Tables A-28 — A-36, we find by comparing our field data for 1966 with those in Table 22, that a small underestimation of Negro employment is evident. The trend is again upward, and again Negro representation in converting plants is substantially larger than in mills, which, given the locational factors in the region, is hardly surprising. In the Midwest, we find little Negro representation in salaried employment, and in contrast to the Middle Atlantic area, no significant difference in this regard between mills and converting plants is discernible.

The Far West includes mills in the Northwest woods, where probably no Negroes were employed prior to 1960, as well as the many converting plants in the San Francisco Bay, Los Angeles, and other metropolitan areas. Table 24 shows the 1966 EEOC data for this

TABLE 23. *Paper and Allied Products Industry*
Percent Negro Employment by Occupational Group
Total Industry, Mills, and Converting Plants
Midwest Region, 1964-1968

Occupational Group	Total Industry			Pulp, Paper, and Paperboard Mills			Converting Plants		
	1964	1966	1968	1964	1966	1968	1964	1966	1968
Officials and managers	0.1	0.2	0.2	—	0.1	0.2	0.3	0.3	0.3
Professionals	*	0.2	0.2	0.1	0.2	0.2	—	—	0.2
Technicians	0.3	0.3	0.8	0.3	0.5	0.6	0.3	—	1.3
Sales workers	0.1	—	0.3	—	—	—	0.1	—	0.4
Office and clerical	0.5	1.1	0.9	0.6	1.1	0.7	0.4	1.1	1.0
Total white collar	0.3	0.5	0.5	0.3	0.5	0.4	0.3	0.5	0.6
Craftsmen	1.6	2.2	2.3	0.8	0.9	1.0	2.9	5.1	3.7
Operatives	2.4	3.4	4.6	1.4	1.7	2.2	4.0	6.5	7.8
Laborers	3.3	5.9	6.4	2.4	2.7	2.6	4.1	10.0	10.5
Service workers	8.4	8.0	8.1	8.3	5.6	6.4	8.7	15.1	11.2
Total blue collar	2.6	3.9	4.7	1.7	1.8	2.2	3.9	7.5	7.7
Total	2.0	3.2	3.9	1.3	1.6	1.9	3.0	6.0	6.1

Source: Tables A-28 — A-36.
*Less than 0.05 percent.

TABLE 24. *Paper and Allied Products Industry*
Employment by Race, Sex, and Occupational Group
238 Establishments
Far West Region, 1966

Occupational Group	All Employees			Male			Female		
	Total	Negro	Percent Negro	Total	Negro	Percent Negro	Total	Negro	Percent Negro
Officials and managers	3,890	4	0.1	3,842	4	0.1	48	—	—
Professionals	1,777	4	0.2	1,738	4	0.2	39	—	—
Technicians	925	5	0.5	842	5	0.6	83	—	—
Sales workers	1,734	5	0.3	1,655	5	0.3	79	—	—
Office and clerical	4,806	46	1.0	1,489	12	0.8	3,317	34	1.0
Total white collar	13,132	64	0.5	9,566	30	0.3	3,566	34	1.0
Craftsmen	10,439	141	1.4	10,183	139	1.4	256	2	0.8
Operatives	18,806	634	3.4	15,405	504	3.3	3,401	130	3.8
Laborers	8,778	337	3.8	6,156	276	4.5	2,622	61	2.3
Service workers	588	80	13.6	545	77	14.1	43	3	7.0
Total blue collar	38,611	1,192	3.1	32,289	996	3.1	6,322	196	3.1
Total	51,743	1,256	2.4	41,855	1,026	2.5	9,888	230	2.3

Source: U.S. Equal Employment Opportunity Commission, *Job Patterns for Minorities and Women in Private Industry, 1966.* Report No. 1 (Washington: The Commission, 1968), **Part II.**

Note: For regional definitions, see Table 4, p. 15.

area. Negroes are less well represented in the Far West than in any region except New England, which again is about what one would expect, given the population and locational factors.

Table 25 summarizes our field data from Appendix Tables A-37 — A-45. Again, judging from a comparison of Table 24 with the 1966 data in Table 25, our data slightly underestimate the proportion of Negroes in the region. Table 25 shows the usual northern paper industry syndrome: a much higher percentage of Negroes in converting plants than in mills, very slight representation of Negroes in the salaried group, and a general upward trend in the Negro employment ratio from 1964 to 1968.

TABLE 25. *Paper and Allied Products Industry
Percent Negro Employment by Occupational Group
Total Industry, Mills, and Converting Plants
Far West Region, 1964-1968*

Occupational Group	Total Industry			Pulp, Paper, and Paperboard Mills			Converting Plants		
	1964	1966	1968	1964	1966	1968	1964	1966	1968
Officials and managers	0.1	—	0.2	0.1	—	0.1	—	—	0.3
Professionals	—	0.1	0.4	—	0.2	0.4	—	—	0.5
Technicians	0.3	0.3	0.4	0.4	0.3	0.5	—	—	—
Sales workers	—	0.3	0.5	—	—	0.4	—	0.4	0.6
Office and clerical	0.6	0.3	0.6	0.8	0.2	0.4	0.3	0.6	1.0
Total white collar	0.3	0.2	0.4	0.4	0.1	0.3	0.1	0.3	0.6
Craftsmen	1.1	0.9	1.0	1.0	0.7	0.6	1.3	1.5	2.4
Operatives	1.8	2.2	3.7	1.0	0.9	2.7	3.8	5.8	7.3
Laborers	2.3	4.4	5.6	3.0	2.5	5.1	1.6	7.6	7.2
Service workers	12.1	14.5	9.9	7.9	10.5	2.5	19.2	23.3	25.2
Total blue collar	1.9	2.4	3.4	1.5	1.2	2.6	2.6	5.4	6.1
Total	1.6	2.0	2.9	1.3	1.0	2.2	2.1	4.3	5.0

Source: Tables A-37—A-45.

Summary of Regional Analysis

To sum up this brief analysis of regional racial employment characteristics in the industry, only in the Middle Atlantic region was there a significant proportion of Negroes working in mills in 1968.

There the percentage was 6.0—almost three times the proportion in the next highest region. Only in the Middle Atlantic region was progress even slightly significant for Negro salaried employees.

All regions showed improvement over the four-year period. All regions also had a substantially higher Negro ratio in converting plants than in mills. Undoubtedly this is a function primarily of locational factors. It does mean, however, that Negroes are concentrated in all regions in the less skilled and less well paying sector of the industry. The major exception was the progress of Negroes in mill salaried jobs in the Middle Atlantic states, which probably include central office and research centers as well.

SOUTHERN DEVELOPMENTS

Throughout the 1960's, significant developments have been occurring in the southern pulp and paper industry, but they do not show up dramatically in the statistics. Thus Table 26 shows that 12.3 percent of the 145,614 employees in 507 establishments reporting to the Equal Employment Opportunity Commission in 1966 were Negroes. For 1960, the census data (Table 13, p. 34) showed 13.9 percent of the 144,459 employees were Negroes. These data, as we have noted, cannot be strictly compared for a number of reasons, especially the differences in reporting and coverage. Nevertheless, the similarity of the percentages indicates that probably no great change in Negro representation in the southern paper industry took place in the first half of the decade.

Likewise within the occupational groups, the *status quo* appears to have been maintained in that Negroes in 1966 were virtually unrepresented in the salaried positions, but comprised half the service workers, nearly 30 percent of the laborers, and 13.7 percent of the operatives. Of the 17,933 Negroes reported in southern plants, 43 percent were laborers. On the other hand, the reported 3.4 percent Negro craftsmen is larger than indicated by this author's field work in southern mills. Undoubtedly it reflects the better position of Negroes in converting plants.

Table 27, which summarizes Appendix Tables A-46—A-54, based upon our field sample, supports the theory that progress in increasing Negro representation in southern mills has been slow. Granting that our data may slightly underestimate the Negro ratio (11.7 percent

TABLE 26. Paper and Allied Products Industry
Employment by Race, Sex, and Occupational Group
507 Establishments
South Region, 1966

Occupational Group	All Employees			Male			Female		
	Total	Negro	Percent Negro	Total	Negro	Percent Negro	Total	Negro	Percent Negro
Officials and managers	10,195	27	0.3	10,064	26	0.3	131	1	0.8
Professionals	4,543	2	*	4,448	2	*	95	—	—
Technicians	2,696	12	0.4	2,191	10	0.5	505	2	0.4
Sales workers	1,969	2	0.1	1,885	2	0.1	84	—	—
Office and clerical	10,951	167	1.5	3,989	129	3.2	6,962	38	0.5
Total white collar	30,354	210	0.7	22,577	169	0.7	7,777	41	0.5
Craftsmen	30,828	1,044	3.4	30,171	1,030	3.4	657	14	2.1
Operatives	55,438	7,608	13.7	45,292	7,053	15.6	10,146	555	5.5
Laborers	26,337	7,723	29.3	22,674	7,494	33.1	3,663	229	6.3
Service workers	2,657	1,348	50.7	2,442	1,218	49.9	215	130	60.5
Total blue collar	115,260	17,723	15.4	100,579	16,795	16.7	14,681	928	6.3
Total	145,614	17,933	12.3	123,156	16,964	13.8	22,458	969	4.3

Source: U.S. Equal Employment Opportunity Commission, Job Patterns for Minorities and Women in Private Industry, 1966. Report No. 1 (Washington: The Commission, 1968, Part II.
Note: For regional definitions, see Table 4, p. 15.
*Less than 0.05 percent.

TABLE 27. *Paper and Allied Products Industry*
Percent Negro Employment by Occupational Group
Total Industry, Mills, and Converting Plants
South Region, 1964-1968

Occupational Group	Total Industry			Pulp, Paper, and Paperboard Mills			Converting Plants		
	1964	1966	1968	1964	1966	1968	1964	1966	1968
Officials and managers	0.1	0.1	0.2	0.1	0.1	0.2	0.1	0.1	0.3
Professionals	*	0.1	0.4	*	0.1	0.5	—	—	—
Technicians	0.3	0.8	1.7	—	0.4	1.8	1.6	2.9	1.2
Sales workers	—	—	0.3	—	—	—	—	—	0.3
Office and clerical	1.3	2.5	3.3	1.3	2.6	3.7	1.3	2.4	2.3
Total white collar	0.5	1.0	1.5	0.5	0.9	1.6	0.6	1.2	1.1
Craftsmen	1.5	2.1	2.8	1.1	1.6	2.1	2.8	4.2	6.9
Operatives	13.2	13.7	16.9	12.5	12.5	15.3	14.6	16.8	23.1
Laborers	36.9	33.2	34.4	45.0	37.6	36.8	24.9	24.2	28.9
Service workers	49.4	47.1	45.5	45.5	45.4	45.0	56.2	52.6	48.7
Total blue collar	15.8	14.6	16.3	15.7	13.9	15.0	15.9	16.5	21.7
Total	12.6	11.7	13.2	12.6	11.2	12.2	12.6	13.0	17.1

Source: Tables A-46 — A-54.
*Less than 0.05 percent.

Negro in 1966 as compared with EEOC's 12.3 percent), the very slow movement over the four years indicates little change for mills. The declining Negro percentage of laborers and the increase in operatives do indicate upgrading, and some improvement occurred in the salaried area, particularly among the office and clerical group, and in the craftsmen category, but the changes otherwise were not very significant.

On the other hand, southern converting plants, which had the same ratio as mills in 1964, had increased that percentage by almost 40 percent four years later. These plants are heavily concentrated in the new industrial areas of the South, including major southern cities, which have experienced remarkably high employment in the 1960's. Negroes have been extensively recruited by southern converting plants, as they have in all regions. This progress, however, has been almost entirely in the blue collar occupations. The percentage of Negro operatives increased from 14.6 percent in 1964 to 23.1 percent in 1968, and craftsmen from 2.8 percent to 6.9 percent. The latter figure is truly significant, representing one of the highest proportions of Negro craftsmen in southern industry, or for that matter, in any industry in any region. Undoubtedly, it has involved a substantial upgrading of Negro operatives as well as considerable recruiting.

Mill Recruiting and Hiring 1967

The slow numerical progress up to 1968 in increasing the proportion of Negroes in southern mills, and in improving their occupational status has been affirmed by another private survey, which the author has authenticated, but which cannot otherwise be identified.[55] This study analyzed data for 54 southern mills, of which 40 reported complete occupational figures for 1966, and 47 for 1967. In 1966, 6,117 of the 50,037 employees covered, or 12.2 percent were Negroes; in 1967, 7,088 of the 57,834 employees, or 12.3 percent were black.

Between January 1 and June 30, 1967, 52 mills reported new hires. Table 28, which categorizes these hires by race and sex, shows that 760 of the 5,480 new hires, or 13.9 percent, were Negro. This was slightly higher than the ratio of existing Negro employment. Moreover, operatives and laborers accounted for 701, or 92.2 percent, of the 760 Negro hires. Of the 995 salaried employees hired, 2.9 percent were Negroes. Most of these were office and clerical workers, but even so, this percentage was substantially above the then existing Negro salaried ratio.

We noted that some Negroes were upgraded in this period, particularly from laborer to operative. Table 29 shows transfers during the first six months of 1967 for 45 companies in this survey. Total transfers numbered 1,967 of whom 273, or 13.9 percent, were Negroes. The largest number of transfers were operatives, 1079, of whom 205, or 19.0 percent were Negro. Of the 273 salaried employee transfers, 9, or 3.3 percent were Negroes.

Of special interest were the results of this study in regard to the presence of Negroes in key lines of progression. Seventeen mills in the South provided racial breakdowns. As of June 1967, only 22 (1.6 percent) of the 1,418 employees in the paper machine line of progression were Negroes. The highest paying and most prestigious work thus remained almost entirely in white hands.

---
55. All data cited in regard to this study are in the author's possession.

TABLE 28. *Paper and Allied Products Industry*
Pulp, Paper, and Paperboard Mills
Number of Hires by Race, Sex, and Occupational Group
52 Establishments
South Region, January 1—June 30, 1967

Occupational Group	All Employees			Male			Female		
	Total	Negro	Percent Negro	Total	Negro	Percent Negro	Total	Negro	Percent Negro
Officials and managers	203	2	1.0	203	2	1.0	—	—	—
Professionals	261	3	1.1	256	3	1.2	5	—	—
Technicians	152	2	1.3	131	2	1.5	21	—	—
Sales workers	26	—	—	18	—	—	8	—	—
Office and clerical	353	22	6.2	70	10	14.3	283	12	4.2
Total white collar	995	29	2.9	678	17	2.5	317	12	3.8
Craftsmen	624	12	1.9	596	10	1.7	28	2	7.1
Operatives	1,135	174	15.3	963	124	12.9	172	50	29.1
Laborers	2,691	527	19.6	2,671	519	19.4	20	8	40.0
Service workers	35	18	51.4	35	18	51.4	—	—	—
Total blue collar	4,485	731	16.3	4,265	671	15.7	220	60	27.3
Total	5,480	760	13.9	4,943	688	13.9	537	72	13.4

Source: Unpublished study in author's possession.

TABLE 29. Paper and Allied Products Industry
Pulp, Paper, and Paperboard Mills
Number of Transfers by Race, Sex, and Occupational Group
45 Establishments
South Region, January 1—June 30, 1967

Occupational Group	All Employees			Male			Female		
	Total	Negro	Percent Negro	Total	Negro	Percent Negro	Total	Negro	Percent Negro
Officials and managers	119	1	0.8	119	1	0.8	—	—	—
Professionals	35	—	—	35	—	—	—	—	—
Technicians	48	7	14.6	48	7	14.6	—	—	—
Sales workers	2	—	—	1	—	—	1	—	—
Office and clerical	69	1	1.4	62	1	1.6	7	—	—
Total white collar	273	9	3.3	265	9	3.4	8	—	—
Craftsmen	289	6	2.1	289	6	2.1	—	—	—
Operatives	1,079	205	19.0	1,072	198	18.5	7	7	100.0
Laborers	233	45	19.3	233	45	19.3	—	—	—
Service workers	20	7	35.0	20	7	35.0	—	—	—
Total blue collar	1,621	263	16.2	1,614	256	15.9	7	7	100.0
Apprentices	73	1	1.4	73	1	1.4	—	—	—
Total	1,967	273	13.9	1,952	266	13.6	15	7	46.7

Source: Unpublished study in author's possession.

In other progressions, Negroes were doing better: 68, or 14.2 percent of the 480 employees in the powerhouse line of progression and 55, or 7.4 percent of the 742 employees in the maintenance line were black. What position Negroes held in these lines was not noted by this study. Only one Negro apprentice was transferred (Table 29) by these mills, indicating that movement to the top in the maintenance crafts was still slow.

In general, this study found the efforts to recruit Negroes were "meager." Results of change were obviously slow to be felt. Yet change was occurring. The following analysis of specific company situations indicates how barriers were being knocked down in southern mills.

Bogalusa and the Crown Zellerbach Case

In the mill town of Bogalusa, Louisiana, home of one of the oldest paper mills in the South, events developed in the 1960's that are altering the racial policies of the southern paper industry. How these developments occurred, why they required massive governmental intervention, and why they are likely to progress slowly, can best be understood by a brief review of Bogalusa history and background.

Bogalusa was historically an isolated community located near the Mississippi state border, sixty miles north of New Orleans. Separated from New Orleans by Lake Pontchartrain and thick forests, residents of Bogalusa had little contact with the "big city" until the 1930's when Governor Huey P. Long began his bridge and road building program which included a causeway over the large, shallow Lake.

Bogalusa was developed by northern entrepreneurs as the headquarters of the Great Southern Lumber Company, which in the early 1900's boasted the largest lumber mill in the world, a major paper mill, a creosoting plant, and shops of the New Orleans Great Northern Railroad. Great Southern provided the services, owned the houses, utilities, newspapers, and virtually the town itself.[56]

Like most southern paper mills, Great Southern employed Negroes for unskilled work. The tradition of separate locals for white and Negro employees was followed in organizing attempts by the Carpenters' union during the World War I period, but the Great Southern

---

56. The background material on Bogalusa is based on Huey Latham, Jr., *A Comparison of Union Organization in Two Southern Paper Mills.* Unpublished M.A. thesis, Louisiana State University, 1962.

company opposed unions, race issues divided the white and colored workers, and after a gun battle in which several unionists died, union organization disappeared from Bogalusa until 1933.

The paper mill at Bogalusa was originally a relatively minor operation built to utilize the waste from the lumber operation. In the 1930's, however, as the great trees of the forests were less and less available, and the potential for paper from southern pine became apparent, the lumber mill was closed and the pulp and paper operations were expanded. The paper unions chartered local unions in 1933, but Great Southern did not follow the lead of International Paper in recognizing unions. Management continued to dominate the town, as in the past until 1938 when the Gaylord Container Corporation, then a major paper converter, purchased Great Southern in order to insure raw materials for its converting units.

The Gaylord regime led to a complete shift in union relations, community relations, and inevitably presaged a hardening of race relations in Bogalusa. Gaylord welcomed the unions and made no effort to fill the community leadership role which Great Southern management had maintained over the years. This vacuum was filled by the white unionists and other working and lower middle-class whites. Bogalusa became a highly unionized town, with its politics run by this group, and the union hall used as a meeting place not only for unions, but "for a church, music school, Boy Scouts and fraternal organizations"[57] without charge, and completely segregated. It was analogous to the post-reconstruction era following the removal of federal troops when the poor whites took over the state reins of government once held by the plantation aristocracy.

The Bogalusa mill is one of the few where the United Papermakers and Paperworkers does not share bargaining rights with the Pulp and Sulphite Workers. Except for a craft local of the International Brotherhood of Electrical Workers, UPP has exclusive jurisdiction in the mill. Over the years, however, three converting plants were added to the paper manufacturing complex: a box plant, a grocery bag plant, and a multiwall bag plant. The Pulp and Sulphite Workers obtained bargaining rights for these converting facilities. The traditional separate locals and confinement of Negroes to the yard and common labor jobs were present in the mill. The multiwall bag plant, about 40 percent of whose employees were female, was traditionally

---

57. Latham, *loc. cit.*

all white in Bogalusa except for one or two Negro porters. The grocery bag plant had a larger complement of Negroes, but segregation did exist. The box plant, which like the mill, had separate locals, also confined its Negro employees to particular jobs.

In 1955, Gaylord Container was merged into Crown Zellerbach, the leading West Coast paper company, the fifth largest forest products company, and in paper alone, probably second only to the International Paper Company. Crown, which had long cultivated a reputation as an employer desirous of having friendly union relations,[58] continued Gaylord's union relation policies at Bogalusa and perhaps even more than Gaylord, adopted a strict hands-off policy in community affairs. Crown's top officials were known to be sympathetic to Negro aspirations for social and economic improvement, and the Company was one of only four paper companies to join Plans for Progress at an early point in this organization's life.[59] Like other Plans for Progress members, Crown promised to take affirmative action in increasing Negro employment opportunities, but it had had no experience in the South prior to acquiring the Gaylord operations and it obviously was reluctant to break with its unions on this issue. It did, however, commence to integrate some facilities in 1961.

Crown's difficulties in Bogalusa were compounded by obsolete and inefficient equipment and methods which it set out to alter in the late 1950's and early 1960's. The company pumped capital into new equipment which reduced the need for people but increased the caliber of people required. The resultant layoffs and downgradings caused a bitter strike. This increased the Company's reluctance to dispute with the unions over the seniority system and at the same time hardened the determination of the whites in Bogalusa against making any concessions to Negroes.

The situation in the early 1960's in Bogalusa was thus set for a classic confrontation. What was extraordinary is that the battleground was largely confined to administrative agencies and courts. It did not start that way. Both the Congress of Racial Equality and the Ku Klux Klan paraded, agitated, and some violence did ensue for several months. The Negro local, however, and their allies had appealed to the President's Committee on Equal Employment Oppor-

---

58. Crown Zellerbach's labor relations policies are discussed in Levinson, note 15 and in Northrup and Young, note 19.
59. The others were Mead, Scott, and St. Regis.

tunity, established by the late President Kennedy, to supervise a more aggressive nondiscrimination policy among government contractors. As a result of pressure by the PCEEO, Crown opened up all jobs to all persons in 1964. This, however, proved more a theory than a fact, because of the extra-board situation. Moreover, in 1963 Crown instituted a testing program which caused Negroes to have great difficulty in meeting hiring and transfer qualifications.

Prior to this period, separate white and Negro extraboards had been established. Those who were without permanent jobs reported to the employment office and filled in for other employees in the plant, but always on a segregated basis. Employees who had worked in a job and were on the extraboard had prior claim to permanent openings on that job, depending upon the time worked there, in accordance with the occupational seniority system. Since there were quite a few employees on layoff, and since the extraboard were segregated prior to May 1964, Negroes who aspired to formerly exclusive white jobs thereafter found that whites had prior claims in many cases.

In July 1965, Title VII of the Civil Rights Act of 1964 became effective, and soon thereafter the Equal Employment Opportunity Commission, established by Title VII, became involved in the Crown Bogalusa case. The prime issue before EEOC was how the segregated lines of progression were to be merged. Subsidiary issues involved integration of the cafeteria, sanitary and eating facilities, and locker rooms. Integration of all was required by the Title VII of the Civil Rights Act, but how this was to be accomplished stirred bitter dispute. As late as December 1965, for example, Crown was proposing for incumbent employees a "horizontal intermeshing of the present white and Negro progression lines into one line of progression" which would have retained existing white and Negro designations so that promotion of whites would have required a "leapfrogging" around Negro jobs and promotion of Negroes a "leapfrogging" around white jobs. Moreover, in such merged progressions, the top five job categories would have been closed to Negroes until all the whites then in the line had been afforded the opportunity to advance.[60]

At this point, Franklin D. Roosevelt, Jr., first chairman of EEOC, entered the case and produced a much heralded agreement between the company and the union which provided for the merger, by inter-

---

60. The facts for this case are based on documents and materials found, unless otherwise noted, in the record of the case, *United States v. Local 189, United Papermakers and Paperworkers, et al.,* 282 F. Supp. 39 (E.D. La., 1968).

meshing of the eleven progression lines, and for the opening of every job classification within each promotion line to all employees without discrimination.[61] The Negro local of the United Papermakers and Paperworkers (Local 189A) at the meetings with Mr. Roosevelt indicated acceptance of this agreement, but later opposed it. Since the white (Local 189) and colored locals voted jointly, and the whites outnumbered the Negroes 1250 to 250, the agreement was deemed accepted.

Why the Negro local voted against the Roosevelt agreement soon became clear. The "leap-in" rights of whites who had gained occupational seniority were maintained, but Negroes who had been excluded from such jobs prior to May 1964 were still required to start at the bottom of an occupational line. This limited upward movement of Negroes. Moreover, since the "intermeshing" of seniority in fact largely tacked the former Negro progressions on the bottom of former white lines, an added security "cushion" was given to whites. For example, those who by virtue of extraboard service won jobs above the point where the former Negro line was added, could, in case of layoff, then bump down into the former Negro jobs. This was possible because the company-union agreement provided for such downgrading in case of layoffs.

By mid-1966, the Office of Federal Contract Compliance, the successor agency to the President's Committee on Equal Employment Opportunity, was charging the company with continued restrictions in Negro employment and upgrading. Moreover, it was maintaining that facilities, although technically desegregated, were *de facto* segregated. Negotiations continued between OFCC and the company through 1966 and 1967. The company made a number of concessions. It abolished its testing program, actively recruited Negroes, upgraded some, and genuinely attempted to satisfy the government, provided such satisfaction did not involve unilateral action which it deemed would violate the Taft-Hartley Act and which most certainly would involve a rupture of its union relations. OFCC kept up the pressure on the company, but adopted a view that union relations were none of its concern—the company, not the union, was the government contractor. How the company was to alter its union contract unilaterally without violating the National Labor Relations Act, as

---

61. The Roosevelt agreement and explanatory press release are found in the Bureau of National Affairs, Inc., *Daily Labor Report,* December 1965, No. 245, pp. A-1—A-4.

amended (Taft-Hartley Act) which specifically proscribes such unilateral action, was left largely to the company by the OFCC attitude
and policy.

In 1967, Crown negotiated a new contract with UPP. It was under
pressure from OFCC to come up with an acceptable seniority agreement, but no such agreement was possible given the adamant attitude
of the white local (Local 189). Moreover, at this time any pressure
from the United Papermakers and Paperworkers, as will be discussed
in greater detail below, tended to strengthen the will to resist integration. Accordingly, Crown and the UPP settled their contract by
agreeing on everything except seniority, and by providing that after a
reasonable time for further negotiations, Crown could, upon fifteen
days notice, institute a new seniority system unilaterally, but that
following ten days after such notice, the union could legally strike.
The parties did reach agreement in December 1967, but the OFCC
found their agreement "probably" unsatisfactory.

At this point, OFCC apparently decided to circulate a "consulting
memorandum" to the heads of all agencies requiring that contracting
officers consult with OFCC before awarding contracts to Crown. A
previous such memorandum, issued in May 1967, and withdrawn one
month later, caused Crown to lose some business.[62] No public
hearing had been held nor would the OFCC provide any, although
OFCC regulations required one prior to final disbarment. OFCC's
rationale was that its "consult memorandum" was only a preliminary
action.

Crown appealed to the Federal District Court of the District of
Columbia for an injunction restraining the OFCC and the Department
of Labor, of which OFCC is a part, from issuing its consult memorandum without a hearing. The court found that the government had
"not made any showing of a public interest that requires summary
suspension of Crown's business with the government and government
contractors;" and that Crown was caught between the demands of the
OFCC and its obligations under the Taft-Hartley Act, and would

---

62. It should be noted that the proposed government sanctions would not only bar
Crown from direct government business but also would prevent all other government contractors from dealing with Crown. Moreover, all of Crown's operations would have been proscribed, not just Bogalusa. The massive nature of
such a penalty explains why it has never been used. The fact that the system
derives from an Executive Order, not an Act of Congress, has also raised grave
questions concerning its propriety.

suffer irreparable injury if the government issued its memorandum. The injunction was therefore granted pending "a hearing in which the question of whether Crown is in compliance with Executive Order No. 11246 can be received."[63]

Having won this restraining order on January 2, 1968, Crown nevertheless the very next day made an agreement with the OFCC that it would install unilaterally the totally new and unique seniority system demanded of it by the OFCC since March 1967 under which promotions, demotions, and layoffs within lines of progression were governed by the total of an individual's mill plus job seniority rather than by his job (occupational) seniority.[64] This was an entirely new system developed by OFCC personnel without careful analysis of its potential impact, but with the thought that it would tend to equalize the position of Negroes who had been discriminated against with whites. Crown then advised the UPP of its intention to install this new seniority system on February 1, 1968, whereupon Local 189, UPP and the IBEW voted to strike on January 30. At this point the U.S. Department of Justice obtained an injunction against the strike on the grounds that its purpose was unlawful (violation of Title VII). The new seniority system went into effect, pending a trial, as the union respected the injunction and the employees remained at work.

After one month in operation, the mill-plus-job seniority system proved very upsetting to the intraplant movement of employees without accomplishing its objective of improving the ability of formerly discriminated against Negroes to compete for better jobs. Thus between February 1 and March 3, 1968, 59 cases of plant movement occurred in which the mill-plus-job seniority was decisive in determining who obtained a job. In 43 of these, or 73 percent, one white employee received the promotion instead of another white who would have received it under the regular occupational seniority system; in eight instances a black employee obtained a promotion at the expense of another black who would have received it under the regular

---

63. *Crown Zellerbach Corp. v. Wirtz,* 281 F. Supp. 337, (Dis. Ct., D.C., 1968).
64. The text of the Crown-OFCC agreement is found in Bureau of National Affairs, Inc., *Daily Labor Report,* January 25, 1968, No. 18, pp. F-1—F-3. The UPP was so incensed at Crown's sudden turnaround that it sought to have the company found in contempt for violating the injunction which the company had obtained. Crown for its part felt that it preferred to reach an accommodation with OFCC rather than to force the public hearing which seemed to be OFCC's next, and final step, prior to actual debarment from government contracts.

system; and in only eight other cases, or 13.6 percent of the total, did the mill-plus-job system, thought up by OFCC personnel, obtain the results that it sought—the promotion of formerly discriminated against Negroes over previously favored whites.[65]

The experience of the OFCC created mill-plus-job seniority system led to its abandonment by the government at the ensuing hearing. The government instead proposed, and the federal District Court for the Eastern District of Louisiana, accepted in its decision and order, that first, the remedy be confined to the "affected class"—that is those Negroes employed prior to January 16, 1966, when all jobs were indisputably opened to Negroes; and second, when those Negroes in the affected class are involved, promotion, demotion, and layoffs should be determined by mill, rather than job seniority, but otherwise the regular occupational seniority system negotiated by the company and union, and universally practiced in the industry, should apply. In any case, an employee would be required to have the ability to do the job, and, subject to the grievance procedure, the company retains the right to judge qualifications.

The decision by the court thus accepted the proposition that the Civil Rights Act of 1964 permits, or even requires, that persons once discriminated against should be offered their "rightful place" in the seniority hierarchy. This idea, originally given judicial backing in a case involving the tobacco industry,[66] has been litigated in a number of federal jurisdictions. The *Crown* case was appealed to the United States Court of Appeals for the Fifth Circuit, which unanimously affirmed the District Court on July 29, 1969.[67] In the Bogalusa mill, what it has meant is that where one or more Negroes in the affected class are involved, total length of service in the mill, regardless of time on the job, determines who is promoted, demoted, or laid off provided the ability to perform the job exists. The use of mill seniority in such cases, it is argued, equalized the situation among whites who were favored and Negroes who were discriminated against. Those who

---

65. These data are found in the trial record of the case cited in note 60 and reproduced in Appendix B. The list of persons, dates, and jobs is in the author's possession.

66. *Quarles v. Philip Morris, Inc.*, 279 F Supp. 505 (E.D. Va. 1968).

67. *United States v. Local 189, United Papermakers and Paperworkers, et. al.*, 282 F. Supp. 39 (E.D. La., 1968). Affirmed, U.S. Court of Appeals, Fifth Circuit, July 29, 1969. Both the District and Circuit Court decisions are reproduced in Appendix B.

oppose it point out that where any upgrading has occurred, no one has the same mill as job seniority.[68] It does, however, give a decided credit to those who were once denied promotion rights and is easily understood. And by being confined to the "affected class," it does not upset the entire plant personnel relationships, nor outlaw the rational system in effect when that system is applied on a nondiscriminatory basis.

A second trial involving the same parties was scheduled to settle such matters as how long a person would be required to remain in various jobs before he would be qualified to exercise his mill seniority. Agreement was reached on most of these questions and orders were proposed to the judge in the spring of 1968. Not till June 1969, did he issue a decision. In it, a lengthy document reproduced in Appendix B with the earlier district court decision and the appeals court decision, the length of time which is required in each job before mill seniority can be exercised is set forth, together with the details of promotions and progressions. Where these matters were not agreed to in the stipulation, the judge, seemingly without exception, accepted the proposed order of the Department of Justice. Prior to this, the same judge issued another order installing the same type of mill seniority in the box plant for those in the affected class;[69] and he approved a stipulation providing for the merger of white Local 189 and Negro Local 189A in which the Negro group is guaranteed a vice-presidency and other representation for a number of years.

Meanwhile, the parties in the mill are learning to live with the seniority system as modified by the court, many whites undoubtedly after their brief experience with the mill-plus-job creation of OFCC, grateful that what the court ordered is not more upsetting of the *status quo*. A number of Negroes are being promoted who would otherwise not have been, but many find educational and training disabilities, age or motivational difficulties too great to overcome in spite of the fact that Crown provides remedial education classes free of charge. The parties worked out most details of length of time on job, training needs, etc., prior to the June 1969 court decision and

---

68. This author, as an expert witness in the case, opposed mill seniority for this reason, but proposed instead a seniority credit system for the affected class based upon average job seniority in each classification at the time of the hearing.

69. *Robert Hicks v. Crown Zellerbach et. al.*, U.S. District Court, E.D. La., Civil Action No. 16638, Section B, April 8, 1968.

these details were accepted by the judge. The past in Bogalusa is dead, although the statistics are not dramatic, and given the slow turnover and intraplant movement in mills, will not be so for many years. Nevertheless, progress is being made. Negroes now occupy several supervisory positions in the Bogalusa mill and box plant and such other salaried positions as assistant personnel supervisor, chemist, and data processing technician.

The impact has spread beyond Bogalusa. Crown, for example, has increased its efforts elsewhere. It opened a box plant in Memphis with Negroes in 50 percent of the wage and 39 percent of the salaried jobs. It now has 22 Negroes in sales and sales service and is transferring Negroes where possible to plants which are expanding so that their promotions will accelerate. Nationally, Crown pledged and filled 390 jobs under the first year's activity of the National Alliance of Businessmen program.

Beyond Crown, the impact of the Bogalusa case has been even greater. This the ensuing discussion will make clear.

International Paper's Agreement

With the Crown Zellerbach case under its belt, the government, through OFCC primarily, next turned to the giant of the industry, International Paper Company's Southern Kraft Division, and demanded that IP install immediately the same seniority system that the court had imposed on Crown Zellerbach's Bogalusa plant. IP, however, declined to react unilaterally. It successfully insisted that OFCC recognize, at long last, that unions, as well as companies, were involved and that amendment of the labor agreement required joint company-union action. Meanwhile, IP opened a new mill at Vicksburg, Mississippi, on a thoroughly integrated basis, with Negroes in the paper machine progression, in the mechanical crafts, and in salaried and managerial jobs.

International paper, it will be recalled, has, besides Vicksburg, ten mills in the South which are covered by a multiunit agreement with the two paper and various craft unions. All of these mills had a traditional southern paper discriminatory seniority and job segregation pattern. In many of the communities, such as Springhill, Louisianna, and Natchez, Mississippi, considerable agitation, threats of violence, actual violence, and Ku Klux Klan and White Citizens Council agitation occurred against any improvement in the economic, social, or political position of Negroes. Against this background, IP moved cautiously toward integration. A number of lines of progression in the various mills were merged, separate facilities consolidated, and all jobs opened to Negroes. International Paper had been developing other aspects of an equal employment program for some time. Its IFCO foundation had for a number of years devoted large sums and considerable talent in an effort to improve secondary education in areas where the company had plants, and much of this went to Negro schools. Its new employees were also given a clear orientation regarding equal employment policies, and it participates in the National Alliance of Businessmen JOBS program in some areas.

Nevertheless, by early 1968, the traditional racial-occupational segregation pattern of the industry predominated in IP plants, although a number of Negroes, in addition to those at Vicksburg, had been upgraded in the job hierarchies once reserved for whites. IP had experienced a shut down of all its southern mills in 1965. Although it attributed this (its first major southern) strike primarily to intraunion political problems arising out of the secession of the West Coast locals to a new independent union, company officials believed that the racial situation added fuel to the fires.

The court decision in the Crown case not only made it clear to the unions that maintenance of the existing progression system would not be permitted, but in addition provided the formula for change. In addition, the resignation in 1968 of Paul L. Phillips, a native southerner and vigorous opponent of change, as president of the United Papermakers and Paperworkers, and his replacement by Harry D. Sayre, a moderate in such matters, aided the resolve for peaceful settlement. Delegates from the locals of the two paper unions and the IBEW met with company officials in Jackson, Mississippi, in June 1968. Present also was Leonard J. Biermann, Senior Compliance Officer of OFCC, who had handled the paper industry investigations, and whose forthright analysis of what the government required to be done, did much to insure the "we have no other choice" attitude of the white local delegates. An agreement was reached, and promptly ratified by the local union memberships, which is reproduced in Appendix C, and which provides in part :

1. The mill seniority requirement as a test for advancement within progressions where the "affected class" of Negroes compete with whites. The "affected class" was defined as Negroes employed prior to September 1, 1962, or hired

subsequent thereto and placed in a job or progression formerly limited to
Negroes. After five years, mill seniority will no longer apply.
  2. The IP agreement does not cover maintenance crafts.
  3. "Red circling" or maintenance of wage rates, for transferees earning less
than $3.00 per hour for period of first transfer.
  4. Merger of all segregated progression lines within 90 days.
  5. Qualifications of employees for transfer or advancement to be determined
by qualifications "as high as the minimally qualified employee currently working in the line."

The IP agreement is thus in some ways more limiting, and in others
more liberal than the court order in the Crown case. IP's agreement
limits the mill seniority provision to five years although this limitation is "subject to the approval of the appropriate governmental agency,
if any"; it does, however, specify qualifications at a level of the lowest
qualified employee now on the job, thus permitting Negroes to advance
on qualifications which presumably would have been in effect at a
time when the Negro employees might have been eligible for the job
except for discriminating restrictions then in effect. IP's agreement
also specifically permits transfers without loss of pay for those desiring
to obtain work where a greater future, but less immediate remuneration exists.

As of December 1968, the impact of the IP agreement was already
being felt. IP sought to interview all its Southern Kraft Negro employees and to ascertain their interest in advancement. Negroes have
moved up especially in the pulp mills, and thirteen, some to fifth hand,
in the paper mills as well as in other departments. Again progress is
held back, not only because of slow turnover but because nearly
every IP mill in the South has less employees today than it did ten
years ago. On the other hand, some of the training periods specified
in the Crown Zellerbach court order appear to require a longer stay
on the job that IP has insisted upon in the early stages of the administration of its agreement. It is likely that movement in the future will
not be rapid, but it undoubtedly will continue. What is much more
important, however, was that the International Paper agreement, even
more than the Crown court case, set the standards for reform of the
southern mill seniority system.

St. Regis Paper Company

St. Regis Paper Company had acquired a mill in Pensacola, Florida,
and built one in Jacksonville, Florida, prior to 1960. Both followed
traditional southern mill seniority and union relations practices. Then

in 1962, St. Regis became one of the first paper companies to join Plans for Progress. It set out to eliminate separate facilities and to integrate its progression lines in the two Florida mills. This proved a long, difficult task, as it has in other southern mills. Meantime, however, St. Regis grasped the opportunity afforded by the construction of a new mill at Monticello, Mississippi, forty miles south of Jackson, to make a new and different beginning.

On May 26, 1965, St. Regis announced plans for "the construction of a $100 million pulp, paper, and paperboard complex near Monticello." Included in the press release were these paragraphs:

Recognizing the current emphasis expressed in the civil rights movement, William R. Adams, president, commented that in 1961 he signed for St. Regis the Equal Employment Opportunity pledge with the then Vice President Lyndon B. Johnson stating its policy of compliance with the principles of non-discrimination in recruiting, training, promotion and transfer of employees without regard to race, creed, color or national origin.

In 1962, St. Regis further stated its accord with this principle by signing the Plans for Progress enunciating the national policy that qualified persons regardless of race, creed, color or national origin are entitled to equal employment opportunity.

Mr. Adams emphasized that plans for the new mill and plant will provide fully integrated facilities, and that the principles of providing employment to all qualified persons in accordance with Title VII of the Civil Rights Act of 1964 will be followed to the best of management's ability.[70]

St. Regis set out to implement this policy with a vigorous recruiting program that added Negro chemists and accountants, a personnel trainee, as well as hourly rated employees in the paper machine lines, as apprentices and in most other key departments. All facilities and activities were fully integrated from the inception in the mill, which has some of the largest and most automated papermaking equipment in the country.

In order to insure maximum employee cooperation, St. Regis required each employee hired at Monticello (and later at other facilities) to sign the "Equal Opportunity Understanding" reproduced in Figure 6. For two years prior to the opening of the mill, the personnel director worked not only to recruit, but to achieve effective community acceptance of company policy. As a result, motel and restaurant facilities were available for visiting Negro recruits and government employees without incident.

---

70. *St. Regis General Bulletin* No. 1996, May 26, 1965, contains the text of the press release.

FIGURE 6

ST. REGIS

EQUAL OPPORTUNITY UNDERSTANDING

Name of Applicant _____
(or Transferring Employee)

I understand that St. Regis Paper Company believes in and follows the principle of non-discrimination in employment, and intends to comply with all Federal and applicable State laws concerning Civil Rights. I, also, intend to comply with such laws.

I understand that the Company is a participant in "Plans for Progress" and is an Equal Opportunity Employer.

I understand that all facilities provided by the Company are to be used by all employees without regard to race, creed, color or national origin.

I understand that all jobs in progression and all promotional opportunities shall be filled by the Company without regard to race, creed, color or national origin.

I understand that by accepting any employment the Company may offer me, I accept the conditions explained in this statement.

I understand and accept these conditions and I agree that if during the course of my employment with the Company I commit any act or engage in any activity against equal opportunity in any respect, the Company may immediately discharge me without recourse.

Witnessed by: _____   Signed: _____

Date: _____

Despite its intensive efforts, St. Regis had difficulty in finding qualified Negro personnel. With Negroes in all lines of progression, however, and in key salaried positions, the number of those qualified will undoubtedly steadily grow.

While its Monticello experience was well underway, St. Regis moved to integrate more fully its Jacksonville and Pensacola facilities. All progression lines had been opened to Negroes beginning in 1962, and slowly a few Negroes moved into formerly white preserves. At Jacksonville in 1965, the company proposed a merger of the lines of progression. It won agreement from Local 749 of the Pulp, Sulphite and Paper Mill Workers, representing white employees, but was unable to convince Local 757 representing the Negro employees. The company offered to "red circle" all rates where a reduction of pay could be involved and to protect the Negro group's seniority in case of cutbacks. Essentially the proposal would have protected the Negroes' rights while opening up new opportunities to them, but their local rejected it.

After the International Paper Company negotiated the agreement described above, St. Regis proposed a similar contract to its unions at Pensacola and Jacksonville. It was accepted without incident at the former place, and by all locals but the Negro local at Jacksonville. By this time, a sizable number of the black employees there had entered former white lines of progression and joined the white local. At this point, the international union officials were pressing a merger of the white and Negro locals as requested by the OFCC. When the contract which was aimed at compensating Negroes for past discrimination was turned down by the black group but approved by the whites, the international president of the Pulp, Sulphite union revoked the charter of the former. The black group meanwhile appealed to the Equal Employment Opportunity Commission, complaining of the attempts to merge the two locals. EEOC began an investigation of the complaint which alleged, among other things, that the company and international union were doing what another government agency clearly required them to do.

A principal difference between the International Paper and St. Regis agreements is that the former has been interpreted to cover temporary promotions. The top jobs on all paper machines (except in new mills) are occupied by long seniority personnel who are eligible for vacations of four to six weeks. This affords great opportunities for temporary upgrading of long duration, and means that in this regard, the IP agreement provides more opportunities for Negroes to work in higher classifications.

As this is being written, EEOC is continuing its investigation of the St. Regis Jacksonville mill. The company is continuing its upgrading and integration program there and elsewhere, and in addition, is extremely active in the JOBS program of the National Alliance of Businessmen, and in other affirmative action policies. Later in this chapter we shall return to the questions raised by the pressure to merge white and Negro locals and the ambivalent, if not contradictory positions of government agencies on this and other matters.

Scott Paper Company

Scott Paper Company is one of the few paper manufacturing companies, and certainly the largest, which markets consumer products under its own name. Perhaps this is a key reason why Scott has long been sensitive to its relations to the Negro community. Another may be its "home" plant location in Chester, an industrial city in southeastern Pennsylvania, which has had a large Negro population since World War I, and which today has about 50 percent black population, many heavily disadvantaged. In 1956, Scott employed its first Negro salesman, perhaps the first in the industry. By 1970, Scott should score another first—the first black machine tender in a southern mill. In between these events, Scott has moved steadily forward as a leader in minority integration in the industry.

In the 1950's Scott acquired Hollingsworth & Whitney, and thereby a large southern mill in Mobile, Alabama, directly adjacent to the International Paper Company mill there. Since then Scott has moved to integrate these facilities, and has made particular progress since 1961 when the company decided that it would be required to take steps out of line with the southern paper industry tradition.[71] Specifically, Scott began actively seeking Negro personnel who would be clearly capable of moving into lines of progression in which they had been barred. Scott's early affirmative action put it into a position of leadership, when combined with several fortuitous circumstances.

The Scott Mobile mill has been expanded a number of times, with the addition of new paper machines, additional pulping capacity and related equipment. This has opened up many new jobs at a time when employment in other key mills has been declining because of automation and methods and mechanical improvements. Then in 1966, an illegal strike occurred at the Scott Mobile plant, apparently engendered by supporters of the Association of Western Pulp and Paper Workers, allegedly with Teamsters' support. The strike failed because Scott reacted vigorously, discharging sixteen key employees. Several others voluntarily resigned, opening up faster promotions to lower-rated personnel, including Negroes.

---

71. A Scott official toured southern plants for ideas on integration at this time. He felt that only two companies were sympathetic. Of course not all companies were visited. The author did learn from other sources that the most sympathetic companies were St. Regis and West Virginia Pulp and Paper. Both remain leaders in integration today.

Scott's recruiting efforts in Mobile have been aided by its early start and by the Mobile location. Scott has justly acquired the reputation as *the* place to apply for work in the Negro community. Moreover, it not only began its recruiting for skilled jobs earlier than its neighbor, International Paper, but in addition the Scott plant has been expanding while the IP plant has seen employment contracting. Because Mobile's school system, although traditionally segregated, has proved much superior to those in rural towns where so many paper mills are located, Scott has found qualified personnel.

In 1968, when Scott signed a labor agreement similar to the one negotiated by St. Regis, Scott already had one Negro back tender (the next to the top job on the paper machine) and one third hand. When the new machine now being installed is operative, the black back tender will be able, as a member of the "affected class," to exercise his mill seniority for a machine tender's job, the Negro third hand will be able to do the same thing to become a back tender, and after a period of training, will in turn become the number one in line for a machine tender's job.

In addition, Scott has a Negro power plant employee, whom it recruited from the Navy in 1959, and who is now first in line for a job as turbine operator, or head fireman as a result of the new agreement. This man will be one of a very few in the South—perhaps alone—to achieve this status in jobs under the jurisdiction of the International Brotherhood of Electrical Workers.

Except for Scott, the author knows of no other Negroes in paper machine progressions who were higher than number four hands (St. Regis, Monticello) in December 1968 or number five hands (several at International Paper). Scott's leadership at Mobile puts it not only ahead in the South, but probably in the country, except for small waste paper mills, which often have only a four man crew. In some of these around Philadelphia, the author has noted all Negro crews. Wage rates for such machines, which trim off rolls at 50 to 80 inches in width, are about one-half those of the big southern machines which produce rolls up to 374 inches wide. In large northern or western mills, like Scott's at Chester, progress in key positions is well below that of the Scott Mobile mill.

Other Company Activities

Scott and St. Regis have not been used as examples of affirmative action to imply that they alone are engaged in such efforts, nor has the review of their activities been complete. Both have developed training, motivational, and special employment programs for minorities and both are strong supporters of the JOBS program of the National Alliance of Businessmen, as is Crown Zellerbach. Westvaco (formerly West Virginia Pulp and Paper) and Union Camp, integrated their seniority rosters and successfully promoted the merger of local unions prior to OFCC directives; Continental Can has developed a program for basic literacy teaching of laborers at its Hodge, Louisiana, plant; and Georgia Kraft Company, jointly owned by Mead and Inland Container, has embarked on an ambitious program financed by the Ford Foundation through the American Paper Institute, to motivate and to train Negro yard laborers so that they may become eligible for promotion to paper machine, pulp mill, and maintenance lines of progression. In addition, Mead, an early member of Plans for Progress, is engaged in numerous other affirmative action programs, including an ambitious one in Atlanta converting plants to recruit and to train the hard core as effective plant operatives. The affirmative action activities of Crown Zellerbach and International Paper have already been noted.

From such activity, the racial occupational pattern of the southern mills will change. Yet change will come slowly, given the relatively low turnover, the great educational disabilities of Negroes, especially in many rural areas where so many mills are found, the undoubted reluctance of managements in many companies to risk change which might cause expensive loss of production, and the opposition of white union members.

UNION IMPACT ON RACIAL POLICIES

Union policies, as we have already noted, which were developed in the South during the 1930's, institutionalized the racial occupational pattern of that period, and aided considerably in maintaining that pattern in the ensuing years. Thus union policies strengthened management's segregated hiring practices, exclusion of Negroes from key lines of progression and better jobs, and segregated facilities. Unions added separate locals and coalition bargaining, with fragmented union structures. Craft union exclusion strengthened management exclusion so that Negroes in maintenance work in the mills, except as laborers or helpers, have been, and continue to be, very rare.

During the period between World War II and 1960, certain subtle changes occurred in union policies in the southern mills and other changes occurred partly as a result of union policies. The Negro locals became forums in which their members learned to handle their affairs and to press for their rights. One company personnel executive stated:

When I went South for the first time in 1948, the Negro delegates sat in the back of the room and did not open their mouths until the end of the negotiations at which time they haltingly and nervously requested two items. The international union representative winked at me and said: "Give the Niggers number one; forget number two."

I was appalled, but local management opposed any change.

Eight years later when I again participated in this mill's negotiations the Negro delegates sat at the conference table, took part in general negotiations and pressed their demands with effective arguments. The same international representative, if his attitude was no different, certainly did not show it. He was courteous in language and demeanor, and certainly supported their demands.[72]

During this period, delegates from Negro locals appeared at the regional and national union conferences and took part in discussions. Their participation was bolstered by a rising number of Negro delegates from northern and midwestern converting plants, and the two paper unions appointed Negro international representatives to their staffs. Neither paper union, however, did anything significant to alter the racial occupational pattern. Moreover, their policies of pushing effectively for large wage increases provided additional incentive to the companies to automate. The impact was felt especially on jobs held by Negroes, with the already noted sharp decline in the proportion of Negroes in southern mills between 1950 and 1960.

The policy of the paper unions in maintaining the racial occupational *status quo* undoubtedly had the support of most southern white mill employees. It was also furthered by the nature of leadership in both unions. The Pulp, Sulphite and Paper Mill Workers was led by a man who held on to his post until an octogenarian, and even then had to be forced from office by a regional union revolt. Men in their

---

72. Interview, November 1968.

late sixties and seventies predominated in other key union offices. Change is never likely in an organization so led.

The United Papermakers and Paperworkers has far fewer Negroes among its members than does its sister union. The Pulp and Sulphite union has jurisdiction over mill yards where most Negroes in mills work, and has organized many more converting plants as well. Moreover, the UPP has jurisdiction over the traditional lily white paper machine crews. The UPP president from 1948 to 1968 was Paul L. Phillips, a former employee of International Paper's Camden, Arkansas, mill, once the chief organizer of southern mills and later a vicepresident of the organization. He remained throughout a strong proponent of the existing seniority system and related policies and fought to perpetuate them.

The winds of change hit the paper unions from an unexpected source in 1964, when the West Coast locals revolted and successfully wrested bargaining rights for the mills there for the new independent, the Association of Western Pulp and Paper Workers. Repercussions of this debacle led to a constitutional amendment in 1966 by the Pulp and Sulphite Workers prohibiting the holding of union office after age 65. The wholesale elimination of union officials which this change produced placed in office younger men more conducive to change.

Before new officers took over in the Pulp and Sulphite Workers, a wave of strikes hit the industry, prompted no doubt by a fear of further revolts and internal union political unrest. These strikes include the one in 1965 which shut down all southern mills of International Paper. The race issue was raised in these strikes, as the government was then definitely moving toward opening up new jobs for Negroes, but race was not the prime issue or cause.

The Association of Western Pulp and Paper Workers complicated union racial policies in the South by campaigning for support on a racist platform, often couched in such phrases as "protecting the seniority of long-time employees." Besides its already noted efforts at the Scott Mobile plant, it obtained a National Labor Relations Board bargaining election in Bogalusa, but lost the vote to UPP. The Association scored no successes for its efforts in the South, although its campaigns were led by dissident ex-officials of the two AFL-CIO paper unions.

In early 1968, Paul Phillips resigned as president of the UPP and was succeeded by Harry D. Sayre, onetime president of the former CIO union that merged into the older papermaker's organization. Sayre, much more flexible and more sympathetic to the rights of Negroes, played a strong role in aiding the culmination of the key International Paper agreement. Undoubtedly, both Sayre and his Pulp, Sulphite counterpart, Joseph Tonelli, are much more conducive to change than their predecessors. Their white southern memberships today are, at best, probably resigned to change but not very happy about sharing their job opportunities with Negroes or being by-passed by Negroes who have greater mill, but less occupational seniority. Moreover, the national leadership of the two paper unions has generally not been as strong as in some unions in the control over local union policies. Rather much of the leadership has centered in regional organizations, which in the South play an important role. Given these factors, it is not expected that the paper unions will play a strong leadership role in the industry's racial policies. Rather one may expect in the future less "stand patism," some support for improving Negro rights, but no position of positive leadership that may severely alienate southern white members or become targets of intraunion political attacks.

The Segregated Locals

For more than a decade, the paper unions have been under great pressure from civil rights organizations and government to eliminate their segregated local unions. In recent years, companies, mindful of this pressure and correctly believing that they, as well as the unions, are subject to criticism where such locals exist, have added their pressure. Thus Union Camp successfully made consolidation of locals at Franklin, Virginia, and Savannah, Georgia, a contract renewal precondition in 1963; Westvaco also successfully added its pressure to achieve this in Charleston, South Carolina in 1968. As a result, neither union will today charter a separate local. None exists in such new mills as, for example, St. Regis, Monticello, or International Paper, Vicksburg, both in Mississippi; or the Alabama Kraft division of Georgia Kraft at Mahrt or Union Camp, Prattville, both in Alabama. On the other hand, separate locals do remain at many of the older mills, and are likely to endure for several reasons.

It should again be emphasized that the separate local system, although devised as a discriminatory institution, has not been totally adverse to the welfare of Negroes. The racial occupational pattern has been no different in the older southern mills where no segregated locals existed than in those where they are found. These separate locals became the training ground and the focal points of the Negro unionists' fight against discrimination by providing leaders and leadership training, by giving them representation and a voice, however outnumbered, in the national and regional union conferences and conventions. Merger in most cases with white locals means being swallowed up by a larger group, loss of representation to national and regional meetings, and loss of the prestige and power of union office. Said one white local president:

> The government is pressing the colored local to merge with us, the company wants it, and we'll be happy to have them. But I'll be damned if I can see anything that they are getting out of it, or why they should do it.[73]

Actually, today most Negro locals in the paper industry are reluctant to give up their identity unless they obtain specific agreement for local union officerships. Under court order, the merger of the Bogalusa locals of the UPP grants the Negro group a vice-presidency for a number of years. The Charleston, South Carolina, locals at Westvaco made the same deal by agreement, but the Negro locals in the Franklin, Virginia, and Savannah, Georgia, plants of Union Camp merged without such officer representation.

At the Mobile plant of Scott, the Negro local of the Pulp, Sulphite group is larger than the white one, probably a unique situation. Here the Negro local is much more anxious to merge than is the white one. The shoe is on the other foot.

Under today's arrangements and integration, when Negroes work in jobs under the jurisdiction of a white local, they become officially represented by, and may join the white local; the reverse is true for whites. Quite a few Negroes are joining former white locals; few if any whites are joining Negro locals. As such situations increase, as some Negro locals do agree to merge, and as new mills are unionized on an integrated basis, the problem should lessen in scope. Yet throughout the country, the emphasis on integration has been questioned by members of the black community. In many plants, despite

---

73. Interview, March 1969.

legal or union representation rights, Negroes are in fact still represented by a black committee and the legalities are winked at by all concerned. Where the Negro local has been abolished or merged, there is often deep dissatisfaction by the Negro employees, and considerable pressure on management, as well as on union leadership, to set up greater or special Negro representation in collective bargaining.

Perhaps it would be wise if the pressure to eliminate the separate locals were eased as long as other vestiges of discrimination and jim crowism are not being perpetuated thereby. The large numbers of Negroes in the converting plants is adding to their power in the unions, and in time may lessen their hostility to integration. In any case, it certainly is unseemly for one agency of the government to demand the elimination of segregated locals and for another agency, as in the St. Regis Jacksonville case, to entertain a complaint that discrimination exists on the part of the company and union because they are attempting to do just that!

GOVERNMENT POLICIES

That the impact of government policies on the racial policies of the paper industry has been great is indisputable. It is inconceivable that the policies of the industry would be so changed without government pressure. The court proceedings pursuant to the Civil Rights Act of 1964 permitted change at Bogalusa. What might have been a bloody racial confrontation appears, after initial strife, to have been settled peacefully. Government pressure, and government presence made the International Paper agreement possible and set the stage for the settlement of the seniority question in an equitable manner. Presidential Executive Orders and civil rights legislation induced companies in all parts of the country to re-examine their employment and upgrading policies and to alter their concepts of Negro labor utilization. Moreover, such orders and laws gave companies support when they desired to engage in "affirmative action." Finally, through the National Alliance of Businessmen, companies such as Mead, St. Regis, and Scott are expanding their hard core hiring in converting plants with training grants from the U.S. Department of Labor.

If the government has been both the carrot and the stick—and especially, and necessarily, the latter—it has also been irritatingly inconsistent and complex. The confusion over separate locals at the St. Regis Jacksonville mill has already been noted. Consider also the chronology of events at Crown Zellerbach's Bogalusa plant:

1. The General Services Administration the Company's main source of government business, sent in examiners who (extraordinarily) gave Crown a clean bill of health.

2. The President's Committee on Equal Employment Opportunity, established by the late President Kennedy, ordered a new investigation which found considerable discrimination.

3. The Equal Employment Opportunity Commission entered the picture and made an agreement to settle the case, which its chairman heralded widely.

4. The office of Federal Contract Compliance, President Johnson's successor to the PCEEO, pointed out the deficiencies in the EEOC agreement, and ordered the company to install unilaterally, regardless of its obligations under the Taft-Hartley Act, a new seniority system under which promotions were governed by a combination mill and job seniority.

5. Crown secured an injunction from the U.S. District Court, District of Columbia against OFCC's attempts to bar it prematurely from government contracts, but promptly agreed to install OFCC's mill plus job seniority system anyway.

6. Local 189, UPP, filed an unfair labor practice with the National Labor Relations Board charging the company with altering unilaterally the terms and conditions of employment in violation of the Taft-Hartley Act. The general counsel of the NLRB dismissed the charge several months later.

7. The U.S. Department of Justice obtained an injunction against the union at Bogalusa from striking over the company-OFCC agreement.

8. The U.S. District Court in New Orleans ordered the company and union to abolish mill plus job seniority installed at OFCC's insistence and to install instead mill seniority for the "affected class."

9. The company, unions, Negro group, and the Department of Justice agreed on administration of the new seniority system, submitted it and some related questions to the Judge, who took more than one year to sign the order and to issue his decision.

In directing a program so revolutionary in concept as that involved in civil rights legislation, conflicts, discrepancies, and cross-purpose currents are difficult to avoid. The civil rights program, however, undoubtedly suffers from an overabundance of agencies working not only without coordination, but almost, it would seem, actively seeking to avoid coordination. When, for example, the Equal Employment Opportunity Commission investigator arrived at the St. Regis plant, Jacksonville, Florida, to investigate the charge against merging the segregated locals, a Department of Defense compliance officer was already there for a follow up of a compliance review. (DOD is the principal St. Regis government customer, or "principal interest agency," as was GSA for Crown.) The company proposed a joint investigation by the two agencies. The EEOC investigator absolutely refused. Two separate and distinct investigations of company employment, testing, upgrading, promotion, etc., have ensued—and unfortunately this is typical in all industry. The point, of course, is not a plea for less effective civil rights enforcement, but less such harassment and more effective utilization of resources to get the job done.

CHAPTER VI

Some Problems of Equal Opportunity

The changed rules and mores required by the civil rights laws and regulations were certain to cause problems of adjustment. In addition, the impact of large numbers of Negroes employed in converting plants has significance. These and other issues are discussed in this chapter.

IMPACT ON WHITE EMPLOYEES

In southern mills, the white employees undoubtedly deeply resent the change in seniority rules and the integration of progression lines. Of this, there can be no doubt. Some of the local unions had been bastions of the Ku Klux Klan. Other white unionists have actively supported white citizens councils and groups opposing school or other public institutions, as well as plant, integration. There have been incidents of terrorism against which companies had to issue stern warning to suppress.

We have already noted that in small towns opening up better jobs to Negroes involves social as well as economic change. The roots go deep, and the reactions are harsh. There continues to be incidents of hostility between the races in the work force, although they are quickly suppressed now. There is also a sort of "underground" opposition among employees to the type of special agreements signed by International Paper, St. Regis, Scott, and others which could manifest itself in such ways as voting down wage agreements or even going on strike, ostensibly on other issues, but actually over the seniority rules negotiated to give Negroes an opportunity to achieve their "rightful place." It is likely that many white employees will continue to pull, haul, and balk for many years. On the other hand, the high earnings of paper mill employees and the lack of alternative employment opportunity has offset some of the reluctance of white employees to working side by side with Negroes.

In the South, where the government has pushed integration on the job, white reaction has been varied. In some cases white employees have bid on, and won, jobs formerly reserved for Negroes just as

Negroes have bid on formerly all-white jobs. This has caused considerable bitterness among Negroes who feel that they can lose as many jobs as they gain. On the other hand, it is difficult to see how some jobs can be reserved for Negroes and all others opened to them without discrimination. Yet it is true, that if all jobs are available on a competitive basis, Negro educational and experience disadvantages make it difficult for them to win a proportionate share.

In the case of janitorial or certain all laboring or service jobs that have traditionally been associated with Negroes, integration attempts in the South have been generally quite unsuccessful. If whites are employed in such jobs, they do not remain long. The stigma of a "Negro job" is often an effective deterrent to the recruitment of whites. Of course, in times of high unemployment that deterrent could be less operative.

Facility Integration, Nature and Impact

Compulsory segregation of facilities is, in terms of economic theory, a method of distinguishing the Negro work force from the white, and thereby making it either more costly to employ Negroes, or if they are employed, to integrate Negroes throughout the plant. By hiring no Negroes in a segregated economy, the plant would need only one set of time clocks, drinking fountains, locker rooms, toilets, and eating facilities. If Negroes were employed, but confined to segregated departments, the number of duplicate facilities could be kept at a minimum. On the other hand, if a plant were totally mixed under the segregation laws, then the most expensive setup would be required, for facilities throughout the plant would have to be duplicated. The basic economics of segregation were thus carefully designed to limit the ability of Negroes to compete with whites for jobs by making it more costly to employ Negroes and most expensive to employ them on an integrated basis. These laws were, of course, designed by southern states between 1880 and World War I, at a time when the white lower, or nonplantation classes came to power. Segregation in education, transportation, housing, and political disenfranchisement, of course, added to the economic burden of Negroes by giving them inferior training, inferior location for and access to jobs, and impotency to alter the situation. The impact of decades of required segregation and inferior treatment still depreciates the ability of Negroes to compete for work on an even basis with whites.

The elimination of all segregated facilities has been a determined goal of the Office of Federal Contract Compliance, and it has firmly demanded that this occur in all southern mills and plants. (The author knows of no such segregation in northern paper facilities.) The response of the white paper workers has been one of opposition, with some violence and much boycotting, especially of locker room facilities. Enforcement of *de facto* segregation of facilities, either by custom, boycott, fear, or harassment, is not uncommon.

The humorist-philosopher, Harry Golden, has often said that integration in the South would be furthered by the custom of "stand up eating." He proposed when the early lunch counter sitdowns occurred, to remove all seats, opining that whites did not seem to object to standing as they did to sitting with Negroes while eating. Faced with boycotted eating facilities and consequent financial losses, paper manufacturers and other employers have turned to this concept with the use of vending machines in southern plants. The impersonality of the machine seems to remove the heat from racial integration. Since people usually carry the products of machines to tables where their friends are, generally Negroes and white eat in the same room but not at the same tables, and the boycotts subside.

A similar gimmick satisfies the drinking fountain problem. Paper cups supplied seem to end fountain damage and sabotage. The individual cup apparently satisfies the segregation psychosis of the racists and permits all to drink from one set of fountains, which incidentally tap water from one supply.

Locker rooms are the last bastion of the boycott in all once segregated plants. Most whites, at least initially, refuse to use them and instead change and shower at home. In time perhaps, the sweaty odor of the unbathed husband will induce his wife and family to pressure him to discover that a shower and fresh clothes in an integrated environment are preferable to sweat, smell, and dirt in the segregation of the home.

Both the Equal Employment Opportunity Commission and the Office of Federal Contract Compliance have been criticized for concentrating too much of their efforts on integrating facilities. Insofar as such efforts might detract from those most directly concerned with opening new job opportunities, this is a valid point. On the other hand, the segregation laws were enacted in order to make it more costly to employ Negroes and they do in fact label Negroes as second-class citizens unfit to associate with whites. Moreover, segregated facilities frequently are built around segregated work locations. Maintaining such segregation places an added burden on Negroes desiring to advance to former all-white jobs. Elimination of segregated facilities is not as important as opening up new jobs, but it is undoubtedly a necessary concomitant of the same process.

Converting Plants

It is not uncommon in a converting or wastepaper plant in a northern city to find that the labor force is either predominantly black or nearly so. As the Negro complement has increased in such plants, the tendency is for white labor not to apply, or if employed, to leave promptly. Moreover, the existing white labor force then tends to drift away.

Some of the white reluctance to work in plants with a heavy Negro complement is attributable to Negro efforts to jostle, ostracize, or even to brutalize the white minority. These are difficulties Negroes have had, and they occur also when the racial balance is turned heavily against whites. For the most part, however, the white reluctance to work in a heavily black labor force is voluntary. Just as neighborhoods which are moving toward Negro concentration seem soon to result in the whites leaving, so it seems to occur in industrial employment.

This is not a phenomenon peculiar to the paper industry. In our study of the automobile industry, we noted that this was occurring, and that the trend was accentuated in periods of a tight labor market.[74] In the automobile industry, however, the pay is high and existing employees tend to remain on the payroll even if new ones of their race do not apply. In the converting plants, the rates are low and the tendency of many whites is to leave. The effect, of course, is to deprive the employer of a share of the labor force but there seems to be little possibility that the trend can be changed, at least as long as jobs are so plentiful.

---

74. Herbert R. Northrup, *The Negro in the Automobile Industry,* The Racial Policies of American Industry, Report No. 1 (Philadelphia, Industrial Research Unit, Wharton School of Finance and Commerce, University of Pennsylvania, 1968), pp. 58-59.

EFFICIENCY AND TURNOVER

In the mills, employees are carefully selected. Even though turnover rises in times of full employment, it does not become large. In the southern mills, turnover is heavier in the lower-rated jobs than in higher ones. Since these jobs are largely filled with Negroes, their turnover is likely to be higher than whites. But turnover is always higher for low-rated, or entry jobs, than higher, better paying ones. The large number of long service Negro employees in southern mills attests to the fact that their turnover—or for that matter absenteeism and tardiness—is not a problem.

In converting plants, and in many small wastepaper operations, turnover is simply unbelievably high, and absenteeism and tardiness equally large. These plants are hiring marginal employees, largely Negroes, who have little or no industrial experience and great difficulty in adapting to industrial life. Paper companies, like many others, have been slow to realize the need for special training and indoctrination for such employees who find the factory a strange and bewildering place. It is easy for such workers to become discouraged, to "blow their paycheck" on one weekend and to miss Monday because of a hangover, or to purchase an inadequate used car and break down on the way to work.

Inexperience in industry, poor educational backgrounds, lack of motivation as a result of lack of belief in or experience with equal opportunity, are all factors in absentee, tardiness, and turnover rates. It would be surprising if the new Negro employees did not fall behind in these measures. Those who survive six months or one year usually adapt to the requirements of industrial life, take advantage of their earnings, and move toward the stability of other experienced employees.

The distinction between those with experience, and new employees is vividly illustrated by data from a wastepaper mill in the Philadelphia area. It employs a blue collar work force of 36, a majority of whom are black. In 1968, to maintain this work force, it employed 110 people. Yet it ended the year with 29 of its original 36 blue collar workers. In other words, all the turnover involved seven jobs!

Several companies, including Mead, St. Regis, and Scott, have attacked this problem with special training programs under grants from the U.S. Department of Labor, pursuant to the JOBS program of the National Association of Businessmen. These programs give recruits special training in basic communications and arithmetic skills and, in shop mores and behavior and attempt to motivate them before giving them on-the-job training. Although it is too early to be certain, preliminary findings indicate that the attendance, punctuality, and performance of these trainees are superior, and their turnover less than employees hired during the same period without such training.

This should not be surprising. Given the current labor market and the relatively low wage rates in the converting plants, there is not likely to be much difference between those certified as "hard core" and those dropping in converting plant employment offices. Hence, the ones trained should turn out better. Perhaps the industry would find it profitable to reorient its hiring procedures and to provide vestibule training and motivation in order to reduce the turnover, tardiness, and motivational problems in its converting plants.

EFFICIENCY AND GOVERNMENT PRESSURE

Although some mill managements claim that they are now employing persons of less caliber than they require, the numbers involved are not great and there is no evidence that efficiency has been impaired. Of course, it is not possible to integrate Negroes or any inexperienced group, into the work force without cost. Yet it is very likely that some standards have been established unreasonably high and have, purposely or not, excluded Negroes without adding substantially to efficiency.

Testing has been a source of conflict in the industry. It is still widely used although some mills, like Crown Zellerbach at Bogalusa, suspended it under OFCC pressure, and later, after study, at all of its locations as a condition for employment in hourly rated jobs. International Paper validated its tests at every southern plant to OFCC's satisfaction and surprise and other companies are attempting to do likewise. EEOC and OFCC have issued different testing regulations, another area where a little agency coordination and less rivalry and duplication could achieve much.

A final aspect of government pressure is the tendency of some Negroes to appeal any discipline to the Equal Employment Opportunity Commission. This is, of course, understandable, especially in view of the failure of the paper unions to protect Negro employee rights any better than they have. Moreover, in many instances these complaints are valid.

On the other hand, EEOC investigators often tend to approach problems with a conviction that redress is in order regardless of the circumstances, without careful investigation and sometimes where inefficiency, poor workmanship, or bad behavior may be at the root of the problem. The result is considerable employer and white worker anguish and ill-feeling, and the reluctance of foremen to discipline Negroes. White employees are heard to claim that a double standard exists—that Negroes "get away" with behavior that they cannot. A "double standard" is troublesome, whomever it favors.

SOME PERSPECTIVES

Changing racial-occupational patterns in southern mills and the heavy influx of Negroes into urban paper converting plants have naturally caused problems. Yet despite some initial violence, the change has been quite peaceful. Government forces have complicated the problems by their lack of coordination, yet change has been initiated, forced, and peacefully effected by government. In retrospect, both the problems have been less severe and the progress greater than thoughtful observers could have predicted, or even hoped.

CHAPTER VII

Determinants of Industry Policy

A number of factors have been noted throughout this study which have contributed to the racial policies of the pulp and paper industry. These and others are discussed in this chapter.

THE DEMAND FOR LABOR

Throughout their history in industry, Negroes have made their greatest gains in periods of labor shortage. The converting branch of the paper industry is an excellent example of this generalization— Negroes came into converting plants in force during World War II, and dramatically increased their share of these jobs during the 1960's. It seems incontrovertible that Negro participation in the labor force of these plants has been heavily a function of the state of the labor market, given the basically unskilled nature of the work and the relatively low wages.

In the mills, no such shortage of labor has existed, except in wastepaper mills located in metropolitan areas. The mills using primary fibers are generally located in small communities where they pay the highest wages and provide the steadiest employment. These mills have been able to set high employment standards and still obtain sufficient employees without difficulty.

The stress on civil rights and minority group employment, or on employment of the disadvantaged, requires that the mill managements re-examine their employment standards in order to distinguish the criteria which are essential for proper job performance and those which are not so essential but permit them to take full advantage of their ability to employ the very best personnel available. To do otherwise will continue to contribute to the exclusion of the disadvantaged, largely Negroes, from mill employment.

In the South, labor market factors first aided Negro employment, then hindered it. When the industry entered the South in force during the 1930's, it needed a large supply of unskilled labor, and Negroes were available for such jobs in abundance. Then as methods and machine improvements occurred during the 1950's, Negroes were disproportionately affected. Not only were they concentrated in jobs which were eliminated, but they were excluded from competing in other areas by management-union rules governing the racial-occupational pattern in the industry. Now that the jobs from which they were excluded have been opened, Negroes find themselves at a disadvantage because of their disproportionate lack of education and experience. In view of the ability of the mill section of the industry to pay the wages which it does, it is likely to continue to attract an abundance of well-qualified labor to man the ever more complicated, instrumented, and automatic equipment. Negroes will, therefore, continue to find the job competition in mills to be severe.

THE JOB STRUCTURE

The job structure in converting plants is very favorable to disadvantaged persons because of the high percentage of unskilled labor still required which necessitates little training. The success of a few key companies in utilizing hard core personnel attests to the ability of converting plants to absorb personnel with minimum education and virtually no industrial experience.

This, of course, may not always be true. The Industrial relations executive of a converting group wrote the author after reading the draft:

> I would . . . like to point out an area of possible concern for further opportunity for the uneducated Negro in converting operations, particularly paperboard packaging. Our operating people have found some 41 separate material handling tasks necessary to manufacture and ship folding cartons. Most of these tasks are performed by under educated blacks. And as you point out, there is a higher ratio of low skilled to skilled jobs in converting. Unions in converting are being more and more controlled by the membership in low skilled positions. Collective bargaining pressure is therefore being concentrated on these positions causing an accelerated increase in labor rates. Management response will and must be automation in order to keep unit costs down. As of this point in time, the equipment people have not recognized this need, but they will. As these material handling tasks are eliminated, so will opportunity for the under educated white and black in converting.[75]

Unskilled jobs are already fast disappearing from the mills. Entry jobs often do not require much skill, but the occupational seniority

---

75. Letter, July 11, 1969.

system means that employees taking entry jobs in a progression must have the capacity to learn the top jobs in that line. This is how persons are trained to man the machines. It is difficult to conceive of a different method of training given the nature of the equipment, its cost, size, and complexities.

Since the mills must have employees capable of progressing up the occupational ladder, and since the wages paid attract an abundance of qualified personnel, the industry must make special efforts to employ and to upgrade Negroes if it is to fulfill its civil rights obligations. This study indicates that several key companies are doing just that, but the statistics also indicate that the impact in terms of numbers is small. The industry, as a whole, therefore has been slow to alter basic employment practices.

GOVERNMENT PRESSURE

We have already noted that government pressure has been *THE* prime motivating force in altering the practices of the southern mills and in moving them toward a more equalitarian stance. Such pressures have not been required in the converting plants where basic labor market factors have been the prime determinant of the racial employment labor force mix. In the southern mills, however, it required the full authority of the legislative, the executive, and the judicial branches of government to alter the practices of an industry. The author knows of a mill opened in South Carolina in 1962 whose only Negro employee was (and perhaps still is) a porter; and another being built in Texas in 1966 with segregated facilities until the architectural plans were altered at the insistence of an executive of a concern having a minor stock interest. Certainly there is little evidence that the industry as a whole, despite some outstanding exceptions, was moving very fast toward equal employment practices until the federal government became directly and emphatically involved.

UNIONISM AND SENIORITY

Some discriminatory practices have been uncovered in converting plant union contracts and practices. Some southern multiwall bag plants had segregated departments and seniority lists; some box plants kept Negro "take off" men off the regular press progressions; Negroes have been assigned only heavy duty and dirty jobs in corrugating facilities. In general, however, such segregation was not a regular practice, but varied throughout both North and South. Of significance is the fact that the paper unions have generally accepted this practice. There was no evidence uncovered that they sought to eliminate discriminatory policies in effect in converting plants, although where Negroes are a majority or a large minority of such plants, this may well have happened by virtue of membership pressures on local and interested union officials.

In the South, the unions, as repeatedly noted, institutionalized the *status quo* of the 1930's, and regularly reflected the desires of the predominantly white membership to deny improvement to Negroes. The national leadership of both paper unions has generally been weak, leaving much authority to regional and local union bodies. Loss of the West Coast group to an independent union accentuated the national officers' fear of other defections. The West Coast Association's attempt to spread into the South and its racist appeals increased the tendency of the national union officers to oppose changes in the racial barriers.

The replacement of the current Pulp, Sulphite officials by younger, more vigorous, and modern leadership, and the resignation of the president of the United Papermakers and Paperworkers who was committed to a southern *status quo* that he had a large part in organizing, in favor of a man with a more flexible and liberal approach, have been significant. Both new presidents aided in the achievement of the key International Paper agreement of 1968 and its ratification by the southern local unions.

The insistence of Negroes in retaining many of their segregated locals is basically a reflection of their distrust of the white dominated unions. The record indicates much to support that distrust. Time will determine the extent of improvement in union treatment of its black members.

The seniority system in the paper mills is the codification of a logical on-the-job training and upgrading system which arose out of the industry's practices and requirements. In the South it was perverted by race discrimination. The perversion need not blind us to the fact that the system is not *per se* discriminatory. The adoption by the court in the Crown Zellerbach litigation and by International

Paper, Scott, St. Regis, and other companies of the mill-in-job seniority criterion gives the "affected class" its opportunity to achieve its "rightful place." When this corrective measure works itself out, there is no reason why the job seniority system cannot remain in effect provided it is administered without discrimination and with non-discriminatory hiring policies.

The nature of training, promotion, and seniority, however, insures that movement up the occupational ladder for Negroes will be a time consuming process. It is not likely that the overall statistics for the industry will demonstrate marked change in the occupational status of Negroes for a number of years. Nevertheless, now that the bars are down, steady improvement may be expected to manifest itself slowly.

LOCATIONAL AND REGIONAL FACTORS

Locational and regional factors play an important role in the racial policies of the industry. We have already noted that the racial composition of converting plant labor forces is heavily dependent on the plant's location. Those in cities with a sizable Negro population have a much larger percentage of black employees than those located in suburbs or in areas of sparse Negro population. Similarly, wastepaper mills are usually found in city areas in order to assure a supply of raw materials, and they too have a high percentage of Negro employees if the city's population is significantly black.

The primary fiber mills had few Negroes before the industry moved South. The Maine woods, and those of the Midwest and Far West are regions where almost no Negroes dwell. Only in the South, where in the 1930's Negroes were concentrated, was there an available Negro labor force. The great bulk of Negroes working in mills is still found in the South.

MANAGERIAL POLICY

There remains, when all other factors are accounted for, differences in the racial policies of companies which are located in the same area, operate in the same industry, deal with the same unions, and are constrained by identical government laws, regulations, and pressures. Such differences can be attributable to different marketing orientations or managerial postures which guide the companies.

Few paper companies are consumer oriented. They sell primarily, often exclusively, to other manufacturers, without brand names or product differentiation. The thought that their employment policies were a matter of public interest and concern was not a part of the industry's general outlook. Events, such as those in Bogalusa, and the outcry when Hammermill Paper announced jointly with Governor George Wallace of Alabama at the time of the demonstrations in Selma, Alabama, that it would build a mill there, literally surprised and shocked most executives in the industry. Indeed, a prime difficulty encountered by the industry is reflected by such events as Crown Zellerbach joining Plans for Progress and apparently being unaware of the full implications of the meaning of nondiscrimination insofar as the Bogalusa facilities were concerned. Public pressures which consumer oriented concerns have long been aware of in other aspects of business seem to have had a massive impact on most paper companies in civil rights matters for the first time. Their response has reflected surprise and concern, and their reactions have often been hesitant until the full import of the issue has been made clear.

A basic research hypothesis of The Racial Policies of American Industry series is that consumer oriented industries and companies are more likely to be aware of external pressures, such as those engendered by civil rights, and to take action which will satisfactorily meet such pressures. The record of the paper industry tends to support this thesis. Moreover, a major company in the industry which *does* have a consumer orientation, and which *does* market to consumers products under its corporate name, Scott Paper Company, was an early leader in Negro integration and affirmative action. It is difficult to believe that this is coincidental. Rather it reflects a sound understanding of marketing needs.

Managerial philosophy has also played a key role in differentiating corporate civil rights policies. Companies such as St. Regis, Scott, and Mead are headed by people whom this author has found honestly concerned. Racial policies developed in some of their mills were profoundly and personally embarrassing to them as contradictory to their personal philosophies. A changed governmental stance gave them the opportunity for change, and they have attempted to move toward change as rapidly as possible. While St. Regis and International Paper were developing plans for fully integrated mill labor forces in the heart of Mississippi, another management was blithely (and illegally) building a mill with segregated facilities in a far more integrated area of Texas. The difference was management philosophy, concern, and direction.

Even the most concerned manager, however, must operate within constraints. In view of the pressures from large customers to avoid interruptions of sales and service, the great capital investments in mills and the costs of lost time, pressures from white employees, often institutionalized and enlarged by unions, company managements must move cautiously, as they have. The difference is the degree of emphasis put on civil rights, and this varies tremendously. Except for a few leaders, however, the industry in general has stressed civil rights largely only when failure to do so threatened sales or operational stability.

Another factor which accounts for the industry's slow movement in the civil rights area is the degree of autonomy of many southern operations. Many southern mills operate as completely decentralized departments, with little headquarters direction as long as the paper and profits are produced. The large number which are jointly owned by two or more concerns and/or produce strictly for captive markets accentuates this factor. Managers of southern mills are paid to produce paper at the lowest cost. Unless central headquarters requires them to consider the racial implications of their actions, mill management cannot be expected to do so. For many paper companies, it is only within the last few years that such control and direction have been forthcoming, or at least stressed.

CHAPTER VIII

Concluding Remarks

The racial occupational employment pattern in southern mills kept Negroes out of the better paying jobs until massive government intervention altered the *status quo* in the mid-1960's. The nature of the industry's training and seniority system, despite its modification to assist Negroes once discriminated against, insures that change will occur slowly. Nevertheless, change is occurring and Negroes will gradually move up the occupational ladder as they are already doing in some companies.

For mills outside of the South, except for city located wastepaper plants, the dearth of Negro population in areas of mill concentration indicates little change in the future racial composition of the labor force. Wastepaper mills, which pay lower wages than larger mills, will continue to have a relatively high concentration of Negroes in their labor force if located in Negro population centers. The converting plants will probably tend to increase their already high Negro concentration because of labor market pressures, locational factors, and the relatively low wages paid. The extent to which this is so will, of course, vary in accordance with competitive job opportunities, and the degree of mechanization. If the wages are substantially increased in converting, the industry will undoubtedly substitute machinery for men. These jobs could then both decrease and be more attractive to whites. At the present time, alternative job opportunities seem more and more to induce whites to leave jobs in paper converting plants to Negroes in areas where Negroes dwell in large numbers.

APPENDIX A

Basic Statistical Tables, 1964, 1966, and 1968

TABLE A-1. *Paper and Allied Products Industry*
Employment by Race, Sex, and Occupational Group
60 Companies, 521 Establishments
Total United States, 1964

Occupational Group	All Employees			Male			Female		
	Total	Negro	Percent Negro	Total	Negro	Percent Negro	Total	Negro	Percent Negro
Officials and managers	13,703	24	0.2	13,590	23	0.2	113	1	0.9
Professionals	7,879	6	0.1	7,648	6	0.1	231	—	—
Technicians	3,843	20	0.5	3,318	15	0.5	525	5	1.0
Sales workers	4,729	8	0.2	4,524	8	0.2	205	—	—
Office and clerical	18,113	163	0.9	6,862	107	1.6	11,251	56	0.5
Total white collar	48,267	221	0.5	35,942	159	0.4	12,325	62	0.5
Craftsmen	43,114	646	1.5	42,393	636	1.5	721	10	1.4
Operatives	76,428	5,304	6.9	64,888	5,075	7.8	11,540	229	2.0
Laborers	37,065	5,681	15.3	30,412	5,507	18.1	6,653	174	2.6
Service workers	3,824	950	24.8	3,494	857	24.5	330	93	28.2
Total blue collar	160,431	12,581	7.8	141,187	12,075	8.6	19,244	506	2.6
Total	208,698	12,802	6.1	177,129	12,234	6.9	31,569	568	1.8

Source: Data in author's possession.

TABLE A-2. Paper and Allied Products Industry
Employment by Race, Sex, and Occupational Group
46 Companies, 564 Establishments
Total United States, 1966

Occupational Group	All Employees			Male			Female		
	Total	Negro	Percent Negro	Total	Negro	Percent Negro	Total	Negro	Percent Negro
Officials and managers	17,238	36	0.2	17,086	35	0.2	152	1	0.7
Professionals	7,085	5	0.1	6,905	4	0.1	180	1	0.6
Technicians	4,682	30	0.6	3,949	22	0.6	733	8	1.1
Sales workers	3,916	8	0.2	3,648	7	0.2	268	1	0.4
Office and clerical	19,301	280	1.5	7,870	227	2.9	11,431	53	0.5
Total white collar	52,222	359	0.7	39,458	295	0.7	12,764	64	0.5
Craftsmen	55,524	1,068	1.9	54,676	1,050	1.9	848	18	2.1
Operatives	98,363	7,399	7.5	84,754	6,912	8.2	13,609	487	3.6
Laborers	44,805	6,877	15.3	37,031	6,517	17.6	7,774	360	4.6
Service workers	4,418	1,107	25.1	4,063	1,018	25.1	355	89	25.1
Total blue collar	203,110	16,451	8.1	180,524	15,497	8.6	22,586	954	4.2
Total	255,332	16,810	6.6	219,982	15,792	7.2	35,350	1,018	2.9

Source: Data in author's possession.

TABLE A-3. *Paper and Allied Products Industry
Employment by Race, Sex, and Occupational Group
51 Companies, 599 Establishments
Total United States, 1968*

Occupational Group	All Employees			Male			Female		
	Total	Negro	Percent Negro	Total	Negro	Percent Negro	Total	Negro	Percent Negro
Officials and managers	19,162	63	0.3	18,999	61	0.3	163	2	1.2
Professionals	7,405	25	0.3	7,118	24	0.3	287	1	0.3
Technicians	4,841	58	1.2	4,220	45	1.1	621	13	2.1
Sales workers	3,467	12	0.3	3,208	11	0.3	259	1	0.4
Office and clerical	19,003	339	1.8	6,931	213	3.1	12,072	126	1.0
Total white collar	53,878	497	0.9	40,476	354	0.9	13,402	143	1.1
Craftsmen	57,632	1,274	2.2	56,925	1,251	2.2	707	23	3.3
Operatives	101,367	9,380	9.3	87,523	8,531	9.7	13,844	849	6.1
Laborers	48,332	7,352	15.2	39,932	6,834	17.1	8,400	518	6.2
Service workers	4,419	967	21.9	4,000	894	22.4	419	73	17.4
Total blue collar	211,750	18,973	9.0	188,380	17,510	9.3	23,370	1,463	6.3
Total	265,628	19,470	7.3	228,856	17,864	7.8	36,772	1,606	4.4

Source: Data in author's possession.

TABLE A-4. Paper and Allied Products Industry
Employment by Race, Sex, and Occupational Group
Pulp, Paper, and Paperboard Mills
23 Companies, 174 Establishments
Total United States, 1964

Occupational Group	All Employees			Male			Female		
	Total	Negro	Percent Negro	Total	Negro	Percent Negro	Total	Negro	Percent Negro
Officials and managers	8,670	9	0.1	8,612	8	0.1	58	1	1.7
Professionals	5,933	6	0.1	5,764	6	0.1	169	—	—
Technicians	3,010	14	0.5	2,590	11	0.4	420	3	0.7
Sales workers	2,144	6	0.3	2,068	6	0.3	76	—	—
Office and clerical	11,045	120	1.1	4,259	75	1.8	6,786	45	0.7
Total white collar	30,802	155	0.5	23,293	106	0.5	7,509	49	0.7
Craftsmen	30,436	306	1.0	29,978	302	1.0	458	4	0.9
Operatives	48,358	3,006	6.2	43,353	2,931	6.8	5,005	75	1.5
Laborers	20,518	3,825	18.6	18,044	3,799	21.1	2,474	26	1.1
Service workers	2,591	585	22.6	2,325	507	21.8	266	78	29.3
Total blue collar	101,903	7,722	7.6	93,700	7,539	8.0	8,203	183	2.2
Total	132,705	7,877	5.9	116,993	7,645	6.5	15,712	232	1.5

Source: Data in author's possession.

TABLE A-5. *Paper and Allied Products Industry*
Employment by Race, Sex, and Occupational Group
Pulp, Paper, and Paperboard Mills
46 Companies, 239 Establishments
Total United States, 1966

Occupational Group	All Employees			Male			Female		
	Total	Negro	Percent Negro	Total	Negro	Percent Negro	Total	Negro	Percent Negro
Officials and managers	11,584	17	0.1	11,505	16	0.1	79	1	1.3
Professionals	5,597	5	0.1	5,470	4	0.1	127	1	0.8
Technicians	3,881	19	0.5	3,255	14	0.4	626	5	0.8
Sales workers	1,417	2	0.1	1,290	2	0.2	127	—	—
Office and clerical	12,221	184	1.5	5,300	154	2.9	6,921	30	0.4
Total white collar	34,700	227	0.7	26,820	190	0.7	7,880	37	0.5
Craftsmen	42,455	534	1.3	41,974	528	1.3	481	6	1.2
Operatives	68,340	4,234	6.2	61,387	4,038	6.6	6,953	196	2.8
Laborers	27,858	4,395	15.8	24,662	4,356	17.7	3,196	39	1.2
Service workers	3,355	786	23.4	3,067	715	23.3	288	71	24.7
Total blue collar	142,008	9,949	7.0	131,090	9,637	7.4	10,918	312	2.9
Total	176,708	10,176	5.8	157,910	9,827	6.2	18,798	349	1.9

Source: Data in author's possession.

TABLE A-6. Paper and Allied Products Industry
Employment by Race, Sex, and Occupational Group
Pulp, Paper, and Paperboard Mills
47 Companies, 259 Establishments
Total United States, 1968

Occupational Group	All Employees			Male			Female		
	Total	Negro	Percent Negro	Total	Negro	Percent Negro	Total	Negro	Percent Negro
Officials and managers	12,777	36	0.3	12,688	34	0.3	89	2	2.2
Professionals	5,939	23	0.4	5,741	23	0.4	198	—	—
Technicians	3,831	50	1.3	3,328	38	1.1	503	12	2.4
Sales workers	1,014	2	0.2	938	2	0.2	76	—	—
Office and clerical	11,828	240	2.0	4,533	171	3.8	7,295	69	0.9
Total white collar	35,389	351	1.0	27,228	268	1.0	8,161	83	1.0
Craftsmen	42,255	634	1.5	41,999	627	1.5	256	7	2.7
Operatives	70,870	5,730	8.1	62,921	5,286	8.4	7,949	444	5.6
Laborers	29,309	4,565	15.6	25,769	4,428	17.2	3,540	137	3.9
Service workers	3,270	764	23.4	2,922	707	24.2	348	57	16.4
Total blue collar	145,704	11,693	8.0	133,611	11,048	8.3	12,093	645	5.3
Total	181,093	12,044	6.7	160,839	11,316	7.0	20,254	728	3.6

Source: Data in author's possession.

TABLE A-7. *Paper and Allied Products Industry*
Employment by Race, Sex, and Occupational Group
Converting Plants
57 Companies, 347 Establishments
Total United States, 1964

Occupational Group	All Employees			Male			Female		
	Total	Negro	Percent Negro	Total	Negro	Percent Negro	Total	Negro	Percent Negro
Officials and managers	5,033	15	0.3	4,978	15	0.3	55	—	—
Professionals	1,946	—	—	1,884	—	—	62	—	—
Technicians	833	6	0.7	728	4	0.5	105	2	1.9
Sales workers	2,585	2	0.1	2,456	2	0.1	129	—	—
Office and clerical	7,068	43	0.6	2,603	32	1.2	4,465	11	0.2
Total white collar	17,465	66	0.4	12,649	53	0.4	4,816	13	0.3
Craftsmen	12,678	340	2.7	12,415	334	2.7	263	6	2.3
Operatives	28,070	2,298	8.2	21,535	2,144	10.0	6,535	154	2.4
Laborers	16,547	1,856	11.2	12,368	1,708	13.8	4,179	148	3.5
Service workers	1,233	365	29.6	1,169	350	29.9	64	15	23.4
Total blue collar	58,528	4,859	8.3	47,487	4,536	9.6	11,041	323	2.9
Total	75,993	4,925	6.5	60,136	4,589	7.6	15,857	336	2.1

Source: Data in author's possession.

TABLE A-8. *Paper and Allied Products Industry*
Employment by Race, Sex, and Occupational Group
Converting Plants
31 Companies, 325 Establishments
Total United States, 1966

Occupational Group	All Employees			Male			Female		
	Total	Negro	Percent Negro	Total	Negro	Percent Negro	Total	Negro	Percent Negro
Officials and managers	5,654	19	0.3	5,581	19	0.3	73	—	—
Professionals	1,488	—	—	1,435	—	—	53	—	—
Technicians	801	11	1.4	694	8	1.2	107	3	2.8
Sales workers	2,499	6	0.2	2,358	5	0.2	141	1	0.7
Office and clerical	7,080	96	1.4	2,570	73	2.8	4,510	23	0.5
Total white collar	17,522	132	0.8	12,638	105	0.8	4,884	27	0.6
Craftsmen	13,069	534	4.1	12,702	522	4.1	367	12	3.3
Operatives	30,023	3,165	10.5	23,367	2,874	12.3	6,656	291	4.4
Laborers	16,947	2,482	14.6	12,369	2,161	17.5	4,578	321	7.0
Service workers	1,063	321	30.2	996	303	30.4	67	18	26.9
Total blue collar	61,102	6,502	10.6	49,434	5,860	11.9	11,668	642	5.5
Total	78,624	6,634	8.4	62,072	5,965	9.6	16,552	669	4.0

Source: Data in author's possession.

TABLE A-9. *Paper and Allied Products Industry*
Employment by Race, Sex, and Occupational Group
Converting Plants
34 Companies, 340 Establishments
Total United States, 1968

Occupational Group	All Employees			Male			Female		
	Total	Negro	Percent Negro	Total	Negro	Percent Negro	Total	Negro	Percent Negro
Officials and managers	6,385	27	0.4	6,311	27	0.4	74	—	—
Professionals	1,466	2	0.1	1,377	1	0.1	89	1	1.1
Technicians	1,010	8	0.8	892	7	0.8	118	1	0.8
Sales workers	2,453	10	0.4	2,270	9	0.4	183	1	0.5
Office and clerical	7,175	99	1.4	2,398	42	1.8	4,777	57	1.2
Total white collar	18,489	146	0.8	13,248	86	0.6	5,241	60	1.1
Craftsmen	15,377	640	4.2	14,926	624	4.2	451	16	3.5
Operatives	30,497	3,650	12.0	24,602	3,245	13.2	5,895	405	6.9
Laborers	19,023	2,787	14.7	14,163	2,406	17.0	4,860	381	7.8
Service workers	1,149	203	17.7*	1,078	187	17.3	71	16	22.5
Total blue collar	66,046	7,280	11.0	54,769	6,462	11.8	11,277	818	7.3
Total	84,535	7,426	8.8	68,017	6,548	9.6	16,518	878	5.3

Source: Data in author's possession.
*This low percentage of service workers in 1968 as compared with previous years is undoubtedly the result of a sampling error and should be disregarded for purposes of analysis.

TABLE A-10.   *Paper and Allied Products Industry*
Employment by Race, Sex, and Occupational Group
12 Companies, 28 Establishments
New England Region, 1964

Occupational Group	All Employees			Male			Female		
	Total	Negro	Percent Negro	Total	Negro	Percent Negro	Total	Negro	Percent Negro
Officials and managers	748	—	—	742	—	—	6	—	—
Professionals	238	—	—	228	—	—	10	—	—
Technicians	115	—	—	97	—	—	18	—	—
Sales workers	172	—	—	152	—	—	20	—	—
Office and clerical	870	1	0.1	279	1	0.4	591	—	—
Total white collar	2,143	1	*	1,498	1	0.1	645	—	—
Craftsmen	2,191	11	0.5	2,181	11	0.5	10	—	—
Operatives	4,097	61	1.5	3,161	42	1.3	936	19	2.0
Laborers	2,236	20	0.9	1,958	19	1.0	278	1	0.4
Service workers	196	2	1.0	188	2	1.1	8	—	—
Total blue collar	8,720	94	1.1	7,488	74	1.0	1,232	20	1.6
Total	10,863	95	0.9	8,986	75	0.8	1,877	20	1.1

Source: Data in author's possession.
Note: For regional definitions, see Table 4, p. 15.
*Less than 0.05 percent.

TABLE A-11. *Paper and Allied Products Industry*
Employment by Race, Sex, and Occupational Group
22 Companies, 51 Establishments
New England Region, 1966

Occupational Group	All Employees			Male			Female		
	Total	Negro	Percent Negro	Total	Negro	Percent Negro	Total	Negro	Percent Negro
Officials and managers	1,442	2	0.1	1,424	2	0.1	18	—	—
Professionals	581	—	—	566	—	—	15	—	—
Technicians	568	2	0.4	432	2	0.5	136	—	—
Sales workers	321	1	0.3	285	1	0.4	36	—	—
Office and clerical	1,897	3	0.2	704	1	0.1	1,193	2	0.2
Total white collar	4,809	8	0.2	3,411	6	0.2	1,398	2	0.1
Craftsmen	5,452	27	0.5	5,371	27	0.5	81	—	—
Operatives	9,030	140	1.6	7,078	112	1.6	1,952	28	1.4
Laborers	4,032	107	2.7	3,385	98	2.9	647	9	1.4
Service workers	421	7	1.7	379	7	1.8	42	—	—
Total blue collar	18,935	281	1.5	16,213	244	1.5	2,722	37	1.4
Total	23,744	289	1.2	19,624	250	1.3	4,120	39	0.9

Source: Data in author's possession.
Note: For regional definitions, see Table 4, p. 15.

TABLE A-12. Paper and Allied Products Industry
Employment by Race, Sex, and Occupational Group
21 Companies, 46 Establishments
New England Region, 1968

Occupational Group	All Employees			Male			Female		
	Total	Negro	Percent Negro	Total	Negro	Percent Negro	Total	Negro	Percent Negro
Officials and managers	1,415	1	0.1	1,397	1	0.1	18	—	—
Professionals	582	1	0.2	562	1	0.2	20	—	—
Technicians	524	1	0.2	436	1	0.2	88	—	—
Sales workers	203	—	—	179	—	—	24	—	—
Office and clerical	1,588	5	0.3	529	1	0.2	1,059	4	0.4
Total white collar	4,312	8	0.2	3,103	4	0.1	1,209	4	0.3
Craftsmen	5,683	38	0.7	5,598	38	0.7	85	—	—
Operatives	7,591	156	2.1	5,803	111	1.9	1,788	45	2.5
Laborers	3,236	78	2.4	2,961	73	2.5	275	5	1.8
Service workers	390	5	1.3	349	5	1.4	41	—	—
Total blue collar	16,900	277	1.6	14,711	227	1.5	2,189	50	2.3
Total	21,212	285	1.3	17,814	231	1.3	3,398	54	1.6

Source: Data in author's possession.

Note: For regional definitions, see Table 4, p. 15.

TABLE A-13. *Paper and Allied Products Industry*
Employment by Race, Sex, and Occupational Group
Pulp, Paper, and Paperboard Mills
7 Companies, 12 Establishments
New England Region, 1964

Occupational Group	All Employees			Male			Female		
	Total	Negro	Percent Negro	Total	Negro	Percent Negro	Total	Negro	Percent Negro
Officials and managers	458	—	—	457	—	—	1	—	—
Professionals	157	—	—	148	—	—	9	—	—
Technicians	57	—	—	55	—	—	2	—	—
Sales workers	21	—	—	16	—	—	5	—	—
Office and clerical	389	—	—	142	—	—	247	—	—
Total white collar	1,082	—	—	818	—	—	264	—	—
Craftsmen	1,377	1	0.1	1,376	1	0.1	1	—	—
Operatives	2,149	15	0.7	1,870	5	0.3	279	10	3.6
Laborers	1,332	3	0.2	1,299	3	0.2	33	—	—
Service workers	137	1	0.7	136	1	0.7	1	—	—
Total blue collar	4,995	20	0.4	4,681	10	0.2	314	10	3.2
Total	6,077	20	0.3	5,499	10	0.2	578	10	1.7

Source: Data in author's possession.
Note: For regional definitions, see Table 4, p. 15.

TABLE A-14. Paper and Allied Products Industry
Employment by Race, Sex, and Occupational Group
Pulp, Paper, and Paperboard Mills
15 Companies, 27 Establishments
New England Region, 1966

Occupational Group	All Employees			Male			Female		
	Total	Negro	Percent Negro	Total	Negro	Percent Negro	Total	Negro	Percent Negro
Officials and managers	949	—	—	948	—	—	1	—	—
Professionals	500	—	—	490	—	—	10	—	—
Technicians	490	—	—	364	—	—	126	—	—
Sales workers	135	—	—	115	—	—	20	—	—
Office and clerical	1,280	—	—	532	—	—	748	—	—
Total white collar	3,354	—	—	2,449	—	—	905	—	—
Craftsmen	4,241	5	0.1	4,166	5	0.1	75	—	—
Operatives	6,413	12	0.2	5,498	9	0.2	915	3	0.3
Laborers	2,724	10	0.4	2,492	10	0.4	232	—	—
Service workers	303	3	1.0	275	3	1.1	28	—	—
Total blue collar	13,681	30	0.2	12,431	27	0.2	1,250	3	0.2
Total	17,035	30	0.2	14,880	27	0.2	2,155	3	0.1

Source: Data in author's possession.

Note: For regional definitions, see Table 4, p. 15.

TABLE A-15. *Paper and Allied Products Industry*
Employment by Race, Sex, and Occupational Group
Pulp, Paper, and Paperboard Mills
14 Companies, 25 Establishments
New England Region, 1968

Occupational Group	All Employees			Male			Female		
	Total	Negro	Percent Negro	Total	Negro	Percent Negro	Total	Negro	Percent Negro
Officials and managers	1,028	—	—	1,016	—	—	12	—	—
Professionals	476	1	0.2	461	1	0.2	15	—	—
Technicians	485	1	0.2	403	1	0.2	82	—	—
Sales workers	97	—	—	82	—	—	15	—	—
Office and clerical	1,129	1	0.1	361	—	—	768	1	0.1
Total white collar	3,215	3	0.1	2,323	2	0.1	892	1	0.1
Craftsmen	4,598	7	0.2	4,529	7	0.2	69	—	—
Operatives	5,332	39	0.7	4,349	30	0.7	983	9	0.9
Laborers	1,855	12	0.6	1,765	12	0.7	90	—	—
Service workers	289	3	1.0	254	3	1.2	35	—	—
Total blue collar	12,074	61	0.5	10,897	52	0.5	1,177	9	0.8
Total	15,289	64	0.4	13,220	54	0.4	2,069	10	0.5

Source: Data in author's possession.
Note: For regional definitions, see Table 4, p. 15.

TABLE A-16. *Paper and Allied Products Industry*
Employment by Race, Sex, and Occupational Group
Converting Plants
9 Companies, 16 Establishments
New England Region, 1964

Occupational Group	All Employees			Male			Female		
	Total	Negro	Percent Negro	Total	Negro	Percent Negro	Total	Negro	Percent Negro
Officials and managers	290	—	—	285	—	—	5	—	—
Professionals	81	—	—	80	—	—	1	—	—
Technicians	58	—	—	42	—	—	16	—	—
Sales workers	151	—	—	136	—	—	15	—	—
Office and clerical	481	1	0.2	137	1	0.7	344	—	—
Total white collar	1,061	1	0.1	680	1	0.1	381	—	—
Craftsmen	814	10	1.2	805	10	1.2	9	—	—
Operatives	1,948	46	2.4	1,291	37	2.9	657	9	1.4
Laborers	904	17	1.9	659	16	2.4	245	1	0.4
Service workers	59	1	1.7	52	1	1.9	7	—	—
Total blue collar	3,725	74	2.0	2,807	64	2.3	918	10	1.1
Total	4,786	75	1.6	3,487	65	1.9	1,299	10	0.8

Source: Data in author's possession.

Note: For regional definitions, see Table 4, p. 15.

TABLE A-17. *Paper and Allied Products Industry*
Employment by Race, Sex, and Occupational Group
Converting Plants
12 Companies, 24 Establishments
New England Region, 1966

Occupational Group	All Employees			Male			Female		
	Total	Negro	Percent Negro	Total	Negro	Percent Negro	Total	Negro	Percent Negro
Officials and managers	493	2	0.4	476	2	0.4	17	—	—
Professionals	81	—	—	76	—	—	5	—	—
Technicians	78	2	2.6	68	2	2.9	10	—	—
Sales workers	186	1	0.5	170	1	0.6	16	—	—
Office and clerical	617	3	0.5	172	1	0.6	445	2	0.4
Total white collar	1,455	8	0.5	962	6	0.6	493	2	0.4
Craftsmen	1,211	22	1.8	1,205	22	1.8	6	—	—
Operatives	2,617	128	4.9	1,580	103	6.5	1,037	25	2.4
Laborers	1,308	97	7.4	893	88	9.9	415	9	2.2
Service workers	118	4	3.4	104	4	3.8	14	—	—
Total blue collar	5,254	251	4.8	3,782	217	5.7	1,472	34	2.3
Total	6,709	259	3.9	4,744	223	4.7	1,965	36	1.8

Source: Data in author's possession.
Note: For regional definitions, see Table 4, p. 15.

TABLE A-18. Paper and Allied Products Industry
Employment by Race, Sex, and Occupational Group
Converting Plants
11 Companies, 21 Establishments
New England Region, 1968

Occupational Group	All Employees			Male			Female		
	Total	Negro	Percent Negro	Total	Negro	Percent Negro	Total	Negro	Percent Negro
Officials and managers	387	1	0.3	381	1	0.3	6	—	—
Professionals	106	—	—	101	—	—	5	—	—
Technicians	39	—	—	33	—	—	6	—	—
Sales workers	106	—	—	97	—	—	9	—	—
Office and clerical	459	4	0.9	168	1	0.6	291	3	1.0
Total white collar	1,097	5	0.5	780	2	0.3	317	3	0.9
Craftsmen	1,085	31	2.9	1,069	31	2.9	16	—	—
Operatives	2,259	117	5.2	1,454	81	5.6	805	36	4.5
Laborers	1,381	66	4.8	1,196	61	5.1	185	5	2.7
Service workers	101	2	2.0	95	2	2.1	6	—	—
Total blue collar	4,826	216	4.5	3,814	175	4.6	1,012	41	4.1
Total	5,923	221	3.7	4,594	177	3.9	1,329	44	3.3

Source: Data in author's possession.
Note: For regional definitions, see Table 4, p. 15.

TABLE A-19. *Paper and Allied Products Industry*
Employment by Race, Sex, and Occupational Group
25 Companies, 86 Establishments
Middle Atlantic Region, 1964

Occupational Group	All Employees			Male			Female		
	Total	Negro	Percent Negro	Total	Negro	Percent Negro	Total	Negro	Percent Negro
Officials and managers	2,212	14	0.6	2,185	13	0.6	27	1	3.7
Professionals	1,798	4	0.2	1,719	4	0.2	79	—	—
Technicians	869	12	1.4	717	10	1.4	152	2	1.3
Sales workers	1,418	7	0.5	1,390	7	0.5	28	—	—
Office and clerical	3,623	44	1.2	1,308	21	1.6	2,315	23	1.0
Total white collar	9,920	81	0.8	7,319	55	0.8	2,601	26	1.0
Craftsmen	6,070	123	2.0	5,822	119	2.0	248	4	1.6
Operatives	12,135	750	6.2	9,854	634	6.6	2,281	96	4.2
Laborers	5,272	326	6.2	4,447	298	6.7	825	28	3.4
Service workers	579	95	16.4	487	72	14.8	92	23	25.0
Total blue collar	24,056	1,294	5.4	20,610	1,143	5.5	3,446	151	4.4
Total	33,976	1,375	4.0	27,929	1,198	4.3	6,047	177	2.9

Source: Data in author's possession.
Note: For regional definitions, see Table 4, p. 15.

TABLE A-20. *Paper and Allied Products Industry*
Employment by Race, Sex, and Occupational Group
30 Companies, 85 Establishments
Middle Atlantic Region, 1966

Occupational Group	All Employees			Male			Female		
	Total	Negro	Percent Negro	Total	Negro	Percent Negro	Total	Negro	Percent Negro
Officials and managers	2,302	21	0.9	2,258	20	0.9	44	1	2.3
Professionals	901	—	—	874	—	—	27	—	—
Technicians	682	8	1.2	594	4	0.7	88	4	4.5
Sales workers	791	6	0.8	748	5	0.7	43	1	2.3
Office and clerical	2,739	22	0.8	1,224	16	1.3	1,515	6	0.4
Total white collar	7,415	57	0.8	5,698	45	0.8	1,717	12	0.7
Craftsmen	7,112	192	2.7	6,907	186	2.7	205	6	2.9
Operatives	14,686	1,148	7.8	12,309	976	7.9	2,377	172	7.2
Laborers	6,274	596	9.5	5,277	541	10.3	997	55	5.5
Service workers	687	113	16.4	590	93	15.8	97	20	20.6
Total blue collar	28,759	2,049	7.1	25,083	1,796	7.2	3,676	253	6.9
Total	36,174	2,106	5.8	30,781	1,841	6.0	5,393	265	4.9

Source: Data in author's possession.
Note: For regional definitions, see Table 4, p. 15.

TABLE A-21. *Paper and Allied Products Industry*
Employment by Race, Sex, and Occupational Group
28 Companies, 86 Establishments
Middle Atlantic Region, 1968

Occupational Group	All Employees			Male			Female		
	Total	Negro	Percent Negro	Total	Negro	Percent Negro	Total	Negro	Percent Negro
Officials and managers	2,222	30	1.4	2,183	29	1.3	39	1	2.6
Professionals	802	2	0.2	770	2	0.3	32	—	—
Technicians	719	13	1.8	584	7	1.2	135	6	4.4
Sales workers	552	3	0.5	521	3	0.6	31	—	—
Office and clerical	2,462	38	1.5	965	23	2.4	1,497	15	1.0
Total white collar	6,757	86	1.3	5,023	64	1.3	1,734	22	1.3
Craftsmen	5,898	182	3.1	5,768	178	3.1	130	4	3.1
Operatives	12,500	1,157	9.3	10,355	1,007	9.7	2,145	150	7.0
Laborers	6,035	718	11.9	4,821	628	13.0	1,214	90	7.4
Service workers	681	99	14.5	589	80	13.6	92	19	20.7
Total blue collar	25,114	2,156	8.6	21,533	1,893	8.8	3,581	263	7.3
Total	31,871	2,242	7.0	26,556	1,957	7.4	5,315	285	5.4

Source: Data in author's possession.
Note: For regional definitions, see Table 4, p. 15.

TABLE A-22. Paper and Allied Products Industry
Employment by Race, Sex, and Occupational Group
Pulp, Paper, and Paperboard Mills
12 Companies, 30 Establishments
Middle Atlantic Region, 1964

Occupational Group	All Employees			Male			Female		
	Total	Negro	Percent Negro	Total	Negro	Percent Negro	Total	Negro	Percent Negro
Officials and managers	1,345	6	0.4	1,328	5	0.4	17	1	5.9
Professionals	1,442	4	0.3	1,373	4	0.3	69	—	—
Technicians	749	11	1.5	609	9	1.5	140	2	1.4
Sales workers	764	6	0.8	752	6	0.8	12	—	—
Office and clerical	2,446	42	1.7	841	20	2.4	1,605	22	1.4
Total white collar	6,746	69	1.0	4,903	44	0.9	1,843	25	1.4
Craftsmen	4,451	56	1.3	4,216	52	1.2	235	4	1.7
Operatives	7,017	344	4.9	5,981	287	4.8	1,036	57	5.5
Laborers	3,094	73	2.4	2,757	73	2.6	337	—	—
Service workers	467	84	18.0	389	63	16.2	78	21	26.9
Total blue collar	15,029	557	3.7	13,343	475	3.6	1,686	82	4.9
Total	21,775	626	2.9	18,246	519	2.8	3,529	107	3.0

Source: Data in author's possession.
Note: For regional definitions, see Table 4, p. 15.

TABLE A-23. *Paper and Allied Products Industry*
Employment by Race, Sex, and Occupational Group
Pulp, Paper, and Paperboard Mills
18 Companies, 34 Establishments
Middle Atlantic Region, 1966

Occupational Group	All Employees			Male			Female		
	Total	Negro	Percent Negro	Total	Negro	Percent Negro	Total	Negro	Percent Negro
Officials and managers	1,376	12	0.9	1,345	11	0.8	31	1	3.2
Professionals	673	—	—	656	—	—	17	—	—
Technicians	586	8	1.4	521	4	0.8	65	4	6.2
Sales workers	401	2	0.5	380	2	0.5	21	—	—
Office and clerical	1,680	18	1.1	802	13	1.6	878	5	0.6
Total white collar	4,716	40	0.8	3,704	30	0.8	1,012	10	1.0
Craftsmen	5,276	96	1.8	5,154	90	1.7	122	6	4.9
Operatives	9,849	589	6.0	8,524	513	6.0	1,325	76	5.7
Laborers	3,774	205	5.4	3,252	199	6.1	522	6	1.1
Service workers	563	87	15.5	477	68	14.3	86	19	22.1
Total blue collar	19,462	977	5.0	17,407	870	5.0	2,055	107	5.2
Total	24,178	1,017	4.2	21,111	900	4.3	3,067	117	3.8

Source: Data in author's possession.
Note: For regional definitions, see Table 4, p. 15.

TABLE A-24. Paper and Allied Products Industry
Employment by Race, Sex, and Occupational Group
Pulp, Paper, and Paperboard Mills
16 Companies, 30 Establishments
Middle Atlantic Region, 1968

Occupational Group	All Employees			Male			Female		
	Total	Negro	Percent Negro	Total	Negro	Percent Negro	Total	Negro	Percent Negro
Officials and managers	1,160	19	1.6	1,134	18	1.6	26	1	3.8
Professionals	480	2	0.4	463	2	0.4	17	—	—
Technicians	414	12	2.9	350	6	1.7	64	6	9.4
Sales workers	195	1	0.5	175	1	0.6	20	—	—
Office and clerical	1,221	20	1.6	493	12	2.4	728	8	1.1
Total white collar	3,470	54	1.6	2,615	39	1.5	855	15	1.8
Craftsmen	3,348	77	2.3	3,239	73	2.3	109	4	3.7
Operatives	7,667	589	7.7	6,494	507	7.8	1,173	82	7.0
Laborers	2,867	257	9.0	2,325	240	10.3	542	17	3.1
Service workers	456	83	18.2	375	68	18.1	81	15	18.5
Total blue collar	14,338	1,006	7.0	12,433	888	7.1	1,905	118	6.2
Total	17,808	1,060	6.0	15,048	927	6.2	2,760	133	4.8

Source: Data in author's possession.
Note: For regional definitions, see Table 4, p. 15.

TABLE A-25. *Paper and Allied Products Industry*
Employment by Race, Sex, and Occupational Group
Converting Plants
20 Companies, 56 Establishments
Middle Atlantic Region, 1964

Occupational Group	All Employees			Male			Female		
	Total	Negro	Percent Negro	Total	Negro	Percent Negro	Total	Negro	Percent Negro
Officials and managers	867	8	0.9	857	8	0.9	10	—	—
Professionals	356	—	—	346	—	—	10	—	—
Technicians	120	1	0.8	108	1	0.9	12	—	—
Sales workers	654	1	0.2	638	1	0.2	16	—	—
Office and clerical	1,177	2	0.2	467	1	0.2	710	1	0.1
Total white collar	3,174	12	0.4	2,416	11	0.5	758	1	0.1
Craftsmen	1,619	67	4.1	1,606	67	4.2	13	—	—
Operatives	5,118	406	7.9	3,873	367	9.5	1,245	39	3.1
Laborers	2,178	253	11.6	1,690	225	13.3	488	28	5.7
Service workers	112	11	9.8	98	9	9.2	14	2	14.3
Total blue collar	9,027	737	8.2	7,267	668	9.2	1,760	69	3.9
Total	12,201	749	6.1	9,683	679	7.0	2,518	70	2.8

Source: Data in author's possession.
Note: For regional definitions, see Table 4, p. 15.

TABLE A-26. Paper and Allied Products Industry
Employment by Race, Sex, and Occupational Group
Converting Plants
20 Companies, 51 Establishments
Middle Atlantic Region, 1966

Occupational Group	All Employees			Male			Female		
	Total	Negro	Percent Negro	Total	Negro	Percent Negro	Total	Negro	Percent Negro
Officials and managers	926	9	1.0	913	9	1.0	13	—	—
Professionals	228	—	—	218	—	—	10	—	—
Technicians	96	—	—	73	—	—	23	—	—
Sales workers	390	4	1.0	368	3	0.8	22	1	4.5
Office and clerical	1,059	4	0.4	422	3	0.7	637	1	0.2
Total white collar	2,699	17	0.6	1,994	15	0.8	705	2	0.3
Craftsmen	1,836	96	5.2	1,753	96	5.5	83	—	—
Operatives	4,837	559	11.6	3,785	463	12.2	1,052	96	9.1
Laborers	2,500	391	15.6	2,025	342	16.9	475	49	10.3
Service workers	124	26	21.0	113	25	22.1	11	1	9.1
Total blue collar	9,297	1,072	11.5	7,676	926	12.1	1,621	146	9.0
Total	11,996	1,089	9.1	9,670	941	9.7	2,326	148	6.4

Source: Data in author's possession.
Note: For regional definitions, see Table 4, p. 15.

TABLE A-27. *Paper and Allied Products Industry Employment by Race, Sex, and Occupational Group Converting Plants 20 Companies, 56 Establishments Middle Atlantic Region, 1968*

Occupational Group	All Employees			Male			Female		
	Total	Negro	Percent Negro	Total	Negro	Percent Negro	Total	Negro	Percent Negro
Officials and managers	1,062	11	1.0	1,049	11	1.0	13	—	—
Professionals	322	—	—	307	—	—	15	—	—
Technicians	305	1	0.3	234	1	0.4	71	—	—
Sales workers	357	2	0.6	346	2	0.6	11	—	—
Office and clerical	1,241	18	1.5	472	11	2.3	769	7	0.9
Total white collar	3,287	32	1.0	2,408	25	1.0	879	7	0.8
Craftsmen	2,550	105	4.1	2,529	105	4.2	21	—	—
Operatives	4,833	568	11.8	3,861	500	13.0	972	68	7.0
Laborers	3,168	461	14.6	2,496	388	15.5	672	73	10.9
Service workers	225	16	7.1	214	12	5.6	11	4	36.4
Total blue collar	10,776	1,150	10.7	9,100	1,005	11.0	1,676	145	8.7
Total	14,063	1,182	8.4	11,508	1,030	9.0	2,555	152	5.9

Source: Data in author's possession.
Note: For regional definitions, see Table 4, p. 15.

TABLE A-28. Paper and Allied Products Industry
Employment by Race, Sex, and Occupational Group
25 Companies, 152 Establishments
Midwest Region, 1964

Occupational Group	All Employees			Male			Female		
	Total	Negro	Percent Negro	Total	Negro	Percent Negro	Total	Negro	Percent Negro
Officials and managers	4,611	5	0.1	4,569	5	0.1	42	—	—
Professionals	2,191	1	*	2,105	1	*	86	—	—
Technicians	1,127	3	0.3	1,002	2	0.2	125	1	0.8
Sales workers	1,939	1	0.1	1,834	1	0.1	105	—	—
Office and clerical	6,249	34	0.5	2,333	13	0.6	3,916	21	0.5
Total white collar	16,117	44	0.3	11,843	22	0.2	4,274	22	0.5
Craftsmen	11,596	182	1.6	11,463	177	1.5	133	5	3.8
Operatives	23,491	560	2.4	20,786	502	2.4	2,705	58	2.1
Laborers	12,214	397	3.3	9,297	349	3.8	2,917	48	1.6
Service workers	1,355	114	8.4	1,219	104	8.5	136	10	7.4
Total blue collar	48,656	1,253	2.6	42,765	1,132	2.6	5,891	121	2.1
Total	64,773	1,297	2.0	54,608	1,154	2.1	10,165	143	1.4

Source: Data in author's possession.
Note: For regional definitions, see Table 4, p. 15.
* Less than 0.05 percent.

TABLE A-29. *Paper and Allied Products Industry*
Employment by Race, Sex, and Occupational Group
31 Companies, 182 Establishments
Midwest Region, 1966

Occupational Group	All Employees			Male			Female		
	Total	Negro	Percent Negro	Total	Negro	Percent Negro	Total	Negro	Percent Negro
Officials and managers	4,944	8	0.2	4,915	8	0.2	29	—	—
Professionals	1,138	2	0.2	1,091	1	0.1	47	1	2.1
Technicians	928	3	0.3	845	2	0.2	83	1	1.2
Sales workers	1,523	—	—	1,396	—	—	127	—	—
Office and clerical	5,279	59	1.1	2,172	44	2.0	3,107	15	0.5
Total white collar	13,812	72	0.5	10,419	55	0.5	3,393	17	0.5
Craftsmen	11,888	263	2.2	11,712	262	2.2	176	1	0.6
Operatives	27,783	952	3.4	24,572	844	3.4	3,211	108	3.4
Laborers	14,671	865	5.9	11,506	736	6.4	3,165	129	4.1
Service workers	1,266	101	8.0	1,166	90	7.7	100	11	11.0
Total blue collar	55,608	2,181	3.9	48,956	1,932	3.9	6,652	249	3.7
Total	69,420	2,253	3.2	59,375	1,987	3.3	10,045	266	2.6

Source: Data in author's possession.
Note: For regional definitions, see Table 4, p. 15.

TABLE A-30. Paper and Allied Products Industry
Employment by Race, Sex, and Occupational Group
32 Companies, 209 Establishments
Midwest Region, 1968

Occupational Group	All Employees			Male			Female		
	Total	Negro	Percent Negro	Total	Negro	Percent Negro	Total	Negro	Percent Negro
Officials and managers	5,623	13	0.2	5,584	12	0.2	39	1	2.6
Professionals	1,374	3	0.2	1,299	2	0.2	75	1	1.3
Technicians	1,079	9	0.8	1,024	6	0.6	55	3	5.5
Sales workers	1,510	5	0.3	1,389	5	0.4	121	—	—
Office and clerical	5,490	48	0.9	1,992	19	1.0	3,498	29	0.8
Total white collar	15,076	78	0.5	11,288	44	0.4	3,788	34	0.9
Craftsmen	12,078	283	2.3	11,933	280	2.3	145	3	2.1
Operatives	28,831	1,331	4.6	25,371	1,176	4.6	3,460	155	4.5
Laborers	16,780	1,073	6.4	13,244	895	6.8	3,536	178	5.0
Service workers	1,363	111	8.1	1,211	104	8.6	152	7	4.6
Total blue collar	59,052	2,798	4.7	51,759	2,455	4.7	7,293	343	4.7
Total	74,128	2,876	3.9	63,047	2,499	4.0	11,081	377	3.4

Source: Data in author's possession.
Note: For regional definitions, see Table 4, p. 15.

TABLE A-31.   *Paper and Allied Products Industry*
Employment by Race, Sex, and Occupational Group
Pulp, Paper, and Paperboard Mills
16 Companies, 45 Establishments
Midwest Region, 1964

Occupational Group	All Employees			Male			Female		
	Total	Negro	Percent Negro	Total	Negro	Percent Negro	Total	Negro	Percent Negro
Officials and managers	2,787	—	—	2,759	—	—	28	—	—
Professionals	1,541	1	0.1	1,488	1	0.1	53	—	—
Technicians	797	2	0.3	702	1	0.1	95	1	1.1
Sales workers	1,042	—	—	995	—	—	47	—	—
Office and clerical	3,789	24	0.6	1,384	9	0.7	2,405	15	0.6
Total white collar	9,956	27	0.3	7,328	11	0.2	2,628	16	0.6
Craftsmen	7,457	63	0.8	7,389	63	0.9	68	—	—
Operatives	14,418	195	1.4	13,664	192	1.4	754	3	0.4
Laborers	6,074	146	2.4	4,727	138	2.9	1,347	8	0.6
Service workers	919	76	8.3	813	69	8.5	106	7	6.6
Total blue collar	28,868	480	1.7	26,593	462	1.7	2,275	18	0.8
Total	38,824	507	1.3	33,921	473	1.4	4,903	34	0.7

Source: Data in author's possession.
Note: For regional definitions, see Table 4, p. 15.

TABLE A-32.   *Paper and Allied Products Industry*
Employment by Race, Sex, and Occupational Group
Pulp, Paper, and Paperboard Mills
27 Companies, 68 Establishments
Midwest Region, 1966

Occupational Group	All Employees			Male			Female		
	Total	Negro	Percent Negro	Total	Negro	Percent Negro	Total	Negro	Percent Negro
Officials and managers	2,994	2	0.1	2,979	2	0.1	15	—	—
Professionals	819	2	0.2	783	1	0.1	36	1	2.8
Technicians	644	3	0.5	595	2	0.3	49	1	2.0
Sales workers	513	—	—	451	—	—	62	—	—
Office and clerical	3,053	34	1.1	1,373	25	1.8	1,680	9	0.5
Total white collar	8,023	41	0.5	6,181	30	0.5	1,842	11	0.6
Craftsmen	8,112	69	0.9	8,040	69	0.9	72	—	—
Operatives	17,980	310	1.7	16,723	284	1.7	1,257	26	2.1
Laborers	8,227	219	2.7	6,981	202	2.9	1,246	17	1.4
Service workers	948	53	5.6	871	47	5.4	77	6	7.8
Total blue collar	35,267	651	1.8	32,615	602	1.8	2,652	49	1.8
Total	43,290	692	1.6	38,796	632	1.6	4,494	60	1.3

Source: Data in author's possession.

Note: For regional definitions, see Table 4, p. 15.

TABLE A-33. *Paper and Allied Products Industry*
Employment by Race, Sex, and Occupational Group
Pulp, Paper, and Paperboard Mills
23 Companies, 75 Establishments
Midwest Region, 1968

Occupational Group	All Employees			Male			Female		
	Total	Negro	Percent Negro	Total	Negro	Percent Negro	Total	Negro	Percent Negro
Officials and managers	2,958	5	0.2	2,942	4	0.1	16	1	6.2
Professionals	878	2	0.2	839	2	0.2	39	—	—
Technicians	687	4	0.6	649	2	0.3	38	2	5.3
Sales workers	287	—	—	272	—	—	15	—	—
Office and clerical	2,479	18	0.7	1,044	8	0.8	1,435	10	0.7
Total white collar	7,289	29	0.4	5,746	16	0.3	1,543	13	0.8
Craftsmen	6,070	63	1.0	6,066	63	1.0	4	—	—
Operatives	16,559	370	2.2	15,375	346	2.3	1,184	24	2.0
Laborers	8,708	229	2.6	7,581	210	2.8	1,127	19	1.7
Service workers	874	56	6.4	758	53	7.0	116	3	2.6
Total blue collar	32,211	718	2.2	29,780	672	2.3	2,431	46	1.9
Total	39,500	747	1.9	35,526	688	1.9	3,974	59	1.5

Source: Data in author's possession.
Note: For regional definitions, see Table 4, p. 15.

TABLE A-34. Paper and Allied Products Industry
Employment by Race, Sex, and Occupational Group
Converting Plants
23 Companies, 107 Establishments
Midwest Region, 1964

Occupational Group	All Employees			Male			Female		
	Total	Negro	Percent Negro	Total	Negro	Percent Negro	Total	Negro	Percent Negro
Officials and managers	1,824	5	0.3	1,810	5	0.3	14	—	—
Professionals	650	—	—	617	—	—	33	—	—
Technicians	330	1	0.3	300	1	0.3	30	—	—
Sales workers	897	1	0.1	839	1	0.1	58	—	—
Office and clerical	2,460	10	0.4	949	4	0.4	1,511	6	0.4
Total white collar	6,161	17	0.3	4,515	11	0.2	1,646	6	0.4
Craftsmen	4,139	119	2.9	4,074	114	2.8	65	5	7.7
Operatives	9,073	365	4.0	7,122	310	4.4	1,951	55	2.8
Laborers	6,140	251	4.1	4,570	211	4.6	1,570	40	2.5
Service workers	436	38	8.7	406	35	8.6	30	3	10.0
Total blue collar	19,788	773	3.9	16,172	670	4.1	3,616	103	2.8
Total	25,949	790	3.0	20,687	681	3.3	5,262	109	2.1

Source: Data in author's possession.
Note: For regional definitions, see Table 4, p. 15.

TABLE A-35. *Paper and Allied Products Industry*
Employment by Race, Sex, and Occupational Group
Converting Plants
23 Companies, 114 Establishments
Midwest Region, 1966

Occupational Group	All Employees			Male			Female		
	Total	Negro	Percent Negro	Total	Negro	Percent Negro	Total	Negro	Percent Negro
Officials and managers	1,950	6	0.3	1,936	6	0.3	14	—	—
Professionals	319	—	—	308	—	—	11	—	—
Technicians	284	—	—	250	—	—	34	—	—
Sales workers	1,010	—	—	945	—	—	65	—	—
Office and clerical	2,226	25	1.1	799	19	2.4	1,427	6	0.4
Total white collar	5,789	31	0.5	4,238	25	0.6	1,551	6	0.4
Craftsmen	3,776	194	5.1	3,672	193	5.3	104	1	1.0
Operatives	9,803	642	6.5	7,849	560	7.1	1,954	82	4.2
Laborers	6,444	646	10.0	4,525	534	11.8	1,919	112	5.8
Service workers	318	48	15.1	295	43	14.6	23	5	21.7
Total blue collar	20,341	1,530	7.5	16,341	1,330	8.1	4,000	200	5.0
Total	26,130	1,561	6.0	20,579	1,355	6.6	5,551	206	3.7

Source: Data in author's possession.
Note: For regional definitions, see Table 4, p. 15.

TABLE A-36. Paper and Allied Products Industry
Employment by Race, Sex, and Occupational Group
Converting Plants
26 Companies, 134 Establishments
Midwest Region, 1968

Occupational Group	All Employees			Male			Female		
	Total	Negro	Percent Negro	Total	Negro	Percent Negro	Total	Negro	Percent Negro
Officials and managers	2,665	8	0.3	2,642	8	0.3	23	—	—
Professionals	496	1	0.2	460	—	—	36	1	2.8
Technicians	392	5	1.3	375	4	1.1	17	1	5.9
Sales workers	1,223	5	0.4	1,117	5	0.4	106	—	—
Office and clerical	3,011	30	1.0	948	11	1.2	2,063	19	0.9
Total white collar	7,787	49	0.6	5,542	28	0.5	2,245	21	0.9
Craftsmen	6,008	220	3.7	5,867	217	3.7	141	3	2.1
Operatives	12,272	961	7.8	9,996	830	8.3	2,276	131	5.8
Laborers	8,072	844	10.5	5,663	685	12.1	2,409	159	6.6
Service workers	489	55	11.2	453	51	11.3	36	4	11.1
Total blue collar	26,841	2,080	7.7	21,979	1,783	8.1	4,862	297	6.1
Total	34,628	2,129	6.1	27,521	1,811	6.6	7,107	318	4.5

Source: Data in author's possession.
Note: For regional definitions, see Table 4, p. 15.

TABLE A-37. *Paper and Allied Products Industry Employment by Race, Sex, and Occupational Group 15 Companies, 60 Establishments Far West Region, 1964*

Occupational Group	All Employees			Male			Female		
	Total	Negro	Percent Negro	Total	Negro	Percent Negro	Total	Negro	Percent Negro
Officials and managers	1,211	1	0.1	1,204	1	0.1	7	—	—
Professionals	604	—	—	592	—	—	12	—	—
Technicians	322	1	0.3	299	1	0.3	23	—	—
Sales workers	515	—	—	498	—	—	17	—	—
Office and clerical	1,562	9	0.6	551	2	0.4	1,011	7	0.7
Total white collar	4,214	11	0.3	3,144	4	0.1	1,070	7	0.7
Craftsmen	5,610	61	1.1	5,454	61	1.1	156	—	—
Operatives	8,017	148	1.8	6,580	117	1.8	1,437	31	2.2
Laborers	4,238	98	2.3	2,997	86	2.9	1,241	12	1.0
Service workers	264	32	12.1	251	30	12.0	13	2	15.4
Total blue collar	18,129	339	1.9	15,282	294	1.9	2,847	45	1.6
Total	22,343	350	1.6	18,426	298	1.6	3,917	52	1.3

Source: Data in author's possession.
Note: For regional definitions, see Table 4, p. 15.

TABLE A-38. *Paper and Allied Products Industry*
Employment by Race, Sex, and Occupational Group
17 Companies, 69 Establishments
Far West Region, 1966

Occupational Group	All Employees			Male			Female		
	Total	Negro	Percent Negro	Total	Negro	Percent Negro	Total	Negro	Percent Negro
Officials and managers	1,669	—	—	1,660	—	—	9	—	—
Professionals	822	1	0.1	811	1	0.1	11	—	—
Technicians	376	1	0.3	341	1	0.3	35	—	—
Sales workers	344	1	0.3	330	1	0.3	14	—	—
Office and clerical	1,796	6	0.3	691	1	0.1	1,105	5	0.5
Total white collar	5,007	9	0.2	3,833	4	0.1	1,174	5	0.4
Craftsmen	5,823	55	0.9	5,766	55	1.0	57	—	—
Operatives	10,955	237	2.2	9,587	203	2.1	1,368	34	2.5
Laborers	4,402	194	4.4	3,380	180	5.3	1,022	14	1.4
Service workers	235	34	14.5	215	33	15.3	20	1	5.0
Total blue collar	21,415	520	2.4	18,948	471	2.5	2,467	49	2.0
Total	26,422	529	2.0	22,781	475	2.1	3,641	54	1.5

Source: Data in author's possession.
Note: For regional definitions, see Table 4, p. 15.

TABLE A-39. *Paper and Allied Products Industry*
Employment by Race, Sex, and Occupational Group
21 Companies, 81 Establishments
Far West Region, 1968

Occupational Group	All Employees			Male			Female		
	Total	Negro	Percent Negro	Total	Negro	Percent Negro	Total	Negro	Percent Negro
Officials and managers	2,523	4	0.2	2,510	4	0.2	13	—	—
Professionals	1,261	5	0.4	1,227	5	0.4	34	—	—
Technicians	670	3	0.4	631	3	0.5	39	—	—
Sales workers	443	2	0.5	412	1	0.2	31	1	3.2
Office and clerical	2,412	14	0.6	824	7	0.8	1,588	7	0.4
Total white collar	7,309	28	0.4	5,604	20	0.4	1,705	8	0.5
Craftsmen	9,588	100	1.0	9,480	96	1.0	108	4	3.7
Operatives	16,129	593	3.7	14,182	492	3.5	1,947	101	5.2
Laborers	7,584	426	5.6	5,991	345	5.8	1,593	81	5.1
Service workers	424	42	9.9	360	40	11.1	64	2	3.1
Total blue collar	33,725	1,161	3.4	30,013	973	3.2	3,712	188	5.1
Total	41,034	1,189	2.9	35,617	993	2.8	5,417	196	3.6

Source: Data in author's possession.
Note: For regional definitions, see Table 4, p. 15.

TABLE A-40.   *Paper and Allied Products Industry*
Employment by Race, Sex, and Occupational Group
Pulp, Paper, and Paperboard Mills
8 Companies, 24 Establishments
Far West Region, 1964

Occupational Group	All Employees			Male			Female		
	Total	Negro	Percent Negro	Total	Negro	Percent Negro	Total	Negro	Percent Negro
Officials and managers	817	1	0.1	817	1	0.1	—	—	—
Professionals	345	—	—	336	—	—	9	—	—
Technicians	251	1	0.4	236	1	0.4	15	—	—
Sales workers	279	—	—	267	—	—	12	—	—
Office and clerical	828	7	0.8	302	1	0.3	526	6	1.1
Total white collar	2,520	9	0.4	1,958	3	0.2	562	6	1.1
Craftsmen	3,784	38	1.0	3,679	38	1.0	105	—	—
Operatives	5,593	56	1.0	4,780	52	1.1	813	4	0.5
Laborers	2,150	65	3.0	1,737	62	3.6	413	3	0.7
Service workers	165	13	7.9	154	12	7.8	11	1	9.1
Total blue collar	11,692	172	1.5	10,350	164	1.6	1,342	8	0.6
Total	14,212	181	1.3	12,308	167	1.4	1,904	14	0.7

Source: Data in author's possession.
Note: For regional definitions, see Table 4, p. 15.

TABLE A-41. *Paper and Allied Products Industry*
Employment by Race, Sex, and Occupational Group
Pulp, Paper, and Paperboard Mills
12 Companies, 31 Establishments
Far West Region, 1966

Occupational Group	All Employees			Male			Female		
	Total	Negro	Percent Negro	Total	Negro	Percent Negro	Total	Negro	Percent Negro
Officials and managers	1,173	—	—	1,172	—	—	1	—	—
Professionals	641	1	0.2	635	1	0.2	6	—	—
Technicians	342	1	0.3	313	1	0.3	29	—	—
Sales workers	100	—	—	94	—	—	6	—	—
Office and clerical	1,140	2	0.2	424	1	0.2	716	1	0.1
Total white collar	3,396	4	0.1	2,638	3	0.1	758	1	0.1
Craftsmen	4,296	32	0.7	4,287	32	0.7	9	—	—
Operatives	8,129	73	0.9	7,275	62	0.9	854	11	1.3
Laborers	2,773	70	2.5	2,232	69	3.1	541	1	0.2
Service workers	162	17	10.5	147	16	10.9	15	1	6.7
Total blue collar	15,360	192	1.2	13,941	179	1.3	1,419	13	0.9
Total	18,756	196	1.0	16,579	182	1.1	2,177	14	0.6

Source: Data in author's possession.
Note: For regional definitions, see Table 4, p. 15.

TABLE A-42. Paper and Allied Products Industry
Employment by Race, Sex, and Occupational Group
Pulp, Paper, and Paperboard Mills
14 Companies, 42 Establishments
Far West Region, 1968

Occupational Group	All Employees			Male			Female		
	Total	Negro	Percent Negro	Total	Negro	Percent Negro	Total	Negro	Percent Negro
Officials and managers	1,792	2	0.1	1,785	2	0.1	7	—	—
Professionals	1,073	4	0.4	1,054	4	0.4	19	—	—
Technicians	569	3	0.5	542	3	0.6	27	—	—
Sales workers	263	1	0.4	244	1	0.4	19	—	—
Office and clerical	1,722	7	0.4	557	5	0.9	1,165	2	0.2
Total white collar	5,419	17	0.3	4,182	15	0.4	1,237	2	0.2
Craftsmen	7,121	42	0.6	7,106	39	0.5	15	3	20.0
Operatives	12,545	333	2.7	11,434	280	2.4	1,111	53	4.8
Laborers	5,586	283	5.1	4,666	240	5.1	920	43	4.7
Service workers	285	7	2.5	230	6	2.6	55	1	1.8
Total blue collar	25,537	665	2.6	23,436	565	2.4	2,101	100	4.8
Total	30,956	682	2.2	27,618	580	2.1	3,338	102	3.1

Source: Data in author's possession.
Note: For regional definitions, see Table 4, p. 15.

TABLE A-43. *Paper and Allied Products Industry*
Employment by Race, Sex, and Occupational Group
Converting Plants
13 Companies, 36 Establishments
Far West Region, 1964

Occupational Group	All Employees			Male			Female		
	Total	Negro	Percent Negro	Total	Negro	Percent Negro	Total	Negro	Percent Negro
Officials and managers	394	—	—	387	—	—	7	—	—
Professionals	259	—	—	256	—	—	3	—	—
Technicians	71	—	—	63	—	—	8	—	—
Sales workers	236	—	—	231	—	—	5	—	—
Office and clerical	734	2	0.3	249	1	0.4	485	1	0.2
Total white collar	1,694	2	0.1	1,186	1	0.1	508	1	0.2
Craftsmen	1,826	23	1.3	1,775	23	1.3	51	—	—
Operatives	2,424	92	3.8	1,800	65	3.6	624	27	4.3
Laborers	2,088	33	1.6	1,260	24	1.9	828	9	1.1
Service workers	99	19	19.2	97	18	18.6	2	1	50.0
Total blue collar	6,437	167	2.6	4,932	130	2.6	1,505	37	2.5
Total	8,131	169	2.1	6,118	131	2.1	2,013	38	1.9

Source: Data in author's possession.
Note: For regional definitions, see Table 4, p. 15.

TABLE A-44.   Paper and Allied Products Industry
Employment by Race, Sex, and Occupational Group
Converting Plants
13 Companies, 38 Establishments
Far West Region, 1966

Occupational Group	All Employees			Male			Female		
	Total	Negro	Percent Negro	Total	Negro	Percent Negro	Total	Negro	Percent Negro
Officials and managers	496	—	—	488	—	—	8	—	—
Professionals	181	—	—	176	—	—	5	—	—
Technicians	34	—	—	28	—	—	6	—	—
Sales workers	244	1	0.4	236	1	0.4	8	—	—
Office and clerical	656	4	0.6	267	—	—	389	4	1.0
Total white collar	1,611	5	0.3	1,195	1	0.1	416	4	1.0
Craftsmen	1,527	23	1.5	1,479	23	1.6	48	—	—
Operatives	2,826	164	5.8	2,312	141	6.1	514	23	4.5
Laborers	1,629	124	7.6	1,148	111	9.7	481	13	2.7
Service workers	73	17	23.3	68	17	25.0	5	—	—
Total blue collar	6,055	328	5.4	5,007	292	5.8	1,048	36	3.4
Total	7,666	333	4.3	6,202	293	4.7	1,464	40	2.7

Source: Data in author's possession.
Note: For regional definitions, see Table 4, p. 15.

TABLE A-45. *Paper and Allied Products Industry*
Employment by Race, Sex and Occupational Group
Converting Plants
14 Companies, 39 Establishments
Far West Region, 1968

Occupational Group	All Employees			Male			Female		
	Total	Negro	Percent Negro	Total	Negro	Percent Negro	Total	Negro	Percent Negro
Officials and managers	731	2	0.3	725	2	0.3	6	—	—
Professionals	188	1	0.5	173	1	0.6	15	—	—
Technicians	101	—	—	89	—	—	12	—	—
Sales workers	180	1	0.6	168	—	—	12	1	8.3
Office and clerical	690	7	1.0	267	2	0.7	423	5	1.2
Total white collar	1,890	11	0.6	1,422	5	0.4	468	6	1.3
Craftsmen	2,467	58	2.4	2,374	57	2.4	93	1	1.1
Operatives	3,584	260	7.3	2,748	212	7.7	836	48	5.7
Laborers	1,998	143	7.2	1,325	105	7.9	673	38	5.6
Service workers	139	35	25.2	130	34	26.2	9	1	11.1
Total blue collar	8,188	496	6.1	6,577	408	6.2	1,611	88	5.5
Total	10,078	507	5.0	7,999	413	5.2	2,079	94	4.5

Source: Data in author's possession.
Note: For regional definitions, see Table 4, p. 15.

TABLE A-46. Paper and Allied Products Industry
Employment by Race, Sex, and Occupational Group
47 Companies, 195 Establishments
South Region, 1964

Occupational Group	All Employees			Male			Female		
	Total	Negro	Percent Negro	Total	Negro	Percent Negro	Total	Negro	Percent Negro
Officials and managers	4,921	4	0.1	4,890	4	0.1	31	—	—
Professionals	3,048	1	*	3,004	1	*	44	—	—
Technicians	1,410	4	0.3	1,203	2	0.2	207	2	1.0
Sales workers	685	—	—	650	—	—	35	—	—
Office and clerical	5,809	75	1.3	2,391	70	2.9	3,418	5	0.1
Total white collar	15,873	84	0.5	12,138	77	0.6	3,735	7	0.2
Craftsmen	17,647	269	1.5	17,473	268	1.5	174	1	0.6
Operatives	28,688	3,785	13.2	24,507	3,760	15.3	4,181	25	0.6
Laborers	13,105	4,840	36.9	11,713	4,755	40.6	1,392	85	6.1
Service workers	1,430	707	49.4	1,349	649	48.1	81	58	71.6
Total blue collar	60,870	9,601	15.8	55,042	9,432	17.1	5,828	169	2.9
Total	76,743	9,685	12.6	67,180	9,509	14.2	9,563	176	1.8

Source: Data in author's possession.

Note: For regional definitions, see Table 4, p. 15.

* Less than 0.05 percent.

TABLE A-47. *Paper and Allied Products Industry Employment by Race, Sex, and Occupational Group 35 Companies, 177 Establishments South Region, 1966*

Occupational Group	All Employees			Male			Female		
	Total	Negro	Percent Negro	Total	Negro	Percent Negro	Total	Negro	Percent Negro
Officials and managers	6,881	5	0.1	6,829	5	0.1	52	—	—
Professionals	3,643	2	0.1	3,563	2	0.1	80	—	—
Technicians	2,128	16	0.8	1,737	13	0.7	391	3	0.8
Sales workers	937	—	—	889	—	—	48	—	—
Office and clerical	7,590	190	2.5	3,079	165	5.4	4,511	25	0.6
Total white collar	21,179	213	1.0	16,097	185	1.1	5,082	28	0.6
Craftsmen	25,249	531	2.1	24,920	520	2.1	329	11	3.3
Operatives	35,909	4,922	13.7	31,208	4,777	15.3	4,701	145	3.1
Laborers	15,426	5,115	33.2	13,483	4,962	36.8	1,943	153	7.9
Service workers	1,809	852	47.1	1,713	795	46.4	96	57	59.4
Total blue collar	78,393	11,420	14.6	71,324	11,054	15.5	7,069	366	5.2
Total	99,572	11,633	11.7	87,421	11,239	12.9	12,151	394	3.2

Source: Data in author's possession.
Note: For regional definitions, see Table 4, p. 15.

TABLE A-48. Paper and Allied Products Industry
Employment by Race, Sex, and Occupational Group
40 Companies, 177 Establishments
South Region, 1968

Occupational Group	All Employees			Male			Female		
	Total	Negro	Percent Negro	Total	Negro	Percent Negro	Total	Negro	Percent Negro
Officials and managers	7,379	15	0.2	7,325	15	0.2	54	—	—
Professionals	3,386	14	0.4	3,260	14	0.4	126	—	—
Technicians	1,849	32	1.7	1,545	28	1.8	304	4	1.3
Sales workers	759	2	0.3	707	2	0.3	52	—	—
Office and clerical	7,051	234	3.3	2,621	163	6.2	4,430	71	1.6
Total white collar	20,424	297	1.5	15,458	222	1.4	4,966	75	1.5
Craftsmen	24,385	671	2.8	24,146	659	2.7	239	12	5.0
Operatives	36,316	6,143	16.9	31,812	5,745	18.1	4,504	398	8.8
Laborers	14,697	5,057	34.4	12,915	4,893	37.9	1,782	164	9.2
Service workers	1,561	710	45.5	1,491	665	44.6	70	45	64.3
Total blue collar	76,959	12,581	16.3	70,364	11,962	17.0	6,595	619	9.4
Total	97,383	12,878	13.2	85,822	12,184	14.2	11,561	694	6.0

Source: Data in author's possession.
Note: For regional definitions, see Table 4, p. 15.

TABLE A-49. *Paper and Allied Products Industry*
Employment by Race, Sex, and Occupational Group
Pulp, Paper, and Paperboard Mills
15 Companies, 63 Establishments
South Region, 1964

Occupational Group	All Employees			Male			Female		
	Total	Negro	Percent Negro	Total	Negro	Percent Negro	Total	Negro	Percent Negro
Officials and managers	3,263	2	0.1	3,251	2	0.1	12	—	—
Professionals	2,448	1	*	2,419	1	*	29	—	—
Technicians	1,156	—	—	988	—	—	168	—	—
Sales workers	38	—	—	38	—	—	—	—	—
Office and clerical	3,593	47	1.3	1,590	45	2.8	2,003	2	0.1
Total white collar	10,498	50	0.5	8,286	48	0.6	2,212	2	0.1
Craftsmen	13,367	148	1.1	13,318	148	1.1	49	—	—
Operatives	19,181	2,396	12.5	17,058	2,395	14.0	2,123	1	*
Laborers	7,868	3,538	45.0	7,524	3,523	46.8	344	15	4.4
Service workers	903	411	45.5	833	362	43.5	70	49	70.0
Total blue collar	41,319	6,493	15.7	38,733	6,428	16.6	2,586	65	2.5
Total	51,817	6,543	12.6	47,019	6,476	13.8	4,798	67	1.4

Source: Data in author's possession.
Note: For regional definitions, see Table 4, p. 15.
* Less than 0.05 percent.

TABLE A-50.   Paper and Allied Products Industry
Employment by Race, Sex, and Occupational Group
Pulp, Paper, and Paperboard Mills
34 Companies, 79 Establishments
South Region, 1966

Occupational Group	All Employees			Male			Female		
	Total	Negro	Percent Negro	Total	Negro	Percent Negro	Total	Negro	Percent Negro
Officials and managers	5,092	3	0.1	5,061	3	0.1	31	—	—
Professionals	2,964	2	0.1	2,906	2	0.1	58	—	—
Technicians	1,819	7	0.4	1,462	7	0.5	357	—	—
Sales workers	268	—	—	250	—	—	18	—	—
Office and clerical	5,068	130	2.6	2,169	115	5.3	2,899	15	0.5
Total white collar	15,211	142	0.9	11,848	127	1.1	3,363	15	0.4
Craftsmen	20,530	332	1.6	20,327	332	1.6	203	—	—
Operatives	25,969	3,250	12.5	23,367	3,170	13.6	2,602	80	3.1
Laborers	10,360	3,891	37.6	9,705	3,876	39.9	655	15	2.3
Service workers	1,379	626	45.4	1,297	581	44.8	82	45	54.9
Total blue collar	58,238	8,099	13.9	54,696	7,959	14.6	3,542	140	4.0
Total	73,449	8,241	11.2	66,544	8,086	12.2	6,905	155	2.2

Source: Data in author's possession.
Note: For regional definitions, see Table 4, p. 15.

TABLE A-51. *Paper and Allied Products Industry*
Employment by Race, Sex, and Occupational Group
Pulp, Paper, and Paperboard Mills
33 Companies, 87 Establishments
South Region, 1968

Occupational Group	All Employees			Male			Female		
	Total	Negro	Percent Negro	Total	Negro	Percent Negro	Total	Negro	Percent Negro
Officials and managers	5,839	10	0.2	5,811	10	0.2	28	—	—
Professionals	3,032	14	0.5	2,924	14	0.5	108	—	—
Technicians	1,676	30	1.8	1,384	26	1.9	292	4	1.4
Sales workers	172	—	—	165	—	—	7	—	—
Office and clerical	5,277	194	3.7	2,078	146	7.0	3,199	48	1.5
Total white collar	15,996	248	1.6	12,362	196	1.6	3,634	52	1.4
Craftsmen	21,118	445	2.1	21,059	445	2.1	59	—	—
Operatives	28,767	4,399	15.3	25,269	4,123	16.3	3,498	276	7.9
Laborers	10,293	3,784	36.8	9,432	3,726	39.5	861	58	6.7
Service workers	1,366	615	45.0	1,305	577	44.2	61	38	62.3
Total blue collar	61,544	9,243	15.0	57,065	8,871	15.5	4,479	372	8.3
Total	77,540	9,491	12.2	69,427	9,067	13.1	8,113	424	5.2

Source: Data in author's possession.
Note: For regional definitions, see Table 4, p. 15.

TABLE A-52. Paper and Allied Products Industry
Employment by Race, Sex, and Occupational Group
Converting Plants
43 Companies, 132 Establishments
South Region, 1964

Occupational Group	All Employees			Male			Female		
	Total	Negro	Percent Negro	Total	Negro	Percent Negro	Total	Negro	Percent Negro
Officials and managers	1,658	2	0.1	1,639	2	0.1	19	—	—
Professionals	600	—	—	585	—	—	15	—	—
Technicians	254	4	1.6	215	2	0.9	39	2	5.1
Sales workers	647	—	—	612	—	—	35	—	—
Office and clerical	2,216	28	1.3	801	25	3.1	1,415	3	0.2
Total white collar	5,375	34	0.6	3,852	29	0.8	1,523	5	0.3
Craftsmen	4,280	121	2.8	4,155	120	2.9	125	1	0.8
Operatives	9,507	1,389	14.6	7,449	1,365	18.3	2,058	24	1.2
Laborers	5,237	1,302	24.9	4,189	1,232	29.4	1,048	70	6.7
Service workers	527	296	56.2	516	287	55.6	11	9	81.8
Total blue collar	19,551	3,108	15.9	16,309	3,004	18.4	3,242	104	3.2
Total	24,926	3,142	12.6	20,161	3,033	15.0	4,765	109	2.3

Source: Data in author's possession.
Note: For regional definitions, see Table 4, p. 15.

TABLE A-53. *Paper and Allied Products Industry Employment by Race, Sex, and Occupational Group Converting Plants 22 Companies, 98 Establishments South Region, 1966*

Occupational Group	All Employees			Male			Female		
	Total	Negro	Percent Negro	Total	Negro	Percent Negro	Total	Negro	Percent Negro
Officials and managers	1,789	2	0.1	1,768	2	0.1	21	—	—
Professionals	679	—	—	657	—	—	22	—	—
Technicians	309	9	2.9	275	6	2.2	34	3	8.8
Sales workers	669	—	—	639	—	—	30	—	—
Office and clerical	2,522	60	2.4	910	50	5.5	1,612	10	0.6
Total white collar	5,968	71	1.2	4,249	58	1.4	1,719	13	0.8
Craftsmen	4,719	199	4.2	4,593	188	4.1	126	11	8.7
Operatives	9,940	1,672	16.8	7,841	1,607	20.5	2,099	65	3.1
Laborers	5,066	1,224	24.2	3,778	1,086	28.7	1,288	138	10.7
Service workers	430	226	52.6	416	214	51.4	14	12	85.7
Total blue collar	20,155	3,321	16.5	16,628	3,095	18.6	3,527	226	6.4
Total	26,123	3,392	13.0	20,877	3,153	15.1	5,246	239	4.6

Source: Data in author's possession.
Note: For regional definitions, see Table 4, p. 15.

TABLE A-54.   *Paper and Allied Products Industry Employment by Race, Sex, and Occupational Group Converting Plants 26 Companies, 90 Establishments South Region, 1968*

Occupational Group	All Employees			Male			Female		
	Total	Negro	Percent Negro	Total	Negro	Percent Negro	Total	Negro	Percent Negro
Officials and managers	1,540	5	0.3	1,514	5	0.3	26	—	—
Professionals	354	—	—	336	—	—	18	—	—
Technicians	173	2	1.2	161	2	1.2	12	—	—
Sales workers	587	2	0.3	542	2	0.4	45	—	—
Office and clerical	1,774	40	2.3	543	17	3.1	1,231	23	1.9
Total white collar	4,428	49	1.1	3,096	26	0.8	1,332	23	1.7
Craftsmen	3,267	226	6.9	3,087	214	6.9	180	12	6.7
Operatives	7,549	1,744	23.1	6,543	1,622	24.8	1,006	122	12.1
Laborers	4,404	1,273	28.9	3,483	1,167	33.5	921	106	11.5
Service workers	195	95	48.7	186	88	47.3	9	7	77.8
Total blue collar	15,415	3,338	21.7	13,299	3,091	23.2	2,116	247	11.7
Total	19,843	3,387	17.1	16,395	3,117	19.0	3,448	270	7.8

Source: Data in author's possession.

Note: For regional definitions, see Table 4, p. 15.

Appendix B

1. Decision of the District Court in the matter of *United States v. Local 189, United Papermakers and Paperworkers, Crown Zellerbach Corp., et al.*, 282 F. Supp. 39 (E.D. La., 1968).

2. Decision of the District Court in the matter of *United States v. Local 189, United Papermakers and Paperworkers, Crown Zellerbach Corp., et al.*, 301F. Supp. 906 (E.D. La., 1969).

3. Decision of the Court of Appeals for the Fifth Circuit in the matter of *Local 189, United Papermakers and Paperworkers, et al., v. United States*, U.S. C.A., 5th Cir., July 28, 1969.

UNITED STATES DISTRICT COURT
EASTERN DISTRICT OF LOUISIANA
NEW ORLEANS DIVISION
UNITED STATES OF AMERICA
by RAMSEY CLARK,
Attorney General
         versus
CIVIL ACTION
No. 68–205
Section B

LOCAL 189, UNITED PAPERMAKERS AND PAPERWORKERS, AFL - CIO, CLC; UNITED PAPERMAKERS AND PAPERWORKERS, AFL - CIO, CLC; and CROWN ZELLERBACH CORPORATION

ORDER

This cause having come on for hearing on the motion of the United States for a preliminary injunction against the defendants, as well as a trial on the merits of the complaints of the United States and the plaintiff-intervenors, Anthony Hill, David Johnson, Sr., and Local 189a, United Papermakers and Paperworkers, for permanent injunctive relief.

IT IS NOW THE ORDER OF THE COURT that, for the reasons assigned, the relief sought be, and the same is hereby, GRANTED to the following extent:

(a) The defendants Crown Zellerbach Corporation and Local 189, United Papermakers and Paperworkers, AFL-CIO, CLC, and United Papermakers and Paperworkers, AFL-CIO, CLC, their officers, agents, employees, servants and all persons and organizations in active concert or participation with them, are hereby ENJOINED and RESTRAINED, pending the further orders of this Court, from discriminating against the Negro employees of the defendant Crown Zellerbach Corporation's paper mill at Boga-

lusa, Louisiana, in violation of Title VII of the Civil Rights Act of 1964, and in particular, the defendants are hereby ORDERED to ABOLISH forthwith the system of "job seniority" and any other seniority system designed to discriminate against the Negro employees at said plant or having the effect of so discriminating, insofar as such systems may apply to the promotion, demotion, or selection for training of Negro employees hired prior to January 16, 1966 in competition with employees of the opposite race; and the said defendants are ORDERED to ESTABLISH, with respect to such promotions, demotions and selection for training, and in the place of such "job seniority" or similar systems, a system of "mill seniority" as follows:

(1) Total mill seniority (i.e., the length of continuous service in the mill) alone shall determine who the "senior" bidder or employee is for purposes of permanent or thirty-day promotions, or for purposes of demotion in all circumstances in which one or more of the competing employees is a Negro employed hired prior to January 16, 1966;

(2) For jobs which operate only one shift per day, promotions to fill casual or vacation vacancies will be made on the same basis as permanent and thirty-day promotions;

(3) For jobs which operate more than one shift per day, promotions because of casual or vacation vacancies will be awarded to the senior (as determined in [1] above) qualified man on the shift and/or machine where the vacancy exists;

(4) Promotions and demotions above shall not affect persons who have formal

189

written waivers in effect at that time. Persons promoted shall go around a waived position in any job slot, and persons demoted shall likewise go around such a position on the way down;

(5) Qualified employees shall be selected for training on the same basis as for promotion described above.

The provisions of this decree pertaining to the implementation by the defendants of a system of "mill seniority" shall be placed into effect within ten days from the entry of this order; prior to the implementation of the said "mill seniority" system, the defendants are ENJOINED and RESTRAINED from interfering and failing to comply with the agreement of March 19, 1967, as modified by the agreements of June 16, 1967 and January 3, 1968, between the defendant Crown Zellerbach Corporation and the Office of Federal Contract Compliance of the United States Department of Labor.

(b) The defendant Local 189, United Papermakers and Paperworkers, AFL-CIO, CLC, and United Papermakers and Paperworkers, AFL-CIO, CLC, their officers, agents, members, employees, servants, and all persons and organizations in active concert or participation with them, are ENJOINED and RESTRAINED, pending the further orders of this Court, from interfering with or hindering, by striking, threatening to strike, or otherwise, the compliance by the defendants with the foregoing provisions of this order.

REASONS

This action was filed by the Attorney General on behalf of and in the name of the United States on January 30, 1968, against Local 189 of the United Papermakers and Paperworkers, AFL-CIO, CLC (all the members of which are of the white race), its parent union, the United Papermakers and Paperworkers, AFL-CIO, CLC, and Crown Zellerbach Corporation, seeking relief for violations of Title VII of the Civil Rights Act of 1964, 42 U.S.C. 2000e *et seq.*, and from interference with the implementation of Executive Order 11246, 30 F. R. 12319 (September 28, 1965), forbidding racial discrimination in employment opportunities by government contractors. On February 15, 1968, Local 189a, United Papermakers and Paperworkers, AFL-CIO, CLC, (all the members of which are Negroes), David Johnson, Sr., and Anthony Hill, both of whom are Negro employees of Crown Zellerbach and members of Local 189a, filed a motion for leave to intervene as parties plaintiff herein and as class representatives.

It is undisputed—in fact the ultimate facts compelling the conclusion have been stipulated by all parties—that prior to May 1964 Crown followed an active program of discrimination in employment opportunities against its Negro employees at its Bogalusa plant, and that not until January 1966 were considerations of race fully obliterated with respect to the job opportunities of the employees at the plant. Although not equally responsible for this situation, the white local was in good measure at fault: the discrimination against Negro employees was possible because Local 189 was all white, and Negro employees excluded from that local had an organization of their own, Local 189a; discrimination was arranged by the device of granting "jurisdiction" over the more attractive lines of progression and the more lucrative jobs to the white local.

In the circumstances of this case, the seniority and recall system which defendant unions and defendant Crown maintained in effect at the Crown, Bogalusa, Louisiana paper mill prior to February 1, 1968, perpetuates the consequences of past discrimination, and is unlawful under Title VII of the Civil Rights Act of 1964, and under Executive Order 11246 and the contractual clauses required thereby. Obviously, that seniority system was not a bona fide seniority system within the meaning of §703(b) of Title VII. See *Quarles v. Philip Morris,* 279 F. Supp. 505 (E. D. Va. 1968).

The government and plaintiff-intervenors have pressed the Court the injustice of the "job seniority" system, its contribution to discrimination at Crown's Bogalusa plant, and the advantages of "mill seniority" over "job seniority." Although we agree with the application of these arguments to the situation involved here, we think it important to correctly express the underlying basis of this approach. "Job seniority" is certainly not *inherently* prejudicial to Negroes; there is nothing about "job seniority" systems themselves to make them necessarily offensive; nor do we think "mill seniority" necessarily a better system. It is not the job seniority system in and of itself, but rather the continuous discrimination practiced by the defendants within the framework of that system, which now requires that the system be abolished in this case. Within the framework of a "job seniority" system, Negro employees have been forced into the inferior lines of progression and the less desirable jobs. The defendants claim that active discrimination against Negroes has now ceased. But the fact that Negroes who, under the present liberalized policy, have only recently entered formerly white progression lines are forced to compete with white employees for promotion on the basis of "job seniority" continues, in each case of such competition, the discriminatory effect of the long history of the relegation of those Negroes to other, less desirable lines.

We cannot accept the Union's contention that such discrimination is not prohibited by Title VII and that Title VII cannot be used in any way to alter or affect seniority systems. Where a seniority system has the effect of perpetrating discrimination, and concentrating or "telescoping" the effect of past years of discrimination against Negro employees into the *present* placement of Negroes in an inferior position for promotion and other purposes, that present result is prohibited, and a seniority system which operates to produce that present result must be replaced with another system. We agree wholeheartedly with the conclusion in *Quarles v. Philip Morris, Inc.*, 279 F. Supp. 505 (E.D. Va. 1968), that present discrimination cannot be justified under Title VII simply because Title VII refers to an effective date and because present discrimination is caused by conditions in the past. "Congress did not intend to freeze an entire generation of Negro employees into discriminatory patterns that existed before the act." *Quarles, supra*, at .....

We find that "mill seniority" is at least as good, if not better, than "job seniority" as the basis for regulating promotion, demotion and selection of employees for training. The contention that mill seniority does not allow full consideration of employee experience as one of the qualifications for promotion is, on its face, without merit, since the government seeks at this time only to supplant the test for promotion of employees to vacant "job slot" from the job slots directly below the vacant slot in the same line of progression. In this situation, all employees competing for the vacant job will have had some previous experience in the progression line. Moreover, we by no means deny Crown the right to require that the competing employees have the fundamental qualifications necessary to fill the vacant position.

The Union asserts that the Court should stay its hand to give the white local a chance to bargain with Crown for a system which would produce a result fair to Negro employees. We cannot sympathize with this approach. This defendant Union bears some responsibility for the past discrimination and the present plight of the Negro employees under the "job seniority" system. The "mill seniority" system required by the Court would mitigate the harshness of this situation. The defendant Union does not seriously attack mill seniority as unfair, but principally questions the right of this Court to order any particular seniority system into effect.

As we have indicated, we do not hold that "mill seniority" is per se required under Title VII. But we do hold that, where, as here, "job seniority" operates to continue the effects of past discrimination, it must be replaced by some other, nondiscriminatory, system, and that mill seniority is an appropriate system in this case. We do not deny, by our present order, the right of Crown to urge some other equally acceptable system, if there be any, by which to control the flow of employee promotion and demotion, or the right of Local 189 to bargain for any such system. But we cannot permit the plaintiffs herein to remain without a remedy to present and continuing discrimination merely because the remedy called for involves matters which may be subject to the bargaining efforts of unions. Title VII provides for the correction of discriminatory practices by any remedial order which may be necessary; the scope of the remedy is not restricted to matters outside the jurisdiction of labor organizations. 42 U.S.C. §2000e-6. Should an acceptable system other than "mill seniority" be proposed by any interested party, nothing herein would prohibit the Union from bargaining for it or Crown from implementing it, subject, of course, to the approval of the Court.

Because the defendant Union was unwilling to consent to a further extension of the Court's temporary restraining order pending a full-scale hearing of all issues in this case, only the two issues mentioned above were submitted to the Court at the hearing on March 20.

By orders of February 21, 1968 and March 8, 1968, this Court granted such leave and a complaint in intervention was filed. On March 20, 1968, this cause came on for hearing on plaintiff's motions for preliminary injunctions against defendant unions and against defendant Crown, and on the prayers for permanent injunctions by plaintiff and plaintiff-intervenors. By stipulation of the parties pursuant to Rule 42(b), the hearing was limited to the following issues:

"(a) Whether, under the facts and circumstances of this case, the job seniority system which was in effect at the Bogalusa paper mill prior to February 1, 1968, was unlawful?

"(b) If the answer to the above question is in the affirmative, what is the necessary or appropriate standard or guideline for identifying the seniority of employees for purposes of promotion and demotion?"

All other issues in this case were not submitted to the Court but were expressly reserved for the hearing which all parties agree will commence on April 30, 1968.

We find, as a matter of fact, (1) that Crown and the white local actively engaged, prior to January 1966, in a pervasive pattern of discrimination against the Negro employees at Crown's Bogalusa paper mill with respect to employment opportunities of promotion, demotion and selection for training; (2) that the continuation of the "job seniority" system, or any seniority system which incorporates job seniority as a substantial factor in promotion, demotion and selection for training, operates, because of the situation engendered by the pervasive past discrimination by the defendants at Crown's Bogalusa paper mill, to effectively presently discriminate against Negro employees at the mill whenever Negro employees hired prior to January 1966 compete against white employees for promotion, demotion or selection for training; (3) that a system of "mill seniority," as defined in the Collective Bargaining Agreement between Crown and the local unions presently in force at the Bogalusa plant, would not have such a continuing discriminatory effect against the Negro employees; and (4) that "job seniority," as a consideration in the promotion and demotion of employees within a particular line of progression and in the selection of employees for training, is not necessitated by safety or efficiency factors, nor for any other reason is "job seniority" objectively a better or more desirable basis than "mill seniority" for promotion, demotion or selection for training of employees within the context of the present lines of progression in force at Crown's Bogalusa paper mill.

As a matter of law, we hold that this Court has jurisdiction of this action under 42 U.S.C. §2000e-6(b) and 28 U.S.C. §1331 and §1345, and that discrimination against Negroes with respect to employment opportunities at this mill is properly subject to attack by the government pursuant not only to Title VII of the Civil Rights Act of 1964,[1] but also

---

1. The parties have stipulated that Crown is an employer within the meaning of 42 U.S.C. §2000e(b) and is engaged in an industry affecting commerce within the meaning of 42 U.S.C. §2000e(h), and that local 189 and its parent union are labor organizations within the meaning of 42 U.S.C. §2000e (d) and are engaged in an industry affecting commerce within the meaning of 42 U.S.C. 2000e (e).

under §209 of Executive Order 11246.[2] That order, like the order in *Farkas v. Texas Instrument, Inc.*, 375 F. 2d 629, 632, (5th Cir. 1967), is to be accorded the force and effect of statutory law . 375 F. 2d 632, n. 1 and text.

The white local is not immune from suit or injunctive process of this Court by reason of the general terms of the Norris-LaGuardia Act, 29 U.S.C. § 101, *et seq.* Even prior to the enactment of Title VII, the Supreme Court had held that racial discrimination by a union was not sanctioned or protected from corrective court orders by the Norris-La-Guardia Act. *Virginian R. Co. v. System Federation*, 300 U.S. 515 (1937); *Graham v. Brotherhood of Firemen*, 338 U.S. 232 (1949); *Brotherhood of Railroad Trainmen v. Howard*, 343 U.S. 768, 774 (1952). These decisions were not predicated on any peculiarity in the anti-discrimination provisions of the Railway Labor Act, *Textile Workers Union of America v. Lincoln Mills*, 353 U.S. 448, 458 (1957), and we find the holdings of these cases equally applicable to the provisions of Title VII and Executive Order 11246. Merely because §706 of Title VII, 28 U.S.C. §2000e-5(h), (authorizing private suits for the correction of Title VII violations), contains an express exemption from the anti-injunction provisions of the Norris-LaGuardia Act, while §707, 280 S.C. §2000e-6, (authorizing civil actions by the Attorney General), does not, fails to influence our holding. Section 707 provides, in the broadest possible language, for the protection of Title VII rights by suit by the Attorney General seeking "permanent or temporary injunction, restraining order or other order against the person or persons responsible . . . as [may be] necessary to insure the full enjoyment of Title VII rights." 42 U.S.C. §2000e-6 (a). This language cannot be read to prohibit the remedy against unions which may be responsible for Title VII violations. Title VII read as a whole forbids such a restrictive interpretation. Section 2000e(a) defines "person" to include "one or more individuals, *labor unions*, . . ."; 2000e-2(c) specifically lists the acts of labor organizations which constitute "unlawful employment practices" under Title VII; §2000e-2(c) (3) makes it unlawful for a labor organization "to cause or attempt to cause an employer to discriminate against an individual in violation of [Title VII]." To hold such unlawful union practices subject to injunctive remedies sought by individuals under §706 and not to the Attorney General seeking to correct what will usually be much more serious and pervasive "patterns or practices of resistance" under §707 would be inconsistent and irrational, and destructive to the national achievement of the basic aims of Title VII.

All parties agreed to try the remaining issues before the Court on April 30, 1968. Because of the limited nature of the March 20 hearing, the basic relief required in view of the Court's findings with respect to the two issues submitted at that hearing may reasonably be expected to require some modification to accommodate whatever findings may be forthcoming after the more extensive hearing on April 30. The relief we grant by the present order we think adequately protects the plaintiffs with respect to the two limited issues which have been presented to us; but the relief granted should in no way operate to prejudice the outcome of the more extensive hearing to be held on the remaining issues so closely related to those already presented.

/s/Frederick J. R. Heebe

UNITED STATES DISTRICT COURT
New Orleans, Louisiana
March 26, 1968—At 7:00 P.M.

---

2. The parties have stipulated that, "since at least 1961, the defendant, Crown, has supplied materials under government contracts and subcontracts, which contain equal employment opportunity clauses similar to or the same as those appearing [in] the Executive Order 11246 and Executive Order 10925, to the extent required by those orders."

UNITED STATES DISTRICT COURT
EASTERN DISTRICT OF LOUISIANA
NEW ORLEANS DIVISION

UNITED STATES OF AMERICA
by RAMSEY CLARK, Attorney General

Plaintiff

LOCAL 189A, UNITED PAPER-
MAKERS AND PAPERWORKERS,
AFL-CIO, CLC;
DAVID JOHNSON, SR., and
ANTHONY HILL   CIVIL ACTION

Plaintiff-Intervenors   No. 68-205

versus   SECTION B

LOCAL 189, UNITED PAPERMAKERS
AND PAPERWORKERS, AFL-CIO,
CLC; UNITED PAPERMAKERS AND
PAPERWORKERS, AFL-CIO, CLC;
and CROWN ZELLERBACH
CORPORATION

Defendants

DECREE

This cause having come for a hearing
on the merits of the complaints of the
plaintiff, United States, and the plaintiff-
intervenors, Anthony Hill, David Johnson, Sr., and Local 189A, United Papermakers and Paperworkers, AFL-CIO,
CLC,

IT IS NOW THE ORDER OF THE
COURT that, for the reasons assigned,
the relief sought should be, and the
same is hereby, GRANTED as follows:

The defendants, Crown Zellerbach
Corporation, Local 189, United Papermakers and Paperworkers, AFL-CIO,
CLC, and the United Papermakers and
Paperworkers, AFL-CIO, CLC, their
officers, agents, employees, servants
and all persons and organizations
in active concert or participation
with them, are hereby permanently EN-
JOINED and RESTRAINED from discriminating against the Negro employees
of the defendant Crown Zellerbach Corporation's paper mill at Bogalusa, Louisiana, in violation of Title VII of the
Civil Rights Act of 1964, and in violation of the obligations imposed pursuant
to Executive Order 11246, and in particular,

IT IS ORDERED that the defendants'
prior system of "job seniority," and any
other seniority system designed to discriminate against Negro employees at
said paper mill, or having the effect of
so discriminating, shall remain permanently ABOLISHED insofar as such systems may apply to the temporary and
permanent job assignment, the temporary
and permanent promotion and demotion,
and the selection for training of the
following class of employees in competition with other employees at said
paper mill:

I. *Affected Class:*

(1) All Negro employees hired prior
to January 16, 1966, shall have all
rights contained in this Decree.

(2) All Negro employees hired after
January 16, 1966, and prior to February 14, 1968, except such of those employees whose initial permanent positions were in job classifications formerly
within the exclusive jurisdiction of
Local 189, shall have the rights set
forth in paragraphs II, III, IV, V, VI
and VII herein while such employee
remains in the line of progression, if
any, in which he permanently held a
permanent position as of the date of
this Decree or while he is in the first
line of progression to which he voluntarily transfers or, if currently a member of the Extra Board (labor pool),
to which he bids within three years
from the date of this Decree, and;

II. The said defendants are permanently
ORDERED to CONTINUE in the place
of such "job seniority" or similar systems, a system of "mill seniority," with
respect to such casual temporary and
permanent job assignments, temporary
and permanent demotions, and selection
for training of Negro employees in the
above affected class, as follows:

(1) Total mill seniority (i.e., the
length of continuous service in the
mill) alone shall determine who the
"senior" bidder or employee is for
purposes of permanent or thirty-day
promotions, or for purposes of demotion in all circumstances in which one
or more of the competing employees

is a Negro employee in the specified class;

(2) For jobs which operate only one shift per day, promotions to fill casual or vacation vacancies will be made on the same basis as permanent and thirty-day promotions;

(3) For jobs which operate more than one shift per day, promotions because of casual or vacation vacancies will be awarded to the senior (as determined in (1) above) qualified man on the shift and/or machine where the vacancy exists;

(4) Except as otherwise provided by this order the waiver provisions set forth in the labor agreement shall remain in effect. Persons promoted shall go around a waived position in any job slot, and except as set forth in ¶ XII below, persons demoted shall likewise go around such a position on the way down;

(5) Qualified employees shall be selected for training on the same basis as for promotion described above.

IT IS THE FURTHER ORDER OF THE COURT that the following shall apply:

III. *Residence*

(1) The jobs in the paper mill for which residence requirements are valid, and the appropriate residence requirements for each are listed in attached Appendix A.

(2) Time spent on jobs on casual or temporary assignments shall be counted toward residency for those jobs if such time is equal to, or exceeds, 64 hours in any calendar month, in which event the total hours actually worked shall be counted; provided, however, that time spent on temporary or casual assignments within any calendar month which does not amount to 64 hours or more on any job shall count toward satisfying the residence requirement, if any, of the job to which the employee is permanently assigned.

(3) Time worked on a job on a permanent basis, or casual or temporary basis as defined in (2) above, shall satisfy residency requirements as follows:

a) 173 ⅓ hours actually worked shall satisfy one month of residency.

b) 40 hours actually worked shall satisfy one week of residency.

(4) Where none of the candidates being considered for the promotion has fulfilled the residency and/or Job Instruction Training requirements, the company may fill such positions with the candidate who has completed the greatest percentage of such requirements.

IT IS THE FURTHER ORDER OF THE COURT that, with respect to the affected class as defined in ¶ I, the following shall apply:

IV. *Lines of Progression*:

Except as provided below, promotions shall be in accordance with the presently constituted lines of progression:

A. *Bypassing Jobs*

(1) With respect to permanent promotions and temporary and casual setups, employees if qualified who are members of the affected class may bypass the following job classifications in the indicated lines of progression:

(a) *Brown Stock Washers*:
Second Washer Operator

(b) *Digesters*:
One, but not both, Gas Off Man or No. 1 Gas Off Man
One, but not both, Capper New Digester or Capper Old Digester

(c) *Finishing Department*:
All jobs from Spare Hand up to and including Five-Day Jitney Operator, provided however that the employee must have served a total of four weeks as a Spare Hand and/or in another job up to Five-Day Jitney Operator
All or any of the following when bidding on the Crane Operators job:
Cutter Operator
Trimmer Operator
Roll Wrap Machine Operator and No. 11 Rewinder Operator
plus two, but not all of the following:
Roll Wrap Machine First Helper or No. 9 Rewinder Operator or Cutter Helper
In that branch of the Finishing Department progression line which con-

tains the jobs of Cutter Operator, Trimmer Operator and First Cutter Helper, an employee may bypass the job of Trimmer Operator. In that branch of the Finishing Department progression line which contains the jobs of Roll Wrap Machine Operator, No. 11 Rewinder Operator, No. 9 Rewinder Operator and Roll Wrap Machine First Helper, an employee may bypass Roll Wrap Machine First Helper provided he also bypasses Roll Wrap Machine Operator, or he may bypass No. 9 Rewinder Operator provided he also bypasses No. 11 Rewinder Operator.

(d) *Paper Machine, Nos. 1, 2 and 4*: Four, but not all of the following:
No. 1, Rewinder Helper
No. 2, Fifth Hand
No. 1, Finisher
No. 1, Felt Checker, or
No. 4, Fifth Hand,
provided that the employee has served as a Spare Hand and/or in one or more of the above jobs other than Spare Hand for a total of seven months, at least six of which must have been served in one of the above listed jobs other than Spare Hand.

(e) *Paper Machines, Nos. 5, 6 and 7*: Two, but not all of the following:
Utility Man
Shaft Tailer
Shaft Puller
provided that the employee has served as a Spare Hand and/or in one of the above jobs for a total of five months, at least four of which must be as a Shaft Tailer or Shaft Puller.

(f) *Stock Preparation*:
One, but not both:
No. 2 Blend Tank Man or
No. 1 Blend Tank Man

(g) *Technical Department*:
One, but not both:
5, 6 and 7 Wet End Tester or
1, 2 and 4 Wet End Tester

(h) *Utilities Department*:
Outside Operator

(i) *Wood Room*:
One, but not both:
Chip Storage Operator or
Assistant Chip Storage Operator

and one, but not both:
Wood Unloader-Flume or
Wood Unloader-Chain

(2) When a permanent, temporary or casual vacancy occurs in a job, the following employees, if qualified, are eligible to fill it:
(a) any incumbents in the job immediately below the vacant job.
(b) and any member of the affected class who is eligible to bypass all of the jobs between the job to which he is permanently assigned and the job in which the vacancy exists.
(3) Mill seniority, as set forth in II (1-4) shall determine the selection of the employee to fill the vacancy from the above eligible employees if a qualified member of the affected class is eligible to bid for the vacancy.

B. *Entry to Progression Lines*
(1) With respect to permanent assignments, members of the affected class may bid for entry into the following indicated progression lines at points above the normal entry point only at the jobs listed below or if a vacancy in a line initially occurs in a job below the listed jobs, members of the affected class may bid for entry at the position where that vacancy occurs:

(a) *Brown Stock Washer*: Third Washer (Swenson) Helper
(b) *Digesters*: Capper — New Digester
(c) *Paper Machine 1, 2, 4*: Spare Hand
(d) Stock Preparation: Payloader Man
(e) *Technical Department*: Pulp Mill Tester
(f) *Utilities*: First Bark Boiler Helper
(g) *Wood Room*: Utility Flume

(2) When members of the affected class are entitled to bid for entry into a progression line above the normal entry point as provided in ¶ 1, above, the following persons are eligible to bid:
(a) all members of the affected class whether or not they are then in progression lines.

(b) all employees permanently assigned to the job immediately below the vacant job.

(3) When a member of the affected class bids, mill seniority as set forth in II (1) shall determine among qualified bidders in the competition contemplated in (2) above.

C. *Residency by Virture of Temporary Assignments*

(1) A member of the affected class may bid for a vacancy above an intermediate job through which, in accordance with the terms of this order, he would otherwise be required to progress provided:

(a) he has fulfilled the residency and Job Instruction Training (J.I.T.) requirements for the job he currently holds.

(b) he has fulfilled the residency and J.I.T. requirements for the above-mentioned intermediate job.

(c) he has served on temporary assignment in the job for which he is bidding a sufficient time to meet one-third of the residency requirements for such job. Such one-third residency shall not be required on jobs which have not customarily involved any training in that job while permanently assigned to the lower job.

(2) Only one intermediate job as defined in ¶ 1 above at a time may be passed in this manner, but jobs which are blocked by waivers shall not be counted for this purpose.

(3) For purposes of this section only, in the Utilities Department line of progression the First and Second Bark Boiler Helper jobs shall be considered as one job for the purpose of determining eligible bidders for higher jobs in this line.

(4) Members of the affected class who are eligible to bid for a vacancy under this ¶ C shall bid on the basis of mill seniority in competition with all other persons eligible to bid for the vacancy.

V. *Extra Board Assignments*

A. Crown shall post two copies of the list of available jobs at least twenty minutes prior to the start of the shift. Extra Board requests coming in after posting will be noted at the end with the time the request came in. The company will endeavor to have all requests received prior to making any assignments.

B. Such lists will show the available jobs in order of decreasing rate of pay.

C. No offers of assignments will be made until ten minutes after the posting of the lists.

D. Immediately after the posting of the lists and prior to any assignments being made, employees meeting the shift who have recall rights to any job listed must indicate to the clock room attendant whether or not they wish to exercise such recall rights. Employees may be required to stay on vacation and weekly line-ups as is the present practice, in which case those jobs will not be available for assignment if the employee filling them meets the shift.

E. The senior man meeting the shift, in terms of mill seniority, will be given the choice of all the then available jobs.

F. Succeeding offers will be made to those meeting the shift in order of their decreasing mill seniority.

G. As each employee accepts a job, he shall sign his name beside the job he accepts and write in the number which shows the order in which he was called (e.g., 1st, 2nd, etc.).

H. Requests coming in after posting of the lists and the start of assignments shall be immediately made available to those meeting the shift who have not already received assignments.

VI. *Red Circling*

A. Members of the affected class who qualify to transfer will be allowed to transfer to jobs in other lines of progression for a period of three years from the date of this Decree with rate of pay protection as follows:

(1) When a member of the affected class transfers to a job in another line of progression in which the highest paying job exceeds the rate for the highest paying job in the line transferred from,

He shall continue to be paid the straight time hourly rate of pay he was receiving in his permanent position immediately prior to transfer (herein called "Red Circle Rate") unless or until:

(i) he is permanently assigned to a position paying a higher rate, or

(ii) he waives or is disqualified from promotion.

In either event, all "Red Circle" rights cease.

(2) In no event shall such "Red Circle Rate" exceed $3.00 per hour nor shall the privileges of this ¶ VI be available to employees transferring to the Yard or Utilities Departments.

(3) Members of the affected class in the Utilities Department and Yard Department may receive their "Red Circle Rate" if they successfully bid (i.e., they are the senior qualified bidder), into another line of progression where the top job has a rate of more than $3.26 per hour.

(4) The "Red Circle Rate" shall apply only to one voluntary transfer for each member of the affected class.

(5) However, if by shutdown or other event over which he has no control, a "Red Circled" member of the class is "bumped" out of the line to which he transferred, excluding the Technical Department, he shall retain his "Red Circle Rate" subject to (1) (i) and (ii) above, and he may

(a) if the "bump" is temporary, return to the Extra Board where he may:

(i) exercise his recall rights, if he meets the shifts, to temporary work in the line of progression transferred to; or failing that, he shall

(ii) for a period of two years from date of transfer based on mill seniority, if he meets the shifts, work in the entry level job in the line he transferred from, or

(b) if within a period of two years from date of transfer the "bump" is permanent, immediately return to the position from which he transferred and/or transfer to another line of progression in which the highest paying job exceeds the rate for the highest paying job in the line originally transferred from, subject to

(3) above if he is transferring from the Utilities or Yard Departments.

VII. *Training*

A. Crown will provide training, in order of seniority, to qualified employees for all jobs to which they are eligible for permanent, temporary or casual assignments.

B. Members of the affected class will be given the training necessary to allow them to bid for jobs for which they would otherwise be eligible. Such training for each successive job will in any case commence no later than completion of 50% of the residency requirements in the job below such job for which training is to be given, provided there is reasonable likelihood that the employee's seniority will allow him to fill such job on a casual, temporary or permanent basis once the training has commenced.

VIII. *Publicity and Records*

Defendant Crown Zellerbach Corporation shall publish and post the terms of this Decree in prominent places throughout the Plant, and will take reasonable steps to explain it to its employees. Such defendant shall also maintain appropriate record of personnel assignments and actions for inspection at reasonable times, after 15 days written notice by the plaintiff or plaintiff-intervenors.

IX. *Qualifications*

The present right of defendant Crown Zellerbach Corporation to refuse promotions to unqualified employees is not affected by this Decree.

X. *Recall*

Recall and J.I.T. provisions as set forth in the letters of agreement between defendant Crown Zellerbach Corporation and the OFCC will continue to apply.

XI. *Limitation of Relief*

The terms and provisions of this Decree shall apply only to Crown Zellerbach Corporation's paper mill at its Bogalusa division. Plaintiff and plaintiff-intervenors are not entitled to any other relief in this case on this record in addition to that specified in this Decree.

XII. *Waivers*

1. Waiver provisions of the collective bargaining agreement will continue to apply except that in the case of demotion, if the man in the higher job is senior in terms of mill seniority to the man below him who has previously waived, the employee in the higher job will not be required to demote around the man who waived but will be considered senior where a member of the affected class is involved.

2. Any employee of the affected class who elects to follow the established line of progression and not bypass a job as provided in ¶ IV above shall not be considered to have waived promotion and need not sign a waiver.

3. An employee who has established rights around another employee higher in such progression line due to a waiver situation shall not prevent the promotion of the waived employee, who has subsequently been reinstated, unless the employee who established rights around the waived employee would next be entitled to the promotion on the basis of his mill or job seniority, whichever is applicable.

XIII. *Demotions*

In case of demotion all employees shall demote straight down the lines of progression they are in, except that where an employee in the affected class has bypassed any of the jobs listed below and has not completed the J.I.T. and Residency requirements for them, then he shall bypass such jobs on the way down upon demotion.

1. *Finishing Department*
Cutter Operator
Trimmer Operator
Roll Wrapping Machine Operator
No. 11 Rewinder Operator

2. *Utilities Department*
Outside Operator

3. *1, 2 and 4 Paper Machines*
No. 1 Felt Checker

XIV. The waivers to the job of Wood Unloader-Flume signed in January 1966 by persons in the affected class who are permanently assigned to the job of Wood Unloader-Chain (J. Harris, A. Brown and T. Brown, Sr.) shall from the date of this order be of no further force and effect and all future training, promotion and demotions, casual, temporary or permanent, shall be made on the basis of mill seniority as provided in ¶ ¶ II, IV and VII of this Decree.

XV. *Union Agreement and OFCC Agreement*

The collective bargaining agreement now in effect between the defendants shall remain in full force and effect, except insofar as it is inconsistent with this Decree. The defendants are ENJOINED and RESTRAINED from interfering and failing to comply with the agreement of March 19, 1967, as modified by the agreements of June 16, 1967, and January 3, 1968, to the extent that they are applicable to the defendant Crown's Bogalusa paper mill division between the defendant Crown Zellerbach Corporation and the Office of Federal Contract Compliance of the United States Department of Labor to the extent such agreements are not in conflict with this Decree.

XVI. The defendant Local 189, United Papermakers and Paperworkers, AFL-CIO, CLC, and United Papermakers and Paperworkers, AFL-CIO, CLC, their officers, agents, members, employees, servants, and all persons and organizations in active concert or participation with them, are ENJOINED and RESTRAINED from interfering with or hindering, by striking, threatening to strike, harassment or otherwise, the compliance by the defendants with the foregoing provisions of this Decree.

XVII. Plaintiff and plaintiff-intervenors shall recover their costs from the defendants. As part of their costs, plaintiffs-intervenors shall recover from the defendants a reasonable attorneys' fee. If after twenty days the parties have not agreed upon a fee, and its proper allocation among the defendants, the Court will allow it and allocate it upon consideration of a statement of services filed and served upon counsel for the defendants, who shall have ten days to serve and file a response. FREDERICK J. R. HEEBE
UNITED STATES DISTRICT JUDGE
New Orleans, Louisiana
June 26, 1969

UNITED STATES DISTRICT COURT
EASTERN DISTRICT OF LOUISIANA
NEW ORLEANS DIVISION

UNITED STATES OF AMERICA
by RAMSEY CLARK, Attorney General

CIVIL ACTION
NO. 68-205
SECTION B

versus

LOCAL 189, UNITED PAPER-
MAKERS AND PAPERWORKERS,
AFL-CIO, CLC; UNITED PAPER-
MAKERS AND PAPERWORKERS,
AFL-CIO, CLC: and CROWN-
ZELLERBACH CORPORATION

MEMORANDUM OPINION AND FINDINGS OF FACT AND CONCLUSIONS OF LAW

The United States instituted this action on January 30, 1968. The complaint sought, *inter alia*, to enjoin the defendants from violating the provisions of Title VII of the Civil Rights Act of 1964, (42 U.S.C. 2000e *et seq.*), and from interfering with or violating the implementation of Executive Order 11246 forbidding racial discrimination in employment opportunities by government contractors.

On March 26, 1968, this Court decided the two following issues submitted to it by joint stipulation of all parties pursuant to Rule 42 (b) of the Federal Rules of Civil Procedure:

A. Whether, under the facts and circumstances of this case, the job seniority system which was in effect at the Bogalusa paper mill prior to February 1, 1968, was unlawful?

B. If the answer to the above question is in the affirmative, what is the necessary or appropriate standard or guideline for identifying the seniority of employees for purposes of promotion or demotion?

The Court ruled that the job seniority system was discriminatory and unlawful and then ordered the defendants to abolish forthwith the job seniority system and to establish a system of "mill seniority" in those cases where one or more

of the competing employees is a Negro employee hired prior to a certain date.

The remaining issues in this case were reserved for trial beginning April 30, 1963. All counsel by stipulation agreed that the following was a complete list of the issues to be submitted to the Court for its determination at this second hearing:

a) What is the affected class or classes of employees, if any, who may have suffered from discrimination on the grounds of race in assignments, transfers, promotions or demotions?

b) Whether the requirement that an employee in the affected class hold a job on a permanent basis for a specified period of time after he is qualified before he is eligible for promotion to a permanent opening higher in his line of progression is lawful; and if so, for what period for each job?

c) Whether a member of the affected class or classes is entitled by law to promotion, on the basis of the applicable seniority standard for permanent vacancies, more than one job slot in the line of progression above his present job, if the intermediate job or jobs do not afford any training necessary for proper performance in the higher job slot either because the training in the intermediate job or jobs is unrelated to any job higher in the line of progression, or because the training in the intermediate job or jobs would not add significantly to the skills already acquired; and if so, how the class of intermediate jobs which do not afford any training necessary for proper performance in the higher job slots is to be identified?

d) Whether an employee in the affected class or classes is entitled by law to enter certain lines of progression at a point above the established entry point?

e) Whether an employee in the affected class is entitled by law to bid for a permanent job opening in a job slot more than one slot above his present job where, through temporary assignment to the intermediate job, he has complied with the applicable residence requirement for that job?

f) Whether assignments from the Extra Board were unlawfully made on the basis of race subsequent to the merger of the Extra Boards in May 1964; and if so, what relief is appropriate?

g) Whether Negro employees who, on the basis of race, were assigned to jobs not in lines of progression, or to jobs in short lines of progression with relatively low paying rates, are entitled as a matter of law to relief; and if so, what relief is appropriate?

h) Whether the law requires the merger of Local 189 and Local 189A; and if so, what terms are appropriate?

i) Whether the three senior Negro employees in the job slot of Wood Unloader-Chain (Lorrain Crane) in the Wood Room were unlawfully induced to sign waivers which had the effect of making them junior to 11 white employees in the space of three weeks; and if so, what relief is appropriate?

j) Whether employees in the Utilities Department were unlawfully subjected to different requirements based upon their race, to qualify for the job of Boiler Room Helper; and if so, what relief is appropriate?

k) Whether the trainee program, in effect at the Crown paper mill from 1959 to December 1965, operated to discriminate unlawfully against Negro employees; and what relief is appropriate?

In accordance with the stipulation by all the parties hereto, trial was held in this Court commencing April 30, 1968, on all of the remaining issues as described immediately above. The Court now considering the three sets of Stipulation of Facts filed herein, the evidence elicited at the trial, and the briefs and memoranda filed by all counsel, and the entire record herein, now makes and files its:

FINDINGS OF FACTS

1.

This suit was instituted by plaintiff, United States of America, seeking relief for violation of Title VII of the Civil Rights Act of 1964, 42 U.S.C. 2000e *et seq.,* and for interference with the implementation of Executive Order 11246 forbidding racial discrimination in employment opportunities by government contractors. (Stipulation of facts, March 19, 1968)

2.

Defendant, Crown Zellerbach Corporation, is a corporation organized under the laws of the State of Nevada, with principal offices in San Francisco, California. Crown is engaged in the manufacture of lumber and paper products. A division of Crown maintains and operates a pulp and paper mill in Bogalusa, Louisiana. (Stipulation of facts, March 19, 1968)

3.

Defendant Crown is an employer engaged in an industry affecting commerce within the meaning of Sec. 701 (b) of the Civil Rights Act of 1964, 42 U.S.C. 2000e (b). (Stipulation of facts, March 19, 1968)

4.

Since at least 1961, Crown has supplied materials under government contracts and subcontracts which contain equal employment opportunity clauses similar to, or the same as, those appearing in the Executive Order 11246 and Executive Order 10925, to the extent required by those orders. (Stipulation of facts, March 19, 1968)

5.

Defendant International United Papermakers and Paperworkers, AFL-CIO, CLC (hereinafter "the International" or "UPP") is the certified collective bargaining representative of the employees at Crown's Bogalusa Mill, with the exception of approximately 40 white employees who are represented by a local affiliate of the International Brotherhood of Electrical Workers; UPP's principal office is in Albany, New York. It maintains an office in Monroe, Louisiana. (Stipulation of facts dated March 19, 1968)

6.

UPP maintains two local unions for its members at the Bogalusa Mill. All white members belong to the defendant Local 189 of UPP (hereinafter "Local 189"). All Negro members belong to plaintiff-intervenor Local 189A of UPP (Hereinafter "Local 189 A") (Stipulation of facts dated March 19, 1968)

7.

UPP, Local 189 and Local 189A are labor organizations engaged in an industry affecting commerce, within the meaning of Sec. 701 (d) (e) of the Civil Rights Act of 1964, 42 U.S.C. 2000e (d) (e). (Stipulation of facts dated March 19, 1968)

8.

Plaintiff-intervenor David Johnson, Sr., is a Negro employee at the mill in Bogalusa. He is also President of Local 189A and has been employed at Crown's mill in Bogalusa since 1952. At the time of the trial, he was a Boiler Room utility man in the Utilities Department.

9.

Plaintiff-intervenor Anthony Hill is a Negro employee at Crown's Bogalusa mill where he has been employed since 1952. At the time of the trial Hill was a utility man in the Recovery Room. He is also a member of Local 189A

10.

Prior to May 17, 1964, certain jobs in the mill were restricted to white employees or members of Local 189. The remaining jobs were restricted to Negro employees or members of Local 189A. (Stipulation of facts, March 19, 1968)

11.

The jobs restricted to white employees were generally the higher paying jobs in the mill, while the jobs restricted to Negro employees were generally lower paying and less desirable jobs. (Stipulation of facts, March 19, 1968)

12.

Prior to May 17, 1964, two separate labor Boards (herein-after "Extra Boards") were maintained to which newly hired employees were assigned. One of the Extra Boards was restricted to white employees; the other to Negro employees. White applicants for employ-ment were hired on the basis of vacancies on the white Extra Board (i.e., the Extra Board within the jurisdiction of Local 189) and were assigned to that Board. Negro applicants for employment were hired on the basis of vacancies on the Negro Extra Board (i.e., the Extra Board within the jurisdiction of Local 189A) and were assigned to that Board. (Stipulation of facts, March 19, 1968)

13.

Employees on the Extra Board were used to fill temporary and permanent vacancies in the various lines of progression. The members of the Negro Extra Board were eligible only for vacancies in the lines of progression open to Negroes. The members of the white Extra Board were eligible for vacancies within the progression lines open to whites.

14.

On May 17, 1964, the two Extra Boards were merged, and under the terms of the governing agreement between Crown and UPP, each employee on the merged Extra Board was eligible for temporary and permanent vacancies throughout the mill on the same basis as each other Extra Board member. (Stipulation of facts, March 19, 1968)

15.

Notwithstanding this merger of the two Extra Boards on May 17, 1964, the evidence shows that prior to February 14, 1968, the white employees on the merged Extra Board continued to work primarily in jobs formerly restricted to whites and the Negro employees on the merged Extra Board continued to work primarily in jobs formerly restricted to Negroes, or the less desirable jobs. (Stipulation of facts, May 30, 1968)

15a.

Further, under this merger, prior to February 14, 1968, Extra Board employees continued to be assigned to jobs with no choices of available Extra Board assignments being offered. If the employee refused the assignment, he was placed at the bottom of the line and would either receive the least desirable job or no work at all.

15b.

One result of the continuation of racially discriminatory Extra Board assignment methods from May 1964 until February 14, 1968, was to discourage Negroes from bidding into jobs other than traditional Negro jobs. Persons are more likely to bid for jobs in which they have had some experience and familiarity.

15c.

The assignment policies of the Extra Board tended to perpetuate the assignments of Negroes to traditionally Negro jobs and whites to traditionally white jobs.

16.

On January 16, 1966, Crown and UPP merged certain job progression lines formerly restricted to Negroes with other functionally related progression lines formerly restricted to whites. (Stipulation of facts, March 19, 1968)

17.

The basis of this merger of progression lines was the existing pay rates for each job. Therefore, in most cases the effect was to place all the formerly Negro jobs beneath the entry level job in the former white line of progression because the Negroes historically had only been permitted to occupy the least desirable jobs and the lower paying jobs.

18.

Under the recall system in effect prior to February 1, 1968, when there was a reduction in force in a progression line and certain employees were demoted out of the bottom job in the progression line, they normally returned to the Extra Board. Each such employee so demoted, however, would retain a "recall right" to the first opening in the bottom job in the progression line from which he was demoted. (Stipulation of facts, March 19, 1968)

19.

After the merger of the Negro and white progression lines on January 16, 1968, each employee maintaining recall rights to the entry job in a progression line that was formerly restricted to white workers retained a recall right to that job even though after the merger that job was no longer the entry point in the merged line, and some of the Negro workers in the lower jobs in the line were senior in terms of mill seniority. (Stipulation of facts, March 19, 1968)

19a.

From about 1959 to December 1965, Crown had in effect at Bogalusa "a trainee" program. Under this program, employees would be trained for entry level jobs in selected lines of progression. While the program was in effect, Crown trained at least 107 employees, of whom 11 were Negro and 96 were white. Once trained for a particular entry job, the employee (trainee) acquired the first, or trainee, right to that job when it became vacant on a temporary or permanent basis. All of the 96 white trainees were trained for jobs in the white progression lines, while 8 of 11 Negro trainees were trained for jobs in Negro progression lines.

After the merger of progression lines on January 16, 1966, defendants treated employees having "trainee" rights to a job in a white progression line as retaining that right to that job, even though after the merger that job was no longer the entry job in the reconstituted progression line and Negro employees in jobs below that job in the new line were senior to the trainee in length of service in the mill.

Both the system of "recall rights" as it existed prior to February 1, 1968, and the extension of those rights to the substantial number of people, almost all white, who were classified as "trainees," operated to hinder the progress of Negroes into jobs which, prior to the merger of the lines of progression on January 16, 1966, had been held only by whites. Like the system of job seniority described in the order and opinion of March 26, 1968, the recall and trainee systems tended to perpetuate the effects of past discrimination, and result in present discrimination, by preventing Negroes who were qualified to perform formerly white jobs from competing for them on the basis of their qualifications and length of service in the mill.

In addition, a series of incidents and changes in Crown's policy which have occurred since the January 1966 mergers operated to further impede Negroes' progress into formerly barred white jobs. For example, after the January 1966 merger of the lines of Negroes in the merger Utilities line of progression, Negroes were required to make daily written reports on the training they received for the job which had been the white entry job before the merger; no such requirement had been imposed on the whites then in that line.

When these incidents, together with the method of assignments on the Extra Board, the recall and trainee systems, and the job seniority system, and such matters as the waivers to the overhead crane, are considered together, it becomes clear that many of the institutional barriers to equal employment opportunities survived the mergers of lines of progression and continued to make Negroes' progress into and within better paying white lines of progression difficult and almost beyond reach until the institution of this lawsuit.

The fact that the continual effects of discrimination in job assignment and promotion, described above in these findings, continued beyond the date of the merger of the lines of progression demonstrates that the class of employees affected by these discriminatory practices included at least some Negroes hired since January 16, 1966. Since the most recent of the discriminatory practices clearly idendifiable from the record—the matter of temporary assignments from the Extra Board—was corrected on February 14, 1968, the affected class includes all Negroes hired before that date, except for the six Negro employees hired since January 16, 1966, who in fact bid for and received formerly white jobs from the Extra Board.

20.

Prior to February 1, 1968, promotions within lines of progression were on the basis of "job seniority" wherein credit is based upon length of time spent in each job and no credit is given for length of service in the plant. When a vacancy occurred in a job within a progression line, the qualified employee who had spent the greatest length of time in the job immediately below that in which the vacancy occurred was entitled to promotion, unless he waived or was disqualified for promotion, and similarly in each job slot below in the progression line. Demotions were also based on the time spent in a particular job. (Stipulation of facts, March 19, 1968)

20a.

White employees had accrued job seniority in the higher paying jobs at a time when Negroes were, because of their race, denied the opportunity to bid for and hold these higher paying jobs. Consequently, Negroes hired prior to January 1966 were frozen in the lower paying, less desirable jobs to which they had been assigned on the basis of race, while white employees of comparable length of service were assigned to higher paying, more desirable positions.

20b.

In an effort to remedy the discriminatory effects of these systems and to meet Crown's obligation under the contractual clauses required by Executive Order 11246, Crown and the Office of Federal Contract Compliance of the Department of Labor entered into agreements on March 19 and June 16, 1967, which contemplated that promotion to higher jobs at the Bogalusa mill would depend on a combination of job and plant seniority. This system was designed to remove some of the present consequence of the past discrimination by giving some weight to each employee's length of service in the mill.

20c.

Because the combination seniority system in part is dependent on the factor of job seniority, Negro employees who were, on the basis of their race, excluded from assignment in the "white" lines of progression will always be junior to the white employees hired contemporaneously with those who were assigned to the white progression lines earlier on the basis of their race.

20d.

A seniority system which is based in whole or in part upon length of service in a job would cause some qualified Negro employees, previously discriminated against, with greater mill seniority to be unsuccessful in bidding against junior white employees with less mill seniority for available job vacancies higher in the progression lines. The reason for this result is that junior white employees, on the basis of their race and color, had obtained greater job seniority in the jobs from which they seek to move than the senior Negro employees who, on the basis of their race and color, had previously been denied assignments to such jobs.

20e.

A seniority system which is based in whole or in part upon length of service in a job would cause some qualified Negro employees who are senior to white employees in length of service in the plant to remain beneath those employees in terms of pay and place in the lines of progression.

20f.

A seniority system based upon length of service in the mill will not result in so blocking or delaying the opportunities of such Negro employees to compete for and obtain jobs held by white employees of comparable ability and length of service in the mill.

21.

The uniform six-month residency requirement for promotion within lines of progression provided for in the June 16, 1967, Crown-OFCC Agreement was not imposed by Crown prior to the date of that Agreement. When applied uniformly to every job throughout the mill, the six-month residency requirement bears no relationship to the reasonable needs of training and experience. The parties have stipulated to those jobs for which some residence is necessary to provide training and experience for the next higher positions in the lines of progression, and the length of time which may appropriately be required in each. That stipulation is accepted as factual by the Court.

22.

In accordance with the June 16, 1967, agreement between Crown and the OFCC, a six-month residency requirement was imposed before the employee was eligible for promotion to the vacant job immediately above the job to which he was permanently assigned.

23.

The six-month residency requirement is in excess of the amount of time necessary to learn some jobs in the mill and to qualify for promotion to some.

24.

The lengths of time listed in Joint Exhibit III are necessary to learn the jobs there indicated and to be fully qualified for promotion. (Third Stipulation of facts—Paragraph 1)

25.

Jobs listed below in the following lines of progression do not provide training necessary to the proper performance of the jobs higher in the line:

A. *Brown Stock Washers*
   Second Washer Operator

B. *Digesters*
   One, but not both, Gas-off Man or No. 1 Gas-off Man
   One, but not both, Capper New Digester or Capper Old Digester

C. *Finishing Department*
   All jobs from Spare Hand to and including Five-Day Jitney Operator, provided, however, that the person bidding must have served a total of four weeks as a Spare Hand and/or in the other jobs below Five-Day Jitney Operator; and two, but not all of:
   First Cutter Helper
   Roll Wrap Machine Helper No. 9
   Rewinder Operator
   Cutting Operator
   Trimmer Operator
   Roll Wrap Machine Operator and No. 11 Rewinder Operator

D. *Paper Machine, Numbers 1, 2 and 4*
Four, but not all:
No. 1, Rewinder Helper
No. 2, Fifth Hand
No. 1, Finisher
No. 1, Felt Checker, or
No. 4, Fifth Hand, provided that the employee has served as a Spare Hand and/or in one or more of these jobs for a total of seven months

E. *Paper Machine, Numbers 5, 6 and 7*
Two, but not all:
Utility Man
Shaft Tailer
Shaft Puller, provided that employee has served as a Spare Hand and/or in one of those jobs for a total of five months, at least four of which must be as a Shaft Tailer or Shaft Puller

F. *Stock Preparation*
One, but not both:
No. 2 Blend Tank Man or No. 1 Blend Tank Man

G. *Technical Department*
One, but not both:
5, 6 and 7 Wet End Tester or 1, 2 and 4 Wet End Tester

H. *Utilities Department*
Outside Operator

I. *Wood Room*
One, but not both:
Chip Storage Operator or Assistant Chip Storage Operator
And one, but not both:
Wood Unloader Flume or Wood Unloader Chain
(See Second Stipulation of facts dated April 30, 1968)

26.

In accordance with promotional procedures in effect at Crown, no employee may promote to more than one job at a time above the job he permanently occupies. (Stipulation of facts, March 19, 1968)

26a.

It is common practice at Crown's Bogalusa mill for employees to be assigned temporarily to jobs higher in the lines of progression than the jobs to which they are permanently assigned, and regularly to spend substantial amounts of time working temporarily on these higher jobs. Time spent in substantial blocks temporarily in higher positions satisfies the need for training and experience provided by those jobs.

27.

The jobs below the following jobs in the following lines of progression do not provide training which is necessary to the proper performance of the jobs higher in those lines of progression:

A. *Brown Stock Washer:* Third Washer (Swenson Helper)
B. *Digester:* Capper—New Digester
C. *Paper Machine 1, 2, 4:* Spare Hand
D. *Stock Preparation:* Payloader Man
E. *Technical Department:* Pulp Mill Tester
F. *Utilities Department:* First Bark Boiler Helper
G. *Wood Room:* Utility Flume

(Second Stipulation of facts, April 30, 1968)

28.

The current Collective Bargaining Agreement between Crown and UPP and the present structure of the jobs within each line of progression require that all employees enter at the bottom of the progression line.

29.

Under the terms of the Collective Bargaining Agreement, any employee may transfer out of his present line of progression if he successfully bids for a permanent opening in an entry level job in another line of progression.

30.

The entry level jobs are the lowest paid jobs in each line of progression.

31.

Negro workers, employed prior to February 14, 1968, are, in some cases, permanently assigned to jobs not in any line of progression or to jobs in lines of progression in which the highest paid job pays less than the highest paid jobs in progression lines formerly restricted to whites. Some of these Negro jobs pay more than the entry level jobs in some progression lines formerly restricted to whites. In these circumstances, under the prevailing system, a Negro transferring to a formerly all-white line of progression must accept a reduction in pay.

32.

In January of 1966, Jesse Harris, Anderson Brown and Tom Brown, Negro employees holding the job slot of Wood Unloader-Chain (Lorrain Crane) in the Wood Room became eligible by virtue of the January 16, 1966, merger of lines of progression for promotion to the next higher job of Wood Unloader Flume (Electrical Overhead Crane), a job which until that time had been reserved for white employees. The job of Wood Unloader-Chain was the highest paying Negro job in the mill. It was the only Negro job which was placed above a substantial number of white jobs when the lines were merged. Jesse Harris signed a waiver on January 17, 1966. In the course of the several days' training A. Brown and T. Brown received on the Electrical Overhead Crane during the week of January 16, white employees led both to believe that the job involved substantial electrical and mechanical hazards which in fact did not exist; they were also told by a supervisor that the company could not afford to fix the crane since a replacement for it had been ordered.

After approximately three days of training, both men were told by a supervisor that their training had been completed and that they should thereafter operate the Electrical Overhead Crane without assistance. At this point both Anderson and Tom Brown signed waivers to the Electrical Overhead Crane job. One or two days later at a meeting, Mr. Kwasny, the Assistant Superintendent in charge of the Wood Room, told both Browns that if they left their waiver in effect only "two or at most three" people would go around them. However, within three weeks, thirteen white employees who were junior to the Browns in the merged line of progression were treated

by Crown and Local 189 as having acquired seniority over them for purpose of temporary and permanent promotions and demotions to the Wood Unloader-Flume job and all jobs above it in the Wood Room line of progression.

The net result of these waivers and subsequent seniority moves was in effect to place the Negro job and Wood Unloader-Chain at or near the bottom of the formerly all-white line of progression by making the Negro incumbents of that slot "junior" for purposes of promotion to the white employees who "went around this" although they were senior to them in length of service and responsibility.

The operation of the waiver system as applied to casual assignments was not, and is not now, a matter easily understood. Even Crown's personnel director had great difficulty on the witness stand explaining this system and at one point conceded that he really did not understand it which led to a company stipulation that one of the white employees who has been treated as senior to the Browns since the signing of these waivers in January 1966 is not and should never have been considered senior to them.

Further, Crown did not adequately explain the consequences of signing these waivers to the three Negro employees.

CONCLUSIONS OF LAW

1.

The Court has jurisdiction of this action under the provisions of Sec. 707(b) of the Civil Rights Act of 1964, 42 U.S.C. Sec. 2000e-6(b).

2.

The scope of the class who has suffered from discrimination on the grounds of race in assignments, transfers, promotion, demotions and selection for training is as follows:

a) All Negro employees hired prior to January 16, 1966; and
b) All Negro employees hired after January 16, 1966 and prior to February 14, 1968, except such of those employees whose initial permanent assignments were to job classifications formerly within the exclusive jurisdiction of Local 189

while such employee remains in the line of progression, if any, in which he was permanently assigned as of the date of this decree or while he is in the first line of progression to which he voluntarily transfers or, if currently a member of the Extra Board, to which he bids within three years from the date of this decree.

3.

The various employment practices of the defendants, among them the continuation of the "job seniority" system, the operation of the "recall" and "trainee" systems after the merger of lines of progression, the imposition in certain cases of requirements on Negro employees which had not been imposed on comparable white employees, the continuation of an Extra Board assignment system which resulted in racially discriminatory Extra Board assignments, and the failure of the company to prepare Negroes for promotion to white jobs which had previously been barred to them, all tended to perpetuate the results of past racial discrimination and to result in present discrimination, at least until the institution of this suit.

4.

Title VII of the Civil Rights Act of 1964 requires that opportunities to hold better paying jobs be made available to all employees equally without regard to race. So long as there are institutional systems or procedures which deny to Negroes advancement to better paying, more desirable jobs which are held by whites with comparable mill seniority and ability, this legal obligation is not satisfied. The company is not required to forego its legitimate interest in maintaining the skill and efficiency of its labor force. Consistent with these two safeguards, however, removal of any structural impediments which delay the attainment by Negroes of jobs generally as good as those held by their white contemporaries or which force Negroes to pay a price for those opportunities are required by law to be removed.

5.

For positions which provide training and experience which are necessary for the performance of higher jobs in the line of progression, the company may lawfully invoke a reasonable residency requirement—i.e., a period of time which must be served before an employee is eligible to bid for higher jobs in the line of progression. However, as the stipulation of the parties demonstrates, many of the jobs in the mill do not provide any such training and experience, while in others the necessary training and experience can be obtained in less than six months. Accordingly, the residency requirement should not be a fixed period, such as six months for each job in the mill, but should be fixed at the minimum time required to provide necessary training and experience for each job, as stipulated to by the parties. Any longer period would unnecessarily retard the advancement of those in the class discriminated against and would be unlawful.

6.

Negroes in the class discriminated against are entitled to compete for jobs on the basis of their competence and mill seniority, and thus may skip such jobs in the lines of progression which do not provide training and experience necessary to the performance of the job for which they are competing.

7.

For the same reasons, Negroes in the class discriminated against are entitled to compete for jobs in lines of progression on the basis of their competence and mill seniority above the entry level in those lines where the present entry level job does not provide training and experience which are necessary to the performance of higher positions in the lines of progression.

8.

Negroes in the class discriminated against may obtain the training and experience necessary to the performance of higher jobs in the line of progression, by virtue of their temporary assignments, which are common in the mill, at least where such assignments amount to 64 or more hours per month. Accordingly, qualified Negroes in the affected class who have served in a position in such increments for sufficient time to acquire the training and experience necessary for performance of higher jobs in the line of progression are entitled to bid for those jobs on the basis of their mill seniority, notwithstanding they may never have held such a position on a permanent basis.

9.

The system for making Extra Board assignments in use prior to February 14, 1968, resulted in the assignment of Negroes generally to Negro jobs, and whites generally to formerly white jobs, and was in violation of Title VII of the Civil Rights Act of 1964. The system of assignment directed in the decree provides available assignments for jobs to be offered to Extra Board employees on the basis of mill seniority and for them to choose from among the assignments which remain available.

10.

After the merger of January 1966, the defendant Crown failed to take the necessary steps to ensure that the Negro employees in the Wood Unloader-Chain jobs who became newly eligible to bid on the white job of Wood Unloader-Flume were adequately trained for that job, and further, failed to ensure that those Negro employees fully understood the possible consequences of the waivers they signed. The result of this default by Crown—nullification of the only significant integration of jobs brought about by the merger of the Wood Room line of progression—requires that those waivers not be considered in any future setup or promotion made in the Wood Room line of progression.

11.

Any practice, system, procedure or policy that denies a member of the affected class promotion to a vacant job which he is qualified to perform, where he is senior in terms of continuous employment with the company to other eligible employees and where he has not

previously waived or otherwise disqualified himself for promotion or advancement, is a "term, condition and privilege of employment" that discriminates against Negro employees on the basis of race, in violation of Sec. 703(a) of the Civil Rights Act of 1964. For this reason, the following practices are unlawful where they operate to deny promotion to a member of the affected class:

a) A job seniority system of promotion within a line of progression, or any promotional system based on a standard other than total employment seniority in the mill;

b) The prohibition on promotions more than one job slot above the employee's present job, if the intermediate job or jobs do not afford any training necessary for proper performance in the jobs higher in the line of progression;

c) The prohibition on promotions more than one job slot above the employees present job if, through temporary assignments to the intermediate job or jobs, the employee has acquired the necessary training in that job to the proper performance in the jobs higher in the line of progression;

d) The requirement that a member of the affected class enter a line of progression a level below the lowest job which provides training necessary to perform the jobs higher in the progression line;

e) The requirement that a member of the affected class spend any specific period of time in a job in excess of the time necessary to learn the job before he is eligible for promotion.

12.

The policy of the defendants in deterring Negro employees from transferring to formerly all-white lines of progression by requiring these employees to suffer a reduction in wages and the loss of all promotional security as a condition of transfer constitutes a "term, condition and privilege of employment" that discriminates against Negro employees on the basis of race, in violation of Sec.

703(a) of the Civil Rights Act of 1964, 42 U.S.C. Sec. 2000e-2(a).

13.

The maintenance of segregated local unions herein violates Sec. 703(c) of the Civil Rights Act of 1964. A consent decree merging these two unions under certain conditions has been signed on September 11, 1968, and approved by this Court.

14.

The defendants have intentionally engaged in the unlawful employment practices described herein within the meaning of Sec. 706(g) of the Civil Rights Act of 1964, 42 U.S.C. Sec. 2000e-5(g).

15.

None of the unlawful employment practices described herein result from a bona fide seniority or merit system within the meaning of Sec. 703(h) of the Civil Rights Act of 1964, 42 U.S.C. Sec. 2000e-2(h), but rather are the result of a seniority or merit system that discriminates against Negro employees employed by Crown prior to February 14, 1968, on the basis of their race.

FREDERICK J. R. HEEBE
UNITED STATES DISTRICT JUDGE
New Orleans, Louisiana
June 26, 1969

APPENDIX A

ASPHALT DEPARTMENT

Asphalt Machine Operator	18 months total—with minimum of two months on each
Color Machine Operator	
Asphalt Machine First Helper	4 months total on each
Color Machine First Helper	
First Helper—Rewinder	1 month
Second Helper—Rewinder	1 month

AUTO MECHANICS

Auto Mechanic Helper	30 months

ATTRITION MILL & ADDITIVES

Attrition Mill Asst. Operator	6 months
Additives Operator	4 months
Additives Helper	6 months

BROWN STOCK WASHER

Second Washer Operator	1 month
First Helper	12 months
Second Helper	6 months
Third Helper	6 months

CARPENTER CREW

Carpenter Helper	30 months

DIGESTER ROOM

Cook—New Room	1 month
Pandia Operator	8 months
Gas Off Old Digester	9 months
Gas Off New Digester	8 months
No. 1 Gas Off Man	6 months
Gas Off Man	in either
Pandia Helper	4 months
Measuring Tank Man	4 months
Capper—New Digester	3 months
Capper—Old Digester	in either

ELECTRICIANS

Helpers	30 months

EVAPORATOR ROOM

Assistant Operator	3 years

ENGINE MACHINIST CREW

Engine Machinist Helpers	30 months

TINSMITH CREW

Tinsmith Helpers	30 months

FINISHING DEPARTMENT

A

Cutter Operator	1 week
Trimmer Operator	1 week
First Cutter Helper	4 weeks

B

Roll Wrapping Machine Operator	1 week
No. 11 Rewinder Operator	1 week
No. 9 Rewinder Operator	4 months
Roll Wrapping Mach. First Helper	4 weeks
5-Day Jitney Driver	2 weeks
Core Recutter	2 weeks
Spare Hand	2 weeks

INSTRUMENT CREW

Helper	30 months

VALVE REPAIRS

Helper	30 months

Appendix B

LIME RECOVERY & CAUSTIC ROOM

Lime Burner—No. 4 Kiln   12 months
Filter Man   9 months

MACHINE SHOP CREW

Helper   30 months

MILLWRIGHT CREW

Millwright Helper   30 months
Turbine Repair Helper   30 months

MILL SUPPLY PROGRESSION LADDER

Receiving Clerk   6 months
Jr. Receiving Clerk   6 months
Warehouseman   6 months
Jr. Supply Room Clerk   6 months

MACHINE LINE OF PROGRESSION

(1-2-4 Machines)
No. 2, 4, 1 Machine Backtender   18 months
No. 2, 4, Machine Third Hand   12 months
No. 1 Machine Rewinder Man   12 months
No. 2 Machine Fourth Hand   4 months
No. 4 Machine Fourth Hand   8 months
No. 4 Machine Fifth Hand
No. 1 Machine Felt Checker
No. 1 Machine Finisher } 6 months in any
No. 2 Machine Fifth Hand
No. 1 Machine Rewinder Helper
Spare Hand   1 month

MACHINE LINE OF PROGRESSION

(5-6-7 Machines)
No. 5, 6, 7 Bank Tender   18 months
No. 5, 6, 7, Third Hand   14 months
No. 5, 6, 7 Fourth Hand   12 months
No. 5, 6, 7 Fifth Hand   4 months
No. 5, 6, 7 Shaft Tailer }
No. 7 Shaft Puller } 4 months in any
Spare Hand   1 month

PIPEFITTERS

Pipefitter Helper   30 months

RECOVERY ROOM

No. 20 Operator   24 months
No. 20 Asst. Operator   24 months
No. 19 Operator   24 months
No. 18 Operator   24 months
No. 19 Helper   12 months
No. 18 Helper   15 months
Combination Helper   4 months
Utility Man   4 months

SCALES

Stencil Man   4 weeks

SCREEN ROOM

No. 1 Screen Man   12 months
Storage & Thickener Man   6 months

PULP MILL SPARE HANDS

Spare Hands   2 months

SHIPPING & WAREHOUSING

Asst. Shipping Clerk   3 months
Scaleman   6 months
Round Clock Jitney Driver   6 months
Car Bracers   3 months
Shipping Laborer & Jitney Driver   2 weeks
Lead Loader   1 week

STOCK PREPARATION

No. 7 Blend Tank Man   6 months
No. 5 & 6 Blend Tank Man   6 months
No. 2 Blend Tank Man } 6 months
No. 1 Blend Tank Man } in either
Hydrapulper Man   3 months
Payloader Man   3 months
Broke Beater Man 5, 6, 7   1 week
Broke Beater Helper 5, 6, 7   2 weeks

TECHNICAL DEPARTMENT PROGRESSION LADDER

Asst. Bleach Operator   18 months
Bleach Liquor Operator   6 months
Asst. Chemical Plant Operator   6 months
Sulphur Chemicals Hpr.   9 months
Utility Man   1 month
Head Tester 5-6-7   3 months
1-2-3-4 Tester   6 months
5-6-7 Tester   6 months
1-2-3-4 Second Tester   2 months

5-6-7 Wet End Tester	} 2 months
1-2-3-4 Wet End Tester	} in either
Pulp Mill Tester	}
Spare Hands	} 6 months total

TECHNICAL DEPARTMENT

Colorist Technician	24 months
Technical Sample Man	12 months

TRACK CREW MILL

Track Laborer	3 months

LIVINGSTON TRACK

Car Operator	6 months*
Section Man	3 months

TRAIN CREW**

Fireman	GMO-ICC Exams (usually 4-5 years)
Engineer	3 yrs. before going to Engineer Mainline—must pass GMO-ICC Tests
Fireman	18 months plus exams to go to Engineer in yard
Spare Hand	4 months to be qualified for Fireman & Switchman in yard
Brakeman	GMO-ICC Test (usually 4-5 years)
Conductor	3-4 yrs. plus GMO-ICC Exam
Switchman	18 months plus GMO Exams before going to Conductor Yd.

UTILITIES

Turbine Room Operator	6 months
Turbine Operator 900 lb. Plant	4 months
Power House Water Tender	6 months
Gas Boiler Operator	6 months
Bark Boiler Operator	3 months
No. 20 Boiler Water Tender	3 months
Rec. Boiler Water Tender	2 months

*6 months unless longer needed by law, regulation or external obligation (contracts, etc.)

**Subject to law, regulations & external obligation (contracts, etc.). The legal time limit unless there is none, in which case the above applies.

Turbine Room Asst.	6 months
Outside Operator	none
Boiler Room Helper	6 months
1st Bark Boiler Helper	3 months
2nd Bark Boiler Helper	3 months
Boiler Room Utility Man	4 months
Fuel Handler	2 months
Turbine Room Utility Man	2 months

WELDERS

Apprentice Welder	30 months

WOOD ROOM

Asst. Foreman	1 year
Wood Unloader-Flume	} 6 months
Wood Unloader-Chain	} in either
Chip Storage Operator	}
Asst. Chip Storage Operator	} 6 months in either
Chipper Operator	6 months
Chip Dispatcher	10 weeks
Utility Flume	3 weeks
Utility Chain	5 weeks
Day Utility	2 weeks

YARD DEPARTMENT

(Janitor Line)

Janitor	6 months

(Crane Operator Line)

Yard Lead Man	6 months
Mobile Equipment Operator	1 month
Dempster Dompster Driver	1 month
Winch Truck Driver	1 month
Payloader Driver	6 months
Dump Truck Driver	1 month
Winch Truck Helper	1 month
Riggers	6 months
Concrete Finisher	3 weeks
Pavement Breaker	3 weeks

(Clean-Up Pool Line)

Sweeper Operator	7 months total on sweeper and/or cleanup pool before going to Leadman
Clean-up Man	1 month

(Brickmason Line)

Brickmason Helper	30 months

in the
UNITED STATES
COURT OF APPEALS
for the Fifth Circuit

No. 25956

Local 189, United Papermakers and
Paperworkers, AFL-CIO, CLC; United
Papermakers and Paperworkers, AFL-
CIO, CLC; and Crown Zellerbach Cor-
poration,   Appellants,

VERSUS

United States of America, by John
Mitchell, Attorney General,   Appellee.

*Appeal from the United States District
Court for the Eastern District of
Louisiana*

(July 28, 1969)

Before WISDOM and DYER, Circuit
Judges, and KRENTZMAN, District
Judge.

WISDOM, Circuit Judge: Title VII of
the Civil Rights Act of 1964 prohibits
discrimination in all aspects of employment.[1] In this case we deal with one of
the most perplexing issues troubling the
courts under Title VII:[2] how to recon-
cile equal employment opportunity *today* with seniority expectations based on
yesterday's. built-in racial discrimination.
May an employer continue to award
formerly "white jobs" on the basis of
seniority attained in other formerly white
jobs, or must the employer consider the
employee's experience in formerly
"Negro jobs" as an equivalent measure
of seniority? We affirm the decision of
the district court. We hold that Crown
Zellerbach's job seniority system in effect
at its Bogalusa Paper Mill prior to February 1, 1968, was unlawful because by
carrying forward the effects of former
discriminatory practices the system results in present and future discrimination. When a Negro applicant has the

1. Pub. L. No. 88-352, 78 Stat. 241, 42 U.S.C. §§2000e to 2000e(15). For the
legislative history, see Bureau of National Affairs, The Civil Rights Act of 1964;
Vass, Title VII: Legislative History, 7 B.C. Ind. & Com. L. Rev. 431 (1966).
Section 703(a) provides that:

"It shall be an unlawful employment practice for an employer—
(1) to fail or refuse to hire or to discharge any individual, or otherwise
to discriminate against any individual with respect to his compensation, terms,
conditions, or privileges of employment, because of such individual's race,
color, religion, sex or national orgin; or
(2) to limit, segregate, or classify his employees in any way which would
deprive or tend to deprive any individual of employment opportunities or
otherwise adversely affect his status as an employee, because of such individual's race, color, religion, sex, or national origin."

2. In the last two or three years there has been a burst of writing on Title VII and
seniority rights. See, for example, Gould, Seniority and the Black Worker:
Reflections on Quarles and its Implications 48 Tex. L. Rev.   (   );
Cooper & Sobel, Seniority and Testing Under Fair Employment Laws: A General
Approach to Objective Criteria of Hiring and Promotion, 82 Harv. L. Rev. 1598
(1969) (The authors are of counsel in the case before the court and in some of
the other cases mentioned in this opinion); Jenkins, A Study of Federal
Effort to End Job Bias: A History, A Status Report and a Prognosis, 14 How.
L.J. 259 (1968); Gould, Employment Security, Seniority and Race: The Role of
Title VII of the Civil Rights Act of 1964, 13 How. L. J. 1 (1967); Walker,
Title VII: Complaint and Enforcement Procedures and Relief and Remedies,
7 B.C. Ind. & Com. L. Rev. 495, 518 (1966); Vaas, Title VII: Legislative His-
tory, 7 B.C. Ind. & Com. L. Rev. 431 (1966); Note, Civil Rights-Racially Dis-
criminatory Employment Practices under Title VII, 46 N.C.L. Rev. 891 (1968)
(The note is on *Quarles*); Note, Title VII, Seniority Discrimination, and the
Incumbent Negro, 80 Harv. L. Rev. 1260 (1967). (The court in *Quarles*, 279 F.
Supp. 505, heavily relied on this note. In this case we too draw heavily on
Quarles and the note.)

qualifications to handle a particular job, the Act requires that Negro seniority be equated with white seniority.

I.

A. The parties stipulated most of the basic facts. Crown Zellerbach (Crown) runs a paper mill at Bogalusa, Louisiana. The Company employs about 950 white workers and 250 Negro workers. Jobs there have always been organized hierarchically within "lines of progression". The jobs within each line for the most part are related functionally so that experience in one job serves as training for the next.

Until May 1964, the Company segregated the lines of progression by race, reserving some lines to white employees and others to Negroes. Local 189 of the United Papermakers and Paperworkers, the white local, had jurisdiction over the more desirable lines; Local 189-A, the Negro local, had jurisdiction over the left-overs. With very few exceptions, the lowliest white jobs paid more and carried greater responsibility than the most exalted Negro jobs. Promotion within each line was determined by "job seniority"; when a vacancy occurred, the workers in the slot below it could bid for the job, and the one who had worked the longest *in the job slot below* had priority.

The Company put new employees on "extra boards". These boards were labor pools used to fill temporary vacancies within the lines of progression. The senior men had first call on vacancies in the entry jobs at the bottom of the various lines. When lay-offs occurred, those at the bottom of the line were bumped back to the extra board. They had first claim, however, on any vacancies in their old jobs under "rights of recall". Crown segregated its extra boards, like its lines of progression, by race, one for Negroes and one for whites.

The Company merged the extra boards in May 1964. Whoever, regardless of race, had the longest term on the board now gained priority to bid on entry jobs in the white lines. Merger opened up the lines to Negro entrants, and helped the relatively recent Negro employees on the board. It did not help more senior Negroes already in the lines of progression. Moreover, the rights of recall gave any white who had served in a white line preference over others on the board in bidding on his old job. That fact slowed the advance of even newer Negro employees. A "transfer provision" added in 1965 enabled Negroes already in black lines of progression to bid on the bottom jobs in white lines on the basis of their "mill seniority", or time worked at the mill. This change meant that they did not have to become junior men on the extra board in order to bid on the starting job in previously white lines. It also meant that they did not have to surrender certain benefits accruing to mill seniority when they made the transfer.

Title VII went into effect with regard to Crown on July 2, 1965. Section 703 (a) (2) makes it unlawful for an employer

"to limit, segregate, or classify his employees in any way which would deprive or tend to deprive any individual of employment opportunities or otherwise adversely affect his status as an employee because of such individual's race, color, religion, sex, or national origin." 42 U.S.C. §2000e-2 (a) (2).

Later in 1965 the Equal Employment Opportunity Commission discussed with the Company and the Papermakers the effect of Title VII on seniority arrangements. A letter from Herman Edelsberg, the Executive Director of the EEOC, stated that the Commission would be satisfied by the "non-discriminatory application of the seniority agreement established by collective bargaining," i.e. job seniority, provided that Crown discontinue segregation of the progression lines. The Chairman of the Commission, Franklin D. Roosevelt, Jr., met with representatives of the Company and the unions in December 1965 and declared that "application of the seniority system established by collective bargaining" would comply with the statute.

In January 1966 the unions and the Company amended the collective bargaining agreement so as to merge the progression lines within each department on the basis of existing pay rates. Except for one job in the plant, merger by pay rates merely meant tacking the Negro lines to the bottom of white lines. Whites on the extra boards who had rights of recall to jobs formerly entry jobs retained those rights to the same jobs, even though the positions were now in the middle of the merged lines. More importantly, Crown continued to award promotions according to job seniority: the man with the most years in the job slot below the vacancy had first call. Time worked in the mill counted for nothing as such. As a necessary result, Negroes had no seniority in bidding for formerly white jobs except as against each other and new white employees. They could not have such seniority, since the Company had not allowed them into the white progression lines. Crown gave no recognition to years spent in the Negro lines, and continued to make years spent in formerly white jobs the determinative factor in awarding all former white jobs except those previously at the entry level. The system conditioned job advancement upon a qualification that the Company itself had limited racially, *regardless of whether the qualification*—seniority in previously white jobs—*was necessary to do the work*. The legality of that arrangement is the main issue here.

In February 1967, more than a year after the merger of the lines, the Office of Federal Contract Compliance entered the picture. That agency has responsibility for overseeing compliance with Executive Order 11246 requiring non-discrimination assurances from all employers who contract with the federal government.[3] The OFCC attacked what the EEOC had previously seemed to approve, Crown Zellerbach's system of job seniority. In place of job seniority the OFCC proposed an "A + B" system which would combine an employee's time in the job below the vacancy and his total time at the mill in computing seniority. The Company accepted this compromise and tried to get the Papermakers to go along with it. The two locals, 189 and 189-A, both refused, although for different reasons. Crown thus faced a strike if it went ahead with the "A + B" system and the loss of future federal contracts if it did not.[4] In January it notified the unions that it would install the "A + B" system unilaterally on February 1, 1968. Local 189, the white union, responded by voting to strike on that date. Local 189-A, the Negro union, refused to join in on the strike warning, calling the "A + B" system "a step in the right direction".

The Government filed this suit on January 30, 1968, to enjoin the strike as an effort "to perpetuate a seniority and recall system which discriminates against Negro employees". The district court

---

3. Section 202 of the order in part reads as follows:

   ". . . During the performance of this contract, the contractor agrees as follows: (1) The contractor will not discriminate against any employee or applicant for employment because of race, creed, color, or national origin. The contractor will take affirmative action to ensure that applicants are employed, and that employees are treated during employment, without regard to their race, creed, color, or national origin. Such action shall include, but not be limited to the following: employment, upgrading, demotion, or transfer, recruitment or recruitment advertising; layoff or termination; rates of pay or other forms of compensation; and selection for training, including apprenticeship. The contractor agrees to post in conspicuous places, available to employees and applicants for employment, notices to be provided by the contracting officer setting forth the provisions of his nondiscriminatory clause." (3 C.F.R. 1965 Supp. pp. 168.)

4. Crown obtained an injunction from a district court in December restraining the Secretary of Labor from barring the company from federal contracts without a prior hearing. Crown Zellerbach v. Wirtz, D.D.C. 1968, 281 F. Supp. 337.

granted the injunction the next day. The United States then asked the court to strike down the "A + B" system as illegal, and to require that mill experience alone become the standard of seniority. The Government now was asking the court to set aside job seniority in any form, a stronger measure than the one requested earlier by the OFCC, which in turn had gone beyond the original position of the EEOC.[5] Local 189-A and two Negro employees intervened as plaintiffs on behalf of all Negro employees at the mill.

After a three-day hearing on job seniority, the district court issued an order on March 26, 1968, dealing with two issues that had been stipulated by the parties. as severable from the eleven others in the case. The court continued in effect the injunction of January 31. It also held that job seniority "presently discriminate[s] against Negro employees at the mill whenever Negroes hired prior to January 1965 [when progression lines were merged] compete against white employees for promotion, demotion or selection for training". The court also found that job seniority, as a matter of fact, "is not necessitated by safety or efficiency factors. . ." It ordered the abolition of job seniority in favor of mill seniority "in all circumstances in which one or more competing employees is a Negro employee hired prior to January

16, 1966." The decree did not, by its. terms, upset the use of job seniority in bidding that involved only whites or Negroes hired after the merger of the lines of progression.

In explaining its order, the court pointed out that the abolition of job seniority did not mean that affected Negro employees would be able to bid on any job in the mill solely on the basis of their years with the Company. They would still have to move up the lines of progression job-by-job. Among the competitors within the slot below a vacancy, however, time in the mill rather than time in the job would define seniority. As a further qualification of its order, the court disavowed any intention "to deny Crown the right to require that competing employees have the fundamental qualifications necessary to fill the vacant position."

A month after issuing its order, the district court heard testimony and argument on the remaining eleven issues stipulated as severable from the issue of job seniority. The court disposed of one issue by ordering the merger of Local 189 and Local 189-A. The court decided the remaining ten issues on June 26, 1969.[6]

B. The stipulated issues are: "whether, under the facts and circumstances of this case, the job seniority system which was in effect at the Bogalusa paper mill prior

---

5. See Section VI of this opinion.
6. On June 26, 1969 the district court issued its findings of fact and conclusions of law on the remaining issues. (1) The court found that Crown had continued to discriminate in job assignments by appointing whites to traditionally white jobs and Negroes to traditionally Negro jobs. The court added to the aggrieved class Negroes hired since the merger of the progression lines (1966), except for the six Negroes hired since then "who in fact bid for and received formerly white jobs fom the Extra Board". (2) The court concluded that a six-months residency requirement was not necessary to train employees for the next higher job in every instance. The parties, it noted, had stipulated which residency requirements were justified by need. (3) The court also found that certain jobs provide no training for the next higher levels. It therefore held that Negroes within the aggrieved class could skip those jobs in bidding on higher jobs in the merged lines of progression. (4) Finally, the court found that 64 hours of temporary assignment to a job per month provided training equivalent to permanent assignment to the job and should be treated as such for the purposes of bidding. The disposition of these and other issues in the district court's decision of June 26 does not effect our consideration of its earlier findings of fact and conclusions of law.

to February 1, 1968, was unlawful" and, if so, "what is the necessary or appropriate standard or guideline for identifying the seniority of employees for purposes of promotion or demotion?"

The plaintiffs maintain that Crown's practice of awarding jobs on the basis of *job* seniority rather than *mill* seniority discriminates against Negroes, since they had no way of attaining job seniority in "white" slots until the recent desegregation of the plant. When Negroes bid for jobs above the former entry level of white lines of progression, Crown in effect penalized them for not having what it denied them on account of their race until a short time ago — "white" job seniority. Crown's system gives renewed effect to the old racial distinctions without the plaintiffs say, *the justification of business necessity.* The practice of awarding jobs by job seniority would, the plaintiffs assert, amount to present and prospective racial discrimination.

Crown and Local 189, the white union, maintain that Crown ceased to discriminate in 1966 when it merged the white and Negro lines of progression. That change, coupled with the merger of the extra boards in 1964 and the transfer provisions of 1965 removed all explicit racial classification at the Bogalusa mill. What remains, the defendants say, is a racially neutral system of job seniority. The fact that the system continues to prefer whites over previously hired Negroes in filling certain vacancies does not in itself show racial discrimination. That effect, the defendants argue, is merely an ineradicable consequence of extinct racial discrimination. They point to evidence that Congress meant Title VII to apply prospectively only. Competitive seniority has an honorable place in the history of labor,[7] and portions of the legislative history of the Act seem to immunize accrued rights of seniority against remedial measures. Thus Title VII §703(h) specifically protects "bona fide seniority systems" from the operation of the Act. The defendants also maintain that insistence upon mill seniority would effectively bestow preferential treatment upon one race, which the Act by its terms positively forbids.

I.

No one can quarrel with the broad proposition that Title VII operates only prospectively. By specific provision, the Act did not become effective at all until one year after the date of enactment. The central operative provision, § 703 (a), declares that "it *shall* be an unlawful employment practice" for an employer to discriminate. (Emphasis added.) Section 701 (b) and (e) provide that for staggered effective dates: The Act applied on July 2, 1965, only to employers of 100 employees or more, extending to employers of 75, 50, and 25 at successive yearly intervals. The dispute is whether a seniority system based on pre-Act work credit constitutes present discrimination.

7. Cooper and Sobel, fn. 2: "The use of competitive status seniority to govern promotions, demotions, and layoffs in a fundamental aspect of industrial relations in this country. In nearly all businesses of significant size whose employees are organized, a seniority system plays some role in determining the allocation of the work. Such systems are commonly accompanied by lines of progression or promotional ladders which establish an order of jobs through which employees normally are promoted.

Seniority may be measured by total length of employment with the employer ("employment," "mill," or "plant" seniority), length of service in a department, ("departmental seniority"), length of service in a line of progression ("progression line" seniority), or length of service in a job ("job" seniority). Different measures of seniority sometimes are used in the same plant for different purposes. The variations and combinations of seniority principles are very great, but in all cases the basic measure is length of service, with preference accorded to the senior worker. Similarly, construction craft unions, which control the allocation of local work in their craft, have adopted referral rules based on length of service."

Although the effect of Title VII provoked considerable debate in Congress, the legislative history of the title is singularly uninstructive on seniority rights. Opponents of the Act warned that Title VII would destroy hard-earned seniority rights; proponents responded that it would. not affect accrued seniority.[8] In *Quarles v. Phillip Morris, Inc.*, E.D. Va. 1968, 279 F. Supp. 505, after a careful review of the legislative history, Judge John D. Butzner, Jr. concluded:

Several facts are evident from the legislative history. First, it contains no express statement about departmental seniority. Nearly all of the references are clearly to employment seniority. None of the excerpts upon which the company and the union rely suggests that as a result of past discrimination a Negro is to have employment opportunities inferior to those of a white person who has less employment seniority. Second, the legislative history indicates that a discriminatory seniority system established before the act cannot be held lawful under the act. The history leads the court to conclude that Congress did not intend to require "reverse discrimination"; that is, the act does not require that Negroes be preferred over white employees who possess employment seniority. It is also apparent that Congress did not intend to freeze an entire generation of Negro

employees into discriminatory patterns that existed before the act.

Perhaps the strongest argument for the *Quarles* construction of the Act is § 703(h):

Section 703(h) expressly states the seniority system must be *bona fide*. The purpose of the act is to eliminate racial discrimination in covered employment. Obviously one characteristic of a *bona fide* seniority system must be lack of discrimination. Nothing in §703(h), or in its legislative history suggests that a racially discriminatory seniority system established before the act is a *bona fide* seniority system under the act. Quarles v. Philip Morris, Incorporated, E.D. Va., 1968, 279 F. Supp. 505, 517.

We agree with this view.

II.

The defendants assert, paradoxically, that even though the system conditions future employment opportunities upon a previously determined racial status the system is itself racially neutral and not in violation of Title VII. The translation of racial status to job-seniority status cannot obscure the hard, cold fact that Negroes at Crown's mill will lose promotions which, *but for* their race, they would surely have won. Every time a Negro worker hired under the old segregated

---

8. "Title VII would have no effect on seniority rights existing at the time it takes effect" Justice Department statement, Cong. Record, April 8, 1964, p. 6986. "If a rule were to state that all Negroes must be laid off before any white man, such a rule could not serve as a basis for a discharge subsequent to the effective date of the title . . . but, in the ordinary case, assuming that seniority rights were built up over a period of time during which Negroes were not hired, these rights would not be set aside by taking effect of Title VII. Employer and labor organizations would simply be under a duty not to discriminate against Negroes because of their race. Any differences in treatment based on established seniority rights would not be based on race and would not be forbidden by the title." Ibid. "Title VII would have no effect on established seniority rights. Its effect is prospective and not retrospective. Thus, for example, if a business has been discriminating in the past and as a result has an all-white working force, when the Title comes into effect, the employer's obligation would be simply to fill future vacancies on a non-discriminatory basis. He would not be obliged—or indeed, permitted—to fire whites in order to hire Negroes, or to prefer Negroes for future vacancies, or, once Negroes are hired, to give them special seniority rights at the expense of the white workers hired earlier." Memorandum by Senators Clark and Case. Bureau of National Affairs Operations Manual, The Civil Rights Act of 1964, p. 320. See Cooper and Sobel, fn. 2, 1607-1614.

system bids against a white worker in his job slot, the old racial classification reasserts itself, and the Negro suffers anew for his employer's previous bias. It is not decisive therefore that a seniority system may appear to be neutral on its face if the inevitable effect of tying the system to the *past* is to cut into the employees *present* right not to be discriminated against on the ground of race. The crux of the problem is how far the employer must go to undo the effects of past discrimination. A complete purge of the "but-for" effects of previous bias would require that Negroes displace white incumbents who hold jobs that, but for discrimination, the Negroes' greater mill seniority would entitle them to hold. Under this *"freedom now"* theory,[9] allowing junior whites to continue in their jobs constitutes an act of discrimination.

Crown and Local 189 advance a *"status quo"* theory: the employer may satisfy the requirements of the Act merely by ending explicit racial discrimination.[10] Under that theory, whatever unfortunate effects there might be in future bidding by Negroes luckless enough to have been hired before desegregation would be considered merely as an incident of now extinguished discrimination.

A *"rightful place"* theory [11] stands between a complete purge of "but-for" effects maintenance of the status quo. The Act should be construed to prohibit the *future awarding* of vacant jobs on the basis of a seniority system that "locks in" prior racial classification. White incumbent workers should not be bumped out of their *present* positions by Negroes with greater plant seniority; plant seniority should be asserted only with respect to new job openings. This solution accords with the purpose and history of the legislation.

Not all "but-for" consequences of pre-Act racial classification warrant relief under Title VII. For example, unquestionably Negroes, as a class, educated at all-Negro schools in certain communities have been denied skills available to

their white contemporaries. That fact would not, however, prevent employers from requiring that applicants for secretarial positions know how to type, even though this requirement might prevent Negroes from becoming secretaries.

This Court recently struck down a nepotism membership requirement of a "white" union which shortly before had ceased overt discrimination. *Local 53 v. Vogler*, 5 Cir. 1969, 407 F.2d 1047. Under the nepotism rule, only the sons of members or close relatives living with members could become "improvers", and only "improvers" could be accepted into the union. Relationship to a member as a prerequisite to admission had the necessary effect of locking non-whites out of the union. The union argued that the desire to provide family security was a rational non-racial basis for the rule and that since the nepotism requirement excluded all persons unrelated to members, regardless of their race, it could not, therefore, be called a racial classification. This court held that the rule served no purpose related to ability to perform the work in the asbestos trade and that it violated Title VII:

> The District Court did no more than prevent *future* discrimination when it prohibited a continuing exclusion of negroes through the application of an apparently neutral membership provision which was *originally* instituted at least in part because of racial discrimination and which served no significant trade-related purpose. While the nepotism requirement is applicable to black and white alike and is not on its face discriminatory, in a completely white union the present effect of its continued application is to forever deny to negroes and Mexican-Americans any real opportunity for membership.

In *Vogler* this Court made the point, citing *Quarles*, that "where necessary to insure compliance with the Act, the District Court was fully empowered to elimi-

9. See Note, Harv. L. Rev., fn. 2 1268.
10. Id.
11. Id.

nate the present effects of past discrimination." *Vogler*, however, does not mesh completely with the facts in this case. The nepotism rule there, as the court pointed out, had scant relation to the operation of the business. It also had the inevitable effect of assuring the lily-white status of the union for all time. Nevertheless, the decision does support the position that reliance on a standard, neutral on its face, is no defense under the Act when the effect of the standard is to lock the victims of racial prejudice into an inferior position.

The controlling difference between the hypothetical typing requirement and the nepotism rule rejected in *Vogler is business necessity*. When an employer or union has discriminated in the past and when its present policies renew or exaggerate discriminatory effects, those policies must yield, unless there is an overriding legitimate, non-racial business purpose. Secretaries must be able to type. There is no way around that necessity. A nepotism rule, on the other hand, while not unrelated to the training of craftsmen,[12] is not essential to that end. To be sure, skilled workers may gain substantial benefits from having grown up in the home of a member of the trade. It is clear, nonetheless, that the benefits secured by nepotism must give way because of its effective continuation and renewal of racial exclusion. That much was decided in *Vogler*.

The decisive question then is whether the job seniority standard, as it is now functioning at the Bogalusa plant, is so necessary to Crown Zellerbach's operations as to justify locking Negroes, hired before 1966, into permanent inferiority in their terms and conditions of employment. The record supports the district court's holding that job seniority is not essential to the safe and efficient operation of Crown's mill. The defendants' chief expert witness, Dr. Northrup, made it clear that he considered mill seniority "disastrous" only to the extent that it allowed *all* men in a slot to bid on the basis of their time at the mill. He stated

that mill seniority in that sense would create labor unrest because its main effect would be to allow whites to "jump" other whites and Negroes to "jump" other Negroes. He also expressed fears about allowing anyone to bid on any vacancy in a line of progression, without requiring that he first advance job-by-job through the various levels below it. That problem might be solved, he stated, by imposing a residency requirement for training purposes. Dr. Northrup explicitly stated that job seniority does *not* provide the only safe or efficient system for governing promotions. He suggested, in fact, an alternative "job credit" system that would give certain fractional seniority credit to victims of discrimination for the years in which they had been excluded from the white progression lines.

The court took account of Dr. Northrup's apprehensions in fashioning its decree. In place of job security the court ordered the institution of a mill seniority system carefully tailored to assure that no employee would have a right to a job that he could not perform properly. The court's decision put the emphasis where it belongs: absent a showing that the worker has the ability to handle a particular job, the entry job is the proper beginning for any worker. Under the court's decree, employees still must move up through the various lines of progression job-by-job.[13] As a further restraint, if a certain minimum time is needed in one job to train an employee for the next, a residency requirement may be imposed that will slow the rise of Negro employees. Under the system that is in effect at the mill now, and that is unaffected by the decree, that residency period is six months. To meet the problem of labor unrest that might result from "jumping" unrelated to racial issues, the court specifically limited its decree to instances in which Negroes hired before 1966 were among the bidders. Finally, and most importantly, both the court's decree and the existing collective bargaining agreement give Crown Zellerbach the right to deny

12. See Kotch v. River Port Pilot Commrs, 1947, 330 U.S. 552, 67 S.Ct. 910, 91 L.Ed. 1093.
13. See footnote 6.

promotions to employees who lack the ability or qualification to do the job properly.

All these precautions, we think, bear out the plaintiffs' assertion that there are satisfactory alternatives to job seniority at the Bogalusa mill. They lead us to conclude that the imposition of a system that perpetuates and renews the effects of racial discrimination in the guise of job seniority is not necessary or justified at Bogalusa. Job seniority, embodying as it does, the racially determined effects of a biased past, constitutes a form of present racial discrimination.

This case is not the first case to present to courts in this circuit the problem of dealing with a change in system that is apparently fair on its face but in fact freezes into the system advantages to whites and disadvantages to Negroes. In *United States v. State of Louisiana,* E.D.La. 1963, 225 F. Supp. 353, a three-judge court had before it a new citizenship test adopted by the State Board of [Voters] Registration. The test was fair on its face and, perhaps, capable of fair administration. But it was a test that white voters, almost all of whom were registered, had not had to take. It was a difficult test for eligible Negroes, most of whom were not registered. The court enjoined the State from administering the test. "The promise of evenhanded justice in the future does not bind our hands in undoing past injustices." 225 F. Supp. at 396. The court said:

> The cessation of prior discriminatory practices cannot justify the imposition of new and onerous requirements, theoretically applicable to all, but practically affecting primarily those who bore the brunt of previous discrimination. An appropriate remedy therefore should undo the results of past discrimination as well as prevent future inequality of treatment. A court of equity is not powerless to eradicate the effects of former discrimination. If it were, the State could seal into permanent existence the injustices of the past.

The Supreme Court affirmed, adding: "the court has not merely the power but the duty to render a decree which will so far as possible eliminate the discriminatory effects of the past as well as bar like discrimination in the future." *Louisiana v. United States,* 1965, 380 U.S. 145, 85 S.Ct. 817, 13 L.Ed.2d 709. See also *Meredith v. Fair,* 5 Cir. 1962, 298 F.2d 696, 702, cert. denied; *United States v. Dogan,* 5 Cir. 1963, 314 F.2d 767; *United States v. Atkins,* 5 Cir. 1963, 323 F.2d 733; *United States v. Penton,* M.D.Ala. 1962, 212 F. Supp. 193. *Cf. Guinn v. United States,* 1915, 238 U.S. 347, 35 S.Ct. 926, 59 L.Ed. 1340; *Lane v. Wilson,* 1939, 307 U.S. 268, 59 S.Ct. 872, 83 L.Ed. 1281; *Goss v. Board of Education,* 1963, 373 U.S. 683, 688, 83 S.Ct. 1405, 1409, 10 L.Ed. 2d 632, 636.

It might be said that in these cases the courts focussed on the unlawfulness of the prior discrimination. In *Gaston County v. United States,* 1969, U.S.   ,   S.Ct.   ,   L.Ed.2d   , however, the Court's refusal to approve a voter literacy test was based on the inferior education inherent in segregated schooling. The automatic "triggering" provisions of the 1965 Voting Rights Act of 1965 had suspended Gaston County's literacy test because certain indicia chosen by Congress raised the presumption that the tests were being used to discriminate against Negroes seeking to register. In order to reinstate its test under the Act, Gaston County had to show that it had not used the test in the preceding five years "for the purpose or with the effect of denying or abridging the right to vote on account of race or color." The district court found, as a fact, that Gaston County's Negro schools had not provided educational opportunities equal to those available to whites. That alone, said the Supreme Court, would make the imposition of a literacy test an act of continuing discrimination. Neither the fair administration of the test, nor its legitimate public purpose could save it from condemnation under the Act.

III.

With specific regard to employment opportunities under Title VII, decisions by at least two district courts support our conclusion that facially neutral but needlessly restrictive tests may not be imposed where they perpetuate the effects of previous racial discrimination.

In *Quarles v. Philip Morris, Inc.*, E.D. Va. 1968, 279 F. Supp. 505, the first case to challenge the legality of a promotion system under Title VII, the employer had segregated the races by departments at its plant. The employer desegregated the plant but prohibited transfers from one department to another. It also required that the transferor bid on vacancies according to his departmental seniority, rather than his seniority at the plant. The effect was to deny to Negroes promotion into the better paying jobs, because they could not accumulate seniority in the fabrication and warehouse departments, where the better jobs lay. Quarles, a Negro employed in the prefabrication department, could not become a truck driver, a higher-rung position in an all-white department. The court held that the new arrangement violates the statute (279 F. Supp. at 519):

> "The present discrimination resulting from historically segregated departments is apparent from consideration of the situation of a Negro who has worked for ten years in the prefabrication department. . . . [He is required] to sacrifice his employment seniority and take new departmental seniority based on his transfer date. Thus a Negro with ten years employment seniority transferring . . . from the prefabrication department to the fabrication department takes an entry level position with departmental seniority lower than a white employee with years less employment seniority. These restrictions upon the present opportunities for Negroes result from the racial pattern of the company's employment practices prior to January 1, 1966. The restrictions do not result from lack of merit or qualification. A transferee under any plan must satisfy ability and merit requirements regardless of his seniority.
>
> . . .
>
> The court finds that the defendants have intentionally engaged in unlawful employment practices by discriminating on the ground of race against

Quarles, and other Negroes similarly situated. This discrimination, embedded in seniority and transfer provisions of collective bargaining agreements, adversely affects the conditions of employment and opportunities for advancement of the class."

In *Dobbins v. Local 212*, IBEW, S.D. Ohio 1968, 292 F. Supp. 413, the union had formerly excluded non-whites from membership. The effects of this practice had been doubly serious, since the union controlled hiring referrals within a certain geographic area. After opening its apprenticeship programs and membership to Negroes the union continued to prefer applicants who had previously worked under union contracts. This preferential referral system contained no explicit racial classification or discriminatory purpose. The court looked, nonetheless, to its inevitable discriminatory effect:

> "A policy of giving priority in work referral to persons who have experience under the Local's Collective Bargaining Agreement is discriminatory when competent N[egroe]s have previously been denied the opportunity to work under the referral agreement by reason of their race." 292 F. Supp. at 445.

When the defendant's conduct evidences an "economic purpose" there is no discrimination under Title VII: "The limitation of either union or apprenticeship membership to a number far below the number necessary for the particular trade would be a discriminatory practice and pattern in context involving an all ["W]hite union membership with a previous history of discrimination. *Louisiana v. United States*, 1965, 380 U.S. 145. However, on a showing by a defendant that the limitation has nothing to do with any discriminatory intention but is related to reasonable economic purpose, the limitation in number is not unlawful." The court went on to hold the referral system illegal:

> "Preference to union members in work referral is a violation of Title VII if that preference operates after July, 1965, to continue to restrict the employment opportunities of N's who have been excluded from membership

and work under union auspices because of their race. United States by Clark v. Local 189, United Papermakers and Paperworkers, 282 F. Supp. 39 (D.C. La., 1968); Quarles v. Philip Morris, Inc., 279 F. Supp. 505 (D.C. Va., 1968)." 292 F. Supp. at 446.

Nothing that we said in *Whitfield v. United Steelworkers, Local 2708,* 5 Cir. 1958, 263 F.2d 546, cert. denied 360 U.S. 902, compels a different result. In that case Negro workers challenged a plan, negotiated through collective bargaining, purporting to do away with segregated lines of progression in a steel mill. There was no issue in *Whitfield* as to the measure of promotion from one job to another. *Quarles* distinguishes *Whitfield* (279 F. Supp. at 518):

> *Whitfield* does not stand for the proposition that present discrimination can be justified simply because it was caused by conditions in the past. Present discrimination was allowed in *Whitfield* only because it was rooted in the Negro employees' lack of ability and training to take skilled jobs on the same basis as white employees. The fact that white employees received their skill and training in a discriminatory progression line denied to the Negroes did not outweigh the fact that the Negroes were unskilled and untrained. Business necessity, not racial discrimination, dictated the limited transfer privileges under the contract.

In *Whitfield* the company had organized functionally-related jobs into two separate lines of progression, Line 1 (the skilled jobs) for whites and Line 2 (the unskilled jobs) for Negroes. Advancement in a line was based on knowledge and experience acquired in the next lower job. The company opened both lines on a non-racial basis, and added that Negroes in Line 2 would in the future have preference over new whites in applying for vacancies in Line 1. Except for variations in pay, the change had the effect of merging the lines into one, with the formerly white line on top. In *Whitfield,* unlike

the present case, the two lines were not so functionally related that experience at the top of the formerly black line could provide adequate training for the bottom jobs in the white line. The company therefore required that men moving into the formerly all-white Line 1 take a qualification test, one that the white incumbents had not been required to take. (The company had previously required 260 hours "probationary" experience instead.) Negroes objected to the test requirement on the ground that whites already working in Line 1 did not have to take the test to advance or remain in the line. The company also required, as we have said, that employees bidding into Line 1 from Line 2 start at the bottom job. Negroes in Line 2 protested that this requirement also discriminated against them because it meant that Negroes would have to take a wage cut in moving from the top job in Line 2 to the bottom job in Line 1. The plaintiffs brought the complaint under the *Steele* doctrine,[14] which requires certified unions to represent members of the bargaining unit on a non-discriminatory basis.

This Court rejected both of the plaintiffs' objections. We held that the qualification test was the " 'minimum assurance' the Company could have of efficient operations", and that the company and union had gone "about as far as they could go in giving negroes preference in filling Number 1 line vacancies consistent with being *fair to incumbents and consistent with efficient management.*" 263 F. 2d at 550 (emphasis added.) The requirement that entrants into Line 1 start at the bottom job was justified as a business necessity:

> *Such a system was conceived out of business necessity,* not out of racial discrimination. An employee without proper training and with no proof of potential ability to rise higher, cannot expect to start in the middle of the ladder, regardless of plant seniority. It would be unfair to the skilled, experienced, deserving employee to give a

14. See Steele v. Louisville & Nashville R. Co., 323 U.S. 192, 65 S.Ct. 226, 89 L.Ed. 173, and Syres v. Oil Workers International Union, Local 23, 1955, 350 U.S. 892, 76 S.Ct. 152, 100 L.Ed. 785.

top or middle job to an unqualified employee. It would also destroy the whole system of lines of progression *to the detriment of efficient management* and to the disadvantage of negro as well as white employees having a stake in orderly promotion." 263 F.2d at 550.

In *United States v. H. K. Porter Co.,* N.D. Ala. 1968, 296 F. Supp. 40, 90, the court rejected an attack by the Government upon "the procedure that the first man to get a job is the first man to advance", *i.e.* job seniority, super-imposed, as here, upon a history of racial discrimination. The court found, as a matter of fact, that it was not "permissible" to assume "on the record in this case" that

> "with less than the amount of on-the-job training now acquired by reason of the progression procedure, employees could move into jobs in the progression lines and perform those jobs satisfactorily and—more importantly—without danger of physical injury to themselves and their fellow employees." 290 F. Supp. at 91.

In other words, the record in that case, as the district court viewed it, showed that safety and efficiency, the component factors of business necessity, would not allow relaxation of the job seniority system. We see no necessary conflict between *Porter's* holding on this point and our holding in the present case.

We have also considered two district court decisions cited by the defendants, *United States v. Sheet Metal Workers,* E.D. Mo. 1968, 280 F. Supp. 719, and *Griggs v. Duke Power Co.,* M.D. N. C. 1968, 292 F.2d 243. In *Sheet Metal Workers,* the defendant white unions had adopted a referral system giving priority to men with previous referrals. They had also discriminated racially before the effective date of the Act as had the union in Dobbins. On the other hand, they had adopted positive measures to encourage minority-group membership. The district court could find no person who had actually suffered on account of his race under the referral preference system and no "pattern or practice" of discrimination. (The sole plaintiff was the United States.) On the

contrary, it found that "in every instance, qualified Negroes applying for union membership and/or apprenticeship training since July 2, 1965, have been admitted therein." 280 F. Supp. 729. Among union members, of course, the referral preference system might well have had the effect of favoring whites, since they would have had a greater chance to amass time under the collective bargaining agreement. On the other hand, if there was more than enough work to go around, the discriminatory tendency inherent in the referral rule might not have asserted itself. The opinion is silent on that critical fact, noting only that "the record is devoid of any specific instance of discrimination". 280 F. Supp. 730.

In *Griggs* the defendant employer had in the past limited Negroes to jobs in the labor department, excluding them from better work in other departments. The plaintiffs sought to overturn a requirement of ten years standing that any employee transferring into one of the formerly white departments have a high school education or passing marks on a qualification test. The court found that both the tests and the education requirements were not racially motivated, but were part of the company's effort to upgrade its work force. It took note of a specific provision in Title VII, §703 (h), that exempts from the operation of the Act the use of "any professionally developed ability test . . . not designed . . . to discriminate because of race" and went on to strike down an EEOC interpretation of that provision which would limit the exemption to tests that measure ability *"required* by the *particular job* or class of jobs which the applicant seeks". (Emphasis added.) The court concluded that the defendant had not violated the Act, since it had not discriminated after July 2, 1965.

When an employer adopts a system that necessarily carries forward the incidents of discrimination into the present, his practice constitutes on-going discrimination, unless the incidents are limited to those that safety and efficiency require. That appears to be the premise for the Commission's interpretation of §703 (h). To the extent that *Griggs* departs from that view, we find it unpersuasive.

IV.

The defendants maintain that Congress specifically exempts seniority system such as Crown's from the operation of Title VII. In support of their assertion the defendants cite that portion of §703 (h) which allows an employer to "apply different standards of compensation, or different terms, conditions, or privileges of employment *pursuant to a bona fide seniority* or merit system . . . provided that such differences are not the result of an intention to discriminate because of race, color, religion, sex, or national origin".

No doubt, Congress, to prevent "reverse discrimination" meant to protect certain seniority rights that could not have existed but for previous racial discrimination. For example a Negro who had been rejected by an employer on racial grounds before passage of the Act could not, after being hired, claim to outrank whites who had been hired before him but after his original rejection, even though the Negro might have had senior status but for the past discrimination. As the court pointed out in *Quarles*, the treatment of "job" or "department seniority" raises problems different from those discussed in the Senate debates: "a department seniority system that has its genesis in racial discrimination is not a bona fide seniority system." 297 F. Supp. at 554.

It is one thing for legislation to require the creation of *fictional* seniority for newly hired Negroes, and quite another thing for it to require that time *actually worked* in Negro jobs be given equal status with time worked in white jobs. To begin with, requiring employers to correct their pre-Act discrimination by creating fictional seniority for new Negro employees would not necessarily aid the actual victims of the previous discrimination. There would be no guaranty that the new employees had actually suffered exclusion at the hands of the employer in the past, or, if they had, there would be no way of knowing whether, after being hired, they would have continued to work for the same employer. In other words, creating fictional employment time for newly-hired Negroes would comprise preferential rather than remedial treatment. The clear thrust of the Senate debate is directed against such preferential treatment on the basis of race. That sentiment was codified in an important portion of Title VII, §703(j):

"(j) Nothing contained in this subchapter shall be interpreted to require any employer, employment agency, labor organization, or joint labor-management committee subject to this subchapter to grant preferential treatment to any individual or to any group because of the race, color, religion, sex, or national origin of such individual or group on account of an imbalance which may exist with respect to the total number or percentage of persons of any race, color, religion, sex, or national origin employed by any employer, referred or classified for employment by any employment agency or labor organization, admitted to membership or classified by any labor organization, or admitted to, or employed in, any apprenticeship or other training program, in comparison with the total number or percentage of persons of such race, color, religion, sex, or national origin in any community, State, section, or other area, or in the available work force in any community, State, section, or other area." 42 U.S.C. §2000e-2(j).

No stigma of preference attaches to recognition of time actually worked in Negro jobs as the equal of white time. The individual victims of prior discrimination in this case would necessarily be the ones—the only ones—to benefit by the institution of mill seniority, as modified in the decree. We conclude, in agreement with *Quarles*, that Congress exempted from the anti-discrimination requirements only those seniority rights that gave white workers preference over junior Negroes. This is not to say that *Whitfield* and *Quarles* and Title VII prohibit an employer from giving compensatory training and help to the Negro workers who have been discriminated against. Title VII's imposition of

an affirmative duty on employers to
undo past discrimination permits compensatory action for those who have
suffered from prior discrimination.

V.

We find unpersuasive the argument
that, whatever its operational effects,
job seniority is immune under the statute because not imposed with the *intent*
to discriminate. Section 703(h), quoted
earlier, excludes from the strictures of
Title VII different working terms dictated by "bona fide" seniority systems
"provided that such differences are *not
the result of an intention to discriminate
because of race* . . . "[15] Here, however,
if Crown did not intend to punish
Negroes as such by reinstituting job
seniority, the differences between the
job status of Negroes hired before 1966
and whites hired at the same time would
have to be called the "result" of Crown's
earlier, intentional discrimination. *Quarles*
put it this way:

"The differences between the terms and
conditions of employment for white
[sic] and Negroes about which plaintiffs complain are the result of an intention to discriminate in hiring policies
on the basis of race before January
1, 1966. The differences that originated
before the act are maintained now. The
act does not condone present differences
that are the result of intention to
discriminate before the effective date

of the act, although such a provision
could have been included in the act
had Congress so intended. The court
holds that the present differences in
departmental seniority of Negroes and
white [sic] that result from the company's intentional, racially discriminatory hiring policy before January 1,
1966 are not validated by the *proviso*
of §703 (h)" 279 F.Supp. 517-518.

Section 706(g) limits injunctive (as
opposed to declaratory) relief to cases
in which the employer or union has
"intentionally engaged in" an unlawful
employment practice. Again, the statute,
read literally requires only that the
defendant meant to do what he did,
that is, his employment practice was not
accidental. The relevant legislative history, quoted in the margin, bears out
the language of the statute on that point.

Section 707(a) allows the Attorney
General to enforce the Act only where
there is a "pattern or practice of resistance to the full enjoyment of any of
the rights secured by this subchapter"
and where the pattern or practice "is
intended to deny the full exercise of the
rights herein described". Defendants
contend that no such condition existed
here. The same point arose in *Dobbins*.
The court rejected it (297 F. Supp. at
448):

"In reviewing statutes, rules or conduct which result in the effective

---

15. "In determining the meaning of 'intentional,' resort must be had almost entirely
to legislative history. In its original form, 706(g) contained no such requirement;
it was amended by Senator Dirksen's proposal, probably in response to opposition pressure. The first draft of the amendment contained the word 'willfully'
instead of 'intentionally'; interpretative material was introduced into the record
by Senator Dirksen:
   The words 'willful and willfully' as ordinarily employed, mean nothing more
   than that the person, of whose actions or default the expressions are used,
   knows what he is doing, intends what he is doing, and is a free agent. . .
   The terms are also employed to denote an intentional act . . . as distinguished
   from an accidental act. . .
   This is precisely the situation which might exist if the words are not added. . .
   Accidental, inadvertent, heedless, unintended acts could subject an employer
   to charges under the present language.
For reasons that are not apparent, this version was not enacted, and not until
some time later was the amendment with the present language passed. The only
significant difference between the two versions is the substitution of 'intentionally' for 'willfully' and there is no indication that any strengthening of the requirement was meant. It may be concluded that the Dirksen Amendment does
not greatly narrow the coverage of section 706(g)." Note, Legal Implications of
the Use of Standardized Ability Tests in Employment and Education, 68 Col.
L. Rev. 691, 713 (1968).

denial of equal rights to Negroes or
other minority groups, intention can
be inferred from the operation and
effect of the statute or rule or from
the conduct itself. The conduct of defendant in the present case 'by its very
nature' contains the implications of the
required intent. Local 357, Intern.
Broth. of Teamsters, etc. v. National
Labor Relations Board, 365 U.S. 667
at 675, 81 S.Ct. 835, 6 L.Ed.2d 11
(1961) citing Radio Officers' Union,
etc. v. National Labor Relations Board,
347 U.S. 17, 45, 74 S.Ct. 323, 98 L.Ed.
455 (1954). See also the remarks of
then Senator Humphrey, 110 Cong.
Rec. 14270 in reference to Title VII,
'Intention could be proved by or inferred from words, conduct or both.'
Thus the Attorney General has a cause
of action when the conduct of a labor
organization in relation to N's or other
minority groups has the effect of
creating and preserving employment
opportunities for W's only. Section
707(a) of the Civil Rights Act of
1964."

Here, as in *Dobbins,* the conduct
engaged in had racially-determined effects. The requisite intent may be inferred from the fact that the defendants
persisted in the conduct after its racial
implications had become known to them.
Section 707(a) demands no more.

VI.

The defendants contend that the letters and statements made by EEOC
officials approving the merger of Crown's
progression lines acted as a bar under
§713(b) of the Act to suit by either
the Government or by the private plaintiffs Johnson, Hill, and Local 189-A.
The relevant portion of §713(b) reads
as follows: "In any action or proceeding based on any alleged unlawful employment practice, no person shall be
subject to any liability or punishment
for or on account of (1) the commission by such person of an unlawful
employment practice if he pleads and
proves that the act or omission complained of was in good faith, in con-

formity with, and in reliance on any
written interpretation or opinion of the
Commission".

The key phrase in this provision is
"written opinion or interpretation of the
Commission". The EEOC published its
own interpretation of the phrase in the
Federal Register in June 1965, *before
Title VII took effect and some six
months before the public statements at
issue here:* "Only (a) a letter entitled
'opinion letter' and signed by the General Counsel on behalf of the Commission or (b) matter published and so
designated in the Federal Register may
be considered a 'written interpretation
or opinion of the Commission' within
the meaning of section 713 of Title
VII." 29 C.F.R. §1601.30.

The statements that Crown relied
upon to its supposed detriment in this
case do not fall within either of the
defined categories. They appeared neither
as portions of the Federal Register or
as designated "opinion letters" over the
signature of the General Counsel. We
have merely a letter from Mr. Edelsberg, Executive Director, and a statement of Mr. Roosevelt, the Chairman
of the Commission. Mr. Edelsberg was
not General Counsel, nor did his letter
bear the "opinion letter" label. Mr.
Roosevelt issued his statement orally.
The regulation clearly requires more.

Courts give great weight to an agency's interpretation of the statute that
it administers.[16] The regulation here
gives reasonable scope to the statutory
provision. A broader reading might bind
the Commission to informal or unap-
proved opinions volunteered by members
of its staff.

We cannot help sharing Crown Zellerbach's bewilderment at the twists and
turns indulged in by government agencies in this case. We feel compelled to
hold, however, that neither the statement by Chairman Roosevelt nor the
letter by Executor Director Edelsberg
provides a legal defense to the present
suit.

16. Zemel v. Rusk, 1965, 380 U.S. 1, 85 S.Ct. 1271, 14 L.Ed.2d 179; Udall v. Tall-
man, 1965, 381 U.S. 1, 85 S.Ct. 792, 13L.Ed.2d 616; Oower Reactor Development Corp. v. Int. U. of Elec., 1960, 367 U.S. 396, 81 S.Ct. 529, 6 L.Ed.2d 924.

VII.

Our main conclusions may be summarized as follows: (1) Crown's job seniority system carries forward the discriminatory effects integral to the company's former employment practices. (2) The safe and efficient operation of Bogalusa mill does not depend upon maintenance of the job seniority system. (3) To the extent that Crown and the white union insisted upon carrying forward exclusion of a racially-determined class, *without business necessity*, they committed, with the requisite intent, in the statutory sense, an unfair employ-ment practice as defined by Title VII.

The district court thoughtfully worked a decree studded with provisos to protect the employer from the imposition of unsafe or inefficient practices and at the same time prevent racial discrimination. The decree also specifically provides that job seniority may still apply to bidding between one white employee and other. By making the decree applicable only to bidding that involves Negroes hired before 1966, the district court limited the remedy to the scope of the illegal conduct. The judgment of the district court is AFFIRMED.

Appendix C

Agreement between International Paper Company and unions representing its Southern Kraft Division employees, concluded under the auspices of the Office of Federal Contract Compliance, Jackson, Mississippi, 1968..

MEMORANDUM OF UNDERSTANDING

In response to the compliance requirements given by the Office of Federal Contract Compliance the parties have agreed to the following:

The following provisions are applicable to Production Lines of Progression only.

1. A. Acceptance of mill seniority as the test for advancement or demotion within progression lines or recall to progression lines or transfer from one progression line to another, or layoff, whenever Negro employees compete with other employees.

   B. (1) Retention of contract seniority whenever Whites compete against each other in any of the above situations.

   (2) Retention of contract seniority whenever Negroes compete against each other in any of the above situations.

   C. The acceptance of mill seniority, as outlined above, as the guiding principle when Whites and Negroes compete shall be subject to agreement with the Company as follows:

(1) All employees in the affected class as identified in Item C (4) below will be contacted for the purpose of discussion with them their desires for transfer to some other line of progression or advancement into a line of progression. Written applications will be prepared for those expressing an interest in such transfer or advancement. When vacancies occur all employees in or out of the affected class having applied for transfer or advancement will be considered on the basis of seniority and qualifications as otherwise provided for herein. Permanent vacancies in the beginning job of lines of progression will be posted on bulletin boards in all departments for at least one week with the understanding that a copy of the notice will be given to each local union.

(2) *All* current employees will be allowed to transfer to or advance into any line of progression if his qualifications are as high as the minimally qualified employee currently working in the line.

(3) Red circling of rates to be provided for first transfer of any current employee under the following conditions:

(a) The employee must have a permanent rate of less than $3.00 per hour.

(b) The employee must have made application for the transfer involved as provided in Paragraph 1. C (1) above within 6 months of the date of this Memorandum.

(c) (1) Red circling shall end for an employee who is transferred to or advanced into a line of progression if such employee fails to qualify after a reasonable trial period.

(2) Red circling shall end for an employee who waives a promotion in the line of progression to which he transfers or if the employee is disqualified for promotion, temporary or permanent, to a higher job to which he would otherwise move.

(4) The "affected class" for purposes of determining mill seniority competition shall be limited to:

(a) Negroes employed prior to September 1, 1962, and

(b) Negroes employed since September 1, 1962 but initially placed in a job or a line of progression formerly considered as an all Negro job or line of progression.

(5) Mill seniority provisions governing the competition between Negroes and Whites shall be terminated in five (5) years subject to the approval of the appropriate government agency, if any.

2. The proposed retroactive seniority for former rejected applicants for employment should be abandoned as unfair to current Negro and White employees.

3. As to Items 11 and 12, these items shall be referred to negotiations at the mill level between local management and local unions, such negotiations to involve the following items in the order of their priority:

A. Merging progression lines. Agreement to be reached within 90 days following ratification of this Memorandum.

B. Within 30 days after the lines of progression have been merged, the appropriate representatives of the local unions and the Company shall meet to examine the shortening of lines of progression and determine those jobs, if any, which may be skipped in advancing within or transferring between lines of progression.

4. If any Federal Court of Appeals or the Supreme Court of the United States shall hereafter determine that the government may not lawfully impose seniority standards upon the parties to a collective bargaining agreement, this Memorandum of Understanding shall immediately revert to the terms of the June 1, 1967 Labor Agreement.

Recommended by the Joint Group Unions and the Company.
International Brotherhood of Pulp, Sulphite and Paper Mill Workers
United Papermakers and Paperworkers
International Brotherhood of Electrical Workers
International Paper Company
June 25, 1968

Index

232

Index

Quarles v. Philip Morris, Inc., 102n.

Racial employment policies
  determinants of, 127-133
    demand for labor, 127-128
    job structure, 128-129
    government pressure, 129
    seniority, 129-131
      unionism and seniority, 129-131
    locational factors, 131
    regional factors, 131
    managerial policy, 131-133
Racial policies
  government policies, 117-119
  restrictions on intraplant movement,
    74-79
  union impact, 112-117
    segregated locals, 115-117
Recruiting and hiring
  South, 92-95
  tests and qualifications, 51-52
Regional comparisons, 80-95
  North, 80-84
    New England, 80-82
    Middle Atlantic, 82-84
  Midwest, 84-86
  Far West, 86, 87-88
  South, 89-95
Risher, Howard W., Jr., 53n, 54n, 69n
Rittenhouse, William, 2
Robert Hicks v. Crown Zellerbach, et al.,
  103n
Roosevelt, Franklin D., Jr., 98, 99, 99n
Roosevelt, President Franklin D., 35
Rowan, Richard L., 67n

San Francisco Employers' Council, 206
Sayre, Harry D., 105, 115
Scott Paper Co., 14, 58, 65, 71, 82, 97n,
  117, 120, 124, 131, 132
  in the South, 110-111, 112, 114, 116
Seniority, 35, 54, 57-58, 75, 97, 102-103,
  111, 112
  discriminatory systems, 39-42, 78-79
  impact of, 42, 48-51, 77-78
  rationale, 76-77
South Carolina Department of Labor, 71
St. Regis General Bulletin, 107n
St. Regis Paper Co., 58, 65, 97n, 110n,
  111, 117, 120, 124, 131, 132
  Equal Opportunity Understanding, 107,
    108
  in the South, 4, 106-109, 112, 115, 118

Strikes, 114
  International Paper, southern plants,
    54
  Scott Paper, 110

Taft-Hartley Act, 99, 100, 118
  Title VII, 101
Teamsters, Chauffeurs, Warehousemen
    and Helpers of America, Inter-
    national Brotherhood of, 26,
    28, 110
Tests, 51-52, 57
Tonelli, Joseph, 115
Truman, President Harry, 52
Turnover, 24-26, 75

Union Camp Corp., 71
  in the South, 112, 115, 116
Unionization, 26-30, 35
Union policies
  in converting plants, 42, 44-45
Union pressure, 69
Union racial policies, 30, 35-37
Unions
  in Bogalusa, 95-96
United Mine Workers
  see District 50
U. S.: Bureau of the Census, 31, 58
  Court of Appeals, 102
  Department of Defense, 119
  Department of Justice and Crown Zel-
    lerbach, 101, 103, 118
  Department of Labor, 100, 117, 124
  District Court (D. C.), 118
  District Court (New Orleans), 118
  Supreme Court, 27
  *United States v. Local 189, United Paper-
    makers and Paperworkers, et
    al.*, 98n, 102n
Upgrading, 54

Wagner Act, 27, 36
Wallace, Governor George, 132
Wall Street Journal, 56n
Western Pulp and Paper Workers, Asso-
    ciation of, 28, 110, 114, 130
Westvaco, 110n
  in South, 112, 115, 116
West Virginia Pulp and Paper Co.
  see Westvaco
Weyerhaeuser Co., 9
Wharton, Vernon Lane, 16n
White Citizens Council, 56, 56n, 104

Young, Harvey A., 30n, 97n

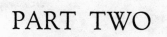

PART TWO

PART·TWO

THE NEGRO
IN THE LUMBER INDUSTRY

by

JOHN C. HOWARD

TABLE OF CONTENTS

LIST OF TABLES

LIST OF FIGURES

CHAPTER I

Introduction

The lumber and wood products industry has been the largest industrial employer of Negroes in the South for many years. Although the lumber industry is not a rapidly growing industry and does not offer great added potential employment for Negroes in the future, it is important because it most perfectly exemplifies the characteristics that have traditionally proved important to the industrial acceptance of Negro labor. A thorough examination of the Negro in the lumber industry clearly reveals the importance of regional factors, locational factors, wage scale, skill requirements, and job characteristics as determinants of racial employment policies in an industry.

This study will examine the industry's current racial policies after describing the structure of the industry and the changes in the extent of Negro participation as an employee prior to 1960. Much use was made of Census data in the investigation to 1960. More current data were collected between 1968 and 1969 and supplemented by visits to lumber mills in the South and West.

CHAPTER II

The Lumber and Wood Products Industry

Lumbering was one of the earliest of American industries. The first settlers found wood to be abundantly available in most portions of the New World and immediately made use of this material for construction of shelters, forts, ships, wine and rum casks, and for use as firewood. The ample supply of pine and hardwoods they found in the southern region of this country is particularly significant in studying Negro employment because of the large number of Negro slaves that were soon to be accumulated there.

Lumber production in the United States from 1799 to 1968 and the per capita consumption of lumber from 1889 to 1968 are shown in Table 1. Maximum per capita consumption of lumber was reached in about 1904 at 504 board feet per person, and the highest production level was reached about 1909 at 44,510 million board feet. The decline in lumber production and consumption since the early 1900's has been largely the result of a widespread shift to stone, brick, and reinforced concrete buildings. Other important factors have been the displacement of wood trim by plaster trimming and the simplification of trim under the impact of modern architecture, the use of steel sashes and doors, and concrete floors with composition covering.[1]

Much of this substitution of other products for wood has resulted from the increased cost of wood related to other materials of construction. Lumber prices have increased because of increased stumpage costs and lower productivity of labor. Although there have been some significant developments in recent years (mobile tree sheers that cut trees to 14 inches in diameter and drag them from the woods; new handling, sorting, slashing, and bucking machines; and automatic layup systems for plywood plants), advances in mechanization and automation in the industry have been inadequate to compensate for the decreasing size and availability of raw material.

---

1. Vernon H. Jensen, *Lumber and Men* (New York: Farrar and Rinehart, Inc., 1945), p. 25.

TABLE 1.   *Lumber and Wood Products Industry*
Lumber Production and Per Capita Consumption
Selected Years, 1799 to 1968

Year	Softwoods	Hardwoods	Total	Per Capita Consumption (In board feet)
	(In millions of board feet)			
1799	263	37	300	n.a.
1829	702	148	850	n.a.
1859	5,802	2,227	8,029	n.a.
1889	20,025	7,014	27,029	434
1909	33,897	10,613	44,510	477
1919	27,407	7,145	34,552	324
1929	30,836	7,909	38,745	268
1939	23,291	5,464	28,755	194
1949	27,197	5,704	32,901	225
1959	30,509	6,657	37,166	226
1968	30,134	6,960	37,094	214

Source: 1799-1939:   U. S. Department of Agriculture, *Lumber Production in the United States, 1799-1946*, Miscellaneous Publication No. 669, October 1948, p. 10; and American Forest Products Industries, Inc., *Facts About the Nation's Lumber Industry, 1965-1966*, p. 13.

1949-1964:   National Forest Products Association, *Forest Products Industry Facts, 1966*, pp. 11 and 22.

1968:   National Forest Products Association, *Fingertip Facts and Figures*, No. 132, May 1969, Table 1.

Note: Per capita consumption calculated by dividing the estimated domestic consumption of lumber in 1968 (43,048 million board feet, from National Forest Products Association, *Fingertip Facts and Figures*, No. 132, May 1969) by the estimate of the population for that year (201,152,000, from U. S. Bureau of the Census, *Current Population Reports*, Series P-25, No. 418, March 14, 1969).

THE PRODUCTION PROCESSES

Logging is the term used for the series of processes involved in the harvesting of forest crops. Felling the standing timber, the first step in this process, is performed by "fallers" who work in pairs with power saws. "Buckers" trim off the branches and cut the trees into conventional lengths for transporting and sawing. The logs are then assembled at a common point, an operation known as "bunching," "yarding," or "skidding." This operation is normally performed by cable yarders, which haul in the logs by means of a cable wound onto a rotating drum, or by tractors, which tow the logs over the ground. Once the logs are assembled, they are loaded onto railroad cars or trucks by mechanical loaders or manpower and hauled to the mill.[2]

The American Forest Products Industries, Inc. has briefly and accurately described current sawmill operations as follows:

When the logs arrive at the sawmill they are stored in huge piles or in ponds until they are needed. Water storage is preferred because it protects the logs from end checking and insect damage, washes off dirt, and logs are easier to sort.

Logs are pulled lengthwise into the mill by a bull chain or jack ladder. At sawmills which do not have water storage facilities, logs are moved by crane to the bull chain for hauling up into the mill and onto the sawing deck. At some mills the bark is removed before sawing.

On the deck, logs are rolled one at a time to the carriage where the sawyer takes over. One of the most important men in the mill, the sawyer, knows lumber grades and trade requirements. He knows how to get the largest amount of high quality lumber out of each log. He does it by controlling the movements of the headrig, where logs are slabbed and cut into boards or into timbers called cants or flitches.

Smaller mills usually have a circular headsaw which is flat and has teeth on its entire circumference. In most large mills, however, the head saw is a band saw. As the carriage moves forward the log is carried straight into the saw's sharp teeth. When the saw has passed through the log from one end to the other, the carriage shoots back and the position of the log is shifted for a second cut.

In large mills cants and flitches cut from the log by the headsaw are moved away on power rollers to either the gang saw or resaw, where they are cut into lumber of various thicknesses. In some mills the entire log is cut into rough lumber of standard sizes at the headsaw. Farther along the production line, an edger saws the boards into desirable widths, and trimmer saws cut the boards to proper lengths.

The next step is the "green chain." This is a conveyor belt or chains on which boards are moved out into a long sorting shed, where trained workmen grade each board. The "green" refers to the sapmoisture in the freshly cut lumber, not its color.

Most lumber is then seasoned, or dried. Some of the lumber is stacked in the yard for air drying. Other lumber is placed in dry kilns. Method and drying time depend on species, thickness and requirements of the final product.

Larger sawmills usually have a planing mill section in which the rough lumber is finished by passing through a set of rotating knives, which give it a smooth surface. Boards are also made into flooring, siding, moulding and other forms of building "trim" in a planing mill. There are also separate planing mills which buy rough lumber

---

2. For a vivid description of early logging practices, see Manuel Conrad Elmer, *Timber* (Boston: Christopher Publishing House, 1961), Chapter V.

from small mills and sell the finished product, called "surfaced lumber." Finished lumber is again graded before it is shipped.[3]

Much physical handling of the logs and lumber is still required; the work with the open saws, rolling logs, and log ponds is hazardous; and most of the workers are exposed to the elements.[4] The nature of the work has been extremely important in structuring the racial employment policies of the industry. Negroes have been used extensively wherever available for such jobs as block setters, chokermen, loaders, stackers, pondmen, and machine off bearers. These jobs are described in detail in Appendix A.

INDUSTRIAL CHARACTERISTICS

Table 2 sets forth employment, payrolls, capital expenditures, and other industrial data for the lumber and wood products industry and its important subdivisions for 1967, by the federal government's Standard Industrial Classification (SIC) system of data collection. The lumber industry constitutes virtually the entire salable product of lumber producers. Since the transportation of heavy lumber products from sawmills to distant finishing mills is expensive, much of the reworking and finishing of lumber products is carried on near the sawmills, and integration of the industry is relatively extensive.[5] Even in integrated establishments the sawmill is easily distinguishable. Data on sawmill operations are usually kept separate from that of other manufacturing activity.[6]

The data show that sawmills and planing mills constitute the largest industry group with almost one-half of the total employment. The sawmill and planing mill segment contributes less than one-half of the total cost of materials and value of shipments because much of the sawmill and planing mill production is purchased by other components of the lumber industry for remanufacture as millwork, wooden containers, etc.

---

3. American Forest Products Industries, Inc., *The Story of Lumber* (Washington: 1968), pp. 5-7.

4. For a comprehensive description of the methods used and the machinery employed in the manufacture and merchandising of lumber, see Nelson Courtlandt Brown and James Samuel Bethel, *Lumber* (New York: John Wiley & Sons, Inc., 1958).

5. "Earnings in the Lumber Industry," *Monthly Labor Review*, Vol. 53, No. 1 (July 1941), p. 189.

6. Joseph Zaremba, *Economics of the American Lumber Industry* (New York: Robert Speller and Sons, Publishers, Inc., 1963), p. 8.

TABLE 2. *Lumber and Wood Products Industry*
Employment, Payroll, Capital Expenditures, and Other Data
by Standard Industrial Classification, 1967

	Lumber and Wood Products (SIC 24)	Logging Camps and Logging Contractors (SIC 241)	Sawmills and Planing Mills (SIC 242)	Millwork, Plywood, and Related Products (SIC 243)	Wooden Containers (SIC 244)	Misc. Wood Products (SIC 249)
			Thousands of Employees			
All Employees	563	72	227	152	34	78
			Millions of Dollars			
Payroll	2,760	329	1,037	873	147	374
Value added by manufacture	4,828	735	1,744	1,427	255	667
Cost of materials	6,026	704	2,176	2,084	317	745
Value of shipments	10,875	1,411	3,938	3,531	574	1,421
Capital expenditures, new	394	90	151	89	18	46

Source: *U. S. Census of Manufactures, 1967*, Series MC 67(P)-1, Summary Series, Preliminary Report, April 1969.

For each industry group, the cost of materials seems to comprise about one-half, and wages about one-fifth, the value of shipments. Labor comprises about one-seventh of the value of shipments for manufacturing industries as a whole. As this indicates, lumber manufacture is a labor intensive industry. Productivity per worker cannot be higher because of lack of sufficient mechanization and automation to compensate for diminishing size and quality of raw material. Table 2 shows that the capital expenditures (new) for the lumber industry in 1967 were $394 million which, for 563,000 employees, means a ratio of $700 per employee. The capital expenditure to employee ratio for all manufacturing industries was $1,045 per employee.[7] The great difference between these two ratios probably exaggerates the degree to which the industry is labor intensive because of the lack of growth in the lumber industry compared to manufacturing industries as a whole.

Industrial Structure

"The lumber industry is one of the few large American industries which approximates the classical concept of competition. Firms are numerous; entry into the industry, particularly for the small producer, is relatively easy; and no one firm produces enough output to influence lumber prices significantly."[8] The majority of the companies have only one mill and it generally produces less than one million board feet annually. There are, however, also some very large companies, including those which are primarily producers of paper and allied products, which are listed on pp. 10-11 of the paper study of this Series. Georgia-Pacific and Boise-Cascade produce building materials and Evans Products and Boise-Cascade produce factory-built houses. Diamond International and Evans Products also produce metal and plastic products.

The existence of a few large prospering lumber producers does not hide the fact that the concentration of production in the lumber industry is almost the lowest in the economy. In 1957 congressional report entitled *Concentration in American Industry* in which 448 industries were studied, sawmills and planing mills were ranked 435th.[9] The predominance of small

7. Capital expenditures of $20,268,000,000 and total employment of 19,398,800 from *U.S. Census of Manufactures, 1967*, Series MC 67(P)-1, Summary Series, Preliminary Report, April 1969.

8. Zaremba, *op. cit.*, p. 7.

9. *Ibid.*, p. 19.

family-owned firms in the South has largely precluded the movement of Negroes into white collar jobs, but the poor profit structure of the firms has forced the companies to pay low wages and accept the only inexpensive labor available in quantity: that of Negroes.

Industrial Growth

Extrapolation of the data in Table 1 leads to a rather bleak prediction for the future of lumber in the United States. There are, however, some particular lumber industry products that show great growth potential. Foremost of these products is plywood, which since 1950 has increased from 2,676 million square feet (⅜ inch basis) to 15,500 million square feet while the per capita consumption has increased from 17.6 to 72.5 square feet per year. The 1968 mill value of softwood plywood shipped exceeded one billion dollars, an all time high.[10] Growth of the plywood industry has been particularly great in the South in recent years and offers great potential for the employment of Negroes in that area.

Another lumber industry product, particleboard (a member of the miscellaneous wood products segment, SIC 249), ranked fifth among the two hundred fastest growing product classes based on the 1958-1966 shipment growth.[11] Since 1958 particleboard products have increased from 125 to 1,350 million square feet (¾ inch basis), and are expected to reach 1,425 million square feet this year.[12] This is another industry segment that has been expanding most rapidly in the South and should offer great employment potential for Negroes.

Particleboards are made in panel form from dry wood particles that have been coated with a binder, and are formed and bonded to shape by pressure and heat. They are known by several names, including chipboard, chipcore, core board, synthetic lumber, and composition board.[13]

---

10. U. S. Bureau of Defense Services Administration, *U. S. Industrial Outlook, 1969*, p. 15.

11. U. S. Bureau of Defense Services Administration, *Industry Trend Series 1*, October 1968.

12. U. S. Bureau of Defense Services Administration, *U. S. Industrial Outlook, 1969*, pp. 17 and 18.

13. U. S. Forest Service, *Particle Board*, Research Note, FPL-072 (Madison, Wisconsin: Forest Products Laboratory, September 1964).

Two more slowly growing but quite important wood products are insulating boards and hardboards (both also in the miscellaneous wood products segment of the industry). These are made from the residue of other forest products industries, repulped wastepaper, and other cellulosic materials, such as bagasse.[14] Insulation board production has grown from 1,602 million square feet (½ inch basis) in 1949 [15] to 3,590 million square feet in 1968.[16] Hardboard production has increased from 533 square feet (⅛ inch basis) in 1949 [17] to 4,162 million square feet in 1968.[18] Because production of these boards does not require large sticks of timber, they can be produced from the southern wood supply, and therefore offer employment opportunities for Negroes.

INDUSTRIAL LOCATION

Until about 1840, the manufacture of lumber was largely a local industry concentrated in New England. As the westward migration of the population spread to the prairie and plain states where there was insufficient timber to meet the requirements of the people, lumber commerce became significant. As the depletion of the virgin timber of the North progressed, the industry turned its attention to the yellow pine forests of the South. Lumbering had been carried on in the South since colonial days, but did not become a large scale industrial enterprise until the last decade of the nineteenth century.[19] After the completion of the Northern Pacific Railway in 1882, the lumber industry resumed its movement westward to the Pacific Coast.[20]

Much of the changing regional character of the industry is shown in Table 3. By 1869, the Northeast had already lost the

---

14. U. S. Forest Service, *Insulating Board, Hardboard, and Other Structural Fiberboards*, Research Note, FPL-077 (Madison, Wisconsin: Forest Products Laboratory, August 1965).

15. National Forest Products Association, *Forest Products Industry Facts, 1966*, p. 17.

16. Herb Lambert, "Board Production Up Across the Board in the U. S. and Canada," *Forest Industries*, July 1969, p. 25.

17. National Forest Products Association, *loc. cit.*

18. Lambert, *loc cit.*

19. John G. Glover and William B. Cornell, *The Development of American Industry* (New York: Prentice-Hall, Inc., 1946), p. 107.

20. Alfred J. Van Tassel, *Mechanization in the Lumber Industry*, National Research Project, Report No. M-5 (Philadelphia: Works Project Administration, March 1940), Chapter 2.

TABLE 3. *Lumber and Wood Products Industry*
Lumber Production by Region, 1869-1963
(Millions of Board Feet)

Year	Total United States Production	Percent of Total	South Region Production	Percent of Total	Northeast Region Production	Percent of Total	Midwest Region Production	Percent of Total	Far West Region Production	Percent of Total
1869	12,756	100.0	1,898	14.9	4,443	34.8	5,795	45.4	620	4.9
1879	18,125	100.0	3,448	19.0	4,511	24.9	9,319	51.4	847	4.7
1889	27,039	100.0	6,496	24.0	5,271	19.5	12,811	47.4	2,461	9.1
1899	35,078	100.0	13,839	39.5	5,490	15.7	12,259	34.9	3,490	9.9
1909	44,510	100.0	23,854	53.6	4,874	11.0	7,543	16.9	8,239	18.5
1919	34,552	100.0	18,287	52.9	2,443	7.1	3,662	10.6	10,160	29.4
1929	38,745	100.0	18,415	47.5	1,577	4.1	2,700	7.0	16,053	41.4
1939	28,755	100.0	13,164	45.8	1,706	5.9	1,814	6.3	12,071	42.0
1947	35,404	100.0	14,749	41.7	2,136	6.0	2,182	6.2	16,337	46.1
1954	36,356	100.0	12,815	35.2	1,873	5.2	1,688	4.6	19,980	55.0
1958	33,384	100.0	10,620	31.8	1,504	4.5	1,559	4.7	19,701	59.0
1963	34,706	100.0	11,236	32.4	1,479	4.3	1,676	4.8	20,315	58.5

Source: 1869-1989: U.S. Department of Agriculture, *Lumber Production in the United States, 1799-1946*, Miscellaneous Publication No. 669, October 1948, Table 4, pp. 11-18.

1947-1963: *U.S. Census of Manufactures:*

1947: Vol. II, *Statistics by Industry*, Table 6-D, p. 263.

1954: Vol. II, *Industry Statistics*, Part 1, Table 6-C, pp. 24A-16—24A-18.

1958: Vol. II, *Industry Statistics*, Part 1, Table 6-C, p. 24A-17.

1963: Vol. II, *Industry Statistics*, Part 1, Table 6-E, p. 24A-27.

Regional Definitions:

South: Alabama, Arkansas, Delaware, District of Columbia, Florida, Georgia, Kentucky, Louisiana, Maryland, Mississippi, North Carolina, Oklahoma, South Carolina, Tennessee, Texas, Virginia, West Virginia.

Northeast: Connecticut, Maine, Massachusetts, New Hampshire, New Jersey, New York, Pennsylvania, Rhode Island, Vermont.

Midwest: Illinois, Indiana, Iowa, Kansas, Michigan, Minnesota, Missouri, Nebraska, North Dakota, Ohio, South Dakota, Wisconsin.

Far West: Arizona, California, Colorado, Idaho, Montana, Nevada, New Mexico, Oregon, Utah, Washington, Wyoming.

lead in yearly production to the Midwest region which was producing 45.4 percent of the total. The South gradually took the
lead until it reached its peak in 1909 with almost 54 percent of
the total United States production. At that time the Far West
was producing only 18.5 percent of the total. In 1963 (the most
recent data available) the Far West's share of the total production had grown to almost 59 percent, and almost 91 percent of
the lumber was produced in the Far West and South. For this
reason and because of the large supply of Negro labor in the
South, this study will concentrate on these two regions with primary focus on the South.

South Region

In 1968, timber cut in the South was estimated at 5.7 billion
cubic feet (2.5 billion for sawlogs, veneer, and plywood; 2.1 billion for pulpwood; and 1.1 billion for other uses). Net growth
was estimated at 8.2 billion cubic feet (one-half softwood and
one-half hardwood).[21] With this excess of timber growth over
timber consumption, the South promises to be the answer to
many of the nation's future wood problems. The South has a
rainfall and temperature pattern which permits long growing
seasons. Most of the soil is also favorable with a balanced mineral content that makes fertilizing unnecessary. The mild cli-
mate permits almost year around logging and the topography
allows the economic logging of younger stands.[22]

The nature of the southern timber stand has imposed certain
characteristics on lumbering in this region, however. Timber in
this area is generally second or third growth, and until tree
farming became prevalent in recent years the timber was found
principally in small scattered tracts. As a result there were a
large number of small producers in the region and the use of
heavy, highly mechanized equipment was greatly limited. Much
of the logging and sawing was carried on by farmers as a part-
time activity supplementary to agriculture. These small mills
differed not only in size, but in basic type, from the larger mills.
Generally speaking, a mill cutting fewer than a million board
feet a year was a portable mill and was commonly referred to

---

21. "Resource Analysis," *Forest Industries*, Vol. 96, No. 7 (June 1969),
p. 35.

22. "How the Third Forest in the South will be Managed," *Pulp and Paper*,
Vol. 43, No. 4 (April 1969), p. 111.

as a "peckerwood" mill. They operated in the midst of a small lumber stand until the supply was depleted, and then moved to another stand. They had no seasoning or planing facilities and produced solely rough green lumber. Today the small peckerwood mills have almost disappeared. They were dependent upon a ready supply of cheap labor of which they have been deprived by minimum wage legislation.[23]

Between 1947 and 1967, the number of sawmills in the South dropped from 24,000 to 5,000.[24] The remaining mills are the larger ones which normally operate their own seasoning and planing facilities and are generally managed on a sustained yield basis (the amount of lumber cut each year being held in balance with the amount of growth). These mills pay higher wages and require a more dependable work force.

The growth cycle of the southern pine is such that the fiber production per acre can be maximized by cutting the trees at about twenty years of age. This is the major reason for the rapid expansion of the pulp and paper industry in the South in recent years. The pulpwood harvest in the South has increased steadily during the past ten years, and the production of hardboard, which does not rely on large trees, has doubled in the past decade.[25] New methods that make use of smaller logs in the production of plywood have allowed great expansion of this industry in the South. The first plywood plant was built in the South in 1963. The Southern Forest Experiment Station of the U. S. Forest Service estimates that by 1975 the South will be producing at least six billion square feet of plywood annually —30 percent of the nation's projected requirements.[26] There are no data yet available, but it appears that the plywood industry will be a great potential source of employment for the Negroes of the South.

Far West Region

Because of the great concentration of the timber stands and the large size of the trees, western operations are more highly

23. Field notes, 1969.

24. Southern Forest Resource Analysis Committee, *The South's Third Forest,* 1969, p. 4.

25. *International Woodworker,* Publication of the International Woodworkers of America, Vol. 34, No. 7 (April 9, 1969), p. 1.

26. "South's Plywood Future Assured," *Southern Lumberman,* Vol. 219, No. 2718 (July 15, 1969), p. 6.

mechanized than operations in other regions. As a result, productivity of western labor is also far greater.

The density of the timber stands, the large size of the trees, and the rugged topography of much of the Far West make both logging and sawmilling more complicated than in other regions. More use is made of railroad cars for transporting logs to the mills; bandsaws rather than circular saws are used almost exclusively for headsaws (often with teeth on both edges so the log can be cut both coming and going); gigantic hydraulic debarkers, which knock the bark off the logs with a stream of high pressure water, are often used instead of the mechanical debarkers; and, of course, most of the equipment up to the lumber stage of production is larger and more costly.

MANPOWER

Lumber employment has fluctuated with lumber production in this century. Although employment in all manufacturing increased from 7,514,000 to 19,398,000 between 1914 and 1967, as shown in Table 4, employment in the lumber industry decreased from 717,727 to 563,000. In 1960, employment in the lumber and wood products industry constituted only 3.9 percent of the total employment of the manufacturing industries in the United States. In the South, however, lumber employment is much more significant. In 1960 lumber and wood products made up 8.2 percent of the total southern industrial employment. The industry was the fourth largest southern industry in number of employees, with 326,905 employees, and the leading employer of Negroes. Almost 27 percent of all Negroes employed in manufacturing in the South were employed by the lumber industry. There were 135,887 Negro employees, 41.6 percent of the work force.[27]

Occupational Distribution

Table 4 shows that employment in the lumber industry has been overwhelmingly blue collar—much more so than the average manufacturing industry. This is a result of the lack of significant technological advancement in the form of increased automation and mechanization.

---

27. *U. S. Census of Population, 1960*, PC(1) 1D, *U. S. Summary*, Table 260.

TABLE 4. *Lumber and Wood Products Industry and All Manufacturing*
Total and Production Worker Employment
United States, 1914-1967

Year	Lumber and Wood Products			All Manufacturing		
	All Employees	Production Workers	Percent Production Workers	All Employees	Production Workers	Percent Production Workers
	(In Thousands)			(In Thousands)		
1914	717,727	671,580	93.6	7,514	6,602	87.9
1919	714,592	663,414	92.8	9,837	8,465	86.1
1925	725,762	674,217	92.9	9,142	7,871	86.1
1929	651,259	603,426	92.7	9,660	8,370	86.6
1935	414,455	384,160	92.7	8,262	7,204	87.2
1947	641,799	601,412	93.7	14,294	11,918	83.4
1954	645,963	581,920	90.1	15,645	12,372	79.1
1958	585,372	508,883	86.9	15,423	11,681	75.7
1963	563,135	497,409	88.3	16,235	12,232	75.3
1967	563,000	500,000	88.8	19,398	13,975	72.0

Source: *U. S. Census of Manufactures:*
1914-1963: Vol. II, *Industry Statistics*, Part 1.
1967: MC67(P)-1, *Summary Series*, Preliminary Report, April 1969.

Extensive use will be made of Equal Employment Opportunity Commission (EEOC) data in later chapters. The occupational distribution of lumber industry employees based on 1966 EEOC data is shown in Table 5. The EEOC data were obtained from companies which employed 100 or more employees or which had contracts with the federal government.[28] Many of the small mills and logging contractors do not meet either of these criteria. Nevertheless, the data do show the occupational characteristics of the industry—an overwhelming blue collar concentration, heavily in the lower classification. The largest group in the white collar classification is officials and managers—obviously the result of the large number of small establishments. Operatives and laborers make up most of the blue collar workers. There are few bars of education or training to block entry to the industry.

TABLE 5. *Lumber and Wood Products Industry Employment by Occupational Group 1,348 Establishments Total United States, 1966*

Occupational Group	Employees	Percent of Total
Officials and managers	12,470	5.2
Professionals	2,781	1.2
Technicians	2,639	1.1
Sales workers	3,239	1.4
Office and clerical	12,090	5.0
Total white collar	33,219	13.9
Craftsmen	36,295	15.1
Operatives	84,139	35.1
Laborers	83,146	34.7
Service workers	2,793	1.2
Total blue collar	206,373	86.1
Total	239,592	100.0

Source: U. S. Equal Employment Opportunity Commission, *Job Patterns for Minorities and Women in Private Industry, 1966*, Report No. 1 (Washington: The Commission, 1968), Part II.

28. EEO-1 reports for 1966 were submitted by employers subject to Title VII of the Civil Rights Act of 1964 with 100 or more employees, and by employers holding federal government contracts or first subcontracts or purchase orders of $50,000 or more with 50 or more employees.

Education

One would expect that an industry that employed a larger-than-average percent of manual laboring workers would also hire individuals that are, on the average, less well educated. For the lumber industry this has been markedly the situation. Table 6 shows the number and percent of the experienced work force in 1960 that had attained different levels of formal education for all manufacturing industries together and for the lumber industry alone. It also shows the cumulative percent, i.e., the percent of the work force that has attained each educational level or one higher. It can be seen that while 13.9 percent of the labor force of the manufacturing industries have some college education, only 5.8 percent of the lumber industry labor force can claim this achievement. Likewise, 41.6 percent of the manufacturing labor force have completed high school compared with 22.7 percent of the lumber work force. Even more important is the comparison of elementary school graduates—82.5 percent for manufacturing and 62.2 percent for the lumber industry.

Table 6 also shows the level of formal education attained by the Negro work force of the lumber industry. Only 28.5 percent of the Negro labor force completed the eighth grade compared with 59.7 percent for Negroes in all manufacturing and 82.5 percent for all employees in all manufacturing.

The lower educational level of the lumber industry work force is particularly significant for purposes of this study. Since the industry has not become highly mechanized or automated, it is still possible to hire workers who would not meet the educational requirements of many industries. This characteristic of the industry coupled with its heavy concentration in the South largely explain the racial employment practices of the industry.

Female Employment

Women have never been a very significant component of the lumber industry work force. Table 7 shows the percent female employment in 1968 for all the manufacturing industries as a group and for the lumber industry and its components. The striking difference between the concentration of women in manufacturing (27.7 percent) and in the lumber industry (9.8 percent) is due primarily to the nature and location of the work. Most logging camps and many mills are located in isolated areas. Much of the work is physically difficult and dirty. Lumber work-

TABLE 6. Lumber and Wood Products Industry and All Manufacturing Years of School Completed for the Experienced Civilian Labor Force by Race, 1960

School Years Completed	Total Labor Force						Negro Labor Force					
	All Manufacturing			Lumber and Wood Products			All Manufacturing			Lumber and Wood Products		
	Number	Percent of Total	Cumulative Percent	Number	Percent of Total	Cumulative Percent	Number	Percent of Total	Cumulative Percent	Number	Percent of Total	Cumulative Percent
College												
5 or more	319,050	1.7	1.7	2,749	0.4	0.4	2,913	0.2	0.2	—	—	—
4	773,193	4.2	5.9	10,765	1.4	1.8	8,647	0.7	0.9	110	0.1	0.1
1 to 3	1,480,636	8.0	13.9	29,725	4.0	5.8	47,461	3.7	4.6	895	0.6	0.7
High school												
4	5,132,568	27.7	41.6	126,195	16.9	22.7	214,694	16.7	21.3	7,242	4.8	5.5
1 to 3	4,472,737	24.1	65.7	151,234	20.2	42.9	316,199	24.7	46.0	20,631	13.6	19.1
Elementary school												
8	3,121,581	16.8	82.5	144,299	19.3	62.2	174,998	13.7	59.7	14,187	9.4	28.5
5 to 7	2,379,306	12.8	95.3	160,129	21.4	83.6	295,459	23.1	82.8	45,865	30.4	58.9
less than 5	880,990	4.7	100.0	122,211	16.4	100.0	220,162	17.2	100.0	62,135	41.1	100.0
Total	18,560,061	100.0		747,307	100.0		1,280,533	100.0		151,065	100.0	

Source: *U. S. Census of Population, 1960,* PC(2) 7F, *Industrial Characteristics,* Table 21, pp. 98-100, and Table 15, pp. 187-190.

TABLE 7. *Lumber and Wood Products Industry and All Manufacturing Total and Female Employment, 1968*

Standard Industrial Classification	Industry	All Employees	Female Employees	Percent Female
	All manufacturing	19,740,000	5,476,000	27.7
24	Lumber and wood products	601,600	59,000	9.8
241	Logging camps and logging contractors	80,700	3,600	4.5
242	Sawmills and planing mills	233,800	12,600	5.4
243	Millwork, plywood, and related products	165,300	17,800	10.8
244	Wooden containers	36,600	6,500	17.8
249	Misc. wood products	85,200	18,600	21.8

Source: *Employment and Earnings*, Vol. 15, No. 9 (March 1969), Tables B-2 and B-3.

ers have a reputation of using rather rough language and the safety record of the industry has been rather poor. Generally speaking, as the Standard Industrial Classification for the components of the lumber industry increases, the sizes of the pieces of wood to be handled become smaller. This would appear to explain the increasing percentage of female workers as the SIC increases. It is easier to envision a woman packing toothpicks in boxes than loading logs on a rail car.

Wages and Turnover Data

Wage rates in the lumber industry are low. Table 8 shows that the average weekly and hourly earnings of production workers in the lumber industry are lower than both durable and nondurable goods manufacturing averages. Generally, there is an inverse relationship between the wage rate and the turnover rate, i.e., as wages go up, turnover goes down. The lumber industry, however, is a notable exception. Although it does not pay the very lowest wages of all industry, it does have the high-

TABLE 8. *Lumber Industry and All Manufacturing*
Production Workers
Average Earnings and Hours Worked, 1968

	Average Weekly Earnings	Average Hourly Earnings	Average Weekly Hours
All manufacturing	$122.51	$3.01	40.7
Durable goods	132.07	3.19	41.4
Nondurable goods	109.05	2.74	39.8
Lumber and wood products	103.68	2.56	40.5
Sawmills and planing mills	100.28	2.47	40.6
Millwork, plywood, and related products	112.06	2.72	41.2
Wooden containers	86.33	2.18	39.6
Miscellaneous wood products	92.52	2.29	40.4

Source: *Employment and Earnings*, Vol. 15 (March 1969), Table C-2.

est turnover rate (Table 9).[29] This is a result of the poor working and living conditions, the number of workers who do not depend on the lumber industry as their sole source of income, and the seasonability of the logging operations in many areas.

In private correspondence, Professor William A. Duerr, Chairman of the Department of Forestry Economics at Syracuse University, made the following statement:

The lumber industry, which is a sick industry and, indeed, has been in ill health for a great many years, has relied rather heavily upon subsidy from its labor in the form of low wage rates. Amongst the little mills which are exceedingly prominent in this industry, family labor is common and the firm resembles, in many ways, the subsistence farm family. In those segments of the industry which use employed labor, there has been some tendency to gravitate toward rural areas which are depressed or which, for some other reason, offer a supply of cheap labor.[30]

---

29. See the Paper and Tobacco studies in this Series for comparable data.

30. Letter from Dr. William A. Duerr, Chairman, Department of Forestry Economics, State University College of Forestry at Syracuse University, January 22, 1969.

TABLE 9. *Lumber and Wood Products Industry Turnover 1958 and 1968*

Per 100 Employees	Year	Lumber and Wood Products (SIC 24)	Sawmills and Planing Mills (SIC 242)	Millwork, Plywood, and Related Products (SIC 243)	Wooden Containers (SIC 244)	Misc. Wood Products (SIC 249)
Accessions	1958	4.8	3.9	3.9	4.8	3.8
	1968	6.5	5.9	5.8	7.3	6.3
New hires	1958	2.9	2.5	2.6	2.4	2.1
	1968	5.5	5.2	5.2	6.1	5.3
Separations	1958	4.9	4.1	3.8	5.1	4.3
	1968	6.4	5.7	5.6	7.4	6.2
Quits	1958	1.7	1.7	1.4	1.5	1.3
	1968	4.2	4.1	3.9	4.5	4.1
Layoffs	1958	2.6	1.9	1.8	3.1	2.3
	1968	1.2	0.8	0.8	1.7	1.0

Source: U. S. Bureau of Labor Statistics, *Employment and Earnings Statistics for the United States,* Bulletin No. 1312-6, pp. 71-93 and *Employment and Earnings,* Vol. 15 (April 1969), Table D-2.

Note: No data available for SIC 241, Logging Camps and Logging Contractors.

The low level of productivity, the minimum skill and educational requirements of much of the work, the poor profit position of the industry, the high concentration of employment in the South, the availability of Negro labor in the South, and the lack of union strength (especially in the South) all have contributed to the poor earnings position of the lumber worker.

Lumber industry wages are lower in the South than in the Far West. Table 10 shows the wage rates for different logging, sawmill, and planing mill occupations for the South in 1965 and for the Far West in 1964. Despite the fact that the Bureau of Labor Statistics data for the Far West are for a period one year prior to that of the southern data, the southern workers doing the same job received just over one-half the pay of their western counterparts.

Because wage rates in the southern lumber industry have been so low, they have been markedly affected by minimum wage legislation. When the Fair Labor Standards Act (FLSA) minimum of 25 cents an hour became effective in 1938, the average wage rate in southern lumber rose from 27 to 31 cents per hour.[31] When the National War Labor Board set the 50 cent per hour minimum in 1943, lumber industry pay in Texas was 44 cents per hour.[32] When the FLSA minimum of 75 cents became effective in 1950, southern lumber wages immediately rose 11 cents to 80 cents per hour.[33] One reason that lumber wages fell so far behind manufacturing wages in the South is that for many years the small logging crews of less than a dozen men were exempted from minimum wage legislation because of the problems of keeping records on them.[34] This encouraged the small logger to use the cheapest labor he could locate—usually the Negro.

Unionization

The major labor organizations in the industry are the International Woodworkers of America (IWA) and the Lumber and Sawmill Workers (LSW), affiliated with the United Brotherhood

31. "Earnings in Southern Lumber," *Monthly Labor Review*, Vol. 76, No. 10 (October 1953), pp. 1077-1081.

32. Ruth Alice Allen, *East Texas Lumber Workers* (Austin: University of Texas Press, 1961).

33. "Earnings in Southern Lumber," *loc. cit.*

34. Albert W. Wilson, "Forest Industries, the Government and the Public Interest," *The MBA*, December 1968, p. 24.

TABLE 10. *Sawmill, Planing Mill, and Logging Wages*
Selected Occupations
South Region, 1965 and Far West Region, 1964

	South, 1965		Far West, 1964	
Occupation	Number of Workers	Average Hourly Earnings	Number of Workers	Average Hourly Earnings
Sawmills and Planing Mills				
Block setters	802	$1.38	183	$2.66
Carrier drivers	573	1.35	1,311	2.53
Cutoff-saw operators	1,951	1.34	255	2.46
Edgermen	3,141	1.37	1,200	2.74
Firemen	2,179	1.30	807	2.43
Graders, lumber (green chain)	681	1.49	582	2.73
Graders, planed lumber	1,109	1.48	1,231	2.86
Head-saw operators, band saw	470	2.70	860	3.51
Loaders, car and truck	2,529	1.29	1,768	2.92
Log deckmen	1,981	1.30	302	2.41
Lumber stackers, air dry or storage	5,657	1.29	364	2.72
Lumber stackers, kiln drying	1,956	1.30	682	2.83
Off-bearers, machine	7,838	1.29	676	2.34
Planer operators				
Feed only	1,500	1.31	818	2.44
Set up and operate	1,093	1.78	525	2.84
Pondmen	143	1.35	1,177	2.45
Sorters, green chain	2,748	1.28	4,391	2.47
Trimmermen	2,402	1.31	1,098	2.57
Watchmen	1,340	1.27	651	2.20
Logging				
Cat drivers, skidding	1,191	1.44	732	2.97
Chokermen	641	1.31	1,795	2.59
Fallers and burkers	2,033	1.37	2,213	4.77
Ground loaders	743	1.30	144	2.64
Truckdrivers	1,600	1.34	1,527	2.70

Source: U. S. Bureau of Labor Statistics, *Industry Wage Survey, West Coast Sawmilling,* June 1964, Bulletin No. 1455 and *Southern Sawmills and Planing Mills,* October 1965, Bulletin No. 1519.

Note: For regional definitions, see Table 3; for occupational definitions see Appendix A.

of Carpenters and Joiners of America (UBCJA, primarily a construction workers union). Both unions are affiliated with the AFL-CIO—the IWA being a former member of the old Congress of Industrial Organizations and the UBCJA a longtime member of the American Federation of Labor. In the Far West, the LSW predominates in the western pine region, while the IWA is strong in the Douglas fir and redwood regions.[35] The South is much less unionized than the Far West. In 1958 the lumber and wood products industry was rated next to the last in a listing of 19 southern industries in order of their degree of unionization based on percent of collective bargaining coverage. The one industry that ranked lower was the textile industry.[36] In 1965, sawmills and planing mills with a labor-management contract covering a majority of their production workers accounted for only one-eighth of the workers in the industry. Unionization in the South is highest in the southwestern states of the region.[37]

Unions have found it difficult to organize the many small, privately-owned logging contractors, sawmills and planing mills, plywood plants, etc. Nine-tenths of the workers in union mills in the South are in establishments employing 100 or more workers.[38] Many of the logging contractors and mill operators are rather rugged individualists who refuse to give up any of their decision-making authority. Many of the managers and workers are only part-time lumbermen and depend on agriculture or some other occupation for their main source of income. Also, the fact that many of the workers are from an agrarian background where unionization has always been rather limited has probably increased worker resistance.

---

35. U. S. Bureau of Labor Statistics, *Industry Wage Survey, West Coast Sawmilling*, Bulletin No. 1455, June 1964, p. 2.

36. H. M. Douty, "Collective Bargaining Coverage in Factory Employment, 1958," *Monthly Labor Review*, Vol. 85, No. 4 (April 1962).

37. U. S. Bureau of Labor Statistics, *Industry Wage Survey, Southern Sawmills and Planing Mills*, Bulletin No. 1519, October 1965, p. 3.

38. *Ibid.*

CHAPTER III

Negro Employment to 1960

This chapter traces the progress of the Negro in the lumber industry from slavery to 1960.

FROM SLAVERY TO WORLD WAR II

Negro labor has been used in the lumber industry since the time of slavery. As Pinchbeck explains:

Carpenters and coopers were probably the most numerous of the Virginia colonial slaves trained in the crafts. The widespread presence of slaves versed in these and other crafts involving wood work was probably due to the fact that not only the houses of the early planters but practically all of their general equipment was made of wood. The products of the colony demanded barrels and other wooden containers. The river craft and barges were constructed of wood. In most instances sleds or crude wooden wagons were used to transport articles about the plantations. In the absence of power sawmills, Negro slaves with the use of rip saws sawed boards from logs or hewed beams with the use of adzes. Thus, the operation of the large plantations constantly demanded the services of coopers, sawyers, carpenters, and joiners.

Current records of the time reveal a great number of sawyers among Virginia colonial slaves. The majority of the large plantations had their own slave sawyers. However, not infrequently, planters hired the services of the slave sawyers from other planters.[39]

Phillips also makes reference to the use of Negro slaves as helpers to sawyers in the South.[40] Negro slaves were not utilized solely in southern lumber manufacture; Turner refers to their use as coopers in Pennsylvania[41] and Greene states that Negro

---

39. Raymond B. Pinchbeck, *The Virginia Negro Artisan and Tradesman* (Richmond: William Byrd Press, 1926), p. 32.

40. Ulrich B. Phillips, *Life and Labor in the Old South* (Boston: Little, Brown, and Company, 1939), p. 307.

41. Edward R. Turner, *The Negro in Pennsylvania, 1639-1861* (Washington: American Historical Association, 1911), p. 41.

slaves were employed to a minor degree in lumbering even in New England.[42]

Negro labor was probably used more extensively in the early logging operations that more closely resembled the agricultural work to which most slaves were accustomed than in the saw and planing mill facilities. This type of work is simpler, physically more strenuous, and more easily supervised. Sydnor reports that slaves often helped wood-cutters along the Mississippi River to chop and stack wood along the river bank for the steamboats. Some of these Negroes were fugitive slaves to which the wood-cutters gave refuge.[43] Hired-out slaves were probably most often used for heavy logging operations.

The Civil War to 1910

The Civil War cost the South much of its prime labor through war casualties. Reconstruction brought with it a great demand for labor of all kinds and also a demand for lumber for rebuilding. The timber supply of the Lake States was rapidly diminishing and the lumber industry started its shift to the South. Table 11 shows that by 1890 there were 17,276 Negroes employed in sawmills. Most of these Negroes had been field hands on the old southern plantations. In the Delta region of Mississippi, western capitalists purchased a million acres of timberland and brought Negro slave laborers from the decadent plantations. A number of freedmen also set themselves up as independent enterprisers to supply wood to steamboats from yards along the banks of the Mississippi River.[44]

The story was similar in South Carolina. Around the turn of the century many Negroes were left without work because of the decline in rice planting. When the Atlantic Coast Lumber Company moved into Georgetown, South Carolina, many Negroes went to the city to work in the mill, and many others stayed in the country to cut timber for the company's use.[45]

---

42. Lorenzo J. Greene, *Negro in Colonial New England, 1620-1776* (New York: Columbia University Press, 1942), p. 111.

43. Charles Sackett Sydnor, *Slavery in Mississippi* (New York: D. Appleton-Century Company, Inc., 1933), p. 8.

44. Vernon Lane Wharton, *The Negro in Mississippi, 1865-1890* (New York: Harper and Row, 1965), pp. 125-126.

45. George Brown Tindall, *South Carolina Negroes, 1877-1900* (Columbia: University of South Carolina Press, 1952), p. 127.

TABLE 11. Sawmills and Planing Mills
Employment by Race and Sex
Total United States, 1890–1960

Year	All Employees			Male Employees			Female Employees		
	Total	Negro	Percent Negro	Total	Negro	Percent Negro	Total	Negro	Percent Negro
1890	138,678	17,276	12.5	138,386	17,247	12.5	292	29	9.9
1900	161,624	33,266	20.6	161,251	33,156	20.6	373	110	29.5
1910	466,624	111,223	23.8	462,981	110,453	23.9	3,643	770	21.1
1930	454,503	113,862	25.1	444,782	112,264	25.2	9,721	1,598	16.4
1940	435,559	113,029	26.0	427,072	112,208	26.3	8,487	821	9.7
1950ᵃ	586,360	143,096	24.4	566,304	140,882	24.9	20,056	2,214	11.0
1960ᵃ	416,136	76,369	18.4	395,855	75,085	19.0	20,281	1,284	6.3

Source: *U. S. Census of Population:*

1890 and 1900: *Occupations,* Chapter II, Table 3, p. xliv; Table 33, p. cvii; Table 34, p. cix; and *Negroes in the United States,* Census Bulletin No. 8, 1904, Table 63, p. 58.

1910: Vol. IV, *Occupation Statistics,* Table 6, p. 360.
1930: Vol. V, *General Report of Occupations,* Chapter VII, Table 2, p. 504.
1940: Vol. III, *The Labor Force,* Part 1, Table 76, p. 188.
1950: Vol. II, *Characteristics of the Population,* Part 1, Table 133, p. 288.
1960: PC(2) 7F, *Industrial Characteristics,* Table 3, p. 7.

Note: 1920 Census gives racial employment data for laborers and operatives only.
ᵃ Includes millwork; 1960 includes Alaska and Hawaii.

By 1910 the Negro had become a critical constituent of the work force of the lumber and wood products industry. Negro workers comprised 23.8 percent of the sawmill workers in the country (Table 11). Table 12 shows that 15.1 percent of the logging employees were Negro; census figures indicate that 9.0 percent of those employed in wooden box factories were Negro (17,987 employees; 1,611 Negro employees).[46]

Lumber industry Negro workers increased more than five-fold between 1890 and 1910 and "in 1910 represented more than one-fifth of all Negroes in industry. This was due in part to the ruthless exploitation of the vast forests of the South about which there was much complaint followed by the usual inaction. . . . The Negroes, because of the heavy, rough work to be performed were generally preferred as common laborers. In this capacity it was said that they had no superior. This hard work, too, was distasteful to the whites. The small wages, 50 cents to 75 cents a day, however, partly account for this monopoly of the Negroes in these factories." [47]

In sawmills and planing mills, however, many of the exslaves had progressed far beyond the laboring categories of employment by 1910 (Table 13). Fourteen percent of the operatives and almost 6 percent of the craftsmen were Negroes. Many of the 533 Negro officials and managers were owners. Of the 169 other white collar workers, more than one-half were in the lowest category. In 1910, 2.5 percent of the owners and managers of logging camps were Negroes (Table 12). This was a result of the very low cost of land in the South after the Civil War as the plantations died out.

World War I to the Depression

At the same time that Negroes were migrating North to find employment in industries expanding as a result of World War I, the lumber industry started its move westward. Between 1909 and 1929, lumber production in the South fell from 23,854 to 18,415 million board feet and in the Far West it increased from 8,239 to 16,053 million board feet. (See Table 3, p. 10.)

---

46. U. S. Bureau of the Census, *Negro Population in the United States, 1790 to 1915*, Table 22, p. 531.

47. L. J. Greene and C. G. Woodson, *The Negro Wage Earner* (Washington: Associated Publishers, Inc., 1930), pp. 124-125.

TABLE 12. *Logging Operations*

Total and Negro Employment by Occupational Group
United States, 1910-1930

Occupational Group	1910			1920			1930		
	Total	Negro	Percent Negro	Total	Negro	Percent Negro	Total	Negro	Percent Negro
Owners and managers	7,931	195	2.5	8,410	122	1.5	6,899	66	1.0
Foremen and overseers	4,798	111	2.3	6,090	118	1.9	3,910	92	2.4
Teamsters and haulers	15,038	2,465	16.4	17,106	1,930	11.3	9,243	1,917	20.7
Lumbermen, raftsmen, and woodchoppers	141,432	22,720	16.1	179,775	23,395	13.0	146,896	22,429	15.3
Inspectors, scalers, and surveyors	n.a.	n.a.	n.a.	2,344	44	1.9	2,184	32	1.5
Total	169,199	25,491	15.1	213,725	25,609	12.0	169,132	24,536	14.5

Source: *U. S. Census of Population:*

1910: Vol. IV, *Occupational Statistics,* Table 1, p. 91; and *Negro Population in the United States, 1790-1915,* Table 19, p. 523.

1920: Vol. IV, *Occupations,* Chapter III, Table 5, pp. 342-343.

1930: Vol. V, *General Report on Occupations,* Chapter II, Table 3, p. 76.

TABLE 13.   *Sawmills and Planing Mills*
Total and Negro Employment by Occupational Group
United States, 1910

Occupational Group	Total	Negro	Percent Negro
Officials and managers[a]	39,997	533	1.3
Professional, technical, sales, office, and clerical workers[a]	8,905	169	1.9
Craftsmen[a]	65,526	3,830	5.8
Operatives	66,060	9,322	14.1
Laborers	260,142	91,887	35.3
Other and not classified[a]	25,994	5,482	21.1
Total	466,624	111,223	23.8

Source: *U. S. Census of Population, 1910*, Vol. IV, *Occupational Statistics*,
Table 1, p. 91; and *Negro Population in the United States, 1790-
1915*, Tables 19 and 22, pp. 523, 542.

[a] Estimated from analysis of occupational listings in *Negro Population*, Table
22. Officials and managers consist of manufacturers, proprietors, officials,
managers, superintendents, foremen, and overseers.

Professional, technical, sales, office, and clerical consist of bookkeepers,
cashiers, accountants, clerks, designers, draftsmen, purchasing agents, and
messenger, errand, and office boys.

Craftsmen consist of blacksmiths, boilermakers, cabinetmakers, carpenters,
coopers, electricians, stationary engineers, machinists, mechanics, mill-
wrights, painters, plumbers, and sawyers.

One might expect that, in the face of these conditions, Negro
employment in the lumber industry would have fallen. To the
contrary, while employment in sawmills fell from 466,624 in
1910 to 454,503 in 1930, Negro employment increased from 111,-
223 to 113,862—from 23.8 to 25.1 percent (Table 11). Whites as
well as Negroes were leaving the South and the sawmill owners
were forced to make greater use of the large pool of Negro
labor remaining.

The Depression to World War II

During the period from 1930 to 1936, almost one-half of the
skilled Negro males in the nation were displaced from their

usual types of employment.[48] The Bureau of Labor Statistics reported in 1931 that there was a tendency to substitute white for colored workers, i.e., whites were taking over forms of work hitherto held as properly belonging to Negro workers.[49]

Considering the economic conditions of the time, one would expect to find a decrease in the utilization of Negroes in the lumber industry during the period from 1930 to 1940. Although production of lumber in 1939 was about 10 million board feet less than in 1929 (see Table 1, p. 3), Negro employment did not suffer disproportionately.

During the slow recovery from the depression, some industries began to shift their operations to the South. Lumber's sister industry, paper and allied products, began a large-scale movement to the South in the 1930's.[50] Recent interviews with some southern lumber producers revealed a general sentiment that the growth of the high wage paper industry had drained off the supply of skilled labor. It appears that as economic conditions began to improve in the late 1930's, many of the white skilled lumber workers who had been laid off found employment in other industries, and the less skilled and less well educated Negroes returned to the lumber industry.

Table 11 shows that Negro employment in sawmills increased about one percent between 1930 and 1940. In logging, Negro employment increased from 14.5 to 17.2 percent during the decade (Tables 12 and 14). These figures probably underestimate the true increase in Negro representation because, beginning in 1940, data include other, less numerous skilled occupations (such as mechanics, machinists, and engineers) in which Negroes have been poorly represented.

World War II to 1960

Between 1940 and 1944, the Negro worker made significant employment advances. "Over a million entered civilian jobs. They moved from the farm to the factory. The number of Negroes employed at skilled jobs doubled. . . . The war gave many Negroes their first opportunity to demonstrate ability to

48. Robert C. Weaver, *Negro Labor* (New York: Harcort, Brace and Company, 1946), p. 9.

49. "The Negro in the Industrial Depression," *Monthly Labor Review*, Vol. 32, No. 6 (June 1931), p. 60.

50. See the paper industry study in this Series, p. 31.

TABLE 14. Logging Operations
Employment by Race and Sex
United States and Regions, 1940–1960

Year	All Employees			Male			Female		
	Total	Negro	Percent Negro	Total	Negro	Percent Negro	Total	Negro	Percent Negro
Total United States									
1940	141,495	24,315	17.2	140,233	24,165	17.2	1,262	150	11.9
1950	171,897	34,263	19.9	169,700	33,951	20.0	2,197	312	14.2
1960a	168,360	47,500	28.2	165,762	47,125	28.4	2,598	375	14.4
South									
1940	61,427	24,048	39.1	61,035	23,902	39.2	392	146	37.2
1950	80,584	33,826	42.0	79,757	33,530	42.0	827	296	35.8
1960	97,949	47,163	48.2	96,925	46,796	48.3	1,024	367	35.8
Northeast									
1940	16,935	65	0.4	16,783	62	0.4	152	3	2.0
1950	17,413	132	0.8	17,199	127	0.7	214	5	2.3
1960	13,682	113	0.8	13,435	109	0.8	247	4	1.6

						Midwest		
1940	16,428	139	0.8	16,258	138	0.8	170	1	0.6
1950	16,364	170	1.0	16,079	164	1.0	285	6	2.1
1960	15,056	117	0.8	14,741	113	0.8	315	4	1.3
						Far West		
1940	46,705	63	0.1	46,157	63	0.1	548	—	—
1950	57,536	135	0.2	56,665	130	0.2	871	5	0.6
1960	41,673	107	0.3	40,661	107	0.3	1,012	—	—

Source: *U. S. Census of Population:*

1940: Vol. III, *The Labor Force*, Part 1, Tables 76 and 77.

1950: Vol. II, *Characteristics of the Population*, Part 1, Tables 133 and 161.

1960: PC(1) 1D, *U. S. Summary*, Tables 213 and 260.

Note: For regional definitions, see Table 3.

ᵃ Includes Alaska and Hawaii.

perform basic factory operations of skilled, single-skilled, and semi-skilled types in a wide range of industries and plants."[51] In the lumber industry, however, there was a negligibly small decrease in Negro employment, from 23.8 percent in 1940 to 23.4 percent in 1950.[52] This occurred through a decrease in the sawmill segment from 26.0 to 24.2 percent (Table 11) and an increase in the logging segment from 17.2 to 19.9 percent (Table 14).

Much of the decreased representation of Negroes in sawmills and planing mills may be explained by the movement of lumber production to the Far West. The South's share of total lumber production decreased from 45.8 percent in 1939 to 35.2 percent in 1954. During this period, the western share of lumber production rose from 42.0 to 55.0 percent (Table 3).[53] Both of these trends continued through 1960.

If the lumber industry was shifting to the Far West, why did Negro employment in the logging segment of the industry increase? There were two causes: an increase in utilization of Negroes in logging in the South, and a movement of the logging operations to the South. Table 14 shows that percent Negro employment in the South increased from 39.1 to 48.2 percent between 1940 and 1960, and Table 15 shows that during this same period the percent of the nation's logging employment located in the South increased from 43.4 to 58.2 percent. This was a result of the growth of the pulp and paper industry in this region, which produced 60.8 percent of all wood pulp in 1964.[54]

Despite the various movements of components of the industry, the geographical distribution of lumber industry employment changed very little between 1940 and 1950. Table 15 shows that the South's share of total lumber employment barely changed from 1940 to 1950. The geographical shift between 1950 and

---

51. Weaver, *op. cit.*, p. 78.

52. *U. S. Census of Population, 1940*, Vol. III, *The Labor Force*, Part 1, Tables 76 and 77; and *1950*, Vol. II, *Characteristics of the Population*, Part 1, Tables 133 and 161.

53. Another explanation for the decreased Negro representation between 1940 and 1950 in sawmills and planing mills may be that the Census started including millwork in this category. White employment in this segment might be greater because the work is cleaner and lighter and the pay is higher (Table 8).

54. American Paper Institute, *Statistics of Paper, 1967 Supplement* (Washington: The Institute, 1968), p. 7.

TABLE 15. *Lumber and Wood Products Industry and Logging Employment by Region, 1940-1960*

	1940		1950		1960	
	Employees	Percent of Total	Employees	Percent of Total	Employees	Percent of Total
All Lumber and Wood Products						
Total United States	712,902	100.0	860,512	100.0	690,558a	100.0
South	363,096	50.9	458,219	53.3	326,905	47.4
Northeast	88,110	12.4	89,276	10.4	71,785	10.4
Midwest	111,795	15.7	108,856	12.6	92,732	13.4
Far West	149,901	21.0	204,161	23.7	199,136	28.8
Logging Operations Only						
Total United States	141,495	100.0	171,897	100.0	168,360a	100.0
South	61,427	43.4	80,584	46.9	97,949	58.2
Northeast	16,935	12.0	17,413	10.1	13,682	8.1
Midwest	16,428	11.6	16,364	9.5	15,056	8.9
Far West	46,705	33.0	57,536	33.5	41,673	24.8

Source: *U. S. Census of Population:*

1940: Vol. III, *The Labor Force,* Part 1, Tables 76 and 77.
1950: Vol. II, *Characteristics of the Population,* Part 1, Tables 133 and 161.
1960: PC(1) 1D, *U. S. Summary,* Tables 213 and 260.

Note: For definitions of regions, see Table 3.

a Includes Alaska and Hawaii.

1960 was reflected in a reduction in employee concentration in the South to 47.4 percent. As a result Negro employment in the industry decreased slightly.

Although there are no occupational data available for this period, it should be noted that the percent of farm woodland in the South held by nonwhites decreased from 9.7 percent in 1939 to 5.3 percent in 1959.[55] While Negro employment in logging in the South increased from 39.1 percent in 1940 to 48.2 percent in 1960 (Table 14), it appears that the trend of decreasing Negro owners and managers between 1910 and 1930 continued through 1960.

The data discussed for Negro employment in the lumber industry between 1940 and 1960 indicate a very strong relationship between regional location of the industry and the percent Negro employment.

Other factors such as World War II did not have a noticeable effect. It appears that by 1940 a saturation point had been reached in terms of Negro employment in the lumber industry. Not that it was impossible to hire more Negroes in the industry, but there were very few "Negro jobs" left to be filled in locations where there were Negroes available and willing to work. Weaver said that "once Negroes enter a type of work, they, as a group, tend to remain in it. Conversely, if it is traditional to exclude Negroes from certain jobs, these occupations become accepted as white men's work. Any move to substitute black labor or to introduce that labor in the occupation is opposed as a departure from the color occupational pattern."[56] Except for the almost total exclusion of Negroes from white collar jobs, there has never been as precise a separation of jobs into "white men's" jobs, and "Negro jobs" in the lumber industry as in many other industries. Since 1940 there has been a slight increase in the degree of representation of Negroes in the higher skilled jobs in the lumber industry. This increase is due to Negroes' great educational advancements since then making them, no doubt, better qualified to fill the more responsible positions.

---

55. *U. S. Census of Agriculture:*

      1940: Vol. III, *General Report*, Table 3, p. 147.
      1959: Vol. II, *General Report*, Chapter X, Table 15, p. 1041.

56. Weaver, *op. cit.*, p. 97.

FEMALE NEGRO EMPLOYMENT

Table 11 shows that during the Great Depression the Negro female suffered greater losses in lumber mill employment than did white females (percent Negro female employment dropped from 16.4 to 9.7). During the tight labor market of World War II, percent Negro female employment increased to 11.0. Between 1950 and 1960, as total mill employment decreased from 586,360 to 416,136, Negro females suffered disproportionately with a decrease from 2,214 to 1,284 employees (from 11.0 to 6.3 percent).

In logging, however, the determining factor has been the growth of the pulp and paper industry in the South. As Negro employment in logging in the United States increased steadily from 17.2 to 19.9 to 28.2 percent (1940, 1950, 1960), Negro female employment increased from 11.9 to 14.2 to 14.4 percent (Table 14).

Although percent Negro employment in the total lumber and wood products industry decreased from 23.8 percent in 1940 to 20.6 percent in 1960, Negro female employment increased slightly from 10.0 to 12.4 percent.[57] A logical explanation is the increased production of certain miscellaneous products in the South. Because the production of particleboard, hardboard, and insulating board does not require large sticks of timber, much of the growth of this segment of the industry has been in the South where the highest concentration of Negroes exists. Table 7 (p. 19) shows that the miscellaneous wood products segment of the industry employed the largest number of females in 1968.

SOUTH CAROLINA DATA

The Department of Labor of the State of South Carolina is unique among the fifty states in that for many years it has reported annually the race of employed persons by industry and sex. Unfortunately lumber is one of the few industries on which the Department of Labor chose to discontinue reporting this information in 1946, probably because of the difficulty in obtaining data from the many small lumbering and logging operations. (At that time there were many of the small peckerwood mills

---

57. *U. S. Census of Population, 1940,* Vol. III, *The Labor Force,* Part 1, Tables 76 and 77; and *1960,* PC(1) 1D, *U. S. Summary,* Tables 213 and 260.

scattered throughout the South.) Reports have been made, however, on one segment of the lumber industry—the barrel, basket, box, and veneer industry (components of SIC 243 and SIC 244). Data for this segment of the lumber industry and the available data for the whole lumber industry are shown in Table 16.

TABLE 16. *Lumber and Wood Products Industry*
Total and Negro Nonsalaried Workers
Two Sectors, South Carolina, 1940-1968

Year	Lumber and Timber			Barrel, Basket, and Veneer		
	Total	Negro	Percent Negro	Total	Negro	Percent Negro
1940	8,360	6,224	74.4	3,301	1,980	60.0
41	10,608	7,790	73.4	4,040	2,654	65.7
42	9,640	7,243	75.1	3,925	2,611	66.5
43	9,112	6,944	76.2	4,507	2,991	66.4
44	5,999	4,486	74.8	4,647	3,112	67.0
1945	5,026	3,545	70.5	4,326	2,842	65.7
46	n.a.	n.a.	n.a.	4,911	3,032	61.7
47	n.a.	n.a.	n.a.	5,597	3,368	60.2
48	n.a.	n.a.	n.a.	6,098	3,732	61.2
49	n.a.	n.a.	n.a.	4,527	2,732	60.3
1950	n.a.	n.a.	n.a.	4,854	2,836	58.4
51	n.a.	n.a.	n.a.	5,496	3,247	59.1
52	n.a.	n.a.	n.a.	4,920	2,819	57.3
53	n.a.	n.a.	n.a.	5,167	3,127	60.5
54	n.a.	n.a.	n.a.	4,429	2,555	57.7
1955	n.a.	n.a.	n.a.	4,983	2,897	58.1
56	n.a.	n.a.	n.a.	5,685	3,187	56.1
57	n.a.	n.a.	n.a.	5,075	2,529	49.8
58	n.a.	n.a.	n.a.	4,529	2,306	50.9
59	n.a.	n.a.	n.a.	4,734	2,426	51.2
1960	n.a.	n.a.	n.a.	4,348	2,354	54.1
61	n.a.	n.a.	n.a.	3,592	2,157	60.1
62	n.a.	n.a.	n.a.	3,705	2,141	57.8
63	n.a.	n.a.	n.a.	4,054	2,239	55.2
64	n.a.	n.a.	n.a.	4,346	2,351	54.1
1965	n.a.	n.a.	n.a.	4,465	2,433	54.5
66	n.a.	n.a.	n.a.	4,698	3,086	65.7
67	n.a.	n.a.	n.a.	4,282	2,824	66.0
68	n.a.	n.a.	n.a.	4,218	2,718	64.4

Source: *Annual Reports*, Department of Labor of the State of South Carolina, 1940-1968.

From the data on barrels, baskets, boxes, and veneers, it can be seen that percent Negro employment in this segment of the industry has changed very little in South Carolina in the past 28 years. This substantiates the notion that by 1940 the "Negro jobs" were already saturated with Negroes. The very high percentage Negro employment (as high as 67.0 percent in 1944) appears to verify the following statement by Green and Woodson: "In the smaller woodworking plants, such as barrel or stave factories, Negroes were frequently employed in preference to the whites. In some instances this was due to the fact that the managers found the Negroes more reliable as workmen than the whites."[58] Negro employment in the lumber and timber products industry appears to follow a similar pattern to that of barrels, baskets, boxes, and veneer.[59]

UNIONISM BEFORE 1960

A number of attempts were made to organize southern lumber workers during World War I, but most of them foundered, as did those in western lumber areas. The radical Industrial Workers of the World (IWW) which originated in the West, also attempted organization in the South, bringing both whites and blacks into its fold. But neither it nor the less equalitarian Carpenters' Union could overcome employer opposition and the use of racial antagonism and violence to thwart employee free choice.[60]

In later years, the International Woodworkers and the Carpenters were able to unionize the western lumber workers, but the South has remained heavily nonunion. Negroes and whites, where unionized in the South, are usually in the same locals but neither union is sufficiently strong to exert an impact on company racial policies involved in hiring or upgrading. There is, however, some evidence that the unions did insist on equal pay for equal work where once racial wage differences were not uncommon.

---

58. Green and Woodson, *op. cit.*, p. 126.

59. See the Paper and Textile studies in this Series for details about Negro employment in these industries.

60. See F. Ray Marshall, *Labor in the South* (Cambridge: Harvard University Press, 1967), pp. 93-94; and Sterling D. Spero and Abram L. Harris, *The Black Worker* (New York: Columbia University Press, 1931), pp. 329-337.

CHAPTER IV

The Impact of Civil Rights and Full Employment, 1960-1969

In recent years there has been a marked improvement in the number and kinds of jobs held by black Americans. In the lumber industry, however, the decade has been largely static in so far as Negro employment has been concerned.

NEGRO EMPLOYMENT IN THE LUMBER INDUSTRY, 1966

Racial employment data for the lumber and wood products industry provided by the Equal Employment Opportunity Commission (EEOC) for 1966 are shown in Table 17. For comparison purposes similar data for all industries are displayed in Appendix B, Table B-12. Comparisons over time cannot be made until regional characteristics are discussed,[61] but a comparison can be made between the lumber industry and all industries on an occupation-by-occupation basis for both males and females.

White Collar Jobs

In no white collar job is the Negro as well represented in the lumber industry as he is in American industry as a whole (Table 17 and B-12). Negroes held 0.6 percent of the white collar jobs in lumber compared to 2.6 percent for all industries. This seems very strange considering that Negroes hold 15.1 percent of all lumber industry jobs compared to 8.2 percent for Negroes in all industries. The bottom-heavy Negro occupational pattern which has always existed in American industry and has become of great concern in recent years is probably most striking in the lumber industry, an industry of high Negro employment.

---

61. EEOC and Census data are not comparable on a national scale for the lumber industry because a much larger percentage of the southern producers are exempt from reporting to the EEOC because of their small size.

TABLE 17. Lumber and Wood Products Industry
Employment by Race, Sex, and Occupational Group
1,348 Establishments
Total United States, 1966

Occupational Group	All Employees			Male			Female		
	Total	Negro	Percent Negro	Total	Negro	Percent Negro	Total	Negro	Percent Negro
Officials and managers	12,470	67	0.5	12,256	67	0.5	214	—	—
Professionals	2,781	4	0.1	2,719	4	0.1	62	—	—
Technicians	2,639	21	0.8	2,504	20	0.8	135	1	0.7
Sales workers	3,239	10	0.3	2,949	7	0.2	290	3	1.0
Office and clerical	12,090	104	0.9	4,040	71	1.8	8,050	33	0.4
Total white collar	33,219	206	0.6	24,468	169	0.7	8,751	37	0.4
Craftsmen	36,295	1,903	5.2	35,974	1,862	5.2	321	41	12.8
Operatives	84,139	11,540	13.7	78,325	10,793	13.8	5,814	747	12.8
Laborers	83,146	22,043	26.5	75,676	19,831	26.2	7,470	2,212	29.6
Service workers	2,793	496	17.8	2,402	384	16.0	391	112	28.6
Total blue collar	206,373	35,982	17.4	192,377	32,870	17.1	13,996	3,112	22.2
Total	239,592	36,188	15.1	216,845	33,039	15.2	22,747	3,149	13.8

Source: U. S. Equal Employment Opportunity Commission, *Job Patterns for Minorities and Women in Private Industry, 1966*, Report No. 1 (Washington: The Commission, 1968), Part II.

Note: Totaling the establishments and employees for the different regions shown in Tables 21 and B-1, B-2, and B-4 results in slightly smaller figures than are shown on this table for the total United States because the EEOC did not publish data for those states with less than 10 reporting establishments unless the state had at least 5 establishments and a total of at least 2,000 employees.

The poor representation of Negroes in white collar jobs can be attributed to many factors. The lack of growth in the industry has resulted in slow white collar employee turnover. As Negroes have become better educated and more highly qualified for professional, technical, managerial, sales, and clerical pursuits, few white collar jobs have opened up in this industry. The structure of the industry is such that many small firms are passed down through the family from one generation to the next. Only family and very close friends are accepted into the management of the organization. Also, there are few Negroes who possess the education and experience in white collar work who choose to seek employment in the lumber industry because there are so many more financially rewarding opportunities open to them in the government and in higher paying industries. Finally, discrimination has existed, and undoubtedly has not been totally eliminated.

In the ratios of percent Negro employment in lumber to the percent Negro employment in all industries for the different white collar occupations, the Negro representation in the officials and managers occupational group in lumber comes closest to equalizing that in all industries (0.5 to 0.9 percent). This is largely a result of the number of Negroes in rural areas of the South who buy or obtain access to a truck and who cut and haul timber to the sawmills and pulp mills. The small amount of capital required to cut and haul a few logs each year makes it possible for many Negroes to enter this business.

Blue Collar Jobs

Comparing percent Negro employment in the blue collar jobs between the lumber industry and all industries gives an entirely opposite view of the industry. The lumber industry employs significantly larger percentages of Negro craftsmen, operatives, and laborers than are employed in all American industry. In terms of total blue collar employment, the lumber industry has 17.4 percent Negro workers compared with 12.4 percent for all industries. As in earlier years, the high percent Negro employment has been a result of this industry's regional concentration in the South, the low educational and skill levels required for employment, the low pay, and the rough, dirty, hot, and hazardous nature of much of the work. Three occupations—craftsmen, operatives, and laborers—possess these characteristics. There is no reason to believe that white collar jobs in the lumber industry have any particular characteristics that would make them more or less open to or suited to Negroes, and consequently, despite the regional concentration in the South, Negroes are poorly represented in these jobs. Also, as one would expect, as the jobs become more strenuous and dirtier, as necessary educational and skill levels are reduced, and as the pay diminishes between jobs, the percent Negro employment increases—from 5.2 percent for craftsmen, to 13.7 percent for operatives, to 26.5 percent for laborers.

Service workers have been ignored to this point because they are a special case. The regional data in the next section will show that percent Negro employment in service jobs in the South is essentially the same for the lumber industry as it is for all industries in that region. Then why the lower percent Negro employment figure for the lumber industry in the country as a whole? This is a result of the primarily urban location of the Negro in regions other than the South and the rural concentration of the lumber industry. Although most urban industries of the North and Far West have an ample source of unskilled Negro labor upon which to draw, there are few available for employment in the lumber industry.

Female Employment

In 1966 there were essentially no Negro women in white collar jobs in the lumber industry except for 33 Negro clerical workers (0.4 percent). In all industries the percent Negro employment of female clerical workers was 3.6 percent—nine times larger than in the lumber industry (Tables 17 and B-12). When asked to explain this unusually low utilization of Negroes in clerical jobs, southern lumber producers have generally replied that although there was some discrimination in years past, the problem today is to find Negro women with the necessary education and experience. The clerical staffs of most wood products operations are quite small—usually just one or two secretaries. The managers of such operations must hire experienced clerical personnel because there are few or no other secretaries available in the office to train them. Most Negro women with the necessary talent live in cities and work for higher paying industries.

Nepotism is another important factor that helps to explain the poor representation of Negroes in clerical work. When there is a job available that an inexperienced secretary could perform, it is likely that one of the officials or managers in the firm has a daughter or niece or cousin who is just graduating from college and would like the job. In blue collar jobs in the lumber industry the Negro woman is far better represented than in blue collar jobs in industry as a whole. The Negro woman has been able to obtain blue collar employment in the lumber industry for the same reason as the Negro man—it is difficult for lumber industry management to find workers to do the many dirty, low-paying, strenuous jobs.

Regional Factors

Table 18 summarizes the Negro regional and national occupational patterns for the lumber industry and all industries respectively. Although the percent Negro employment in the South is much higher in the lumber industry than percent Negro employment in all industries (42.1 percent for lumber compared to 12.9 percent for all industries), percent Negro employment in all other regions is significantly higher for all industries than for the lumber industry. This trend is generally consistent among the states within each region as well. (See Appendix Tables B-6—B-9.) The cause of this difference in racial employment characteristics for the lumber industry between the South and other regions was discussed briefly in the previous section in reference to service workers. Negroes in the North and West are concentrated in urban areas while the wood products industry is concentrated in rural areas. On the other hand, in most areas of the South, both rural and urban, there are enough unskilled Negroes available to meet the needs of the lumber industry. (Locational factors will be discussed further in a later section.)

The occupational patterns in the different regions shown in Table 18 allow some informative comparisons. In only one white collar occupation in only one region (officials and managers in the South) is the percent Negro employment as high as it is for all industries together. The reasons set forth in the previous section for low Negro white collar employment in lumber can be applied here also. The lower Negro employment figures for blue collar workers in the lumber industry in the Northeast, Midwest, and Far West regions can again be explained by the absence of Negroes in the rural North and West. The higher percent Negro employment in blue collar jobs in the South in lumber than most industries results from the nature of the work and the compensation. The very similar figures for the

TABLE 18. Lumber and
Wood Products Industry and All Industries
Percent Negro Employment by Occupational Group
United States and Regions, 1966

Occupational Group	Lumber and Wood Products					All Industries				
	Total United States	South	Northeast	Midwest	Far West	Total United States	South	Northeast	Midwest	Far West
Officials and managers	0.5	1.2	—	0.3	0.2	0.9	1.1	1.0	0.8	0.5
Professionals	0.1	0.2	0.4	—	0.1	1.3	1.6	1.5	1.2	0.9
Technicians	0.8	3.2	—	0.4	—	4.1	5.3	4.3	3.7	2.9
Sales workers	0.3	0.8	0.6	—	—	2.4	2.9	2.3	2.2	1.8
Office and clerical	0.9	2.4	0.7	0.2	0.3	3.5	2.7	4.6	3.4	2.7
Total white collar	0.6	1.6	0.4	0.2	0.2	2.6	2.5	3.1	2.4	1.9
Craftsmen	5.2	17.0	2.7	2.1	0.4	3.6	4.8	3.4	3.2	2.4
Operatives	13.7	42.4	3.0	4.0	0.7	10.8	14.1	8.1	11.3	6.2
Laborers	26.5	61.3	8.1	8.6	1.2	21.2	38.8	14.2	14.8	9.3
Service workers	17.8	37.3	3.5	6.1	3.5	23.2	37.6	18.4	20.4	13.0
Total blue collar	17.4	47.8	4.8	5.6	0.8	12.4	19.2	9.4	11.1	6.8
Total	15.1	42.1	4.0	4.5	0.7	8.2	12.9	6.4	7.6	4.3

Source: Tables 17 and 21 and Appendix B, Tables B-1, B-2, B-4, B-12, and B-13.

Note: For regional definitions, see Table 3.

service workers in the South (37.6 percent for all industries and 37.3 percent for lumber) should be expected considering that the nature of this work is similar in all manufacturing industries. Service worker experience must be almost perfectly transferable between industries.

Examination of these data by occupational distribution of workers rather than percent Negro employment in each occupation gives a clearer view of the differences between the occupational patterns for the lumber industry in different regions. The occupational distribution of all employees and Negro employees in the lumber industry for the United States and each region are exhibited in Table 19. One cannot meaningfully compare the occupational distribution of Negroes in different regions without giving consideration to the differences in the all-employee occupational distribution between regions. Since the timber in the Far West is much larger and is found in denser stands, the industry is more highly mechanized and a greater percentage of the work force is employed in the more highly skilled jobs.

White collar workers make up 12.3 percent of the lumber industry employees in the South and 11.8 percent in the Far West (Table 19). These percentages are quite comparable and one would expect to find equally comparable figures for Negroes employed in the lumber industry in these two regions. The table shows, however, that only 0.5 percent of Negro workers in the lumber industry in the South are engaged in white collar occupations while the related figure for the Far West is 2.7 percent. Why is the figure higher for the Far West? One's first thought is discrimination in the South. Perhaps those factors already discussed, such as (1) past discrimination, (2) low white collar turnover rate, (3) family ownership, (4) lack of desire of Negroes to enter these jobs or own lumber operations, and (5) lack of an available source of Negro female clerical help in the rural South have been the major causes. Southern lumber operators explained the causes as (1) more equal education for Negroes in the West and (2) higher level of education and motivation among most of the Negroes who migrated from the South. This latter suggestion would seem to be substantiated by McClelland and Winter. Their study of the forces that motivate people found that migrants are apt to have a higher need to achieve.[62]

---

62. David McClelland and David Winter, *Motivating Economic Achievement* (New York: MacMillan, 1969), p. 6.

TABLE 19. Lumber and Wood Products Industry
Percent Occupational Distribution of Total and Negro Employees
United States and Regions, 1966

Occupational Group	All Employees					Negro Employees				
	United States	South	Northeast	Midwest	Far West	United States	South	Northeast	Midwest	Far West
Officials and managers	5.2	5.6	5.3	6.2	4.5	0.2	0.2	—	0.4	1.0
Professionals	1.2	0.7	1.5	1.1	1.5	*	*	0.2	—	0.3
Technicians	1.1	0.7	1.5	2.2	1.0	0.1	0.1	—	0.2	—
Sales workers	1.4	1.2	3.0	2.8	0.7	*	*	0.4	—	—
Office and clerical	5.0	4.1	8.0	8.8	4.1	0.3	0.2	1.4	0.4	1.4
Total white collar	13.9	12.3	19.3	21.1	11.8	0.6	0.5	2.0	1.0	2.7
Craftsmen	15.1	12.6	10.9	11.1	19.4	5.2	5.1	7.5	5.2	11.0
Operatives	35.1	31.6	39.3	34.5	37.4	31.9	31.8	30.1	30.9	35.3
Laborers	34.7	42.1	28.7	32.0	30.6	60.9	61.3	58.8	61.2	47.2
Service workers	1.2	1.4	1.8	1.3	0.8	1.4	1.3	1.6	1.7	3.8
Total blue collar	86.1	87.7	80.7	78.9	88.2	99.4	99.5	98.0	99.0	97.3
Total	100.0	100.0	100.0	100.0	100.0	100.0	100.0	100.0	100.0	100.0

Source: Calculated from data shown in Tables 5, 17, and 21 and Appendix B, Tables B-1, B-2, and B-4.

Note: For regional definitions, see Table 3.

* Less than 0.05 percent.

THE 1964-1968 FIELD SAMPLE

The data published by the Equal Employment Opportunity Commission for 1966 are deficient for our purposes in several respects: they are based on the period immediately after the effective date of Title VII of the Civil Rights Act of 1964 (July 1965), and therefore cannot be used to detect significant later developments; and they do not distinguish logging from mill and plant operations, urban from rural operations, small plants from large plants, or small companies from large companies.

Accordingly, data were gathered for this study for two years: 1964 and 1968. In contrast to most industries previously studied in this Series, the lumber industry is made up of many small firms. In industries with only a few large companies such as steel, rubber tires, aerospace, and automobiles, it was not difficult to obtain data for the same companies in different years.

In the lumber industry, however, there is no one company or group of companies that is large enough to dominate the policies of the industry. Because of the many companies involved, the author had to choose between obtaining a small consistent sample or obtaining as much data as were available for each year. In order to meet requirements of statistical significance, the author chose the latter course. As it turned out, however, the data appear not only to be very representative of the industry, but highly comparable as well.

Efforts were made to secure data on a national basis, but only for the two most important regions—the South and Far West—were enough data obtained to yield meaningful results. The data for the South region for 1964, 1966, and 1968 are shown in Tables 20, 21, and 22. (For the Far West, see Appendix Tables B-3, B-4, and B-5.) Despite the fact that in 1964 the southern sample consisted of only 28 companies compared to 64 companies for 1968, there is little difference in the overall percent Negro (42.0 percent for 1964 and 42.5 percent for 1968). Likewise, for the West the figures are also quite similar—0.7 percent in 1964 and 0.6 percent in 1968.

Occupationally the only changes between 1964 and 1968 that can be detected were in the South as follows: (1) minor increases in Negro representation in the white collar jobs (0.5 to 1.6 percent), (2) increased use of Negroes in craftsmen jobs (13.3 to 20.0 percent), and (3) increased use of Negro laborers (58.7 to 64.1 percent), or more accurately, decreased use of laborers in general with a disproportionately large reduction

TABLE 20. *Lumber and Wood Products Industry*
Employment by Race, Sex, and Occupational Group
28 Companies
South Region, 1964

Occupational Group	All Employees			Male			Female		
	Total	Negro	Percent Negro	Total	Negro	Percent Negro	Total	Negro	Percent Negro
Officials and managers	620	3	0.5	607	3	0.5	13	—	—
Professionals	207	—	—	206	—	—	1	—	—
Technicians	141	3	2.1	137	3	2.2	4	—	—
Sales workers	129	—	—	119	—	—	10	—	—
Office and clerical	582	3	0.5	211	2	0.9	371	1	0.3
Total white collar	1,679	9	0.5	1,280	8	0.6	399	1	0.3
Craftsmen	1,589	211	13.3	1,589	211	13.3	—	—	—
Operatives	3,148	1,392	44.2	3,085	1,385	44.9	63	7	11.1
Laborers	6,513	3,822	58.7	5,760	3,534	61.4	753	288	38.2
Service workers	156	61	39.1	141	48	34.0	15	13	86.7
Total blue collar	11,406	5,486	48.1	10,575	5,178	49.0	831	308	37.1
Total	13,085	5,495	42.0	11,855	5,186	43.7	1,230	309	25.1

Source: Data in author's possession.

Note: For regional definitions, see Table 3.

TABLE 21. Lumber and Wood Products Industry
Employment by Race, Sex, and Occupational Group
477 Establishments
South Region, 1966

Occupational Group	All Employees			Male			Female		
	Total	Negro	Percent Negro	Total	Negro	Percent Negro	Total	Negro	Percent Negro
Officials and managers	4,421	54	1.2	4,320	54	1.2	101	—	—
Professionals	534	1	0.2	516	1	0.2	18	—	—
Technicians	571	18	3.2	553	18	3.3	18	—	—
Sales workers	926	7	0.8	849	6	0.7	77	1	1.3
Office and clerical	3,199	77	2.4	1,213	67	5.5	1,986	10	0.5
Total white collar	9,651	157	1.6	7,451	146	2.0	2,200	11	0.5
Craftsmen	9,849	1,678	17.0	9,764	1,640	16.8	85	38	44.7
Operatives	24,743	10,496	42.4	22,909	9,902	43.2	1,834	594	32.4
Laborers	32,977	20,231	61.3	29,836	18,233	61.1	3,141	1,998	63.6
Service workers	1,133	423	37.3	1,035	340	32.9	98	83	84.7
Total blue collar	68,702	32,828	47.8	63,544	30,115	47.4	5,158	2,713	52.6
Total	78,353	32,985	42.1	70,995	30,261	42.6	7,358	2,724	37.0

Source: U. S. Equal Employment Opportunity Commission, Job Patterns for Minorities and Women in Private Industry, 1966, Report No. 1 (Washington: The Commission, 1968), Part II.

Note: For regional definitions, see Table 3.

TABLE 22. *Lumber and Wood Products Industry*
Employment by Race, Sex, and Occupational Group
64 Companies
South Region, 1968

Occupational Group	All Employees			Male			Female		
	Total	Negro	Percent Negro	Total	Negro	Percent Negro	Total	Negro	Percent Negro
Officials and managers	2,742	41	1.5	2,718	41	1.5	24	—	—
Professionals	918	4	0.4	912	4	0.4	6	—	—
Technicians	643	30	4.7	634	30	4.7	9	—	—
Sales workers	305	—	—	265	—	—	40	—	—
Office and clerical	1,538	24	1.6	483	21	4.3	1,055	3	0.3
Total white collar	6,146	99	1.6	5,012	96	1.9	1,134	3	0.3
Craftsmen	5,227	1,045	20.0	5,198	1,031	19.8	29	14	48.3
Operatives	11,138	5,210	46.8	10,577	4,963	46.9	561	247	44.0
Laborers	14,876	9,538	64.1	13,144	8,273	62.9	1,732	1,265	73.0
Service workers	392	174	44.4	337	130	38.6	55	44	80.0
Total blue collar	31,633	15,967	50.5	29,256	14,397	49.2	2,377	1,570	66.0
Total	37,779	16,066	42.5	34,268	14,493	42.3	3,511	1,573	44.8

Source: Data in author's possession.

Note: For regional definitions, see Table 3.

in white laborers. Other differences which can be seen in the data between the years were either too small or not sufficiently consistent to warrant drawing conclusions as to trends. Although Negro employment during the 1960's improved quantitatively and qualitatively in most industries, in southern lumber—and indeed throughout the entire lumber industry—the status quo was largely maintained.

NEGRO EMPLOYMENT IN LOGGING AND MILLS, 1968

When a small, one-mill company that does its own logging reports racial employment data, it often combines the figures for the logging, milling, and finishing operations into one report. Logging contractors, large lumber companies, and large paper companies often report separate data for logging operations. The 1968 data have been separated, as accurately as possible, into two groups—one for logging and woods operations and one for all factory operations—for the South and the Far West. The results are displayed in Table 23 for the Far West and Table 24 for the South.

It is difficult to extract much information about differences in Negro employment in the different occupations between the two groups in the Far West because there are so few Negroes in any one occupation in either group. Generally, it can only be concluded that in the Far West there are fewer Negroes in logging than in the mills and plants (0.5 percent compared to 0.7 percent). Such a situation would be expected because some of the mills and plants are located near cities, but logging operations by their very nature are confined to rural areas in which few Negroes reside.

Much more can be learned from examination of the southern data (Table 24), including an insight into the nature of these data and how they differ from Census data. Census data show a higher percent Negro employment in logging in the South in 1960 (48.2 percent) than in the lumber and wood products industry as a whole (41.6 percent).[63] This is attributed to the large number of Negroes who either run their own small logging operations or several times a year cut some pulpwood or sawlogs off their own land or that of a neighbor and sell it to a nearby mill. These Negroes may occupy most of their time in agri-

---

63. *U. S. Census of Population, 1960*, PC(1) 1D, *U. S. Summary*, Tables 213 and 260.

TABLE 23. Lumber and Wood Products Industry
Total and Negro Employment in Logging and Mills and Plants
Far West Region, 1968

Occupational Group	Logging Operations (SIC 241)			Mills and Plants (SIC 242-249)		
	Total	Negro	Percent Negro	Total	Negro	Percent Negro
Officials and managers	272	—	—	2,149	1	*
Professionals	148	1	0.7	426	2	0.5
Technicians	85	2	2.4	260	1	0.4
Sales workers	1	—	—	194	—	—
Office and clerical	147	—	—	1,270	4	0.3
Total white collar	653	3	0.5	4,299	8	0.2
Craftsmen	1,580	—	—	8,640	47	0.5
Operatives	2,095	14	0.7	16,366	112	0.7
Laborers	1,002	10	1.0	13,052	112	0.9
Service workers	66	—	—	327	1	0.3
Total blue collar	4,743	24	0.5	38,385	272	0.7
Total	5,396	27	0.5	42,684	280	0.7

Source: Data in author's possession.

* Less than 0.05 percent.

TABLE 24. Lumber and Wood Products Industry
Total and Negro Employment in Logging and Mills and Plants
South Region, 1968

Occupational Group	Logging Operations (SIC 241)			Mills and Plants (SIC 242-249)		
	Total	Negro	Percent Negro	Total	Negro	Percent Negro
Officials and managers	676	—	—	2,066	41	2.0
Professionals	541	2	0.4	377	2	0.5
Technicians	335	3	0.9	308	27	8.8
Sales workers	6	—	—	299	—	—
Office and clerical	438	5	1.1	1,100	19	1.7
Total white collar	1,996	10	0.5	4,150	89	2.1
Craftsmen	555	82	14.8	4,672	963	20.6
Operatives	1,223	217	17.7	9,915	4,993	50.4
Laborers	1,410	674	47.8	13,466	8,864	65.8
Service workers	50	29	58.0	342	145	42.4
Total blue collar	3,238	1,002	30.9	28,395	14,965	52.7
Total	5,234	1,012	19.3	32,545	15,054	46.3

Source: Data in author's possession.

cultural pursuits or perhaps are idle a great portion of the year, but during a Census interview many of these men state their occupation as logging. They do not show up on the employer reports, however, and consequently the compilation of the data on these reports do not indicate the large percentage of Negroes participating in this industry segment. Table 24 shows the percent Negro employment in logging based on these reports to be only 19.3 percent compared to that for mills and plants of 46.3 percent.

In addition, a comparison of the occupational data shows an even greater emphasis on the lower skilled jobs for Negroes in logging than in mills and plants. For example, although the percent Negro employment in southern logging operations is about one-half that in mills and plants, percent Negro employment in the white collar jobs is about one-quarter of that in mills and plants. This paints a dismal picture for the future of the Negro in southern logging. As more and more emphasis is placed on tree farming and the "third forest" becomes reality, there is going to be increased logging by the large companies using highly mechanized harvesting equipment. Unless the rural Negroes are willing to make the transition and the pulp and lumber manufacturers are willing to train these men to operate the new harvesting machines, there may come a day when 19.3 percent Negro employment in southern logging will be a better approximation of the true proportion than the 48.2 percent given by the Census for 1960.

INFLUENCE OF LOCATION AND SIZE

Low Negro employment in the North and West was explained as a matter of location: lumber is primarily a rural industry and the Negro population is concentrated in the urban communities of these regions. If this is truly the reason, there should be greater percent Negro employment in those few urban lumber operations than for the average. Data for urban lumber operations in the Northeast and Midwest regions could not be located, but some data were found for a few operations in the Far West and South. Table 25 gives the Negro employment for these two regions and for the operations located in cities. In both the South and the Far West, Negro employment is higher in the urban areas (in the West, 3 times higher).

TABLE 25. *Lumber Mills and Plants*
Employment by Race
South and Far West Regions and Urban Areas, 1968

	Region			Urban Area [a]		
	Total Employees	Negro	Percent Negro	Total Employees	Negro	Percent Negro
South	32,545	15,054	46.3	3,881	2,270	58.5
Far West	42,684	280	0.7	1,138	24	2.1

Source: Data in author's possession.

Note: For regional definitions, see Table 3.

[a] Plants in the following cities are included in these data:

South: Houston, Little Rock, Louisville, Memphis, Mobile, Montgomery, Nashville, and Richmond.

West: Fresno, Portland, Sacramento, Tacoma.

Professor Northrup found a similar situation in paper converting plants (Far West region—5.0 percent Negro; urban areas in the Far West—8.0 percent Negro; South region—17.1 percent Negro; urban areas in the South—25.3 percent). He voiced concern over the fact that throughout the country "industry is tending to move out of the cities to rural areas or to suburban industrial parks and other locations. Inevitably the corrugated box plants will do likewise. Thus, despite their strong position in the industry, Negroes could see their jobs reduced unless they can and will move with them." [64] This current migration of industry out of the cities will have little or no effect on the future of the Negro in the lumber industry because so little of the industry is presently located in urban areas.

Efforts have been made by western lumber manufacturers to bring Negroes into their operations. One large producer of lumber in the Pacific Northwest went into "hard-core" areas of two of the large cities to hire men for the sawmills and logging operations. When the Negroes reached the work sites and observed the rough and dirty nature of the work, most refused to start and some even refused to get off the bus. Several freely stated that they preferred to stay on relief. In another attempt, Negroes in a large city were hired to work in a sawmill about

---

64. See the Paper study in the Series, pp. 73-74.

forty minutes from the city. A bus service was provided by the company at first, but white workers complained of inverse discrimination. They felt that they, too, should be picked up and brought to and from work. The Negroes were encouraged to establish motor pools, which they did, but unsuccessfully. In the driver's haste to leave the mill after work, he often left one or more of the black workers behind. The foremen ended up running a taxi service to take these stranded men home at night. Eventually all the Negro workers got discouraged and quit.[65]

Plant Size

The 1964 and 1968 data were broken down into three plant size groups: (1) those plants with 100 or less employees, (2) those with greater than 100 and less than 200 employees, and (3) those with 200 or more employees. The employment by race for the two regions by plant size is shown in Table 26. In the South there were no significant differences in percent Negro employment for the three plant sizes in either year. In the Far West there appears to be some slight increase in Negro employment in the middle size plant range for the 1964 data, but this condition does not carry over to the 1968 data and the increase is certainly small enough to be attributed to random deviation in the samples. Plant size is apparently not a determinant of racial employment policy in the lumber industry.

Company Size

Racial employment data for eight of the ten largest forest products companies are shown in Appendix Tables B-10 and B-11 for the South and Far West regions. The percent Negro employment data for all employees from these tables are shown in Table 27, along with comparable figures for each region as a whole.

In the Far West the large companies employ the same proportion of Negro white collar workers as all companies (large and small) together, but a slightly lower proportion of Negro blue collar workers (0.4 percent compared to 0.7 percent for the whole Far West region). In the South the white collar Negro employment for the large companies is again about equal to that for all the companies (1.5 percent compared to 1.6 per-

---

65. Field notes, 1969.

TABLE 26. Lumber Mills and Plants
Total and Negro Employment by Plant Size
South and Far West Regions, 1964 and 1968

| Region | Year | Number of Employees | | | | | | | | | | | |
| | | 100 or less | | | More than 100 and less than 200 | | | 200 or more | | |
		Total	Negro	Percent Negro	Total	Negro	Percent Negro	Total	Negro	Percent Negro
South	1964	1,763	777	44.1	2,320	1,086	46.8	8,072	3,492	43.3
	1968	2,573	1,180	45.9	7,625	3,494	45.8	22,347	10,380	46.4
Far West	1964	1,918	10	0.5	4,032	61	1.5	29,975	211	0.7
	1968	2,021	19	0.9	6,876	80	1.2	33,787	181	0.5

Source: Data in author's possession.

Note: For regional definitions, see Table 3.

TABLE 27. *Lumber and Wood Products Industry*
Percent Negro Employment by Occupational Group
South and Far West Regions, 1968

	South		Far West	
Occupational Group	64 Companies	8 of 10 Largest Companies	66 Companies	8 of 10 Largest Companies
Officials and managers	1.5	1.9	*	—
Professionals	0.4	0.4	0.5	0.5
Technicians	4.7	3.2	0.9	0.6
Sales workers	—	—	—	—
Office and clerical	1.6	1.3	0.3	0.2
Total white collar	1.6	1.5	0.2	0.2
Craftsmen	20.0	18.7	0.5	0.1
Operatives	46.8	39.8	0.7	0.4
Laborers	64.1	56.8	0.9	0.7
Service workers	44.4	57.6	0.3	—
Total blue collar	50.5	43.8	0.7	0.4
Total	42.5	35.3	0.6	0.4

Source: Tables 21, B-5, B-10, and B-11.

Note: For regional definitions, see Table 3.

* Less than 0.05 percent.

cent for all companies). In blue collar employment, however, the large companies employ a lower percentage of Negroes (43.8 percent compared to 50.5 percent for all companies).

This is opposite to what most people would expect. Should not the large companies be more concerned with their national image and less concerned with local sentiments? In one case, one of the Big Ten companies had a Negro salaried employee in a large mill in a small southern town. The company was scheduled to have a dinner for salaried personnel at a local club, but was informed that the Negro and his wife would not be allowed to enter. The company avoided publicity, but let it be known to the club's management that if the Negro couple were not allowed to attend the dinner, the company would hold no more activities at the club. The club, being the only such facility in any reasonable distance, might have resisted, but

submitted without incident. This is just a minor example of
many such occurrences, but it helps to demonstrate the power
of a large company in a small rural community. The point is,
if large lumber companies have the power to affect the racial
behavior of a community, they certainly have good control over
racial practices within the firm and can utilize and advance
Negroes to any position which they are capable of handling.

The question of why large companies in the South employ a
smaller percentage of Negroes than the rest of the companies
was posed to both large and small lumber companies with rather
unsatisfactory results. No consistent reply was received, but a
few credible explanations were offered. One suggestion was that
the large companies have better access to capital and consequently have more highly automated plants that require more
highly skilled personnel. Although this seems quite plausible,
the data in Tables 22 and B-10 show that the large companies
do not employ a more highly skilled labor force. For both large
companies and the industry as a whole, about 14 percent of the
employees are craftsmen and about 30 percent are operatives.
Even if the work force were more highly skilled, this would
not explain the generally lower percentage of Negro employment
in each occupational group for large companies.

Another suggestion which perhaps possesses more validity is
that the entrance requirements for jobs in large companies are
greater. In small companies the general hiring policy is for
the foreman to tell his men that he needs another man. One
worker may say that he knows someone who would like the
job, in which case the foreman tells the worker to bring him
in and he will put him to work. Otherwise, his men spread
the word to their families and friends. If an applicant turns
up who seems reasonably fit, the foreman will hire him.

Many of the large lumber companies are also pulp and paper
companies. Pulp and paper manufacture is a highly technical
process, and most of these manufacturing operations have minimum criteria that an applicant must meet in order to be considered for employment, e.g., tests and high school diplomas.
These same criteria may be carried over to the hiring of lumber
mill employees.

POLICY FACTORS

From the data that has been presented, one would feel confi-
dent in making the statement that it is and has been for many

years the policy of lumber industry managers in the South to employ Negroes on a large scale, especially for blue collar jobs. By presenting the data in aggregate form, as has been done up to this point, it is not possible to detect any particular plants that have not conformed to this pattern.

To determine individual company differences in the lumber industry, the percentage of Negro employment in each southern establishment in the field sample was calculated. All logging operations, mills, and plants for which the county location was not known, and all those mills and plants for which the data were combined into singular reports were excluded. The percentage of Negro employment against percentage of Negro population in the county population was then plotted (Figure 1). All those points that fall above the 45 degree line represent plants or mills which employ a greater percentage of Negroes than exist in the county in which located. Seventy-five percent fall into this category. The plants that fall below the line are mostly in the lower percent Negro population areas.

The availability of Negro labor seems to be almost the sole determinant of the racial employment practices of a lumber operation. If there are Negroes available, the lumber industry will hire them. Except for minor fluctuations, there should be almost a straight line relationship between percent Negro employment and percent Negro population. Most of the deviations from some imagined line starting from zero and proceeding toward some point around 100 percent employment at 60 percent Negro population are caused by the fact that the county Negro population is not a good measure of the Negro population of the labor market of the mill or plant. A lumber mill's labor market generally covers much less area than a county and there are often extreme fluctuations in percent Negro population throughout a county. Also, a mill may be built near the border of two counties with entirely different racial mixes.

It appears, then, that all those plants shown in Figure 1 except one have what can be considered reasonable Negro employment in light of the Negro population in the area in which located. The one exception is a plant with 21.1 percent Negro employment in a county of 77.9 percent Negro population. This plant just happens to be one owned by a foreign firm headquartered in a country with very few Negroes. Perhaps this has affected the employment policies of that company.

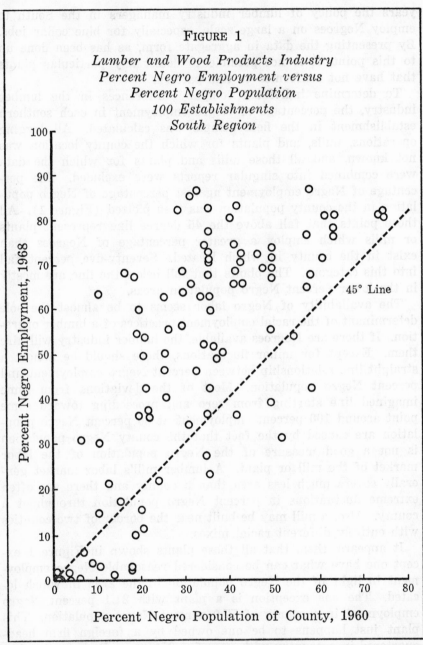

FIGURE 1

Lumber and Wood Products Industry
Percent Negro Employment versus
Percent Negro Population
100 Establishments
South Region

Source: Employment data: in author's possession.

Population data: *U. S. Census of Population, 1960*, Supplementary
Report PC(S1)-52, *Negro Population by County, 1960 and 1950*,
Table 2.

CHAPTER V

Some Problems of Equal Opportunity

Even in an industry such as lumber and wood products in which Negro labor has been highly valued, the changes in practices required by the civil rights laws and regulations were certain to cause problems of adjustment. The nature of these problems and how have they been resolved is the subject of this chapter.

IMPACT ON WHITE EMPLOYEES

The impact on and reaction of white employees to equal rights for Negroes in the lumber industry can be divided into two areas of consideration: employment and facilities.

Employment

Resentment of white employees to the advancement of Negroes has been very slight in the lumber industry. Many Negroes have been moved into supervisory and skilled craft positions. Many of these Negro supervisors have white employees working under their direction without opposition or resentment. Lumber mill operators claim that they would have been fearful of the white workers' reactions if they had tried to make some of the Negro promotions a few years ago. They further feel that the civil rights legislation has made the process of upgrading the Negro much easier, because the workers realize that the employer has no choice in the matter.

The low pay in the lumber industry makes it difficult to recruit and retain qualified skilled workers. Consequently, the company officials of this industry cannot afford to pass over a qualified man just because he is black. One lumber mill operator in the South said that he would "run right out and hug a Negro sawyer if he could find one." He went on to say how he would find the man and his family a home, move them into it, and help them get settled.

A sawmill is a rather tightly-knit community. Nearly everyone has general knowledge of how others perform. There are no seniority rules or lines of progression. When a job opening appears that involves a promotion, the man who is considered best qualified gets the job. Turnover in the more desirable, higher-paying jobs is very slow and the foremen have ample time to evaluate their subordinates. A decision is normally made without regard to the man's color, and there is little resentment afterward because there is normally little disagreement about who was best qualified.

Of course, not all attempts at Negro advancement have been successful. Certainly great harm can be done to a man by placing him in a job requiring greater skill, training, or education than he possesses. One southern lumber company employed a Negro ex-serviceman who, according to his Air Force personnel files, was trained in electrical equipment repair. After a year of on-the-job training as an electrician, he had made little progress toward grasping the essential requirements of the job. He did not have the necessary background to learn this trade. It was probably a very wise decision of management to utilize this man in a less technical job.

Integration of Facilities

Most lumber operations in the South are too small to justify such facilities as cafeterias. Only if a sawmill is operated in conjunction with a large pulp mill are there enough personnel to warrant these additional facilities. Of course, some mills do have locker rooms, and all have rest rooms and drinking fountains. With the recent government pressure, these facilities have all been integrated; at least, all those in plants visited by the writer. This integration, however, has not taken place completely without resistance. For considerable lengths of time after the "white" or "colored" signs were removed, both races continued to use the same segregated drinking fountains and rest rooms as before. Plant operators report that gradually both races are starting to make use of the most conveniently located facilities, rather than the ones previously designated for their use.

The locker rooms presented a somewhat greater problem for a while. It was necessary to build larger locker rooms or join existing facilities by knocking out walls. At first the white workers refused to use the integrated facilities and waited until they were home to shower and change clothes. But gradually a combination of the inconvenience and complaints from the wives had forced them to start using the integrated locker rooms.

The lumber industry has a set of facility integration problems that are common only to a few other industries. The problems concern housing, and are a result of the rural nature of the industry. As the lumber industry in a region expends the supply of timber near the urban areas for which the finished products are demanded or from which they are shipped, it is forced to move its operations nearer to the raw material. A study made in 1930 stated that "When a sawmill is located some miles from a town or village, it is an absolute necessity that the company furnish some sort of housing facilities." [66] Jensen stated in his appraisal of the southern pine industry in 1945 that "Company housing is still provided nearly everywhere." A survey at that time of 132 companies showed 12,717 houses owned and rented to both white and Negro workmen.[67] Many of these houses are still owned by the lumber companies. The difficulties which are involved in owning such houses in the South are well illustrated by the American Can Company's experience in Alabama. Following are excerpts from the statement by the American Can Company to the U. S. Commission on Civil Rights:

The Allison Lumber Company was acquired by the American Can Company on May 26, 1960. Among the acquired assets were . . . 172 houses in the immediate vicinity of the sawmill, 38 houses located elsewhere on Company property . . . .

The Allison sawmill, which probably is the largest southern pine mill east of the Mississippi, currently produces approximately 60MM board feet of lumber per year . . . . The company currently employs approximately 303 hourly and approximately 31 salaried employees at the Allison sawmill plant. . . .

At the present time, the average home occupied by a white employee consists of 6.2 rooms, has a book value of approximately $6,000, and rents for $41.00 per month. The average home occupied by a Negro employee consists of 3.4 rooms, has a book value of approximately $1,200, and rents for $14.85 per month. . . . All white residences have inside running water and sewer outlets; eight of the Negro residences have these same facilities. Water supply for the remaining residences is available from convenient outside faucets, and toilet facilities for such homes are the usual out-door types.

Although within the Bellamy community the houses that are occupied by white employees are grouped together, these houses are in some instances immediately adjacent to homes occupied by Negro fam-

---

66. Abraham Berglund, George T. Starnes, and Frank T. deVyer, *Labor in the Industrial South* (Charlottesville: Institute for Research in the Social Sciences, University of Virginia, 1930), p. 54.

67. Vernon H. Jensen, *Lumber and Men* (New York: Farrar and Rinehart, Inc., 1945), p. 80.

ilies. Negro employees are free to and frequently do walk through the area of homes occupied by white employees. No Negro employee has ever sought to rent a house previously rented to a white employee in Bellamy, and no white employee has ever sought to rent a home previously rented to a Negro employee in Bellamy during American Can Company's ownership.

In July, 1967 the American Can Company concluded that it should investigate the possibilities of divesting itself of its Bellamy housing properties. Since the housing operation was consistently unprofitable, the Company sought to determine whether a reasonable program for the divestment of the housing and community facilities could be developed without creating undue hardships on the tenants in the Bellamy community. . . .

At the time the American Can Company acquired the Allison Lumber Company, there existed upon the property a swimming pool which had been built by and at the expense of the white tenants in Bellamy. The swimming pool was and continues to be operated by a committee of white tenants.

At the request of Negro residents of the Bellamy community, the American Can Company within the first year of ownership, at its expense, built another swimming pool, larger than the one previously built by the white tenants. This pool cost the Company approximately $23,000 and is currently operated by a committee of Negro residents of the Bellamy community. To the Company's knowledge, no Negro has ever sought admission to the swimming pool built by the white tenants and no white has ever sought admission to the swimming pool built by the American Can Company.

Two churches are located on Company property adjacent to the sawmill. Negroes attend one church and whites attend the other. . . .[68]

After intervention of the Office of Federal Contract Compliance, the company worked out a program leading to peaceful desegregation. Undoubtedly, the addition of the civil rights problem to others inherent in company housing will encourage concerns to dispose of such holdings whenever possible.

EFFICIENCY AND TURNOVER

Lumber industry employees have very high turnover rates (Table 9, p. 21). Some might try to establish a relationship between the high turnover rate and the high percent Negro employment in the industry. In reply to such an accusation, the following statement was made in 1935: "Negroes are as a rule hired to do unpleasant work which is frequently casual and they are also marginal laborers with slight hold on their jobs. These

---

68. *Hearings Before the United States Commission on Civil Rights*, Montgomery, Alabama, April 27 to May 2, 1968, pp. 1067-1075.

facts, in addition to the fact that the type of labor which falls to the lot of colored workers is of the kind that ordinarily has a higher turnover, regardless of the race of those doing such labor, throw considerable light on the tendency toward irregularity." [69] Such a large portion of the lumber industry labor force consists of manual laborers who do not identify with a particular firm or even industry and whose few skills are highly transferable between industries, that it is this skill mix of the industry, not the racial mix, that is the primary cause of the high turnover rates.

A large portion of the turnover in parts of the South (especially the Negro turnover) is not a result of either the employee's or the employer's desire for the employee to leave, but the result of social conditions. As a result of the rural nature of the industry, many of the employees live on small farms. Some own their own farms and some rent farmhouses from the owners. Those who own farms will often quit work at the lumber mill each spring for planting and again in the fall for harvesting. Those who rent farms often pay their rent by planting and harvesting the crops of the owner. Because of the difficulty of obtaining competent labor, the local lumber company will continue to rehire these men season after season.

Lumber company officials report little or no consistent difference in tardiness between white and black workers of the same job level. The rural southern Negro is accustomed to rising early because of his close tie with agriculture. In fact, one lumber operator reported better punctuality among his Negro workers than his white workers.

Absenteeism is a greater problem. It is not uncommon for a new employee to work diligently until he receives his first pay, then disappear and never return. Many southern rural Negroes have never seen so much money at one time. They feel that they are rich and do not need to work. It is also more common for the Negroes than the whites to use their paycheck for a "wild weekend" and have it run over into Monday. In order to avoid this excessive Monday absenteeism some employees have tried paying the men on Thursday, but that only increased Friday absenteeism. Others have tried to pay the men less often but this only increases the number of men requesting advances on

69. "Relative Efficiency of Negro and White Workers," *Monthly Labor Review*, Vol. 40, No. 2 (February 1935), p. 337.

their pay because they ran out of money before the end of the pay period.

Unlike the paper industry, there is little formal training of lumber industry recruits or employees because of the small size of the operations and the low skill level required for most jobs. There is one company-sponsored training program in the South in which the sawmill is operated in conjunction with a large pulp mill and the courses available are of a general nature, i.e., concentration is on the "three R's." It is too soon to determine if this program will increase job performance or reduce turnover, absenteeism, or tardiness.

IMPACT OF GOVERNMENT PRESSURE

Companies in some industries claim that the government is forcing them to employ Negroes and as a result they are compelled to utilize persons of lower caliber than they require. Both the Equal Employment Opportunity Commission and the Office of Federal Contract Compliance have been very active in reducing job entrance requirements which they feel are excessive and used to preclude the movement of Negroes into these jobs.

Lumber manufacturers have had little difficulty complying with the wishes of these government agencies, and the government apparently has not challenged the employment policies of any firms in connection with their employment practices in their lumber or wood products operations. This is because of the widespread utilization of Negroes in the southern lumber industry and the common lack of entrance requirements.

Likewise, there have been few complaints by white workers of inverse discrimination. The complaints by white workers in the Far West of the special treatment of Negroes, when the company provided bus service for the Negroes to and from the cities to work, was one example of such a complaint. These, however, have been few. No general feeling was found among the white employees that Negro employees receive preferential treatment or that they "get away" with prohibited behavior.

Some lumber industry managers feel that although government pressure has not been a factor in reducing efficiency in this industry, government aid programs have been such a factor. Wages in the southern lumber industry are so low that employers must compete with welfare to obtain workers. Mr. Blanton, past President of the Southeastern Lumber Manufacturers Association, said that the sawmill operator's inability to secure enough labor to operate at full capacity is attributable to these factors: "A lot of men do not work when they can draw almost as much under the welfare programs not to work. A lot of men do not work when they can exploit the food stamp program. A lot of men do not and will not work when society will shoulder the load of feeding them." [70]

SOME PERSPECTIVES

Compared to most industries, government pressures have caused few problems in the lumber industry. Legislation has made it easier for employers to upgrade Negro workers, but resentment by white workers to the advancement of qualified Negroes has never been as acute a problem as in most other industries. The lumber and wood products manufacturers have been forced by law to take action in the area of desegregation of facilities. Such action, however, does relatively little in the way of improving the welfare of the race as compared to economic progress. Since the southern lumber industry is already a heavily Negro employing industry, there is little that legislation or government pressure can accomplish for the Negro in this industry except perhaps some increase in white collar jobs.

---

70. *Southern Lumberman,* Vol. 218, No. 2715 (June 1, 1969), p. 14.

Determinants of Industry Policy

A number of factors have been noted throughout this study which have contributed to the racial policies of the lumber and wood products industry. These and others are discussed in this chapter.

THE DEMAND FOR LABOR

The lumber industry's racial employment policy has not conformed with this characteristic pattern. The lumber industry has always had a great need for the unskilled and uneducated and because the work is not conducive to female employment the industry has had to rely on the minority group members who are less well equipped for employment in other industries. As a result there has been little change in the racial employment practices as the economy has moved through periods of rapid expansion and decline. Also, the expansions and contractions of the lumber industry have not coincided with that of the economy as a whole. Lumber and wood products demand is closely tied to residential construction which is more subject to changes in interest rates than moves in the nation's economy. Therefore, surges in the demand for labor in the lumber industry have not generally corresponded with surges in the demand for labor in the economy.

THE JOB STRUCTURE

Except for the industry's high regional concentration in the South, the job structure of the lumber industry has been the greatest reason for the high utilization of Negroes. The lumber industry is characterized by a job structure in which the large majority of jobs require little education, skill, or training; pay poorly; and are not conducive to female labor. In other words, the lumber industry has jobs for the man whom few other industry can utilize. The logging portion of this industry is even more highly characterized by this type of job structure.

There has been some mechanization and minor examples of

automation in the manufacture of lumber and wood products which have resulted in slight increases in white collar and skilled jobs and slight decreases in laboring jobs. The movement in this direction has not been nearly so great as in most industries and consequently there has been relatively little threat to Negro jobs in this industry. Employers do not need to make special efforts to attract Negro workers: there are few whites interested in the low pay and poor working conditions which the lumber industry offers.

In the white collar jobs, there is a different racial employment pattern. Negroes are very poorly represented in these jobs. Most of the white collar personnel in the southern wood products operations are close friends or members of the same family. The turnover of white collar jobs is very low and there is no reason to believe that many Negroes with the necessary qualifications are interested in securing white collar employment in this industry. It is not likely that there will be much increase in the small number of Negroes engaged in this type of work.

GOVERNMENT PRESSURE

Contrary to the situation in most industries, government pressure has not been a prime motivating force in altering the practices of the lumber industry. Negroes have been a highly valued asset to the southern lumber industry almost since they first arrived in this country as slaves. As the industry moved South, greater use was made of Negroes, and when other industries also began to expand in the South and draw upon the supply of white workers, the lumber industry's use of Negroes increased further. Government pressure has resulted in only two small changes within this industry: (1) promotion of a Negro into a supervisory or skilled position is less likely to receive opposition from the white workers and (2) the industry has been forced to defy the established sentiments and wishes of the majority of whites in the community and desegregate facilities.

UNIONISM AND SENIORITY

Few of the southern lumber and wood products operations are unionized. Many of those that are unionized are owned by the large pulp and paper companies who have grown to accept unions over the many years that they have been strong in the paper industry. Some of the unionized lumber operations are, in fact, represented by paper workers' unions, such as the Pulp, Sulphite, and Paper Mill Workers and the United Papermakers and Paperworkers. Most prominent in the industry are the International Woodworkers of America (IWA) and the United Brotherhood of Carpenters and Joiners of America (UBCJA), both affiliated with the AFL-CIO. None of these unions possess powerful influence in the southern lumber industry.

It does not appear that unions have ever worked to encourage exclusion of Negroes from employment or advancement in the lumber industry. Moreover, in neither union nor nonunion lumber operations are there defined seniority lines of any significance. Promotions are based on management decision about who is best qualified. In view of their weakness in the South, unions have virtually no control over the situation.

LOCATIONAL AND REGIONAL FACTORS

Locational and regional factors are unquestionably very important determinants of Negro employment in the lumber industry. None of the industries studied in this Series more vividly demonstrates the importance of joint regional and locational characteristics in influencing the racial employment pattern of an industry. Certainly the most clearly defined observation to be made from this study is that when there exists an industry with low skill and educational requirements that pays poorly and offers physically strenuous work (e.g., the lumber industry) in a region and location where there is a high concentration of a disadvantaged minority group (the Negro in the rural South), there results a high representation of this group in that industry (42.5 percent for the Negro in the southern lumber industry in 1968—Table 22). Conversely, if the same industry exists in a region of moderate minority group concentration (the Negro in the West), but in a location of low concentration (the Negro in the rural West), an industry with very low minority group representation results (0.6 percent for the Negro in the western lumber industry in 1968—Appendix Table B-5—which is far lower than for most industries in that region). Both region and location are important; neither alone solely determines the availability of the minority group labor supply. This adds reinforcement to Dr. Northrup's concern for the future of Negro employment in industries that are moving out of the urban areas in the North and West.

MANAGERIAL POLICY

Managerial policy in the lumber industry regarding racial employment has evolved out of necessity. Lumber manufacturers are not consumer oriented firms. Only the very large companies like Weyerhaeuser mark their product so that it can be differentiated. The product is basically homogeneous and is sold to agents or brokers and sometimes to retailers, but rarely directly to the consumer. Except in the immediate vicinity of the plant, the company's employment policies are usually not considered a matter of public concern.

Legislation and government pressure have not been factors influencing managerial policy. Most lumber companies in the South are so small that the likelihood of government intervention in their employment policies is small. At least in the immediate future, the probability is quite small because there are too many other industries toward which the government could more beneficially devote its time and efforts.

The management of lumber companies visited by the writer seemed honestly concerned with finding methods of employing and upgrading the Negro labor force. This concern arose primarily from their own needs. The southern lumber industry depends heavily on the Negro labor supply. This dependency has increased in recent years with the increasing influx of higher paying industries into the South. Most lumber industry managers feel very strongly that a dramatic improvement is necessary in the formal education offered southern Negro children, especially in rural areas. Many also say that they feel that in general the Negro does not possess the degree of motivation to learn, to work, or to achieve that exists in most white men. Whether this is fact or fiction, and whether motivation is an inherited or a learned trait, these beliefs exist and indicate a maintenance of the status quo.

It has been the general managerial policy in the lumber industry to employ the best work force obtainable from the existing supply of labor within the severe low-pay restraint. As other industries and the government have expanded operations in the South, lumber industry wages have declined relative to the other employment opportunities available. Years ago most lumber industry managers recognized that they could not afford the luxury of racial discrimination. Consequently, today the Negro is well

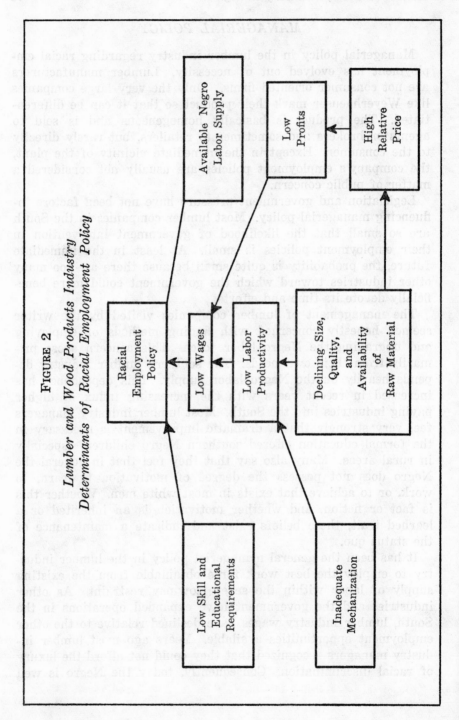

FIGURE 2

*Lumber and Wood Products Industry
Determinants of Racial Employment Policy*

represented in all blue collar jobs, albeit he is most highly represented in the lower skilled jobs.

Figure 2 relates the factors that have molded managerial policy in the lumber industry. Inadequate mechanization coupled with a decline in size, quality, and availability of timber have resulted in low labor productivity. These raw material factors plus lower productivity of labor have resulted in high prices (compared to other materials of construction). High prices have resulted in increased usage of substitute goods and, therefore, sales at less than capacity and low profits. Low profits and low labor productivity have resulted in low wages. The low wages coupled with lack of necessity for highly skilled or highly educated workers, and the ample supply of Negro labor in the rural South have caused management to choose its present policy of making maximum utilization of the Negro labor in blue collar jobs.

CHAPTER VII

Concluding Remarks

Civil rights legislation, government pressure, and full employment have had little effect on the racial employment pattern in the lumber and wood products industry. The low wages, lack of entrance requirements, and low skill and educational level necessary for employment have resulted in an industry ideally suited for utilization of a disadvantaged minority group. The high concentration of this industry in the South has led this industry in the direction of high Negro employment. The Negro has been a critical component in the southern lumber industry since before the turn of the century.

Most changes in the degree of Negro representation in the lumber industry on a national scale have resulted from geographical shifts in the industry. The Negro has always been represented in all blue collar occupations. He has further improved his hold over the more highly skilled jobs through the years, but the change has been very gradual. This trend will, no doubt, continue as white workers are continually drawn to the higher paying industries and government jobs. Few Negroes are employed as white collar employees, and because of this industry's structure, there is little hope for change. The growth of the "third forest" in the South promises to bring more job opportunities for the southern rural Negro, but the move toward substitute materials for wood may in turn dampen these prospects.

Appendix A

OCCUPATIONAL DESCRIPTIONS

Block Setter (block placer, ratchet setter, setter)

Rides on log carriage of headsaw and on signal by head sawyer moves lever to adjust position of log on carriage so that planks of desired thickness are cutoff as carriage passes saw; pulls lever which moves carriage blocks toward center of carriage to make room for log; moves lever to advance log toward edge of carriage to cutting position; and advances log after each return of carriage.

Carrier Driver

Operates a special truck which is used to lift, transport, and deposit piles of lumber from one place to another within the plant. Drives truck into position; moves levers which hook under and lift piles of lumber; drives carrier to designated location with lumber slung underneath; and releases levers lowering lumber to the ground.

Cat Driver, Skidding

Operates a gasoline- or diesel-powered tractor to pull logs out of the woods to a loading platform.

Chokerman (choke setter, choker, choker-hooking)

Maneuvers logs into skidding position with peavey and fastens choker (noose or wire, rope, cable, or chain) about each log by which the log is dragged to the loading platform. May level butt end of log with an ax to make it skid more easily.

Cutoff-saw Operator

Operates a swinging or treadle-operated cutoff saw to cut wooden stock to desired lengths, and grades and cuts stock to best advantage, eliminating knots and other defects.

Edgerman (edging-machine operator)

Adjusts spacing of the several saws of an edging machine in order to obtain the maximum number of standard width, quality boards from each plank; feeds the planks into the feed rollers that grasp and carry them through the machine; and raises or lowers, by handwheel, the feed rollers to accommodate planks of different thicknesses.

Faller and Bucker, Power (bucker, chopper, crosscutter, faller, feller, log cutter, timber cutter, timber faller, tree faller)

Working with partner, uses power-saw equipment to fell trees; may saw the felled trees into log lengths; may saw and chop limbs from felled trees to prepare them for cutting into logs for skidding.

Fireman, Stationary Boiler

Fires stationary boilers to furnish the establishment in which employed with heat, power, or steam. Feeds fuel to fire by hand or operates a mechanical stoker, gas or oil burner; and checks water and safety valves. May clean, oil, or assist in preparing boiler-room equipment.

Grader, Lumber

Examines and sorts milled or rough-sawed lumber according to designated standards; as milled lumber passes on conveyor belt or is placed on table, examines it on all sides for defects, such as knots, faulty edges, stains, and unsatisfactory machine work; routes faulty pieces to workers who dispose of them; removes satisfactory pieces and places them in proper bin or truck; sorts them into classes which are determined by the presence of blemishes, such as worm holes, small knots, or off-coloring. May scale board footage in each piece and record results. In some establishments the grader marks each satisfactory piece with a number that indicates its grade and sends it to the sorter, who places it in proper bin.

Ground Loader (hooker, tongs hooker, tongs puller)

Stationed on the ground and assists in loading logs upon railway cars, trucks, or other vehicles, or assists in rolling logs onto a log deck. Work involves maneuvering log into position with a peavey and fastening tongs, chains, or other devices about the log by which the log is loaded, or guiding log with peavey as the log is pulled up on skids and onto log deck, sled, truck, or other vehicle. Includes ground loader employed on mechanical loading operations and workers who load logs manually.

Headsaw Operator (sawyer, head sawyer)

Supervises and directs activities of the entire head rig crew while operating a band headsaw or a circular headsaw, which cuts logs into rough lumber; is responsible for maintaining efficient work performance, high rates of production, and for keeping waste to a minimum.

Loader, Car and Truck (car storer, car stower, carman, freight-car loader, train loader, vehicle loader)

Loads railway car or motortruck with lumber products using handtrucks, skids, bars, chutes, hand hoists, jacks or similar equipment; places products in a compact load which will not shift or be damaged in transit and will permit unloading in desired order. May secure load with ropes, metal straps, or other fastening; and may also unload incoming shipments.

Log Deckman (deckman, log handler, rampman, sawmill-deck laborer)

Arranges logs on sawmill log deck in convenient order for accessibility to carriage of head saw; rolls logs from conveyor, tram car, or motortruck into position, using a cant hook; or guides loads of logs being moved by crane or derrick, and releases lashings from logs after they are lowered to the deck, using a cant hook to roll logs into position. May operate mechanical equipment in pulling logs up an incline from the log pond. May remove stones or nails embedded in the bark of the logs with pick or ax.

Lumber Stacker (piler, stacker, kiln loader, kiln pusher)

Piles rough-sawed or planed lumber in large stacks for air drying or loads kiln cars and pushes them into steam-heated kilns for seasoning. Stacks lumber manually or with the aid of mechenical equipment, separating layers with "stickers" to increase air circulation and expedite drying. Usually works in a team.

Off-Bearers, Machine

Stationed at the discharge end of a saw or machine to receive wooden parts as they come off the machine; and piles or loads materials on a conveyor for transfer elsewhere.

Planer Operator (facer operator, planer, surfacer operator, wood planer operator)

Operates a single or double surface planer to level off irregularities and cut a smooth surface on rough stock, reducing it to specified thickness. Planer operators may be classified on the basis of whether they: *Operate only*—by feeding stock into the machine; or *set up and operate*—by adjusting table for depth of cut and thickness of stock; adjusting pressure bar; inserting, guiding, and checking stock; and changing dull blades.

Pondman (boatman, boomman, hoister, log chain feeder, log rider, poler, pond monkey, sinkerman, sinker puller, swingman)

Performs any of the following duties connected with the storage of logs in a pond and their selection and delivery to log chute for sawing: Selects logs and drives them to log chute, working from catwalk, flatboat, raft, or from floating logs; guides logs with pike pole onto log chain that carries them up to log deck, working from bank near foot of log chute; raises sunken logs; and operates a powered winch on pond bank to haul cable with which sunken or jammed logs are raised or released.

Sorter, Green Chain (green-chain tailer, green chainman)

Removes newly sawed lumber from conveyor, handtruck, etc., and stacks it in piles according to size and grade marked on each piece by grader.

Trimmerman (double-end-trimmer operator, equalizer-machine operator, trim sawyer, trimming machine operator, multisaw trimmer operator)

Operates a machine equipped with two or more cutoff saws mounted on a common horizontal shaft to cut wooden stock to desired lengths. The saws may be adjustable and are spaced by handwheel to obtain desired lengths of stock. Stock is fed to the saws either by placing individual lengths on a conveyer belt or chain that feeds stock into the saws, or on a movable table that is pushed past the saws. This type of saw is used in a sawmill to square stock ends, to cut stock to standard lengths, and to trim out defects.

Truckdriver, Logging

Hauls logs on a log truck (a two-wheeled trailer with long tongue and regular truck) from forest over highways to a landing or log pond. Aids in loading and unloading logs and fastens chains around logs on truck. Includes drivers of all types of trucking equipment used in hauling logs.

Source: U. S. Bureau of Labor Statistics, *Industry Wage Survey, West Coast Sawmilling*, June 1964, Bulletin No. 1455, and *Southern Sawmills and Planing Mills*, October 1965, Bulletin No. 1519.

Appendix B

BASIC STATISTICAL TABLES

TABLE B-1. *Lumber and Wood Products Industry, Employment by Race, Sex, and Occupational Group*
132 Establishments, Northeast Region, 1966

Occupational Group	All Employees			Male			Female		
	Total	Negro	Percent Negro	Total	Negro	Percent Negro	Total	Negro	Percent Negro
Officials and managers	947	—	—	930	—	—	17	—	—
Professionals	259	1	0.4	252	1	0.4	7	—	—
Technicians	264	—	—	241	—	—	23	—	—
Sales workers	531	3	0.6	486	1	0.2	45	2	4.4
Office and clerical	1,408	10	0.7	398	1	0.3	1,010	9	0.9
Total white collar	3,409	14	0.4	2,307	3	0.1	1,102	11	1.0
Craftsmen	1,932	53	2.7	1,877	53	2.8	55	—	—
Operatives	6,936	211	3.0	5,543	167	3.0	1,393	44	3.2
Laborers	5,077	412	8.1	3,769	346	9.2	1,308	66	5.0
Service workers	315	11	3.5	281	10	3.6	34	1	2.9
Total blue collar	14,260	687	4.8	11,470	576	5.0	2,790	111	4.0
Total	17,669	701	4.0	13,777	579	4.2	3,892	122	3.1

Source: U.S. Equal Employment Opportunity Commission, *Job Patterns for Minorities and Women in Private Industry, 1966*, Report No. 1 (Washington: The Commission, 1968), Part II.

Note: For regional definitions, see Table 3.
Data for South Region, 1964, 1966, and 1968 are in Tables 20-22 of text.

TABLE B-2. *Lumber and Wood Products Industry*
Employment by Race, Sex, and Occupational Group
203 Establishments
Midwest Region, 1966

Occupational Group	All Employees			Male			Female		
	Total	Negro	Percent Negro	Total	Negro	Percent Negro	Total	Negro	Percent Negro
Officials and managers	1,978	5	0.3	1,949	5	0.3	29	—	—
Professionals	356	—	—	348	—	—	8	—	—
Technicians	713	3	0.4	691	2	0.3	22	1	4.5
Sales workers	882	—	—	819	—	—	63	—	—
Office and clerical	2,773	5	0.2	1,053	—	—	1,720	5	0.3
Total white collar	6,702	13	0.2	4,860	7	0.1	1,842	6	0.3
Craftsmen	3,506	74	2.1	3,374	72	2.1	132	2	1.5
Operatives	10,937	440	4.0	9,397	340	3.6	1,540	100	6.5
Laborers	10,163	870	8.6	8,687	725	8.3	1,476	145	9.8
Service workers	410	25	6.1	327	18	5.5	83	7	8.4
Total blue collar	25,016	1,409	5.6	21,785	1,155	5.3	3,231	254	7.9
Total	31,718	1,422	4.5	26,645	1,162	4.4	5,073	260	5.1

Source: U.S. Equal Employment Opportunity Commission, *Job Patterns for Minorities and Women in Private Industry, 1966,* Report No. 1, Washington: The Commission, 1968), Part II.

Note: For regional definitions, see Table 3.

TABLE B-3. Lumber and Wood Products Industry
Employment by Race, Sex, and Occupational Group
76 Companies
Far West Region, 1964

Occupational Group	All Employees			Male			Female		
	Total	Negro	Percent Negro	Total	Negro	Percent Negro	Total	Negro	Percent Negro
Officials and managers	1,391	—	—	1,383	—	—	8	—	—
Professionals	535	—	—	522	—	—	13	—	—
Technicians	360	—	—	340	—	—	20	—	—
Sales workers	293	1	0.3	238	—	—	55	1	1.8
Office and clerical	1,662	21	1.3	593	2	0.3	1,069	19	1.8
Total white collar	4,241	22	0.5	3,076	2	0.1	1,165	20	1.7
Craftsmen	7,869	16	0.2	7,863	16	0.2	6	—	—
Operatives	14,465	111	0.8	14,223	111	0.8	242	—	—
Laborers	12,589	130	1.0	12,397	129	1.0	192	1	0.5
Service workers	453	6	1.3	355	4	1.1	98	2	2.0
Total blue collar	35,376	263	0.7	34,838	260	0.7	538	3	0.6
Total	39,617	285	0.7	37,914	262	0.7	1,703	23	1.4

Source: Data in author's possession.

Note: For regional definitions, see Table 3.

TABLE B-4. *Lumber and Wood Products Industry*
Employment by Race, Sex, and Occupational Group
467 Establishments
Far West Region, 1966

Occupational Group	All Employees			Male			Female		
	Total	Negro	Percent Negro	Total	Negro	Percent Negro	Total	Negro	Percent Negro
Officials and managers	4,608	8	0.2	4,550	8	0.2	58	—	—
Professionals	1,572	2	0.1	1,543	2	0.1	29	—	—
Technicians	1,023	—	—	951	—	—	72	—	—
Sales workers	740	—	—	640	—	—	100	—	—
Office and clerical	4,256	11	0.3	1,208	2	0.2	3,048	9	0.3
Total white collar	12,199	21	0.2	8,892	12	0.1	3,307	9	0.3
Craftsmen	20,020	85	0.4	19,974	84	0.4	46	1	2.2
Operatives	38,563	273	0.7	37,831	267	0.7	732	6	0.8
Laborers	31,604	365	1.2	30,545	364	1.2	1,059	1	0.1
Service workers	823	29	3.5	657	10	1.5	166	19	11.4
Total blue collar	91,010	752	0.8	89,007	725	0.8	2,003	27	1.3
Total	103,209	773	0.7	97,899	737	0.8	5,310	36	0.7

Source: U.S. Equal Employment Opportunity Commission, *Job Patterns for Minorities and Women in Private Industry, 1966*, Report No. 1 (Washington: The Commission, 1969), Part II.

Note: For regional definitions, see Table 3.

TABLE B-5. Lumber and Wood Products Industry
Employment by Race, Sex, and Occupational Group
66 Companies
Far West Region, 1968

Occupational Group	All Employees			Male			Female		
	Total	Negro	Percent Negro	Total	Negro	Percent Negro	Total	Negro	Percent Negro
Officials and managers	2,421	1	*	2,404	1	*	17	—	—
Professionals	574	3	0.5	557	3	0.5	17	—	—
Technicians	345	3	0.9	332	3	0.9	13	—	—
Sales workers	195	—	—	164	—	—	31	—	—
Office and clerical	1,417	4	0.3	517	3	0.6	900	1	0.1
Total white collar	4,952	11	0.2	3,974	10	0.3	978	1	0.1
Craftsmen	10,220	47	0.5	10,183	47	0.5	37	—	—
Operatives	18,461	126	0.7	18,187	126	0.7	274	—	—
Laborers	14,054	122	0.9	13,469	121	0.9	585	1	0.2
Service workers	393	1	0.3	342	1	0.3	51	—	—
Total blue collar	43,128	296	0.7	42,181	295	0.7	947	1	0.1
Total	48,080	307	0.6	46,155	305	0.7	1,925	2	0.1

Source: Data in author's possession.

Note: For regional definitions, see Table 3.

* Less than 0.05 percent.

TABLE B-6. *Lumber and Wood Products Industry and All Industries Employment by Race for States South Region, 1966*

State	Lumber and Wood Products			All Industries		
	Total	Negro	Percent Negro	Total	Negro	Percent Negro
Alabama	5,772	2,957	51.2	380,040	62,668	16.5
Arkansas	10,557	3,711	35.2	157,130	17,070	10.9
Florida	2,757	1,594	57.8	557,067	74,036	13.3
Georgia	8,801	4,286	48.7	579,851	91,995	15.9
Kentucky	2,755	390	14.2	309,049	21,255	6.9
Louisiana	6,727	3,874	57.6	303,150	55,173	18.2
Mississippi	7,800	3,864	49.5	172,442	30,884	17.9
North Carolina	7,179	2,661	37.1	694,758	87,335	12.6
South Carolina	3,679	2,118	56.7	330,473	47,671	14.4
Tennessee	7,280	3,028	41.6	506,572	52,965	10.5
Texas	7,617	1,905	25.0	1,102,349[a]	102,856	9.3
Virginia	6,169	2,596	42.1	486,600	77,630	16.0
West Virginia	1,260	1	0.1	190,752	5,960	3.1

Source: U.S. Equal Employment Opportunity Commission, *Job Patterns for Minorities and Women in Private Industry, 1966*, Report No. 1 (Washington: The Commission, 1968), Part II.

[a] Figure obtained by adding males and females.

TABLE B-7.   *Lumber and Wood Products Industry and All Industries*
Employment by Race for States
Northeast Region, 1966

State	Lumber and Wood Products			All Industries		
	Total	Negro	Percent Negro	Total	Negro	Percent Negro
Maine	4,761	3	0.1	108,749	161	0.1
Massachusetts	1,546	6	0.4	884,604	25,664	2.9
New Jersey	1,874	405	21.6	932,420	91,055	9.8
New York	3,801	72	1.9	2,499,613	189,757	7.6
Pennsylvania	5,687	215	3.8	1,892,646	116,443	6.2

Source: U.S. Equal Employment Opportunity Commission, *Job Patterns for Minorities and Women in Private Industry, 1966*, Report No. 1 (Washington: The Commission, 1968), Part II.

TABLE B-8. *Lumber and Wood Products Industry and All Industries*
Employment by Race for States
Midwest Region, 1966

State	Lumber and Wood Products			All Industries		
	Total	Negro	Percent Negro	Total	Negro	Percent Negro
Illinois	5,417	986	18.2	1,827,733	201,562	11.0
Indiana	7,271	170	2.3	844,688	51,762	6.1
Michigan	2,373	105	4.4	1,372,598	145,569	10.6
Minnesota	2,172	4	0.2	430,480	5,018	1.2
Missouri	1,914	42	2.2	669,660	54,616	8.2
Ohio	3,217	91	2.8	1,717,341[a]	122,207	7.1
Wisconsin	9,354	24	0.3	582,905	18,497	3.2

Source: U.S. Equal Employment Opportunity Commission, *Job Patterns for Minorities and Women in Private Industry, 1966*, Report No. 1 (Washington: The Commission, 1968), Part II.

[a] Figure obtained by adding males and females.

TABLE B-9.   *Lumber and Wood Products Industry and All Industries*
Employment by Race for States
Far West Region, 1966

State	Lumber and Wood Products			All Industries		
	Total	Negro	Percent Negro	Total	Negro	Percent Negro
Arizona	1,467	182	12.4	157,753	3,430	2.2
California	20,905	481	2.3	2,350,188	129,365	5.5
Idaho	3,702	—	—	44,556	94	0.2
Montana	4,383	1	*	46,056	80	0.2
Oregon	43,710	39	0.1	210,772	3,391	1.6
Washington	29,042	70	0.2	334,039	6,734	2.0

Source: U.S. Equal Employment Opportunity Commission, *Job Patterns for Minorities and Women in Private Industry, 1966*, Report No. 1 (Washington: The Commission, 1968), Part II.

* Less than 0.05 percent.

TABLE B-10. *Lumber and Wood Products Industry*
Employment by Race, Sex, and Occupational Group
8 of the 10 Largest Companies
South Region, 1968

Occupational Group	All Employees			Male			Female		
	Total	Negro	Percent Negro	Total	Negro	Percent Negro	Total	Negro	Percent Negro
Officials and managers	1,232	23	1.9	1,223	23	1.9	9	—	—
Professionals	480	2	0.4	478	2	0.4	2	—	—
Technicians	312	10	3.2	308	10	3.2	4	—	—
Sales workers	130	—	—	111	—	—	19	—	—
Office and clerical	695	9	1.3	211	9	4.3	484	—	—
Total white collar	2,849	44	1.5	2,331	44	1.9	518	—	—
Craftsmen	1,977	370	18.7	1,958	366	18.7	19	4	21.1
Operatives	4,303	1,712	39.8	4,186	1,668	39.8	117	44	37.6
Laborers	5,006	2,845	56.8	4,529	2,601	57.4	477	244	51.2
Service workers	99	57	57.6	71	33	46.5	28	24	85.7
Total blue collar	11,385	4,984	43.8	10,744	4,668	43.4	641	316	49.3
Total	14,234	5,028	35.3	13,075	4,712	36.0	1,159	316	27.3

Source: Data in author's possession.

Note: For regional definitions, see Table 3.

TABLE B-11. Lumber and Wood Products Industry
Employment by Race, Sex, and Occupational Group
8 of the 10 Largest Companies
Far West Region, 1968

Occupational Group	All Employees			Male			Female		
	Total	Negro	Percent Negro	Total	Negro	Percent Negro	Total	Negro	Percent Negro
Officials and managers	1,492	—	—	1,486	—	—	6	—	—
Professionals	365	2	0.5	353	2	0.6	12	—	—
Technicians	173	1	0.6	166	1	0.6	7	—	—
Sales workers	79	—	—	72	—	—	7	—	—
Office and clerical	814	2	0.2	294	2	0.7	520	—	—
Total white collar	2,923	5	0.2	2,371	5	0.2	552	—	—
Craftsmen	6,160	6	0.1	6,154	6	0.1	6	—	—
Operatives	11,685	52	0.4	11,525	52	0.5	160	—	—
Laborers	7,762	53	0.7	7,373	52	0.7	389	1	0.3
Service workers	203	—	—	177	—	—	26	—	—
Total blue collar	25,810	111	0.4	25,229	110	0.4	581	1	0.2
Total	28,733	116	0.4	27,600	115	0.4	1,133	1	0.1

Source: Data in author's possession.

Note: For regional definitions, see Table 3.

TABLE B-12. All Industries, Employment by Race, Sex, and Occupational Group 116,901 Establishments, Total United States, 1966 (thousands)

Occupational Group	All Employees			Male			Female		
	Total	Negro	Percent Negro	Total	Negro	Percent Negro	Total	Negro	Percent Negro
Officials and managers	2,078	18	0.9	1,882	14	0.7	196	4	2.2
Professionals	1,690	22	1.3	1,454	12	0.8	236	10	4.3
Technicians	1,138	47	4.1	784	17	2.2	354	29	8.3
Sales workers	1,797	42	2.4	1,100	17	1.6	696	25	3.6
Office and clerical	4,265	151	3.5	1,178	39	3.3	3,087	112	3.6
Total white collar	10,967	280	2.6	6,398	99	1.6	4,569	181	4.0
Craftsmen	3,626	131	3.6	3,396	115	3.4	230	16	6.8
Operatives	6,499	702	10.8	4,700	542	11.5	1,799	160	8.9
Laborers	2,466	524	21.2	1,877	434	23.1	589	90	15.3
Service workers	1,952	452	23.2	1,108	259	23.4	844	193	22.9
Total blue collar	14,544	1,809	12.4	11,081	1,350	12.2	3,462	458	13.2
Total	25,511	2,089	8.2	17,479	1,449	8.3	8,031	640	8.0

Source: U.S. Equal Employment Opportunity Commission, Job Patterns for Minorities and Women in Private Industry, 1966, Report No. 1 (Washington: The Commission, 1968), Part II.

Note: Figures may not add due to rounding. Percentages are based on unrounded figures for greater accuracy. Table excludes Alaska and Hawaii.

TABLE B-13. All Industries

Employment by Race, Sex, and Occupational Group
by Regions, 1966
(thousands)

Occupational Group	South			Northeast			Midwest			Far West		
	Total	Negro	Percent Negro	Total	Negro	Percent Negro	Total	Negro	Percent Negro	Total	Negro	Percent Negro
Officials and managers	525	6	1.1	594	6	1.0	647	5	0.8	312	2	0.5
Professionals	361	6	1.6	546	8	1.5	442	5	1.2	342	3	0.9
Technicians	247	13	5.3	377	16	4.3	325	12	3.7	189	5	2.9
Sales workers	468	13	2.9	481	11	2.3	565	13	2.2	282	5	1.8
Office and clerical	928	26	2.7	1,389	63	4.6	1,265	44	3.4	683	19	2.7
Total white collar	2,530	64	2.5	3,386	105	3.1	3,243	78	2.4	1,808	34	1.9
Craftsmen	1,005	48	4.8	950	33	3.4	1,140	37	3.2	531	13	2.4
Operatives	1,898	268	14.1	1,623	131	8.1	2,341	264	11.3	638	39	6.2
Laborers	746	289	38.8	602	86	14.2	820	122	14.8	299	28	9.3
Service workers	512	192	37.6	551	102	18.4	575	117	20.4	314	41	13.0
Total blue collar	4,160	797	19.2	3,725	351	9.4	4,877	540	11.1	1,782	121	6.8
Total	6,689	860	12.9	7,112	456	6.4	8,119	618	7.6	3,590	155	4.3

Source: U. S. Equal Employment Opportunity Commission, Job Patterns for Minorities and Women in Private Industry, 1966, Report No. 1 (Washington: The Commission, 1969), Part II.

Note: For regional definitions, see Table 3.

Index

Absenteeism, 67-68
American Can Company, 65-66
American Forest Products Industries, 4, 5n
American Paper Institute, 34n
Atlantic Coast Lumber Company, 26
Automation, mechanization, and technological change, 2, 7, 14, 16, 70, 75

Berglund, Abraham, 65n
Bethel, James Samuel, 5n
Blanton, President of Southeastern Lumber Manufacturers Association, 68-69
Boise-Cascade Corporation, 7
Brown, Nelson Courtlandt, 5n

Carpenters' union *see* United Brotherhood
Civil Rights Act of 1964, 16n, 48
Cornell, William B., 9n

deVyer, Frank T., 65n
Diamond International Corporation, 7
Douty, H. M., 24n
Duerr, William A., 20n

East Texas Lumber Workers, 22n
Educational requirements, 17, 22, 70
Elmer, Manuel Conrad, 4n
Employment, 7, 14
    female, 17, 19, 37
Equal Employment Opportunity Commission, 16, 40, 48, 68

Evans Products Company, 7
Fair Labor Standards Act, 22
Field sample, 1964-1968, 48-52
Forest Industries, 12n
Forests, 8, 75, 76

Georgia-Pacific Corporation, 7
Glover, John G., 9n
Greene, Lorenzo J., 25, 26n, 28n, 39, 39n

Harris, Abram L., 39n

Industrial characteristics, 5-9
    growth, 8-9
    production process, 3-5
    profits, 22, 75
    regional concentration, 42, 72
Industrial location, 9-14, 22, 72
    effect on Negro employment, 43-44, 55-57
    Far West, 9, 12, 34
        production, 28
        nature of work, 13-14
        occupational distribution, 57
        technology, 14
        and unions, 24
        wages, 22
    geographical shifts, 26, 31, 34-36, 76
    Midwest, 12
    Northeast, 9
    South, 9, 12-13, 26, 31, 34-36
        forests, 8, 12
        miscellaneous wood products in, 8-9
        production, 8, 12-13, 28
        sawmills, 12-13
        and unions, 39
        wages in, 22
Industrial structure, 7-8, 42
    company size, 20, 57-60
    concentration, 7-8
    demand for labor, 70
    family ownership, 20, 43-44
    integration, 5
    plant size, 5
Industrial Workers of the World, 39
International Woodworker, 13n
International Woodworkers of America, 22, 24, 72

Jensen, Vernon H., 2n, 65n

Labor force, 8, 14-24, 60
    demand for, 70
    educational attainments, 17
    effect of location on, 61
    skill requirements, 22, 42, 60, 70
Lambert, Herb, 9n

95

PART THREE

THE NEGRO
IN THE TOBACCO INDUSTRY

by

HERBERT R. NORTHRUP

TABLE OF CONTENTS

LIST OF TABLES

viii   *List of Tables*

CHAPTER I

Introduction

The tobacco industry has employed Negroes since its inception in colonial Virginia. This study is primarily concerned with the course of Negro employment and industry racial policies in those branches of the industry processing, manufacturing, selling, and distributing cigarettes and "manufactured tobacco"—that is, smoking and chewing tobacco and snuff. Throughout this study, this will be known as the "tobacco industry," as distinct from the "cigar industry." The latter involves quite different manufacturing processes, industrial location, and industry policies, and is included in this study only incidentally. Our concern is with the industry which has had the longest continuous record of factory employment of Negroes in the United States, and which is today concentrated not only in the three southern states of Kentucky, North Carolina, and Virginia, but within these states, in seven cities—Louisville, Kentucky; Durham, Greensboro, Reidsville, and Winston-Salem, North Carolina; and Petersburg and Richmond, Virginia.

An analysis of the racial policies of the tobacco industry affords an opportunity to analyze the impact on such policies, over a long period of time, of such factors as the southern location, employment opportunities following new products and new technologies, mechanization and automation, union attitudes and policies, and governmental restraints. In order to put these matters into perspective, the characteristics of the industry and its structure will be briefly decribed in Chapter II.

1

CHAPTER II

The Tobacco Industry

When Columbus discovered America, he found the natives growing and processing tobacco for smoking, chewing, and snuff. Led by John Rolfe, at Jamestown, the English colonists later found that tobacco culture was their most profitable enterprise. A large part of the wealth of colonial Virginia and Maryland, and later of other states of the upper South, was based upon export of tobacco, which by the Revolution was about 100 million pounds.[1]

As tobacco was grown in various colonies and in the West Indies, it became apparent that different soils and climates caused many and noticeable differences in the characteristics of the product. The varying properties of the leaf were conducive to its use in many manufactured forms. This realization gave impetus to the importance of the domestic manufacturing of tobacco.

By 1790, 29 million pounds were used in manufacturing by small factories. The product was in the form of a roll or twist from which a portion was cut for chewing or smoking or grated for snuff. The manufacture of cigars began in the early 1800's. Initially, imported Cuban leaf was used, but then domestic products, grown first in Massachusetts and Connecticut and later in Pennsylvania and Wisconsin, were combined with the Cuban imports.[2]

During the first half of the nineteenth century, tobacco manufacturing was concentrated in Virginia and North Carolina. Negro slaves were the principal form of labor. Their masters, the upper class plantation proprietors and some of the bourgeoisie, hired them out to the tobacco manufacturers.[3]

---

1. U.S. Department of Agriculture, Consumer and Marketing Service, *Tobacco in the United States*, Miscellaneous Publication No. 867 (Washington: Government Printing Office, 1966), pp. 1-2.

2. *Ibid.*

3. The extent of Negro labor in these early factories is examined in Chapter III.

CIGARETTES AND THE PRODUCTION PROCESS

Prior to the Civil War, cigarettes were either unknown or confined to use by a small segment of society. They were introduced from Europe soon after the war and Negroes were taught to make them by hand rolling after the industry first experimented using immigrant Jews. By 1884, however, a cigarette machine was introduced which could produce 120,000 cigarettes per day as compared with 2,500, at most, by a hand operator. White, largely female, machine operators replaced Negro hand operators, as has so often been the case, with Negroes remaining in the processing (premanufacturing) jobs. A racial-occupational segregation pattern gradually became rigid. The following detailed description describes how it has operated over the years and explains the work traditionally performed by men and women, blacks and whites. Today, most of the hand operations have been eliminated. The racial-occupational segregation pattern began to crumble in the 1960's.

In the manufacture of cigarettes, four major departments are of importance in characterizing the work for men and women, whites and Negroes. These are the leaf handling, making, packing, and boxing departments. The tobacco leaf that goes into the cigarette is delicate and requires careful and skilled attention. From harvesting to the finishing process, a period ranging from a year to three years may elapse.

The leaf is first removed from the auction room.[4] This was traditionally a male Negro job. The redrying machine was originally operated by white men and the tobacco was fed into it by Negro men. Now this process is largely automatic. Going to a

---

4. The auctioned tobacco is obtained from the following areas: Burley tobacco, 90 percent of which is used in the domestic production of cigarettes, is grown principally in Kentucky and Tennessee, although Ohio, Indiana, Virginia, North Carolina, West Virginia, and Missouri also produce this product. Flue-cured tobacco, 95 percent of which is used in American cigarettes and the rest for smoking and chewing tobaccoes, is grown in Virginia, North Carolina, South Carolina, Georgia, Alabama, and Florida.

Maryland broadleaf, a light air-cured tobacco similar to burley, is used predominantly in cigarettes. Fired-cured, found in Virginia, Tennessee, and Kentucky, is utilized in making snuff, roll, and plug chewing tobacco, strong cigars, and heavy smoking tobacco.

Dark air-cured tobacco, grown in Kentucky, Tennessee, and Virginia, is used mainly for chewing tobacco and snuff, but, to some extent, for smoking tobacco and cigars. Pennsylvania, Wisconsin, and Connecticut grow cigar leaf tobacco. (U.S. Department of Agriculture, *op. cit.*, pp. 3-5.)

cooling chamber, the tobacco is packed into hogsheads and stored in the warehouses, usually by Negro men. This rehandling process is frequently carried on outside the large factory in separate establishments which are open for three or four months only, following the tobacco season. To preserve the tobacco, a large supply of labor must be readily available at this season. At the end of the season, these rehandling plants close down.

After aging, the tobacco is taken to the factory for the first stages of preparation. Negro women traditionally performed the next operations. Before mechanization the "pickers" opened up the "hands" of tobacco or untied the bunched tobacco to pick out the trash or gave it a shake to remove dust before putting it on the moving belt. The "orderers" took up the leaves, tied them in bunches, and hung them on racks before they went into the steamer. Today this is a highly mechanized operation, but Negro women still predominate.

The moist leaves are then ready for stemming. Formerly "shakers" removed and shook out the leaves and placed them on trays. After "sorters" arranged them by size and spread them out, the leaf was ready to stem. Originally done by hand, this is now almost completely mechanized. It has always been a female job.

In hand stemming, which, as indicated, was done almost exclusively by Negro men and women, but very largely by women, the mid rib was deftly removed with the least possible damage to the leaf. In machine stemming, a knife cuts out the vein and the leaves must be so stacked as to avoid damage. The machine at first required an operator, two feeders, and two searchers, but gradually improved mechanization reduced the complement. One of the "feeders" fed to the belt, and the other to the machine. The "searchers" watched the strips as they returned from the machine to complete the stemming if the machine had failed to remove the stem entirely. They also watched the stems to prevent leaves from being taken along with the stems.

The leaves are next prepared for blending and flavoring. This has been a Negro male job and has been regarded as skilled. If for cigarettes, the leaf then goes to the cutting machine, which was traditionally fed by a Negro man, and is shredded to the desired fineness. If the leaves are for smoking or chewing tobacco, the process varies from the point of stemming.

The shredded tobacco is then sent to the making machines, traditionally operated by white women. The "feeder" keeps the shredded tobacco flowing evenly into the machines which roll it in paper. The operator of the machine has traditionally been a white man or woman depending, to some extent, upon the machine. The "catcher" receives the made cigarettes in a tray to be sent to the packing room. The foremen, inspectors, and mechanics have been white men. The "weighers," who test the weight of the cigarettes, and the "counters" have traditionally been white women. The sweepers and cleaners are Negro men. As a rule the white and Negro workers were engaged in different operations and were on different floors or in different buildings.

The various operations of packing have also been jobs for both white men and women. The cigarettes are wrapped in foil, packed, sealed, and labelled by machine, and the revenue stamp affixed. "Watchers" for defective packages, "labelers," "stampers," "belt feeders" who send cartons to be wrapped, "salvagers" and "repairers" who remove parts of damaged packages all have been traditionally white men or women.

The process after stemming varies somewhat for smoking, chewing, and snuff tobacco. For chewing, the tobacco is flavored with mixtures which include licorice, cane sugar, and molasses. This was a job traditionally held by Negro men and women who had some skill. The weighers and dividers who prepared it for the mould were traditionally white as were workers who put on the outside leaf wrapper and operated the hydraulic pressure which gives shape to the plugs. The plugs are tagged and packed into wooden boxes, a job once reserved for white women. In the auxiliary work of making box containers and in removing these boxes for shipment to the market, Negro men have been used.[5]

Negroes historically have done the janitorial, porter, and outside work; whites have held the skilled maintenance jobs. Except for these groups, the segregation has been quite complete, not only occupationally, but also physically. Most Negroes have been employed in the stemming, blending, and shredding departments, which, because of atmospheric requirements, are housed in separate buildings, or at least on separate floors from other operations.

---

5. This outline is essentially an updating of the excellent description found in Charles S. Johnson, "The Tobacco Worker," National Recovery Administration, Division of Review, Industrial Studies Section, 1935, 2 vols., MS in U. S. Archives, Washington, D. C. (copy in author's possession), Vol. I, pp. 14-17.

INDUSTRIAL CHARACTERISTICS

Table 1 sets forth employment, payrolls, capital expenditures, and other industrial data for the various subdivisions of the tobacco industry for 1967 by the federal government's standard industrial classification system (SIC) of data collection. These data, first of all, make it very clear that the tobacco industry is not a large employer, having only 75,000 employees in 1967, according to the Census of Manufactures.[6] About two-thirds of these are in the branches of the industry covered by this study.

The cigarette sector of the industry is by far the largest employer, the chewing, smoking, and snuff (manufactured tobacco) sector, which has been declining on a secular basis for many years, the smallest. Tobacco stemmeries and redrying facilities include two types: manufacturers (captive) and independents. The former are owned by the manufacturing companies and operated for their own use throughout the year according to their needs in the manufacture of the products. Thus, despite some seasonal variations, these stemmeries provide year around employment for their workers, most of whom are Negroes.

Independent stemmeries, on the other hand, are operated by leaf tobacco dealers, the middlemen who purchase "green" leaf tobacco from farmers and sell it to manufacturers. These leaf dealers also age and redry tobacco and stem it for smaller companies and for export. Some of the leaf dealers have large storage facilities and can operate all year around, but most of them confine their operations to the late summer and fall months after the tobacco crop has been harvested.

Tobacco stemmeries are located in small towns throughout the tobacco-growing regions. They employ about twice as many persons—mostly Negro women—at peak season as they do on average during a year. About 90 percent of the employment in stemmeries serving the non-cigar tobacco industry is found in Kentucky, North Carolina, and Virginia.[7]

Tobacco manufacturing is today a highly mechanized series of operations. Payrolls are relatively small, cost of materials and value added by manufacturing are high. As will be shown

---

6. Census of Manufactures data are constructed quite differently from those of the U. S. Bureau of Labor Statistics, utilized below, and the two are not comparable.

7. Herbert R. Northrup, *Organized Labor and the Negro* (New York: Harper & Bros., 1944), pp. 108-109.

TABLE 1. Tobacco Industry

Employment, Payroll, Capital Expenditures, and Other Data by Standard Industrial Classification, 1967

	Tobacco Industry (SIC 21)	Cigarettes (SIC 2111)	Cigars (SIC 2121)	Chewing and Smoking Tobacco (SIC 2131)	Tobacco Stemming and Redrying [a] (SIC 2141)
Thousands of Employees					
All employees	75	37	19	4	15
Millions of Dollars					
Payroll	377	219	73	22	63
Value added by manufacture	2,011	1,615	199	89	108
Cost of materials	2,898	1,385	177	66	1,270
Value of shipments	4,957	3,036	374	156	1,391
Capital expenditures, new	53	32	5 [b]	2	14

Source: *U. S. Census of Manufacturers, 1967*, Series MC 67(P)-1, Summary Series, Preliminary Report, April 1969.

[a] Data subject to further checking and revision.

[b] Limited reliability.

in the examination of the racial employment trends in the industry, the trend since the development of the cigarette machine until recent years has featured increased productivity which permitted greater production either without materially adding to employment or actually reducing employment. In recent years, at least until 1960, Negroes have been disproportionately affected by these trends.

Industrial Structure

The development of the cigarette-making machine changed the industry from one of small shops to one in which the economies of scale all but eliminated the small producer. James B. Duke materially aided the process. In the age of trusts he had welded together by 1890 nearly all cigarette manufacturing except R. J. Reynolds, and the bulk of manufactured tobacco [8] into one great combine, The American Tobacco Company.

In 1911, The American Tobacco Company was dissolved by order of the United States Supreme Court.[9] The four successor companies are still a dominant part of the tobacco industry almost 60 years later. R. J. Reynolds, American Tobacco (which has changed its name to American Brands to reflect its broader product range), P. Lorillard, and Liggett & Myers were the "Big Four" of the industry until the latter two were passed in sales by Brown & Williamson, a subsidiary of British-American Tobacco Company, and by Philip Morris.

These six companies produced all but a tiny fraction of American-made cigarettes in 1969, as shown in Table 2. (They also produced an overwhelming, but somewhat smaller percentage of all the manufactured tobacco in the United States.) Reynolds and American together produced more than one-half of the 513.3 billion cigarettes sold in 1969. At the other end of the scale, small independent companies held a minute market share, accounting for just 0.3 percent of all the cigarettes sold. The other four major companies each held between about 6 and 15 percent of the sales.

---

8. Duke failed to achieve a similar monopoly in the cigar industry, which remained a handicraft operation with little or no economies of scale until the development of the cigar-making machine around World War I. He secured control of R. J. Reynolds a few days before the Supreme Court ordered his combine dissolved, but never had effective control of this company.

9. *United States* v. *American Tobacco Company*, 221 U. S. 106 (1911).

TABLE 2.   *Tobacco Industry*
Domestic Cigarette Sales by Company, 1969

Company	Domestic Sales Billions of Cigarettes
R. J. Reynolds	163.6
American Tobacco [a]	108.0
Brown & Williamson [b]	81.3
Philip Morris	77.1
P. Lorillard [c]	47.0
Liggett & Myers	35.0
All others	1.3
Total	513.3

Source: *Business Week*, December 13, 1969, p. 82.

[a] Name changed to American Brands in 1969.

[b] Subsidiary of British-American Tobacco.

[c] Absorbed by Loew's Theaters, 1968.

Table 3 sets forth statistics for five of the six major tobacco companies, those for Brown & Williamson, the number three producer, not being available. All are giant corporations and are taking on more and more the aspects of conglomerates. In recent years, for example, R. J. Reynolds acquired McLean Industries, Inc., operators of Sea-Land Service, and P. Lorillard merged into Lowe's Theaters. Philip Morris, Liggett & Myers, and American are all actively expanding into other areas, spurred by the continuing attacks on smoking as a cause of cancer, heart, and respiratory diseases, and the consequent decline in cigarette and tobacco sales.

The data in Table 3 thus reflect corporate activity in areas other than tobacco products. Nevertheless, they again demonstrate the industry's relatively small employment in relation to invested capital and sales. Of the companies, R. J. Reynolds, the only one with headquarters where its main operations are, is the largest and most profitable.

In addition to the six major concerns, there are a number of thriving smaller ones. Such companies are found mostly in the manufactured tobacco segment of the industry, and in the independent processing business. They, like the majors, are located primarily in Virginia, North Carolina, and Kentucky and follow the same general employment policies.

TABLE 3. *Five of the Six Major Tobacco Companies, 1968 Statistics*

Company and 1968 Rank Among Industrial Corporations		Headquarters	Sales	Assets	Net Income	Invested Capital	Number of Employees	Net Income as a Percent of	
								Sales	Invested Capital
			Thousands of Dollars						
R. J. Reynolds	(74)	Winston-Salem, N. C.	1,264,681	1,197,107	150,045	938,609	21,332	11.9	16.0
American Tobacco	(85)	New York	1,117,419	1,512,061	92,911	712,100	40,540 [a]	8.3	13.0
Philip Morris	(147)	New York	675,408	786,578	48,866	314,496	20,000	7.2	15.5
Liggett & Myers	(219)	New York	438,248	507,385	24,066	318,104	8,265	5.5	7.6
P. Lorillard	(255)	New York	359,180	363,363	30,714	209,586	7,000	8.4	14.3

Source: *Fortune*, Vol. LXXIX (May 15, 1969), pp. 170-177.

Note: Data include non-tobacco business. Since 1968, Reynolds has acquired McLean Industries, the 29th largest transportation company, Lorillard has been acquired by Loew's Theaters, and American Tobacco has changed its name to American Brands, Inc. Data for Brown & Williamson, the number three producer, are not available.

[a] *Fortune* figure may be an error. Tobacco employment in 1968 was about 14,000.

Industrial Location

The history of the tobacco industry has been one of steady industrial concentration of factories into the seven cities of three southern states. In the late twenties and early thirties, Liggett & Myers and American Tobacco abandoned their New York and Philadelphia plants and concentrated their production in the South. The last major northern plant was closed in 1956 when P. Lorillard moved its operations from Jersey City, New Jersey, to Greensboro, North Carolina. Table 4 lists the major company

TABLE 4. *Tobacco Industry*
Major Plant Locations
and Negro Percent of Population Estimates
1965 and 1970

City and State	Estimated Negro Population Percentage		Companies with Major Facilities[a]
	1965	1970	
Louisville, Kentucky	21	24	American [b] Brown & Williamson P. Lorillard Philip Morris
Durham, North Carolina	36	36	American Liggett & Myers
Greensboro, North Carolina	28	30	P. Lorillard
Reidsville, North Carolina	34 [c]	35 [c]	American
Winston-Salem, North Carolina	36	34	R. J. Reynolds Brown & Williamson
Petersburg, Virginia	47	49	Brown & Williamson
Richmond, Virginia	47	51 [d]	American Liggett & Myers Philip Morris

Source: Company annual reports and The Center for Research in Marketing, Inc., *The Negro Population: 1965 Estimates and 1970 Projections* (Peekskill, New York: The Center, 1966).

[a] Excludes stemmeries and warehouses or cigar factories not associated with other plants.

[b] American announced the closing of its Louisville facilities in late 1969; it will concentrate production in other areas.

[c] Author's estimates. In 1960 Negro population was 33 percent of total.

[d] The City of Richmond is now litigating the annexation of certain contiguous areas. An effect could be a reduction in the over-all percentage of Negroes in the city.

plant locations and the estimated percentage of the Negro population in each for 1965 and 1970. Obviously, the industry is concentrated in areas where a sizeable proportion of Negroes dwell and are available for employment.

The degree of concentration of the industry in these three states in terms of employees is shown in Table 5. In 1967, two-thirds of all tobacco workers and over 90 percent of cigarette employees were employed in the three southern states, with North Carolina accounting for more than one-half of the tristate employment. Data for manufactured tobacco and tobacco stemming and redrying are not available, but 80-90 percent of employees in these industry branches are certainly also located in the three states. Indeed, the only significant group of non-cigar tobacco employees not found in Kentucky, North Carolina, and Virginia are the central office employees in New York City, where all the major domestic companies except Reynolds maintain corporate headquarters.

MANPOWER

The tobacco industry, as already noted, is not a large employer. Moreover, as Table 6 shows, employment in several branches has actually declined in many periods as a result of technology or habit changes. For example, between 1919 and 1939, the production index of the cigarette industry (with 1929=100) rose from 43.4 to 147.7; but so great was the increase in productivity, that the employment index fell from 131.5 to 101.7 during this period.[10]

In more recent years, employment in the cigarette sector has increased, although declining cigarette sales in the last two or three years have apparently reversed this trend; employment for a number of years in the cigar branch has declined precipitously; that in manufactured tobacco has continued a long secular decline; and that in tobacco stemming and redrying has also declined. With Negroes concentrated in the latter two branches or in jobs in the cigarette industry that have been easy to automate, these trends have been inimical to Negro employment. The recent decline in cigarette smoking may reduce employment in that sector of the industry in the future.

---

10. U. S. Department of Labor, Wage and Hour Division, "The Tobacco Industry" (Mimeo., 1941), pp. 92-93.

TABLE 5. *Tobacco Industry*
Total Industry and Cigarette Employment
United States and Major Tobacco Manufacturing States, 1967

	Tobacco Industry (SIC 21)	Cigarettes (SIC 211)	Percent of Total Employment in Tobacco Industry	Percent of Total Employment in Cigarettes
Kentucky	13,000	9,400	14.9	22.5
North Carolina	30,700	19,200	35.2	46.1
Virginia	14,500	9,600	16.6	23.0
Total	58,200	38,200	66.7	91.6
Total United States	87,300	41,700	100.0	100.0

Source: U.S. Bureau of Labor Statistics, *Employment and Earnings Statistics for the United States, 1909-68*, Bulletin 3, No. 1312-6 (Washington: Government Printing Office, 1968) ; and *ibid.*, *Employment and Earnings Statistics for the States and Selected Areas, 1939-67*, Bulletin 180, No. 1370-5 (Washington: Government Printing Office, 1968).

Occupational Distribution

Employment in the tobacco industry is heavily production-worker oriented. Thus in 1967, almost 86 percent of all tobacco workers and more than 90 percent of all cigarette employees were classified as "production workers." [11]

Table 7 provides a more detailed occupational distribution for employees of the six major companies as of 1968. More than 50 percent of all employees are classified as semiskilled (operatives or lower) with the operative group comprising more than one-third of the total work force. Professional and technical representation in the labor force is very low, with total white collar, buoyed by a large sales force, less than 30 percent of the total.

11. Data based on U. S. Bureau of Labor Statistics figures.

TABLE 6. *Tobacco Industry*
Employment by Standard Industrial Classification
Selected Years, 1914-1967

Year	Tobacco Manufacturers (SIC 21)	Cigarettes (SIC 2111)	Cigars (SIC 2121)	Chewing and Smoking Tobacco (SIC 2131)	Tobacco Stemming and Redrying (SIC 2141)
1914	195,694		164,163[a]	31,531	n.a.
1919	172,776		150,633[a]	22,143	n.a.
1923	162,076		142,668[a]	19,408	n.a.
1933	90,790	23,816	56,195[b]	10,779	n.a.
1937	97,851	27,655	58,910	11,286	n.a.
1939	96,035	30,803	54,262	10,970	n.a.
1947	111,782	27,674	47,068	11,139	25,901
1952	93,175	29,342	40,165	7,764	15,904
1954	94,862	29,987	38,494	7,535	18,846
1958	84,467	33,832	29,350	6,348	14,937
1960	81,247	36,513	26,319	4,398	14,017
1961	77,456	36,102	23,415	4,654	13,285
1962	75,966	35,434	22,161	4,649	13,722
1963	77,330	35,568	20,731	4,058	16,973
1964	78,838	34,843	22,988	5,054	15,953
1965	74,555	35,924	21,041	4,437	13,153
1966	72,363	35,602	19,357	4,339	13,065
1967	75,000[c]	37,000	19,000	4,000	n.a.

Source: *U. S. Census of Manufactures:*

1947: Vol. II, *Statistics by Industry*, pp. 147-149 (for 1914-1939).

1963: Vol. II, *Statistics by Industry*, Part 1, pp. 21-3, 21A-6, 21A-7 (for 1947-1963).

1967: Series MC67 (P)-1, Summary Series, Preliminary Report, April 1969.

Annual Survey of Manufactures, 1964-1966.

[a] Cigarettes and cigars combined as one industry.

[b] Coverage of "Cigars" was incomplete in 1933.

[c] Includes uncorrected SIC 2141 data.

TABLE 7. *Tobacco Industry
Employment by Occupational Group
Six Companies, 1968*

Occupational Group	All Employees	
	Number	Percent
Officials and managers	4,814	7.6
Professionals	1,473	2.3
Technicians	1,456	2.3
Sales workers	5,411	8.6
Office and clerical	5,658	8.9
Total white collar	18,812	29.7
Craftsmen	6,095	9.6
Operatives	21,781	34.4
Laborers	14,560	23.0
Service workers	2,104	3.3
Total blue collar	44,540	70.3
Total	63,352	100.0

Source: Data in author's possession.

Note: Data include non-tobacco employees employeed by tobacco companies, but overwhelmingly reflect the tobacco occupational distribution.

Female Employment

The tobacco industry almost from its inception employed a considerable number of females and still does. In 1968, for example, over one-third of the more than 60,000 employees of the major companies were females.[12] Much of the work is either light machine tending or requires manual dexterity of a type in which women excel. Female employment has long been a practice in the industry and is likely to continue in view of the nature of the operations.

Wages

The tobacco industry is not a high paying one. Table 8 compares average weekly and hourly earnings of production workers in the industry with those in durable and nondurable goods manufacturing, and with two nondurable groups, food and kindred products and textile mill products. It is apparent that cigar

12. Based on data in the author's possession.

manufacturing is the lowest of the group,[13] with cigarette production worker earnings somewhat above the nondurable goods average and substantially above textile mill products and cigars, but just slightly below food and kindred products. (The cigarette data include some lower paid prefabrication wages.) The all-manufacturing average, buoyed by the high paying durable goods group, exceeds that of cigarettes or any other nondurable product represented in Table 8.

Separate data for the manufactured tobacco and stemming and redrying segments of the industry are not available, but rates therein have always been substantially lower than in cigarettes. Stemming wages, as those in cigar manufacturing, do not usually exceed the minimum wage by substantial amounts. Actually few Negroes have traditionally been employed in cigarette manufacturing, the top earnings sector of the tobacco industry, execpt in the lower paying prefabricating departments.

The earnings picture in the tobacco industry seems to reflect a number of factors. Among the most significant are probably the lack of high skills required, the large number of female jobs, and the abundance of female and Negro labor available in the southern locations. On the other hand, with labor costs so small

TABLE 8. *Tobacco and Selected Industries*
Average Weekly and Hourly Earnings
Production Workers, 1968

	Average Weekly Earnings	Average Hourly Earnings
All manufacturing	$122.51	$3.01
Durable goods	132.07	3.19
Nondurable goods	109.05	2.74
Tobacco manufacturers	93.87	2.49
Cigarettes	113.93	3.03
Cigars	75.00	2.00
Food and kindred products	114.24	2.80
Textile mill products	91.05	2.21

Source: *Employment and Earnings*, Vol. 15, No. 9 (March 1969), Table C-2.

13. The reasons for the low wages in cigar manufacturing have not been investigated by this author. The decline in employment noted in Table 6 may well be a key factor, for it involves continued mechanization which eliminates most of the last vestiges of skill in a once craft occupation.

a percentage of the value added by manufacturing, tobacco companies are paying cigarette manufacturing employees substantially more in wages than are textile manufacturers who are faced with the same general conditions, but who have a much higher proportion of labor costs with which to contend. Related both to relative wages and to the proportion of labor costs in the two industries is, undoubtedly, the general absence of unionization in textile manufacturing and its presence in all but one major company in the tobacco industry.

Unionization

Today nearly all tobacco manufacturers are unionized by one organization—the Tobacco Workers International Union. The outstanding exception is the huge R. J. Reynolds complex in Winston-Salem, North Carolina, which was unionized by the TWIU during World War I and by a rival union during World War II, but which today operates on a nonunion basis.[14] Today, the TWIU has a membership of about 34,000.

Most of the TWIU contracts date from the mid-1930's. Before that period, the union existed only on the fringes of the industry by virtue of making common ground with the small manufacturers. In return for permitting the union label to be placed on products, a few small companies in effect unionized their employees. Twice before the 1930's, the TWIU attempted to organize the major companies and even succeeded at Reynolds during World War I. Its eventual failure there, and later that of a rival union, has left Reynolds nonunion.

As might be expected, the TWIU accepted the racial-occupational segregation pattern by having separate locals on the basis of race. This tended to institutionalize the racial-occupational status quo and make it more difficult for the unionized companies to integrate their work forces in the 1960's. On the other hand, even after the separate locals policy was abandoned by the TWIU, the practice of departmental seniority added to the barriers against equal employment and strong local union autonomy restricted opportunities for change. The story of the union role in affecting Negro employment will be recounted within the appropriate time sequences of the following chapters.

---

14. The history of the TWIU is found in Herbert R. Northrup, "The Tobacco Workers International Union," *Quarterly Journal of Economics*, Vol. LVI (August 1942), pp. 606-626; and Northrup, *Organized Labor and the Negro, op. cit.*, Chapter IV.

CHAPTER III

Negro Employment — from the Colonial Period to 1960

As noted in the previous chapter, Negroes have been employed in the tobacco industry of the South since the colonial period of America—longer than in any other manufacturing industry. This chapter surveys racial employment trends from their colonial inception to 1960.

COLONIAL TIMES TO THE GREAT DEPRESSION

The plantation was, by necessity, a self-sufficient economy which produced to satisfy its own needs and utilized available labor. The tobacco-producing plantations of Virginia realized at an early date that it would be profitable to process some of their products for sale in the colonies, and Negro slaves were trained for this work. The need to be self-sufficient and to market their products locally was greatly magnified when war cut off the colonies from their English markets. Consolidation of duplicating efforts "led to slight commercial ventures with the use of Negroes in the manufactures. Planters who could not economically use all their slaves found it profitable to hire out not only slave laborers but trained slave artisans either to companies or to individual artisans and entrepreneurs. These latter were often to be found at the crossroads or in the small towns." [15]

Negroes trained as pressmen, twisters, stemmers, and "eventually coopers" were in demand in the cities by 1800.[16] Throughout the first half of the Civil War period, they were not only widely used in the tobacco factories of Richmond, Petersburg, and Lynchburg, but made up this labor force almost exclusively until the 1850's, when the "higher prevailing wages paid Negroes

---

15. Raymond B. Pinchbeck, *The Virginia Negro Artisan and Tradesman*, University of Virginia, Phelps-Stokes Fellowship Papers, No. 7 (Richmond: William Byrd Press, Inc., 1926), pp. 45-46.

16. *Ibid.*, p. 54.

are said to have been the cause leading to the employment of white women in the lighter processes of the manufacture of tobacco." [17]

The Virginia tobacco factories employed not only male Negro slaves, but also females, and in addition utilized a large proportion of that Commonwealth's free Negroes, both male and female:

Regardless of sex, and regardless of residence in town or country, one line of employment excelled all others with reference to the number of free Negroes it attracted—namely, the tobacco industry. The history of the cultivation of tobacco in Virginia makes evident the very high place which Negro labor, slave and free, held in this industry. Contrary to his position in the cotton industry, in which he was confined largely to cultivation, the Negro was important in the manufacture, as well as in the cultivation, of tobacco. In its manufacture many women workers were engaged. In the factories of Petersburg, where the women were about half as numerous as men, they worked as stemmers, while the men worked as twisters. According to the report on manufactures in Virginia of the 1860 census, there were at this time 261 tobacco establishments employing 11,382 workers at an annual cost of $2,123,732. At least 2,500 of this number were free Negroes, who lived chiefly in Richmond, Petersburg, and Lynchburg, the leading centers of tobacco manufacture, and who worked side by side with slaves. In Lynchburg most of the free Negroes worked in the tobacco factories during the manufacturing season, "and then," said a public official of that town, "the males do whatever comes in their way the balance of the time." In Farmville likewise the five tobacco establishments absorbed many more free Negroes than did any other line of employment. Richmond factories, for some reason, made so little use of women that during the fifties there were about 125 free Negro washerwomen in Richmond and only thirty-nine in Petersburg. The women of the latter place found their opportunity in tobacco factories rather than as washerwomen. [18]

Professor Jackson also affirms that Richmond was the center of the "slave for hire" market, and that the tobacco factories in this city and nearby Petersburg were principal employers of hired-out slave labor as late as 1860. [19]

In North Carolina and Kentucky, there is little evidence of the use of Negroes in tobacco factories probably because such factories did not exist there at that time. An economic history of slaveholding in North Carolina reports considerable agitation

---

17. *Ibid.*, p. 57. See also pp. 54-58.

18. Luther Porter Jackson, *Free Negro Labor and Property Holding in Virginia* (New York: Atheneum, 1969), pp. 94-95.

19. *Ibid.*, pp. 176-177.

about the use of Negro slaves in cotton mills (but little actual
such utilization) and much contracting out of slaves for turpen-
tine harvesting and as building artisans and railroad labor; but
it makes no mention of tobacco manufactures.[20] North Carolina's
rise to first place in the industry occurred after the cigarette
became fashionable, for North Carolina's "bright yellow" tobacco
proved especially suited for cigarettes. North Carolina tobacco
towns owe their start in manufacturing to the inability of farmers during the Civil War to transport their crop to Richmond
and the need to manufacture nearer the source of supply.

Reconstruction and the Advent of Cigarette Manufacturing

The immediate post-Civil War reconstruction era saw no di-
minution in the utilization of Negroes in Virginia tobacco factories. During the period 1800-1875, according to A. A. Taylor,
"Practically all travelers saw the blacks at work in the tobacco
factories." [21] Moreover, the introduction of machinery in factories in Virginia did not result in the displacement of blacks
by whites. Both men and women worked in these plants, and
in some cases Negro and white men worked side by side, but
white women were not part of any mixed work force. The supervisors, however, were generally white.[22]

In 1879, a Virginia United States Senator asserted that Negroes constituted "the bulk of the labor used in the manufacture
of Virginia's great staple—tobacco." Other officials in this period
found Negroes "quite free from trade unionism" and "less liable
to strikes and interruptions. . . ." But A. A. Taylor's evidence
indicates that Negro tobacco workers attempted to form unions
and that strikes for higher wages in tobacco factories were not
so uncommon.[23]

A British visitor to Virginia stated of the freed men that
"Tobacco seems to be specially their vocation . . . [but] cigars,

---

20. Rosser Howard Taylor, *Slaveholding in North Carolina: An Economic
    View*, The James Sprunt Historical Publications, Vol. 18 (Chapel Hill:
    University of North Carolina Press, 1926), pp. 38-40, 42, 74-80.

21. A. A. Taylor, *The Negro in the Reconstruction of Virginia* (Washington:
    The Association for the Study of Negro Life and History, Inc., 1926),
    p. 116.

22. *Ibid.*, pp. 116-118.

23. *Ibid.*, pp. 119-120.

it seems, are not made by blacks. It is one of the skilled things that they do not do." [24]

When cigarettes were first introduced from abroad, Negroes appeared about to break through the barrier for similar work. After first experimenting with Jewish immigrants who had learned the trade abroad, American tobacco manufacturers in the South turned to Negroes. But then in the 1880's came the introduction of the cigarette machine which could produce 120,-000 cigarettes per day as compared with 2,500 by the most efficient hand rollers. (Machine production has increased many fold since then.) The tobacco industry, following custom of the day, employed white females as machine operatives, white males as mechanics and set-up men. Whites remained as supervisors and as white collar workers. As machines were developed to make manufactured tobacco (smoking, chewing, and snuff), jobs were likewise divided up on a racial basis. By 1900, the racial-occupational segregation pattern, described in the previous chapter, was thoroughly effectuated in southern tobacco factories.

Although Negro workers lost out in the competition for jobs in the modern tobacco manufacturing processes, they continued to hold a large, and for a long period, increasing share of the total jobs in the industry, once the influx of white machine operators, mechanics, supervisors, and office employees had stabilized. Because of the low wages paid in the stemming and processing jobs, companies made little or no effort to mechanize them prior to 1932. On the other hand, mechanization in the cigarette manufacturing area, and mechanization and declining demand in the manufactured tobacco sector, tended either to restrain advances in the white-designated jobs or even to reduce the number of such jobs. In addition, the economies of large scale, the consolidations effected by the "tobacco trust" and its successor companies, and the impetus given the industry to move South in order to maximize the advantages of nearness to raw materials and of cheap labor, all tended to increase job opportunities for Negroes during the last decades of the nineteenth and first ones of the twentieth centuries.

Both the traditional headquarters of the industry—Richmond, Virginia—and the newer industrial cities of North Carolina and Kentucky were well ensconced as tobacco manufacturing centers before the turn of the century. Thus a reporter noted in 1899:

---

24. Quoted by *ibid.*, p. 118.

The colored people of Richmond are employed principally in all branches of the tobacco business, with the exception of cigarette making, cigar making and cheroot rolling. About 8,000 men, women and children are employed in the factories; of this number about 2,000 might be classified as skilled laborers.[25]

According to Greene and Woodson, "Negro workers increased, too, with the spread of this industry into North Carolina, Kentucky and Missouri. Among the centers of the industry were Winston-Salem, Durham, Louisville and St. Louis, where about two-thirds of the employees were Negroes." [26] Tradition was a factor in maintaining these jobs for Negroes (as well as denying them jobs in cigarette factories), but poor working conditions—dust particles and humid atmosphere—and low wages contributed also. Nevertheless, it remained for Negroes virtually the only significant factory work and factory employer of women in the South prior to World War I.

World War I to the Great Depression

By and large, Negroes maintained their position in the tobacco industry during the first three decades of the twentieth century. The continued increase in cigarette sales was largely offset by improved equipment so that employment in cigarette manufacturing did not increase. On the other hand, the processing work for that manufacturing remained low paid, largely hand labor performed by Negroes. As the demand for tobacco products—mainly cigarettes—grew, the need for more processing labor increased. Moreover, the remaining major plants in the North, with only a few exceptions, were closed and consolidated in the South by 1930. Finally, the demand for labor during World War I brought proportionately more opportunities for whites than Negroes, and tended to reinforce the dependence of tobacco companies on Negroes for the processing work, with Negro women in the South having, by 1930, still very few, if any, manufacturing job opportunities elsewhere.

Table 9 shows the number and proportion of operatives and laborers in the three principal tobacco manufacturing states,

---

25. *Proceedings, Hampton Conference,* July 1902, p. 43, quoted by Lorenzo J. Greene and Carter G. Woodson, *The Negro Wage Earner* (Washington: The Association for the Study of Negro Life and History, Inc., 1930), p. 152.

26. Greene and Woodson, *loc. cit.* St. Louis has since lost its position in the industry.

TABLE 9.   *Tobacco Industry*
Laborer and Operative Employment by Race
Major Tobacco Manufacturing States, 1910-1930

	1910			1920			1930		
	Total	Negro	Percent Negro	Total	Negro	Percent Negro	Total	Negro	Percent Negro
Kentucky	8,896	4,046	45.5	14,719	8,521	57.9	7,006	3,534	50.4
North Carolina	7,735	5,716	73.9	20,006	14,852	74.2	19,756	15,049	76.2
Virginia	12,397	8,948	72.2	15,520	10,457	67.4	11,104	7,142	64.3
Total	29,028	18,710	64.5	50,245	33,830	67.3	37,866	25,725	67.9

Source: *U. S. Census of Population:*

1910:   Vol. IV, *Occupations,* Table 7.
1920:   Vol. IV, *Occupations,* Table 1.
1930:   Vol. IV, *Occupations,* Table 11.

1910-1930. More than 90 percent of all Negroes in the non-cigar tobacco industry were then, as now, found in these three states. Although these data include a few cigar workers, the number producing cigars in these states has been insignificant.

On the other hand, the proportion of Negroes in the tobacco industry during these twenty years was less than is indicated by Table 9. The term "operative" as then defined by the census excludes certain highly skilled personnel as well as supervisory, managerial, and other salaried groups, nearly all of whom were then white. Thus in 1930, when 67.9 percent of the laborers and operatives in these states were black, only 58.7 percent of all gainful workers (that is, those employed or actively seeking work) were Negro. Nevertheless, in view of the overwhelming proportion of the work force of the industry that is classified as "production," "operative," or "semiskilled," the data in Table 9 do present a good picture of the racial employment trends for the period.

Looking at Table 9, we find that Negroes actually increased their proportion of factory jobs between 1910 and 1930, especially during the first of these two decades. The most substantial proportional increase came in Kentucky between 1910 and 1920, but was lost there during the following decade when black workers were disproportionately hurt in an exodus of work from Kentucky. In terms of numbers of jobs, North Carolina tripled both its tobacco work force and its Negro work force between 1910 and 1920, and then during the next decade added slightly to its black tobacco worker complement while its total work force declined slightly. In Virginia, both the total work force and the Negro work force increased slightly between 1910 and 1920, but in the following decade, both the total work force and the Negro proportion thereof suffered losses of jobs.

The principal reasons for these racial employment trends have already been noted. One was the continued decline in the sales and the production of manufactured tobacco. More significant was the consolidation of the industry in the three southern states. About four-fifths of the tobacco factories operating in 1914 were closed by the middle of the next decade; the number of tobacco workers declined by 178,872 in 1914 to 132,132 in 1925; the number of establishments declined from 13,951 to 2,623. While this occurred, value of product sold increased from $490 million to nearly $1.1 billion.[27]

---

27. *Ibid.*, pp. 287-288 quoting U. S. Department of Commerce, *Statistical Abstract of the United States*, 1926, p. 749.

Although most of these changes reflect the development of new cigar-making equipment, they also include the impact of continued consolidation of plants and mechanization in the cigarette manufacturing sector. More facilities were abandoned in the North than in the South. Meanwhile continued mechanization occurred in the cigarette sector of the industry:

Using 1929 as a base of 100, the index of output per wage earner per year in the cigarette branch rose from 32.8 in 1920 to 112.8 in 1930 and that of output per man-hour, from 28.7 to 105.3. Although the production of cigarettes increased from 47.4 billion in 1920 to 123.8 billion in 1930, the percentage increase in production was less than that in labor productivity. Thus the rate of mechanization not only prevented the cigarette branch from compensating for the decline in employment due to the decrease in the production of manufactured tobacco, but it was also so rapid that it caused unemployment within the cigarette branch itself.[28]

While this was occurring, the segregated Negro work areas paid such low wages that for them laborsaving equipment was either not economical or not even considered.[29]

During these two decades the Women's Bureau of the U. S. Department of Labor made a number of studies of the tobacco industry. It reported that the racial-occupational pattern was fixed and strong; that the clean, machine work was performed by white women whose "working conditions and wages were in striking contrast to those of Negro women workers. Their separation and isolation to prevent any contrast was apparent in the 16 establishments in which both races were employed." [30]

In regard to the condition of Negro workers, the Women's Bureau reported:

In tobacco factories conditions were particularly unsatisfactory. Sometimes the fumes were so strong that they were stifling and provoked incessant coughing from persons not accustomed to such conditions. Frequently the women wore handkerchiefs tied over their noses and mouths to prevent inhaling the heavy tobacco dust diffused throughout the room. One manager said new workers often suffered from nausea and loss of appetite, but as soon as they got used to the tobacco they did not mind it. Dust was thick in the air in many

28. Herbert R. Northrup, *Organized Labor and the Negro* (New York: Harper & Bros., 1944), pp. 105-106.

29. Tobacco manufacturers told the author in the 1940's that it may well have been economical to install machinery during this period but in view of the low wages of Negroes, they never considered the potential of mechanization.

30. Quoted by Greene and Woodson, *op. cit.*, p. 285.

of the factories, especially those in which the screener was operated in the general workroom without exhaust systems. In 18 factories these conditions were so bad that ventilating systems to purify the air were needed. A strong contrast was noted in one factory; the dust was taken off by electric fans, while humidifiers and a system of washing the air kept it pure and fresh.[31]

As for wages, Negro medians for women were $4.00 to $5.00 per week in the mid-1920's, those of whites as high as $13.20 per week. Hours were long—55 to 60 per week—and employment in the Negro jobs often seasonal.[32]

THE NEW DEAL TO 1960

The thirty-year period between 1930 and 1960 saw whites clearly emerge as the dominant employee group in the tobacco industry. Despite continued increased sales of tobacco products, particularly cigarettes, during this period and further (almost complete) consolidation of the industry in the three southern states, Negro employment declined as a percentage of total employment in each of the three decades. The reasons are indisputable: government imposition of minimum wages, employer response by mechanizing jobs in the stemmeries and in other areas where Negroes were employed, failure on the part of employers and unions to open up jobs in the white sectors of the industry to displaced Negroes, and failure of the dominant union to challenge the status quo in behalf of its eroding black membership.

The NRA Period

In his endeavors to lift the country out of the Great Depression, President Franklin D. Roosevelt obtained legislation, known as the National Industrial Recovery Act, which permitted employers to combine for the purpose of regulating production, wages, and hours under "Codes of Few Competition" or "NRA codes." While the codes were being hammered out, industries were requested to reduce hours, raise wages, and hopefully increase employment. The major tobacco companies cooperated in the hours reduction and wage increase part, spurred like all industry not only by a desire to do their part, but also by the

---

31. *Ibid.*, p. 286.

32. *Ibid.*, quoting various U. S. Women's Bureau bulletins.

stirrings of organized labor which also had been promised new rights by the NRA.

Expanded employment was yet another matter, for to increase labor costs and at the same time to raise employment certainly is at variance with the economic facts of life. As a result of the increased labor costs, hand stemming no longer was economical for the major companies. Studies by the U. S. Bureau of Labor Statistics and by the U. S. Women's Bureau found that hours in manufacturers' stemmeries declined from 50 or 55 to 40 between 1933 and 1935, and that wages rose substantially, from an average of 19.4 cents in March 1933 to 32.5 cents two years later.[33] Faced with rising wages, the tobacco companies rushed to install stemming machines and to commence a mechanization program which continued for at least two decades, and which within a few years halved employment in many manufacturers' stemmeries.

Impact of the Fair Labor Standards Act

The independent stemmeries escaped coverage by the NRA, but the impact of minimum wages on their activities was soon felt. In 1938, Congress enacted the Fair Labor Standards Act which set the minimum wage for covered employment at 25 cents per hour. After successive amendments over the years, the minimum now stands at $1.60. The imposition of each new minimum has affected the wage policies and employment practices of the independent stemmeries, with the original 25 cent minimum having had a drastic effect.

In 1937, a study by the U. S. Bureau of Labor Statistics reported:

Negro workers in independent or dealers' tobacco stemmeries, who comprise virtually the entire working force in these establishments, are among the lowest paid employees in the country. In September 1935, the average earnings of these workers amounted to 16 cents per hour. With an average of 43.4 hours of employment per week, their weekly earnings average $6.92.

The independent stemmeries were never subject to code regulations under the National Recovery Administration . . . their earnings were much smaller and their hours longer than those of corresponding

---

33. "Earnings in Cigarettes, Snuff and Chewing and Smoking Tobacco Plants," *Monthly Labor Review*, Vol. XLII (May 1936), p. 1331. See also Caroline Manning, *Hours and Earnings in Tobacco Stemmeries*, Bulletin No. 127, U. S. Women's Bureau (Washington: Government Printing Office, 1936).

workers in the manufacturers' stemmeries . . . [which] are far more important in the industry than are the independent stemmeries.[34]

In a study conducted during the period from August 1940 to February 1941, the Bureau of Labor Statistics found that average hourly earnings of the employees of independent stemmeries had risen to 34.3 cents.[35]

A comparison of the average hourly and weekly earnings of Negro workers employed in 11 identical establishments in 1935 and 1940 indicates that in this 5-year period earnings almost doubled. The increase in earnings has been accompanied by a marked increase in the mechanization of stemming operators. . . .

The advent of minimum hourly earnings under the Fair Labor Standards Act has had important repercussions in the industry. . . . In 1935, for illustration, the Bureau of Labor Statistics secured wage data from a group of stemmeries, 10 of which employed no machine stemmers. In 1940-41 the identical 10 plants reported that 54 of their stemmery employees were employed on automatic stemming machines.[36]

In some of the largest stemmery establishments, employment increased, but overall it declined as many smaller ones went out of business or drastically curtailed employment. The impact of the NRA on manufacturers' stemmery employment and of the Fair Labor Standards Act on that of independent stemmeries is noted in the census data set forth in Table 10, which compares the percentage of laborers and operatives by race, 1930 and 1940, for the three key tobacco manufacturing states.

In Virginia and North Carolina, Negroes retained a majority of the laborer and operative jobs during this decade, but they were disproportionately affected by the declining employment in the industry. In Kentucky, total employment in the decade fell by approximately 2,000; Negro employment declined by *2,500*. In other words, white employment increased while Negro employment fell so the proportion of Negro laborers and operators in the state declined from 50.4 percent to 18.4 percent. The reasons for this drastic drop in Negro employment appears to be the decline in the number of stemmeries and the decline in stemmery employment in the state while one plant employing an all-white labor force expanded. In the three states, the propor-

---

34. Jacob Perlman, "Earnings and Hours of Negro Workers in Independent Tobacco Stemmeries in 1933 and 1935," *Monthly Labor Review*, Vol. XLIV (May 1937), p. 1153.

35. "Hours and Earnings of Employees of Independent Leaf-Tobacco Dealers," *Monthly Labor Review*, Vol. LIII (July 1941), p. 215.

36. *Ibid.*, pp. 215-216.

TABLE 10. *Tobacco Industry
Laborer and Operative Employment by Race
Major Tobacco Manufacturing States, 1930 and 1940*

	1930			1940		
	Total	Negro	Percent Negro	Total	Negro	Percent Negro
Kentucky	7,006	3,534	50.4	5,052	932	18.4
North Carolina	19,756	15,049	76.2	17,078	11,063	64.8
Virginia	11,104	7,142	64.3	11,049	6,169	55.8
Total	37,866	25,725	67.9	33,179	18,164	54.7

Source: *U. S. Census of Population:*
  1930:   Vol. IV, *Occupations*, Table 11.
  1940:   Vol. III, *The Labor Force*, Parts 3, 4, and 5, Table 20.

tion of Negro laborers and operatives declined in the 1940's from 67.9 percent to 54.7 percent.

In terms of total tobacco industry employees (rather than only laborers and operatives), only North Carolina showed a majority of Negroes by 1940, and for the first time the proportion of Negro employment in the three key states dropped below 50 percent, being 45.8 percent in 1940 (Table 11) and compared with 58.7 in 1930. The jobs already open to Negroes in the industry were yielding to mechanization but no new jobs were being opened to them.

From World War II to 1960

During World War II the racial pattern in the industry was not basically changed. One company—R. J. Reynolds in Winston-Salem—upgraded a few Negroes to operative jobs on cigarette machines following the war, but generally otherwise the status quo was maintaind insofar as the racial-occupational employment pattern was concerned. Moreover, the trend of employment was up in the nearly all white cigarette manufacturing sector, but down in stemming and redrying, which has a nearly all black work force, and down in smoking, chewing, and snuff in which a sizeable proportion of the employees has always been Negro.

The declining employment in stemmeries came as a result of further mechanization. This involved not only improvement in existing equipment, but the development of new machinery, in particular a tipping and threshing machine. According to Professor Donald Dewey, who studied employment in sixteen tobacco plants in 1950-1951, this was the prime cause of the decline in Negro employment in the period around 1950.[37] In addition, the investment required to install modern stemming equipment has been beyond the means of most independents. Probably a majority of these concerns had gone out of business by 1960 and the larger ones had consolidated their operations in a few establishments. No longer do seasonal stemmeries dot the landscape in the tobacco growing states. Table 11 shows that in 1950, even North Carolina had for the first time a less than 50 percent black labor force in tobacco. Kentucky slightly reversed the downward Negro trend in the industry as Negroes gained back just a few of the jobs lost in the previous decade. In the three states, the proportion of Negro employment in the industry declined from 45.8 percent in 1940 to 37.2 percent ten years later.

The 1960's saw the declining trend of Negro employment in the industry continued despite small beginnings of a break in the racial-occupational segregation pattern. We have already noted that the R. J. Reynolds Company placed a few Negroes on cigarette machines following World War II. In 1951, Dewey reports, 6 percent of that company's cigarette machine operators were black,[38] certainly the largest Negro representation in the industry at that time and undoubtedly the first in such jobs.

Then in the mid-1950's, under pressure by the President's Committee on Government Contracts (known as the "Nixon Committee" because it was chaired by the then Vice-President), which handled equal employment issues under government contracts during the Eisenhower Administration, both Liggett & Myers and American Tobacco negotiated with locals of the Tobacco Workers International Union, then organized on a segregated basis,[39] to open up a few formerly all-white jobs to Negroes. Both companies won agreement from white locals to upgrade a limited number of Negroes—about 25 by Liggett &

---

37. Donald Dewey "Negro Employment in Sixteen Tobacco Plants," in *Selected Studies of Negro Employment in the South*, Report No. 6, NPA Committee of the South (Washington: National Planning Association, 1955), pp. 177-178.

38. *Ibid.*, pp. 170-171. Dewey does not mention Reynolds by name, but refers to a nonunion company. Only Reynolds fits this description.

39. See the ensuing section of this chapter for a discussion of TWIU policies.

TABLE 11. Tobacco Industry
Total and Negro Employment
Major Tobacco Manufacturing States, 1940-1960

	1940			1950			1960		
	Total	Negro	Percent Negro	Total	Negro	Percent Negro	Total	Negro	Percent Negro[a]
Kentucky	7,172	1,015	14.2	7,457	1,328	17.8	9,342	1,298	13.9
North Carolina	21,489	11,797	54.9	22,251	9,407	42.3	27,465	8,666	31.6
Virginia	13,799	6,626	48.0	10,955	4,384	40.0	12,103	3,166	26.2
Total	42,460	19,438	45.8	40,663	15,119	37.2	48,910	13,130	26.8

Source: *U. S. Census of Population:*

1940: Vol. III, *The Labor Force*, Parts 3, 4, and 5, Table 18.
1950: Vol. II, *Characteristics of the Population*, Table 83.
1960: PC(1) D, *Detailed Characteristics*, State Volumes, Table 129.

[a] For estimate basis and probable overstatement of Negro ratio, see Appendix A.

Myers in Durham and 50 by American Tobacco in Richmond. Both these concerns (and most others in the industry) had few openings to which displaced Negroes could be transferred, even if they had desired to breech the racial segregation pattern further. Continued mechanization in cigarette manufacturing and loss of market position kept job levels relatively constant for these concerns.

Few other changes were made in the racial-occupational employment pattern. P. Lorillard opened its highly automated factory in Greensboro in 1956 with only about 10 percent of the approximately 1,000 jobs going to Negroes. Continued automation increased the demand for professional and technical employees, and craftsmen, but reduced the need for unskilled labor. Although employment in cigarette manufacturing increased by about one-third between 1950 and 1960 (Table 6, p. 14), Negroes enjoyed none of the fruits of this increase for several reasons. First, the introduction and improvement of a variety of material handling devices in cigarette factories reduced the already small Negro complement in these plants. Second, in manufactured tobacco plants, where Negroes have traditionally enjoyed a much larger share of the work, declining product demand and mechanization cut the work force by about 50 percent. In addition, mechanization continued to reduce the need for unskilled labor in the stemmery departments where Negroes have traditionally been employd. Finally, in two companies where a small dent in the racial-occupational employment pattern had been made, Liggett & Myers and American, layoffs were occurring and few if any new employees were hired between 1953 and 1960.

The extent of Negro job loss in the tobacco industry during the 1950's must be estimated from the Census of Population because, for reasons that surely defy explanation, tobacco employment by race in North Carolina, Virginia, and Kentucky was not computed; instead, it was combined with two leather categories in "all other non-durable goods." [40] Even by assuming that *all* Negroes in this catch-all category worked in tobacco plants, the proportion of Negroes shows a substantial decline. Thus, for the three states combined, the decline in Negro employment would be 13.2 percent while total tobacco employment increased 20.3 percent. Table 12 shows the percentage changes for the three states, assuming again that none of the 2,264

---

40. See Appendix A for details of the estimate and its probable understatement of Negro job losses.

TABLE 12. *Tobacco Industry*
Percentage Increase in Total and Decrease in Negro Employment
Major Tobacco Manufacturing States, 1950-1960

	All Employees		Actual Percent Increase	Negro Employees [a]		Minimum Percent Decrease
	1950	1960	1950-1960	1950	1960	1950-1960
Kentucky	7,457	9,342	25.3	1,328	1,298	2.3
North Carolina	22,251	27,465	23.4	9,407	8,666	7.9
Virginia	10,955	12,103	10.5	4,384	3,166	27.8
Total	40,663	48,910	20.3	15,119	13,130	13.2

Source: Table 11.

[a] Negro employment in 1960 is estimated by assuming that *all* Negroes reported in the "All other non-durable goods" category worked in tobacco plants. This probably overstates Negro employment in 1960 and understates the percentage decrease during the decade. See Appendix A.

leather workers were black. Hence the decline shown for the Negor labor force is the absolute minimum and actually could have been substantially more, as explained in Appendix A.

Thus Negroes who had monopolized employment in the tobacco industry from colonial times to the latter part of the nineteenth century, and who from the nineteenth century to 1932 held a clear majority of this industry's jobs, found in 1960 that they possessed only one-fourth the employment therein as their share. A rigid racial-occupational employment pattern, only slightly dented by 1960, discriminatory hiring and employment policies, changing product demand, and the uneven impact of technological progress had all combined to work against Negroes, particularly since 1932. To this must be added union policies which, as shall be documented below, served to institutionalize the difficulties of Negro members, rather than to work to overcome them.

THE IMPACT OF UNIONISM TO 1960

Unionism in tobacco manufacturing existed only on the fringes of the industry before the 1930's. The Tobacco Workers' International Union, unable to dent the antiunion policies of the tobacco "trust" or the four major successor companies, American, Liggett & Myers, Lorillard, and Reynolds, bought recogni-

tion from some smaller companies in exchange for granting
these companies the right to use the union label.[41] With management in effect unionizing its employees to obtain the label
in small companies and with the TWIU unable to penetrate the
bulk of the industry, unionism probably had no impact on employer racial policies prior to World War I.

During World War I, membership in the TWIU tripled to
15,000, largely as a result of winning recognition from R. J.
Reynolds in Winston-Salem. Negro organizers had been used
with excellent results. Following the war, however, Reynolds
reduced wages without consulting the union, which offered no
overt resistance. After membership declined to 1,500 in 1925,
the TWIU decided to attempt to unionize Reynolds a second
time. Some 7,000 employees were enrolled, but when Reynolds
refused to recognize the union, it again took no overt action to
redeem its campaign promises. The resultant distrust of the
TWIU by Reynolds employees, and apparently especially the
feeling on the part of Negro employees that they had been
victimized in the two unionization attempts, has plagued TWIU's
efforts to organize Reynolds ever since.

In December 1933, the unionization of three Brown & Williamson plants by a union label sale touched off a revolt within the
union. The revolt was led by workers who received just about
enough in wage increases to pay the compulsory union dues.
The leader of the TWIU since its founding in 1895 was deposed,
and the TWIU was converted from a label-selling organization
into a typical business union. Meanwhile, the bulk of the industry, except for Reynolds, was unionized.

Most of the TWIU locals in the South were organized on a
separate racial-local basis prior to 1946. This method of organizing was, of course, facilitated by the racial-occupational segregation pattern in the industry. The Negro locals had full rights
as locals, and usually negotiated on a joint basis with the white
locals. At Liggett & Myers Durham plants, for example, there
was one white local having jurisdiction over most employees in
the cigarette operations, a Negro local with jurisdiction over
Negro employees attached to these operations, and a second
Negro local with jurisdiction over stemming, storage, and blend-

---

41. The history of the TWIU prior to 1942 is based on Herbert R. Northrup,
    "The Tobacco Workers International Union," *Quarterly Journal of Eco-
    nomics*, Vol. LVI (August 1942), pp. 606-626; and Northrup, *Organized
    Labor and the Negro, op. cit.*, Chapter IV.

ing plant employees. These three locals, together with the one Negro and one white local in the same company's Richmond plant, negotiated a joint contract with Liggett & Myers. Likewise, three white and three Negro locals representing employees at American's Durham, Reedsville, and Richmond plants negotiated jointly.

By running their segregated locals, the Negro tobacco workers developed leadership and were insured a voice at national union meetings as well as representation on local or company-wide bargaining sessions. Negroes also have played a role in the national leadership. Negro representatives served on the national executive board of the TWIU between 1897 and 1900. Then after a forty-year hiatus, George Benjamin, a Negro, was elected a vice-president. He retained that post until he retired in 1968 and was succeeded by Oliver Shaw, who is also black. A second vice-presidency has been held by a Negro since 1944, and other Negroes have served as organizers, committeemen, local presidents, etc.

Despite some advantages of the separate local system and despite efforts of the TWIU leadership to represent their Negro membership, the separate local system had definite disadvantages for Negroes. It institutionalized the status quo, adding another barrier which maintained the racial-occupational segregation pattern, and did so in a period when Negroes were disproportionately losing jobs to mechanization. Moreover, in some instances, separate locals prevented Negroes, who initially comprised a majority of a company's employees, from controlling a local bargaining situation.

The separate local system also maintained racial exclusiveness by providing contacts only for local leaders. In some areas, such as Durham, there was good cooperation among Negro and white leadership. In Richmond, however, the union movement affiliated with the American Federation of Labor was at first quite antagonistic to Negroes. The Central Labor Union denied TWIU locals affiliation in the 1930's, but the white TWIU locals were able to join it. TWIU leaders in this area largely ignored Negroes, attempting for a time to organize only whites. This opened the way for a challenge by a rival union.

Rival Unionism in Tobacco

Employees of independent stemmeries, like most seasonal workers, are difficult and expensive to organize. The labor force of a facility can vary from year to year and employees are easily replaceable. Hence the TWIU at first did not exert a major effort to unionize these employees. In 1937 in Richmond, however, a strike at two independent stemmeries was given leadership by the Southern Negro Youth Congress "controlled by the Communist Party." [42] Union recognition was secured and three other contracts obtained. These locals then affiliated with what was then called the United Cannery, Agricultural and Allied Workers of America, a CIO affiliate which later changed its name to the Food, Tobacco and Allied Workers (FTA). This union, which sedulously adhered to the Communist Party line throughout its life, employed the Southern Negro Youth Congress personnel as organizers and began a drive to enroll tobacco workers in Richmond. Its support came largely from Negroes, in contrast to the white-employee oriented TWIU leadership in Richmond. The TWIU emerged victorious in National Labor Relations Board representation elections in Richmond plants, leaving the CIO affiliate only its stemmery locals, which in time also apparently became extinct.[43]

It was in Winston-Salem, however, that the FTA scored its greatest victory, winning a NLRB election in 1944. Unquestionably, as before, its support came principally from Negroes. The TWIU withdrew from the election contest after an earlier indecisive election showed it to have an insufficient following, but again one that was much stronger among whites than Negroes.[44]

The FTA's success was short lived. In 1948, it lost bargaining rights following a long strike. The FTA's position among employees had been materially weakened by its leaders' refusal to sign the non-Communist affidavits required by the Taft-Hartley Act of 1947,[45] and by their militant concern with, and adherence to, Communist Party policies, such as foreign policy issues, at

---

42. F. Ray Marshall, *Labor in the South* (Cambridge: Harvard University Press, 1967), p. 217.

43. These locals seem to have lasted through World War II, but apparently disappeared as unions when, as explained below, the parent union also disintegrated. This has been the fate of most stemmery locals. The TWIU now has 24 locals in 19 independent stemmeries, but between 1945 and 1969, it chartered 87 locals, most in independent stemmeries, most of which are no longer in existence. (Interview, Washington, D.C., December 3, 1969.)

44. Northrup, *Organized Labor and the Negro, op. cit.*, pp. 115-117.

45. This requirement was altered by the Landrum-Griffin Act of 1959.

the expense of local collective bargaining problems.[46] Soon after this strike, the FTA, along with several other unions, was expelled from the CIO on charges of Communist domination. Afterwards it completely disintegrated.[47]

The TWIU, the FTA, and the United Transport Service Employees (then a CIO union led by and comprising mainly porters at railroad stations), attempted to organize Reynolds employees in 1950. Since the employees were split both on racial lines and on union adherence, and since unionism had left a bad taste of strife and failure for Reynolds employees since World War I, the attempt was a failure.[48] As a result, Reynolds remains today a nonunion concern, a fact which has had an important effect on its ability to move away from the racial-occupational job pattern during the 1960's.

Impact of Rival Unionism

The departure of effective rival unionism left the field to the TWIU. Unfortunately for Negroes, the union which had promised, and indeed practiced, equalitarian policy beyond that of the TWIU had been decisively handicapped by ideological subservience to extraneous policies, and therefore could have little direct impact. Undoubtedly, however, the FTA did force the TWIU to liberalize its policies. As already noted, the FTA presence forced the TWIU to concern itself effectively with the Negro tobacco employees of Richmond. And in 1946, following the loss of Reynolds employees to the FTA, the TWIU resolved not to organize any local plants on a segregated basis.

In 1956, when Lorillard moved its operation from Jersey City, New Jersey, to Greensboro, North Carolina, the TWIU organized the plant on a single local basis. Only 10 percent of the

---

46. Based on interviews, review of FTA papers, etc.

47. The FTA and another Communist-led organization affiliated with Local 65, which had disaffiliated from Retail, Wholesale and Department Store Employees, CIO. Local 65 later broke with the Communists, and returned to the CIO. In 1969, it disaffiliated again, this time from the AFL-CIO to join the Alliance for Labor Action. Most FTA locals which survived, however, left FTA and joined other unions. See F. S. O'Brien, "The 'Communist Dominated' Unions in the United States Since 1950," *Labor History,* Vol. IX (Spring 1968), especially pp. 189-193.

48. F. Ray Marshall, *The Negro and Organized Labor* (New York: John Wiley & Sons, 1965), p. 189. In this book, Professor Marshall correctly places the year of the FTA's last strike at Reynolds as 1948. His *Labor in the South, op. cit.,* p. 217, incorrectly refers to the year as 1946.

employees hired at Lorillard's highly automated plant were Negroes, however, and they found that their integrated local had few advantages. The company and union negotiated a contract with strict departmental seniority which was a carryover from the Jersey City plants. With Lorillard adhering to the traditional racial-occupational segregation pattern in its hiring policies, Negroes found that they were as rigidly confined to traditional jobs (the few that remained) as they were in older plants where segregated locals prevailed. For under departmental seniority, no one had promotion or layoff rights except in his department or job grouping.

Craft Unions in Tobacco Plants

An additional barrier to Negro upward mobility in tobacco plants was erected in the early days of unionism. A number of craft unions, especially the International Brotherhood of Electrical Workers, the International Association of Machinists, and others varying from plant to plant, won bargaining rights for craftsmen. These unions were traditionally antagonistic to Negro employment and upgrading and therefore tended to reinforce the racial-occupational segregation pattern.[49] Negroes desiring opportunities to transfer to craftsmen jobs or to train as apprentices in plants so unionized in the tobacco industry, as in other industries, would have encountered the organized hostility of these unions and their members in addition to the other difficulties traditionally inherent in the tobacco industry's employment patterns and policies.

In Louisville, the Teamsters' Union organized the stemmery of American Tobacco, while the TWIU organized the manufacturing facility. This gave Negroes no rights in the latter and added an additional union barrier to Negro upgrading. The abandonment of those operations by American in 1970 came before this interunion issue was resolved.

Union Impact on Racial Policies Prior to 1960—Final Comment

A study of the tobacco industry's racial policies in the 1950's, which noted that the proportion of Negro employment had steadily declined, contained this contradictory paragraph:

---

49. For analysis of craft union policies in this era, see Northrup, *Organized Labor and the Negro, op. cit.,* Chapters I-II.

Nevertheless, in view of the large number of other circumstances that affect (or in the absence of union organization could affect) the conditions of Negro employment in the industry, one cannot fairly assert that the union policy of segregation has adversely affected the interest of its Negro members. In established plants, union policy discourages, if it does not preclude the upgrading of Negro workers; in the event of falling employment, it would block the transfer of Negro jobs to white workers. As yet, the tobacco firms probably have a free hand in staffing new plants.[50]

One must agree that employers have prime responsibility for the racial-occupational segregation pattern in the industry, and they indeed do the hiring with a free hand. Moreover, the proportion of Negroes declined in the nonunion, as well as the union labor force from 1932 to 1960. The TWIU completely acquiesced to maintaining the pattern of employment and therefore represented its white members well to the detriment of, and at the expense of, its Negro members. New white workers were employed while black TWIU members were laid off with little or no union opposition. Even token integration in the 1950's was initiated by the companies under government pressure, with the union, which could exert little control over its local affiliates, merely acquiescing. Integration at nonunion Reynolds, though token, was ahead of unionized plants. Surely it is not possible to equate union protection against layoffs with lack of opportunity for transfers and promotions in a situation in which the brunt of the layoffs was borne by Negroes while cigarette employment was expanding in jobs open almost exclusively to whites.

To repeat, the prime responsibility for the disadvantaged position of Negro tobacco workers and their steadily worsening proportion of job opportunities rested with the tobacco companies. The TWIU, and particularly its local unions and its dominant white membership, aided in the enforcement of the racial-occupational segregation pattern and seemed to institutionalize and support the denial of jobs to black union members even when these members were being laid off and new white workers hired.

---

50. Dewey, *op. cit.*, p. 177.

CHAPTER IV

The 1960's – Attempting to End Segregation

The racial-occupational segregation pattern in tobacco manufacturing, which endured for nearly a century after the mechanization of cigarette manufacturing, finally began to crumble in the 1960's under the impetus of governmental intervention and civil rights legislation. By then, however, the proportion of Negroes in the industry was the lowest since colonial times. This chapter discusses developments in the decade of the 1960's and analyzes the changes which have occurred since the 1960 Census of Population.

QUALITATIVE IMPROVEMENT, QUANTITATIVE STABILITY

In the 1950's the efforts of the President's Committee on Government Contracts (Nixon Committee) resulted in a few small dents in the racial-occupational segregation pattern, and even earlier, R. J. Reynolds Company had moved some Negroes into traditionally all-white jobs. Then when the Kennedy Administration created the President's Committee on Equal Employment Opportunity (PCEEO) to replace the Nixon Committee and gave the newer committee stronger authority, complaints poured in from nearly every major tobacco facility. By the time Title VII of the Civil Rights Act became effective in July 1965, changes were well underway.

Despite the favorable qualitative developments of the 1960's, our data show little or no quantitative improvement in the Negro employment ratio. Continued mechanization and automation and the linkage of smoking and health problems with consequent decline in domestic tobacco consumption have precluded employment expansion. Moreover, during the first few years of the decade, Negroes continued to be barred from most traditionally white departments and were disproportionately affected by the continued technological and productivity improvements as they had been since the early 1930's.

The initial government response under PCEEO to charges of discrimination in the tobacco industry was to pressure the com-

panies to open up all departments to all races and to pressure
the TWIU and the companies to abolish separate racial-locals
and bargaining arrangements. The response of the companies
to the former was to tack the Negro seniority list on the bottom
of former white jobs, and vice-versa. Since few openings occurred, there was little upward movement, and the complaints
of Negro employees to the government continued. Meanwhile,
Reynolds opened a new plant in Winston-Salem on a fully integrated basis and then moved to desegregate its older facilities;
in other companies the Negro local unions were merged into the
white locals, and later new seniority arrangements were either
worked out or litigated. The details and problems involved in
these changes vary among companies and are discussed later in
this chapter, following an analysis of the basic statistics for the
period.

The 1966 Equal Employment Opportunity Commission Data

Data by race, collected from employers of 100 or more, have
been published by the Equal Employment Opportunity Commission for 1966. In the three key tobacco manufacturing states,
these data show that 25.6 percent of all employees in 71 tobacco
plants were Negro (Table 13). As noted in previous studies,
EEOC data are not strictly comparable to those of the Census
of Population. The exclusion of plants which have less than 100
employees from EEOC coverage could eliminate some small stemmeries which have an all-Negro labor force and which were included in census data. More significant, of course, is that census
data are based on responses by people to interrogators, while
EEOC reports are filed by employers from payroll figures. On
the other hand, both the census and the EEOC data for the three
states do include the few cigar employees working there.

A further complication is the failure of the census to report
tobacco employees by race for the three key states since 1950.
Table 11 (p. 31) therefore estimated the maximum percentage
of Negroes in 1960 as 26.8 of the total employment. Remarkably, Table 13 shows that percentage to be 25.6 percent in 1966.
In fact, these figures support the author's impressions, based
upon field interviews, that the precipitous decline in the ratio of
Negro tobacco employment, which began with the NRA minimum
wage codes in the early 1930's, had been slowed, or possibly
halted, by 1966.

TABLE 13. Tobacco Industry
Employment by Race, Sex, and Occupational Group
Kentucky, North Carolina, and Virginia, 1966

Occupational Group	All Employees			Male			Female		
	Total	Negro	Percent Negro	Total	Negro	Percent Negro	Total	Negro	Percent Negro
Officials and managers	3,688	42	1.1	3,583	42	1.2	105	—	—
Professionals	872	8	0.9	825	6	0.7	47	2	4.3
Technicians	1,103	31	2.8	855	27	3.2	248	4	1.6
Sales workers	2,025	44	2.2	1,951	42	2.2	74	2	2.7
Office and clerical	3,352	166	5.0	1,267	57	4.5	2,085	109	5.2
Total white collar	11,040	291	2.6	8,481	174	2.1	2,559	117	4.6
Craftsmen	4,963	137	2.8	4,835	129	2.7	128	8	6.2
Operatives	19,716	3,133	15.9	11,022	2,473	22.4	8,694	660	7.6
Laborers	18,792	9,572	50.9	10,843	6,298	58.1	7,949	3,274	41.2
Service workers	2,070	1,353	65.4	1,618	1,012	62.5	452	341	75.4
Total blue collar	45,541	14,195	31.2	28,318	9,912	35.0	17,223	4,283	24.9
Total	56,581	14,486	25.6	36,799	10,086	27.4	19,782	4,400	22.2

Source: U. S. Equal Employment Opportunity Commission, Job Patterns for Minorities and Women in Private Industry, Report No. 1 (Washington: Government Printing Office, 1966), Part II.

Tables 14-16 show the same EEOC data for the three states individually. Comparing again (with due regard for the limitations of such comparisons) the data in these tables with those in Table 11, we find that both North Carolina and Virginia show similar percentages in both years—the former down 2.6 percentage points in 1966, the latter up 1.8. Kentucky is up 4.1 percentage points in 1966 over 1960, apparently as a result of a large increase in stemmery operations reporting there.

The 1964-1968 Field Sample

The EEOC data reported in Tables 13-16 are based on the period immediately after the 1965 effective date of Title VII of the Civil Rights Act of 1964 and therefore, as noted in other studies in this Series, do not reflect significant later developments. Accordingly, as was done for other studies, data were gathered for the three years 1964, 1966, and 1968. Although these data include most establishments of all major concerns, they do not, unlike those of the EEOC or Census of Population, include any independent stemmeries or the few cigar facilities in the three key states. Thus the sample data for 1966 report 47,382 employees as compared with 56,581 in the EEOC data of the same year (Tables 13 and 18).

Given the dissimilarities in coverage, and especially the absence of the nearly all black independent stemmery labor force from the author's sample, it is not surprising that the percentage of Negroes for 1966 shown in Table 18 is only 21.8 as compared with 25.6 in Table 13. It should be borne in mind, therefore, that by reason of the exclusion of data for independent stemmeries from the author's sample, the number and ratio of Negro employees for 1964, 1966, and 1968 are understated. On the other hand, the occupational analysis which follows is enhanced by comparing the trend over the three years.

OCCUPATIONAL CHANGE, 1964-1968

Historically Negroes have occupied few jobs above that of operative in the tobacco industry, and have been heavily concentrated in the lowest skill jobs—laborers and service workers. By 1960 there had been very little change. A few Negroes had been employed for special sales work—largely sales promotion among members of their own race—and some Negroes were employed as supervisors in stemmeries, but the concentration of blacks in the lowest level jobs remained.

TABLE 14. Tobacco Industry
Employment by Race, Sex, and Occupational Group
Kentucky, 1966

Occupational Group	All Employees			Male			Female		
	Total	Negro	Percent Negro	Total	Negro	Percent Negro	Total	Negro	Percent Negro
Officials and managers	902	8	0.9	877	8	0.9	25	—	—
Professionals	132	1	0.8	126	—	—	6	1	16.7
Technicians	217	3	1.4	131	2	1.5	86	1	1.2
Sales workers	610	17	2.8	610	17	2.8	—	—	—
Office and clerical	1,025	28	2.7	378	8	2.1	647	20	3.1
Total white collar	2,886	57	2.0	2,122	35	1.6	764	22	2.9
Craftsmen	983	32	3.3	964	32	3.3	19	—	—
Operatives	5,253	547	10.4	2,524	434	17.2	2,729	113	4.1
Laborers	6,645	2,108	31.7	4,212	1,336	31.7	2,433	772	31.7
Service workers	487	179	36.8	329	118	35.9	158	61	38.6
Total blue collar	13,368	2,866	21.4	8,029	1,920	23.9	5,339	946	17.7
Total	16,254	2,923	18.0	10,151	1,955	19.3	6,103	968	15.9

Source: U. S. Equal Employment Opportunity Commission, *Job Patterns for Minorities and Women in Private Industry*, Report No. 1 (Washington: Government Printing Office, 1966), Part II.

TABLE 15. Tobacco Industry
Employment by Race, Sex, and Occupational Group
North Carolina, 1966

Occupational Group	All Employees			Male			Female		
	Total	Negro	Percent Negro	Total	Negro	Percent Negro	Total	Negro	Percent Negro
Officials and managers	1,922	14	0.7	1,917	14	0.7	5	—	—
Professionals	452	3	0.7	438	2	0.5	14	1	7.1
Technicians	644	23	3.6	579	21	3.6	65	2	3.1
Sales workers	1,407	26	1.8	1,333	24	1.8	74	2	2.7
Office and clerical	1,707	100	5.9	643	29	4.5	1,064	71	6.7
Total white collar	6,132	166	2.7	4,910	90	1.8	1,222	76	6.2
Craftsmen	2,933	85	2.9	2,824	77	2.7	109	8	7.3
Operatives	9,204	1,603	17.4	6,033	1,340	22.2	3,171	263	8.3
Laborers	8,302	5,295	63.8	4,352	3,472	79.8	3,950	1,823	46.2
Service workers	1,156	880	76.1	919	655	71.3	237	225	94.9
Total blue collar	21,595	7,863	36.4	14,128	5,544	39.2	7,467	2,319	31.1
Total	27,727	8,029	29.0	19,038	5,634	29.6	8,689	2,395	27.6

Source: U. S. Equal Employment Opportunity Commission, Job Patterns for Minorities and Women in Private Industry, Report No. 1 (Washington: Government Printing Office, 1966), Part II.

TABLE 16. Tobacco Industry
Employment by Race, Sex, and Occupational Group
Virginia, 1966

Occupational Group	All Employees			Male			Female		
	Total	Negro	Percent Negro	Total	Negro	Percent Negro	Total	Negro	Percent Negro
Officials and managers	864	20	2.3	789	20	2.5	75	—	—
Professionals	288	4	1.4	261	4	1.5	27	—	—
Technicians	242	5	2.1	145	4	2.8	97	1	1.0
Sales workers	8	1	12.5	8	1	12.5	—	—	—
Office and clerical	620	38	6.1	246	20	8.1	374	18	4.8
Total white collar	2,022	68	3.4	1,449	49	3.4	573	19	3.3
Craftsmen	1,047	20	1.9	1,047	20	1.9	—	—	—
Operatives	5,259	983	18.7	2,465	699	28.4	2,794	284	10.2
Laborers	3,845	2,169	56.4	2,279	1,490	65.4	1,566	679	43.4
Service workers	427	294	68.9	370	239	64.6	57	55	96.5
Total blue collar	10,578	3,466	32.8	6,161	2,448	39.7	4,417	1,018	23.0
Total	12,600	3,534	28.0	7,610	2,497	32.8	4,990	1,037	20.8

Source: U. S. Equal Employment Opportunity Commission, Job Patterns for Minorities and Women in Private Industry, Report No. 1 (Washington: Government Printing Office, 1966), Part II.

Tables 17-19 show, with one minor exception, that the occupational representation of Negroes improved in the 1964-1968 period. In each of the white collar classifications, the ratio of Negroes rose between 1964 and 1968, except for professionals, where a minute rise in 1966 was cancelled out in 1968. Likewise, the proportion of Negroes in the craftsman and operative classifications increased over this four-year period. On the other hand, the proportion of Negroes working as laborers declined slightly, and those employed as service workers declined substantially. This would indicate both upgrading of Negroes and employment of whites for once all-Negro jobs.

White Collar Jobs in the Three Southern States

In the three states, the total number of salaried positions in 1968 was only 10,140, of which Negroes held 279. Thus small increases in Negro representation result in relatively large percentage changes—101 additional Negro salaried employees resulted in an increase in the ratio from 1.8 to 2.8 percent. In view of the fact that white collar personnel of most companies are likely to be in New York offices instead of southern factories, these data also understate such Negro representation as does exist. This should be borne in mind in the subsequent discussion.

In the officials and managers group, the number of Negroes more than doubled—from 25 to 64. Most of these are, to be sure, first line supervisors and a sizable number are in the processing departments where the labor force is all or nearly all black. There have, however, been some higher rated appointments, including several in personnel departments.

Professionals and technical employees are not numerous in the industry, which now finds attracting blacks very difficult. Qualified Negro professionals and technical personnel have numerous opportunities for good jobs. The tobacco industry has neither glamor nor an historical record of fair employment. Moreover, its southern location is frequently considered "out of bounds" for northern-born Negroes who often do not want to chance the environment there. While the number of Negro professional employees has remained about the same, the number of technicians has increased from 18 in 1964 to 34 in 1968, 3.0 percent of all technical employees.

TABLE 17. Tobacco Industry
Employment by Race, Sex, and Occupational Group
6 Companies
Kentucky, North Carolina, and Virginia, 1964

Occupational Group	All Employees			Male			Female		
	Total	Negro	Percent Negro	Total	Negro	Percent Negro	Total	Negro	Percent Negro
Officials and managers	2,806	25	0.9	2,798	25	0.9	8	—	—
Professionals	828	6	0.7	782	4	0.5	46	2	4.3
Technicians	1,170	18	1.5	928	13	1.4	242	5	2.1
Sales workers	1,917	38	2.0	1,870	38	2.0	47	—	—
Office and clerical	3,305	91	2.8	1,280	40	3.1	2,025	51	2.5
Total white collar	10,026	178	1.8	7,658	120	1.6	2,368	58	2.4
Craftsmen	4,950	82	1.7	4,760	82	1.7	190	—	—
Operatives	18,072	2,368	13.1	10,139	1,783	17.6	7,933	585	7.4
Laborers	12,385	5,926	47.8	7,128	4,536	63.6	5,257	1,390	26.4
Service workers	1,993	1,355	68.0	1,608	1,069	66.5	385	286	74.3
Total blue collar	37,400	9,731	26.0	23,635	7,470	31.6	13,765	2,261	16.4
Total	47,426	9,909	20.9	31,293	7,590	24.3	16,133	2,319	14.4

Source: Data in the author's possession.

TABLE 18. Tobacco Industry
Employment by Race, Sex, and Occupational Group
6 Companies
Kentucky, North Carolina, and Virginia, 1966

Occupational Group	All Employees			Male			Female		
	Total	Negro	Percent Negro	Total	Negro	Percent Negro	Total	Negro	Percent Negro
Officials and managers	3,021	37	1.2	2,939	37	1.3	82	—	—
Professionals	838	8	1.0	791	6	0.8	47	2	4.3
Technicians	1,040	23	2.2	802	20	2.5	238	3	1.3
Sales workers	1,986	44	2.2	1,913	42	2.2	73	2	2.7
Office and clerical	2,891	100	3.5	1,018	48	4.7	1,873	52	2.8
Total white collar	9,776	212	2.2	7,463	153	2.1	2,313	59	2.6
Craftsmen	4,542	86	1.9	4,441	86	1.9	101	—	—
Operatives	18,186	2,670	14.7	10,367	2,086	20.1	7,819	584	7.5
Laborers	12,962	6,114	47.2	7,459	4,515	60.5	5,503	1,599	29.1
Service workers	1,916	1,262	65.9	1,512	965	63.8	404	297	73.5
Total blue collar	37,606	10,132	26.9	23,779	7,652	32.2	13,827	2,480	17.9
Total	47,382	10,344	21.8	31,242	7,805	25.0	16,140	2,539	15.7

Source: Data in the author's possession.

TABLE 19. *Tobacco Industry*
Employment by Race, Sex, and Occupational Group
6 Companies
Kentucky, North Carolina, and Virginia, 1968

Occupational Group	All Employees			Male			Female		
	Total	Negro	Percent Negro	Total	Negro	Percent Negro	Total	Negro	Percent Negro
Officials and managers	3,326	64	1.9	3,247	64	2.0	79	—	—
Professionals	966	7	0.7	884	5	0.6	82	2	2.4
Technicians	1,124	34	3.0	884	29	3.3	240	5	2.1
Sales workers	1,319	41	3.1	1,272	41	3.2	47	—	—
Office and clerical	3,405	133	3.9	1,127	42	3.7	2,278	91	4.0
Total white collar	10,140	279	2.8	7,414	181	2.4	2,726	98	3.6
Craftsmen	4,841	107	2.2	4,814	107	2.2	27	—	—
Operatives	19,880	3,438	17.3	11,130	2,581	23.2	8,750	857	9.8
Laborers	13,127	6,175	47.0	8,099	4,664	57.6	5,028	1,511	30.1
Service workers	1,973	1,090	55.2	1,632	862	52.8	341	228	66.9
Total blue collar	39,821	10,810	27.1	25,675	8,214	32.0	14,146	2,596	18.4
Total	49,961	11,089	22.2	33,089	8,395	25.4	16,872	2,694	16.0

Source: Data in the author's possession.

In sales, tobacco has only a few Negroes, but it is by no means behind the general industry pattern. Tobacco companies have been utilizing Negro route salesmen and promotion men for many years, at first to increase their sales among Negroes, and more recently in general sales work and promotion. Most of these salesmen are not based in the three states. Office and clerical personnel, on the other hand, were almost all white in the three southern states, both in tobacco plants and others, prior to 1960. As in other large industries, tobacco companies are now doing extensive recruiting and training to increase their share of Negroes in these jobs.

Three State Differences

Some surprising differences are apparent when comparing field data for Kentucky, North Carolina, and Virginia, especially for total employment and for white collar jobs. Table 20 shows the percentage distributions in the three states, based upon Tables 17-19 and Appendix Tables B-1 to B-9. First, there is the relative stability of North Carolina over the four-year period, and in contrast, the jump in the Negro proportion in Kentucky and Virginia. The latter state, for the first time in this century, had a larger proportion of Negro tobacco workers than did its neighboring state just to the south.

Kentucky also saw surprising gains in the ratio of Negro employment, but most of its gains were concentrated in the lower rated jobs. Both Virginia and North Carolina Negro tobacco workers scored qualitative gains by increasing their proportion of salaried jobs and of the top two blue collar jobs. The gains in salaried positions for Negroes were especially impressive in Virginia, where the proportion of officials and managers, technicians, and office and clerical employees not only rose but substantially exceeded those groups in other states. Nor were any sales workers reported for Kentucky in 1968.

Virginia no longer boasts the headquarters of major tobacco companies, so no sales workers were recorded there. The proportion of Negro white collar employees was 2.6 percent in Kentucky, 2.4 percent in North Carolina, and 4.0 percent in Virginia. The 3.1 ratio in North Carolina for this group in effect is the industry figure for the three states and probably reflects local sales personnel of the one company headquartered there.

TABLE 20. Tobacco Industry
Percent Negro Employment by Occupational Group
Major Tobacco Manufacturing States
1964, 1966, 1968

Occupational Group	Total			Kentucky			North Carolina			Virginia		
	1964	1966	1968	1964	1966	1968	1964	1966	1968	1964	1966	1968
Officials and managers	0.9	1.2	1.9	0.8	0.9	1.8	0.6	0.8	1.3	2.4	2.5	3.4
Professionals	0.7	1.0	0.7	0.9	0.8	—	0.4	0.7	1.0	1.3	1.5	0.6
Technicians	1.5	2.2	3.0	1.1	1.6	1.4	1.8	2.5	3.3	1.0	2.1	3.6
Sales workers	2.0	2.2	3.1	2.6	2.9	—[a]	1.7	1.9	3.1	—[a]	20.0[b]	—[a]
Office and clerical	2.8	3.5	3.9	3.1	3.0	4.0	2.2	3.0	3.2	4.4	5.8	5.9
Total white collar	1.8	2.2	2.8	2.1	2.1	2.6	1.5	1.8	2.4	2.8	3.3	4.0
Craftsmen	1.7	1.9	2.2	0.8	1.0	0.6	2.1	2.3	2.8	1.0	1.4	2.1
Operatives	13.1	14.7	17.3	5.6	8.8	10.2	15.2	16.1	18.9	15.6	17.5	22.9
Laborers	47.8	47.2	47.0	22.7	30.3	27.9	54.3	54.4	53.9	52.7	50.1	55.8
Service workers	68.0	65.9	55.2	36.0	35.3	36.9	79.2	78.3	61.2	67.1	67.2	60.9
Total blue collar	26.0	26.9	27.1	11.9	17.4	16.5	30.6	30.5	29.8	27.9	28.9	33.9
Total	20.9	21.8	22.2	9.7	14.0	14.2	23.6	24.1	23.2	24.6	24.9	29.2

Source: Tables 17-19 and Appendix Tables B-1 to B-9.
[a] No sales personnel of either race reported.
[b] One Negro of a total of five.

The gains made by Negroes in Virginia tobacco plants during the 1960's are probably the result both of labor market and civil rights factors. Richmond and Petersburg, where the Virginia tobacco industry is concentrated, have both become heavily black populated cities in which Negroes are clearly close to a majority. (See Table 4, p. 11.) Richmond in particular has been in a full employment situation for the entire decade. With most tobacco factories located in heavily Negro neighborhoods, and with continued pressure for fair employment, the pressures and the needs have coincided.

In North Carolina, there is more competition for tobacco plant jobs between whites and Negroes, with at least two newer plants attracting many applicants for the available jobs. Despite the affirmative action, particularly of one, but also of other companies, the percentage of Negroes, at an all-time low in 1960, has not increased substantially since then.

Louisville, Kentucky, has attracted several major employers— International Harvester, General Electric, and DuPont, for example—which pay much higher wages than does the tobacco industry. It is quite likely that jobs have opened to Negroes in Louisville tobacco plants as whites have been attracted elsewhere. How the closing of the American plant in Louisville will affect these data remains to be seen. Since some of the work will be moved to American's three North Carolina plants, it could improve Negro employment there.

White Collar Jobs in the Total Tobacco Company Employment

For a comparison with other industries, it is appropriate to look at tobacco white collar employment, not only in the three key manufacturing states, but also in the companies as a whole, and (for the four companies which maintain them) in their New York offices. Table 21 summarizes the total occupational group breakdown by race and sex for the six major tobacco companies for 1968, and Table 22 provides the data for the New York offices of four.

As pointed out in Chapter II, the tobacco companies are more and more either becoming conglomerates or are being absorbed by such diversified concerns. Hence the data in Tables 21 and 22 include employees of non-tobacco aspects or divisions of these companies' businesses. The bulk of their employees as of 1968 were, however, directly concerned with the tobacco industry.

TABLE 21. *Tobacco Industry*
Employment by Race, Sex, and Occupational Group
Consolidated Report Data, 6 Companies, 1968

Occupational Group	All Employees			Male			Female		
	Total	Negro	Percent Negro	Total	Negro	Percent Negro	Total	Negro	Percent Negro
Officials and managers	4,814	91	1.9	4,691	90	1.9	123	1	0.8
Professionals	1,473	13	0.9	1,326	10	0.8	147	3	2.0
Technicians	1,456	46	3.2	1,193	34	2.8	263	12	4.6
Sales workers	5,411	195	3.6	5,325	194	3.6	86	1	1.2
Office and clerical	5,658	241	4.3	1,797	72	4.0	3,861	169	4.4
Total white collar	18,812	586	3.1	14,332	400	2.8	4,480	186	4.2
Craftsmen	6,095	144	2.4	6,008	137	2.3	87	7	8.0
Operatives	21,781	3,822	17.5	11,497	2,692	23.4	10,284	1,130	11.0
Laborers	14,560	6,600	45.3	8,786	4,916	56.0	5,774	1,684	29.2
Service workers	2,104	1,156	54.9	1,717	895	52.1	387	261	67.4
Total blue collar	44,540	11,722	26.3	28,008	8,640	30.8	16,532	3,082	18.6
Total	63,352	12,308	19.4	42,340	9,040	21.4	21,012	3,268	15.6

Source: Data in the author's possession.

TABLE 22. *Tobacco Industry*
Employment by Race, Sex, and Occupational Group
4 Companies, New York Offices, 1968

Occupational Group	All Employees			Male			Female		
	Total	Negro	Percent Negro	Total	Negro	Percent Negro	Total	Negro	Percent Negro
Officials and managers	564	5	0.9	554	5	0.9	10	—	—
Professionals	161	6	3.7	155	5	3.2	6	1	16.7
Technicians	38	3	7.9	37	3	8.1	1	—	—
Sales workers	801	29	3.6	766	28	3.7	35	1	2.9
Office and clerical	1,574	101	6.4	406	26	6.4	1,168	75	6.4
Total white collar	3,138	144	4.6	1,918	67	3.5	1,220	77	6.3
Craftsmen	10	2	20.0	8	2	25.0	2	—	—
Operatives	9	4	44.4	7	2	28.6	2	2	100.0
Laborers	—	—	—	—	—	—	—	—	—
Service workers	21	5	23.8	18	5	27.8	3	—	—
Total blue collar	40	11	27.5	33	9	27.3	7	2	28.6
Total	3,178	155	4.9	1,951	76	3.9	1,227	79	6.4

Source: Data in the author's possession.

It is apparent that Negro white collar employment is higher in all categories in the consolidated reports than in those pertaining to plants in the three key states except for the officials and managers group. This last includes supervisors who are, of course, in the plants. Total Negro white collar employment of 1968 was 3.1 percent in the consolidated reports, 2.8 percent for the three state plant compilation (Table 19). Undoubtedly, the companies' greater success in recruiting salaried personnel for the New York and other northern big city offices is a factor in this. Table 22 shows a 4.6 salaried employment figure for the New York offices, buttressed by a 6.4 percent office and clerical representation. In Virginia, the overall salaried figure for 1968 was 4.0 percent; for office and clerical, 5.9 percent (Table 20).

One can conclude this discussion of white collar employment by noting that in the South, all of the tobacco companies are attempting to recruit Negro salaried employees, and are not far behind other industry in this regard. They have had greater success in sales personnel than in professional or technical employees. In New York City, they have maintained a stance that is near average.[51]

Blue Collar Employment

As already noted, the occupational structure has improved for Negroes since 1964. The percentage of craftsmen rose from 1.7 to 2.2 (Tables 17-19); that of operatives from 13.1 to 17.3; meanwhile, Negro representation in the unskilled laborer category remained constant and that in service workers declined from 68 to 55.2 percent. Change is not rapid. Job openings are relatively few and production has recently been constant only because foreign sales have been making up for declining domestic consumption. In addition, continued automation increases pro-

---

51. In 1966, an Equal Employment Opportunity Commission survey saw Negro participation rates in New York City for officials and managers at 0.7 percent for 100 corporations, 0.5 percent for cigarettes; for professionals, the 100 corporation average was 0.7 percent, but cigarettes stood first at 2.8 percent. For all white collar employees, the rates for the 100 corporations were 2.6 percent, for cigarettes, 2.5 percent. See *Hearings before the U.S. Equal Employment Opportunity Commission on Discrimination in White Collar Employment in New York* (Washington: Government Printing Office, 1968), pp. 648, 662, and 664. The EEOC obviously used "cigarettes" as synonomous with "tobacco" in defining the industry.

ductivity, resulting in an expanded capacity to produce with no increase in personnel, or even with a decreased labor force.

In the craft situation, not only are few Negroes qualified, but those that are continue to find intense white worker opposition to their advancement, often solidified and strengthened by craft unions. The potential for a faster rate of improvement in upgrading Negroes is not too great even with the support of the courts for special "make-up" seniority provisions, which will be discussed later in this chapter. Whether Negroes are therefore likely to continue to be concentrated in the lower rated jobs in the industry for many years to come will depend on the capacity of company affirmative action to overcome these difficult problems.

Female Employment

As noted in previous chapters, the tobacco industry has always employed a sizeable proportion both of white and Negro women. Approximately one third of the employees are women, and the industry for many years was the only which employed Negro women in large numbers.

Mechanization of the stemmeries substantially reduced Negro female job opportunities prior to 1960. The decline in the proportion of Negroes after 1932 was in part attributable to the greatly reduced employment of black women stemmery employees. In 1930 the census reported that 65.6 percent or 14,000 of the 21,444 tobacco female "laborers and operatives" in the three key states were Negro; by 1940, the total females in these classifications had declined to 17,953 and Negro women to 9,465, or 52.7 percent.[52]

Negro women continued to lose out in the tobacco industry during the next twenty years. Total tobacco employment for women in the three states (not just laborers and operatives) in 1940 was 19,485, of whom 9,770, or 50.2 percent were black; by 1950, these figures had declined to 16,234 total and 5,977 Negro, or 36.8 percent,[53] again demonstrating the disproportionate impact on Negro female employment of stemmery mechanization and rigid segregation.

52. *U. S. Census of Population, 1930*, State Volumes, Table 11; *1940*, State Volumes, Table 20.

53. *Ibid., 1940*, State Volumes, Table 18; *1950*, State Volumes, Table 83.

The decade of the 1950's saw a continued decline in Negro female employment, but an actual slight increase in total female jobs in the three states. Thus 18,190 female tobacco workers were reported by the 1960 census, but it is estimated that an absolute maximum of only 25 percent were black.[54]

The decline in Negro female representation in the tobacco industry probably leveled off in the 1960's, as did that of males. The EEOC data presented in Table 13 (p. 42) show Negro females comprising 22.2 percent of all female employees in the three key states as compared with an overall black ratio of 25.6 percent. Even at this figure, it is not likely that many other manufacturing industries have a larger black female share of jobs.[55] Insofar as occupational distribution is concerned, however, only 117 of the 4,400 Negro women, 2.7 percent, were salaried, whereas 82.1 percent were classified as laborers or service workers. By 1966, there was thus little change in the occupational role of the black female tobacco employee.

Table 23 shows the percentage of Negro women in each major occupational group for the three key states for the years 1964, 1966, and 1968, based upon the field sample. Again the reader should bear in mind that this sample did not include any independent stemmeries in which Negro women traditionally make up the bulk of the labor force. Hence the data underestimate the proportion of Negro females as indicated by the figure of 22.2 percent for Negro female employment in 1966 shown by Table 13 based upon the EEOC data in 1966 as compared with 15.7 percent in Table 23 for the same year, based upon the field sample.

Table 23 does show that Negro women made some gains between 1964 and 1968 both quantitatively and qualitatively in the three states. But only a very few were employed as salaried employees other than in office and clerical jobs, and the great bulk in the plants were still listed as laborers and especially service employees in 1968.

---

54. See Appendix A. The Negro female percentage has always been below that of males. Hence, 25 percent is probably an overestimate.

55. The poultry sector of the meat industry probably has a higher black ratio. See Walter A. Fogel, *The Negro in the Meat Industry,* The Racial Policies of American Industry, Report No. 12 (Philadelphia: Industrial Research Unit, Wharton School of Finance and Commerce, University of Pennsylvania, 1970).

TABLE 23. Tobacco Industry

Percent Negro Female Employment by Occupational Group

Major Tobacco Manufacturing States

1964, 1966, 1968

Occupational Group	Total			Kentucky			North Carolina			Virginia		
	1964	1966	1968	1964	1966	1968	1964	1966	1968	1964	1966	1968
Officials and managers	—	—	—	—	—	—	—	—	—	—	—	—
Professionals	4.3	4.3	2.4	25.0[b]	16.7[c]	—	6.2	7.1	4.4	[a]	—	—
Technicians	2.1	1.3	2.1	2.7	1.2	1.9	3.3	1.7	4.1	—	1.1	—
Sales workers	—	2.7	—	[a]	[a]	[a]	—	2.7	—	[a]	[a]	[a]
Office and clerical	2.5	2.8	4.0	3.8	3.5	4.7	1.9	2.1	3.2	2.8	3.7	5.3
Total white collar	2.4	2.6	3.6	3.8	3.2	4.1	1.9	2.1	3.2	2.1	2.6	4.1
Craftsmen	—	—	—	—	[a]	[a]	—	—	—	—	[a]	[a]
Operatives	7.4	7.5	9.8	3.5	4.8	7.6	10.1	7.8	10.3	7.2	9.5	11.5
Laborers	26.4	29.1	30.1	18.6	30.3	27.8	24.6	26.3	26.6	37.1	34.2	38.8
Service workers	74.3	73.5	66.9	26.2	36.9	51.0	98.2	94.5	77.4	94.4	97.1	57.1
Total blue collar	16.4	17.9	18.4	8.5	15.5	15.7	19.5	19.1	18.4	17.4	18.5	21.4
Total	14.4	15.7	16.0	7.7	13.6	13.9	16.6	16.5	15.5	15.9	16.6	19.3

Source: Tables 17-19 and Appendix Tables B-1 - B-9.

[a] None reported of either race.

[b] One Negro of four.

[c] One Negro of six.

The consolidated reports of the tobacco companies (Table 21) show a larger number, although still very few, in salaried positions other than office and clerical, but about the same blue collar service employment and laborer concentration. The four New York City based concerns, as already noted (Table 22), have a higher office and clerical representation of Negroes than is found in the three key manufacturing states, but only 77 employees, including two Negroes in other classifications.

COMPANY DIFFERENCES

Although the tobacco companies have followed much the same path toward trying to eliminate the traditional racial-occupational segregation pattern, there have been significant variations in policies and practices. These have resulted from a variety of factors including different governmental legal tactics and pressures, union policies, civil rights actions, managerial policies, etc. Since much of what has occurred and is continuing is a matter of record, individual company names can be utilized.

R. J. Reynolds

That Reynolds is a leader in the integration of the tobacco factory work forces appears indisputable. Nevertheless, the proportion of Negroes employed at Reynolds has declined sharply over the years, and difficulty has been experienced even in the 1960's. The accomplishments and the problems at Reynolds are in some ways unique and in others typical of the industry.

Reynolds had three significant factors in its favor which aided the integration process. First, it had made several breakthroughs in the integration process in the past. As in other tobacco companies, Negroes have been employed in unskilled jobs and in the processing department all along. But over the years, Negroes have also been given the opportunity for semiskilled jobs in the white departments. The plug (chewing) and leaf departments, as well as a section of the cigarette department, became predominantly Negro. The smoking tobacco department and the remainder of the cigarette department were integrated, but the job classifications were predominantly segregated; the Negroes held the lower-classified jobs and the higher-classified jobs were reserved for the whites. Skilled Negroes had been used in segregated production rooms since 1919, and a few Negroes have been employed on cigarette machines since World War II. Thus integration in the 1960's was not totally new.

A second factor aiding the company has been its active role in the community and the strong feeling of community responsibility with which its management is imbued. Reynolds is not only the largest employer in Winston-Salem, North Carolina, but also maintains its corporate headquarters there. Company officials take an active role in community affairs, and have been strong leaders in community desegregation activities. Prior to legislation requiring the elimination of segregated state and municipal facilities, Winston-Salem integrated all public facilities except a park which had been willed to white residents and which required a court suit to open to blacks.[56]

While community desegregation was in progress; company officials met with Negro leaders in the community and laid out a program to desegregate its factories. The company's participation in community desegregation gave it additional credibility here. Moreover, the Negro leaders were aware of what in this case was Reynolds' third advantage in the movement toward desegregation—it had no union, and therefore, the status quo of the 1930's was not institutionalized, nor was there a vehicle for organized white worker opposition to desegregation which could easily be backed up by strike action or threats thereof.[57]

Perhaps, however, the fundamental reason why Reynolds was willing to move forward was that its management, realizing that it was both sound business and the right thing to do, had the foresight to seize the opportunity when it was presented. In March 1961, President Kennedy signed Executive Order 10925 strengthening the requirements for nondiscrimination by government contractors. A short time thereafter, Reynolds was scheduled to move its main production facility from downtown Winston-Salem and to start production in a new, modern, $32,000,000 plant in Whitaker Park, located just outside of that city. This plant was to be the largest cigarette manufacturing facility in the world, covering an area larger than twelve football fields, and it was planned as a showplace for the public. Each cigarette-making machine would be capable of producing more than 2,000

56. See "Company F. A Southern Tobacco Company" [obviously Reynolds] in Stephen Habbe, *Company Experience with Negro Employment*, Studies in Personnel Policy No. 201 (New York: National Industrial Conference Board, 1966), pp. 124-127; and Clarence N. Patrick, "Desegregation in a Southern City," *Phylon*, Vol. XXV (Fall 1964), pp. 263-269.

57. The role of the TWIU in desegregation is discussed below. That unions are not always antagonistic to civil rights progress is of course obvious, and has been pointed out in many reports in this Series.

cigarettes per minute and more than 200 packs per minute would
be produced by each packaging machine. Reynolds decided that
the easiest way to comply with Executive Order 10925 would be
to integrate the production lines upon opening Whitaker Park.

This, then, is what was done. Each worker from the old plant
who was to be transferred and each new hiree was informed of
the new system in detail. So when production began in April,
Negroes and whites were holding the same jobs at the same rates
of pay in the same production lines. There was some apprehen-
sion among the workers, but few protested against the new system. In part, this can be attributed to the positive attitude of
the community and the company toward integration. Also, there
were no unions with segregated locals or departmental seniority
rights. In addition, most employees desired strongly to work in
the new and pleasant surroundings of the Whitaker Park facility;
they preferred to stay in an integrated plant rather than quit
just to escape integration.

As the Whitaker Park plant was being opened, a schedule was
established to desegregate the facilities at the older plants. Drinking fountain signs were removed, walls separating the eating
areas taken down, a single cafeteria line was established, and
finally toilets and locker rooms were desegregated. Job integration meanwhile proceeded in the older, in town, facilities.

The company planned and monitored these personnel policies
and programs through a strong centralized personnel department
which does all personnel screening and placement and, in addition, makes frequent visits and checks to ascertain whether operating departments are adhering to these policies. Civil rights
and industrial race relations have thus been given careful scrutiny. The personnel department also carefully reviews all discharges so that if discrimination is involved, it can be detected
prior to final action.

In the early years of the desegregation policy, there was no
specific policy to recruit or to promote Negroes into better jobs.
Rather, they were promoted on the basis of qualifications in competition with other qualified personnel. In the early 1960's, this
resulted in limited progress. Negro women were promoted to
foremen on the machines and checked the output of Negro and
white operators. Seven Negro technicians on the payroll and
eleven Negro craftsmen were upgraded; and Negro receptionists
and secretaries were employed in the corporate offices.

Most of the janitor force remained Negro as did the shipping department, which was almost 100 percent Negro with the exception of white foremen. Although the company strove to remove all-white and all-Negro teams on the machines, it did not succeed in several instances in the making and packing departments. Also, Negroes still tended to be segregated by aisle in the machine departments or within an area of machines in the department. In other departments, such as filter-making and glue, only a token representation of Negroes was found as late as 1965.

Mechanization and improved methods continued to eat into jobs at Reynolds in the early 1960's, with traditional Negro jobs disproportionately affected. As a result, the long term decline in Negro representation in the company's (and the state's) tobacco labor force had not ceased by 1965. Two years later, the declining percentages of blacks was turned around for the first time in three decades, but the Negro concentration in the lowest rated jobs continued. Reynolds decided to attempt to resolve these inequities by an entirely new, affirmative approach.

First, all employees were encouraged to fill out a thirty-six page questionnaire revealing skills, educational background, talents, interests, and aptitudes (but not race). This was worked into a computerized skills inventory which is carefully kept up to date. Then the company identified 225 job classifications and 52 lines of progression. It formalized a procedure that requires promotion of the most senior qualified person. If no qualified person is available, the Reynolds procedure requires a supervisor to select for training the most senior man who is trainable.

The program is carefully audited at the personnel department level. A supervisor who does not promote or offer training to the most senior man must file a detailed report explaining his action and obtain approval for it. In addition, supervisors must counsel employees on a regular basis and file personnel performance and development reports with the personnel department with a notation showing that the report has been discussed with the employee. Employees are also urged and counselled to enter training programs, and supervisors are regularly cautioned to increase minority representation in jobs formerly all white.

To monitor this program, Reynolds employed a native North Carolinian, Marshall B. Bass, who had entered the U.S. Army as a recruit, gone through college and Officer Candidate School, and worked up to become a colonel. Mr. Bass, a Negro, was appointed Manager, Personnel Development. He has full authority to approve or disapprove all promotions, training assignments, and policies relating to all non-officer employees, and is especially directed to see to it that no discrimination occurs.

Since this program was effectuated minority representation in all white collar jobs has risen steadily, and in the lowest rung blue collar occupations it has declined. The downturn in total Negro ratio has also been halted. Although the proportion of Negroes employed by Reynolds is now only about one-half of that which existed before stemmeries were mechanized, it remains about 25 percent—the highest of any company in the industry.

R. J. Reynolds has thus vigorously moved toward equality of opportunity. Yet many problems remain. The more skilled Negroes are difficult to recruit. More often than not, whites seeking jobs have better schooling and/or experience. Mechanization and the uncertain demand for tobacco products limit opportunities for upgrading. It will take many years to offset the long history of the racial-occupational segregation pattern.

American Brands, Inc.

American Brands, until 1969 known as American Tobacco Company, has its headquarters in New York. It operates major tobacco facilities in Richmond, Virginia, Durham and Reidsville, North Carolina, and is phasing out its operations in Louisville, Kentucky. Like all tobacco concerns, American traditionally employed whites and Negroes in accordance with the racial-occupational segregation pattern and, like all but Reynolds, it was unionized in the 1930's by the Tobacco Workers' International Union on a segregated local union basis. Moreover, American's corporate organization followed the same pattern, since a separate division, American Suppliers, processed the tobacco and then "sold" it to American tobacco for manufacturing. Since the stemmeries were operated by American Suppliers, most Negroes worked for one corporate division and whites for another within the total corporation. As already noted, in Louisville this division was compounded because the Teamsters represented the stemmery workers, and the TWIU, the manufacturing unit.

In the previous chapter, it was noted that under pressure from the President's Committee on Government Contracts (Nixon Committee), American had upgraded a few Negroes at its Richmond and Durham facilities during the 1950's. Since, however, neither of these facilities had done any hiring during most of this decade, no more progress was made, and, as a result of modernization programs, some of those upgraded (as well as many whites) were downgraded during this period.

A master contract governs relations between American and the six TWIU locals (three of each race) in Durham, Reidsville, and Richmond, with a separate agreement covering the Louisville plant. (In addition, a number of craft unions hold separate agreements at the various plants.) In 1962, the master contract governing North Carolina and Virginia plants provided for promotions and demotions on the basis of seniority, but made no mention of seniority districts or scope—that is, whether plant, job, departmental, or some other method of determining seniority prevailed.[58] In actual fact, by either agreement of the locals or custom, job seniority had always prevailed. Separate locals on the basis of race insured that promotion, transfer, and demotion were confined to the groups of classifications under the jurisdiction of each separate local. There was no provision in the labor-management agreement for transfer from one local jurisdiction to another, and by tradition there was, in fact, little or no interjurisdictional mobility except in the few instances in which management transferred employees from the operation at American Suppliers to the cigarette factory operation. Seniority areas were classified by male and female, white and Negro, and by the fabrication departments and the pre-fabrication departments.

The modernization program inaugurated by the company in the 1950's was preceded by an agreement with the TWIU not to lay off anyone because of automation. This saddled the company with considerable excess labor which had prior rights to the better jobs before Negroes or others in lower rated positions could assert upgrading rights.

A number of complaints were made to the newly created President's Committee on Equal Employment Opportunity (PCEEO) by Negro employees of American in early 1962. Government investigators placed heavy pressure on the company and TWIU to merge the local unions [59] and to eliminate separate seniority and separate facilities. The locals were merged by January 1964,

---

58. "Agreement between the American Tobacco Company and Local Nos. 182, 183, 191, 192, 204, and 216 of the Tobacco Workers' International Union, AFL-CIO, effective January 1, 1962," mimeo., Article 8.

59. The merger of local unions and the issues relating thereto are discussed in a subsequent section of this chapter.

and the separate facilities eliminated some time earlier. Seniority, however, continued to be a problem.

In the American tobacco plants, opportunities for promotions continued to be relatively infrequent. Seniority was widened and many seniority lists combined in all plants, and Negroes were promoted to once all-white jobs. Indeed, this occurred with enough frequency in Richmond that white employees charged Negroes were favored at their expense. On the other hand, Negroes, particularly in Reidsville and Durham, have charged that the existence of American Suppliers as a quasi-separate entity has acted as a barrier to their progress by providing the basis for separate seniority systems, and particularly has denied seasonal employees the opportunity to transfer to better jobs. Company and union officials deny this, pointing out that seasonal employees in American plants actually have preferential rights for open jobs in all associated tobacco manufacturing plants.

The facts appear to be that American has opened up all jobs to blacks, but that declining sales and continued automation preclude any significant opportunity for advancement. The transfer of Louisville jobs to the three other plants could create some movement. As the situation now stands, seasonal employees (mostly Negroes) are governed by a separate agreement from that covering year around employees, but seasonal workers do have prior rights to open jobs. If they accept such jobs, they give up their seasonal seniority and begin as new employees.

A court case is now pending involving the Reidsville operations, in which Negro seasonal employees are asking for transfer with full seniority rights from the seasonal operation to the full-time facility. They are basing this claim on the decision in the Philip Morris litigation [60] discussed below, which clearly did not, however, grant this privilege.

American Suppliers has been abolished as a separate entity, but the manufacturing plants and stemmeries continue under separate managements. These report to different middle managers whose supervision is unified only in the person of the Vice-President—Manufacture and Leaf in New York. Seasonal employees not only have preference for manufacturing jobs but also for any disadvantaged or hard-core training programs.

---

60. *Quarles* v. *Philip Morris, Inc.*, 279 F. Supp. 505 (E. D. Va., 1968). The pending American case in the U.S. District Court, Middle District, Greensboro Division, is *Russell et al.* v. *The American Tobacco Company*, Civil Action No. C-2-G-68.

Within manufacturing plants, American and the TWIU have agreed to plantwide seniority which does tend to favor long service but once discriminated against black employees. Thus, except where there is an agreed upon and extensive progression and learning period necessary to qualification, as in the case of machine adjusters or craftsmen, anyone with the requisite plant-wide seniority can successfully bid on a job. The company is required to train that person even though previously qualified and trained persons, including those once downgraded from the open job, are available but have less plantwide seniority. The only qualification required is the capacity to perform reasonably the duties of the job after training.

At the present time, lines of seniority at American plants are merged and Negroes are working in jobs formerly reserved for whites. The company, like others in the industry, has attempted, with some success, to employ Negroes in higher rated jobs, particularly in white collar and sales jobs. Employment is not expanding, however, and, as in the rest of the industry, integration occurred after many Negroes had been eliminated from the company's work force by a combination of automation, segregation, and job denial over a long period. Today, American's Negro work force is about 20 percent of the total, putting it slightly below Reynolds and Liggett & Myers in this regard.

Liggett & Myers

Liggett & Myers' principal tobacco manufacturing operations are in Richmond and Durham. Its past history is quite like that of American, with employment historically segregated in accordance with the industry's pattern, and, since the 1930's, union relations characterized by segregated locals and seniority. Similarly, Liggett & Myers broke the segregation pattern and upgraded a few Negroes to formerly all-white jobs under pressure from the Nixon Committee in the 1950's, but its declining employment has precluded the potential for great change.

The local unions at the Liggett & Myers Richmond and Durham plants, as at American facilities, bargained jointly. One Negro and one white local existed at Richmond, but at Durham there were two Negro locals and one white. One Negro local (No. 194) represented seasonal employees and others in the processing department, the other (No. 208), represented those in the manufacturing department and other full-time employees. In 1937, Local 194 had approximately 2,800 members; No. 208

had 800 members; and No. 176, the white local, 1,600 members. In this situation (and probably others), union segregation was, among other things, initially a device to preserve white hegemony.

In the late 1940's and early 1950's, Negroes were laid off in large numbers, particularly at the Durham works, but also in Richmond, while jobs under the jurisdiction of the white local increased. Thus a statement of Local 208 claimed that in 1950:

. . . approximately 1,800 Negroes, members of local 194, were laid off. Cut-offs and layoffs did not affect many of the white employees, members of local 176. . . . Instead there was an actual increase in the number of white employees. Negroes with more than 20 years of seniority were cut-off while whites were being hired into the tobacco industry for the first time in jobs at a higher classification and at a higher rate of pay, but equivalent in skill to those from which Negroes had been cut-off.[61]

What actually occurred was that Liggett & Myers began moving its major stemmery operations out of Durham in 1950, operating only on a short seasonal basis between 1950 and 1964. Stemmery operations were closed permanently in 1964. In addition, it abolished the night shift in the blending operation in 1962. All these actions, although dictated by business conditions, substantially reduced Negro employment.

These reductions led to the pressures which first brought the Nixon Committee and later the PCEEO into the picture. At the insistence of the latter agency, Liggett & Myers opened up all jobs to Negroes and whites, and with the national officials of the TWIU, pressured the local unions to merge.

The Richmond locals of the TWIU at Liggett & Myers did merge, but at Durham one Negro local held out. In 1962 new seniority agreements had been negotiated at Durham which in effect gave existing employees rights to jobs in departments other than those for which their local union bargained on the basis of seniority *after* incumbents, as follows:

1. Local 176—The names of all regular employees on the seniority lists of Locals 208 and 194 were combined in order of

---

61. From a statement by Local No. 208 to a special fact finder appointed by PCEEO. Much of our material comes from this proceeding, which was continued by the Office of Federal Contract Compliance, successor to PCEEO. Additional facts were obtained from interviews with Liggett & Myers and TWIU officials, Durham and Washington, D.C., November 14 and December 3, 1969, and from court proceedings cited in note 62, below.

employment dates and added to the bottom of the seniority list for Local 176 jobs.

2. Local 208—Locals 176 and 194 seniority lists were combined in order of employment dates and added to the seniority list of Local 208 jobs.

3. Local 194—Locals 176 and 208 seniority lists were combined in order of employment dates and added to the seniority list of Local 194 jobs.

Prior to this action, strict local union seniority had prevailed at Liggett & Myers, except that members of Local 194, the Durham Negro local in processing, had preference for open jobs under the jurisdiction of Local 208, the other Durham Negro local, which members of the latter did not desire, or could not fill. This allowed seasonal employees to obtain full year jobs.

The national TWIU and Liggett & Myers officials had hoped that the 1962 agreement would lead to a merger of the locals. Local 208 officials, however, declined to accept merger on this basis. There then began a long legal battle involving the company, the union, and several civil rights and government agencies.

The company was on the spot because the PCEEO and its successor, the Office of Federal Contract Compliance (OFCC), took the position that Liggett & Myers was in noncompliance with Executive Order No. 10925, and therefore, potentially ineligible for government contracts if it dealt with segregated local unions. The officers of TWIU felt that segregated locals were an embarrassment, as we shall discuss later in this chapter. Nevertheless, aided by attorney Floyd McKissick, later president of the Congress on Racial Equality (CORE), Local 208 resisted pressure for merger until it could secure what it regarded as a more satisfactory arrangement on seniority and on representation in local union offices. Meanwhile Local 194 was merged into Local 176 at a sparsely attended meeting. Litigation over this was threatened but apparently did not materialize. Alleged participation of Local 176 officials in White Citizens' Council activities in Durham certainly did not decrease the apprehensions of blacks concerning local union mergers.

In 1964, the international TWIU officials ordered Local 208 to merge with Local 176, and served notice that a trusteeship would be imposed if it did not do so. Local 208 officials obtained an ex parte injunction restraining the international officials from lifting Local 208's charter. On the subsequent hearing, the injunction was modified and extended until Local 208 could exhaust its internal remedies. This it did, first with a hearing presided over by George Benjamin, who was then the senior Negro officer of the TWIU. Mr. Benjamin, then the TWIU president, and finally the 1964 TWIU convention, all upheld the action which proposed to put Local 208 into trusteeship, then lift its charter and merge it with Local 176.[62]

In the meantime, Liggett & Myers was faced with bargaining demands by Local 176, which now claimed to represent all bargaining unit employees in Durham. Given the predominance of white employees and a split among Negroes over the merger question, Local 176 easily proved majority status by signed authorization cards. Anxious to see the end of the racial local situation and believing that a National Labor Relations Board election campaign would only exacerbate existing racial tensions, the company recognized Local 176 as exclusive bargaining agent for all Durham represented employees. A joint contract for Richmond and Durham was negotiated with Locals 176 and 177 (Richmond). One Negro from Richmond was on the bargaining committee, but none from Durham. Local 208 officials then filed a charge with the National Labor Relations Board charging the company and the union with unfair labor practices. The District Court then continued the injunction against lifting 208's charter until the NLRB had exhausted jurisdiction over the local's charges.

At this point, the President's Committee on Equal Employment Opportunity, whose simplistic view that the abolition of separate racial locals must, of itself, improve Negro job opportunities resulted in the controversy reaching its high pitch, appointed veteran labor relations arbitrator and mediator, Ronald W. Haughton, to try to resolve the dispute. The NLRB took no action on Local 208's charges while the Haughton proceeding was pending.

---

62. Transcipt and order in *Daye* v. *Tobacco Workers International Union*, Civil Action No. 1924-64, U.S. Dist. Ct., D.C., August 6, 14, 17, 1964, February 11, 1966, and April 1, 1968. See also "Negro Seniority Fight Raises Broad Rights Issue," *New York Times*, December 13, 1964. According to this story, a member of the TWIU at the convention told the reporter that "if we ever merge locals 176 and 208, it will be the first organization in the world composed of Negroes, members of the White Citizens Council and the Ku Klux Klan." The *Times* reporter obviously was unaware of similar situations in the paper, rubber, automobile, steel, textile, building trades, and many other local unions in the South.

After initial investigations, Mr. Haughton, whose appointment was continued by the Office of Federal Contract Compliance, successor to the PCEEO, held hearings over a nine-month period in 1965, and issued his report on April 8, 1966. In it, he found that the seniority article noted above, which tied together the former seniority arrangements of the prior segregated era were not discriminatory on their face, but that they tended to perpetuate past seniority practices and to maintain a kind of super-seniority for whites in the better jobs. Instead, he recommended that jobs be assigned in the future on the basis of seniority regardless of former local union jurisdiction (that is, plantwide seniority), except in machine line progressions where orderly on-the-job training required that job seniority prevail in promotion from the bottom job to the next higher, etc. Under this recommendation, plant seniority would, of course, govern openings on the bottom machine progression job. In order to facilitate integration, Mr. Haughton proposed a system of maintaining or "red-circling" wages so that Negroes who entered the bottom of a machine progression as a means of qualifying for top jobs would not have to accept a reduction in pay.

Following receipt of the Haughton report, a long series of bargaining conferences took place. An agreement was finally reached which actually went beyond the Haughton recommendations. It provided for plantwide seniority except for two ladders of progression—one on packing machines, the other on cigarette making machines. The senior employee, regardless of race or sex, can bid on any job outside the two progression ladders. Moreover, once an employee successfully bids into the bottom job of either progression ladder and works in this capacity for 160 days or more, he moves up the progression ladder by plant seniority.

White employees were induced to accept this agreement because the TWIU and Liggett & Myers agreed to "red circle" any employee bumped out of position as a result of the agreement up to a maximum of 23 cents per hour. Local 208 officials had an additional inducement to agree because they had been losing their members to Local 176 and the local was close to the TWIU constitutional minimum of ten members by the time that it agreed to merge. If its membership had fallen below the ten member minimum, its charter would have been subject to automatic forfeiture.

The last segregated local in the TWIU—Local 208—thus merged with Local 176. On May 31, 1967, the merger and the above summarized agreement were noted in a telegram from the Director of the Office of Federal Contract Compliance which stated that as a result thereof, Liggett & Myers was in compliance with Executive Order 11246. The National Labor Relations Board's General Counsel dismissed Local 208's charge and the United States District Court dissolved the restraining order.

Unfortunately, the civil rights litigation at Liggett & Myers did not end. The Equal Employment Opportunity Commission, after receiving a complaint, demanded that Liggett & Myers supply it with information dating back to the period when the PCEEO (later OFCC) was investigating the matter. The company demurred, pointing out that it was found in compliance with the executive order on May 31, 1967, and proposing that the EEOC confine its investigation to the period since that date. The EEOC refused and won a court order that the company produce its files.[63] That order is presently being appealed. Given the EEOC's backlog of complaints and the long litigation that ensued involving another governmental civil rights agency, together with its successor, its special fact finder, the National Labor Relations Board, and a United States District Court, one can well wonder what purpose is being fulfilled by a rehash of the matter.

Another reason why the EEOC's insistence on an investigation of matters prior to June 1967 is not easily comprehended, is that few jobs are in fact at stake. Liggett & Myers in Durham has not employed anyone since 1956 and few, if any, in Richmond since then. The situation is not likely to change since the company has been losing market position for a number of years and is increasing the speed of its cigarette machines and introducing other improvements. Like other companies, it has attempted to employ Negro sales personnel and other white collar employees, with limited success. Liggett & Myers now has a Negro complement of about 20 percent, which is approximately equal to American and slightly below Reynolds. Given the lack of job openings, the Negro employees of Liggett & Myers are likely to continue to be concentrated in the lower rated jobs for the forseeable future.

---

63. *Equal Employment Opportunity Commission* v. *Liggett & Myers Tobacco Company*, U.S. Dist. Ct., Mid. Dist., N.C., No. C-126-D-69, September 30, 1969

Brown & Williamson

Brown & Williamson operates major plants in Petersburg, Virginia and Louisville, Kentucky, with a smaller facility in Winston-Salem. Petersburg is a city moving toward a majority Negro population, and Brown & Williamson there has a sizeable Negro labor force—about one-third of the total. At Louisville, however, less than 10 percent of the work force is black. Separate locals existed at Petersburg (but not at Louisville) with the usual racial job division, separate seniority, etc.

When locals of Brown & Williamson in Petersburg were merged, the Negro local survived—one of only two situations where this occurred. (The other was at United States Tobacco, Richmond.) Moreover, the president of the former black local, Oliver Shaw, became president of the new body and in 1968 was also elected an international vice-president.

Of special interest is the fact that the Petersburg locals were able to merge on a basis that set the stage for the Haughton proposal and the subsequent Liggett & Myers settlement. In 1964, these locals merged and agreed with the company on a seniority arrangement which opens up all but machine progression jobs on the basis of plantwide seniority. After an employee has been on a job for three months, he can utilize plant seniority for promotion to open jobs. On layoffs, plant seniority governs in all cases.

This agreement was worked out with no outside assistance in a plant that has as large a black ratio as any in the industry except stemmeries. Undoubtedly, the fact that the company has been gaining a large share of the market, and hiring instead of laying off, has helped. Negro representation in the total company is, however, only about one-half that of the Petersburg plant and considerably less than that of the companies previously discussed.

P. Lorillard—Departmental Segregation and Seniority

The major facilities of P. Lorillard are in Greensboro, North Carolina, where the company transferred its former Jersey City, New Jersey operations in 1956, and in Louisville. The former plant now has a Negro complement of about 20 percent, the latter, less than one-fourth that. Yet it was problems at the former which generated the most heat and led to the most improvement.

At Jersey City, Lorillard followed the occupational pattern of the industry despite the location of its plant until directed to cease violating New Jersey civil rights laws in 1951. Thus the files of the then New Jersey Division Against Discrimination contain this note from the Division's assistant director:

We did discover . . . the existence of a form of racial segregation which the union and the employees have permitted to exist from the very beginning of this plant's operations.[64]

By 1954, this same official wrote the company noting considerable progress in integration, but still a heavy concentration of Negroes in the leaf and cutting departments and an equally heavy ratio of whites in making and packing.[65] Soon thereafter, of course, the company began its move South, where it again firmly adhered to southern customs, as it had continued to do in Louisville. It set up the new plant on a strictly segregated basis and set the stage for rigid departmental seniority contract provisions —a provision that is inherently discriminatory when combined with a discriminatory hiring pattern, but which would not necessarily be so when employment is conducted without discrimination. At its Greensboro plant, Lorillard employed Negroes only for jobs in leaf processing, blending, cutting, stripping, receiving, and service departments.[66] The last named included janitors and sweepers and therefore departmental lines prevented Negroes employed in these occupational roles from advancing to better jobs.

The Greensboro Lorillard plant was organized by the TWIU soon after its establishment. On instructions from the TWIU general president, it was organized on an integrated basis and two Negroes were represented on the first seven-man negotiating committee.[67] But the white majority on the TWIU negotiating committee proposed, and the company accepted, seniority provisions which limited movement to occupational groups within

64. From the files of the New Jersey Division, in the author's possession.

65. *Ibid.* The situation in Jersey City was confirmed by the testimony of Carl Fieg, formerly factory manager at the Jersey City plant of P. Lorillard, and later director of manufacturing for the company in *Robinson et al.* v. *P. Lorillard et al.*, U.S. Dist. Ct., Mid. Dist., N.C., Case No. C-14-G-66, May 5-7, 1969; transcript of testimony, pp. 248-260, 265-268.

66. See especially the testimony of the then personnel manager of the Lorillard plant, *Robinson* v. *P. Lorillard, op. cit.*, pp. 239-247. Helping to maintain segregation was the North Carolina Employment Service, then also racially segregated and highly discriminatory.

67. *Ibid.*, testimony of Lionel J. Dugas, TWIU organizer, p. 355

departments. White members of the negotiating committee and former local union officials later testified that this proposal emanated from the desire to prevent Negroes from advancing to better jobs.[68] This allegation was denied by the first local union president, but in fact, the white members of the negotiating committee did meet for lunch at a cafeteria which Negroes were not allowed to use, and there strategy was apparently determined to accomplish their purpose.[69]

In addition to the issue of Negro rights, the departmental seniority issue at Lorillard's Greensboro plant involved a fundamental divergence of views among the white employees. Lorillard's "Old Gold" brand was the company's biggest seller when it opened the Greensboro plant. Then on 9 July 1958, the *Reader's Digest* carried an article which seemed to indicate that Lorillard's new "Kent" filter cigarette had the most effective restraint against harmful tars and nicotine. "Kent" sales and production expanded rapidly. Since then, "Old Gold" sales have continued to decline, and "Kent" has been the company's best seller.[70] The result has been that employees in the "Old Gold" making department, including some who came South with the company and who once saw departmental seniority to their advantage, soon joined forces with the Negro employees in demanding plantwide seniority. The filter department employees, however, were a clear majority, and so the departmental seniority was maintained until governmental intervention following numerous complaints.

The first complaints were made to the Nixon Committee in 1958 by Negroes. This resulted in two Negroes being upgraded to then all-white departments prior to 1960. Further complaints to the PCEEO in 1961 resulted in eleven more upgradings, this time of Negro women. Then in the 1961-62 negotiations, the company and the TWIU abolished job seniority, but retained the strict departmental seniority. By this time, the company had ceased to confine Negroes and whites to segregated departments.

---

68. *Ibid.*, testimony of Lois N. Burnside, pp. 104-126; Sterling Caviness, pp. 126-133; and James R. Lee, Jr., pp. 133-147. Also affidavits filed with the National Labor Relations Board in the author's possession.

69. *Ibid.*, and testimony of Albert W. Thompson, *Robinson* v. *P. Lorillard*, *op. cit.*, pp. 301-316.

70. In 1969, "Kent" ranked seventh among all cigarette brands in sales, "Old Gold," nineteenth, and "Newport," another Lorillard filter, twenty-first. In 1968, "Newport" sales led "Old Gold." *Business Week* (December 1969), p. 83.

If, however, a person elected to transfer from one department to another, he would still be required under this agreement to give up all seniority in his old department and begin as a new employee in the department to which he transferred.

Under strong pressure from PCEEO, the company unilaterally granted employees the right to return to former departments with seniority intact if they elected to transfer to another department and then were laid off because of lack of work. The TWIU protested this action, took it to arbitration and won the case. In the 1965 negotiations, however, the TWIU agreed to this transfer provision. Employees who transferred started as the lowest ranking employees in the new department. Employees who were on layoff status were then given preference for any job openings in other departments, but their right to return with accumulated seniority, if recalled to their original department was limited to a two-year period.

While the difficulties over seniority continued, Lorillard, under PCEEO pressure, integrated its cafeteria in 1961, and then after North Carolina abolished its segregation laws in 1963, toilets and locker rooms. White workers boycotted the cafeteria for a time, but no incidents occurred, and the boycott soon lost effectiveness.

Throughout the period from 1963 to 1966, Negroes continued to lodge complaints with PCEEO, its successor, the Office of Federal Contract Compliance (OFCC), and with the Equal Employment Opportunity Commission, and also with the National Labor Relations Board. The EEOC found "probable cause" that discrimination existed, and the already-noted court case was filed, which led to the seniority system being declared discriminatory and the substitution of plantwide seniority therefor.[71]

White employees of the "Old Gold" departments also complained to the NLRB, charging, as did the Negroes, that the seniority arrangements represented lack of fair representation by their bargaining agent, the TWIU and its Local No. 317. Actually, movements of Negroes out of traditional jobs were occurring by 1966, as black employees took advantage of the new provision which permitted them to transfer without loss of seniority rights in their original departments. Transfers, however, were limited not only by what may have been a lack of enthusiasm on the part of the company to upset its collective bargaining relationships, but also by a lack of job openings. As a matter of fact,

---

71. *Robinson* v. *P. Lorillard, op. cit.*, transcript, pp. 323-354. The final court decision was issued on March 11, 1970.

one government investigator interviewed emphasized that even with plantwide seniority, there would be little movement of Negroes, since layoffs and low turnover kept new plant jobs at a minimum.[72]

Nevertheless, by 1968, Lorillard had made considerable progress in integration of Greensboro. It doubled its percentage of Negroes over the former ratio of 10 percent. Employing Dr. Julius Thomas, former industrial secretary of the National Urban League as a consultant, Lorillard added a number of white collar employees to its staff at Greensboro and in the New York office, and began an apprentice program in order to train potential Negro craftsmen. The bulk of its Negro employees, however, continued to remain in the lowest classifications.

Lorillard opened a new plant in the mid-1950's on the assumption that a racial-occupational segregation pattern, already under strong attack, would nevertheless endure. Its lack of foresight provided for a smooth initial relationship with its white-dominated local union, but resulted in much difficulty later on, not only with the Negro minority, but also with senior white employees. They, like the Negroes, were locked into less advantaged employment situations by a rigid departmental seniority system that could not be defended on the basis of job requirements or in-plant training needs.

As so often seems to happen, Lorillard's major problems did not occur at the plant in which the poorer integration situation existed. The ratio of Negroes at its Louisville plant in 1968 remained about 5 percent, one-fourth that at its Greensboro operation. Nor had the Louisville plant made any meaningful progress in upgrading blue collar workers nor employing Negro salaried personnel. Yet agitation for change, or involvement of government agencies therein, was as conspicuous by its absence at Louisville as by its presence in Greensboro.

Philip Morris—the "Rightful Place" Doctrine

Philip Morris operates several major facilities in Richmond and Louisville. As of 1968, Philip Morris' Negro employment was the lowest of the major producers, the only one below 15 percent. In both Louisville and Richmond plants, however, Negro employment was considerably above that figure. In its

---

72. Interview, March 1967. Since then Lorillard sales, and presumably jobs, have further declined.

Richmond plants, aided by a tight labor market and the fastest expanding sales of any cigarette company, there was a Negro ratio well over 15 percent. It was in Richmond that a key court case was generated, of great significance not only for the tobacco industry, but for industry generally.[73]

Essentially, Philip Morris followed the same employment practices as did other tobacco manufacturers. In 1955, as a result of President Eisenhower's Executive Order No. 10599, which established the Nixon Committee, the first thirteen Negroes were assigned to the Richmond plant's fabrication department. As a result of Executive Order No. 10925 of 1961 and the work of the PCEEO, Philip Morris began to move toward nondiscriminatory hiring by what the District Court termed "token hiring of Negroes in fabrication" from 1963 to 1967. On the other hand, the court noted that

Negroes have been appointed foremen in the stemmery, the blended leaf section, the wrapping section and the storage and dressing section of the company's 20th Street plant [Richmond]. Other Negroes have been placed as in export superintendent and in the quality control sections. The company has recruited Negroes from colleges to enter its management trainee program. Negroes are employed at the executive level in the sales program.[74]

Philip Morris' Richmond employees were originally represented by segregated locals. In 1963, they merged. Negroes have been represented on the bargaining committee of the merged local, but not as officers.

Prior to 1957, the wages of Negroes and whites employed in the same occupations but in different departments were unequal. Wages were equalized between 1957 and 1959, with two exceptions for which the District Court ordered equalization. Beyond these two wage rate situations, the court found no extant discrimination. It did find, however, that "the restrictive departmental transfer and seniority provisions of the collective bargaining agreement are intentional, unlawful employment practices because they are imposed on a departmental structure that was organized on a racially segregated basis." [75] Through this

---

73. *Quarles* v. *Philip Morris, Inc., loc. cit.* Our facts are based largely on the briefs and decision in this proceeding.

74. *Ibid.*

75. *Ibid.* The intellectual basis of the court's decision is found in note, "Title VII, Seniority Discrimination and the Incumbent Negro," *Harvard Law Review*, Vol. LXXX (April 1967), pp. 1260 ff.

decision, the stage was set for a challenge of seniority arrangements in other tobacco plants, for the successful challenge to seniority provisions in the paper industry, discussed in the paper study of this Series, and probably for similar challenges elsewhere.

Originally, Philip Morris operated under strict departmental seniority, which was first modified for whites, then eventually for Negroes. Because its Richmond facilities are in seven locations within that city, departmental seniority was a natural development, and, in the absence of discriminatory employment practices, would not have been considered invidious in any manner. But the court concluded that the Civil Rights Act "does not require that Negroes be preferred over white employees who possess employment seniority. It is also apparent that Congress did not intend to freeze an entire generation of Negro employees into discriminatory patterns that existed before the act." [76] Accordingly, the court did not disturb the departmental seniority system as such. Moreover, it excluded seasonal stemmery employees from relief on the grounds that they were temporary employees. It provided that all other Negro employees employed prior to January 1, 1966, who were not hired directly into, or who were not transferred in a nondiscriminatory manner into, formerly all white departments, "shall be given an opportunity to transfer to the fabrication or warehouse, shipping and receiving departments to fill vacancies if they elect to transfer and if they are qualified for the jobs they seek." [77]

To accomplish this purpose, the court ordered the company to screen its Negro employees "of the affected class," and to list those who desire to transfer and are eligible on the same basis as white employees are deemed eligible for such work. When a vacancy occurs, the company is required to offer it to the qualified employee, white or black, with the greatest company (Richmond area) seniority. Members of the affected class "shall have departmental seniority computed from their employment seniority date." [78] This they carry with them as a seniority credit to make up for past discrimination. If they fail to qualify for promotion or transfer after a fair trial, they can return

---

76. *Quarles* v. *Philip Morris, loc. cit.*

77. *Ibid.*

78. *Ibid.*

to the former jobs, without loss of seniority. The court also provided:

> For every person transferred under these procedures from the prefabrication department, the company may hire a replacement from the street, and to that extent its obligation under the collective bargaining agreement to hire into prefabrication from the semmery is modified. This provision is designed to prevent the company's new labor pool from being restricted to seasonal employees.[79]

No appeal was taken by the company or the TWIU from this decision. Management and the union are apparently living with it without difficulty. Although the *Quarles* decision gave greater opportunities to some of the black Philip Morris employees, it limited those of many others—a fact largely unnoticed to date. For the decision provided that seasonal employees have less rights to full-time jobs than they formerly had (or now have in American or Liggett & Myers plants, for example). Moreover, although the complainants in the *Russell* case involving American are demanding that seasonal employees be included in the "affected class" and given plantwide seniority, such employees were specifically excluded from exercising plantwide seniority by the *Quarles* decision. Finally, *Quarles* gave seasonal employees preferential rights only to every other full-time job opening, whereas previously they had such rights to any such openings. This came out clearly in the second big case involving Philip Morris.

Philip Morris—the "Rightful Place" of Seasonal Employees

Philip Morris' other major location is in Louisville, where in 1944 it acquired the former Axton-Fischer Tobacco Company. The latter concern had almost literally maintained the Tobacco Workers' International Union during the 1920's, being the only concern of size which then recognized the TWIU. Philip Morris took over from Axton-Fischer its labor contracts with TWIU Local 16 (white) and Local 72 (Negro), plus contracts with seven craft unions.[80]

Until 1952, Philip Morris purchased most of its tobacco for the Louisville plant from independent stemmeries. Its employees

---

79. *Ibid.*

80. *Carr et al.* v. *Philip Morris, Inc., et al.*, Complaint No. 103-E, Kentucky Commission on Human Rights, transcript of testimony, September 8-10, 23, 26, 1969, Vol. I, pp. 5-6. Most of our facts are based on this six volume transcript and the pertinent exhibits.

were thus all full time, with Negroes used in some prefabrication work, janitorial duties, and in other traditional jobs, but with more whites than is typical in North Carolina or Virginia utilized in blending and cutting departments. Intraplant movement, as described in the Liggett & Myers situation, was based on local union seniority. Negroes had seniority rights only in Local 72 jobs; whites, in Local 16 jobs. In addition, departmental restrictions on movement also existed.

In 1952, Philip Morris opened a new "green leaf" stemmery to handle tobacco purchased directly after harvesting, and a warehouse. Both were located in Louisville, but at a considerable distance from the main plant. Jurisdiction over the seasonal employees in the stemmery and over the few permanent ones in the warehouse was given to the black local (No. 72). Contracts were negotiated which gave no rights in the main plant to seasonal employees. All employees in the main plant retained their full-time jobs; the labor force, entirely Negro, for the stemmery was all newly recruited.

In 1957, partially as a result of contracts with the Nixon Committee which, it will be recalled, handled equal employment matters during the Eisenhower Administration, Philip Morris agreed to permit some seasonal employees to transfer to the main plant. Since racial segregation was being maintained, such transfers could be made only to jobs within the jurisdiction of Local 72. Transferees obtained seniority in the main plant as of the date of their transfer there, receiving no credit for seasonal employment. They were, however, permitted to bump back into the stemmery if laid off at the main plant.[81]

At first, only men in the stemmery were selected on a seniority basis to be transferred to the main plant. In 1960, at the request of the longtime (now retired) Negro vice-president of the TWIU, George Benjamin, a few women were selected for main plant jobs by the plant manager of the stemmery, with the approval of the Local 72 president. Later all selections were on a seniority basis. The company reserved the right (as it still did in 1969) to employ persons directly into the main plant from the street. Its policy has been to consider stemmery employment needs also and not to restrict its main plant hiring to its seasonal labor force. Thus an employee who was hired

---

81. *Carr* v. *Philip Morris, op. cit.,* testimony of Walter Reeb, stemmery plant manager, Vol. IV, pp. 738-823; Catherine M. L. Northington, former president of Local 72, Vol. III, pp. 730-738; Vol. IV, pp. 471-506.

into the Philip Morris main plant with no previous company experience on December 1, 1968, would have seniority as of that date, whereas an employee who had done seasonal stemmery work since 1962, but did not enter the main plant until December 2, 1968, would have seniority in the main plant from the latter date and could be laid off while the newly-hired worker remained on the job. On the other hand, only the former seasonal employee could bump back into the stemmery during the eight months in which the stemmery was operating.[82]

Beginning in 1961 with the establishment of President Kennedy's President's Committee on Equal Employment Opportunity, successor to the Nixon Committee, Philip Morris began desegregating its Louisville operations and the TWIU commenced pushing for the merger of its locals. In October 1961, the company and the unions agreed to permit employees in other departments to transfer to the cigarette department in stipulated numbers. At that time, all permanent Negro employees in the main plant were in what was called the "sundry department." They, like white employees, were thus permitted to transfer to the preferred department, cigarette making. Moreover, the new understanding provided: "In the event Sundry Job personnel decline transfer to the Cigarette Department, Stemmery male or female, as needed, will be permitted to transfer to the Cigarette Department." [83]

This, of course, was progress, but it discriminated against Negroes in two ways. First, stemmery employees were given preference for cigarette making jobs only if sundry department personnel—that is, other Negroes—declined transfer to such jobs, but were given no such preference when other (white) employees declined transfers. Second, the October 1961 arrangement contained this clause:

When employees transfer outside of the jurisdiction of their respective local unions, their departmental seniority will begin on the date they begin work therein. When employees transfer within the jurisdiction of their respective local unions, they will carry their seniority to the job to which they transfer.[84]

What this clause meant was that transferring white employees carried their Local 16 seniority with them unless they trans-

82. *Ibid.*

83. *Ibid.*, Vol. I, p. 53.

84. *Ibid.*, Vol. I, p. 54.

ferred to the sundry department, which none did. On the other hand, transferring Negro employees were given no credit for their time worked in the sundry department prior to their transfer. This was obviously and invidiously discriminatory.

At this time also, Philip Morris announced that it would hire whites into the stemmery and Negroes into former white jobs in the main plant, but it was not until 1963 that any substantial integration progress was made and the first Negroes employed off the street into anything but the sundry department. In 1963 also, the same employment tests and qualifications were applied to stemmery employment as to that in the main plant. During this period, cafeterias, restrooms, etc. were desegrated as well.[85]

As the company was altering its policies, Locals 16 and 72 were negotiating for a merger. Some members of Local 72 apparently desired to hold out for stemmery employees to obtain seniority credit in the main plant for work performed in seasonal jobs and for assurance of at least one major office in the merged union; others were apparently ready to settle for equal seniority within the main plant by giving sundry department employees the same seniority rights as whites who transferred from one former white department to another. The division within the black local weakened its position. It apparently voted to merge but also to refrain from executing the merger.

While this was occurring, Local 72 failed to comply with the TWIU's constitutional requirement for election of officers. After a hearing, the international union placed Local 72 into trusteeship, appointed a merger committee, and effectuated the merger. Former and existing sundry department employees were given, retroactively, full seniority rights in transfers. Negroes have since served as stewards and bargaining committee members, and as trustee and sergeant-at-arms, but no higher offices in the surviving local, No. 16.[86]

Today, both the main plant and the stemmery are well integrated. Like its Richmond factory, the company's Louisville facility has expanded and increased its proportion of Negroes

---

85. *Ibid.*, testimony of John Cox, Personnel and Labor Relations Manager, Vol. III, pp. 506-592; Vol. IV, pp. 671-710.

86. The merger issue was discussed from all points of view in testimony in *Carr* v. *Philip Morris, op. cit.*, testimony of James Juleson, Vol. II, pp. 350-429; Catherine M. L. Northington, *loc. cit.*; B. T. Curtis, Vol. V, pp. 1041-1119 and Vol. VI, pp. 1237-1252.

to over 20 percent. There is thus no claim of existing discrimination. Rather what the complaints before the Kentucky Commission on Civil Rights are demanding is an extension of the "rightful place" doctrine, enunciated in the *Quarles* case, by applying it to a "class" of seasonal employees. Specifically, they are requesting the Kentucky Commission to give additional seniority rights to Negro seasonal employees hired by the stemmery between its opening in 1952 and October 10, 1961, when Philip Morris began its integration program in Louisville, or to those employed prior to various dates in 1963 or 1964 when alleged discrimination is claimed to have existed.

Whatever date is picked, it is admitted that there is no civil rights case in the denial of main plant seniority to stemmery employees after racial discrimination was no longer a factor. The contention of the complainants, however, is that the before and after time periods are different because those hired during the earlier period were denied opportunities in the main plant because of their race; hence they now carry a present disadvantage based on prior discrimination.

What is at stake is how far the "rightful place" doctrine is to be carried. If it is applied, how far back should it go? Should seasonal employees be compensated for discrimination in hiring and promotion in a period that some complainants say ended four years prior to the effective date of Title VII of the federal Civil Rights Act or even a longer time prior to the very similar Kentucky Act under which the litigation was brought? If so, should they be given full seniority for an average of two-thirds of a year's work? Should they be given proportional credit related to their typical year's service? These are some of the questions before the Kentucky Commission. It is likely that whatever its decision, the issue will be appealed and eventually resolved in court.

TWIU RACIAL POLICIES IN THE 1960's

In the 1960's, the TWIU succeeded in eliminating all its segregated locals, with only the Negro local of Liggett & Myers workers in Durham, North Carolina, offering any strong resistance. TWIU officials had desired to end this embarrassing practice of segregation earlier. No segregated locals were given charters after World War II (few of any type were organized after that date), and as noted, the new Lorillard local in Greensboro was integrated from the start. Moreover, many locals in the border city of Louisville were nearly all integrated from their inception. In a strong editorial in the *Tobacco Worker* in 1957, the president of the TWIU emphasized the union policy:

> America is opportunity, where a man's station in life is what he makes it and not what his birth might indicate . . . America is the conscience that pushes us and those with whom we associate in the world toward greater justice for all men, no matter what their creed or color.[88]

The TWIU national officials also felt that segregated locals divided employees and the union and weakened their bargaining power. Accordingly, when the PCEEO took the position, beginning in 1961, that a company would be ineligible for government contracts if it dealt with segregated locals, the TWIU national officials began their campaign of education, persuasion, and direct action to merge the black and white locals. Companies, anxious to avoid complications in government contracts, added their influence. In two cases already noted—the Brown & Williamson locals in Petersburg and those at United States Tobacco in Richmond—smaller white locals merged into Negro locals with Negro local presidents. In all other cases, the Negro locals disbanded and merged into the white locals. By the time that Title VII of the Civil Rights Act of 1964 became effective, only the black local at Liggett & Myers in Durham held out.

In the paper industry study, it was noted that the integration of racially segregated local unions, the simplistic views of some governmental civil rights functionaries to the contrary notwithstanding, is not necessarily always in the interest of the black unionists. To be sure, the purpose of these segregated locals was originally clearly and avowedly discriminatory—to control the work and opportunities of Negroes, and in some cases, to deny them control of racially mixed unions. Segregated unions added another fence around the industry's segregation pattern and served both to institutionalize it and to make it more difficult to change. Yet, it has been the segregated locals which have developed Negro leadership and provided the mainsprings of protest which have led to the significant changes of the last few years. The fact that some of the white union officials were anxious to merge locals lends some credence to the views ex-

---

88. *Tobacco Worker*, February 1957. (This was Vol. I, No. 7, of a new issue of the oft-started, oft-abandoned journal.)

pressed in 1964 by John H. Wheeler, president of a major
Negro-owned bank in Durham, North Carolina, and then a
member of PCEEO. Stating that the "new policies on racial
matters at the national level" were not being honored by local
unions "because their members still have strong views of an
entirely different nature," Mr. Wheeler declared that in the tobacco industry

. . . the white segregated locals (whose membership lists are overwhelmingly larger than those of the Negro locals) are moving to take
over the Negro locals in order to prevent them from filing complaints
with the President's Committee on Equal Employment Opportunity.
Wherever this operation has been successfully engineered, the Negro
members are out-numbered and are no longer in position to fight
their cause because their treasuries and their bargaining rights have
been taken over by the white locals, leaving them (Negro members)
without representation as officers of the local or as members of the
negotiating, grievance or shop committees.
    In more than one instance, it has been charged that the Inter-
national Union has exerted extreme pressure to eliminate (not merge)
the Negro local while at the same time trying to shut off protests
of discrimination by Negro workers. When one considers that in at
least one large cigarette manufacturing center, several officers of the
formally all-white locals are at the same time said to be officers of
the White Citizens Councils, we may have reason to fear that Negro
workers will be eliminated rapidly from these plants and that their
loss of seniority rights and exclusion from the skilled categories of
employment will not be aggrieved through any affirmative action on
the part of a union dominated by arch segregationists.[89]

In fact, few black locals had many assets to covet. A year
before it merged, Louisville Negro Local 72, at Philip Morris,
was trusteed because it was insolvent. It regained its autonomy,
only to be trusteed again and forcibly merged—on the face of
it, a quite likely high-handed, but from the national union point
of view, understandable action, and one supported by some of
its members and former officials.

Mr. Wheeler's charge that integration of locals was directed
at silencing them certainly was not successful, even if true.
Negro protests continued and the vast federal and state machinery designed to hear such protests, as the research heretofore discussed amply demonstrated, has provided numerous
forums and given ample opportunity for frequent and varied complaints.

---

89. John H. Wheeler, "The Impact of Race Relations on Industrial Relations
    in the South," *Proceedings of the 1964 Spring Meeting*, Industrial Rela-
    tions Racial Association, 1964, p. 477.

In addition to the two locals with Negro presidents, there are some others with additional Negro officials, but for the most part Negro representation is now confined to lesser jobs like departmental steward. Most locals' bargaining committees are represented by a proportional number of Negroes, but usually, since the great majority of the membership is white, the Negroes can be easily defeated on any issue before the bargaining committee.

The experience of Negroes in the integrated locals such as that at the Lorillard works in Greensboro shows how Negroes often find that local union integration can change nothing. It is likewise certain that integration has meant a decided loss of convention representation to the black workers who now comprise about 20 percent of TWIU's membership.

In point of fact, the resolution of the segregation pattern in the tobacco industry depends primarily on the integration of the segregated seniority lists and not on the integration of the locals. This is not to say that these two areas do not go hand in hand but only to point out that the heart of the problem has been the segregated employment and seniority systems. Government pressure and court cases would appear to have ended the latter, and mitigated the former. The problems of shrinking employment resulting from the impact of automation and declining consumer demand would, however, seem to insure that change occurs slowly in most locations.

Within this context, the TWIU remains a relatively minor influence. It is not a large nor a strong union; its locals are relatively independent. Since the one-man rule of E. Lewis Evans was ended in 1940, the TWIU has operated under a constitution which gives national officials very limited power. Local unions are the bargaining agents and hold the real power. Local white leadership, directly dependent on white membership for continuation in office are not, and are rarely likely to be, as concerned with equal rights as are national leaders. The latter are anxious to avoid divisive racial problems which weaken their union; the former often see their job as one of preserving the rights and hegemony of their constituents. The national leaders have attempted to give some constructive leadership to integration and have had some success. Their lack of power, the declining employment, and the long history of segregation and discrimination in the industry seem to limit both their influence and the results achieved even with the best of intentions.

CHAPTER V

The Determinants of Change

Integration occurred in the tobacco industry at the lowest ebb of Negro employment. Integration has caused few problems. Temporary boycotts of cafeterias occurred, but did not persist. The fact that the work is not highly skilled—and indeed, largely low skilled—precluded major problems of qualification.

As the court noted in the *Quarles* case, seasonal stemmery employees are likely to be marginal workers, and upgrading of these will continue to be a problem for years. Yet much of the work in the former all-Negro departments is equal in skill to that in the former all-white departments. If the racial-occupational segregation pattern ever had a rationale other than segregation and discrimination, it has not been apparent since the stemmeries were mechanized in the 1930's.

There are thus few problems worth reviewing which have not been sufficiently examined in previous chapters. It is, however, appropriate to note again the basic factors which have affected Negro employment in the industry.

THE ORIGIN AND LOCATION OF THE INDUSTRY

The southern location and the use of Negro slaves in tobacco plants set the stage for continued Negro employment in the industry. Then the development of the cigarette machine in the post-Civil War reconstruction era led to the racial-occupational segregation pattern which was religiously adhered to even in the last major northern plant. Custom dictated the labor utilization pattern and custom was institutionalized, first by management, then by union and management. This went on generally without question, at least until World War II, with no more than token change to 1960. Meanwhile, the employment base of Negroes eroded, but neither management nor union opted for change until government action compelled, or seemed about to compel, such change.

THE DEMAND FOR LABOR

Tobacco was never a large employer, and is now a small one. The demand for labor is likely to shrink rather than expand

in the future. Because the industry could always obtain ample
white labor, its limited propensity to open up all-white departments to Negroes was never encouraged. In Richmond and
Petersburg, Virginia, the demand of higher paying industries
has siphoned off the white labor supply and afforded Negroes
additional opportunities in the expanding Philip Morris and
Brown & Williamson plants. Automation and declining demand
in other plants have had the opposite effect, and, for the total
industry, employment is expected to decline.

The tobacco industry has been a prime example of the manner
in which technological advancement combined with discriminatory employment practices adversely affect Negroes. The greatly
reduced proportion of Negroes in the industry is the direct
result of mechanization and automation in the stemmeries and
other formerly all-black departments combined with the denial
to Negroes of opportunities to work in formerly all-white areas.
As a result, the industry, which once had a preponderance of
Negroes, now is about 25 percent black at most.

GOVERNMENT PRESSURE

That government pressure was needed to alter the status quo
is indisputable. Except for some movement at Reynolds, the
first breaks came as a result of government committee actions—
the Nixon Committee in the late 1950's, the PCEEO and the
OFCC later. Government pressure and law suits pursuant to
Title VII of the Civil Rights Act of 1964 have clearly precluded
continued reliance on a discriminatory seniority system.

Government action has not always been so helpful. The minimum wage laws and regulations, commencing with the National
Industrial Recovery Act in 1933 and the Fair Labor Standards
Act of 1938, resulted in the continued search for, and installa-
tion of, machinery to replace hand labor. The government did
not give due heed to the impact of such wage determination.
Certainly, minimum wages hurried the displacement process.

Government policy also rushed through the integration of
formerly segregated local unions in the simplistic view that such
integration would automatically reduce discrimination. The long
fight of the black Liggett & Myers local to win a superior *quid
pro quo*, the paucity of Negro local union officials in the integrated locals, and the adherence of some integrated locals to a
discriminatory departmental seniority system, all indicate that

this governmental policy was more concerned with appearance than substance. And the attempt of the Equal Employment Opportunity Commission to reinvestigate the Liggett & Myers settlement is a prime example of duplication and waste of scarce government resources.

Again, however, with all its limitations, one must credit government action with breaking the racial-occupational segregation pattern. Without such pressure, or the threat thereof, it is difficult to believe that much of the progress which has occurred would have materialized.

MANAGERIAL ACTION

With one exception, management has been slow to lead in this industry. Reluctant to antagonize the southern community or to upset existing collective bargaining relationships, tobacco management stayed with the status quo until pushed or prodded by government.

Reynolds took more leadership. Consciously nonunion, it has developed an outstanding personnel department which has great prestige in the company and has been traditionally alert for change. Seeing change in the offing, Reynolds moved carefully, intelligently, and thoroughly when the opening of its new Whitaker Park facility provided the opportunity. The company's leadership in the community, again a function of its alert policies, aided its integration program. Having allowed its proportion of Negro employees to decline precipitously, as did other companies, Reynolds has vigorously attempted to offset the inroads of automation in order to reverse this trend. As the industry leader in sales and market share, it may not suffer in the future the job declines which could well beset the industry, a fact which should be helpful to Negro employment.

Philip Morris also deserves special mention for its successful efforts in both Louisville and Richmond, and its relatively early action to eliminate past discriminatory practices. Negro advancement now is likely to be greatest at the above facilities of Philip Morris and those of Brown & Williamson at Petersburg. A large Negro representation in the labor force and expanding demand have aided these companies in improving their racial policies and Negro representation in their plants.

UNION POLICY

Until recently the Tobacco Workers' International Union accepted and institutionalized the racial-occupational segregation pattern. TWIU negotiations have raised the wages of Negroes, but the union did little on its own initiative to halt the decline of Negro jobs while Negroes were laid off and whites hired, nor otherwise to alter the racial-occupational segregation pattern, nor to eliminate discriminatory practices. Instead TWIU policies institutionalized the existing structure and added barriers against Negro employment opportunity. The strong TWIU support to eliminate racially segregated locals came only after Negroes were no longer a majority in any plant.

Actually, as was pointed out in the previous chapter, the national TWIU is not strong and the locals have considerable independence. In such a situation, the views of the dominant white majority are likely to prevail, and the rights of black minorities are frequently ignored. Negro local union officials and leaders have therefore sought redress outside of their union—through civil rights and government agencies. They saw the TWIU as antagonistic to their aspirations, and the union in turn was usually arguing for the status quo, although the international officials strongly supported the integration of locals, and sought to develop a constructive solution in the final resolution of the big Liggett & Myers case.

Union organization has hindered Negro job opportunities in one other way. The craft unions are strong among maintenance crews in many tobacco plants. Where this occurs, Negroes have found an additional barrier to the many which inhibit opportunities in such jobs.

CONCLUDING REMARKS

The racial-occupational segregation pattern in the tobacco industry endured for nearly a century. When it was finally broken, Negroes, who had once dominated the industry's factory employment, held only 25 percent of the jobs, an all-time low. The industry's sales are not increasing as consumers become wary of the influence of smoking on health and the dangers of crippling disease; moreover, automation is continuing to affect jobs. Thus new opportunities for Negroes may not result in substantial change because of declining labor demand. The only offsetting factors are the strong affirmative action program at the

Reynolds complex in Winston-Salem, the continued affirmative action and expansion of both sales and employment at the Philip Morris plants in Richmond and Louisville, and the increased utilization of Negroes at the Petersburg facility of Brown & Williamson. Since overall employment in the industry, however, is likely to decline, opportunities for Negroes may depend strongly on the extent to which whites prefer jobs elsewhere. Negroes are therefore likely to have their greatest opportunities in the tobacco industry in cities like Louisville and Richmond where a multitude of industries competes for labor and where many often pay considerably more than does the tobacco industry.

Appendix A

ESTIMATE OF NEGRO EMPLOYMENT FOR 1960

The U. S. Census of Population for 1960 did not list the Negroes separately from the whites for tobacco manufacturing in North Carolina, Kentucky, and Virginia as in the previous census. Therefore, a possible minimum and maximum number of Negroes in this industry was obtained in the following manner: Table 127 for each state listed the male and female workers for each detailed industry, one of which was tobacco manufacturing. Table 129 broke down the employed persons by white and Negro only by industry, not detailed industry. Therefore, in the category of "All Other Non-Durable Goods" industries in Table 129, "Tobacco Manufacturing" was combined with "Leather: Tanned, Cured, and Finished" and "Leather Products, except Footwear."

From Table 127, the total labor force in tobacco manufacturing was ascertained by combining the male and female totals. Likewise, total employment figures were computed for the two leather categories. Then, by assuming that all employees in the two leather categories were Negroes, a minimum number of Negroes available for the tobacco manufacturing category was computed. Total Negroes, male and female, from Table 129, less the total employment for the two leather occupations, resulted in a minimum possible number of Negroes in tobacco manufacturing.

This same approach was used to determine the maximum possible number of Negroes in tobacco manufacturing by making an assumption that all the employees in the two leather groups were white.

Even though the figures in Table A-1 are not exact, in comparison with the 1950 data, a definite trend is observable regardless of whether the 1960 minimum or maximum figures for the Negro are used in the comparison.

The wide range of Negroes in Kentucky in 1960 is due to the low total of Negroes (1,298) and the relatively high number of workers (440) in the two leather categories.

TABLE A-1. Tobacco Industry
Total and Negro Employment
Kentucky, North Carolina, and Virginia, 1950 and 1960

	1950		
	Total	Negro	Percent Negro
Kentucky	7,457	1,328	17.8
North Carolina	22,251	9,407	42.3
Virginia	10,955	4,384	40.0
Total	40,663	15,119	37.2

	1960				
	Total	Negro (Minimum)	Negro (Maximum)	Percent Negro (Minimum)	Percent Negro (Maximum)
Total—Kentucky, North Carolina, and Virginia					
All other nondurable goods	51,174	13,130	13,130		
Less: Leather, tanned, curried, & finished	1,332				
Leather products except footwear	932				
Subtotal	2,264	2,264	0		
Total tobacco manufacturing	48,910	10,866	13,130	22.2	26.8

Kentucky

All other nondurable goods	9,782	1,298	1,298		
Less: Leather, tanned, etc.	351				
Leather products	89		0		
Subtotal	440	440			
Total tobacco manufacturing	9,342	858	1,298	9.2	13.9

North Carolina

All other nondurable goods	28,054	8,666	8,666		
Less: Leather, tanned, etc.	337				
Leather products	252		0		
Subtotal	589	589			
Total tobacco manufacturing	27,465	8,077	8,666	29.4	31.6

Virginia

All other nondurable goods	13,338	3,166	3,166		
Less: Leather, tanned, etc.	644				
Leather products	591		0		
Subtotal	1,235	1,235			
Total tobacco manufacturing	12,103	1,931	3,166	15.9	26.2

Source: *U. S. Census of Population:*

   1950: Vol. II, *Characteristics of the Population,* State Volumes, Table 83.
   1960: PC(1)D, *Characteristics of the Population,* State Volumes, Tables 127 and 129.

Appendix B

Basic Statistical Tables, 1964, 1966, and 1968

TABLE B-1. Tobacco Industry
Employment by Race, Sex, and Occupational Group
5 Companies
Kentucky, 1964

Occupational Group	All Employees			Male			Female		
	Total	Negro	Percent Negro	Total	Negro	Percent Negro	Total	Negro	Percent Negro
Officials and managers	589	5	0.8	585	5	0.9	4	—	—
Professionals	106	1	0.9	102	—	—	4	1	25.0
Technicians	190	2	1.1	117	—	—	73	2	2.7
Sales workers	580	15	2.6	580	15	2.6	—	—	—
Office and clerical	782	24	3.1	260	4	1.5	522	20	3.8
Total white collar	2,247	47	2.1	1,644	24	1.5	603	23	3.8
Craftsmen	870	7	0.8	854	7	0.8	16	—	—
Operatives	4,178	236	5.6	2,032	161	7.9	2,146	75	3.5
Laborers	2,372	539	22.7	1,518	380	25.0	854	159	18.6
Service workers	414	149	36.0	288	116	40.3	126	33	26.2
Total blue collar	7,834	931	11.9	4,692	664	14.2	3,142	267	8.5
Total	10,081	978	9.7	6,336	688	10.9	3,745	290	7.7

Source: Data in author's possession.

TABLE B-2. Tobacco Industry
Employment by Race, Sex, and Occupational Group
5 Companies
North Carolina, 1964

Occupational Group	All Employees			Male			Female		
	Total	Negro	Percent Negro	Total	Negro	Percent Negro	Total	Negro	Percent Negro
Officials and managers	1,801	10	0.6	1,797	10	0.6	4	—	—
Professionals	484	2	0.4	468	1	0.2	16	1	6.2
Technicians	777	14	1.8	686	11	1.6	91	3	3.3
Sales workers	1,337	23	1.7	1,290	23	1.8	47	—	—
Office and clerical	2,001	44	2.2	815	22	2.7	1,186	22	1.9
Total white collar	6,400	93	1.5	5,056	67	1.3	1,344	26	1.9
Craftsmen	3,030	65	2.1	2,890	65	2.2	140	—	—
Operatives	9,091	1,384	15.2	5,821	1,055	18.1	3,270	329	10.1
Laborers	7,065	3,834	54.3	3,856	3,046	79.0	3,209	788	24.6
Service workers	1,214	961	79.2	991	742	74.9	223	219	98.2
Total blue collar	20,400	6,244	30.6	13,558	4,908	36.2	6,842	1,336	19.5
Total	26,800	6,337	23.6	18,614	4,975	26.7	8,186	1,362	16.6

Source: Data in author's possession.

TABLE B-3. Tobacco Industry
Employment by Race, Sex, and Occupational Group
5 Companies
Virginia, 1964

Occupational Group	All Employees			Male			Female		
	Total	Negro	Percent Negro	Total	Negro	Percent Negro	Total	Negro	Percent Negro
Officials and managers	416	10	2.4	416	10	2.4	—	—	—
Professionals	238	3	1.3	212	3	1.4	26	—	—
Technicians	203	2	1.0	125	2	1.6	78	—	—
Sales workers	—	—	—	—	—	—	—	—	—
Office and clerical	522	23	4.4	205	14	6.8	317	9	2.8
Total white collar	1,379	38	2.8	958	29	3.0	421	9	2.1
Craftsmen	1,050	10	1.0	1,016	10	1.0	34	—	—
Operatives	4,803	748	15.6	2,286	567	24.8	2,517	181	7.2
Laborers	2,948	1,553	52.7	1,754	1,110	63.3	1,194	443	37.1
Service workers	365	245	67.1	329	211	64.1	36	34	94.4
Total blue collar	9,166	2,556	27.9	5,385	1,898	35.2	3,781	658	17.4
Total	10,545	2,594	24.6	6,343	1,927	30.4	4,202	667	15.9

Source: Data in author's possession.

TABLE B-4. *Tobacco Industry*
Employment by Race, Sex, and Occupational Group
5 Companies
Kentucky, 1966

Occupational Group	All Employees			Male			Female		
	Total	Negro	Percent Negro	Total	Negro	Percent Negro	Total	Negro	Percent Negro
Officials and managers	749	7	0.9	731	7	1.0	18	—	—
Professionals	123	1	0.8	117	—	—	6	1	16.7
Technicians	192	3	1.6	107	2	1.9	85	1	1.2
Sales workers	588	17	2.9	588	17	2.9	—	—	—
Office and clerical	870	26	3.0	296	6	2.0	574	20	3.5
Total white collar	2,522	54	2.1	1,839	32	1.7	683	22	3.2
Craftsmen	784	8	1.0	784	8	1.0	—	—	—
Operatives	4,471	392	8.8	2,243	286	12.8	2,228	106	4.8
Laborers	3,344	1,012	30.3	1,946	589	30.3	1,398	423	30.3
Service workers	453	160	35.3	304	105	34.5	149	55	36.9
Total blue collar	9,052	1,572	17.4	5,277	988	18.7	3,775	584	15.5
Total	11,574	1,626	14.0	7,116	1,020	14.3	4,458	606	13.6

Source: Data in author's possession.

TABLE B-5. Tobacco Industry
Employment by Race, Sex, and Occupational Group
5 Companies
North Carolina, 1966

Occupational Group	All Employees			Male			Female		
	Total	Negro	Percent Negro	Total	Negro	Percent Negro	Total	Negro	Percent Negro
Officials and managers	1,597	13	0.8	1,594	13	0.8	3	—	—
Professionals	441	3	0.7	427	2	0.5	14	1	7.1
Technicians	611	15	2.5	552	14	2.5	59	1	1.7
Sales workers	1,393	26	1.9	1,320	24	1.8	73	2	2.7
Office and clerical	1,521	45	3.0	547	25	4.6	974	20	2.1
Total white collar	5,563	102	1.8	4,440	78	1.8	1,123	24	2.1
Craftsmen	2,804	65	2.3	2,703	65	2.4	101	—	—
Operatives	8,981	1,448	16.1	5,833	1,203	20.6	3,148	245	7.8
Laborers	6,563	3,570	54.4	3,679	2,812	76.4	2,884	758	26.3
Service workers	1,076	842	78.3	856	634	74.1	220	208	94.5
Total blue collar	19,424	5,925	30.5	13,071	4,714	36.1	6,353	1,211	19.1
Total	24,987	6,027	24.1	17,511	4,792	27.4	7,476	1,235	16.5

Source: Data in author's possession.

TABLE B-6. Tobacco Industry
Employment by Race, Sex, and Occupational Group
5 Companies
Virginia, 1966

Occupational Group	All Employees			Male			Female		
	Total	Negro	Percent Negro	Total	Negro	Percent Negro	Total	Negro	Percent Negro
Officials and managers	675	17	2.5	614	17	2.8	61	—	—
Professionals	274	4	1.5	247	4	1.6	27	—	—
Technicians	237	5	2.1	143	4	2.8	94	1	1.1
Sales workers	5	1	20.0	5	1	20.0	—	—	—
Office and clerical	500	29	5.8	175	17	9.7	325	12	3.7
Total white collar	1,691	56	3.3	1,184	43	3.6	507	13	2.6
Craftsmen	954	13	1.4	954	13	1.4	—	—	—
Operatives	4,734	830	17.5	2,291	597	26.1	2,443	233	9.5
Laborers	3,055	1,532	50.1	1,834	1,114	60.7	1,221	418	34.2
Service workers	387	260	67.2	352	226	64.2	35	34	97.1
Total blue collar	9,130	2,635	28.9	5,431	1,950	35.9	3,699	685	18.5
Total	10,821	2,691	24.9	6,615	1,993	30.1	4,206	698	16.6

Source: Data in author's possession.

TABLE B-7. Tobacco Industry

Employment by Race, Sex, and Occupational Group

5 Companies

Kentucky, 1968

Occupational Group	All Employees			Male			Female		
	Total	Negro	Percent Negro	Total	Negro	Percent Negro	Total	Negro	Percent Negro
Officials and managers	821	15	1.8	787	15	1.9	34	—	—
Professionals	180	—	—	166	—	—	14	—	—
Technicians	214	3	1.4	106	1	0.9	108	2	1.9
Sales workers	—	—	—	—	—	—	—	—	—
Office and clerical	949	38	4.0	315	8	2.5	634	30	4.7
Total white collar	2,164	56	2.6	1,374	24	1.7	790	32	4.1
Craftsmen	971	6	0.6	971	6	0.6	—	—	—
Operatives	5,841	593	10.2	3,102	384	12.4	2,739	209	7.6
Laborers	3,712	1,035	27.9	2,195	613	27.9	1,517	422	27.8
Service workers	477	176	36.9	373	123	33.0	104	53	51.0
Total blue collar	11,001	1,810	16.5	6,641	1,126	17.0	4,360	684	15.7
Total	13,165	1,866	14.2	8,015	1,150	14.3	5,150	716	13.9

Source: Data in author's possession.

TABLE B-8. Tobacco Industry
Employment by Race, Sex, and Occupational Group
5 Companies
North Carolina, 1968

Occupational Group	All Employees			Male			Female		
	Total	Negro	Percent Negro	Total	Negro	Percent Negro	Total	Negro	Percent Negro
Officials and managers	1,674	21	1.3	1,668	21	1.3	6	—	—
Professionals	621	6	1.0	576	4	0.7	45	2	4.4
Technicians	689	23	3.3	615	20	3.3	74	3	4.1
Sales workers	1,319	41	3.1	1,272	41	3.2	47	—	—
Office and clerical	1,834	58	3.2	584	18	3.1	1,250	40	3.2
Total white collar	6,137	149	2.4	4,715	104	2.2	1,422	45	3.2
Craftsmen	2,847	80	2.8	2,820	80	2.8	27	—	—
Operatives	9,122	1,720	18.9	5,484	1,344	24.5	3,638	376	10.3
Laborers	5,989	3,227	53.9	3,751	2,632	70.2	2,238	595	26.6
Service workers	1,061	649	61.2	866	498	57.5	195	151	77.4
Total blue collar	19,019	5,676	29.8	12,921	4,554	35.2	6,098	1,122	18.4
Total	25,156	5,825	23.2	17,636	4,658	26.4	7,520	1,167	15.5

Source: Data in the author's possession.

TABLE B-9. Tobacco Industry

Employment by Race, Sex, and Occupational Group

5 Companies

Virginia, 1968

Occupational Group	All Employees			Male			Female		
	Total	Negro	Percent Negro	Total	Negro	Percent Negro	Total	Negro	Percent Negro
Officials and managers	831	28	3.4	792	28	3.5	39	—	—
Professionals	165	1	0.6	142	1	0.7	23	—	—
Technicians	221	8	3.6	163	8	4.9	58	—	—
Sales workers	—	—	—	—	—	—	—	—	—
Office and clerical	622	37	5.9	228	16	7.0	394	21	5.3
Total white collar	1,839	74	4.0	1,325	53	4.0	514	21	4.1
Craftsmen	1,023	21	2.1	1,023	21	2.1	—	—	—
Operatives	4,917	1,125	22.9	2,544	853	33.5	2,373	272	11.5
Laborers	3,426	1,913	55.8	2,153	1,419	65.9	1,273	494	38.8
Service workers	435	265	60.9	393	241	61.3	42	24	57.1
Total blue collar	9,801	3,324	33.9	6,113	2,534	41.5	3,688	790	21.4
Total	11,640	3,398	29.2	7,438	2,587	34.8	4,202	811	19.3

Source: Data in author's possession.

Index

P. Lorillard, 8-9, 11, 32, 33, 73-77
 complaints against, 75-76
 Jersey City plant, 73-74
 market share, 75, 75n, 77n
 Negro proportion of work force, 32
 and unions, 33, 37, 74-76

McKissick, Floyd, 69

Manning, Caroline, 27n
Manpower, 12-17
Marshall, F. Ray, 36n, 37n
Monthly Labor Review, 27n, 28n

National Industrial Recovery Act, 26-
 27, 89
 NRA codes, 26
National Labor Relations Board, 36,
 69, 72, 75n, 76
Negro employment, 1, 24, 40-43
 Colonial period, 18-26
 pre-Civil War, 3, 18-19
 impact of World War I, 22
 World War I to Depression, 22-26
 New Deal to World War II, 26-29
 World War II to 1960, 29-33
 1960's, 40-87
 declines in, 12, 26, 28, 32, 40-43
 hostility of craft unions to, 57
 in independent stemmeries, 27-28
 proportion of work force, 22, 29, 30,
  33, 38, 41-43, 60, 64, 67, 72,
  73, 77-78, 83-84, 89
 slave laborers and artisans, 2, 18-19
Negro female employment
 occupations, 4, 19, 22, 58, 60
 racial-occupational segregation, 25-
  26, 57
 in stemmeries, 6
 wages, 26
New York Times, 70n
Nixon Committee
 see President's Committee on Government Contracts
North Carolina, 12, 43, 51-53
Northington, Catherine M. L., 81n,
 83n
Northrup, Herbert R., 6n, 17n, 25n,
 34n, 36n, 38n

O'Brien, F. S., 37n
Occupational distribution, 3-5, 13, 20-
 22, 41-43, 51-53, 60
 blue collar, 47, 56-57, 63, 78
 craftsmen, 18-19, 76

laborers, 5, 13, 22-24, 29, 43, 58,
 81
 operatives, 13, 22-24 29-30, 58, 60
 service workers, 43, 63, 74, 81
 white collar, 13, 47-51, 53-56, 62, 64,
  76, 78
 office and clerical, 51, 56, 58, 60
 professional and technical, 13, 147
 sales, 51
Office and Federal Contract Compliance, 68, 69, 71, 76, 89

Patrick, Clarence N., 61n
Perlman, Jacob, 28n
Philip Morris, 8, 9, 77-84
 complaints against, 66, 66n, 78-81,
  84
 Negro proportion of work force, 77-
  78, 83-84
 and unions, 78-83
Pinchbeck, Raymond B., 18n, 19n
President's Committee on Equal Employment Opportunity, 40-41,
 65, 68, 68n, 75, 78, 81, 85, 89
President's Committee on Government
 Contracts (Nixon Commit-
 tee), 30, 40, 64, 67, 68, 75, 78,
 81, 89

Quarles v. *Philip Morris, Inc.*, 66n,
 78n, 79n, 90, 80n, 84, 88

Racial employment policies
 departmental segregation, 5, 40-41,
  60, 73-77
 hiring, 33, 38, 83
 impact of governmental pressure
  and civil rights, 40, 53, 61,
  64, 67-69, 75-76, 78, 89-90
 integration of facilities, 62, 66, 76,
  83
 managerial action, 90
 recruiting, 51, 56, 78
 training, 51, 63, 67, 78
 transfers, 78, 80, 82-83
 union influence, 33, 38-39
Racial-occupational segregation, 3-5,
 21, 25, 29-38, 40
 at American, 64-65
 at Liggett & Myers, 67
 at Lorillard, 74
 at Philip Morris, 78-79, 81-82
 at Reynolds, 60
Reeb, Walter, 81n

PART FOUR

THE NEGRO
IN THE BITUMINOUS COAL
MINING INDUSTRY

by

DAROLD T. BARNUM

TABLE OF CONTENTS

Table of Contents

LIST OF TABLES

viii

CHAPTER I

Introduction

The bituminous coal industry has historically been a major employer of Negroes, particularly in four southern states and one border state—Alabama, Kentucky, Tennessee, Virginia, and West Virginia. Since World War II, however, as employment declined precipitiously in the industry, Negro employment declined at a more rapid rate, accelerating a trend that became apparent in the 1930's. The reasons for this loss of jobs by Negroes are discussed in detail in subsequent chapters.

Since its founding in 1890, the United Mine Workers of America has been a significant force in the industry, exercising its greatest strength in the 1935-1950 period. The role of the UMW in the industry's racial employment policies is carefully assessed throughout this study.

The analysis in the following chapters will concentrate on the five aforementioned states—Alabama, Kentucky, Tennessee, Virginia, and West Virginia. This is known as the Southern Appalachian region, where the bulk of Negroes in the industry have always been employed. Some Negroes have worked in northern, midwestern, and other nonsouthern coal fields, but the percentage of Negro miners in any state outside of the Southern Appalachian region has never exceeded 3 percent, and more than 90 percent of the black miners have always been in the five states where the study concentrates.

This monograph will also exclude coverage of anthracite mining, which is located in three northern Pennsylvania counties. Negroes have always been excluded from work in these mines. They came into northern bituminous mines as strikebreakers, but had no such opportunity in the anthracite industry, which settled with the United Mine Workers in the first years of this century and has dealt with the UMW ever since. Moreover, since the mid-1920's, anthracite has been an industry of declining sales, production, and employment, with few opportunities for employment and much more out- than in-migration.

The basic field work for this study was done in the summers of 1968 and 1969, during which employers, union officials, and government personnel in the principal areas studied were visited, and data were collected from the various sources cited in the text. The techniques utilized to offset data shortcomings are summarized in the appendices.

CHAPTER II

The Bituminous Coal Industry

Bituminous coal is the most abundant conventional energy reserve in the United States. It accounts for almost 90 percent of known United States conventional reserves, and at the present rate of consumption could last for over 2,000 years.[1]

Although its importance has declined, bituminous coal production is still a significant segment of United States industry. In the industry as a whole, about 170,000 men produced 545 million tons of coal in 1968. This coal played an important part in energy, steel, and cement production. It generated an estimated 21.4 percent of all United States energy, and 63 percent of all electrical energy. Further, 93 million short tons of coal were used to manufacture coke for steel making.[2]

Bituminous coal is mined in about one-half the states. The five states of the Southern Appalachian region produced 57 percent of coal mined in 1968 and accounted for 66 percent of the average number of men working daily.[3] This background chapter considers both the Southern Appalachian region and the industry as a whole, in order that a proper perspective be obtained. The remaining chapters, however, deal only with Southern Appalachia, except when outside events affect the Appalachian mines.

INDUSTRY CHARACTERISTICS

From the time it was first mined commercially in 1750 until after the Civil War, coal production expanded at a slow pace. The development of steam locomotives and heavy industry after 1860 caused a rapid expansion in coal mining that continued through World War I. In Southern Appalachia, however, the rapid expansion did not begin until the 1890's, but from then on it grew faster than the industry as a whole.[4] Table 1 shows

1. U. S. Bureau of Labor Statistics, *Technological Change and Productivity in the Bituminous Coal Industry 1920-1960*, Bulletin No. 1305 (Washington: U. S. Government Printing Office, 1961), p. 6.

2. U. S. Bureau of the Census, *Statistical Abstract of the United States*, privately published as *The U. S. Book of Facts Statistics and Information* (New York: Washington Square Press, Inc., 1969), pp. 512, 517, and 673.

3. U. S. Bureau of Mines, "Coal-Mine Injuries and Worktime, Monthly," *Mineral Industry Surveys*, May 14, 1969.

4. Herbert R. Northrup, *Organized Labor and the Negro* (New York: Harper & Bros., 1944), p. 158.

TABLE 1. Bituminous Coal Industry
Production, Employment, and Productivity
United States and Southern Appalachia, 1910-1968

| Year | Production (Thousands of Short Tons) | | Employment | | Productivity (Tons per Man-Day) | |
	United States	Southern Appalachia	United States	Southern Appalachia	United States	Southern Appalachia[a]
1910	417,111	106,034	644,500	112,357	3.46	3.59
1920	568,667	159,997	733,936	182,845	4.00	3.94
1930	467,526	204,291	621,661	197,162	5.06	5.14
1940	460,772	212,259	527,025	213,233	5.19	5.00
1950	516,311	261,395	509,673	245,781	5.77	6.19
1960	415,512	232,569	199,735	112,397	12.83	12.02
1965	512,088	289,707	177,000[b]	92,500[c]	17.52	16.14
1968[d]	545,000	308,000	169,000[b]	92,400[c]	19.40	17.90

Source: Production and productivity:

U. S. Bureau of Mines, *Minerals Yearbook, 1911-1967*; and *id.*, "Coal-Mine Injuries and Worktime, Monthly," *Mineral Industry Surveys*, May 14, 1969.

Employment:

U. S. Census of Population, *1910-1940*, in Herbert R. Northrup, *Organized Labor and the Negro* (New York: Harper & Bros., 1944), pp. 156-157; *1950*, Vol. II, *Characteristics of the Population*, U. S. Summary, Table 130; *1960*, PC(1) D, U. S. Summary, Table 211; and U. S. Bureau of Mines, "Coal-Mine Injuries and Worktime, Monthly," *Mineral Industry Surveys*, May 14, 1969.

Note: Alabama, Kentucky, Tennessee, Virginia, and West Virginia comprise Southern Appalachia.

a Weighted averages of the five Southern Appalachian states.

b Figures adjusted upward by 30 percent to correspond with Census figures of "gainfully employed." Bureau of Mines figures are based on "average number of men working daily."

c Figures adjusted upward by 8 percent. See note above.

d Southern Appalachia figures include Georgia and Maryland, but these two states accounted for less than one-half of one percent of that area's production in 1965.

production, employment, and productivity trends from 1910 to 1968.

Production Trends

During the period between the World Wars, production declined in the whole industry, but increased slightly in the Southern Appalachian region. The end of the rapid expansion was partly the result of the increasing use of other fuels, and partly because of general economic stagnation. Output spurted briefly during World War II, but in 1948 it again began to decline in both Southern Appalachia and in the rest of the industry. This decline in production continued through 1961. It was caused by the shift from steam to diesel locomotives, and by declining commercial and retail markets. The decline was partly offset by an expanding electrical utility market.[5] Since 1961, production has increased substantially because of expansion of the utility market.[6]

Markets

The markets for bituminous coal have changed greatly since the 1930's, as shown in Table 2. Railroads used about one-fifth of all

TABLE 2. *Bituminous Coal Industry*
Percent Domestic Consumption by Consumer
1940-1966

Year	Total	Electric Utilities	Coking Coal	Industry and Railroads	Retail
1940	100	11	19	50	20
1945	100	13	17	49	21
1950	100	19	23	39	19
1955	100	33	25	29	13
1960	100	46	21	25	8
1965	100	53	21	22	4
1966	100	54	20	22	4

Source: National Coal Association, *Bituminous Coal Data 1968 Edition* (Washington: National Coal Association, 1969), p. 81.

---

5. William F. Saalbach, *United States Bituminous Coal Markets; Trends Since 1920 and Prospects to 1975* (Pittsburgh: University of Pittsburgh Press, 1960), pp. 31-50.

6. Hubert E. Risser, *The Economics of the Coal Industry* (Lawrence: University of Kansas Bureau of Business Research, 1958), pp. 53-54.

coal consumed up through the mid-forties. By 1960, railroads were responsible for less than 0.5 percent of total coal consumption. Another major market, retail sales, followed a decline similar to the railroads. Up to 1946, the retail market took about one-fifth of total output. It has decreased its consumption since at a steady pace, and accounted for only 4 percent of total consumption in 1965.[7]

The industrial market (excluding railroads) has remained more stable than the previous two, but has declined somewhat. It declined from 30 percent of total coal consumed in the thirties to about 20 percent of total consumption since 1950, as industry has turned to gas and electricity. The market for coking coal has remained at about 20 percent of total consumption since 1940, although the percentage fluctuates with steel production.[8]

Electric utilities provided a rapidly expanding market for coal. The amount of coal bought for electric generators roughly doubled every ten years between 1933 and 1963. During the same period, electrical utilities also increased their share of total coal consumed, going from a share of 8.5 percent in 1933 to 51 percent in 1963.[9] In 1966, electrical utilities bought 54 percent of all coal sold domestically (Table 2).

Mechanization and Productivity

In no other industry has mechanization advanced at so rapid a pace as in coal mining. And in no other industry has it had such an impact on employment in general and Negro employment in particular.

Mechanization was slight in coal mining's early years, the pick and shovel being the primary tools of the trade. By the 1920's, however, the coal operators began facing greater competition from other fuels and increasing labor costs. To remain competitive in spite of higher production costs, the operators introduced labor-saving machinery to increase labor productivity.

The pick-and-shovel miner was rapidly replaced by machines: machines that undercut the coal for blasting, machines that drilled holes and then stuffed in the explosive, and machines that loaded blasted coal onto mechanized conveyors and shuttle cars.

---

7. U. S. Bureau of Mines, *Minerals Yearbook, 1965 Preprint on Coal* (Washington: Department of Interior, 1967), p. 96.

8. *Ibid.*

9. *Ibid.*

Finally came a machine that replaced machines—the continuous miner. Mole-like, it claws coal directly from the vein, and loads it onto a waiting conveyor.

The machines did not come, however, all the same time. The undercutting machine, first introduced in the 1870's, was cutting 80 percent of the underground tonnage by 1930. Machines began loading coal in the mid-twenties and by 1950 70 percent was loaded by machines. Continuous mining machines mined less than 2 percent of United States underground coal in 1950, but mined 33 percent by 1960 and 50 percent by 1967.[10] The Negro was especially hard-hit by mechanization because the jobs eliminated were those in which he was concentrated, and because he did not get his proportional share of the mechanization-created jobs.

Another advance, occurring primarily after World War II, was the increase in strip mining. In the stripping operation, the overburden (dirt above the coal vein) is removed by huge power shovels. Then, somewhat smaller shovels load the coal into waiting trucks. From the standpoint of productivity, stripping is the most efficient method of mining; output per man-day in strip mines is double that of underground mines.[11] Strip-mined coal accounted for 9 percent of United States coal production in 1940. It had increased its share of production to 29 percent by 1960.[12]

From an insignificant position in the thirties, stripping in some of the Southern Appalachian states also increased rapidly. The increasing numbers of strip miners were, however, almost all white. Output per man-hour for the industry increased 23 percent above its 1940 level by 1950, and soared 75 percent above its 1950 level by 1960. (By way of comparison, output per man-hour in the total nonagricultural economy increased 32 percent between 1940 and 1950, and 25 percent between 1950 and 1960.)[13] The number of men needed to mine 100 tons of coal per day dropped from 33 in 1900 to 5 in 1968.[14]

---

10. *Ibid.*, pp. 13, 29, and 62, and National Coal Association, *Bituminous Coal Data, 1967 Edition* (Washington: National Coal Association, 1969), p. 55. (Note that statistics vary somewhat depending on the source.)

11. U. S. Bureau of Mines, *Minerals Yearbook, 1965, op. cit.*, p. 28.

12. *Ibid.*, p. 13.

13. *Ibid.*, pp. 39-42, 49.

14. *Ibid.*, pp. 12-13; and U. S. Bureau of Mines, "Coal-Mine Injuries and Worktime, Monthly," *loc. cit.*

Industrial Structure

In 1967, 5,873 mines were in operation. Of these, 3,968 were underground, 1,507 were strip mines, and 458 were auger mines. The three types produced 63 percent, 34 percent, and 3 percent of coal output, respectively.[15]

Although there are many mines in the industry, it is dominated by a few large operations. Table 3 shows that in 1967, for example, mines producing over half a million tons annually provided 59.1 percent of output, but represented fewer than 5 percent of all mines. On the other hand, mines producing 50 thousand tons or less annually provided only 11 percent of total output but represented 76 percent of all mines.

TABLE 3. *Bituminous Coal Industry Production by Size of Mine Output United States, 1967*

Size of Mine (Tons per Year)	Percentage of Mines	Percentage of Production
Over 500,000	4.8	59.1
200,000 to 500,000	4.2	14.0
100,000 to 200,000	6.2	9.4
50,000 to 100,000	9.2	6.8
10,000 to 50,000	35.4	8.9
Less than 10,000	40.2	1.8
Total	100.0	100.0

Source: National Coal Association, *Bituminous Coal Data, 1968* (Washington: National Coal Association, 1969), p. 19.

Employment is more widely distributed, but still follows the same pattern. Thus, in 1958, mines employing over 500 workers accounted for one percent of the mines but 16 percent of total employment, while mines with under 10 employees accounted for 67 percent of all mines but only 10 percent of employment.[16]

Underground mines tend to have more employees than surface mines. Thus, in 1967, four-fifths of underground production workers were in mines with fifty or more employees, but only

15. National Coal Association, *op. cit.*, pp. 25, 27, and 28.

16. U. S. Bureau of Labor Statistics, *Technological Change, op. cit.*, p. 11.

one-half of strip mine production workers were in mines of that size.[17]

The industry as a whole has gone through several structural changes since the thirties. From 1940 to 1946, small mines proliferated. From 1947 to the late 1950's, the industry lost its middle-sized mines, with the small mines holding a relatively constant share of production. Production became increasingly concentrated in the larger companies. The fifty biggest companies increased their market share from 45 percent in 1947 to 60 percent in 1960. Concentration has continued in the sixties, and the production and number of small mines have been decreasing.[18]

The Southern Appalachian fields have generally followed the trends of the industry. The number of Class 6 mines (mines producing under 10,000 tons annually and generally having less than 10 miners) has, however, followed unique patterns, as will be discussed later.

Industrial Location

Although bituminous coal is mined in over half the states, production is highly concentrated in a relative few. The six states leading in production, West Virginia, Kentucky, Pennsylvania, Illinois, Ohio, and Virginia, accounted for 87 percent of output and 85 percent of employment in 1965.[19]

The five states having both significant coal production and significant proportions of black miners—West Virginia, Kentucky, Virginia, Alabama, and Tennessee—rank first, second, sixth, eighth, and ninth in volume of output. Tennessee is relatively insignificant, however, as in 1965 it accounted for only 1.2 percent of total production.[20]

These five Southern Appalachian states have become an increasingly important part of the industry with each decade of the twentieth century. Between 1910 and 1960, they increased their share of production and miners from about one-quarter to one-half of the industry's total. The proportions from 1890 to 1968 are shown in Table 4.

---

17. U. S. Bureau of Labor Statistics, *Industry Wage Survey, Bituminous Coal Mining*, Bulletin 1583 (January 1967).

18. Interview with Dr. David Brooks, May 1968.

19. U. S. Bureau of Mines, *Minerals Yearbook, 1965, op. cit.*, p. 20.

20. *Ibid.*

TABLE 4. *Bituminous Coal Industry*
Southern Appalachian Proportion of Production and Employment
1890-1968

Year	Percentage of Output	Percentage of Miners
1890	—	16.4
1900	—	21.8
1910	25.4	23.4
1920	35.6	31.8
1930	43.7	41.8
1940	46.0	47.6
1950	50.5	56.4
1960	56.0	61.6
1968	57.0	66.0

Source: U. S. Bureau of Mines, *Minerals Yearbook, 1890-1960;* and U. S. Bureau of Mines, "Coal-Mine Injuries and Worktime, Monthly," *Mineral Industry Surveys*, May 14, 1969, p. 8.

The nature and accessibility of the coal reserve, the availability of a market, and the existence of transport facilities are factors which influence the size of the mines and the pressures for mechanization, which in turn affect the Negro miner. Professor C. L. Christenson has used these factors to divide Southern Appalachian coal mining into four areas.

Western Kentucky has a substantial amount of manufacturing within or near the mining area which provides an industrial fuel market. Its coal reserves are readily accessible but of such low rank that there is strong competition from other forms of fuel and coal from outside the area. This competition necessitates efficient, mechanized coal mining operations in that area.

Alabama has a growing industrial fuel market and coal reserves which are generally higher rank than Kentucky's. Mines in this area with very accessible, high rank coal do not face strong pressures to mechanize; those operating on thinner-seam reserves and away from concentrated markets, however, may be forced to shift to stripping to remain economically viable.

Mechanization is extremely important in West Virginia, which lacks a large industrial market nearby but has enormous accessible deep reserves of high rank coal. Efficient production is necessary to offset shipping costs.

Eastern Kentucky, Virginia, and Tennessee, which comprise the fourth area, also have high rank coal and comparatively limited industrial markets, but most of their reserves are thin seams which are unsuitable for large scale mechanization. Transportation facilities for most of the mines are limited as well, making coal mining a less profitable operation in this area.[21]

A final aspect of coal mine location is its effect on unemployment. With the exception of the Alabama mines which center around Birmingham, coal towns in Southern Appalachia are frequently one-industry towns, and are isolated from industrial and trade centers by mountainous terrain and long distances. Thus, alternate sources of employment are limited.

These limited job alternatives combined with the declining manpower requirements between 1947 and 1961 to cause severe and persistent unemployment in many of the coal mining centers. In West Virginia, for example, unemployment in coal mining exceeded twenty percent in both 1958 and 1959, and the average length of unemployment was over five months. The average unemployment rate of the state's other industries was about one-half that in coal mining.[22]

MANPOWER

Both productivity and tonnage sales had major impacts on employment. Before 1920, tonnage increases offset the relatively modest increases in productivity, and total employment increased. A sharp increase in productivity and decrease in demand caused a large decrease in employment during the 1920's for the industry as a whole, and a leveling off of employment growth in Southern Appalachia. Employment remained generally stable during the 1930's in Southern Appalachia and the rest of the industry. The war years saw an increased demand handled almost entirely by a rapidly increasing productivity rate.

After World War II, productivity increased at an even more rapid rate. Demand, however, first leveled off and then fell. These two factors caused a sharp decline in employment between 1948 and 1961. Although demand for coal has increased some-

---

21. C. L. Christenson, *Economic Redevelopment in Bituminous Coal, The Special Case of Technological Advance in United States Coal Mines, 1930-1960* (Cambridge: Harvard University Press, 1962), pp. 253-254.

22. U. S. Bureau of Labor Statistics, *Technological Change, op. cit.,* p. 48.

what since 1961, total employment has continued downward, since productivity has kept increasing at a rapid pace.[23]

Additional coal miners are now needed however, because of quits, retirements, and expanding sales. A 1967 *Coal Age* survey estimated that nearly 30,000 new men per year would be needed through 1970.[24] In 1969 James McCartney, of Consolidation Coal Company, said that "the industry faces a crisis in manpower" and will need "at least 50,000 new miners within the next five years." [25]

Occupational Structure

The occupational structure, which also plays an important part in Negro miners' opportunities for advancement, has shifted rapidly with the advent of mechanization. Hand loading, once the occupation of over 50 percent of the miners, has now declined to less than 2 percent of all jobs. Maintenance, on the other hand, has grown in importance. In 1967, the percentages of underground miners in selected nonmanagement capacities were roughly as shown in Table 5.

TABLE 5. *Bituminous Coal Industry*
Proportion of Underground Miners in Selected Occupations
United States, 1967

Occupation	Percentage of All Miners
Mechanical cutting and loading	25
Transportation	24
Pick mining, hand loading, etc.	2
Maintenance	23
Other	26
Total	100

Source: U. S. Bureau of Labor Statistics, *Industrial Wage Survey, Bituminous Coal Mining, 1967*, Bulletin No. 1583, January 1967, calculation from Table 7, p. 14.

23. U. S. Bureau of Mines, *Minerals Yearbook 1965, op. cit.*, pp. 39-42, 49.

24. Ivan A. Given, "Manpower for Coal," *Coal Age*, May 1967, p. 60.

25. *New York Times*, August 3, 1969, Section 3, p. 13.

Unionization

The Progressive Miners' Union merged with the Knights of Labor District Assembly Number 135 to form the United Mine Workers of America in 1890. The UMW has always been an industrial union, recruiting all those who worked "in and around the mines, regardless of race, creed, color, or nationality." [26] Although it strenuously attempted to organize the southern fields from its beginning, its influence fluctuated dramatically through 1933, alternating between almost complete organization and almost complete collapse. With the passage of the National Industrial Recovery Act, the union's hand was so strengthened that it was able to organize 90 percent of the nation's miners within three months of the Act's passage. Assisted by the NRA machinery and President Roosevelt, the UMW and company representatives signed an agreement covering the entire Appalachian area in September, 1933.[27] Since the late 1940's the UMW has lost some strength due to the increase of small, nonunion mines, but as of 1967, 80 percent of the underground and 50 percent of the surface workers were working under labor-management contracts. The UMW represented all but 3 percent of the workers in organized mines. The proportion of organized workers varies greatly in different states, however, as shown in Table 6.

TABLE 6. *Bituminous Coal Industry*
Percent Unionization of Production and Related Workers
United States and Southern Appalachian States, 1967

	Unionized Percentage of Workers
United States	75-79
Alabama	90-94
Kentucky	55-59
East Kentucky	45-49
West Kentucky	80-84
Virginia	50-54
West Virginia	90-94

Source: U. S. Bureau of Labor Statistics, *Industry Wage Survey, Bituminous Coal Mining, 1967,* Bulletin No. 1583, January 1967, p. 3.

26. Northrup, *op. cit.*, p. 161.

27. *Ibid.*, p. 165.

The notably lower proportions of unionized employees in East Kentucky and Virginia are the result of the prevalence of many small mines in these areas. Because they often consist of family-and-friend work forces, small mines have always been difficult to organize. Also, it would be impossible for many of the small mines to pay the union scale of wages and benefits. Underground mines with fifty or more employees are almost 100 percent organized, and surface mines of the same size are about 80 percent organized. On the other hand, for mines with fewer than fifty workers, underground operations were only one-third organized and surface mining slightly more than one-fourth organized.[28] It is likely that really small mines (Class 6 as explained above) are almost completely unorganized.

The UMW took all races into the union, and even made special efforts to organize Negro miners. Full racial equality was practiced within the union organization. In the area of upgrading, however, the union's record has been poor; the union's failure to insist on equality in upgrading has permitted the virtual elimination of Negroes from the coal industry.

Wages and Earnings

The wages of coal miners have been generally increasing since 1933. The average hourly wages of coal miners are now among the highest in the United States. In January 1969, average hourly wages of $4.08 were almost one-third greater than the average for all manufacturing industries exceeding the autoworkers' average of $4.07 and the aerospace workers' $3.78.[29] Further augmenting the miners' income are fringe benefits such as a retirement pension, which was $115 per month as of 1967.[30]

---

28. U. S. Bureau of Labor Statistics, *Industry Wage Survey, op. cit.*, p. 3.

29. *Employment and Earnings*, Vol. 15, No. 9 (March 1969) Table C-2.

30. U. S. Bureau of Labor Statistics, *Industry Wage Survey, op. cit.*

CHAPTER III

Negro Employment: Colonial Times to the National Industrial Recovery Act

Negroes have been employed in the coal mines of the South since slavery days. This chapter traces their history from these beginnings to the early thirties, emphasizing the factors which have affected their employment since 1890.

THE EARLY YEARS

Negro employment in coal mines commenced in the eighteenth century in Virginia. Thus Pinchbeck reports:

Soft coal [bituminous] was discovered near Richmond in 1750 and mines in that region were producing regularly by 1787. In 1796 a French traveler described those at Dover as employing five hundred Negroes in the works. South of the James there were said to be larger works.[31]

In Alabama deposits of coal and iron in Jefferson County were noted in 1869. Between 1869 and 1890, mining of both minerals began. Many of the first coal miners were Negroes, and by 1889, Negroes accounted for 46.2 percent of all Alabama coal miners.[32] Negro miners were also used from the beginning in Tennessee, Kentucky, and southern West Virginia.[33]

NEGRO EMPLOYMENT 1890 TO 1933

The Negro miner's work share was influenced by four factors between 1890 and 1933. First, the rapidly increasing demand for labor brought many new Negroes into the mines. Second, operators used Negroes in their attempts to thwart the United Mine Workers' organizing efforts. Third, the union was equali-

---

31. Raymond B. Pinchbeck, *The Virginia Negro Artisan and Tradesman*, University of Virginia, Phelps-Stokes Fellowship Papers, No. 7 (Richmond: William Byrd Press, Inc., 1920), p. 66.

32. Robert D. Ward and William W. Rodgers, *Labor Revolt in Alabama: The Great Strike of 1894* (University: University of Alabama Press, 1965), pp. 19-21.

33. S. O. Spero and A. L. Harris, *The Black Worker* (New York: Atheneum, 1968), pp. 216-217.

tarian in policy, and was partly successful in achieving this goal in practice. Fourth, discrimination was evident, both on the job and in the communities.

Expansion of the Southern Appalachian Coal Fields

Until the late 1890's, the Southern Appalachian coal fields were relatively unexploited. Professor Northrup has given the following explanation:

> Because of their greater distance from the centers of coal consumption, and because of inferior transportation facilities, the rich coal deposits of West Virginia and Kentucky were not exploited on a large scale before 1900. Since then, however, they have been developed at a rapid rate; nor is this difficult to explain. The coal seams of these states are unusually thick and contain an exceptionally high grade of coal. But most important, the southern coal industry was from its inception, and with a few years excepted, for nearly forty years thereafter, strictly non-union; whereas the central competitive field, composed of the mine fields of Illinois, Indiana, Ohio, and Pennsylvania, was to a large extent organized as early as 1900. Since labor costs constitute the principal element in total costs of production, the non-union coal operators in the southern fields were able to encroach steadily on the markets of the union employers in the North by paying lower wages than the union scale.[34]

Employment expanded substantially during the early part of this period. It increased almost 500 percent between 1890 and 1920 for the region as a whole. The growth slowed for the next decade, increasing only 7.9 percent between 1920 and 1930.

Because of their close proximity to the Southern Appalachian coal fields the Negroes provided a ready supply of labor for the expanding demand. As Spero and Harris noted: "The existence of such a store of labor in the southern communities has given the operators in West Virginia . . . an industrial reserve army which may be used . . . to meet an increased demand for labor caused by the expansion of the coal industry."[35] European immigrants also provided labor in the Southern Appalachian region, primarily to supplement native labor.

Turning to census data, it can be seen that the rates of increase for Negro and white miners were quite closely correlated for the region as a whole. Table 7 shows the number of all miners and of Negro miners between 1900 and 1930.

---

34. Herbert R. Northrup, *Organized Labor and the Negro* (New York: Harper & Bros., 1944), pp. 155 and 158.

35. Spero and Harris, *op. cit.*, pp. 215, 220-221.

TABLE 7. Bituminous Coal Industry
Total and Negro Employment
Southern Appalachian States, 1900-1930

	1900[a]			1910			1920			1930		
	Total	Negro	Percent Negro	Total	Negro	Percent Negro	Total	Negro	Percent Negro	Total	Negro	Percent Negro
Alabama	17,898	9,735	54.3	20,779	11,189	53.8	26,204	14,097	53.8	23,956	12,742	53.2
Kentucky	9,299	2,206	23.7	18,310	3,888	21.3	44,269	7,407	16.7	54,307	7,346	13.5
Tennessee	10,890	3,092	28.4	11,094	1,609	14.5	12,226	913	7.5	8,765	578	6.6
Virginia	7,369	2,651	35.9	7,291	1,719	23.6	12,418	2,450	19.8	12,629	1,511	12.0
West Virigina	20,797	4,620	22.2	54,884	11,237	20.5	87,728	17,799	20.3	97,505	22,089	22.7
Total Southern Appalachia	66,253	22,304	33.7	112,358	29,642	26.4	182,845	42,666	23.3	197,162	44,266	22.5

Source: *U. S. Census of Population, 1900-1930*, in Herbert R. Northrup, *Organized Labor and the Negro* (New York: Harper & Bros., 1944), pp. 156-157.

Note: Census did not give breakdown for female mining employment.

[a] All miners and quarrymen.

Although the number of both Negro and white miners increased in each decade through 1930, the number of white miners increased at a faster rate after 1900 so that the Negro proportion of miners declined from 33.7 percent in 1900 to 22.5 percent in 1930.

Regional figures hide significant differences among the states, however. Because these differences are closely tied to the use of Negroes to fight unionization, they are discussed in the next section.

The Use of Negroes to Forestall Unionization

Many companies used Negroes to fight the United Mine Workers. First, the operators engaged them to replace striking miners. Second, they hired "judicious mixtures" of Negroes, native whites, and foreign whites, in attempts to forestall unionism by promoting disunity and playing one group against the others. Third, they used the race issue to arouse public opinion against striking miners.

Ward and Rodgers point out that as early as the 1890's, racial devisiveness between white and Negro miners in Alabama hindered the development of an effective labor movement.

Whatever the common economic interests shared by white and Negro miners, the labor force's mixture often tended to transcend and obscure the more immediate demands of labor solidarity.[36]

The use of Negroes as strikebreakers is clearly evident in the great Alabama coal miners' strike of 1894. For various reasons, the operators had cut the miners' wages and hours several times. After several attempts by the UMW and operators to reach an agreement, the miners' state convention voted to strike on April 14, 1894. The strikers' main target was the Tennessee Company's mines. The company, under the direction of Henry DeBardeleben, almost immediately began employing nonunion Negroes to break the back of the strike, bringing in 100 from Kansas the first week.[37] There were few defections by Negro union members, however.

---

36. Ward and Rodgers, *op. cit.*, p. 21.

37. *Ibid.*, pp. 63, 68, and 89. A short time later, the reverse process occurred. Between 1898 and 1902 about 500 Negroes were brought from Alabama to break a strike in the Oklahoma coal fields. Negroes were also re-

It is likely that the 1894 strike resulted in a permanent increase in the number of Negroes employed in Alabama mines. During the strike, DeBardeleben decided to use only Negroes in the Blue Creek mines because whites had given him so much trouble.[38] The miners eventually lost the strike, and "those that the company was willing to rehire went back to work, but there was no guarantee of re-employment." [39]

Later Alabama strikes, in 1908 and 1920-1921, illustrate the Alabama operators' use of race to arouse public opinion against both black and white strikers. In the 1908 strike, for example,

The tent colony in which the strikers lived after they had been evicted from the company-owned houses, was burned to the ground in order to prevent the "mobilization of Negroes in union camps." In addition, a committee of citizens threatened a race riot unless the president of the UMW ordered the miners to return to work. The UMW executive was informed that "no matter how meritorious the union cause, the people of Alabama would never tolerate the organization and striking of Negroes along with white men." [40]

Similar racial violence occurred in the 1920-1921 strike, in which 76 percent of the strikers were Negro.[41]

Negro strikebreakers were used in West Virginia, Kentucky, and Tennessee. The divergence of Negro employment patterns in Tennessee, Virginia, and West Virginia from their employment patterns for Southern Appalachia as a whole (Table 7) can be explained largely by the movement of Negro strikebreakers during periods of labor unrest. The tremendous early increase and subsequent rapid decrease of Negroes in Tennessee is due to

---

cruited from the Birmingham area to thwart strikes in Southeast Kansas during the late 1890's. See Frederick Lynne Ryan, *The Rehabilitation of Oklahoma Coal Mining Communities* (Norman: University of Oklahoma Press, 1935), pp. 38 and 39; and John M. Robb, *The Black Coal Miner of Southeast Kansas*, History of Minority Groups in Kansas, No. 2 (Topeka: State of Kansas Commission on Civil Rights, 1969), pp. 3 and 4.

38. *Mobile Daily News*, May 5, 1894, cited in Ward and Rodgers, *op. cit.*, p. 74.

39. *Labor Advocate*, September 15, 1894, cited in Ward and Rodgers, *op. cit.*, p. 135.

40. Northrup, *op. cit.*, pp. 162-163.

41. *Ibid.*

the fact that Negroes were used as strikebreakers there only during the 1890's. Spero and Harris report that Negroes were imported during the Tennessee strikes of that decade, but make no reference to their use in later years.[42] Professor Northrup notes in his discussion of strikebreaking during the labor unrest of the 1920's that "In Kentucky, Tennessee, and Virginia, the coal operators found the white 'mountaineers' and recent immigrants from southeastern Europe less likely to catch union contagion, and consequently the number of white employees was increased at the expense of the Negroes in these three states." [43] Between 1930 and 1940 there was a 70 percent decline in Negro miners which might reflect the retirement of Negroes brought into the mines in the 1890's.

In Virginia, there were large declines in numbers of Negro miners between 1900 and 1910, and again between 1920 and 1930 (Table 7). In each decade, the number of Negro miners declined by about 40 percent, or by about 1,000 workers. The number of black miners increased 40 percent, however, in the intervening decade of 1910 to 1920 (Table 7).

The exportation of Virginia Negro miners to replace striking miners in other states offers one explanation for the fluctuations. The number of Negro miners declined as they left for other states to act as strikebreakers during periods of labor unrest, and increased during the relatively peaceful 1910 to 1920 decade.

Finally, although they declined in every other Southern Appalachian state during the 1920's, the number of Negroes increased significantly in West Virginia, during which time the state was experiencing major strikes. The 1925 strike, for example, resulted in a large increase in the number of Negro miners in the northern part of the state. In 1923 there were not more than 2,600 Negro miners in the entire Fairmont district, but by 1926 there were 3,359 Negro miners there. These strikebreakers were primarily natives of Alabama, Mississippi, South Carolina, and Virginia.[44]

The Influence of the United Mine Workers

The UMW, in its early years, worked harder than any other union to recruit Negro miners. O. H. Underwood, a Negro

---

42. Spero and Harris, *op. cit.*, pp. 206-245, 352-382.

43. Northrup, *op. cit.*, p. 159.

44. Spero and Harris, *op. cit.*, pp. 219, 225.

miner, wrote in the early 1900's, "I believe that the United Mine Workers has done more to erase the word white from the Constitution than the Fourteenth Amendment." [45]

The objective of complete equality is clearly stated in the International Constitution: "To unite in one organization, regardless of creed, color or nationality, all workmen . . . employed in and around coal mines." An earlier version of the constitution was even more explicit: "No member in good standing who holds a dues or transfer card shall be debarred or hindered from obtaining work on account of race, creed, or nationality." [46]

The UMW tried to achieve equality in fact as well as in policy. During this period, it employed one national and several district Negro organizers to help organize black miners. In northern West Virginia and other states, Negroes were often elected to offices in their locals, including president. When white miners in eastern Ohio struck against the employment of Negroes, the national executive board of the UMW revoked the charter of the local. Later it placed in the local's district constitution the statement that "Any Local Union that is found guilty of discriminating against a fellow worker on account of creed, color or nationality, said Local Union to be fined not less than $125, for each offense." [47]

Although the UMW was equalitarian in policy and practice, discrimination occurred both in spite of and because of the union. Prior to the 1925 strike, for example, there were few Negro miners in the then almost completely organized northern West Virginia mines. Spero and Harris point out that "where the non-employment of Negroes occurred, prior to the strike, it seemed attributable in some instances to the desire of management to keep out recent immigrant workers and Negroes, and in other instances to the refusal of white workers, especially of native Americans, to work with Negroes." [48] (Organized workers, of course, are more likely to have influence over employment policy than unorganized workers.)

---

45. *Ibid.*, pp. viii, xii.

46. *Ibid.*, p. 355.

47. *Ibid.*, pp. 355 and 375. Richard Wright, in his 1912 study, reported that Negro miners in Pennsylvania were all members of the UMW and that it was "one of the few unions in which the Negroes agree that they receive fair treatment." See Richard R. Wright, Jr., *The Negro in Pennsylvania* (New York: Arno Press, 1969), p. 95.

48. *Ibid.*, p. 227.

The 1925 report of the Bureau of Negro Welfare and Statistics of West Virginia gives support also to the idea that the union provided a method for prejudiced white workers to discriminate against blacks. The report stated that

With few exceptions, white men in strongly organized territory will not permit the employment of Negroes as motormen, brakemen on motors, head-house operators, machine runners, track layers . . . and other higher waged . . . jobs even though the Negroes are members of the union also. . . . [The loss of the 1925 strike] will result in the employment of more Negroes.[49]

In another place, the Bureau's director noted that after the unionization of Fayette and Kanawha counties, Negroes lost their higher jobs in the mines, but regained them when the union later collapsed.[50] Spero and Harris report that "As prevalent as the practice of racial discrimination is claimed to be in union territory, and as great as the Negro miners' opportunity for advancement is in non-union territory, nearly every interview that the authors had with Negro miners in Cabin Creek emphasized the advantages of unionism over non-unionism." [51] (Cabin Creek is in Raleigh County, West Virginia, which was the center of the strongly antiunion counties when the interviews were conducted in 1928.) This finding would seem to indicate that although discrimination was present under union conditions in the early years, in the eyes of the Negro miner the benefits of unionism were greater than its faults.

Discrimination

Overt discrimination by both the companies and white miners was also prevalent during this period. For example, there was much opposition to Negroes serving on mine committees in West Virginia. It was reported that "The West Virginia native white miners dislike serving on committees with 'ignorant niggers who just came from the South.' Sometimes the white miners wouldn't follow the black committeemen's orders." In the same area, the KKK was used to fight the Negroes and foreign whites.[52]

49. *Ibid.*, p. 374.

50. *Ibid.*

51. *Ibid.*, pp. 375-376.

52. *Ibid.*, pp. 238, 371.

The companies also discriminated between black and white miners. In one (nonunion) company, the houses assigned to Negroes were near the road, openly exposed to attacks by union miners. The Negroes were segregated from the whites in the bath houses and dining rooms, and even were served separate food. They were removed from jobs when white workers complained and were not promoted to better jobs.[53]

The number of Negro miners increased between 1890 and 1933 because of the generally high demand for coal miners, and the specific need for strikebreakers. Negroes faced discrimination, however, both on the job and in the communities, despite the equalitarian policies of the UMW.

53. *Ibid.*, pp. 239-241.

CHAPTER IV

Negro Employment: 1933 to 1960

The Southern Appalachian coal industry of the 1890-1933 era could be characterized as a "boom industry," with a generally unorganized, unmechanized, and rapidly expanding work force. The advent of the depression heralded a new era, however. The demand for coal broke and started a long downward trend. With the National Industrial Recovery Act and the Great Depression to aid them, the UMW succeeded in organizing the southern as well as northern fields. Mechanical loaders, the first tool of the mechanical revolution in coal mining, began to load an increasing proportion of Southern Appalachian coal. Finally, the work force increases began tapering off. Chapter IV considers the period that began with these radical changes and ended with the expanding demand of the early 1960's.

FROM DEPRESSION THROUGH WORLD WAR II

Negro employment during the period between 1933 and 1947 was characterized by two factors. First, the number and proportion of Negro miners decreased markedly. Second, Negro miners were still underrepresented in the skilled jobs and overrepresented in the unskilled jobs.

Decrease in Negro Miners

Total coal mining employment in Southern Appalachia increased about 10 percent per decade between 1930 and 1950. The employment changes were, however, quite different for Negro and white miners. Between 1930 and 1950 the number of Negro miners decreased from 44,000 to 26,000, while the number of white miners increased from 153,000 to 217,000. Thus, for every decrease of one Negro, there was an increase of three whites. Consequently, the Negro proportion of total mining employment dropped from 23 percent in 1930, to 16 percent in 1940, to 11 percent in 1950. Variations among the states are shown in Table 8.

TABLE 8. Bituminous Coal Industry
Total and Negro Employment
Southern Appalachian States, 1930, 1940, and 1950

	1930ᵃ			1940			1950		
	Total	Negro	Percent Negro	Total	Negro	Percent Negro	Total	Negro	Percent Negro
Alabama	23,956	12,742	53.2	23,022	9,605	41.7	20,084	6,756	33.6
Kentucky	54,307	7,346	13.5	54,676	5,474	10.0	64,074	2,965	4.6
Tennessee	8,765	578	6.6	9,534	168	1.8	9,323	92	1.0
Virginia	12,629	1,511	12.0	20,086	1,190	5.9	25,006	900	3.6
West Virginia	97,505	22,089	22.7	105,915	18,356	17.3	127,304	15,423	12.1
Total Southern Appalachia	197,162	44,266	22.5	213,233	34,793	16.3	245,791	26,136	10.6

Source: U. S. Census of Population:

1930: Vol. IV, Occupations by States, Table 11.
1940: Vol. III, The Labor Force, Parts 2, 3, and 5, Table 20.
1950: Vol. II, Characteristics of the Population, State Volumes, Table 83.

ᵃ Males only. Census did not give breakdown for mining females, but the number was very small.

Differences in Negro and White Occupational Distribution

As in the earlier period, Negroes were underrepresented in the skilled and desirable jobs, but overrepresentd in the unskilled and undesirable jobs. A 1932 study of twenty West Virginia mines found that 77 percent of the Negro, but only 60 percent of the white miners were hand loaders. On the other hand, 6 percent of the whites, but only 2 percent of the Negroes, were undercutting machine operators. Negroes were overrepresented in the dangerous job of brakeman, but underrepresented in the more desirable outside jobs and indirect labor jobs. Of the 2,411 Negroes studied, only 11 "were in positions which, even by the most liberal stretching of the term could be called positions of authority." [54]

An occupational breakdown by race and state was given in the 1940 Census (Table 9). Only two Negroes were classified as professional or semiprofessional workers in all five Southern Appalachian states, and only five were proprietors, managers, or officials. In clerical and sales positions, Negroes should have had ten times as many jobs, based on their proportion of the total work force. The same situation prevailed among craftsmen and foremen; from 5 to 14 percent of the whites were in these occupations, but in no state was even one percent of the blacks so employed. About 99 percent of the Negroes were in the operative category in all states, while the percentage of whites in these occupations varied between about 80 and 90 percent.

The increasing number of Negro miners between 1890 and 1933 resulted from the need for many unskilled laborers as coal production boomed, and from the use of Negroes to slow unionization. Both these factors were absent during the 1933-1947 period. The rapid growth of the earlier period had leveled off, and the mines were almost completely unionized in 1933, after the passage of the NRA. Although the absence of these factors would be expected to mitigate further *increases* in the number of Negro miners, their absence cannot account for the large *decreases* that actually occurred. A new set of factors—centering around mine mechanization and a change in industry structure—was the primary cause of the decreases.

---

54. James T. Laing, "Negro Miner in West Virginia," *Social Forces*, Vol. XIV (1936), pp. 416-422.

TABLE 9. Bituminous Coal Industry

Employment by Major Occupational Group and Race, Southern Appalachian States, 1940

	Total	Professionals and Semi-professionals		Managers, Proprietors, and Officials		Clerical, Sales, and Kindred		Craftsmen, Foremen, and Kindred		Operatives and Kindred		Other	
		Number	Percent	Number	Percent	Number	Percent	Number	Percent	Number	Percent	Number	Percent
Alabama													
Negro	9,605	1	*	1	*	10	0.1	75	0.8	9,496	98.9	22	0.2
White	13,417	103	0.8	302	2.3	365	2.7	1,945	14.5	10,576	78.8	126	0.9
Kentucky													
Negro	5,474	—	—	1	*	6	0.1	45	0.8	5,411	98.9	11	0.2
White	49,202	234	0.5	696	1.4	961	2.0	3,387	6.9	43,704	88.8	220	0.4
Tennessee													
Negro	168	—	—	—	—	—	—	—	—	168	100.0	—	—
White	9,366	32	0.3	210	2.2	125	1.3	471	5.0	8,491	90.7	37	0.4
Virginia													
Negro	1,190	—	—	—	—	—	—	4	0.3	1,180	99.2	6	0.5
White	18,896	97	0.5	181	1.0	360	1.9	1,290	6.8	16,905	89.5	63	0.3
West Virginia													
Negro	18,356	1	*	3	*	61	0.3	158	0.9	18,076	98.5	57	0.3
White	87,559	614	0.7	964	1.1	2,293	2.6	9,835	11.2	73,554	84.0	299	0.3
Total Southern Appalachia													
Negro	34,793	2	*	5	*	77	0.2	282	0.8	34,331	98.6	96	0.3
White	178,440	1,080	0.6	2,353	1.3	4,104	2.3	16,928	9.5	153,230	85.9	745	0.4

Source: U. S. Census of Population, 1940, Vol. III, The Labor Force, Parts 2, 3, and 5, Table 20.

* Less than 0.05 percent.

Underground Mine Mechanization

One of the most important influences on underground coal mining during this period was the advent of the mechanical loader which loaded 20 percent of Southern Appalachian underground coal by 1940 and over 50 percent by 1950. Mine mechanization especially hurt Negro miners because the jobs in which they predominated were the ones which were eliminated and they were not given a proportionate share of the machine and machine-created jobs.

Augmenting the effect of mechanization on the black miner was the type of seniority system used for laying off workers. Until the late forties, classification seniority was used for determining the order of layoff. Men in jobs eliminated by mechanization were laid off before others having less mine seniority but who were in occupations unaffected by mechanization. Since Negroes were overrepresented in the eliminated jobs, Negro miners were laid off in disproportionate numbers.

Thus, the advent of mechanical loading resulted in a decreasing proportion of Negro miners because it caused a "twist" in labor demand. Demand decreased for hand jobs (in which the Negro was concentrated) and increased for mechanized and mechanization-created jobs (in which the Negro had not received his share).

Although productivity increased during this period, the increase in Southern Appalachia was smaller between 1930 and 1950 than it was between 1910 and 1930. The productivity rate changes during each period are shown in Table 10.

Increase of Small Mines in Kentucky

When laid off, the black miner had a harder time than the white miner in finding work in another mine. The unemployed whites often opened "dog hole" mines. The dog holes were relatively unmechanized compared to the bigger operations. They were either on land leased from a larger operation, or they were on the land of a local entrepreneuer. They usually had ten or fewer employees, and hence fell into the smaller production classes.[55]

---

55. Harry M. Caudill, *Night Comes to the Cumberlands* (Boston: Atlantic Little, 1963), pp. 222-223.

TABLE 10.　*Bituminous Coal Industry
Productivity in Tons per Man-Day
Southern Appalachian States, 1910, 1930, and 1950*

	Tons per Man-Day			Percent Change	Percent Change
	1910	1930	1950	1910-1930	1930-1950
Alabama	2.91	3.38	4.31	16.2	27.5
Kentucky	3.26	4.83	6.39	48.2	32.3
Tennessee	2.65	3.48	4.67	31.3	34.2
Virginia	3.72	4.66	5.54	25.3	18.9
West Virginia	3.94	5.61	6.41	42.4	14.3
Southern Appalachia	3.59	5.14	6.19	43.2	20.4

Source:　U. S. Bureau of Mines, *Minerals Yearbook, 1911, 1931, 1951.*

Dog hole operations were especially common in Kentucky and increased rapidly there between 1940 and 1950. They were mostly in the eastern part of the state, however. In *Night Comes to the Cumberlands,* Caudill tells about such operations in eastern Kentucky.

The indigenous coal miners . . . had inherited or bought small tracts of mountain land . . . . These small plots of rugged earth were the sole estates of thousands of coal-digging mountaineers and inferior though they were, they constituted an all-important collateral. By mortgaging his inheritance to the local bank or the holding company whose coal he proposed to mine, a would-be operator could borrow eight hundred to one thousand dollars. With such modest capital he could go into business for himself. From a mere handful at the beginning, the truck mines increased in number with unbelievable speed. More and still more mountaineers took the plunge, gambling every nickel between themselves and absolute poverty, on the hazard that they knew enough about mining to succeed.[56]

While only 2 percent of the Kentucky coal was produced in Class 6 mines in 1940, 12 percent was produced in Class 6 mines by 1950.[57]

The dog hole mines were manned mainly by primary groups —the operator, his sons, relatives, and close friends. Because of this social composition, Negroes were largely excluded. The un-

56. *Ibid.,* pp. 224-225.

57. U. S. Bureau of Mines, *Minerals Yearbook, 1941,* p. 382; *1951,* p. 319.

employed Negroes could not, or at least did not open many dog holes themselves. Thus, the decreasing employment of white workers in large mines was offset partly by the increasing employment of white workers in the small mines. But since the decreasing employment of Negroes in the large mines was not offset by small mine employment, the number and proportion of Negroes in the Kentucky mines decreased.

Increase of Stripping Operations

The declining proportion of Negroes in coal mining jobs was further augmented by the increase of stripping which had increased to 13 percent of all Alabama coal, 18 percent of all Kentucky coal, 9 percent of all West Virginia coal, and 9 percent of all Virginia coal by 1950.[58] The Negro got virtually no stripping jobs in any of the Southern Appalachian states.[59] There are several possible explanations for this.

A number of the strip operations are quite small and are similar in employee makeup to the small deep mines previously discussed. The large stripping operations also have few, if any, Negro workers, however. One large stripper in Kentucky offered the following explanation, applicable to both the 1933-1947 and later periods:

The heavy and very expensive equipment used on large stripping operations requires skilled and experienced operators. Most of the workers we hire are already trained—often they got their skill as heavy equipment operators in the construction industry. A case in point is a man who came in to apply for a job today. He's working on a road construction job near town right now. He heard we hire experienced dozer operators, and he thought he would like the steady wages and living in one place. The construction operators, mainly those in road building, are a prime source of new workers.[60]

Until recently the construction industry—and its unions—has barred Negoes from apprenticeship programs. Since almost all construction machinery operators were white, and since a major source of strip mining machinery operators was the construction work force, the opportunities for Negroes to enter strip mining were very limited.

A final cause of the small number of Negroes in stripping is that its jobs are in high demand. The stripping industry does

58. *Ibid.*, p. 340.

59. Data in author's possession.

60. Interview, June 1968.

not need black workers because plenty of white workers are available.

The advent of stripping also caused a "twist" in the demand for Negro miners. As the strip mines produced more coal, the underground mines produced less. Lowered underground production resulted in layoffs—a decreased demand for both white and black miners. The increased stripping caused an increasing demand for whites only (although not necessarily the same whites). So, again the demand for those jobs the Negro held declined, and the demand for the jobs he could not get increased. Thus, stripping also had a double impact on decreasing the proportion of Negroes among all miners. Because stripping grew especially fast in Kentucky it also may have been a cause of the rapid decrease in Kentucky's Negro miners between 1940 and 1950.

Natural Attrition of Negro Miners

During the 1930-1950 period, the decrease in the number of Negro miners was about the size that would occur if Negro miners were depleted by natural attrition (mainly retirement) and no new hiring. (The decline in Kentucky between 1940 and 1950 was the major exception.)

The reason for this is easily illustrated. If, for example, a work force is evenly distributed between the ages of 20 and 60, 25 percent will retire every ten years. If their ages range from 15 to 65, 20 percent will retire each decade. Thus, from 20 to 25 percent of a work force will retire each decade.

The decline of Negro miners in Southern Appalachia followed this pattern. The rate ranged from 16 to 30 percent for the individual states, with the exception of the decline in Kentucky between 1940 and 1950. It is thus likely that although the number of Negroes decreased, few Negro miners were permanently thrown out of work during this period.

Causes of Occupational Differences

His unique occupational distribution explains why the Negro was more likely to lose his job than the white. Company managers, union officials, and white miners were directly or indirectly responsible for the hiring, upgrading, and firing patterns of Negro miners. Their actions were guided and restricted by union and company policies, as well as social norms. Of course, the Negro himself—including his ability and values—influenced the occupational distribution of his race. He was, however, generally the dependent variable.

Influence of the Operators

Upgrading and training are by and large managerial prerogatives, although they are within the scope of the grievance process. These decisions are usually made based on both ability and seniority.[61] The reason that Negroes were not placed proportionately in some jobs can be partly explained by lack of education; but a more important reason was that many managers perceived Negroes as being capable only of low-skilled work. Below are some typical statements by management about the qualifications for a loading machine operator, and about their perceptions of Negro miners:

Qualifications for Loading Machine Operators	Perceptions of Negro Miners
"In selecting his (machine loading) crews, men mechanically tuned, industrious, and resourceful will be needed."	"Negroes are irresponsible . . . you can't trust them with a machine, even the educated ones."
"Candidates for mechanical jobs . . . best recommendations are steadiness and a practical turn of mind."	
"Likely candidates can be spotted by noting which of them take an interest in their work and can be trusted to carry out instructions without being watched. . . ."	"They sometimes just take off for a while, and don't show up for two or three days at a time."
"In placing men in machine loading as well as other lines of mine work my experience has been that it is best to talk to your men and learn their aspirations."	Barriers to free communication exist between whites and Negroes. Such subcultures are likely to develop different values, mores, and even different languages.[62]

---

61. Interviews, 1967 and 1968.

62. Joseph E. McGrath, *Social Psychology* (New York: Holt, Rinehart, and Winston, 1965), p. 150.

Qualifications for Loading Machine Operators	Perceptions of Negro Miners
[A loading machine operator] "should be possessed of plenty of confidence and a quick, active mind; his mining experience should include a good mechanical knowledge of machinery and a fairly practical acquaintance with mining methods, especially pertaining to the seam in which he worked. His loyalty to the company and his boss should be unquestioned."	"Let's face it. You can only hire a Negro labor for a Negro laborer's job."

The quotations on the qualifications for a loading machine operator are from letters of employers written to *Coal Age* in response to a query about what a loading machine operator's qualifications should be. As they were published in the latter part of 1929, they are applicable to the period during which mechanical loading showed its most rapid advance—the thirties and forties. It is notable that educational background was not once mentioned. The quotations regarding Negroes were made by mine operators of the thirties and forties during field interviews for this study. They are typical of management personnel's perceptions of Negroes during this period. While such perceptions were by no means universal, it is clear that a substantial number of managers held them.

Influence of the UMW

As in the earlier period, the UMW both preached and practised racial equality. There continued to be local exceptions; but the national officials never condoned such action, and were quick to reprimand individual locals for discriminating. Further, organizing campaigns and day-to-day operations have always been free of racial discrimination in both the North and South.

The way the UMW dealt with racial prejudice in Alabama and West Virginia illustrates how it provided the greatest possible racial equality in each case without unduly antagonizing community mores. Professor Northrup reported in 1944:

When the time came for the election of local officers, the Alabama district leaders advocated the selection of whites as presidents and Negroes as vice-presidents, and this procedure was followed in locals even where the Negroes were in a majority. This device was designed to facilitate good employer-employee relations, for the local president usually heads the "pit committee" which meets with representatives of management for the joint settlement of grievances arising out of working conditions in the mines. It was felt that the employers should be accustomed to the novelty of joint grievance committees before being subject to the still more novel experience of having to deal with Negroes as equals. At the same time, the election of Negro vice-presidents and of other Negro officers provided the colored miners with representation in the policy-making decisions of the locals.

The results of this policy of gradualism are already discernible. According to a number of informants of both races, Negro members of grievance committees, who a few years ago would have risked physical violence had they raised their voices in joint union-management meetings, now argue their cases quite as freely as their fellow white members. Local meetings are no longer featured by such "formal" relationships between the races, as according to Dr. G. S. Mitchell, was the case in 1934-1935. White members no longer hesitate to call a Negro unionist "Brother," or to shake hands with Negro delegates without displaying embarrassment. And now, Negro delegates contribute freely to discussions.

In West Virginia, it was not found necessary to adhere to a policy of strict gradualism. Negroes are usually well represented among the local and district officers and in some cases have been elected local union presidents even though white miners are in the majority. In many mines where there are a large number of foreign-born workmen, it is the custom to elect on a three-man pit committee, one from this group, one native white, and one Negro. By such means, the UMW has been able to weld into a united front that conglomerate mixture of races and nationalities which many coal operators once thought was an insurmountable bar to unionism.[63]

Although overt discrimination was not present, less obvious discriminatory tactics were often "overlooked" by local officials. This was because the UMW, like other unions, is basically a political organization. Its local officials are elected, and so cannot disregard their constituents' wishes. Further, since the local officials are members of the same community as the other miners, they are likely to have similar attitudes. So, although a local official could not ignore open and overt discrimination, he could ignore less obvious methods, and he sometimes did.

Notably, few grievances about racial discrimination were filed. Since a large number of Negroes felt they were discriminated against, it appears the grievance procedure was not used

---

63. Herbert R. Northrup, *Organized Labor and the Negro* (New York: Harper & Bros., 1944), pp. 166-167.

to the extent it should have been. (It should be noted, however, that many of the Negro miners were afraid to complain, and hence did not give the grievance process a chance to be used.)

The lack of grievances about the Negro miners' inability to get their fair share of machine jobs is a very important example of this "discrimination by omission." Professor Northrup discussed the UMW policy as follows:

When loading machines were installed, the employers gave white workers preference as a matter of course. This, of course, is in direct conflict with the equalitarian policies of the UMW, but until recently, the district officials of the union have hesitated to take a firm stand on the question. For the very reason that machine jobs have been traditionally "white man's work," the UMW officials, pursuing a policy of gradualism, did not attempt a quick break with the past.[64]

This occupational discrimination was, however, the major cause of the Negroes' demise in coal mining. Professor Northrup saw the beginnings of the disproportionate displacement of Negroes, due to mechanization, in 1944, and he noted that

This [disproportionate displacement] is particularly likely to occur in instances where machines replace men. These post-war adjustments will put the equalitarian policies of the UMW to their severest test. If Negroes continue to bear the brunt of technological unemployment, the UMW will no longer be able to claim that it adheres to a policy of racial equality as steadfastly as any other American labor union.[65]

As this and the next chapter show, the UMW did not pass this test, and Negroes were largely displaced by mechanization.

Influence of the White Miners

In some cases, the advent of unionism combined with the attitudes of some white miners to increase discrimination. For example, one large commercial Alabama mining company was 22 percent Negro in 1939, but only 4 percent Negro in 1951. According to the company's president, this decrease resulted from the union's insistence on equal advancement opportunity regardless of color. This policy meant the Negro miners would begin to move into job classifications which were previously all white; the white miners, according to the president, rebelled against this, and at one point a delegation of white miners told the company that they refused to work with Negroes. The company stopped

64. *Ibid.*, p. 169.

65. *Ibid.*, pp. 170-171.

hiring Negroes completely at one mine, and greatly reduced hiring them at another. In 1951, it still hired Negroes only in positions that would not cause "friction." [66]

Such cases, however, appear to be the exception rather than the rule. Even in Alabama, overt and prolonged white resistance seemed limited to those mines which had low proportions of Negroes before unionization. Several company officials said they felt that in those mines that were over one-half Negro prior to unionization, the races were already used to working in the same spaces and job occupations.[67] So, white miners were less likely to resist the upgrading of Negroes. On the other hand, in mines where whites were in the great majority before unionization, the Negroes were employed almost exclusively in unskilled laborer jobs. White miners resisted Negro upgrading to a much greater degree in these mines, according to these officials.

Another example appears in a late 1940's study of the Pocahontas coal field in West Virginia. It reported that all electricians and machinists were white, because the men in these jobs refused to work with Negroes.[68] In sum, the uneven distribution of jobs between Negro and white miners was largely the result of the policies and practices of the companies, the union, and the white miners.

Areas of Racial Equality

Although the more desirable jobs were given disproportionately to the white miners, the Southern Appalachian coal industry was outstandingly equalitarian in two respects. First, there was a complete mixing of races in the mines. Second, there were no wage differentials for white and black miners doing the same job.

In a 1936 study of the Negro miner in West Virginia, Dr. Laing reported that "under the stimuli of controlled competition of the company-owned town, the white no longer expects the Negro to receive lower wages or occupy a definitely lower plane. Negroes and whites receive equal pay in the same positions." [69]

---

66. Langston T. Hawley, "Negro Employment in the Birmingham Metropolitan Area," in *Selected Studies of Negro Employment in the South,* Report No. 6, NPA Committee of the South (Washington: National Planning Association, 1955), pp. 238-239.

67. *Ibid.,* p. 239.

68. Laing, *op. cit.,* pp. 416-422.

69. *Ibid.*

Professor Northrup reported similar findings in the early forties. He noted that "the outstanding characteristic of the southern coal industry from a racial-occupational standpoint, is the comparatively high degree of mixing of the races. Besides, since the earnings of piece and day workers are usually about equal, no wage differential based on race is present in the industry." [70]

Finally, in a study conducted during the late forties in the Pocahontas coal field, Professor Minard draws the same conclusions. He also discusses why he thinks equality in the mine occurred.

There is no doubt that the average or typical miner accepts approximate equality of role and status within the mine. This is to be explained by 3 principal factors. There is a sense of community relationship arising from the necessity of sharing common dangers, hardships, obstacles, and class status. Mutual respect is also developed by equality of achievement as measured by the rough standards of evaluation which the miners themselves recognize as criteria of a man's fitness for membership in their group. Finally, there is the standard of efficient performance imposed upon the mine organization by its executive leadership in accordance with which men are selected for preferment upon the basis of their productivity or successful achievement. [71]

Thus, although the coal mining industry of this period contained some outstanding examples of equality, because of unequal treatment in upgrading combined with the advent of mechanization, the Negro proportion of all miners became smaller and smaller.

THE POSTWAR PERIOD TO 1960

The influences on the Negro miner in the postwar period differed mainly in degree from those in the 1933 to 1947 period. Although stripping continued to expand at about the same rate, underground mechanization advanced at a much more rapid pace. Also, the number of small mines in Virginia and West Virginia began to increase, as had Kentucky's in the previous decade. Further, the rapidly increasing productivity was accompanied by a declining output, and large numbers of both white and Negro miners were thrown out of work.

---

70. Northrup, *op. cit.*, p. 160.

71. Ralph D. Minard, "Race Relations in the Pocahontas Coal Field," *Journal of Social Issues*, Vol. VIII (1952), pp. 29-44.

The Negro miners were still concentrated in the jobs being eliminated by mechanization, and they still did not receive their proportionate share of the new jobs created by mechanization. Hence, they were again displaced in disproportionate numbers.

The 1960 Census did not classify the number of coal miners by race, but classified only the number of all miners by race. An explanation of the method used to adjust for this problem can be found in Appendix A.

Decrease of Negro Miners

Although the number of Southern Appalachian coal miners had increased in every decade between 1890 and 1950, the number dropped by more than 50 percent between 1950 and 1960. By 1960, the number of Southern Appalachian coal miners had declined to its 1910 level (Table 11).

Both Negro and white miners decreased rapidly during this period, in contrast to the previous period's 20 percent per decade increase in whites and 20 percent per decade decrease in Negroes. The number of Negroes, however, declined at a much faster rate than did the number of whites. Between 1950 and 1960, the number of white coal miners declined over 50 percent, from 219,655 to 105,289, but the number of Negro coal miners declined almost 75 percent, from 26,136 to 7,108. Consequently, the Negroes' proportion of Southern Appalachian coal miners

TABLE 11. *Bituminous Coal Industry*
Total and Negro Estimated Employment
Southern Appalachian States, 1950 and 1960

	1950			1960		
	Total	Negro	Percent Negro	Total	Negro	Percent Negro
Alabama	20,084	6,756	33.6	7,798	1,983	25.4
Kentucky	64,074	2,965	4.6	30,725	930	3.0
Tennessee	9,323	92	1.0	3,969	39	1.0
Virginia	25,006	900	3.6	16,004	570	3.6
West Virginia	127,304	15,423	12.1	53,901	3,586	6.6
Total	245,791	26,136	10.6	112,397	7,108	6.3

Source: Table 8 and Appendix Table A-3.

decreased from 10.6 percent in 1950 to an estimated 6.3 percent in 1960. This decrease continued the Negroes' decline in numbers and proportions that started in 1930.

Differences in Negro and White Occupational Distribution

The Negroes' place in the occupational structure did not change in this period. They still were relegated largely to the unskilled, underground, blue collar, nonmanagerial jobs, according to all the case histories which the author has seen. Some of the relevant findings of the case studies done during this period are presented below.

In a 1950 study of a West Virginia coal mining community, William Walker found that the whites had the jobs in the machine shops, including most of the best jobs in and around the mines: section boss, tipple boss, machine operator, and so on. Although there were a few Negro machine operators, there were no Negroes above ground in repair shops where the machinists and electricians worked. Walker notes, "when a Negro works in the machine shop, it is as a janitor who sweeps the floor." [72]

In his 1952 study of the southern West Virginia coal mines, Professor Minard noted "a somewhat higher class status is involved [for electricians and machinists] and . . . Negroes have not been employed much in these fields." Although Minard found approximate equality in most nonmanagerial jobs, in management's jobs he found "a horizontal cast line effectively excludes the Negro from recognition." [73]

A 1953 study of segregation patterns in a West Virginia coal camp found that all the highly skilled jobs were filled by white miners. In the captive mine he studied, one-third of the work force was Negro. The top five jobs in the mine, which employed one-fourth of the work force, were "lily-white." These jobs were fireboss, cutting machine operator, loading machine operator, mechanic, and electrician. Thus, all the foremen, craftsmen, and machine operators in this mine were white. Table 12 presents a list of the jobs, wages, and percentage of Negro workers.[74]

---

72. William S. Walker, "Occupational Aspirations of Negro Family Members in a Coal Mining Community," Master's thesis, New York University, 1950, p. 194.

73. Minard, *op. cit.*, pp. 31-32.

74. Jack French, "Segregation Patterns in a Coal Camp," Master's thesis, West Virginia University, 1953, p. 9.

TABLE 12. *Bituminous Coal Industry*
Earnings and Total and Negro Employment by Job Category
One Large Mine, West Virginia, 1953

Job Category	Wage Per Hour	Workers Employed	Percent Negro
Fireboss	$2.90	8	—
Cutting machine operator	2.58	32	—
Loading machine operator	2.58	32	—
Mechanic	2.58	14	—
Electrician	2.58	2	—
Cutting machine helper	2.43	32	50
Loading machine helper	2.43	32	50
Stoker	2.43	24	83
Motorman	2.30	52	35
Trackman	2.28	12	50
Timberman	2.28	10	50
Mechanics' helper	2.28	14	—
Track helper	2.24	12	50
Timber helper	2.24	10	50
Brakeman	2.24	52	35
Total workers		338	33

Source: Jack French, "Segregation Patterns in a Coal Camp," Masters
thesis, West Virginia University, 1953, p. 9.

In a 1955 study of Negro employment in Birmingham that
included the Alabama coal mines, Professor Langston Hawley
found that Negroes "shared in promotional opportunities only to
a limited extent." He found that Negroes were upgraded to
machine jobs only when Negro and white crews worked separately. There were, according to Professor Hawley, apparently
no Negroes in the jobs of hoist engineer, mine electrician, or
maintenance mechanic.[75]

In sum, the Negroes were still concentrated in the lowest job
classifications. The only change in this period from the previous
one was the increase in the types and numbers of jobs in which
Negroes were not receiving their proportionate share.

75. Hawley, *op. cit.*, p. 278.

Mechanization in the 1950's

Just as increased productivity was achieved with the mechanical loader in the 1933-1950 period, it was achieved with the continuous miner in the 1950's. Postwar mechanization differed in several important respects, however.

The first difference was that the continuous miner had a much larger impact on productivity than had the mechanical loader. This difference can be seen by comparing the productivity increases achieved during the implementation of each machine. Between 1930 and 1950, when mechanical loading achieved most of its growth, productivity in Southern Appalachia increased from 5.1 to 6.2 tons per man-day, 20 percent in this 20 year period. The continuous miner began its growth in about 1950, and accounted for 33 percent of United States production by 1960. During this decade, productivity in Southern Appalachia increased from 6.2 to over 12 tons per man-day, or almost 100 percent.[76] Thus, productivity increased five times as much in a period half as long. The doubling of productivity combined with a 10 percent decrease in output to slash the total number of Southern Appalachian miners in half between 1950 and 1960. These factors affected both races.

The second difference in postwar mechanization was that the continuous miner not only eliminated unmechanized jobs, but certain machine jobs as well since it replaced undercutting, drilling, and loading machines. This fact is important because miners with previous machine experience would likely be those retained to operate the new continuous miners. Since the old machine jobs had been mainly filled by whites, it is not surprising that almost all the continuous miner operators were white, also.

Another change was that increased proportions of the employees began working in white collar jobs, in jobs on the surface rather than in the mine, and in maintenance rather than direct production jobs. Although blue collar jobs for all United States coal miners declined over 60 percent between 1947 and 1960, white collar jobs declined only 17 percent. Thus, the proportion of white collar (e.g., nonproduction) workers increased from 5.5 percent in 1947 to 12.3 percent in 1960. Likewise, an increasing proportion of the blue collar workers had surface jobs. Ex-

---

76. U. S. Bureau of Mines, *Minerals Yearbook, 1951*, p. 325; *1960*, Vol. II, p. 61.

panding coal preparation operations and, of course, strip mining contributed to this increase.[77]

Finally, underground miners moved into machine maintenance, transportation, and supervisory occupations. Although no figures that include the Southern Appalachian states are available, Illinois' figures provide a fairly analogous example. In 1947, one-quarter of underground workers were in direct production jobs, such as cutting, shooting, and loading coal. By 1956, only one-sixth of the underground miners were in direct production occupations.[78]

There was another side effect of mechanization that resulted in a decreased proportion of Negroes. The mines that did not replace their hand loaders with mechanical loading machines often had a high proportion of Negro employees.[79] Since many nonmechanized mines were forced to close in the fifties when falling demand radically increased competitive pressure, Negro miners lost jobs.

Underground mechanization in Alabama mines followed a somewhat different pattern than the other Southern Appalachian states. First, almost no continuous miners have been used there, because of the nature of Alabama coal seams. On the other hand, almost 100 percent of the Alabama mines use mechanical loaders.[80]

Second, and most important, the method by which the companies mechanized their operations was unique. Often a company would continue to use hand loading in a mine until it was depleted. Only when the company opened new mines would it install machines. This method of mechanization may be accounted for by the fact that because many of Alabama's mines are captives of steel or utility companies, they were under less competitive pressure to mechanize rapidly.[81]

---

77. U. S. Bureau of Labor Statistics, *Technological Change and Productivity in the Bituminous Coal Industry 1920-1960*, Bulletin No. 1305 (Washington: Government Printing Office, 1961).

78. *Ibid.*

79. Interviews, June 1968.

80. In 1967, 97.2 percent of Alabama's underground production was mechanically loaded. National Coal Association, *Bituminous Coal Data, 1967 Edition* (Washington: National Coal Association, 1969), pp. 27 and 56.

81. Interviews, June 1968.

The effect of Alabama mechanization on the Birmingham Negro was hence different from the effect of mechanization on his more northern counterpart. The influence of classification seniority was lessened, because whole mines were closed and everyone was laid off. But another factor was present. Unlike their more northern counterparts, whites flocked to the new mines.

The new mines attracted whites for several reasons. First, some white miners were forced out of the smaller commercial mines because these mines could not compete with the larger units, and closed down. The displaced miners came to the newly opened mines beginning in about 1948. They got the first machine jobs as the new mines opened up. Also, mechanization, higher wages, and better working conditions turned mining into a fairly attractive occupation. Finally, because of their easy accessibility to a large potential labor supply, the new mines had no trouble attracting white (and likely Negro) applicants.

Whites were hired in the new mines in preference to Negroes. This practice resulted partly from the "tradition" of giving preference to white applicants. It also resulted from the same forces that kept Negroes from getting machine jobs in all mines. A final factor that made it possible for a company to hire whites from outside in preference to Negroes who had worked at another of the company's mines was the lack of a companywide seniority system. (It should be noted that the Birmingham UMW negotiated such a seniority system a number of years before it was adopted nationally; but even here it was not adopted until the late fifties.) A miner laid off at one of a company's mines thus had no seniority at its other mines, and so could not demand employment before outsiders were hired.[82]

In sum, the extremely rapid advances of underground mechanization during this period resulted in large decreases in the numbers of both Negro and white miners. But, because the Negroes continued to be concentrated in those jobs eliminated by mechanization and because they did not get their share of the new jobs created, the proportion of Negroes in the work force continued to fall.

---

82. Interviews, June 1968.

Changing Industrial Structure

In about mid-1952, the number of small mines began a rapid increase in Kentucky, West Virginia, and Virginia. Although the number of small mines in Kentucky decreased after 1957, the number in Virginia and West Virginia continued to increase through 1961. These increases likely occurred as a result of the lay-offs in the large mines. Although both whites and Negroes were laid off, only whites tended to enter the small mines, for reasons already discussed. Thus, as the proportions of workers in the small mines increased, the proportion of Negroes in the work force tended to decrease.

Also, the proportion of coal mined in strip operations increased to almost 20 percent in Alabama, and almost 30 percent in Kentucky and Tennessee.[83] Since Negroes received almost no stripping jobs, this increase in stripping resulted also in a decrease in their proportion.

On-the-Job Treatment

Company and union policies and practices, and white community mores continued to influence the Negro in about the same way as in previous periods. In most mines this continuation meant that the companies chose men for the less skilled positions based on ability. It meant that there was no segregation of the work force in most mines, as white and Negro miners worked and ate side by side. It meant that there was one union for all miners, and that the Negro had and exercised equal political rights within the union organization.

But it also meant that race kept Negroes from promotion to the more skilled and desirable jobs, because many operators felt that the Negroes lacked both ability and dependability. It meant that the union grievance process was seldom used to correct the biased promotional policies. Finally, it meant that the white miners continued to support the status quo. A study of the Birmingham mines during this period illustrates a technique that kept Negroes from getting the better jobs.

Promotion in the Birmingham mines was based on classification seniority and past practices. Labor agreements of individual firms specifically sanctioned past practice, as well as classification seniority, for upgrading decisions. The result of these two

83. U. S. Bureau of Mines, *Minerals Yearbook, 1951* and *1960*.

not uncommon promotional techniques was the establishment of informal lines of promotion. None of these practices are inherently discriminatory, but they became tools for discrimination because Negroes were allowed to start only in certain promotional lines. Furthermore, these lines did not lead to the most desirable jobs. For example, Negroes were often found in the promotional line leading from mine helper to trip rider to motorman, but rarely, if ever, found in the lines leading to such jobs as hoist engineer, mine electrician, or maintenance mechanic. Thus, the Negro miner was unable to get certain jobs because he could not get into the promotional lines in which his seniority would have assured him the better jobs. The study concludes that:

In the majority of firms, then, promotion systems include formal or informal promotion lines. These lines of promotion are commonly established on a color basis, and partly as a result of their operation, the Negro shares in promotional opportunities only to a limited extent.[84]

Some companies, however, appear to have been more equalitarian than others during this period. Several Negro interviewees who had worked in southern West Virginia and Kentucky coal mines during the fifties and sixties said Island Creek Coal Company had been *relatively* equalitarian in its hiring and upgrading policies.[85] The results of these practices are evident in 1968, for although the highly mechanized Island Creek mines did not have as large a proportion of Negroes as did a few of their competitors, they had an unusually high proportion of Negroes for mines with a similar degree of mechanization.[86]

MIGRATION

Another factor accounting for the decreasing percentage of Negro miners was the migration of Negroes from the coal fields. Although both Negroes and whites were leaving the fields, the Negroes left at much faster rates. This migration was caused both by unemployment and by the Negroes' dissatisfaction with the coal industry.

---

84. Hawley, *op. cit.*, p. 238.

85. Interviews, June 1968.

86. Data in author's possession.

The following section examines migration patterns in coal mining counties of Alabama, Kentucky, Virginia, and West Virginia. The concluding section discusses the causes of the migration, and its effect on Negro employment in the coal mining industry.

Data from the United States Censuses show three significant migration trends for the major coal mining counties of the Southern Appalachian states. First, the percentage of Negroes in the population has decreased continuously in all the Southern Appalachian states' coal mining counties since 1930 (Table 13). Second, the number of Negroes in the respective areas' populations has decreased continuously since 1940. Third, young Negroes—those just entering the labor force—have left the coal fields much more rapidly than young whites since 1940. The proportion of young Negroes leaving the fields has increased each decade since 1940.

Migration into the Coal Fields

Although the proportion of Negroes in the population began to decrease at an earlier date, the number of Negroes in the coal fields continued to grow through 1940. The percentage of Negroes in the population decreased only because the number of whites grew faster than the number of Negroes before 1940. (Western Kentucky is an exception, as its number of Negroes has decreased each decade since 1900.)

The data for Alabama are relatively meaningless because they include the Birmingham Standard Metropolitan Statistical Area, and Negroes were migrating to the city for reasons other than to mine coal. Also, coal mining was and is only a small part of Birmingham industry, and so it would affect or be affected by migration only to a minor extent. The data for western Kentucky also provide little information of interest, because relatively few Negroes have been employed in western Kentucky mines in the past.

In the other three areas, eastern Kentucky, Virginia, and West Virginia, the major activity was coal mining, and large numbers of Negroes were employed in the mines. In these three areas a clear pattern of migration is evident. Up through the 1920's, there was a large inflow of Negroes into the coal mining counties. With the slowing of production growth and the advent of mechanization in the 1930's, the growth in the Negro population dropped to almost zero. In the 1940's the number of Negroes began to decline at a rapid pace, and during the 1950's the rate

TABLE 13. Coal Mining Counties
Total and Negro Population
Southern Appalachian States, 1890-1960

State	1890	1900	1910	1920	1930	1940	1950	1960
Alabama								
Total	155,817	225,413	337,977	441,424	582,667	629,129	747,151	830,254
Negro	52,485	82,675	123,822	165,595	204,309	217,100	247,770	262,867
Percent Negro	33.7	36.7	36.6	37.5	35.1	34.5	33.2	31.7
Eastern Kentucky								
Total	84,874	115,416	152,426	242,023	348,776	401,454	413,160	334,323
Negro	2,549	3,848	5,577	11,576	15,220	16,552	13,029	9,415
Percent Negro	3.0	3.3	3.7	4.8	4.4	4.1	3.2	2.8
Western Kentucky								
Total	143,323	169,249	176,548	175,567	176,203	177,764	164,628	155,860
Negro	20,698	23,699	23,208	20,963	18,743	16,545	12,312	11,027
Percent Negro	14.4	14.0	13.1	11.9	10.6	9.3	7.5	7.1

	1890	1900	1910	1920	1930	1940	1950	1960
Virginia								
Total	50,447	68,815	91,781	114,668	125,764	141,958	154,059	134,871
Negro	5,315	6,311	6,713	8,282	6,950	7,058	5,937	3,921
Percent Negro	10.5	9.2	7.3	7.2	5.5	5.0	3.9	2.9
West Virginia								
Total	762,794	958,800	1,221,119	1,463,701	1,729,205	1,901,974	2,005,552	1,860,421
Negro	32,690	43,499	64,173	86,345	114,893	117,754	114,867	89,378
Percent Negro	4.3	4.5	5.3	5.9	6.7	6.2	5.7	4.8

Sources: *U. S. Census of Population:*

1910: Vol. II, Chapter 2, Table 1 (for 1890 and 1900).
1920: Vol. III, *Characteristics of the Population,* State Volumes, Table 9 (for 1910 and 1920).
1940: Vol. II, *Characteristics of the Population,* State Volumes, Table 22 (for 1930 and 1940).
1950: Vol. II, *Characteristics of the Population,* State Volumes, Table 41.
1960: Vol. I, *Characteristics of the Population,* State Volumes, Table 27.

Note: Alabama counties: Jefferson, Tuscaloosa, Walker, Shelby.
Eastern Kentucky: Bell, Boyd, Clay, Floyd, Harlan, Letcher, Perry, Pike.
Western Kentucky: Butler, Henderson, Hopkins, Muhlenberg, Ohio, Union, Webster.
Virginia: Dickenson, Russell, Tazwell, Wise.
West Virginia: all counties.

oı decline became even more rapid. Thus, the large inflow of Negroes into the Southern Appalachian coal fields through the 1920's was followed by an increasingly larger outflow thereafter (Table 13). These migration flows are directly related to the factors affecting the Negro coal miner.

The migration patterns of young Negro men just entering the labor force make the change from immigration to emigration even more clear. Between 1930 and 1940, there was a flow of young Negro men into the coal mining counties of all the Southern Appalachian states, with the exception of western Kentucky. This inflow ranged from a one percent increase in West Virginia to a 16 percent increase in eastern Kentucky. There were either decreases or only small increases in young whites in all areas.[87]

A study of migration of three generations of Negroes, made in Raleigh, West Virginia in 1950, confirms the pattern. It showed that the parents of almost all the Negro miners had been Southerners, born in states other than West Virginia. Of the Negro miners themselves, about 58 percent were born in southern states other than West Virginia, and the rest were born in West Virginia. However, 94 percent of the sons of the miners—high school and young adult age groups—were born in West Virginia.[88] These young Negroes were migrating to the northern cities in large numbers. So, while the Negroes of one generation immigrated to the coal fields from the South, their sons and grandsons are now emigrating from the coal fields to northern cities.

Reasons for Out-Migration

Negroes migrated into and then out of the coal fields for largely economic reasons, either the desire for occupational improvement or because of unemployment. The desire for occupational improvement is key to understanding Negro migration. According to the Raleigh study, the miners and their parents migrated from the South to accept mining jobs because they felt they were bettering themselves by entering the mines. The generation entering the labor force since World War II felt they were bettering themselves by leaving mining. For example, 80 percent of the high schoolers and young adults in the Raleigh study felt

87. *U. S. Census of Population, 1940,* Vol. II, *Characteristics of the Population,* State Volumes, Table 22.

88. Walker, *op. cit.,* pp. 47-60.

"they would make more and have a better chance in life doing work other than mining." [89] Not surprisingly, *none* of the boys wanted to make a career of mining. Furthermore, although many of the black miners entered mining with the idea of improving their occupational status, the majority felt at the time of the study that to move out of mining constituted occupational progress, and most of the miners wanted their sons to enter other occupations. [90]

Most Raleigh Negroes considered mining an undesirable occupation and wanted to leave or stay out of mining jobs because they felt that they had been barred from their "best" jobs, such as mechanic, tipple boss, machine runner, etc. More of the Negro miners said mining would be a good occupation if they could advance as easily as whites, but even then most of the sons of the Negro miners preferred not to enter mining.

Most Raleigh Negroes, however, felt that the only opportunity open to them in West Virginia was mining. [91] So to stay out of mining, they left the state. As Raleigh is typical of many coal mining communities in the West Virginia-Virginia-eastern Kentucky fields, it is likely that similar factors motivated Negroes in all these fields. (During World War II, for example, many eastern Kentucky Negro miners left their jobs to work in defense plants, but did not return after the war. The same thing occurred in northern West Virginia.) [92]

The industry, however, was unable to attract even those Negroes remaining in the coal fields. As the census shows, all young Negroes did not leave. Those remaining did not enter mining for two main reasons.

First, the stigma of mining jobs led many Negroes to accept any other available work first. In fact, some of the young Raleigh Negroes remained unemployed rather than go into the mines; in many cases their parents (who were miners) approved of this behavior. [93]

Second, the young Negroes who remained were often the less able. The Negro migrants from the South (including West Vir-

---

89. *Ibid.*, pp. 133, 170, and 202-203.

90. *Ibid.*, pp. 169-170

91. *Ibid.*

92. Interviews, June 1968.

93. Walker, *op. cit.*, pp. 169-170.

ginia) have usually been the best educated and most skilled. The young Negroes leaving the area, therefore, were the very ones best qualified for the better coal mining jobs. Since mechanization has increased the level of competence needed by a miner, those Negroes remaining were even less able to fill the qualifications for the newer jobs.

White-Negro Differentials

Since 1940, therefore, the desire for occupational improvement led many Negroes—both miners and potential miners—to leave the coal fields. After World War II, however, unemployment was probably the major reason for the outward migration of older Negroes who were already miners. Notably, unemployed Negroes and whites had different migration patterns.

The Southern Appalachian coal fields—other than Alabama's—are in extremely mountainous areas. Coal towns are small, isolated communities. In the period before 1960, local whites were reluctant to leave their home communities, even when out of work. As one operator pointed out, it is difficult to induce an unemployed white native to move even fifty miles for a job.[94] C. W. Davis of the Big Sandy-Elkhorn Coal Operators' Association reported:

The majority (of coal miners) are reluctant to leave their established homes and will remain in the area as long as it is possible for them to exist there. The serious unemployment problem and the reluctance of of the unemployed to seek employment elsewhere is well illustrated by the fact that in Pike County (Kentucky) alone where I reside, more than 22,000 persons out of a population of some 83,000 persons are certified as being eligible to receive Government surplus commodities.[95]

As might be expected, native whites who do leave tend to return if work becomes available. The reluctance of their migration is shown by the fact that even those living in the cities often spend their weekends "back home." Every Friday one can see a heavy flow of cars with Ohio tags heading toward southern Kentucky and Tennessee, and a flow North after the weekend.[96]

---

94. Interview, June 1968.

95. Statement of C. W. Davis, Executive Secretary, Big Sandy-Elkhorn Coal Operators Association, Pikesville, Kentucky, *Senate Hearings* on *the Causes of Unemployment in Coal and Other Industries*, 1955, p. 292.

96. Interviews, June 1968.

But this tendency of whites to remain in their local communities even when out of work and to return if work becomes available is not shared by a majority of the Negroes. As one union official pointed out, "Once Negroes leave, they stay gone."[97]

These white and black migration characteristics, when combined with the fluctuations in coal mining employment, may have affected the declining proportion of Negroes in mining. For although the overall trend in employment has been down, there were some fluctuations, and the trend has been up since 1964. When they were laid off, Negroes left the areas permanently. When laid-off miners were recalled, only whites were left. So although decreases caused both whites and Negroes to be laid off, recalls saw mainly the whites coming back.

Thus, the majority of young Negroes did not want to enter the mines because of occupational discrimination, and unemployed Negro miners tended to leave the area faster than unemployed whites. Both factors help account for the decreasing proportion of Negro miners.

---

97. Interview, June 1968.

CHAPTER V

Negro Employment in the 1960's

The coal industry's treatment of the Negro miner has changed little since 1960. Negroes are still concentrated mainly in the lower job classes, and the proportion of Negro miners has continued to decline. As of June 1968, federal and state efforts to enforce equal opportunity laws have had only a limited effect on the industry. Although no data comparable to Decennial Census data were available after 1960, other sources have been used, including employment estimates for the various coal fields and detailed employment and occupational breakdowns for individual mines, given the author by coal company and union representatives.

MINING EMPLOYMENT

The coal industry's revolutionary changes in mechanization and manpower moderated during the sixties. In fact, total employment began an annual increase in 1965. The trend toward more maintenance and service personnel and away from direct operating personnel has continued. There has been a continued growth in the proportion of coal coming from strip mines and a continued concentration of tonnage in the large companies since 1960. *Coal Age* predicted in 1961 that by 1970 the proportion of deep mining employees in maintenance and services would increase 50 percent, while the proportion of miners working at the face would decrease about 15 percent.[98]

In 1967, a *Coal Age* survey of mining companies showed that to replace separations and provide for production expansion, 30,000 men per year for four years would be needed.[99] The men needed in the greatest proportions were managers, maintenance employees, and machine operators.

Negroes have not shared in the recent growth, however, but have continued to decline as a percentage of total miners. Al-

---

98. "Manpower for Coal's New Growth Era," *Coal Age*, October 1961, pp. 196-199.

99. Ivan A. Given, "Manpower for Coal," *Coal Age*, May 1967, pp. 59-66.

though no census data are available, a survey of sample companies, union officials, and others knowledgeable of the situation shows a general consensus that this is the case. In northern West Virginia, both the number and percentage of Negro miners was reported to have declined since 1960. A union official reported that currently 2 to 3 pecent of the miners are Negro.[100]

The proportion of jobs held by Negro miners has also declined in southern West Virginia. For example, a mine in a heavily Negro populated county had 33 percent Negro employees in 1950 but 20 percent by 1968. This is typical of other mines in southern West Virginia. Decreases also occurred in Kentucky. In eastern Kentucky, there are very few Negroes except in the largest companies. Most interviewees said the proportion of Negro miners had also continued to decline in Virginia and Alabama through 1968, although there was some disagreement in the Birmingham fields.[101]

Although it is not comparable to the 1960 Census, a comparison of a matched sample of mines in 1967 and 1968 shows the trend that is occurring in the 1960's (Table 14). The total number of Negroes decreased and the total number of miners increased. If the changes are expressed as percentage change per decade, the number of Negroes decreases at a rate of 17 percent per decade, and the number of whites increases at a rate of 34 percent per decade. Thus, the change between 1967 and 1968 appears very similar to the trend during the thirties and forties, when the number of Negroes decreased 20 percent per decade and the number of whites increased 20 percent per decade.

A 17 percent per decade rate of decline is about the size that would occur if workers who retired were not replaced. It appears, then, that no young Negroes are entering the mines. This was validated by nearly all union and company men interviewed. A refrain echoed by almost all interviewees was that Negroes have not been applying for the mining jobs. Civil rights groups interviewed tended to agree that few Negroes had been applying for mining jobs in the sixties (but said that Negroes had applied for, but not been given, jobs in the forties and fifties).

---

100. Interviews, June 1968.

101. Interviews, June 1968.

TABLE 14. *Bituminous Coal Industry*
Deep Mine Employment by Race
Southern Appalachia and Selected Areas, 1967 and 1968

	1967			1968		
	Total	Negro	Percent Negro	Total	Negro	Percent Negro
Alabama	1,910	523	27.4	1,874	499	26.6
Eastern Kentucky	3,494	181	5.2	3,456	157	4.5
Western Kentucky	2,384	196	8.2	2,476	215	8.7
Northern West Virginia	5,066	259	5.1	5,037	256	5.1
Southern West Virginia	10,266	782	7.6	10,792	776	7.2
Total Southern Appalachia [a]	23,606	1,957	8.3	24,239	1,915	7.9

Source: Data in author's possession.

[a] Includes areas not shown separately.

The young Negroes are not entering mining in the same proportion as young whites in the sixties for exactly the same reason they did not want to mine during the earlier period. They feel that they cannot get the "better" jobs, and hence, in order to make occupational progress they must not become miners.

OCCUPATIONAL DISCRIMINATION

Racial discrimination has lessened over time in the West Virginia-Virginia-eastern Kentucky coal fields, or at least it has become less obvious. There are no longer grievance cases such as one in the late forties, when a company's defense for not promoting a Negro to loading machine operator was only, "We don't hire Negroes as Joy Loader Operators."

But the West Virginia Human Rights Commission still reported a "general pattern of discrimination in the coal mining industry of West Virginia" in 1968. According to one official, "the companies discriminate by failing to hire, train, and promote Negroes in proportion to whites." Although the Negro can get most jobs in West Virginia, the Commission reported "he must be 'head and shoulders' above his white counterpart to get a job on the same level with him." For example, there are few black foremen, electricians, mechanics, or machine operators, although these positions compose over one-third of the work force.[102] In northern West Virginia, field work indicated that although less than half of the whites were in unskilled jobs, 90 percent of the Negroes were in such positions.[103]

The situation is similar in eastern Kentucky, where Negroes made up over 7 percent of the work force, but had less than 2 percent of the skilled or white collar jobs. In several representative Alabama mines, Negroes were not found in occupations such as loading machine operator or loading machine helper, electrician, machinist, etc.[104]

A complete occupational breakdown by color was obtained for one large, and reportedly representative, southern West Virginia mine. In this mine Negroes were greatly underrepresented in mechanized or mechanization-created jobs, and overrepresented in the low paying jobs as Table 15 shows. According to a Chi-square test, there was less than one-tenth of one percent chance that such results could have occurred by random chance, assuming the distributions for white and Negro miners were really equal.

Negroes are still almost nonexistent in white collar and managerial occupations. A sample taken in 1968 (which represented about one-third of Southern Appalachian miners, or 27,843 workers), showed 3,769 or 13.5 percent of all workers to be white collar personnel. However, only seven Negroes, or about .035 percent of all Negro miners, were in these occupations. Thus, Negroes had only about one-four hundredth of their proportionate representation in white collar or managerial jobs. In many areas, moreover, promotion to the more skilled jobs was still generally a prerogative of the foremen, and the criteria used for selection were also much the same as they had been in the earlier periods. According to a representative of a national operators' association, the foreman is primarily responsible for promotion, and workers are promoted based on "whom they travel with," whether they are "reliable and stable," and whether they have "the necessary background to learn the new processes."

---

102. Interview with George E. Chamberlain, Jr., State of West Virginia Human Rights Commission, Charleston, West Virginia, June 6, 1968.

103. Interview, June 1968.

104. Data in author's possession.

TABLE 15. *Bituminous Coal Industry*
Occupational and Earnings Distribution by Race
Production Workers
One Mine, West Virginia, 1968

	Percent of White Employees	Percent of Negro Employees
Occupation		
Mechanized or mechanization-created jobs[a]	34.3	7.3
Other jobs	65.7	92.7
Total	100.0	100.0
Earnings[b]		
Greater than or equal to $3.50 per hour	61.0	32.0
Less than $3.50 per hour	39.0	68.0
Total	100.0	100.0

Source: Data in author's possession.

[a] Jobs included: armature winder, auger operator, bulldozer operator, electrician, electrician's helper, mechanic, shoval operator, continuous miner operator, continuous miner's helper, loading machine operator, machinery repairman, machinery repairman's helper.

[b] Earnings are based on industry averages in West Virginia from U. S. Department of Labor, *Industry Wage Survey, Bituminous Coal Mining*, Bulletin No. 1583, January 1967, Table 19.

Importantly, this representative also contended that Negroes have a lower educational background and lacked the basic skills necessary to operate the machines.[105] Thus, the situation in 1968 had apparently changed very little from that in the previous two decades.

EFFECTS OF CIVIL RIGHTS LEGISLATION

State and national civil rights laws are beginning to have some effect on the coal industry. Many of the mines, however, have too few employees to be affected. The larger companies have definitely felt the impact, and have begun to take steps to give Negroes a more equal chance. One major commercial producer

---

105. Interview, February 1968.

in West Virginia who has joined the Plans for Progress, reported a slight increase in the proportion of Negroes between 1966 and 1967. Other companies are moving to comply with the laws under threat of court action. Some are complying without such threat, because of the laws. As one Alabama operator said, in effect, "Although we did not treat Negroes equal to whites before 1964, we are now hiring and promoting equally, to stay within the law." [106]

On the other hand, many companies are still following past practices, but often complaints are not filed. For example, many of the West Virginia Negroes are allegedly afraid to complain although they are being discriminated against, according to the state commission. They feel—justly or unjustly—that they will lose their jobs if they are identified. Under the West Virginia Human Rights Act, as in United Mine Workers' grievance procedures, the individual complainants must file charges.[107] (This could explain the very low number of union grievance cases on discrimination.)

Civil rights legislation is thus having an effect on the bigger companies. Because of the large number of small company mines, however, the impact in the coal industry will not be as great as in many more concentrated industries.

THE UNITED MINE WORKERS OF AMERICA

Because of the provision in the contract that uses a form of companywide seniority for layoff purposes, the practice of laying off Negroes at worked-out mines and not rehiring them in newly opened mines has generally been halted. The union itself is moving to place Negroes in positions at the district and national level that they have not held in the past.[108] However, progress has been slow, and the UMW has ceased to be a powerful force for equal treatment.

NEGRO MIGRATION AND THE STIGMA OF MINING

The out-migration of Negroes has continued during the sixties in the West Virginia-Virginia-eastern Kentucky fields. It was

---

106. Interview, June 1968.

107. Interview, June 1968.

108. Interview, June 1968.

reported that neither high school nor college graduates are stay-ing in the area. (No trends were reported in western Kentucky or Alabama.) Of course, a large percentage of the white youth is also leaving, but nearly all the young Negroes are leaving.[109]

This high out-migration of Negroes of prime working age has definitely augmented their decline as a percentage of miners dur-ing the sixties. Few Negroes remained in the coal fields to take the increasing number of jobs. As a result, the jobs have been filled almost exclusively by whites. As of 1968, personnel men report they can find no Negroes even to apply for jobs. In one case, the white to black application ratio was 300 to 1. In sev-eral districts, union representatives said that some companies had come to them in search of Negro applicants, but none had been found. Of course, the company's desire for more black miners may be just for window dressing, but the fact remains that it is very difficult to find Negro applicants. The extra effort on the part of some of the companies to find Negroes, with little success, highlights the lack of interest among Negroes in mining. This bias against mining is a continuation of the earlier trend. It was reported that as of 1968 even the Negroes not migrating were reluctant to go into the mines.[110]

ANALYSIS OF FIELD SAMPLE DATA

The field sample, which was taken during the summer of 1968, makes possible quantitative tests of a few of the rela-tionships discussed in this and earlier chapters. Relationships which proved to be significant are as follows:

1. Negroes are virtually absent from all strip and auger mine work forces (Appendix Table B-1).

2. New mines tend to have lower proportions of Negro em-ployees than old mines (Appendix Table B-2).

3. Mines with high proportions of Negro workers tend to be in counties with high proportions of Negroes in their popu-lations (Appendix Table B-3).

4. Highly mechanized mines tend to have low proportions of Negro miners, and vice versa (Appendix Table B-4).

---

109. Interviews, June 1968.
110. Interviews, June 1968.

The third relationship includes only deep mines, of course, and the fourth relationship was testable only in the southern West Virginia fields. A short discussion of the limitations of the data appears in Appendix B.

Mechanization

Within a given area, the degree of mechanization in a deep mine can be approximated by its productivity rate. Although some variations in productivity will occur as a result of geographic differences, differences in vein thickness, differences in faults, and so on, the main variations in the productivity rate will be caused by the degree and type of mechanization. This relationship will only hold within the given coal field, however, where differences in characteristics other than mechanization are relatively minor.

Of the various coal fields in the Southern Appalachian states, only southern West Virginia had enough mines included in the sample data to meet the statistical sample size requirements. Within this area, the relation between percentages of Negro employees and degree of mechanization was shown by testing the relationship between the mines' productivity and their proportion of Negro employees. A contingency table of the results appears in Appendix Table B-4 which shows that 75 percent of the mines having a productivity rate higher than 4,000 tons per man-year also had a 4 percent or lower proportion of Negro employees. Conversely, 67 percent of those mines that had productivity rates of 4,000 tons per man-year or lower also had more than 4 percent Negro workers. In short, high-productivity mines tended to have low proportions of Negro employees, and low-productivity mines tended to have high proportions of Negro employees. Because higher productivity is caused primarily by more intense mechanization, it is the most highly mechanized mines that have the lowest proportions of Negro workers.

Several important facts, however, should be noted. The sample is too small to be of much validity, and several major producers in the area were not included because their data for individual mines were not available. This finding, however, does offer further evidence for the hypothesis that the proportion of Negroes in the work force has declined as mechanization has increased because Negroes have not received their proportionate share of mechanized or mechanization-created jobs.

CHAPTER VI

Determinants of Industry Policy

A number of factors are responsible for the racial policies of the bituminous coal industry. Although these factors are causally related, interacting with each other and perpetuating themselves over time, they have been discussed in a static setting so that the basic relationships can be seen. These factors are summarized in this concluding chapter.

THE DEMAND FOR LABOR

As in many other industries, Negroes made their greatest gains in bituminous coal mining during periods of labor shortage. Southern Appalachian coal production grew very rapidly between 1890 and 1920. The demand for labor, of course, also increased at a fast pace. Negroes were hired in large numbers to help meet this demand.

Mechanization radically modified the demand for labor during the period following 1930. Between 1930 and 1950, the mines switched from hand to mechanical loading. After 1950, they switched to continuous mining machines, except in Alabama. Concurrently, the highly-mechanized stripping industry grew rapidly, particularly in Alabama and western Kentucky. Mechanization between 1930 and 1950 resulted in a shift in demand from unskilled hand loaders to machine operators, maintenance personnel, and other skilled workers. With the mechanization came a much decreased demand for additional mine labor. The "twist" in demand was even more rapid after 1950, and the effects were made much more severe by a huge decrease in the total number of miners needed.

The Negro miner suffered from the twist in demand because he held a disproportionate share of the unskilled jobs being eliminated, and because he did not obtain his share of the expanding occupations. Not surprisingly, the proportion of Negro coal miners declined continuously after 1930.

Between 1950 and the early sixties, the period marked by both an increased twist in demand and a sharp decrease in the total number of miners needed, the Negro was even more severely affected. Between 1950 and 1960, 75 percent of the Negroes were eliminated from the industry, compared to a 50 percent decrease in the number of white miners.

From 1963 through 1969 a strong demand for new mine labor developed. The need for new miners has, in fact, almost reached crisis proportions. This acute labor shortage has not, however, attracted new Negroes into the mines. Thus, the classic relationship between labor shortages and Negro employment gains has not occurred recently. The reason for this is primarily the result of the Negroes' disenchantment with coal mining and consequent out-migration.

GOVERNMENTAL PRESSURE

As of 1968, governmental pressure has had only a small effect on the industry's racial policies because many of the coal companies do not have enough employees to fall under the law. Also, perhaps because of the declining importance of the industry, the government has brought relatively little pressure to bear on coal companies.

There are, however, significant exceptions. State agencies in West Virginia are moving against some of the larger coal companies in that state, and some captive coal mines in Alabama are feeling governmental pressure. Overall, however, there appeared to be little progress, as of 1968, toward equalizing the industry's racial policies through governmental intervention.

UNIONISM AND OCCUPATIONAL DISTRIBUTION

Unionism and company reactions to it have both had major impacts on Negro job opportunities. Between 1890 and 1930 there were sporadic but persistent attempts of the United Mine Workers to organize the coal miners in Southern Appalachia. The operators hired large numbers of Negroes to combat these organizing efforts. Negroes were used as strikebreakers and to foment racial unrest. Many operators also felt that the Negro miner was more "docile" and less susceptible to organization than his white counterpart.

The UMW directly influenced the Negroes' position in the industry in several ways. It actively recruited all coal miners regardless of race. It maintained political equality within the union organization and it did not permit layoff policies which were obviously discriminatory. But, very importantly, the UMW did not enforce upgrading equality. Moreover, the UMW stood idly by while its Negro members were displaced and not given a fair share of newly opened jobs. Once the most equalitarian of unions, the UMW failed completely to protect its black members during the last twenty years.

Finally, the UMW's bargaining power, wage policy, and policy toward mechanization have all been major factors in the coal industry's rapid mechanization. Mechanization, of course, was a major cause of the Negroes' demise in the industry when combined with discriminatory placement on machines and a union policy that did not see fit to insist on equal treatment.

COMPANY POLICY AND PRACTICES

In the last analysis, it was the operators who were primarily responsible for both the increasing number of Negroes in the early years and the decreasing number of Negroes after 1930. Thus, preceding 1930 it was management that hired the large numbers of Negroes in response to the companies' need for labor and their attempt to prevent unionization. It was also management that was largely responsible for the disproportionate occupational distributions because the operators retained the prerogative of promoting whom they saw fit, subject, of course, to grievance procedures.

Managerial policy toward civil rights is, of course, largely determined by institutional factors, including community mores. Hiring Negroes in a period of labor shortage and not promoting Negroes because of their perceived inferior qualifications are obvious examples. It is important to note, however, that managerial policy can be modified in spite of exogenous variables; and modified managerial policy can have an impact on the Negroes' position in the industry. Island Creek Coal Company is a case in point. Even in such mines, however, the Negroes never achieved complete equality of upgrading to all positions.

OTHER FACTORS

Because they were less attached to the local areas than were the native whites, the unemployed black miners left the coal fields in greater proportions than the unemployed whites, and hence were not available for recall. Also, because the young Negroes during the late forties, the fifties, and the sixties perceived occupational discrimination, they left the coal fields rather than going into mining. So, occupational discrimination caused the proportion of Negro miners to decrease indirectly because young Negroes did not even apply for coal mining jobs. Other factors such as the increasing proportions of strip mines and small family-and-friend mines, resulted in a decrease of the Negro miners, because both types excluded Negroes.

CONCLUSION

If present trends continue, the black man will vanish from the coal mines during the next three decades. Extremely few young Negroes are entering the mines, so, as the current black miners retire, the number of Negroes becomes increasingly smaller. Only a radical change in the Negroes' perception of the industry can alter this picture. And only a radical change in company, union, and government policy can alter that perception.

Appendix A

Estimate of Negro Coal Mining Employment
Southern Appalachia, 1960

Because the 1960 Census did not tabulate the number of coal miners by race, it was necessary to extrapolate these figures from other data. These data classified all miners by race and all miners by type of mining. Tables A-1 and A-2 present the data used.

TABLE A-1. *Employed Miners and Employed Coal Miners by State Southern Appalachia, 1960*

	Alabama	Kentucky	Tennessee	Virginia	West Virginia
Total miners	11,902	37,519	8,794	19,277	59,098
Coal miners	7,798	30,725	3,969	16,004	53,901
Percent coal miners	65.5	81.9	45.1	83.0	91.2

Source: *U. S. Census of Population, 1960,* PC(1) D, *Characteristics of the Population,* State Volumes, Table 127.

TABLE A-2. *Employed Miners by Race and by State Southern Appalachia, 1960*

	Alabama	Kentucky	Tennessee	Virginia	West Virginia
Total miners	11,902	37,519	8,794	19,277	59,098
Negro miners	3,026	1,135	400	687	3,932
White miners	8,876	36,384	8,394	18,590	55,166

Source: *U. S. Census of Population, 1960,* PC(1) D, *Characteristics of the Population,* State Volumes, Table 129.

The approximate numbers of Negro and white coal miners were estimated by multiplying the numbers of Negro and white miners in a state, by that state's total percentage of coal miners. Because Tennessee had such a low proportion of coal miners to

66

total miners, the breakdown between black and white miners was obtained differently. It was simply assumed that the proportion of Negroes among Tennessee coal miners was the same in 1960 as in 1950. In both 1950 and 1960 Tennessee had insignificant numbers of both Negro and white miners, and thus had an extremely small effect on total Southern Appalachia figures. It was included only so that "Southern Appalachia" would be defined the same way for all years.

These estimates, of course, assume that the same percentage of Negroes are employed in all types of mining. This assumption may not be completely valid, however, since a large majority of Southern Appalachian miners are coal miners. (Tennessee, with only 45 percent of its miners in the coal industry, is an exception.) The estimates for the numbers of coal miners by race and state appear in Table A-3.

TABLE A-3. *Employed Coal Miners by Race and State*
Southern Appalachia, 1950 and 1960

State	1950	1960	Percent Change
Alabama			
Negro	6,756	1,983	—70.6
White	13,328	5,815	—56.4
Kentucky			
Negro	2,965	930	—68.6
White	61,109	29,795	—51.2
Tennessee			
Negro	92	39a	—57.6
White	9,231	3,930a	—57.4
Virginia			
Negro	900	570	—36.7
White	24,106	15,434	—36.0
West Virginia			
Negro	15,423	3,586	—76.7
White	111,881	50,315	—55.0
Total Southern Appalachia			
Negro	26,136	7,108	—72.8
White	219,655	105,289	—52.0

Source: Calculations from Table 8 and Appendix Tables A-1 and A-2.

a Tennessee figure for 1960 based on 1950: Negro percent of coal miners was one percent.

Appendix B

Estimate of Negro Coal Mining Employment
Southern Appalachia, 1968

The data are of two types. The first type covers all the mines in the major coal fields, but consists mainly of estimates, with little quantitative data to back them up.

The second type is a sample of the actual number of white and Negro miners in individual mines, but represents only the large mines. Historically the Negroes have been concentrated in the large mines, and field work in the summer of 1968 indicates this is still the case. Therefore, these mines probably give a fairly accurate representation of the effect of certain characteristics of the industry on the Negro. There are two types of comparisons that cannot be made from the mine sample, however. First, the number and proportion of Negroes in the sample cannot be compared to the number and proportion of Negroes in the Decennial Censuses. This is because the percentage of Negroes in the sample is higher than the percentage of Negroes in the coal mining industry as a whole. Almost all the industry's Negroes are concentrated in the large mines. Since the sample covers only large mines, it tends to overrepresent the proportion of miners who are Negro.

Second, comparisons of the occupational classifications of blue collar workers, among mines and geographic areas, cannot be made because no standard system was followed by the mines when classifying blue collar occupations into the categories of craftsmen, operatives, and laborers. Occupations classified as craftsmen in one mine might well have been classified as operatives in another.

The mine sample covers mines in the states of Alabama, Kentucky, Tennessee, Virginia, and West Virginia. It includes one-third of all miners employed in the Southern Appalachian coal fields. The sample size and makeup vary, of course, with the relationship being tested.

TABLE B-1. *Bituminous Coal Industry*
Employment by Type of Mine and Race
Southern Appalachia Field Sample, 1968

Type of Mine	Total	Negro	Percent Negro
Deep	23,336	1,943	7.4
Strip or auger	1,981	4[a]	0.2
Total	28,317	1,947	6.9

Source: Data in author's possession. The type of each mine in the sample was determined from the *1966 Keystone Coal Buyers Manual* (New York: McGraw-Hill, 1966).

[a] Two of the four Negroes were service workers, probably janitors.

TABLE B-2. *Bituminous Coal Industry*
Employment by Age of Mine and Race
Deep Mines, Southern Appalachia Field Sample, 1968

Age of Mine	Total	Negro	Percent Negro
Opened in 1967 or 1968	474[a]	3	0.6
All other mines	25,862	1,943	7.5
Total	26,336	1,946	7.4

Source: Data in author's possession.

[a] Represents five mines or four different companies.

TABLE B-3. *Bituminous Coal Industry*
Percent Negro Employment versus Percent Negro Population
Deep Mines, Southern Appalachia Field Sample, 1968

Percentage Negro Employment	Percent Negro Population of County		
	Less than 3.5	Greater than or equal to 3.5	Total
Less than 2.10	66	33	50
Greater than or equal to 2.10	34	67	50
Total	100	100	100
Number of mines	29	27	56

Source: Calculations from data in author's possession and Table 13.

TABLE B-4. *Bituminous Coal Industry*
Percent Negro Employment by Productivity Rates
Southern West Virginia Field Sample, 1968

Percent Negro Employment	Productivity Rate in Tons Per Man-year		
	Less than or equal to 4,000	Greater than 4,000	Total
Less than or equal to 4 percent	33	75	53
Greater than 4 percent	67	25	47
Total	100	100	100
Number of mines	9	8	17

Source: Calculations from data in author's possession and the *1966 Keystone Coal Buyers Manual* (New York: McGraw-Hill, 1966).

Note: The Chi-square test gives 97 percent confidence that this result could not have occurred by chance. This sample excluded 10 mines in the area that all belonged to one company. Males only.

Index

Alabama, 11
Anthracite mining, 1
Auger mines, 9
Big Sandy-Elkhorn Coal Operators' Association, 52
Brooks, David, 10n

Caudill, Harry M., 29n, 30, 30n
Chamberlain, George E., Jr., 57n
Christenson, C. L., 11-12, 12n
Coal Age, 54n
Consolidation Coal Company, 13

Davis, C. W., 52, 52n
DeBardeleben, Henry, 19-20
"Dog hole" mines, 29-31

Employment, 3-6, 54-56, 63
  before 1948, 12
  1948-1961, 9-10, 12-13
  1961-1969, 13
Employment and Earnings, 15n

French, Jack, 40n

Given, Ivan A., 13n, 54n

Harris, A. L., 16n, 17n, 21, 21n, 22n, 23, 23n, 24n
Hawley, Langston, 37n, 41, 41n, 46n

Industrial location, 1, 3, 10-12
Industrial structure, 3-12, 45
  competition, 7
  concentration, 10
  markets, 6-7
  mine size, 10, 15, 29-31, 45
  production, 3, 6, 9, 61
  productivity, 3-8, 29
Island Creek Coal Company, 46, 64

Kentucky, 11-12, 15, 32
Knights of Labor District Assembly No. 135, 14
Ku Klux Klan, 23

Labor Advocate, 20n
Labor force, 3, 12-15, 44, 54
Laing, James T., 27n, 37n

McCartney, James, 13
McGrath, Joseph E., 33n

Mechanization, 7-8, 25, 29, 42-44, 61
  effect on Negroes, 7-8, 27, 31, 47
  and labor demands, 31, 62
  and occupational segregation, 36, 42
  UMW policies toward, 36, 64
Minard, Ralph D., 38, 38n, 40, 40n
Mobile Daily News, 20n

National Coal Association, 8n, 9n, 43n
National Industrial Recovery Act, 14, 25
Negro employment
  pre-1890, 16
  1890 to 1933, 16-24
  1933 to 1947, 25-38
  1947 to 1960, 38-46
  1960 to 1969, 54-61
  declines and unemployment, 21, 25-28, 38-40, 46
  effect of migration, 46-53, 59-60, 64
  impact of mechanization on, 8, 29, 33, 43, 60-61
  locational factors, 17-19, 60
Negro jobs, 13, 27, 46
  occupational discrimination, 36-37, 39-41, 46, 51, 56-58, 61
  proportions, 19, 36-37, 39-40, 45, 54-55, 62-63
  in Southern Appalachia, 1, 21, 31
  strikebreakers, 1, 19-21, 63
  in surface mines, 29, 32, 60
  in underground mines, 38
Negro migration, 46-53, 64
Negro occupational distribution, 27, 32-33, 63-64
  blue collar, 13, 40-41, 57
  white collar, 57
New York Times, 13n
Northrup, Herbert R., 3n, 14n, 17, 17n, 20n, 21, 21n, 34-35, 35n, 36, 36n, 38, 38n

Occupational distribution, 13, 40-43, 53-54
  blue collar
    craft and forman, 27, 43, 54
    unskilled, 27

71

PART FIVE

THE NEGRO
IN THE TEXTILE INDUSTRY

by

RICHARD L. ROWAN

TABLE OF CONTENTS

LIST OF TABLES

CHAPTER I

Introduction

Textile manufacturing has been a part of America's economic history since 1790 when Samuel Slater established a cotton factory in Pawtucket, Rhode Island. By 1810, over 200 cotton mills were located in the United States and, for over one hundred years, the textile industry was concentrated in New England, New York, and Pennsylvania.[1] This concentration remained until the mid-1920 period when the South emerged as the major textile producing region of the country. Today, almost one million people are employed in the textile industry with the great majority located in the southern states.

The major concern of this study is to examine racial employment policy in the textile industry with particular reference to the southern experience, since so much of the industry and of the black population are in the South. Also, there has been no other systematic study of Negro employment in textile manufacturing. Broadus Mitchell recognized the problem of blacks in the cotton mills in his classic study of 1921, but the subject was not of prime consideration at the time.[2] Negroes were excluded from the textile industry, almost as a matter of policy, from 1880 to 1960. The 1960 period, however, witnessed a virtual revolution in employment in the southern textile plants, with blacks being used in nearly every aspect of manufacturing. This study attempts to facilitate an understanding of the past practices of employers in dealing with the question of black labor and the present process of accommodation where equal employment policies are being designed.

DEFINITION OF THE INDUSTRY

For purposes of the study, the textile industry is defined as closely as possible in terms of the Standard Industrial Classifica-

---

1. Stanley Vance, *American Industries* (New York: Prentice-Hall Inc., 1955), p. 428.

2. Broadus Mitchell, *The Rise of Cotton Mills in the South* (Baltimore: The Johns Hopkins Press, 1921).

tion (SIC) system. The SIC 22 group, Textile Mill Products, is defined as follows: [3]

This major group includes establishments engaged in performing any of the following operations: (1) preparation of fiber and subsequent manufacturing of yarn, thread, braids, twine, and cordage; (2) manufacturing broad woven fabric, narrow woven fabric, knit fabric, and carpets and rugs from yarn; (3) dyeing and finishing fiber, yarn, fabric, and knit apparel; (4) coating, waterproofing, or otherwise treating fabric; (5) the integrated manufacture of knit apparel and other finished articles from yarn; and (6) the manufacture of felt goods, lace goods, bonded-fiber fabrics, and miscellaneous textiles.

Some of the important classifications in the industry include:

221   Broad Woven Fabric Mills, Cotton

222   Broad Woven Fabric Mills, Man-Made Fiber and Silk

223   Broad Woven Fabric Mills, Wool: Including Dyeing and Finishing

224   Narrow Fabrics and Other Smallwares Mills: Cotton, Wool, Silk, and Man-Made Fiber

225   Knitting Mills

226   Dyeing and Finishing Textiles, except Wool Fabrics and Knit Goods

227   Floor Covering Mills

228   Yarn and Thread Mills

2211   Weaving Mills, Cotton

2221   Weaving Mills, Synthetics

2231   Weaving and Finishing Mills, Wool

2241   Narrow Fabric Mills

The most important three digit and four digit classifications in the industry, in terms of employment, are 225 Knitting Mills and 2211 Broad Woven Fabric Mills, Cotton. A detailed breakdown of employment by SIC code is presented in the following chapter.

Employment in SIC 22 was volatile over the period 1939 to 1968, but the general trend was downward. During 1939-1956 employment ranged between 1.0 and 1.3 million with a peak reached in 1942 when 1,342,000 people were employed. In 1957 textile employment dropped below 1.0 million and has not exceeded that figure since. An all time low in employment was reached in 1963 when only 885,000 were employed; however, a new high for the period 1957-1968 was reached in 1968 with

---

3. U.S. Bureau of the Budget, *Standard Industrial Classification Manual,* 1967, pp. 54-64.

employment at 985,000. Even though the percentage of production workers in the industry has declined consistently since 1939, it remained at 88.6 percent in 1968. There has not been significant growth in textile employment in the past decade, but, in comparison to some other industries, such as steel and paper, the textile industry is one of the largest employers in the United States.

RESEARCH METHODOLOGY

This study relies heavily on the techniques of survey and questionnaire. Despite the well-known shortcomings of such an approach, it appears to be adequate in collecting data in an emotionally-charged area of Negro employment in American industry. Subjective elements are unavoidable when an analysis is made of employment problems relating to Negro workers. Progress in minority employment is difficult to measure and quantification reflects only a part of the picture. In regard to the Negro's job situation in industry, for example, it is not enough to know how many are employed in various jobs; it is necessary to explore the reasons why the numbers appear.

Some of the major questions for which answers are sought are as follows:

1. What is the general background of the company or companies under consideration in terms of location and age?

2. What is the total employment picture in terms of blue collar and white collar job categories? How have Negroes fared in employment?

3. What is the company policy in regard to nondiscrimination in employment? How is the policy implemented?

4. How are employees recruited, selected, and trained? What special efforts are made in regard to Negroes?

5. What is the upgrading procedure for employees and for Negroes in particular?

6. What effect does new technology have on employment? Will the introduction of labor saving equipment affect the Negro disproportionately?

7. What influence has the union had in regard to utilization of the Negro in the plant?

8. In terms of job opportunities for Negroes, how effective has equal employment opportunity legislation been?

9. What can be expected realistically in terms of jobs for Negroes in the industry?

The general approach used in collecting data for the study that may shed light on these and other questions involved: (1) a survey of the literature, (2) a search of relevant census material, and (3) a questionnaire-interview process, including plant visits, to gather current company information. There is probably no other area of social science research that presents as many formidable problems and as much frustration as that of Negro employment. The old adage that it is difficult to do research in the midst of revolution takes on real meaning as one attempts to explore the sensitive job territories claimed by whites and blacks in their struggle for economic security.

Company Data

A total of 46 companies and 444 plants, representing about 30 percent of the industry's total employment in 1968, were selected for study. The selection includes 11 of the 15 largest companies in the industry (over 10,000 employees), 20 middle-sized companies (1,000 to 9,999 employees), and 15 small companies (under 1,000 employees). In addition to the 46 companies that represent the traditional textile industry, the study also covers 4 chemical companies (21 plants) and 5 rubber companies (15 plants), which employ together 66,143 southern workers in fiber production.

The emphasis in the study is on the South since most of the country's textile production is conducted in that area. A total of 27 textile plants in New York and New England were covered, but they are relatively insignificant in terms of racial employment problems. Most of the plants outside of the South are located in areas where there are very few or no Negroes in the population. The textile industry is truly a southern industry today; therefore, the study centers on minority employment in plants distributed as shown in Table 1.

In the six southern states studied, the sample included 271,245 employees or about 41 percent of all southern textile employees in 1968. Since the *same* companies and plants are studied in 1966 and 1968, the profile for 1966 would be roughly equivalent to that shown above. The data indicate that the study is broadly representative of the textile industry. An effort was made to include plants of varying size and geographic location within the states to insure a more general view of industrial race relations in the industry.

TABLE 1. *Textile Mill Products Industry*
Distribution of Employees in Research Sample by State
South Region, 1968

State	Employees (in Thousands) Total (SIC 22)	in Sample	Percent Sample of Total	Number of Plants in Sample
Alabama	42.0	25.6	61.0	44
Georgia	116.0	43.3	37.3	62
North Carolina	275.6	101.6	36.9	168
South Carolina	148.4	67.5	45.5	112
Tennessee	32.9	9.1	27.7	11
Virginia	41.5	24.1	58.1	20
Total	656.4	271.2	41.3	417

Source: U.S. Bureau of Labor Statistics, *Labor in the Textile and Apparel Industries*, Bulletin No. 1635, 1968, p. 58 and data in author's possession.

Employer responses to the study were very good and most agreed to cooperate through personal interviews and/or answering questions pertaining to racial employment practices. Ample time was provided to cover topics in an interview pertaining to company background, racial employment data, manpower policy in regard to minority groups, recruitment, selection and training, the union response to company policy, and the government-employer relationship in equal employment opportunity. Plant facilities were made available in most instances for close observation. The cooperation of companies in allowing open discussion relevant to Negro employment and in making available data that have been handled on a confidential basis has made it possible to present a representative picture of racial employment in the textile industry.

Government Data

The government data used are of two major types: (1) census material and special reports of the Department of Labor, and (2) reports of the agencies responsible for implementing civil rights legislation and executive orders. In addition, the State of South Carolina data covering racial employment are included in the appendix tables for comparative purposes. South Carolina is the only southern state that has published employment data by race and industry over a long period of time.

Two principal agencies, whose work deals exclusively with civil rights matters, cooperated in the study. The Equal Employment Opportunity Commission (EEOC) and the Office of Federal Contract Compliance (OFCC) furnished valuable data within the confines of confidentiality requirements. Discussions with staff members of these agencies have enabled us to gain perspective on certain problems.

The EEOC, in cooperation with the OFCC, collects employer reports, EEO-1, showing total employment, male and female, and employment of Negro, Oriental, American Indian, and Spanish American persons, male and female, in nine standard occupational categories. Additional information covering apprentices and on-the-job trainees is also collected. Data gathered by EEOC are used for analytical purposes by OFCC and a voluntary agency, Plans for Progress. Use of the data by private researchers is governed by agency rules and law in order to protect the anonymity of an individual employer or establishment. This means that the information is available for private use only in an aggregate form where no single employer can be identified.

CHAPTER II

The Textile Industry

Industrial structure is important in determining the conditions under which adjustments to equal employment opportunity pressures will be made. An understanding of the industrial environment in which a company or companies operate facilitates an analysis of Negro employment problems. A more realistic appraisal of the Negro's position, both past and present, can be made through a knowledge of an industry's structure. The purpose of this chapter is to discuss the general background of the textile industry with particular reference to production processes, industrial characteristics, and manpower.[4]

THE PRODUCTION PROCESSES

The production processes in the textile industry are relatively simple.[5] Most mills use standard equipment in the various spinning, weaving, and finishing operations, and few skilled employees are required except as loom fixers. The great bulk of work in a textile plant is performed by unskilled or semiskilled employees. Machine operators, classified as semiskilled labor, hold well over one-half of all jobs in most mills. Unskilled employees are assigned to jobs as janitors, sweepers, and outside helpers.

The purpose here is to define some of the principal operations in a typical integrated textile mill as they relate to technology and labor requirements. The kind of jobs in any industry determines the skill level of the employees and suggests the type of problem to be found in recruiting, selecting, and training

---

4. See U.S. Department of Agriculture, *The American Textile Industry*, Agricultural Economic Report No. 58 (Washington: Government Printing Office, 1964); Leonard W. Weiss, *Economics and American Industry* (New York: John Wiley & Sons, Inc., 1961); and Stanley Vance, *American Industries* (New York: Prentice-Hall, Inc., 1955).

5. See U.S. Bureau of Labor Statistics, *Technology and Manpower in the Textile Industry of the 1970's*, Bulletin No. 1578 (Washington: Government Printing Office, 1968).

personnel. While the overall study pertains to Negro employment in the traditional textile industry, an effort has been made to analyze the development of the labor situation in regard to textile-type operations in chemical and rubber companies which produce man-made fibers. The processes described below do not relate specifically to the latter types of operations, but they would require essentially the same kinds of skill requirements as found in textiles.

Textile production generally begins in the opening room where bales of cotton are opened and fed into a machine that loosens and cleans the fiber. The fiber then passes through a blending machine that is used to mix various fibers together. No more than 5 percent of a mill's labor force is used in opening and blending. The work is basically manual and skill requirements are low. Because of the unskilled nature of the opening process, Negroes are used wherever possible. Since the work has been burdensome and difficult to staff on a stable basis, employers have turned to improvement of technology in recent years. Faster machines have diminished the labor requirement and contributed to the production of better quality fibers through more efficient processing.

After the opening process, the cotton or blended fibers are transferred mechanically to pickers for further cleaning and formation into large rolls called laps which weigh between 60 and 90 pounds. The laps are taken from the machine, weighed by the operator, and manually moved to the next machine. Modern technology has improved the picking process and has led to decreased physical handling by the operator. Floor cleaning operations also have been mechanized requiring less labor. As in opening, management has been motivated, in part, to improve technology in this work area because of high turnover of employees who think the job is too arduous or unpleasant. Negroes are used in most picking operations.

The picking process is followed by transferance of lap rolls to carding machines where the fibers pass between slats and a rotating cylinder. This process cleans, straightens, and parallels the fiber into long strands called card slivers that are mechanically coiled into cans for transfer to the next stage of production. Operators feed the laps into the machines, remove the cans of sliver from the cards, and keep the cards free of waste material. Technology has greatly improved the operation of carding machines in the past decade. New machines can produce more than four times the output of the 1950's, and automated cleaning equipment can reduce an operator's cleaning time by at least 50 percent. These improvements have enabled fewer operators to maintain more machines than in the past.

After carding, the slivers are processed on drawing frames to reduce several loose slivers into a single, more compact strand of the same size. The operators, of which about 25 percent are female, must repair broken strands, service the machines, and change fiber cans. Productive capacity in this operation has been increased through automation about six-fold over the past few years and labor input per unit of production has diminished by 75 percent.

The roving machine further reduces the size of strands, gives them a twist, and winds the twisted strands onto bobbins. The work is semiskilled and an operator is required to tie broken ends of sliver, load empty and remove finished bobbins, and keep the machine clean. About 5 percent of a mill's employment is involved in this operation, with few women employed as operators, because machine tending requires some heavy lifting. Pressures under equal employment legislation in regard to both women and Negroes may cause a change in the labor composition of this and other operations in the future.

Spinning is the final operation in yarn manufacture. The strands are drawn out still further and twisted tightly to form yarn which is then wound onto bobbins. The semiskilled spinners constitute about 20 percent of a mill's employment and are mainly female. Operators must keep the frames loaded with roving bobbins, attach the ends of nearly empty bobbins to full ones, repair broken ends of fiber, and clean the machines. Men usually are used as doffers to remove full bobbins and replace them with empties. In some mills, women are replacing men as doffers in response to a tight labor market. Some employers are studying ways to reduce the labor component of doffing in order that more women can be used. Negroes are also making inroads into spinning and doffing jobs. Faster machines and new laborsaving devices can reduce the need for spinning operators, but, at present, there is more demand for than supply of labor for most spinning operations.

Winding and warping processes transfer the yarn from spinning bobbins onto larger units to be used on looms or for use in a knitting operation. About 10 percent of a mill's employment, consisting mainly of women, is involved in these unskilled operations. The winding process has become increasingly automated with such devices as a mechanical bobbin conveyor, and it is conceivable that unit man-hours can be reduced by as much as 60 percent.

The weaving process in a mill consists of mixing crosswise (filling) threads with lengthwise (warp) threads on a loom to form cloth. In an integrated mill, about one-half of all operators are employed as weavers. Both males and females are used in this operation. The work is more skilled than most textile operations, and weavers receive relatively high wages compared to other operators. A weaving room contains many looms and an individual operator may be responsible for a large number. In a spacious weaving room, it is sometimes difficult to see operators on the floor, even though one is aware that they are working. Technological advances in weaving have occurred in two areas: refinement of conventional equipment and the innovation of shuttleless and foreign-made water-jet looms. In conventional looms, operating speeds have been doubled in the last two decades, while, at the same time, more efficient methods of maintenance have reduced down-time. Both the shuttleless and water-jet looms have advantages over older models, but high change-over costs plus some operating defects combined with improvement in existing equipment have so far prevented widespread adoption of the new looms. The noise level is one of the major problems that management is now addressing itself to in weaving operations. Even the newer weaving equipment apparently operates with more noise than government regulations permit.

There is not rapid employee turnover in weaving operations, and it may be that integration of Negroes into this area will be slower than in other divisions of the textile plant. The weaver's job, and particularly a loom fixer's position, are looked upon as some of the more highly skilled and best jobs in the industry, and whites may be more reluctant to accept competition from blacks here than in the less skilled and less desirable jobs.

The finishing process consists of many distinct operations including bleaching, dyeing, and preshrinking. These operations further improve the qualities of a fabric. Finishing work is generally either unskilled or semiskilled with most of it done by men. Women are employed in the inspection phase of the work. A major improvement in finishing operations has been the replacement of less efficient processes with systems which operate continuously, thereby reducing both time and labor costs.

A brief look at the production process in textile manufacturing suggests several important things in direct relation to a study of Negro employment: (1) most of the operations can be classified as those requiring machine tending or auxiliary help such as sweepers and outside laborers; (2) there are few skilled jobs, with the exception of loom fixing, in any textile plant; (3) most jobs can be learned within a six-months time period; (4) technological change has not altered job classifications greatly in the past decade; and (5) many operations can be performed by women. These factors help to explain why Negroes have been able to make significant gains in the southern textile industry in the past few years. Faced with a tight labor market, employers find that to keep the mills running Negro labor has to be used; the industry, with uncomplicated production processes, is one that can accommodate large numbers of unskilled, untrained, and relatively uneducated workers. The following chapters will analyze the process of accommodation.

INDUSTRIAL CHARACTERISTICS

Table 2 shows employment, payroll, capital expenditures, and other industrial data for the textile mill products industry (SIC 22), and major divisions thereof, for 1967. It can be seen readily that cotton and synthetics weaving mills (SIC 2211 and 2221), knitting mills (SIC 225), and yarn and thread mills (SIC 228) are the most significant parts of the industry in terms of the industrial characteristics presented. Operations in these important facets of the industry are comparable in regard to the composition of employment.

The data in Table 2 present several basic characteristics of the industry that are related to the problem of Negro employment. These include: (1) the textile products industry employs a large number of workers, many of whom are unskilled or semiskilled; the industry is highly labor intensive compared to others such as chemicals, petroleum, or even paper and allied products; (2) payroll is relatively small, which indicates low wage-paying in the industry; however, "textile industry payrolls are of particular importance to the economic health of many small communities in nonmetropolitan areas"; [6] and (3) new

---

6. U.S. Bureau of Labor Statistics, *Labor in the Textile and Apparel Industries*, Bulletin No. 1635 (Washington: U.S. Government Printing Office, August 1969), p. 18.

TABLE 2.   *Textile Mill Products Industry*
Employment, Payroll, Capital Expenditures, and
Other Data by Standard Industrial Classification
1967

| Industrial Characteristics | Total (SIC 22) | Weaving Mills | | Weaving and Finishing Mills, Wool (SIC 2231) | Narrow Fabric Mills (SIC 2241) | Knitting Mills (SIC 225) | Textile Finishing Except Wool (SIC 226) | Floor Covering Mills (SIC 227) | Yarn and Thread Mills (SIC 228) |
		Cotton (SIC 2211)	Synthetics (SIC 2221)						
				Thousands of Employees					
All employees	931	204	108	42	26	241	72	42	119
				Millions of Dollars					
Payroll	4,394	943	529	221	127	1,016	400	222	508
Value added by manufacture	8,003	1,603	888	418	222	1,887	688	570	953
Cost of materials	11,765	1,779	1,394	663	236	2,599	1,017	1,131	1,650
Value of shipments	19,767	3,336	2,303	1,085	455	4,472	1,705	1,703	2,616
Capital expenditures, new	710	168	92	30	15	133	47	40	135

Source: U.S. Bureau of the Census, *1967 Census of Manufactures*, Series MC 67(P)-1, Summary Series, Preliminary Report, April 1969.

capital expenditures are quite low compared to other industries such as paper. Most of the capital expenditure for new plant and equipment and research and development is made by a relatively small number of large companies.[7] A combination of the above factors means that the industry is in a position to employ a large number of relatively unskilled people who have a minimum training capability. While technological change has occurred at a slow rate in the industry, with capital expenditures quite low, machine operations remain comparatively simple. As discriminatory barriers are broken down, particularly in the South, and the labor market becomes tight, uneducated and previously unemployed Negroes should find the textile industry a natural source of employment. While wages would appear low generally, as noted by the size of payroll, they may seem high to a Negro male or female who has had only make-shift or domestic employment. The same industrial characteristics that made it possible for poor whites to enter the mills as operatives, during 1880 through 1960, are likely to do the same for Negroes in the future.

Industrial Structure

The contemporary textile industry developed into its present state from a history of small, individually-owned and controlled companies. As late as 1950, Dewey found that in North Carolina, the largest employer had no more than 7 percent of the state's textile workers and most mills employed less than 100 people.[8] This pattern has continued into the 1970's, except that the trend seems to be in the direction of more consolidation, but perhaps at a slower pace.

Mergers, involving both horizontal and vertical integration, have been important aspects of the history of the textile industry in its efforts to improve profit margins and better control product lines. For example, following similar activity in the post-World War II period, there were approximately 1,100 mergers between 1951 and 1968, with about 80 percent of the assets involved being acquired by the eleven largest textile firms in

7. *Ibid.*, p. 31.

8. Donald Dewey, "Negro Employment in Seventy Textile Mills, October 1950-August 1951," National Planning Association Report No. 6, *Selected Studies of Negro Employment in the South* (Washington: National Planning Association, 1955), p. 180.

1967. Horizontal combinations (mergers of two or more firms on the same level of production such as spinning, weaving, finishing, and retailing establishments) represented 42 percent of the total number made by the eleven largest firms.[9] By contrast, "about one-half of the spindles that changed hands in the period 1940-1946 did so as a result of vertical integration [which involves the combination under one management of operating units in two or more stages in the manufacture and distribution of products] while 18 percent of the mergers were horizontal combinations."[10] Even though such activity may lead to restricted entry and competitive problems for small producers, it has helped to achieve some stability in the industry. The combination movement has not seriously affected the nature of employment opportunities in textile mills and a high labor-capital ratio remains.

Table 3 presents statistics for the fifteen largest textile products companies in 1968. Within the industry, Burlington Industries is by far the largest; however, it employed less than 10 percent of the industry's workers in 1968. In fact, the fifteen largest companies together employed far less than one-half of all employees in the same year. This indicates the competitive nature of the textile industry, with many small operations employing relatively few people. Seven of the fifteen largest firms had their headquarters in the South with most of the remainder based in New York. Even though a majority of the companies maintained headquarters in New York for financial and marketing purposes, most of their employees worked in southern mills. As indicated by the financial and employment data in Table 3, textile companies are not industrial giants in the sense of firms in industries such as chemicals, rubber, automobiles, or steel. Taken as an aggregate, however, the textile industry is a prime source of employment and production in the United States.

The industrial structure of the industry has a considerable effect on racial employment policy. Since no one firm has a large number of employees, a leadership role in regard to civil rights matters has not emerged. Although Burlington is the largest employer in the industry and has been reported in various sources to be the leader in integrating its mills, there appears

---

9. "Window on Washington," *Mergers and Acquisitions,* January-February 1969, pp. 42-43.

10. William Hays Simpson, *Some Aspects of America's Textile Industry* (Columbia: University of South Carolina, 1966), p. 57.

TABLE 3. The Fifteen Largest Textile Mill Products Companies, 1968

Company	Rank[a]		Headquarters	Sales	Assets	Net Income	Invested Capital	Number of Employees	Net Income as Percent of	
	1968	1967							Sales	Invested Capital
				(Thousands of Dollars)						
Burlington Industries	52	55	Greensboro, N.C.	1,619,253	1,192,676	78,952	630,547	83,000	4.9	12.5
J. P. Stevens	106	109	New York	963,163	649,613	32,175	374,473	49,300	3.3	8.6
United Merchants & Manufacturers	155	145	New York	651,968	627,168	21,031	223,545	35,000	3.2	9.4
Kayser-Roth	226	224	New York	425,997	297,910	15,184	124,067	29,500	3.6	12.2
Indian Head	252	279	New York	369,531	248,782	12,072	81,541	19,100	3.3	14.8
West Point-Pepperell	262	247	West Point, Ga.	347,075	242,247	14,768	184,428	20,380	4.3	8.0
M. Lowenstein & Sons	270	276	New York	338,267	236,722	8,074	121,938	18,106	2.4	6.6
Cannon Mills	289	280	Kannapolis, N.C.	308,075	246,368	17,748	208,977	18,000	5.8	8.5
Dan River Mills	298	306	Danville, Va.	285,099	282,157	7,523	135,814	19,000	2.6	5.5
Cone Mills	320	300	Greensboro, N.C.	261,854	222,440	3,450	136,647	14,000	1.3	2.5
Springs Mills	331	320	Fort Mill, S.C.	253,089	344,625	1,899	253,002	19,000	0.8	0.8
Kendall	378	374	Boston	209,827	157,135	9,164	94,660	10,800	4.4	9.7
Fieldcrest Mills	384	399	Eden, N.C.	203,732	143,845	9,579	71,551	11,652	4.7	13.4
Collins & Aikman	437	417	New York	167,545	86,668	6,355	49,092	5,600	3.8	12.9
Riegel Textile	450	440	New York	160,953	124,718	4,450	63,399	9,022	2.8	7.0

Note: Reeves Brothers, Number 495 in the 1967 Directory, fell from the list. Beaunit was acquired by El Paso Natural Gas and was also removed from the list.

[a] Rank among industrial corporations.

Source: Fortune, Vol. LXXIX (May 15, 1969), pp. 170-182.

to be little connection between its policies and programs and the
rest of the industry. As will be discussed later, there are major
differences in the industry in regard to the treatment of the
industrial relations or personnel function which usually handles
the development and implementation of racial employment matters as part of company policy. Many of the small textile companies, as well as some of the large ones, have not invested
heavily, if at all, in developing adequate resources for personnel
administration, including recruiting, selecting, training, and upgrading. This, of course, can interfere with solving difficult human problems in industrial race relations.

Industrial Growth

Tables 4, 5, and 6 show the pattern of growth in textile production during the past ten years. The index of industrial production, shown in Table 4, indicates that output of the textile
products industry has increased almost every year from 1959
to 1968, and the overall trend has been in an upward direction.
Compared to total manufacturing, however, the textile industry
has lagged behind since 1960. The growth in individual companies has not always proceeded smoothly, and overproduction
has plagued the industry on many occasions.

TABLE 4. *Textile Mill Products Industry*
Index of Industrial Production, 1959-1968
(1957-1959=100)

Year	All Manufacturing	Textile Mill Products
1959	106.0	109.2
1960	108.9	105.0
1961	109.7	106.9
1962	118.7	115.2
1963	124.9	116.9
1964	133.1	122.9
1965	145.0	134.9
1966	156.8	142.5
1967	159.7	142.0
1968	166.9	151.5

Source: *Survey of Current Business*, Federal Reserve Index of Quantity
Output.

The data in Tables 5 and 6 present the pattern of production
in some of the important subdivisions of the industry between
1958 and 1968. It is clearly shown that: (1) production has
been increasing slightly; (2) cotton broad woven goods production has remained relatively stable; (3) man-made fiber production has increased greatly; (4) silk and woolen and worsted production has declined; and (5) the output of weaving mills and finishing plants has remained stable except for large increases in
the production of man-made fiber gray goods.

TABLE 5. *Textile Mill Products Industry
Broad Woven Goods Production
1958-1968*

Period[a]	Total	Cotton[b]	Man-Made Fiber and Silk Fabrics				Woolen & Worsted Fabrics[c]
			Total	Rayon and Acetate	Non-Cellulosic	Silk and Other	
Millions of Linear Yards							
1958	11,628	8,974	2,383	1,654	694	35	271
1959	12,414	9,603	2,500	1,619	837	44	311
1960	12,056	9,366	2,404	1,434	928	42	286
1961	11,863	9,168	2,408	1,465	908	34	287
1962	12,301	9,248	2,743	1,576	1,131	36	310
1963	12,104	8,759	3,061	1,727	1,301	3	284
1964[d]	12,766	8,966	3,545	1,583*	1,260†	702**	257
1965	13,431	9,238	3,926	1,640*	1,535†	751**	267
1966	13,304	8,841	4,198	1,576*	1,908†	714**	265
1967	12,747	8,284	4,235	1,626*	1,977†	632**	233
1968	12,693	7,454	5,280	1,829*	2,754†	697**	243

Source: U.S. Department of Commerce, Bureau of Census. (From ATMI,
Textile Hi-Lights, March 1969, p. 10); 1968: *Survey of Current
Business*, October 1969.

a Annual production totals are from quarterly data based on 13-week periods
approximating the calendar quarter, except that the fourth quarter, 1958
was for 14 weeks.

b Over twelve inches in width.

c Finished linear yards. Fabrics principally wool, raised wool, or reprocessed
wool by weight, except felts.

d Beginning first quarter 1964, man-made fiber classification revised.

* 100% filament yarn.

† 100% spun yarn. Fabrics and blends chiefly man-made fibers by weight;
excludes blanketing.

** All other.

TABLE 6. *Textile Mill Products Industry*
Weaving Mills and Finishing Plants Production
1963-1968

Period	Weaving Mills (Gray Goods)		Finishing Plants		
	Cotton[a]	Man-Made Fibers[b]	Whites	Plain Colors	Prints
		Thousands of Linear Yards			
1963	168,098	49,842	3,229,861	2,554,143	1,610,975
1964	175,708	61,714	3,453,441	2,667,554	1,456,989
1965	178,133	66,610	3,638,534	2,800,907	1,443,563
1966	170,050	68,474	3,546,574	2,599,380	1,394,310
1967	159,979	67,175	3,331,519	2,447,906	1,341,988
1968	143,769	77,139	2,883,483	2,190,703	1,300,005

Source: U.S. Department of Commerce, Bureau of the Census. (From ATMI, *Textile Hi-Lights*, March 1969, pp. 8, 9, 11.)

[a] According to the source, it may be assumed that the 1965 figures should be lowered by 3 to 4 percent to make them more comparable to 1966 data because of revised classifications.

[b] Gray goods, blanketing, silk, paper, and other specialty fabrics are excluded. Data for 1964 are not completely comparable to prior information. The scope for 1964 was broadened to include drapery fabrics which were excluded in 1963.

One of the major factors relating to the textile industry's overall economic position, and the production problem in particular, has been imports of textile manufactures. Table 7 shows the significant growth of imports in the industry from 1958 to 1968. The problem of civil rights has arisen in the context of difficult problems of over-production, imports, and competition. It would not be unreasonable for the industry to argue for more import protection based on the urgency of solving Negro employment problems in the South. Cutbacks in employment, resulting in part from imports, could affect Negro employment opportunities, more than jobs for whites, as the doors are opened to blacks in the face of a scarce labor supply.

TABLE 7. *United States Imports of Textile Manufactures*
1958-1968

Year	Total[a]	Cotton	Man-Made Fiber[b]	Wool
	Millions	of Equivalent	Square Yards	
1958	610	492	61	57
1959	976	735	151	90
1960	1,314	1,054	149	111
1961	956	720	151	85
1962	1,519	1,165	213	141
1963	1,474	1,101	221	152
1964	1,517	1,058	328	131
1965	2,059	1,313	566	180
1966	2,796	1,823	798	175
1967	2,569	1,485	934	150
1968	3,279	1,648	1,439	191

Source: U.S. Department of Commerce. (From ATMI, *Textile Hi-Lights*, March 1969, p. 27.)

[a] U.S. Department of Commerce, unit import data converted to equivalent square yards.

[b] Figures through 1961 converted by ATMI from pounds to equivalent square yards; from 1962, U.S. Department of Commerce conversion factors used.

Consumer Orientation

Most textile products are not associated by the consumer with the manufacturer's name. There are, of course, exceptions such as Cannon sheets and pillow cases, but usually brand names, such as Wamsutta and Martex, are not identified in the customer's mind with the respective company. Also, many of the items produced by textile mills are sold under department store labels, such as J.C. Penney and Sears, Roebuck and Co. A lack of direct consumer orientation may contribute to the industry's lack of concern in regard to social problems.

The textile industry is a major supplier to the federal government during war periods, and in recent years this has made the industry vulnerable to pressure in civil rights matters. A recent study estimates that there are 41,000 jobs (about 3 percent of all war created employment) in the textile industry directly related to the Vietnam war.[11] The impact of government in opening up job opportunities for Negroes is discussed later in this volume.

Industrial Location

The South is by far the leading producer of textile products in the United States. By 1965, the cotton-growing states of the South had 18,512,000 spindles compared to 756,000 in New England and 64,000 in other states. The South's leadership in textiles dates back to a period in the 1920's. In 1920, New England was still ahead of the South in the number of spindles, but by 1930 the picture had completely reversed itself (see Table 8). The shift of the industry from New England to the South was prompted mainly by lower costs in the form of labor, transportation, and taxes. Other factors, such as modern equipment in southern mills, availability of a docile, white labor force, and weak unions, played a part in the industry's move.[12] For purposes of the study at hand, it is significant to note that the industry has moved into areas with considerable Negro population while leaving behind mills in sections of the country, such as Maine, Rhode Island, and Massachusetts, where there are few Negroes.

North Carolina and South Carolina have become the most important textile-producing states in the South, and in the nation, with Alabama and Georgia occupying significant positions. Tennessee and Virginia also produce fairly large volumes of textiles. Many small towns in North Carolina and South Carolina, as well as the other states mentioned, have textile mills, but a majority of them employ only several hundred people. This complicates the problem of Negro employment since segregation has been deep-rooted in small, rural communities for many years. It would be a mistake, however, to generalize too much about civil rights matters on an industry-wide basis in the South. Problems, and responses to the problems, vary by location within states and certainly between states.

---

11. "How Peace Will Cut Employment," *Business Week*, February 14, 1970, p. 130.

12. F. Ray Marshall, *Labor in the South* (Cambridge: Harvard University Press, 1967), p. 80.

TABLE 8. *Cotton-System Spindles by Region and State*
1910-1965

Thousands of Spindles

Period	United States	Cotton-Growing States	New England	All Other States	Ala.	Georgia	North Car-olina	South Car-olina	Tenn.	Va.	Connec-ticut	Maine	Massachu-setts	R.I.	New Hamp-shire
							South						New England		
1910	29,189	10,801	16,112	2,275	935	1,861	3,124	3,793	271	332	1,333	1,011	9,836	2,455	1,350
1920	35,480	15,231	18,288	1,963	1,215	2,542	4,955	4,974	400	589	1,393	1,127	11,759	2,676	1,444
1930	34,025	19,122	13,479	1,424	1,862	3,240	6,229	5,676	613	688	1,090	1,036	7,828	2,104	1,302
1940	24,750	18,136	5,884	730	1,800	3,211	5,840	5,519	555	640	518	685	3,331	945	307
1950	22,995	18,244	4,332	419	1,693	3,195	5,975	5,679	554	650	490	631	2,263	698	—
1960	19,956	18,311	1,525	120	1,640	2,917	5,713	6,633	466	559	168	370	567	297	—
1965	19,332	18,512	756	64	1,537	2,885	5,971	6,791	451	562	100	224	256	62	—

Source: U.S. Bureau of the Census, *Cotton Production and Distribution, 1910-1965*, Bulletins 110-202.

Note: Table includes both spindles used in 100 percent cotton production and synthetic fiber production. Southern and New England totals for individual states do not sum to regional totals.

Table 9 illustrates the employment impact of the industrial location of textile mills. The statistics show the clear dominance of the South in textile production in 1966. In the total number of employees, 68.3 percent were in the South and 69.8 percent of all production workers in the industry were so located. The largest competitor to the South in textile employment was the Middle Atlantic area, including the states of New Jersey, New York, and Pennsylvania. Even in those states, however, there were only 151,769 people employed in 1966. Various aspects of the manpower situation are discussed below.

TABLE 9. Textile Mill Products Industry
Total and Production Worker Employment by Region
1966

Regions	All Employees		Production Workers	
	Total	Percent	Total	Percent
United States[a]	927,339	100.0	827,992	100.0
South	632,955	68.3	577,766	69.8
New England	100,052	10.8	86,647	10.5
Middle Atlantic	151,769	16.4	129,753	15.7
North Central	31,025	3.3	24,852	3.0
West	10,503	1.1	8,072	1.0

Source: U.S. Bureau of the Census, Annual Survey of Manufactures, 1966, No. 7.1-7.9.

[a] Sections do not add to United States total because of statistical inaccuracies in state-reporting techniques.

MANPOWER

Employment in the textile industry has been relatively stable over the past thirty years as depicted by data in Table 10. A peak of 1,342,000 employees was reached during the World War II period. In 1957 employment fell below one million and since then it has fluctuated between 885,000 and 985,000.

The textile industry ranks high as a major employer compared to industries such as automobiles, steel, and paper. While it is not a rapidly growing industry, it is one that can offer considerable opportunities to Negroes seeking jobs. This factor makes textiles an important one in a study of industrial race relations.

TABLE 10. *Textile Mill Products Industry*
Total and Production Worker Employment
1939-1968

Year	All Employees (in Thousands)	Production Workers (in Thousands)	Percent Production Workers of All Employees
1939	1,193	1,108	92.9
1940	1,177	1,090	92.6
1941	1,336	1,251	93.6
1942	1,342	1,265	94.3
1943	1,295	1,228	94.8
1944	1,197	1,133	94.7
1945	1,139	1,074	94.3
1946	1,264	1,190	94.1
1947	1,299	1,220	93.9
1948	1,332	1,248	93.7
1949	1,187	1,103	92.9
1950	1,256	1,169	93.1
1951	1,238	1,146	92.6
1952	1,163	1,073	92.3
1953	1,155	1,064	92.1
1954	1,042	953	91.5
1955	1,050	962	91.6
1956	1,032	944	91.5
1957	981	893	91.0
1958	919	833	90.6
1959	946	857	90.6
1960	924	835	90.4
1961	893	805	90.1
1962	902	812	90.0
1963	885	793	89.6
1964	892	798	89.5
1965	926	827	89.3
1966	964	859	89.1
1967	957	849	88.7
1968	985	873	88.6

Source: U.S. Bureau of Labor Statistics, *Employment and Earnings Statistics for the United States, 1909-68*, pp. 522-523; and for 1968, *Employment and Earnings*, March 1969, Table B-2.

Occupational Distribution

Production workers, normally classified as blue collar, predominate in the textile industry. In 1968, 88.6 percent of all employees in the industry were production workers. (See Table 10.) The industry's technical requirements are less than those found in the aerospace industry, for example, and many of the occupations are of a semiskilled or operative nature. A textile plant's occupational distribution in terms of production workers would more nearly approximate that of a rubber or automobile plant. In this sense, the Negro's disadvantaged position arising from a rigidly segregated society in the South should not provide strong barriers to employment.

Table 11 shows the distribution by occupational groups for the textile plants included in the survey. The blue collar ratio is 87 percent, with about 61 percent in the operatives category. There is probably no other basic industry in the United States with more employees classified as operatives. For example, in the

TABLE 11. *Textile Mill Products Industry*
Distribution of Employment by Occupational Group
1968

Occupational Group	New England and South Region[a]		South Region[b]	
	Number	Percent	Number	Percent
Officials and managers	15,097	5.2	14,099	5.2
Professionals	2,671	0.9	2,387	0.9
Technicians	2,749	1.0	2,556	0.9
Sales workers	1,490	0.5	500	0.2
Office and clerical	18,141	6.3	15,481	5.7
Total white collar	40,148	13.9	35,023	12.9
Craftsmen	37,835	13.1	36,062	13.3
Operatives	171,736	59.6	164,809	60.8
Laborers	31,833	11.1	29,223	10.8
Service workers	6,592	2.3	6,128	2.2
Total blue collar	247,996	86.1	236,222	87.1
Total	288,144	100.0	271,245	100.0

Source: Tables 25 and A-3.

[a] 46 companies, 444 plants.

[b] 40 companies, 417 plants.

paper industry, about 39 percent of all employees were in the category in 1968. There are actually many skills covered by the operatives category in the textile industry with some requiring more training than others; a weaver, who is described generally as a semiskilled operative, may be considered a skilled employee requiring significant training, whereas a sewing machine operator may be relatively unskilled and require little formal training.

There is not an abundance of job opportunities in white collar areas in the textile industry. Table 11 indicates that in the 417 southern plants studied, only 35,023 white collar employees were found, and 29,580 of these were in the two categories of officials and managers and office and clerical. Many of the officials and managers positions are those related to supervising the work force in the mills. All foremen, for example, are included in this category.

The relatively small number of employees in the technical and professional categories suggests a lack of emphasis on research and development. In 1968, only 2.7 percent of all textile employees were classified in the technical and professional occupational group, compared to 9.6 percent in all manufacturing.[13]

Female Employment

The textile industry employs a large and growing proportion of female workers in almost every division of its operations. Table 12 indicates that 45 percent of all employees in the textile mill products industry in 1968 were female with the heaviest concentration in semiskilled jobs in knitting mills (69 percent), narrow fabric mills (58 percent), yarn and thread mills (47 percent), and cotton weaving mills (40 percent). In the other industry divisions, women workers are also found in large numbers. Indeed, some have suggested that almost all jobs in the textile industry can be performed by female labor. In addition to historical precedent, the large number of women workers may be explained by the fact that "textile production is responsive to wide seasonal and cyclical fluctuation in demand" and "women, more easily than men, can provide a reservoir of labor to meet the peak labor needs of the industry." [14]

---

13. U.S. Bureau of Labor Statistics, Bulletin 1635, *op. cit.*, p. 68.

14. *Ibid.*, p. 24

TABLE 12. *Textile Mill Products Industry*
Total and Female Employment by Standard Industrial
Classification
1967 and 1968

Industry Group	All Employees		Female		Percent Female	
	1967	1968	1967	1968	1967	1968
	(in Thousands)					
Textile Mill Products (SIC 22)	956.9	984.9	427.7	447.1	44.7	45.4
Weaving Mills, Cotton (SIC 221)	236.2	232.9	92.7	93.0	39.2	39.9
Weaving Mills, Synthetics (SIC 222)	101.1	105.1	36.1	37.9	35.7	36.1
Weaving and Finishing Mills, Wool (SIC 223)	43.4	44.2	15.7	16.3	36.2	36.9
Narrow Fabric Mills (SIC 224)	30.5	31.1	17.4	18.0	57.0	57.9
Knitting Mills (SIC 225)	229.7	240.6	157.3	165.8	68.5	68.9
Textile Finishing, Except Wool (SIC 226)	78.5	80.5	19.6	20.5	25.0	25.5
Floor Covering Mills (SIC 227)	45.9	51.4	15.0	17.3	32.7	33.7
Yarn & Thread Mills (SIC 228)	114.4	118.7	52.0	55.6	45.5	46.8
Miscellaneous (SIC 229)	77.2	80.6	21.9	22.8	28.4	28.3

Source: U.S. Bureau of Labor Statistics, *Employment and Earnings for the United States, 1909-68*, Bulletin No. 1312-6 (Washington: U.S. Government Printing Office, 1968), pp. 522-555; and *Employment and Earnings*, March 1969, Tables B-2 and B-3.

The introduction of Negro women into textile mills has been a recent phenomenon and one that will be discussed at a later point in this study.

Earnings and Hours

The textile industry ranks quite low compared with most other manufacturing industries in terms of earnings. Average weekly and hourly earnings are below those in all manufacturing and also in the durable and nondurable goods sectors of industry (see Table 13). Low wages reflect, in large measure, the lack of major skill requirements, low educational attainment of em-

TABLE 13. *Textile Mill Products and
All Manufacturing Industries
Earnings and Hours Worked
Production (Nonsupervisory) Workers, 1968*

Industry	Average Weekly Earnings (Dollars)	Average Hourly Earnings	Average Weekly Hours
All Manufacturing	122.51	3.01	40.7
Durable goods	132.07	3.19	41.4
Nondurable goods	109.05	2.74	39.8
Textile mill products	91.05	2.21	41.2
Weaving mills, cotton	90.01	2.19	41.1
Weaving mills, synthetics	96.98	2.25	43.1
Weaving and finishing mills, wool	97.13	2.28	42.6
Narrow fabric mills	88.94	2.18	40.8
Knitting mills	83.07	2.13	39.0
Textile finishing, except wool	99.17	2.35	42.2
Floor covering mills	97.18	2.26	43.0
Yarn and thread mills	85.70	2.07	41.4
Miscellaneous textile goods	102.79	2.43	42.3

Source: *Employment and Earnings*, March 1969, Table C-2.

ployees, and the absence of unions. Average weekly hours in textiles generally are comparable to those in all manufacturing. Some segments of the industry average longer hours, however, and this indicates overtime for employees working in the continuous process operations of the mills.

Even though textile wages appear to be quite low, they may be high compared to others in an area where few job opportunities exist. For many years, the one company textile town was typical in parts of the South and the mill wage, which appeared low by national standards, was considered quite good by mill workers. This has changed in recent years with the movement of industry into the South. Many textile employees now choose to accept higher wage paying opportunities. New industries in

TABLE 14. Textile Mill Products Industry
Average Hourly Earnings of Production Workers by Standard Industrial Classification Groups United States and Regions, 1966

Region	Textile Mill Products (SIC 22)	Weaving Mills Cotton (SIC 221)	Weaving Mills Synthetics (SIC 222)	Weaving and Finishing Mills, Wool (SIC 223)	Narrow Fabric Mills (SIC 224)	Knitting Mills (SIC 225)	Textile Finishing, Except Wool (SIC 226)	Floor Covering Mills (SIC 227)	Yarn and Thread Mills (SIC 228)	Misc. Textile Goods (SIC 229)
United States	1.99	2.01	2.07	2.10	2.00	1.82	2.23	2.00	1.85	2.29
New England and Middle Atlantic	2.15	2.18	2.25	2.16	2.08	2.04	2.41	2.25	1.91	2.28
North Central	2.30	—	—	1.99	—	1.94	2.08	2.34	1.94	2.78
South	1.92	2.01	2.03	2.06	1.82	1.69	2.11	1.87	1.84	1.97
West	2.45	—	—	2.15	—	—	—	—	—	2.92

Source: *Annual Survey of Manufacturers, 1966, General Statistics for Industry Groups and Industries,* M66 (AS)-1 and *Statistics for States, Standard Metropolitan Statistical Areas, and Large Industrial Counties,* M66 (AS) 7.1-7.9, Parts 1-9, Tables 1 and 3.

Note: Constructed from composite regional data where given; individual state data otherwise.

Definition of Regions:

West: Colorado,* New Mexico,* Arizonia,* Utah, Washington,* Oregon, California, Hawaii,* Wyoming,* Montana,* Idaho,* Nevada, and Alaska.*

New England & Middle Atlantic: Maine, New Hampshire, Vermont, Massachusetts, Rhode Island, Connecticut, New Jersey,* New York, and Pennsylvania.*

North Central: Ohio, Indiana, Illinois, Michigan, Wisconsin, Minnesota, Iowa,* Missouri, Nebraska,* Kansas,* North Dakota,* and South Dakota.*

South: Delaware, Maryland, Virginia, N. Carolina, S. Carolina, Georgia, Florida, W. Virginia, Kentucky, Tennessee, Alabama, Mississippi, Arkansas, Louisiana,* Oklahoma,* and Texas.

* Textile employment not included in source sample.

close proximity to textile towns also attract workers who may have gone into the mills as a first point of employment. In response to these changing conditions, textile employers have begun to use Negro male and female employees. The Negro female, in particular, may view compensation in a mill as very good compared to earnings as a domestic.

Low wages were an important factor in the move of the textile industry from New England to the South. Regional data presented in Table 14 show striking differences between earnings in the South and other parts of the country. For example, in 1966, the average hourly earnings of production workers in textiles in New England and the Middle Atlantic states was $2.15 compared to $1.92 in the South. Earnings in the major subdivisions of the industry are also lower in the South than in other regions. The low wage profile is a source of much difficulty in maintaining a stable work force.

Turnover

Table 15 shows the rates for various measurements of turnover in the textile mill products industry by Standard Industrial Classification for 1958, a recession year with high unemployment, and 1968, a period of prosperity and relatively full employment. As would be expected, the turnover rates for 1968 are higher. Separation rates in textile mills rose sharply between 1958 and 1968. The layoff rate in 1968 was less than half the rate in 1958, but the quit rate was twice as high. The high quit rates and low layoff rates indicate that employees found alternative job opportunities in the 1958-1968 period. Many of the industry's white male workers, in particular, appear to have shifted to higher-paying jobs in other industries. The accession rate in the industry also rose substantially from 1958 to 1968, which reflects increasing labor requirements and apparently the availability of black workers. In recent years, some have argued that turnover among employees constitutes the most serious problem of southern mill managers. Given contemporary labor market conditions, employers in the low wage paying textile industry have been forced to hire many marginal workers, in addition to a large number of blacks who have had no previous industrial experience, and this has led to a very unstable work force.

TABLE 15. Textile Mill Products and all Manufacturing Industries
Labor Turnover by Standard Industrial Classification Groups
1958 and 1968

Per 100 Employees	Period	Total Mfg.	Textile Mill Products (SIC 22)	Weaving Mills Cotton (SIC 221)	Synthetics (SIC 222)	Weaving and Finishing Mills, Wool (SIC 223)	Narrow Fabric Mills (SIC 224)	Knitting Mills (SIC 225)	Textile Finishing, Except Wool (SIC 226)	Floor Covering Mills (SIC 227)	Yarn and Thread Mills (SIC 228)	Misc. Textile Goods (SIC 229)
Accessions	1958	3.6	3.2	2.4	2.4	5.3	3.7	3.9	2.1	3.6	3.5	3.8
	1968	4.6	5.3	4.7	4.9	5.0	4.9	5.5	4.0	5.8	6.9	5.4
New Hires	1958	1.7	1.6	1.4	1.4	1.9	2.0	2.1	1.3	1.7	1.8	1.6
	1968	3.5	4.3	3.7	4.0	4.0	4.1	4.4	3.2	5.0	5.6	4.5
Separations	1958	4.1	3.5	2.8	2.7	5.7	3.6	4.0	2.4	3.8	3.7	4.3
	1968	4.6	5.1	4.9	4.7	5.0	4.7	5.1	4.1	5.3	6.6	5.3
Quits	1958	1.1	1.3	1.3	1.1	1.1	1.2	1.5	0.9	1.0	1.4	1.0
	1968	2.5	3.6	3.7	3.5	3.1	3.2	3.4	2.7	3.8	5.1	3.3
Layoffs	1958	2.6	1.8	1.1	1.2	4.0	2.0	2.2	1.2	2.4	1.8	2.9
	1968	1.2	0.6	0.3	0.3	0.9	0.6	0.9	0.5	0.5	0.4	0.8

Source: U.S. Bureau of Labor Statistics, Employment and Earnings Statistics for the United States, 1909-68, Bulletin No. 1312-6, pp. 524-557 and Employment and Earnings, April 1969, Table D-2.

The problems in the textile industry are likely to remain the same, or become worse, unless management invests in sufficient training and orientation programs to help new employees become better related to the work environment. A large mill, or even a small one, with heavy, noisy equipment can be a frightening experience for a person entering a new job. Some inducement for an employee to remain and overcome his or her fear can be provided by improved supervision and training. It is relatively easy for one who has worked for many years in a mill to overlook the enormous psychological problems of a Negro female, for example, who comes to work and whose only exposure to a piece of equipment has been the kitchen stove. The disciplined life of a factory which depends on regularity of employment is foreign to many employees who are entering southern mills today. A great challenge for management in developing techniques of motivation and worker-job relatedness in trying to cultivate a stable labor force continues to exist in the textile industry.

Unionization

The history of unions in the textile industry has been presented by many writers.[15] In general, the story has been one of frustration and failure based on weak unions with poor financing and ineffective programs and strong employers with the ability to recruit strikebreakers in hostile, antiunion communities. The United Textile Workers (an A.F. of L. affiliate developed in 1901) and the American Federation of Textile Operatives (1916-1942) had limited success in organizing textile workers in New England, but the Textile Workers Organizing Committee (a joint effort of the C.I.O. and U.T.W. in 1937) and the Textile Workers Union of America (founded as a C.I.O. affiliate in 1939) and remnants of the United Textile Workers that remained with the A.F. of L. have achieved little on southern territory. Bitter battles such as those fought at Elizabethton, Tennessee and Marion and Gastonia, North Carolina in 1929, the general strike of 1934, and, more recently, the major confrontation at Henderson, North Carolina in 1958, along with the court's deci-

---

15. See, for example, Tom Tippett, *When Southern Labor Stirs* (New York: Cape and Harrison Smith, 1931); Herbert J. Lahne, *The Cotton Mill Worker* (New York: Farrar and Rinehart, Inc., 1944); George S. Mitchell, *Textile Unionism and the South* (Chapel Hill: University of North Carolina Press, 1931); and F. Ray Marshall, *op. cit.*

sions in cases such as the Deering Milliken Darlington, South Carolina episode (1956-1967), have left the southern textile unions demoralized and generally without members. Marshall was accurate in stating that "The experiences of postwar campaigns suggest that a well-financed campaign would probably not succeed even in the more prosperous 1960's." [16] This same conclusion may be reached for the 1970's, regardless of a rapidly changing labor force. Employers who left New England, in part to escape the unions and high labor costs, are committed to running their southern operations on a unilateral basis.

The racial issue has appeared at various times during the history of southern textile unionism. During sporadic independent union activity in the late 1890's in Georgia, the Negro question was raised. A strike in Rome, Georgia in 1890 occurred when the company employed a Negro to replace a white worker, and the employer was forced to reinstate the white employee. This type of activity, of course, warned the employer that employees felt strongly about Negro employment in the mills and unions would be formed to fight it if necessary. Another strike in Atlanta, Georgia occurred in 1897 when the Fulton Bag and Cotton Mill Company employees walked out to protest the hiring of twenty Negro women to work with whites as spinners. A one-day strike ended with the employer agreeing to discharge the Negroes. The force of organization was felt by the employer again as "Another dispute occurred at this mill when the returning strikers presented an ultimatum to the manager to discharge all Negroes, with the exception of janitors and scrubbers. The manager refused, and the workers went out again. This strike also lasted only one day because the manager agreed to segregate all Negro employees." [17] While the employer was willing to listen to the demands of the employees in regard to Negro workers, he was not sympathetic to other demands and the union soon disappeared.

In the Gastonia strike of 1929, the Communist National Textile Workers Union advocated racial equality, and this position was generally exploited by the local press to arouse hatred among white workers. It became somewhat easy for the employers to relate to the white workers that communism and Negro em-

---

16. Marshall, *op. cit.*, p. 279.

17. *Ibid.*, p. 81. (Approximately 75 years later, this company operates with almost all Negro labor.)

ployees followed in the wake of unionism. Trade union efforts following this period have carefully tried to avoid the racial issue, but it will become increasingly more difficult as Negroes are hired in large numbers by the industry.

Lack of any major organizing in the southern textile industry has made the adjustment by employers to civil rights pressures somewhat less complicated than has been true in heavily unionized industries such as paper and steel. Institutionalized seniority systems, based on departmental units and written into collective bargaining agreements, are not characteristic of the southern textile industry where the Negro is now entering the employment picture. Since Negroes were not generally employed in the industry as operatives prior to 1964, the difficult problems of eliminating the present effects of past discrimination do not confront employers. What the hiring of blacks in the industry, as a result of government pressure and tight labor market conditions, portends for union organization is a subject of much speculation among southern textile mill managers today. While most seem to agree that Negroes, as a class, are more organizable than whites, the prospects for immediate unionization are not great.

It could be that the civil rights movement will do for the textile industry what the labor movement never has accomplished; namely, it may force the employer to develop expertise in the industrial relations function that has been neglected but continues to be needed. The mill superintendent, who at one time was expected to handle employee relations and run the plant, needs expert assistance in solving the difficult problems of recruiting, selection, training, and upgrading of employees in a rapidly changing labor market. The manner in which the industry addresses itself to these matters will determine in large measure whether or not the union gains a foothold.

CHAPTER III

The Negro in the Textile Industry to 1900

The history of the Negro in the southern textile industry reveals an interesting pattern of utilization. From the colonial period to the years following Reconstruction, Negroes were used in the limited textile manufacturing activities. Large plantation owners, who engaged in some cloth production in the antebellum years, trained Negro slaves in the methods of spinning and weaving. After the Civil War, however, and the rise of the industry in the South as a means of economic revival, Negroes were almost totally excluded from employment. This situation remained until the early 1960's when a combination of civil rights pressures and labor market conditions opened abundant opportunities for Negroes. The present chapter is concerned with the following early periods of Negro involvement in textile manufacturing in the South: (1) the colonial and revolutionary periods, covering roughly the years of the late eighteenth and early nineteenth centuries, (2) the agricultural period of 1820 to 1860, and (3) the Civil War and Reconstruction periods of 1861 to about 1880. Later periods are discussed in the chapters to follow.

THE COLONIAL AND REVOLUTIONARY PERIODS

It has been fairly clearly established that there was some production of textiles in the South in the colonial and revolutionary periods. The Negro slave was considered a useful element in the domestic production stage of the textile industry. It was relatively easy for the masters to train captive blacks to produce coarse cotton goods on simple machinery. In the plantation economy, labor was generally scarce and it was not unusual for slaves to be placed at spinning and weaving operations.[18]

In the early period, most manufacturing in the United States was done on a domestic production basis usually within the con-

---

18. Ben F. Lemert, *The Cotton Textile Industry of the Southern Appalachian Piedmont* (Chapel Hill: University of North Carolina Press, 1933), p. 15.

fines of a planter's home or workshop. This was true in small individually controlled textile operations on a southern plantation, as well as in the Philadelphia shops of master cordwainers. Under such a system, a planter in the South stated in 1777 that in three months he "trained thirty negroes to make one hundred and twenty yards of cotton and woolen cloth per week, employing a white woman to instruct in spinning and a white man in weaving, and it was said: 'He expects to have it in his power not only to clothe his own negroes, but soon to supply his neighbors.' " [19] The foregoing indicates that as early as 1777 Negroes were being trained by whites to produce cloth. No doubt the product was coarse and used principally to clothe Negro slaves on a plantation, but the example does suggest that relatively unskilled Negro labor was trained to textile operations. Other examples of early development in the textile industry are noteworthy.

In 1789, a South Carolinian by the name of Hugh Templeton, "seeking inventor's privileges, . . . deposited with State authorities a plan for a carding machine and 'a complete draft of a spinning machine, with eighty-four spindles that will spin with one man's attendance ten pounds of good cotton yarn per day.' " [20] Also, in 1795, the South Carolina legislature "authorized commissioners to project a lottery for the benefit of William Mc-Clure in his effort to establish a cotton manufactory to make 'Manchester wares.' " [21] These activities indicate that the South desired, with the rest of the nation, to develop self-sufficiency and a balanced economic condition after the war with England and cessation of colonial commerce. The latter part of the eighteenth century gave rise to limited manufacturing and it appeared, for a brief period, that the South would mix agriculture with manufacturing in an effort to revive. Cotton cloth was produced for family use in the homes and "larger plantations began to run weaving shops, using free and slave labor to make goods both for their own use and for sale to their neighbors." [22] Poor whites and blacks were used together in some instances in early textile

---

19. Broadus Mitchell, *The Rise of Cotton Mills in the South* (Baltimore: The Johns Hopkins Press, 1921), p. 13.

20. *Ibid.*, p. 11.

21. *Ibid.*

22. Lemert, *op. cit.*, p. 17.

operations when plantation owners discovered that the number of slaves was not sufficient to produce the needed cloth.

THE AGRICULTURAL STAGE

The spurt of activity in textile manufacturing in the late eighteenth century was probably misleading as an indication of things to come. The years between 1820 and 1860 were devoted almost exclusively to the production of cotton in the South. Plantation owners discovered quickly that with the increasing price of cotton, and the slave labor system, large profits could be derived from agricultural pursuits alone. Why manufacture cloth when there was so much to gain in cotton growing itself? New England manufacturers were able and willing to process the cotton if southern planters would grow it. Mitchell's words are clear on this point:

A manufacturing development throughout the Piedmont region of the South might have continued parallel with that which has taken place in Pennsylvania, except for the . . . combined influence of the invention of the cotton gin, the institution of slavery, and the checking of . . . immigration . . . . By Whitney's invention . . . cotton planting became so profitable, that for a period of forty years the price remained above twenty-five cents a pound . . . . As cotton and slavery advanced, the population of free white work people were driven further and further into the mountain country, and thus many of the white industrial workers of 1800 became the poor mountain farmers of 1850 . . . the owners of factories who operated with free white labor in 1800 had become in 1850 the cotton planters operating with black slave labor . . . . When the abolition of slavery removed one great difficulty of industries and the white people who had formerly deserted manufacturers for agriculture went back to the pursuits of their fathers, these mountaineers formed the labor supply.[23]

Thus, manufacturing was abandoned for agriculture except for a few scattered efforts. The mills developed in this period were not in any significant sense real forerunners of those arising after 1880. Mitchell argues that the Civil War did not interrupt a continuous development of the textile industry in the South. The "old" mills of the agricultural period were distinctly different from the "new" ones growing out of the campaign in 1880. One would not put much faith in an observation that "the first cotton mill . . . in North Carolina was built at

_____
23. Mitchell, *op. cit.*, p. 10. (Mitchell quotes D.A. Tompkins, *The South in the Building of the Nation*, Vol. ii, p. 58.)

Lincolnton in 1813 by Michael Schenck. . . . This mill was the forerunner of that remarkable industrial development which has taken place in North Carolina since that time." [24]

The "old" mills of the period 1810-1840 differed from those of a later time in several respects. They were subject to being moved about from one water-power location to another; the manager had an industrial background from New England; there was little public enthusiasm for a textile industry; and Negroes were used in many instances. At the stage of development after 1880, the industry became more localized; management was generally native born; the public realized the value of manufacturing; and Negroes were not used in the industry in operative positions. For the purposes of this study, the important distinction drawn here is that which has to do with the Negro, namely, that the Negro was used in many capacities in the mills prior to 1880 but only in a highly restricted manner afterwards. Concerning a mill in Rocky Mount, North Carolina, it was said that "until 1851 slaves and a few free Negroes were worked in this mill." [25] This suggests that blacks were gradually being eliminated from textile operations even before 1880.

The southern textile industry in the mid-nineteenth century was operating on a small scale compared to New England as shown by the figures in Table 16. As cotton manufacturing was held to a minimum, the number of southern cotton planters increased. Aided by the cotton gin, the plantation owners devoted almost full energies to the growing of the staple that was to make them wealthy and others poor. Out of this blind dedication to a one-crop system grew three social classes: the owners, the slaves, and the poor whites. The cotton gin, slavery, and the masters drove a wedge between blacks and whites that has never been completely bridged.

During the period 1840-1860, "cotton planting engaged the labor and the thought and capital of a directing white class, but the natural operative of the South remained unemployed. . . ." [26] Indeed, the system of slavery forced native, poor white southerners into the hills and out of the economic life of the region and discouraged skilled white immigrants from locating in the area. "In 1860 only 6 per cent of the white population of

24 Mitchell, *op. cit.*, p. 15.

25. *Ibid.*, p. 19.

26. *Ibid.*, p. 23.

TABLE 16. *The Textile Industry*
in the South and New England
1840 and 1850

	Census	Plants	Capital	Operatives	Spindles	Bales Consumption
Virginia	1840	22	$1,299,020	1,816	42,262	17,785
	1850	27	1,908,900	2,963	—	—
North Carolina	1840	25	995,300	1,219	47,934	7,000ᵃ
	1850	28	1,058,800	1,619	531,903	13,617
South Carolina	1840	15	617,450	570	16,353	—
	1850	18	857,200	1,119	—	9,929
Georgia	1840	19	573,835	779	42,589	—
	1850	35	1,736,156	2,272	—	20,230
Southern States	1840	248	4,331,078	6,642	180,927ᵇ	—
	1850	166	7,256,056	10,043	—	78,140
New England	1840	674	34,931,399	46,834	1,497,394	—
	1850	564	53,832,430	61,893	—	430,603

Source: Broadus Mitchell, *The Rise of Cotton Mills in the South*, p. 21.

ᵃ Holland Thompson, *From the Cotton Field to the Cotton Mill* (New York: Macmillan Co., 1906), p. 50.

ᵇ Incomplete summary.

the South was foreign-born, but immigrants made up nearly 20 percent of that of the North. In the decade 1850-1860 the South's quota of foreign-born in the whole country dropped from 14 to 13 per cent. Independent white artisans, so important to the industrial history of the North in this period, avoided competition with slave labor; . . ." [27] In this way, the plantation owners stifled the development of most human resources in the South. As slaves were kept servile, whites were denied their very existence, and the importation of foreign mechanical skills was not allowed.

The cotton plantation was to become a self-contained unit, a closed society, in which manufacturing was discouraged because of limited markets and internal and external pressures for the South to produce cotton and the North to manufacture it.

---

27. *Ibid.*, p. 31.

Strained relations between whites and blacks developed naturally from such a system. "From the point of view of the independent white workman the presence of the negro in slavery held as a far more forcible objection than the presence of the negro in freedom. His killing economic competition and radiated social poison were beyond dispute and beyond prospect of remedy until he was made at least a free producer." [28] The antagonism between the races is clearly indicated in the statement above. Negro slaves were employed on the plantations, while whites were practically excluded; Negroes were producing, while whites were parasites on the land; and the competitive conditions were exclusively beyond the control of the poor whites as long as slavery lasted. As far as the social position of the groups was concerned, the Negro had basic needs met by his master and the white was left outside to fend for himself in a system that had totally excluded him.

In regard to employment, it has been noted that ". . . in the period before the War the mills often employed slaves as the exclusive operatives, in some cases negroes were employed with whites, and finally and more importantly, through Reconstruction years and at the very outset of the cotton mill era the inclination of establishers of factories was frequently to engage negro hands and to induce operatives to come from the North and even from England and the Continent—overlooking the native white population as a useful supply of workers as though it had not been there." [29] This observation places heavy emphasis on the fact that Negroes were used in factories as operatives and that native whites were almost completely overlooked. Apparently, the Negro slave on the plantation was a preferred labor source since he was servile, easily managed, and cheap. Slavery made black labor more valuable than white labor and conflict was inevitable once the system was destroyed by war. At the end of the war, one writer stated that the use of Negroes in the slave economy "has done infinite injury to the South. In the past it brought about a condition which drove the white laborer from the South or into enforced idleness. It is important to reestablish as quickly as possible respectability for white labor." [30]

---

28. *Ibid.,* pp. 24-25.

29. *Ibid.,* p. 25.

30. *Ibid.,* p. 27.

Not all southerners of the period were oblivious to the potential dangers of a commitment to cotton as King. William Gregg,
a South Carolinian who established the Graniteville Manufacturing Company, was a voice crying in the wilderness. His message
to contemporaries was not always heard but it was nevertheless
there. Gregg was quick to see that as long as the individual,
rather than the corporate form of business, prevailed in the
South, the textile industry was doomed to failure. In addressing
the legislature, Gregg insisted upon charters of incorporation,
and pointed to New England as a business model for the South.
It was clear to him that "the textile industry could not be a movement in economic society, . . . so long as investment participation sprang from and ended with individual initiative." [31] Few
listened to these words seriously because the cotton planters were
bound to a single interest of accumulating large profits through
agriculture. One of the strongest attitudes concerning the cotton-
growing system was presented by S. C. Hammond who said:

> . . . would any sane nation make war on cotton? Without firing a gun,
> without drawing a sword, should they make war on us we could bring
> the whole world to our feet . . . . What would happen if no cotton were
> furnished for three years? . . . England would topple headlong and carry
> the whole civilized world with her, save the South. No, you do not
> dare to make war on cotton. No power on earth dares to make war
> upon it. Cotton *is* King.[32]

The case may be overly stated, but it indicates that the slaveholders on cotton plantations were convinced that theirs was the
proper cause.

Slave holding was greater in 1860 than 1850; cultivated land
for cotton production increased by 16.4 percent, and the more
than two billion bale cotton crop of 1859-1860 was the largest
up to that time. Various commercial conventions held in the
South between 1845 and 1860 reflected the tendency toward a
greatly unbalanced economic development. At such conventions,
politicians raved about the virtues of agriculture and railed
against the vices of manufacturing.[33] On the other hand, Hinton
Rowan Helper, the Southern anti-slavery advocate, suggested that:

---

31. *Ibid.*, p. 38.

32. *Ibid.*, pp. 48-49.

33. *Ibid.*, pp. 49-50.

... the stupid and sequacious masses, the white victims of slavery ... believe whatever the slaveholders tell them; and thus it is that they are cajoled into the notion that they are the freest, happiest and most intelligent people in the world, and are taught to look with prejudice and disapprobation upon every new principle or progressive movement. Thus it is that the South, hopefully inert and inventionless, has lagged behind the North, and is now weltering in the cesspool of ignorance and degradation.[34]

THE CIVIL WAR AND RECONSTRUCTION

The antebellum South, devoid of any industrial character, received its greatest external challenge in 1861. As the Civil War moved to end slavery, it also ended the romance of a cotton plantation economy. The air was cleared and "with the removal of political obsession vanished its cohort, slavery; slavery gone, it not only became apparent that the South had to change tactics, but that it could change tactics . . . not just the slaves, but the South as a whole was emancipated." [35] Emancipation was extended not only to blacks on plantations but to whites previously excluded from economic life in the South.

The Reconstruction years were difficult for the South as readjustments between all groups in society had to be accomplished. For a period shortly after the War, the South was to be ruled by "a coalition of former slaves and their northern sympathizers." Such a government was "extravagant, corrupt, and incompetent." [36] Obviously, such political regimes were doomed to failure. Whites who were hurt under this system began to strike back and after President Hayes withdrew the federal troops in 1877, they began to develop ways to disfranchise Negroes permanently.

Reconstruction nurtured concepts of work in the South that had never been developed. Once the slaves were set free, whites understood that they must now work and that they could become competitors. As part of the economic revival in the South, it was now believed that the textile mills should be brought to the cotton fields. Several mills were able to survive the Civil War and around this small nucleus textile manufacturing began to grow. The Graniteville Mill, established by Gregg and referred to earlier, became a major operation by 1880. As the difficult

---

34. *Ibid.*, p. 52.

35. *Ibid.*, p. 54.

36. Donald R. Matthews and James W. Prothro, *Negroes and the New Southern Politics* (New York: Harcourt, Brace & World, Inc., 1966), p. 13.

days of Reconstruction came to a close in the late 1870's, cotton manufacturing was well on its way toward permanent establishment. The figures below indicate the rapid advancement of the southern textile industry between 1870 and 1900.

TABLE 17. *The Southern Textile Industry*
1850-1900

Year	Establishments	Capital (Dollars)	Operatives	Spindles	Looms	Cotton (Pounds)
1850	166	7,256,056	10,043	—	—	—
1860	165	9,840,221	10,152	298,551	8,789	45,786,510
1870	151	11,088,315	10,173	327,871	6,256	34,351,195
1880	161	17,375,897	16,741	542,048	11,898	84,528,757
1890	239	53,821,303	36,415	1,554,000	36,266	250,837,646
1900	401	124,596,874	97,559	4,299,988	110,015	707,842,111

Source: Broadus Mitchell, *The Rise of Cotton Mills in the South,* p. 63.

The growth of the industry in the South is reflected in the great relative increases between 1880 and 1890 in the following factors: establishments, 48.4 percent; capital, 209.7 percent; operatives, 117.5 percent; and spindles, 186.7 percent. Indeed, 1880 was the "take off" period for southern textile manufacturing. The census of 1890 reports that:

In considering the geographical distribution of the cotton manufacturing industry the most important fact is the extraordinary rate of its growth in the South during the past decade . . . . It is only in the period since the close of the civil war that mills have been erected in the South for the purpose of entering the general market of the country with their merchandise, and almost all the progress made in this direction has been effected since 1880.[37]

THE CAMPAIGN OF THE 1880's

As already noted, the year 1880 marked the "real reconstruction" in the South and the rise of the cotton textile industry. The people were ready to go to work and build for the future. Columbus, Georgia, completely burned out during the War, had

---

37. U.S. Census of Manufactures, 1890, as quoted by Mitchell, *op. cit.,* p. 66.

revived; Augusta was bristling with manufacturing activity; Charleston, South Carolina was marking the advent of "the dawn of a new era" with the opening of the Charleston Manufacturing Company, a textile concern; and Atlanta was holding a cotton Exposition. All across the South, spirits were aroused to the possibility of economic revitalization based on the concepts of self-help and white labor. Negroes were shunted off to the cotton fields and whites became the operative class in the cotton mills.

The War years and Reconstruction made it brutally clear that politics and a one-crop agricultural system could not fulfill the needs of a struggling society. As one spokesman noted: "We must have less politics and more work, fewer stump speakers and more stump pullers, less tinsel and show and boast, and more hard, earnest work. . . ." [38] This was a general call for the poor whites, who had been denied work opportunities through a plantation-slavery system, to go to work in the mills that were built partly with their economic well being in mind.

Many reasons could be stated for the development of mills in the 1880's. The president of one mill said:

You cannot find any uniformity in the reasons for the establishment of mills. There were a thousand reasons. Sometimes it was salaries that were wanted; sometimes commission houses that were after the charges; sometimes it was to build up the community; sometimes the profits of one mill that brought another into being; sometimes the machinery men; sometimes it was just because they were . . . fools.[39]

General feeling among the people in various areas about poverty stimulated manufacturing interests: "To help the city of Charleston and the people was the simple reason for starting the Charleston Manufacturing Company." [40] The mill owners of this day were merchants of varied backgrounds. Many of them had no particular knowledge of textile manufacturing, but they had a vision of improved economic conditions for their localities through such activity. Leroy Springs, a general mercantile manager in Lancaster, South Carolina, opened a mill through an accumulation of small capital, and the man who began the Charleston Manufacturing Company was in the ice business. Appar-

---

38. Mitchell, *op. cit.*, p. 89.

39. *Ibid.*, p. 96.

40. *Ibid.*, p. 97.

ently a lack of knowledge of cotton manufacturing proved to be
a disadvantage in some cases:

Gen. Irving Walker, a stationery man, was the first president of the
Charleston Manufacturing Company. He was a nice man, but he knew
nothing about the business. That was at the bottom of nine-tenths of the
failures of cotton mills in this State—the presidents were popular, you
know, everybody liked them, but they were incompetent, with no technical
knowledge.[41]

The press was an important factor in drawing attention to
cotton manufacturing in the South. Dawson of the *Charleston
News and Courier* stressed the slogan "Bring the cotton mills to
the cotton fields" and Grady of the *Atlanta Constitution* extolled
the virtues of manufacturing for a rich economy. These spokesmen were sometimes rebuffed by others, such as Edward Atkin-
son of Boston, who made a concerted effort in speeches to have
the South remain in the cotton-growing business, leaving the
cotton mills in New England. The International Cotton Exposition, held in Atlanta in late 1881, provided a forum for those
who were actively engaged in remaking the industrial order and
gave encouragement to those who were already in business;
furthermore, it made the North aware of investment opportunities in the South.[42]

Community self-interest was a prime motivating factor in the
South's awakening. The record is full of accounts of certain
citizens acting in accord with community betterment. Almost
every town desired to have a cotton mill, and they began to
arise in such places as Albemarle, Salisbury, Spartanburg,
Charleston, and Gaffney.[43] To the central theme of this study,
the following observation by Mitchell stands out in stark relief:
"To give employment to the necessitous masses of poor whites,
for the sake of the people themselves, was an object animating
the minds of many mill builders."[44] The words of a manufacturer in 1902 are important in this regard also: ". . . although
negro labor was feasible, abundant, and would be cheapest, the
managements have recognized the fact that the mill life is the
only avenue open today to our poor whites, and we have with

---

41. *Ibid.*, p. 108.
42. *Ibid.*, pp. 113-122.
43. *Ibid.*, pp. 129-134.
44. *Ibid.*, p. 132.

earnestness and practically without exception kept that avenue open to the white man alone to provide an escape from competition with the blacks." [45]

The depressed condition of cotton prices, in the period of the 1880's and following the depression of 1893, was an adjunct to the rise of the mills. The South was now in the cotton manufacturing business to stay and whites were to dominate the employment scene to the almost total exclusion of blacks until nearly one hundred years later.

THE PARTICULAR PROBLEM OF BLACK AND WHITE

It has been pointed out earlier how "the gin, slavery and cotton formed the wedge that pried a unified population apart" between 1820 and 1860.[46] The manufacturing impulse of the late eighteenth century, which may have provided employment for whites and blacks, was extinguished by the property owners' firm commitment to cotton growing. As plantation life developed, large numbers of whites were dispossessed and denied any real participation in the life of the South; "from the time that cotton began to control until after the period of Reconstruction, these people lapsed into the background." [47] The people retreated to the mountains; however, some who remained in the Piedmont section were occasionally used by a landowner when Negro slave labor was not adequate. Just as the cotton culture of the antebellum days had placed whites on the outside of the economic and social order, cotton mills of the 1880's provided them with a chance to re-enter and build for the future.

The poor white, who had become a victim of his environment, had sunk to a level probably lower than "the ordinary plantation negro" by the Civil War.[48] Olmstead wrote in 1856 that "the slaveholders have . . . secured the best circumstances for the employment of that slave-labor which is the most valuable part of their capital. They need no assistance from the poor white man; his presence near them is disagreeable and unprofitable." [49] Strained relationships between blacks and whites emerg-

---

45. *Ibid.,* pp. 136-137.

46. *Ibid.,* p. 161.

47. *Ibid.*

48. *Ibid.,* p. 164.

49. *Ibid.*

ing in this period can be understood better against a system of slavery that "was responsible for the history of the class of unfortunate whites, whether they were left in the low country, stranded upon the sandhills between coastal plain and Piedmont, or driven into the hills." [50] White people developed bitterness toward the Negro slave who appeared to be "employed" and living under more favorable conditions on plantations than they could support by being generally excluded from the system. On the other hand, the Negro slave looked upon whites as parasites on the land who were unsympathetically characterized as "poor white trash." Immediately after cessation of hostilities between the states, free blacks were considered, in many cases, as far superior to whites for labor purposes. The neglected whites made up a motley crew from which the southern mill owner would draw his labor. Once at the mill these people had to have every need taken care of by the employer. Health facilities, schools, homes, and churches had to be established to meet the requirements of whites coming into the mill life. The construction of the mill village was an absolute necessity to accommodate the white employees.

Those who were to operate the new mills found labor in abundance.

Shut out in so many directions the whites, who now find life a bitter struggle, will gladly turn to the spindle and loom as a means of gaining a livelihood. Manufacturing will be their deliverance . . . . For girls and women who have hitherto had no opportunity to earn money the establishment of factories in every town and village will be an incalcuable blessing.[51]

White women began working in the mills in large numbers. In 1880, the Graniteville and Vaucluse mills employed 775 operatives of whom two-thirds were females 11 years of age and up.[52] Testimony of mill superintendents in Augusta, Winston-Salem, and cities in South Carolina gave evidence that white labor was in aboundant supply. As long as this was the case, blacks would be excluded.

The rise of the immigrant was discussed as a means of replacing the Negro and further insuring an all-white labor force

---

50. *Ibid.*, pp. 166-167.

51. *Ibid.*, p. 178.

52. *Ibid.*, p. 181.

in the mills. It was thought by some that the presence of Negro labor had kept immigrants out of the South and if Negroes could be confined to the cotton fields and whites to the mills, the situation could be remedied. There was not unanimity of thought about these matters and many argued that immigration should not be seriously considered until the poor whites had been taken care of satisfactorily. Col. Boykin, the immigration commissioner in South Carolina seemed to be intent "chiefly upon getting laborers who are able to take the place of the negroes." [53] Any attention to the issue of immigrants, prior to 1900, should not overlook the fact that there was ample local white help for southern mill owners to draw upon. The effort to bring in immigrants was based only on some peculiar notion of making sure that Negroes would not be hired or of perhaps improving the skill levels of white workers.

Negroes were used in the cotton mills prior to the Civil War as indicated earlier. Mitchell finds that this should be "considered . . . a proof of the depressing effect of slavery upon the industry than as supporting a contrary argument." [54] In reference to the early philosophy, he states that "in most cases there must have been no further thought behind the use of negroes than it was convenient, cheap and sufficient for the limited project in hand." [55] William Gregg, the South Carolina mill owner, thought that:

. . . experience has proved that any child, white or black, of ordinary capacity, may be taught, in a few weeks, to be expert in any part of a cotton factory; moreover, all overseers who have experience in the matter, give a decided preference to blacks as operatives.[56]

No doubt Gregg had in mind the fact that Negro labor was cheap and controllable under a slave system. He must have had knowledge of mills operating in Tennessee and Virginia with all Negro (slave) labor which was docile and "employed" at little expense to the owner. It has been estimated that the best Negro worker in 1840 could be maintained for only $170 a year and females for much less.

---

53. *Ibid.*, p. 206.

54. *Ibid.*, p. 209.

55. *Ibid.*, p. 210.

56. *Ibid.*

Thompson found Negroes operating in the Rocky Mount, North Carolina mills from 1820 to 1851 and "in 1849 negroes were the only operatives." [57] A similar experience was found at the Saluda factory in South Carolina in the early 1850's:

> The enterprise was of $100,000 capital, and employed 128 operatives, including children; there were 5,000 spindles and 120 looms, the product being heavy brown shirting and Southern stripe. 'The superintendent is decidedly of the opinion that slave labor is cheaper for cotton manufacture than free white labor. The average cost per annum of those employed in this mill, he says, does not exceed $75. Slaves not sufficiently strong to work in the cotton fields can attend to the looms and spindles in the cotton mills . . . .' [58]

The cost of employing a white operative was about $116, so that great savings would accrue to those using slaves. Reports of the Negro operatives at the Saluda factory indicate that they were trained in spinning and weaving and that they were at least equal in efficiency to their white counterparts. Indeed, one observer said ". . . the sources of profitable employment and support to our rapidly increasing African labor are illimitable. . . ." [59] Some contrary views in regard to the Saluda experience are also found in the literature. One superintendent of the plant claimed that the Negro was not successful and another mill manager found the Negro operatives unsatisfactory because their "fingers were clumsy." [60] The important lesson of the experience for our purposes here is that Negro operatives *were* trained and used in the antebellum cotton mills and, regardless of some disparaging comments, they must have made a contribution to the owner's business. The Saluda mill was destroyed by fire when federal troops entered Columbia, South Carolina during the Civil War.

Negroes were employed in cotton mills in various parts of the South, including Alabama, Georgia, South Carolina, North Carolina, Virginia, and Tennessee, prior to the Civil War, and their work compared favorably with white operatives. The lull between 1865 and 1880 witnessed a few experiments where Negroes were to be employed in the mills, such as the one at Con-

---

57. *Ibid.*, p. 211.

58. *Ibid.*

59. *Ibid.*, p. 212.

60. *Ibid.*

garee Mill in Columbia, South Carolina, but these experiments were short-lived—". . . the rare later efforts to use negroes were considered experimental and watched with doubt by outsiders." [61] Any excitement over the possibiilty of using Negro labor in the postwar period based on prewar experience was subdued after 1880 as the cotton manufacturing industry arose to alleviate the adverse effects of war and slavery on the white population.

A study made in South Carolina in 1880, referred to as the Blackman survey of cotton mills, makes little reference to Negroes in the mills; however, it comments on the all-white nature of employment. Of the Glendale factory, it states: "The factory employs 120 operatives, all of whom are white." [62] Blackman's study attempted to explore the pros and cons of using Negro labor, and "he received answers from which it must have appeared pretty evident that negroes were not destined to play a progressive part in the history of the industry." [63] Negative replies were based on "disbelief in the suitability of working negroes and whites together, on the inadaptability of negroes to the employment, and on the plentifulness of whites offering for service in the mills." [64] These factors appear rather strange in view of prior experience where Negroes had been trained as operatives and worked with whites in some instances. Apparently, the free Negro was a different person than the Negro slave in the mill owner's thinking. The last factor mentioned is probably the most reliable of the three in explaining the Negro's absence in the industry after 1880. Mill owners could find white labor in abundance and if there were no advantages to accrue from slave ownership, whites were preferred as employees. It was generally thought that free Negroes and whites could not be worked together without chaos.

One experimental all-Negro textile operation was that projected by Warren Coleman in Concord, North Carolina, in 1896. Coleman was reported to be an illegitimate son of a prominent North Carolinian. He accumulated some capital in Concord renting shacks to Negroes. Using his own funds as a base and help from the white community, as well as stock subscriptions from

---

61. *Ibid.*, p. 213.

62. *Ibid.*, p. 214.

63. *Ibid.*

64. *Ibid.*

Negroes, Coleman opened a textile plant to be operated as an all-Negro venture. A white superintendent was engaged from Massachusetts, but as the operations got underway with inferior equipment and a depressed yarn market little progress was made. Coleman died in 1904 and the mill closed. The Negro labor factor was not the principal source of failure, as much as "poor machinery, insufficient capital, unaccustomed administration." Poor wages and strict overseeing by harsh Negro managers, however, did not encourage a favorable response by Negro operatives. A manager of the mill thought that ". . . under favorable circumstances . . . a mill could be run successfully with white overseers and colored operatives." [65]

Debate continued as to whether or not the Negro could be used in textiles and, if so, to what extent. In 1880, a South Carolinian, H. P. Hammett, reported that in his judgment Negroes could be used to do coarse yarn work with profit to the owner. In another instance, the Charleston Manufacturing Company, which did not succeed with white labor, decided to experiment with Negro operatives. One involved in that situation stated:

The superintendent of the mill and myself . . . got the colored preachers and a negro ex-policeman down here at the bank and showed them the opportunity for the colored people if they would go into the mill and make good operatives. They saw it too, and as far as we know did all they could, but they couldn't make efficiency where it wasn't. The negroes lost a great opening.[66]

This observer had difficulty in understanding why Negroes would not rush into the mills given the opportunity to do so.

We had everybody exhorting them, telling them now was their opportunity, and that if the experiment succeeded here, mills all over the South would be open to them. But when a circus would come, they would all troop away to it. It was a sight to see them. The negroes, shunning the opportunity of their lives, would go for oysters in the oyster season, and then for strawberries in the strawberry season.[67]

The superintendent of the Charleston plant indicated that he had trained 3,000 Negro operatives, but in any day only about 300 would appear for work. Some reflection on the background

---

65. *Ibid.*, p. 216.

66. *Ibid.*, p. 217.

67. *Ibid.*, pp. 217-218.

that the Negro may bring to the industry would perhaps have enabled this observer to understand the situation. Negroes who had experienced a controlled life under slavery were hard pressed to develop work habits under emancipation without emphasis being placed on the particular circumstances. As the southern cotton industry developed around 1880, the Negro had no reason to believe that he would be allowed to live in a mill village, receive the same wages as whites, and otherwise have his every need attended to as was typical of the white operative. It should not have been surprising that the Negro looked upon textile employment (and other employment in industry) with some discouragement since he was generally considered as an extension of a machine rather than as a human being.

Generalizations were soon drawn upon the experiment at the Charleston mill. Mill owners quickly developed the belief that Negro labor was not suitable for their operations. Some, of course, argued against these hasty conclusions indicating that the experiment was not of sufficient duration to test the feasibility of using Negro labor. Selection was also discussed by some as a reason for failure in using Negroes. A mill president stated the matter succinctly:

. . . there are labor troubles in anything . . . running a shoe factory in New England or in picking prickly apples in the Zulu Islands. . . . if I wanted to operate a mill at . . . Charleston, I would employ negroes. I wouldn't work them as those people worked them. I would not pay them half as much as white labor, but just as much. There is no reason why colored labor will not prove profitable.

One cotton mill expert said: "A negro can run a ginning outfit as well as a white man, and is tickled to death with it. *The great trouble with negro labor for cotton mills is poor adaptability to organization"* [68] (emphasis supplied). This observer was far ahead of his time in specifying that the real challenge in utilizing labor (white or black) would be in adapting labor to the organization. He continued: "If I was going to run a mill with negroes, I would want to be right on the ground and study them, and not follow the experiment of trying to run the mill in Charleston with the president living in Spartanburg." [69] Again, the challenge was made to management to be present and study

---

68. *Ibid.*, p. 219.

69. *Ibid.*

the elements of the work situation so that labor could be adapted to the environment in an efficient manner.

Mill owners at the turn of the century were beginning to explore the idea of using Negro operatives as a shortage of white labor was predicted. Such speculation again stimulated a discussion of the relative merits of the Negro as an employee: "Drawbacks are dislike of the negro of working alone, insufficient ambition and pride in his work; daily association in the same employment might make the negro less respectful to the white man." [70] Mitchell suggests that an important factor explaining the antagonism toward blacks was that of "bitter hatred, born of political and racial fear, that followed the war and Reconstruction." [71] Opinions of authorities of the time vary as to the use of Negro labor. A hosiery manufacturer in 1904 reported the use of Negro labor, but indicated that absenteeism was high among Negroes, even though production was about equal with whites.

70. *Ibid.*, p. 220.

71. *Ibid.*

CHAPTER IV

The Negro in the Textile Industry, 1900 to 1960

The conditions surrounding the employment of Negroes in the textile industry at the close of the nineteenth century carried over into the twentieth century. Table 18 shows the small representation of Negroes in the textile industry from 1890 to 1960. The data indicate that between 1940 and 1960 some change in Negro employment was occurring as a result of the industrialiaztion of the South and the beginning of the civil rights movement. This activity is important in understanding the current situation of minority employment in textiles.

At the turn of the century, rapid increases in southern textile production were occurring with the building of many new mills. Thompson observed that:

It seemed as though nearly every mill was profiitable, and the occasional failures did not seriously check the movement, which developed about 1900 almost into a craze in some parts of the South. In these sections every town talked of building one mill or more.[72]

Northern capital and loans of northern commission houses aided in the establishment of southern plants. High expectations of these money sources may have hampered the use of Negro labor in that high returns and efficiency were demanded of human resources. Time could not be permitted for the adequate development of labor; some argued that if Negroes could operate at only 70 percent efficiency while whites could produce at 85 percent, then whites should be employed. Of course, other factors also were responsible for the development of an all-white labor force in the southern textile industry.

---

72. Holland Thompson, *The New South* (New Haven: Yale University Press, 1921), p. 91.

TABLE 18. *Textile Mill Products Industry*
Total Employed Persons by Race and Sex
United States, 1890-1960

	All Employees			Male			Female		
	Total	Negro	Percent Negro	Total	Negro	Percent Negro	Total	Negro	Percent Negro
1890	482,110	5,638	1.2	241,393	4,731	2.0	240,717	907	0.4
1900	597,059	2,744	0.5	296,196	2,005	0.7	300,863	739	0.2
1910	898,992	11,333	1.3	488,928	9,099	1.9	410,064	2,234	0.5
1920	961,668	24,763	2.6	490,333	17,506	3.6	471,335	7,257	1.5
1930	1,183,429	26,202	2.2	689,122	19,815	2.9	494,307	6,387	1.3
1940	1,170,024	24,764	2.1	692,353	21,286	3.1	477,671	3,478	0.7
1950	1,234,020	44,640	3.6	709,950	35,130	4.9	524,070	9,510	1.8
1960	963,040	43,136	4.5	539,190	33,592	6.2	423,850	9,544	2.3

Sources: *U.S. Census of Population*

1890: Special Reports (1900), *Occupations*, Table IV and *Negro Population in the United States, 1790-1915,* Table 20.

1900: *Special Reports, Occupations*, Tables 1 and 3.

1910: Volume IV, *Occupation Statistics*, Table VI.

1920: Volume IV, *Occupations*, Tables 6, 10 (Semiskilled operators, loomfixers, and laborers).

1930: Volume V, *General Report on Occupations*, Table 2.

1940: Volume III, *The Labor Force*, Part I, Table 76.

1950: P-E No. 1D, *Industrial Characteristics*, Table 2.

1960: PC(2)7F, *Industrial Characteristics*, Table 3.

GROWTH IN THE TEXTILE INDUSTRY, 1900-1930

The first few decades of the twentieth century witnessed advances in the textile industry in the South. Conditions favorable to agriculture, such as rising cotton prices, continued at this time, but they did not cause recourse to the past practice of abandoning manufacturing. Cotton growing was a major activity in the South, but its status as "King" was descending. Textile manufacturing had begun on a permanent basis with new mills being built and old ones expanded.

Between 1890 and 1920, the number of bales of cotton consumed by southern mills increased from 545,000 to 3,714,000, while the number of cotton spindles increased from 1,570,000 to 15,231,000. Comparable figures in the same period for northern mills indicate a slower rate of growth, with the number of bales consumed increasing from 1,780,000 to 3,048,000, and the number of spindles in New England increasing from 10,934,000 to 18,-287,000. Shortly after 1920, the cotton textile industry became a "southern industry." The number of bales of cotton consumed by northern mills dropped to 959,000 and the number of spindles in New England fell to 11,351,000 by 1930. (See Table 19.)

TABLE 19. *The Cotton Textile Industry*
Cotton Consumed and Spindle Activity
United States and Regions, 1890-1930

	Bales of Cotton Consumed		Cotton Spindle Activity		
Year	Southern Mills	Northern Mills	Total U.S.	South	New England
1890	545,000	1,780,000	14,384,000	1,570,000	10,934,000
1900	1,597,000	2,047,000	19,472,000	4,368,000	13,171,000
1905	2,140,000	2,139,000	23,687,000	7,631,000	14,203,000
1910	2,292,000	2,507,000	28,267,000	10,494,000	15,735,000
1915	3,193,000	2,816,000	31,964,000	12,956,000	17,101,000
1920	3,714,000	3,048,000	35,481,000	15,231,000	18,287,000
1925	4,220,000	1,639,000	35,032,000	17,292,000	15,975,000
1930	4,238,000	959,000	31,245,000	18,586,000	11,351,000

Source: Ben F. Lemert, *The Cotton Textile Industry of the Southern Appalachian Piedmont*, pp. 35 and 38.

Lemert comments on several factors that contributed to the rise of the southern textile industry during the first decades of the twentieth century. The first is the growth of the tobacco industry. Washington Duke founded the American Tobacco Company in 1890 and much of the money attracted to the South by this venture went into the textile industry. Another member of the Duke family, James, developed the hydro-electric industry in the Piedmont section which relieved the power problems of textile manufacturers. Prior to this time, the industry had to locate on a stream bank or near railroads for a supply of fuel. Electric power made the use of the ring spindle and the automatic loom feasible.

The second factor is the rise of the furniture industry. Manufacturing of furniture began in High Point, North Carolina in 1888, and the money utilized here stimulated textile development. There was a direct relationship between the labor supply for furniture and textile operations. Labor in a furniture plant generally was male, whereas in textiles it was heavily female. On many occasions a textile plant and a furniture plant would be located in the same community with males working in furniture and their wives working in textiles. This early employment pattern mitigated against Negroes going into textile plants.

The third factor is the abundance of labor. This is the important one for the present study.

The Abundance of White Labor

That there was an abundance of cheap, white labor for textile firms to draw upon in their early development is of major significance in understanding the absence of Negroes in the industry. Throughout the Piedmont, from Virginia to Alabama, small tenant farms stood in close proximity to the cotton mills and "if the white man [did] not farm, he must compete with the Negro for a job and [was] glad to find an industry which [gave] the white man preference." [73] Mountain families would frequently come to the Piedmont in search of employment in the mills. These were the people who had been driven out of the mainstream of economic life in the South through slavery and the plantation system. They became the poor whites who developed deep an-

---

73. Ben F. Lemert, *The Cotton Textile Industry of the Southern Appalachian Piedmont* (Chapel Hill, University of North Carolina Press, 1933), p. 47.

tagonism toward blacks and refused to work with them as equals in the reconstructed textile industry. The condition of the mountaineers is vividly portrayed by a Gaffney, South Carolina mill owner:

Many of our people came from the mountains. They came down to the mills, and for six months or a year were terribly dissatisfied and finally resigned and went home. Back there, they never saw anyone, their kids could not go to school, had no one to play with and their wives had no one to talk to. The men folks had had the novel experience of hearing coins jingle in their own pockets and its hard to find even enough to eat back in those mountains. Almost without exception they write back 'For God's sake send us money to come back to the mill village.' The one trip back weans them away from the mountains and brings them into the mill life for good.[74]

The foregoing comment suggests that the mountain family, once settled at the mill, would produce a generation or two of mill hands.

The Piedmont section and neighboring mountain territory produced more white labor than could be used by the mills for many years. A South Carolina mill superintendent stated: "we usually figure on about five children to a family and usually get three of them into the mill, keeping up a steady labor supply." [75] Since whole families had worked on the farm, it was natural that they would now work in the mill. Technological developments in the late 1920 and early 1930 periods, such as the mechanical cotton picker, also increased the supply of labor.

Population changes between 1920 and 1930 gave additional comparative advantages to white workers as the number of Negroes declined and whites increased in many parts of the South. The population of North Carolina, South Carolina, and Georgia increased 23.9, 3.3, and 0.4 percent, respectively, during 1920-1930, while the white population of North Carolina increased 25.3 percent, South Carolina, 15.3 percent, and Georgia, 8.7 percent. Over the same period, the Negro population of South Carolina and Georgia declined, while in North Carolina it increased by 20.3 percent. There was also no significant increase in the foreign population of these states at this time. Labor in the textile industry in the South continued to be native born, white, and abundant. It has been observed that "between 1925 and 1927 over thirty-four thousand additional textile operatives were re-

---

74. *Ibid.*, p. 48

75. *Ibid.*, p. 134.

58 	The Negro in the Textile Industry

ported. Almost none of these came from outside the South, and most were taken from farming." [76]

Another interesting trend in the 1920's was the urban movement as whites, in particular, began to move to the city. Many Negroes had migrated to northern cities between 1910 and 1920. They had few opportunities in the southern cities, except as common laborers, as manufacturing plants attempted to protect whites from Negro competition. [77]

Trade Union Developments in the 1920's

The trade unions made a concerted effort in the late 1920's to organize southern textile workers, but conditions did not permit a great deal of success in the drives to bring mill employees into the union fold. Wages in most textile plants were low but "sufficient to draw the people from the farms and to hold them at the mills." [78] Even though conditions in the mills were poor, they remained better than those found on the farm or in the mountains. The fact that there was a "great negro labor force" in reserve weakened the strength of the employee vis-a-vis the employer, and union scales were rarely paid. [79] During the years 1924-1931, the United Textile Workers of America (UTWA) reported about 30,000 members and in 1932, approximately 27,500. In 1929, the Bureau of Labor Statistics reported "nineteen [locals] in North Carolina; eleven in South Carolina; seven in Tennessee; seven in Georgia; [and] four in Alabama. . . ." [80]

The American Federation of Labor organized a major drive in southern textile plants in 1929 following a strike by the UTWA at Elizabethton, Tennessee in 1928. Strikes occurred in Gastonia and Marion, North Carolina, and Danville, Virginia, as well as various other plants in North and South Carolina, but the results were generally the same: "no trade agreements, no advance in wages, some checking of the stretchout; perhaps improvement of other conditions, such as arbitrary discharge. . . ." [81] There simply was no tradition of unionism in the South and

---

76. *Ibid.*, p. 54.

77. *Ibid.*, pp. 52-53.

78. Thompson, *op. cit.*, p. 109.

79. Lemert, *op. cit.*, p. 60.

80. *Ibid.*, pp. 60-61.

81. *Ibid.*, p. 62.

most employees could not understand why they should pay dues in an organization once a strike was over. Also, mill workers considered the twelve-hour day spent tying threads in a plant far preferable to the hardships of farm labor where even the coarsest food was scarce. Most mill employees were from the same ethnic stock as the mill owners; they attended the same church; and there was an identification of interests. Even if this were not enough to dissuade the white employees to resist the union, they knew that "always the untried potentiality of a great black labor force looms like a threatening cloud in the background" [82] and employers may turn to Negro labor if unions were accepted to push up wage scales. Mill owners and their white employees combined to keep Negroes out of the plant or, if they did gain entrance, it was as common laborers.

Spero and Harris found in 1931 that the unions had not given very much attention to Negroes in the textile industry. Since Negroes were employed in small numbers and in unskilled and nonstrategic positions in the mills, they were not attractive to the unions except perhaps as part of their social philosophy. The Negro was on the periphery of the industry, and there was no practical reason for the union to address itself to his cause. When the American Federation of Labor began its southern drive in textiles in 1928, the problem of the Negro textile worker appeared. Spero and Harris observe: "The A.F. of L. union, the United Textile Workers, wishing to avoid all unnecessary trouble in a difficult situation, did its best to avoid the race issue, and its rival, the communist National Textile Workers' Union, followed the same course when it first entered the southern field." [83] The communists soon changed their position, however, and tried to interest the Negro worker on the basis of social equality. This move provided the southern press and white employers with a means to frighten whites away from the union. The Gastonia, North Carolina paper wrote:

> Do you want your sisters or daughters to marry a Negro? That is what this Communist controlled Northern Union is trying to make you do. We know that no red-blooded Southern white man is going to stand for anything like that, and when these foreign agitators come down here to insult us with such a policy, our answer to them should be in the good old Southern fashion of riding them out of town on a rail.[84]

---

82. *Ibid.*, p. 64.

83. Sterling D. Spero and Abram L. Harris, *The Black Worker* (New York: Columbia University Press, 1931), p. 350.

84. *Ibid.*

Generally, Negroes were skeptical of what appeared to be a sudden "change of heart on the part of the white workers" and did not respond enthusiastically to the appeal to social justice by the union.

THE DECADE OF THE 1930's

By the 1930's, the pattern had been set in regard to racial composition in the mills. During this period of accelerated activity, Thompson characterized labor as follows:

The laborer employed in the manufacturing enterprises of the South, whether white or black, is native born and Southern born . . . . Speaking broadly, those dealing with complicated machines are white, while those engaged in simpler processes are white or black. We find, therefore, a preponderance of whites in the textile industries . . . . There are some skilled workmen among the negroes, . . . but generally they furnish the unskilled labor.[85]

If Negroes were to be found at all, they were in the unskilled jobs, and they were not found in large numbers in the latter, because there was a limited need for common labor in a textile plant.

At the same time that Negroes were being denied opportunities as operatives in the mills, they maintained the right to work outside of the industry in many of the skilled trades and as manual laborers in most parts of the South. Thompson found numerous cases where Negroes and whites worked together on the farms and as plumbers, carpenters, and masons. Also, Negroes were employed in tobacco factories. One important distinction was made in the labor of Negroes: "A negro man may work with white men indoors or out, but he may not work indoors by the side of white women except in some subordinate capacity, as porter or waiter. Occasionally he works with women out of doors." [86] Indeed, in 1915, the state of South Carolina passed a law making it virtually impossible for whites and blacks to work together as mill operatives:

Be it enacted by the General Assembly of the State of South Carolina, That it shall be unlawful for any person, firm or corporation engaged in the business of cotton textile manufacturing in this State to allow or

---

85. Thompson, op. cit., pp. 106-107.

86. Ibid., p. 135.

permit operatives, help and labor of different races to labor and work together within the same room, or to use the same doors of entrance and exit at the same time, or to use and occupy the same pay ticket windows or doors for paying off its operatives and laborers at the same time, or to use the same stairways and windows at the same time, or to use at any time the same lavatories, toilets, drinking water buckets, pails, cups, dippers or glasses: Provided, Equal accommodations shall be supplied and furnished to all persons employed by said person, firm or corporation engaged in the business of cotton textile manufacturing as aforesaid, without distinction as to race, color or previous condition.

This Act shall not apply to employment of firemen as subordinates in boiler rooms, truckmen, or to floor scrubbers and those persons employed in keeping in proper condition lavatories and toilets, and carpenters, mechanics and others engaged in the repair or erection of buildings.[87]

In later years, when mill owners found this law bothersome in times of labor shortage, it was conveniently ignored.

The Negro's position in southern society was a precarious one since southerners acted upon the assumption that Negroes were inferior to all whites. The doctrines of separate but equal and white supremacy relegated the Negro to a second-class citizenship that has left its scars to the present day. It was because these doctrines had become so firmly implemented by 1920 that Thompson could report, "On the whole there is surprisingly little friction between the blacks and the whites." [88] The Negro had learned his place and as long as he did not venture out of it, as he seldom did, peaceful relationships existed. Such conditioning by society as a whole, of course, made it difficult to bring blacks into operative positions in southern mills. The basic problem in dealing with the question of black labor today developed from this early, irrational position based on racial prejudice. There was no real economic justification for refusing to employ Negroes in cotton mills. It had been demonstrated clearly before the Civil War that blacks could perform well as operatives.

THE DECADE OF THE 1940's

By 1940, Negroes still constituted only about 2 percent of all employees in the textile industry and these were distributed in the states as shown in Table 20. The total number of Negro

---

87. South Carolina, *Acts*, 1915, No. 69, 1916, No. 391 as quoted by Herbert J. Lahne, *The Cotton Mill Worker* (New York: Farrar & Rinehart, Inc., 1944), p. 82.

88. Thompson, *op. cit.*, p. 147.

TABLE 20. Textile Mill Products Industry
Employment by Race and Sex
Selected States, 1940-1960

State	Year	All Employees			Male			Female		
		Total	Negro	Percent Negro	Total	Negro	Percent Negro	Total	Negro	Percent Negro
Alabama	1940	44,710	2,169	4.9	27,257	1,881	6.9	17,453	288	1.7
	1950	53,200	3,373	6.3	30,121	2,720	9.0	23,079	653	2.8
	1960	45,085	2,980	6.6	25,927	2,609	10.1	19,158	371	1.9
Georgia	1940	84,799	4,742	5.6	51,835	4,124	8.0	32,964	618	1.9
	1950	102,342	7,002	6.8	58,503	5,729	9.8	43,839	1,273	2.9
	1960	94,614	5,939	6.3	55,763	4,991	9.0	38,851	948	2.4
North Carolina	1940	189,979	6,121	3.2	111,342	5,665	5.1	78,637	456	0.6
	1950	215,074	8,718	4.1	119,165	7,897	6.6	95,909	821	0.9
	1960	221,726	8,438	3.8	118,353	7,747	6.5	103,373	691	0.7
South Carolina	1940	100,461	4,397	4.4	65,829	4,121	6.3	34,632	276	0.8
	1950	131,611	6,619	5.0	81,765	6,113	7.5	49,846	506	1.0
	1960	132,166	6,855	5.2	85,164	6,471	7.6	47,002	384	0.8
Tennessee	1940	37,364	949	2.5	18,845	802	4.3	18,519	147	0.8
	1950	35,645	978	2.7	16,329	736	4.5	19,316	242	1.3
	1960	31,792	983	3.1	14,334	757	5.3	17,458	226	1.3

Virginia	1940	30,285	1,297	4.3	16,967	954	5.6	13,318	343	2.6
	1950	41,328	2,244	5.4	22,741	1,548	6.8	18,587	696	3.7
	1960	36,587	1,775	4.9	19,632	1,433	7.3	16,955	342	2.0
Connecticut	1940	39,946	102	0.3	27,006	85	0.3	12,940	17	0.1
	1950	36,974	380	1.0	24,247	252	1.0	12,727	128	1.0
	1960	16,461	371	2.3	10,150	276	2.7	6,311	95	1.5
Maine	1940	23,337	4	*	14,382	2	*	8,955	2	*
	1950	25,602	10	*	15,423	5	*	10,179	5	*
	1960	14,923	10	0.1	8,989	—	—	5,934	10	0.2
Massachusetts	1940	126,957	525	0.4	80,336	456	0.6	46,621	69	0.1
	1950	117,491	587	0.5	73,008	451	0.6	44,483	136	0.3
	1960	52,336	556	1.1	34,009	334	1.0	18,327	222	1.2
New Hampshire	1940	15,891	3	*	9,844	1	*	6,047	2	*
	1950	18,805	10	0.1	10,977	5	*	7,828	5	0.1
	1960	12,430	12	0.1	6,881	—	—	5,549	12	0.2
New York	1940	102,325	642	0.6	60,698	487	0.8	41,627	155	0.4
	1950	94,998	2,821	3.0	55,559	1,579	2.8	39,439	1,242	3.1
	1960	71,285	5,082	7.1	38,608	2,790	7.2	32,677	2,292	7.0
Rhode Island	1940	57,202	101	0.2	33,170	78	0.2	24,032	23	0.1
	1950	57,385	183	0.3	32,366	119	0.4	25,019	64	0.3
	1960	28,022	74	0.3	15,919	50	0.3	12,103	24	0.2

Source: *U.S. Census of Population.*

    1940: Vol. III, *The Labor Force,* State Volumes, Table 18.

    1950: Vol. II, *Characteristics of the Population,* State Volumes, Table 83.

    1960: PC(1) D, *Detailed Characteristics,* State Volumes, Table 129.

* Less than 0.05 percent.

employees amounted to 24,764 in 1940 in an industry employing 1,170,024. (See Table 18.) Negro females were almost completely excluded, accounting for only 3,478 positions (0.7 percent) in a total female employment of 477,671.

Lahne, writing in 1944, states that "the South has yet another labor reserve which has been relatively untouched." [89] He was referring to the fact that Negroes had been excluded from almost all aspects of cotton manufacturing except in very menial jobs. This exclusion continued to be explained by the "deliberate discriminatory social and economic structure of the South." [90] Whites who had advanced one step up the economic ladder by moving from the farm to the mill wished to reserve the industry to themselves and leave the Negro in the field. The South Carolina law referred to earlier was an effort to legalize this form of race discrimination.

Occasionally, a mill owner expressed a desire to bring Negroes into the mill, but social, economic, and political pressures usually operated against such experimentation. The law may not permit Negroes and whites to work together and, even if it did, white employees may strike to force the discharge of Negroes. If a Negro was discharged, it became almost impossible for mill owners to get whites to use a mill house formerly occupied by the Negro.[91] Given these conditions, which were sometimes outside their control, mill owners took the safe course of excluding Negroes from their operations except for outside or laboring jobs.

The unions made no real effort to help the Negro in these difficult times. In a day when white workers could scarcely be organized, the unions had "neither the ability nor the inclination to cope with the problem of racial interrelations." [92] The Textile Workers Union of America (TWUA), as the major force in southern textile unionism in the 1940's, "[had] made no public announcement as to its position on the employment of Negroes in mills or their place in the union scheme of things." [93] There were a few Negroes in the TWUA, but local control generally rendered them ineffective in any real sense of participation. The

89. Lahne, *op. cit.*, p. 81.

90. *Ibid.*

91. *Ibid.*, p. 82.

92. *Ibid.*

93. *Ibid.*, p. 83.

union was the victim of a hostile environment that adhered to strict segregation of the races. It was a difficult task to defend a black man's right to equal job opportunity when society had denied him the right to equal education, housing, and public accommodations. Of course, these same conditions made it difficult for an employer who wished to remedy employment discrimination.

Lahne expressed a concern that the Negro's minor position in the textile industry was deteriorating by 1944. The National Recovery Act codes of the mid-1930's permitted lower minimum wages to be paid to groups holding positions, such as outside employees, where Negroes were found in large numbers. On the contrary, the Fair Labor Standards Act of 1938 did not permit such discrimination and mill owners indicated that "they were thinking of replacing the Negro with whites in . . . unskilled occupations—especially when there were unemployed whites available and the juxtaposition of an unemployed white with an employed Negro . . . was not calculated to satisfy the white workers." [94] The record of the 1950's does not support a general movement of this type, but the statistics show that the Negro's position improved only gradually for some time to come. (See Tables 18 and 20.)

The Negro's relative position increased from 2.1 percent to 3.6 percent of total textile employment, with the absolute increase from 24,764 to 44,640, during the period 1940 to 1950. Negro female employment more than doubled from 3,478 to 9,510. (See Table 18.) World War II stimulated growth in the industry and created opportunities in new industries in the South to which whites either shifted or began work. Even though the number of Negroes in the textile plants increased, as shown in Tables 18 and 20, they were still not represented in the operative class.

THE DECADE OF THE 1950's

In 1950-1951, Dewey made a survey of Negro employment in 70 mills owned by 25 firms in Virginia, North Carolina, and South Carolina. Approximately 416,000 employees were found in these states in 1950 and most of them were widely scattered in hundreds of mills. Small, separate plants employing about 100 people were characteristic of the southern textile industry in this period. Dewey's study covered about 65,000 employees or

94. *Ibid.*, p. 84.

approximately 15 percent of the total textile employment in the three states.[95] While the study was not presented as fully representative of the employment situation in the textile industry, the results are indicative of Negro utilization at the time the research was conducted. It may also be assumed that the experience of the upper South was consistent with, if not better than, that of the lower South, including Tennessee, Alabama, and Georgia, in terms of Negro employment.

A number of results were reported in the Dewey study which provide a partial picture of the Negro's position in the industry in 1950. These are: (1) Negroes did not constitute more than 10 percent of any mill's employment but in only two cases was there a total absence of Negro workers; (2) Negro women were almost completely excluded from the mills, and where they were found, they performed jobs such as scrubwoman or maid; (3) no Negroes were working in white-collar office work at all; (4) and none were employed in spinning and weaving departments in jobs such as weaver, spinner, doffer, or slasher. In several cases, Negroes were found on card machines and in more instances they were employed in the picking and opening operations; (5) outside work was performed mostly by Negro males; (6) a few jobs were performed by Negroes and/or whites such as truck driving, sweeping, and machine cleaning; and (7) there were practically no Negroes in supervisory positions.

Summarizing the above, "Negro workers [were] employed as laborers outside the plant or as janitors inside the plant. Most white workers [were] employed in office or production jobs inside the plant."[96] The racial divisions were fairly well established in 1950. Negroes were assigned, if at all, to the unskilled jobs requiring no training and generally within no close proximity to white workers. A few exceptions to the broad generalizations above could be found in the case of several companies employing Negro maintenance painters or electricians, and occasionally a production employee in the picking and carding rooms, but no major effort to utilize Negroes on a substantial or equal basis with whites was reported by Dewey. The 1960 census of employment in the textile industry, as shown in Table 21,

---

95. Donald Dewey, "Negro Employment in Seventy Textile Mills, October 1950-August 1951," in National Planning Association, *Selected Studies of Negro Employment in the South* (Washington: NPA, 1955), pp. 179-189.

96. *Ibid.*, pp. 183-184.

TABLE 21. Textile Mill Products Industry
Total Employed Persons by Color, Sex, and Occupational Group
United States, 1960

Occupational group	All Employees			Male			Female		
	Total	Nonwhite	Percent Nonwhite	Total	Nonwhite	Percent Nonwhite	Total	Nonwhite	Percent Nonwhite
Managers and officials	26,866	103	0.4	24,779	61	0.2	2,087	42	2.0
Professional and technical workers	18,296	122	0.7	14,423	61	0.4	3,873	61	1.6
Clerical workers	71,805	2,397	3.3	26,627	1,770	6.6	45,178	627	1.4
Sales workers	11,288	60	0.5	10,284	40	0.4	1,004	20	2.0
Craftsmen and foremen	115,886	2,445	2.1	110,454	2,343	2.1	5,432	102	1.9
Operatives	640,710	24,401	3.8	291,228	16,480	5.7	349,482	7,921	2.3
Laborers	39,016	8,065	20.7	33,214	7,699	23.2	5,802	366	6.3
Service workers	17,827	5,380	30.2	15,182	4,343	28.6	2,645	1,037	39.2
Occupation not reported	21,346	1,521	7.1	12,999	1,300	10.0	8,347	221	2.6
All Occupations	963,040	44,494	4.6	539,190	34,097	6.3	423,850	10,397	2.5

Source: U.S. Census of Population, 1960, PC (2) 7A, Occupational Characteristics, Table 36.

Note: Nonwhite are about 99 percent Negro and the analysis of the data treats them as synonymous.

further indicates the general lack of participation by blacks in the white collar and skilled jobs.

Several factors may explain the racial division of labor in the 1950's: (1) textile mills were high-wage employers in the locality where they were located and thus had a wide selection of whites; (2) mill villages did not encourage the acceptance of Negroes into work groups. The village was a closed society in many respects and it tended to isolate whites from Negroes and, indeed, from many others outside their own group; (3) most jobs in a textile mill could be performed by females. When there was a shortage of white men, employers resorted to the use of women who were preferred over Negro males.[97]

The foregoing suggests that if the racial division of labor, which rested firmly on the status quo in 1950, was to be changed, several things needed to occur: (1) new high wage paying industry, with improved working conditions attractive to whites, would have to locate in close proximity to southern mill towns; (2) mill villages with company-owned stores and houses would have to be abolished; and (3) the labor market would have to tighten so that white females would be in scarce supply. These conditions were developing in the late 1950's and reached their full impact in the late 1960's. New industry of all types moved into the South; mill houses were sold or torn down by management, and there was practically no unemployment in the Piedmont by 1969. Employers in the textile South turned to Negro employees to keep the plants running.

---

97. *Ibid.*, pp. 187-189.

CHAPTER V

General Employment in the 1960 Period

The decade of the 1960's witnessed the beginning of major changes in the employment of Negroes in the southern textile industry. A combination of factors, including a tight labor market and government pressure, began to open job opportunities to both male and female blacks. The record of Negro employment in textiles in the late 1960's is impressive, particularly if it is compared with the whole period of 1880 to 1960 when blacks were systematically excluded from the industry except in the most menial jobs.

THE EARLY 1960's

Government activity in the field of equal employment opportunity has a long history dating back to the Civil Rights Act of 1866 and to President Roosevelt's Executive Order 8802 in 1941 which created the first Fair Employment Practices Committee. Each president since Roosevelt created a committee, through executive order, to implement programs pertinent to nondiscrimination in employment. The committees have not always been effective and most of them have not been concerned with the textile industry. President Eisenhower's Committee on Government Contracts, operating in the 1950's, under the leadership of the then Vice-President Richard M. Nixon, gave considerable attention to the southern petroleum industry, but little recognition was given to the problems of blacks in other southern industries such as paper and textiles.[98] In at least one investigation of a southern textile company in early 1960, the Nixon committee found that Negroes were not hired as doffers and in other semiskilled jobs. As a result of this finding, Negroes were upgraded in this company. The real impact of government pressure was not felt in the textile industry until later in the 1960's.

---

98. See Herbert R. Northrup, *The Negro in the Paper Industry* (in this series), p. 54.

Following the Nixon Committee, the President's Committee on Equal Employment Opportunity was established by President Kennedy on March 6, 1961 under Executive Order 10925. This was the most important action taken by a president up to that time in an effort to end discrimination in employment. President Kennedy placed full support behind his Committee and indicated that vigorous action would be taken to achieve equal employment opportunity among the nation's contractors. The impact of the investigations of this Committee was felt sharply in the South, particularly in areas such as Birmingham, Alabama, where the large United States Steel facility was ordered to integrate lines of progression and desegregate facilities such as bath houses, drinking fountains, and toilets. Even though textile companies had not been selected as direct targets by the President's Committee, the handwriting was on the wall. The first full impact of government pressure to be felt by the textile industry was to come under the Civil Rights Act of 1964, which created the Equal Employment Opportunity Commission. President Johnson's Executive Order 11246 of September 24, 1965 established the Office of Federal Contract Compliance and it has been directly involved in equal employment matters in the textile industry. The two present operating federal agencies in the area of non-discrimination in employment are the Equal Employment Opportunity Commission (EEOC), which reports to the President, and the Office of Federal Contract Compliance (OFCC), which reports to the Secretary of Labor.

Pursuant to authority established under the Civil Rights Act of 1964, the EEOC conducted public hearings in the textile industry in Charlotte, North Carolina on January 12 and 13, 1967. This was the first experience the Commission had in conducting hearings in private industry. The purpose of the meetng was supposedly to gather information pertinent to the status of employment and utilization of Negroes in the industry in the Carolinas. Many parties were invited to give testimony, including industry representatives, unions, civil rights groups, educators, ministers, and private citizens who may have had difficulty in obtaining employment rights in textile plants. Others were invited as observers at the forum, which was held in the public library,

As a result of what appeared to be poor communication and ineffective planning between the industry and EEOC, only two industry representatives gave testimony at the hearings. The

American Textile Manufacturers Institute stated that the forum might "encourage unfounded and irresponsible accusations" and the simple fact of holding hearings "implied a punitive approach" against the companies.[99] Apparently, the Institute and many of its member companies had been led to believe that the purpose of the hearings was to bring in any person who had a complaint against the industry, and this would only serve to air the industry's dirty laundry before the public. Since most companies refused to testify, the hearing centered around several position papers presented by EEOC staff members and their consultants and testimony from unions and civil rights groups. The textile industry was criticized severely and several of the state's leading newspapers carried the following headlines after the sessions: "Negro and Labor Leaders Vent Wrath On Dixie Mills," "Hiring Bias Charged In Textile Industry," and "Mills Exclude Negroes As Systematic Policy."[100] These stories contained a report of the statements and charges against the industry made by members of such organizations as the NAACP and the Textile Workers Union of America. In view of the activity by many firms in the industry in hiring Negroes in 1967, it is somewhat surprising that they chose not to participate in the government hearing. It is reasonable to expect that some people in the industry regret the stand that was taken since it resulted in a one-sided picture of minority employment problems being presented.

One of the reports prepared by the EEOC staff for the hearings came to the following conclusions: Negro employees are concentrated in the lowest occupational categories; Negroes are not being hired for white collar jobs; Negro females are significantly underutilized in this industry; and both on a headcount basis and on a job quality basis the utilization of Negroes could be vastly improved in the textile industries of North and South Carolina.[101] These conclusions can be examined against the

---

99. *Greensboro Daily News*, January 13, 1967.

100. *Greensboro Daily News*, January 13, 1967; *Charlotte Observer*, January 13, 1967; and *The Greensboro Record*, January 13, 1967.

101. Phyllis A. Wallace and Maria P. Beckles, *1966 Employment Survey in the Textile Industry of the Carolinas*, Equal Employment Opportunity Commission, Research Report 1966-11, December 19, 1966 and Donald D. Osburn, *Negro Employment in the Textile Industries of North Carolina and South Carolina*, Equal Employment Opportunity Commission, Research Report 1966-10, November 2, 1966 (Washington: The Commission, 1967).

record of employment activity in the industry since 1967 as discussed in the following sections of this study.

THE OVERALL PICTURE, 1964-1968

Table 22 shows the percent Negro employment by occupation and sex for 1964, 1966, and 1968 in the southern textile industry based on data gathered in field interviews. In many respects, an examination of the contemporary southern textile industry is an examination of the industry. The latter is particularly true if one is interested in Negro employment. Some finishing and knitting plants remain in the New England states and in New York, New Jersey, and Pennsylvania, but they are generally small operations located in areas where the Negro population is practically nonexistent. Table 11, shows "total industry" figures that include employment in the South, as well as in selected plants in New England. The effect of including areas outside of the South is to reduce the relative employment position of the Negro in textiles by about one percentage point. Since the industry is heavily concentrated in the South, where Negroes are also present in large numbers in many labor markets, the analysis here will be directed toward the minority employment problem in the southern textile industry.

The data in Table 22 cover fifteen companies and 139 plants in 1964 and forty companies and 417 plants in 1966 and 1968. Meaningful comparisons can be made in examining the relative position of Negroes since the same companies and plants covered in 1964 are included in 1966 and 1968. The sample for the latter two years, however, was considerably larger. The 1964 data are included with the understanding that they are not as broadly representative of the industry as those for 1966 and 1968.

Several conclusions emerge from the data in Table 22 in regard to Negro employment: (1) the Negro's overall position relative to whites improved between 1964 and 1968; in every important job category, except for sales, the Negro's relative position increased; (2) the total white collar position of Negroes increased from 0.6 to 1.0 percent with the most change occurring in the technical and office and clerical jobs; (3) the total blue collar positions increased from 7.5 to 15.3 percent with positive increases in the craftsmen, operatives, and laborers classifications; the relative position of Negroes declined in the service

TABLE 22. Textile Mill Products Industry
Percent Negro Employment by Sex and Occupational Group
South Region, 1964-1968

Occupational Group	All Employees			Male			Female		
	1964	1966	1968	1964	1966	1968	1964	1966	1968
Officials and managers	*	0.1	0.2	*	0.1	0.2	—	—	0.5
Professionals	0.1	0.1	0.3	0.1	0.1	0.3	—	1.6	0.8
Technicians	—	0.6	1.0	—	0.7	1.0	—	0.2	0.9
Sales workers	—	0.2	—	—	—	—	—	1.1	—
Office and clerical	1.2	1.2	1.9	3.2	3.1	4.4	0.1	0.3	0.7
Total white collar	0.6	0.6	1.0	0.9	0.8	1.1	0.1	0.3	0.7
Craftsmen	0.7	1.6	2.9	0.8	1.6	2.8	—	2.0	4.1
Operatives	5.3	7.8	12.9	9.5	12.4	18.0	1.0	3.4	8.3
Laborers	25.8	33.0	38.3	28.7	37.9	43.1	10.5	13.8	22.7
Service workers	51.7	37.1	40.8	50.0	36.0	39.0	62.7	41.6	46.8
Total blue collar	7.5	10.7	15.3	10.9	14.9	19.2	1.8	4.5	9.7
Total	6.8	9.5	13.4	9.7	13.0	16.6	1.6	4.0	8.8

Source: Tables 23-25.

Note: 1964: 15 companies; 139 plants.
1966: 40 companies; 417 plants.
1968: 40 companies; 417 plants.

* Less than 0.05 percent.

worker category from 1964 to 1968, but increased during 1966
to 1968; and (4) the data suggest an important change in the
utilization of Negro females in the operative and laborer categories.

A clearer understanding of what the relative improvements
mean can be gained by examining the absolute changes in Negro
employment over the same period. Tables 23-25 show the absolute changes in Negro employment between 1964 and 1968. Since
the same number of companies and plants are covered for 1966
and 1968, the absolute comparisons will be drawn using these
two years. Several general observations can be made from an
examination of the data: (1) total Negro employment increased
more than total employment between 1966 and 1968, rising from
25,065 to 36,413, with total employment increasing from 264,815
to 271,245. This suggests that Negroes were beginning to replace some whites who left the industry; (2) Negro female employment more than doubled during the period under study; (3)
in the white collar jobs, Negroes are practically nonexistent; in
1966, there were 211 Negroes out of 33,017 employed in white
collar jobs, compared to 349 Negroes out of 35,023 in 1968. Almost all of the Negroes holding such jobs in both years were
Negro males in office and clerical positions; (4) in the blue collar
jobs, Negroes were better represented, with their number increasing from 24,854 out of 231,798 jobs in 1966 to 36,064 out
of 236,222 jobs in 1968. The impact of these overall changes
can be understood best by examining the specific movements
within the occupational structure of the industry.

The following section analyzes total and Negro employment by
occupation in 1964, 1966, and 1968. Emphasis is placed on the two
years, 1966 and 1968, since in these years it was possible to
obtain data for the same 40 companies and 417 plants. Companies generally use the same classification scheme in reporting
minority employment data to the Equal Employment Opportunity
Commission, however, certain variations do exist. Foremen will
sometimes be placed in the craftsmen category instead of in the
officials and managers group and occasionally engineers will be
classified as technicians rather than professionals. These differences do not lead to serious discrepancies in the data presented.
The occupational profile as shown in Tables 23, 24, and 25 gives
an excellent summary of the Negro's position in the textile industry. An analysis of the figures follows.

TABLE 23. Textile Mill Products Industry
Employment by Race, Sex, and Occupational Group
15 Companies, 139 Plants
South Region, 1964

Occupational Group	All Employees			Male			Female		
	Total	Negro	Percent Negro	Total	Negro	Percent Negro	Total	Negro	Percent Negro
Officials and managers	2,873	1	*	2,863	1	*	10	—	—
Professionals	768	1	0.1	759	1	0.1	9	—	—
Technicians	684	—	—	505	—	—	179	—	—
Sales workers	182	—	—	160	—	—	22	—	—
Office and clerical	4,311	51	1.2	1,548	49	3.2	2,763	2	0.1
Total white collar	8,818	53	0.6	5,835	51	0.9	2,983	2	0.1
Craftsmen	13,643	101	0.7	12,252	101	0.8	1,391	—	—
Operatives	46,819	2,490	5.3	23,810	2,265	9.5	23,009	225	1.0
Laborers	7,563	1,951	25.8	6,344	1,823	28.7	1,219	128	10.5
Service workers	1,334	690	51.7	1,149	574	50.0	185	116	62.7
Total blue collar	69,359	5,232	7.5	43,555	4,763	10.9	25,804	469	1.8
Total	78,177	5,285	6.8	49,390	4,814	9.7	28,787	471	1.6

Source: Tables A-18 to A-23.

* Less than 0.05 percent.

TABLE 24.   Textile Mill Products Industry
Employment by Race, Sex, and Occupational Group
40 Companies, 417 Plants
South Region, 1966

Occupational Group	All Employees			Male			Female		
	Total	Negro	Percent Negro	Total	Negro	Percent Negro	Total	Negro	Percent Negro
Officials and managers	13,236	16	0.1	13,048	16	0.1	188	—	—
Professionals	2,295	3	0.1	2,234	2	0.1	61	1	1.6
Technicians	2,162	12	0.6	1,609	11	0.7	553	1	0.2
Sales workers	546	1	0.2	458	—	—	88	1	1.1
Office and clerical	14,778	179	1.2	4,941	153	3.1	9,837	26	0.3
Total white collar	33,017	211	0.6	22,290	182	0.8	10,727	29	0.3
Craftsmen	35,712	574	1.6	32,655	512	1.6	3,057	62	2.0
Operatives	161,288	12,525	7.8	78,391	9,720	12.4	82,897	2,805	3.4
Laborers	28,385	9,377	33.0	22,668	8,586	37.9	5,717	791	13.8
Service workers	6,413	2,378	37.1	5,216	1,880	36.0	1,197	498	41.6
Total blue collar	231,798	24,854	10.7	138,930	20,698	14.9	92,868	4,156	4.5
Total	264,815	25,065	9.5	161,220	20,880	13.0	103,595	4,185	4.0

Source: Tables A-11 to A-16.

TABLE 25. *Textile Mill Products Industry*
Employment by Race, Sex, and Occupational Group
40 Companies, 417 Plants
South Region, 1968

Occupational Group	All Employees			Male			Female		
	Total	Negro	Percent Negro	Total	Negro	Percent Negro	Total	Negro	Percent Negro
Officials and managers	14,099	28	0.2	13,880	27	0.2	219	1	0.5
Professionals	2,387	7	0.3	2,267	6	0.3	120	1	0.8
Technicians	2,556	25	1.0	1,892	19	1.0	664	6	0.9
Sales workers	500	—	—	441	—	—	59	—	—
Office and clerical	15,481	289	1.9	4,803	212	4.4	10,678	77	0.7
Total white collar	35,023	349	1.0	23,283	264	1.1	11,740	85	0.7
Craftsmen	36,062	1,063	2.9	32,589	921	2.8	3,473	142	4.1
Operatives	164,809	21,294	12.9	78,448	14,116	18.0	86,361	7,178	8.3
Laborers	29,223	11,207	38.3	22,379	9,654	43.1	6,844	1,553	22.7
Service workers	6,128	2,500	40.8	4,706	1,835	39.0	1,422	665	46.8
Total blue collar	236,222	36,064	15.3	138,122	26,526	19.2	98,100	9,538	9.7
Total	271,245	36,413	13.4	161,405	26,790	16.6	109,840	9,623	8.8

Source: Tables A-4 to A-9.

OCCUPATIONAL DISTRIBUTION

Employers use the standard guidelines developed by the Equal Employment Opportunity Commission in gathering data relevant to Negro employment. The following classification of occupations is used:

White Collar Occupations	Blue Collar Occupations
Officials and managers	Craftsmen (Skilled)
Professionals	Operatives (Semiskilled)
Technicians	Laborers (Unskilled)
Sales workers	Service workers
Office and clerical	

Employment in the white collar occupations is generally direct. A person may be hired as a professional, salesman, technician, or office and clerical employee, and, if a movement upward is made, it likely would be into an official or managerial position. On the other hand, in the blue collar occupations, an employee may begin as a laborer, with the expectation of moving up to a craftsman's position. The progression in the blue collar jobs normally is from unskilled to semiskilled to skilled positions, except that many times in the textile industry an employee will be hired directly as a semiskilled operative and remain in that position for the duration of his employment. A distinguishing feature of employment in blue collar jobs in the textile industry is the lack of upward mobility. Long narrow lines of progression, such as those in the steel industry, do not exist in the textile industry. Within any department in the industry, including spinning, weaving, and finishing, there are few jobs in a promotion sequence, and the great bulk of the work is semiskilled in nature. Any effort to assess the effectiveness of equal employment programs must take the foregoing characteristics into consideration.

The analysis which follows is based on Tables 23-25, which present employment by occupation, sex, and race for the textile industry for the years 1964, 1966, and 1968.

White Collar Occupations

Officials and managers. This job category, at the top of the white collar hierarchy, includes those people in the firm who have the major responsibility of organizing and directing the work force, such as corporate officials, plant managers, and supervisory personnel. Any foreman or supervisor on exempt status is included in the officials and managers classification. Usually an employee shown in this category has gained capabilities through formal education and/or experience and, in the case of supervision, may have been with a company for many years.

The statistical record of Negro employment in the officials and managers category is a dismal one. As late as 1964, there were practically no Negroes represented in this white collar area; in 1966, there were sixteen Negroes in a total of 13,236 employees (0.1 percent), and by 1968 the number increased to twenty-eight in a total of 14,099 (0.2 percent). This means that a total of only twelve additional Negroes were hired or upgraded by the companies studied between 1966 and 1968. The few Negroes found in this classification are in jobs where they supervise mainly other Negroes or occasionally one is found in a personnel department where his function is to assist in recruiting blacks. There are a few notable examples where a Negro male has been assigned to supervise an all-white female department and where a Negro female has been assigned to supervise a predominantly white department using both males and females. These would be exceptional cases in any industry and in any part of the country. The significant lack, of course, is in those areas where one may expect to find Negro males supervising racially mixed departments.

Highly discriminatory social, economic, and political systems in the South have not permitted the development or utilization of the skills of Negroes in supervisory and other managerial positions. Until quite recently, Negroes in textile areas of the South were not afforded equal access to public accommodations or educational opportunities, and adequate housing remains a problem. The educated Negro who can qualify for a managerial position in textiles does not wish to remain in a mill town with a history of discrimination. As is true in some other industries, such as paper, textiles began late in the equal employment field following considerable adverse publicity.

Professional and Technical. Professional jobs in textiles include accountants, chemists, personnel specialists, engineers, lawyers, and purchasing agents. These are people who generally possess an advanced degree in a specialized field. On the technical side, personnel would be employed in laboratories and in

various research and development activities. The small number
of professionals and technicians in the textile industry reflects
the limited resources directed toward research and development
and staff specialists in the corporate organization. In 1966, there
were 2,295 professionals and 2,162 technicians and in 1968, 2,387
professionals and 2,556 technicians. Negro representation was
almost nonexistent in each year and in each category: three
Negro professionals and twelve Negro technicians in 1966, and
seven Negro professionals and twenty-five Negro technicians in
1968. While considerable effort was made by a few companies to
increase the proportion of Negroes, the representation for the
industry as a whole is quite poor.

Given the historical setting of the industry in the South, the
talented Negro's propensity to leave the area, and a lack of
vigorous recruiting activity on the part of management, the
prospects for significant change in these categories are unlikely
for the future. A Negro who is qualified through education and
training to fill jobs in the professional and technical operations
of the industry generally has attractive opportunities outside of
the South or within the South in new industries that have entered in the past decade.

Sales. Less than one percent of total employment in the southern textile industry is in sales. Distribution of textile products
is made generally through brokers, wholesalers, or commission
houses and producers maintain small sales forces. Those who
are employed as salesmen in the industry usually serve within a
highly social and personal context, exploiting new contacts and
maintaining long relationships with purchasing agents.

In the sample covered in this study, no Negroes were found
in the 500 salesmen employed in 1968. Interestingly enough, this
same situation has been evident in industries such as steel and
paper.[102] The Negro has experienced the most direct discrimination in the sales job category than in any other one in the
United States, and there is little reason to expect that the situation will improve greatly in the near future. Negroes, like whites,
do not seek insults in their job search. Rather than be rebuffed,
the qualified Negro will look for job opportunities in those areas

---

102. See *The Negro in the Paper Industry* in this Series and Herbert R.
Northrup, Richard L. Rowan, *et al.*, *Negro Employment in Basic
Industry*, Studies in Negro Employment, Vol. I (Philadelphia, Industrial
Research Unit, Wharton School of Finance and Commerce, University
of Pennsylvania, 1970), Part Four.

where it is at least somewhat clear that the chance for equal treatment is present.

In a certain sense, the Negro's difficulty in obtaining employment in the sales field is a reflection on the broader society that industry serves. Segregated housing and discriminating social institutions, such as the country club, complicate the job environment for blacks in most important white collar fields, but perhaps to the greatest extent in professional sales. The sales job places a person in close contact with the public outside the company. An employer, particularly in textiles, who may wish to utilize Negro salesmen, would find it exceedingly difficult to control all of the outside influences that could lead to failure and frustration for the Negro. Simply stated, the president of a textile company has little control over the action of the purchasing agent in a company his salesmen contact.

Office and Clerical. This category consists of those who work as stenographers, messengers, secretaries, telephone operators, and clerks in all phases of textile operations. It ranks second to officials and managers in terms of employment in the white collar job categories. In 1968, there were 15,481 employees in office and clerical jobs in a total white collar employment of 35,023. Negroes held 289 (1.9 percent) of these jobs in 1968, which represented an increase from 179 (1.2 percent) such jobs in 1966.

Blue Collar Occupations

Craftsmen. Craftsmen include skilled workers in the production and maintenance departments of a textile plant. In the sample studied for 1968, there were 36,062 craftsmen positions in a total employment of 271,245, which represented 13 percent of the total mill force. Skilled craftsmen are important in textile operations, but their relative position is not as significant as found in paper, aerospace, and steel. The skilled employee in textiles works in the mechanical or electrical trades in maintenance and in production he generally would be classified as a loom fixer. A craftsman normally has arrived in his position as a result of completing an apprenticeship program leading to a maintenance job or by training and experience in a production unit.

Any assessment of the Negro's current position as a skilled employee in the textile industry must take into consideration a long history of discrimination from 1880 to the early 1960's.

The cotton plantation owners in the South used Negro slaves to do much of the trades work in the pre-Civil War period, but the situation changed radically after Reconstruction. When the cotton mills came to the cotton fields, Negroes were excluded from almost all jobs and particularly the skilled ones. As late as 1960, only 4.6 percent of all employees in the textile industry were Negroes.

By 1966, Negroes were beginning to appear in the craftsmen job category as a result of changes in the social, economic, and political environment in the South. Pressures from civil rights groups, the government, and particularly a tight labor market began to open the door for Negroes into skilled jobs. Between 1966 and 1968, the total number of craftsmen increased from 35,712 to 36,062, or by 350, while the Negro representation increased from 574 to 1,063, or by 489. On a relative basis, the Negro's position increased from 1.6 percent to 2.9 percent of all craftsmen jobs between 1966 and 1968. While the relative position of Negroes in the industry's skilled job category does not appear to have changed greatly during the years studied, the absolute gains are quite significant. The fact that 489 new skilled positions were held by blacks when the total increase in the category was only 350 indicates considerable progress. Negroes were either upgraded from the operative category or they were hired directly as craftsmen. Opinions vary as to the real importance of the change, but given a background of exclusion of Negroes in the top blue collar jobs, recent improvements appear impressive.

It is conceivable that new plants and equipment will stimulate demand for highly trained employees which will be met by several principal sources: apprenticeship training, upgrading of existing personnel, and new hires. Negroes will participate in the skilled areas to the extent that local upgrading arrangements permit and also by the number to be found in the labor market. Just as in other industries, mill managements are finding that since hiring policies have changed, the supply of qualified labor is limited. If a Negro youth can meet the requirements of a rigorous apprenticeship program, he may prefer to go to college rather than accept an opportunity as a craftsman. Also, in the growing industrial South, where many alternatives for employment currently present themselves, a Negro may avoid the textile industry in favor of industries that have better records in civil rights activities.

Operatives. The operative category includes semiskilled employees who work in a wide variety of jobs, including weaving, spinning, sewing, and knitting. The textile industry probably hires more semiskilled operatives as a percentage of its employment than any other industry in the United States. In 1968, about 61 percent of all employees, and about 70 percent of all blue collar employees surveyed, were classified as operatives. Many employees work as operatives from shortly after they enter the industry until they retire. It is not uncommon for a weaver, spinner, or knitter to consider his or her job as a lifetime proposition. If any upward mobility occurs for the operative, it is generally to a loom fixer's position or perhaps into a craft, and occasionally one will be promoted into a supervisory position.

Up until the mid-1960's, the great mass of semiskilled operatives in the mills were white men and women living in small textile communities. Major changes occurred in the late 1960's bringing large numbers of black employees into semiskilled jobs, and the movement will no doubt continue into the 1970's and the indefinite future. Once again, the combination of government pressure and, most importantly, the scarcity of white labor, has opened job opportunities to Negroes. Now that employers have had a chance to experience the entrance of black workers into their operations, they are beginning to understand the advantages lost in previous years by overlooking this part of the labor supply of the region.

Between 1966 and 1968, the total number of operatives increased by 3,521, from 161,288 to 164,809, while Negroes increased by 8,769, from 12,525 to 21,294. On a relative basis, Negro representation increased from 7.8 percent in 1966 to 12.9 percent in 1968. Both in absolute and relative terms, the Negro made major gains in the operative category. Not only were they hired into the industry for the first time, but in many cases they replaced whites who left the industry. There is reason to believe that if employers had not been able to recruit black workers in the years studied, some of their operations would have been seriously curtailed.

Laborers. The laborers group consists of unskilled workers who hold jobs that require no special training. A laborer, such as a sweeper, has an opportunity to observe general plant practices and operating procedures in the department where he starts to work. An employee who has been hired as a laborer may proceed to an operative position, but he may also remain in the unskilled job all of his working life. Unlike his counterpart in strongly unionized industries, such as steel, a laborer in textiles usually does not enter the mill with expectations of moving up a promotion ladder in regular sequence. Also, in contrast to other mass producing industries, the number of laborers in textiles has increased steadily over the years, and the Negro's relative position in such jobs has improved considerably since 1964. This could be significant for black workers if they are able to move into operative and craftsman positions in the future. Entrance into the industry, even at the lowest level, can provide useful experience for those who have never worked in a plant or factory environment. The textile industry is offering the first step for many southern Negroes from agriculture or no employment into an industrial world. It is ironic that the industry will probably do for the uneducated, untrained Negroes what it did for the poor, unskilled whites during the period 1880 to 1960.

In 1966, there were 28,385 employees classified as laborers, of which 9,377 (33.0 percent) were Negroes; in 1968, in the same companies there were 29,223 laborers, of which 11,207 (38.3 percent) were Negroes. The number of Negro laborers increased more rapidly than the total number of laborers. In the small sample of 1964, there were 7,563 in this group, of which 1,951 (25.8 percent) were Negroes. The statistics indicate further the somewhat rapid advances that Negroes have made in their employment situation in the textile industry within the past few years.

Close scrutiny of the jobs in the laborer category would probably result in some of them being reclassified as semiskilled. There has been no union pressure to upgrade jobs in the textile industry and the nomenclature remains basically the same that it has been since the early 1900's.

Service workers. Service workers include janitors, guards, watchmen, and those normally in nonproduction jobs and responsible for cleaning and protection of plant property. Negroes have always been well represented in this job category, particularly in the outside cleaning jobs and yard work. While the total number of service workers declined from 6,413 to 6,128 between 1966 and 1968, the number of Negroes in the job category increased from 2,378 (37.1 percent) to 2,500 (40.8 percent). All of the increase occurred among Negro females.

Most employees in the service worker classification will not be upgraded during their employment since they are usually hired for rather specific routine low-ability jobs. Such jobs are not in a line of promotion sequence and an employee understands this when he is hired. If Negroes, or other employees, have been assigned to service jobs without a fair appraisal of their ability, they may be a source of unexpected talent for employers to draw upon.

NEGRO EMPLOYMENT CHANGES, SOUTH REGION
1966 TO 1968

Tables 26 and 27 present the change in Negro employment by job category between 1966 and 1968. Several important facts emerge from the statistical summary.

The total number of employees increased by 6,430 (2.4 percent) but Negroes increased by 11,348 (45.3 percent) which indicates that all of the net additions in employment resulted from Negroes entering the industry. On the basis of sex, total males increased by 185 (0.1 percent), while Negro males increased by 5,910 (28.3 percent); total females increased by 6,245 (6.0 percent), while Negro females increased by 5,438 (129.9 percent). The relative overall position of Negroes in textiles improved considerably more than whites during the two-year period from 1966 to 1968.

White Collar Occupations

The actual number of Negroes in all white collar jobs in the textile industry did not change greatly between 1966 and 1968; however, in relative terms, the change was quite large. The total increase was 2,006, 993 males and 1,013 females. Negroes increased by only 138, 82 males and 56 females. In relative terms, the Negro's overall position increased by 65.4 percent, which was considerably larger than the 5.7 percent increase in whites. Negro males rose by 45.1 percent and females by 193.1 percent in comparison to increases of only 4.1 percent and 8.9 percent for white males and females, respectively. The large relative increases in Negro employment occurred because of the small Negro representation in the base year, 1966.

Negro Males. The change in Negro male white collar jobs occurred in the following categories:

TABLE 26.   *Textile Mill Products Industry*
Change in White Collar Employment by Race, Sex, and
Occupational Group
South Region, 1966 to 1968

Occupational Group and Race	All Employees		Male		Female	
	Number	Percent	Number	Percent	Number	Percent
All employees	6,430	2.4	185	0.1	6,245	6.0
Negro	11,348	45.3	5,910	28.3	5,438	129.9
White[a]	—4,918	—2.1	—5,725	—4.1	807	0.8
All white collar	2,006	6.1	993	4.5	1,013	9.4
Negro	138	65.4	82	45.1	56	193.1
White	1,868	5.7	911	4.1	957	8.9
Officials and managers	863	6.5	832	6.4	31	16.5
Negro	12	75.0	11	68.8	1	b
White	851	6.4	821	6.3	30	16.0
Professionals	92	4.0	33	1.5	59	96.7
Negro	4	133.3	4	200.0	—	—
White	88	3.8	29	1.3	59	98.3
Technicians	394	18.2	283	17.6	111	20.1
Negro	13	108.3	8	72.7	5	500.0
White	381	17.7	275	17.2	106	19.2
Sales workers	—46	—8.4	—17	—3.7	—29	—33.0
Negro	—1	b	—	—	—1	b
White	—45	—8.3	—17	—3.7	—28	—32.2
Office and clerical	703	4.8	—138	—2.8	841	8.5
Negro	110	61.5	59	38.6	51	196.2
White	593	4.1	—197	—4.1	790	8.1

Source: Tables 24 and 25.

[a] Includes all employees other than those classified as Negro.

[b] Unable to calculate percentage.

TABLE 27. *Textile Mill Products Industry*
Change in Blue Collar Employment by Race, Sex, and
Occupational Group
South Region, 1966 to 1968

Occupational Group and Race	All Employees		Male		Female	
	Number	Percent	Number	Percent	Number	Percent
All blue collar employees	4,424	1.9	—808	—0.6	5,232	5.6
Negro	11,210	45.1	5,828	28.2	5,382	129.5
White[a]	—6,786	—3.3	—6,636	—5.6	—150	—0.2
Craftsmen	350	1.0	—66	—0.2	416	13.6
Negro	489	85.2	409	79.9	80	129.0
White	—139	—0.4	—475	—1.5	336	11.2
Operatives	3,521	2.2	57	0.1	3,464	4.2
Negro	8,769	70.0	4,396	45.2	4,373	155.9
White	—5,248	—3.5	—4,339	—6.3	—909	—1.1
Laborers	838	3.0	—289	—1.3	1,127	19.7
Negro	1,830	19.5	1,068	12.4	762	96.3
White	—992	—5.2	—1,357	—9.6	365	7.4
Service workers	—285	—4.4	—510	—9.8	225	18.8
Negro	122	5.1	—45	—2.4	167	33.5
White	—407	—10.1	—465	—13.9	58	8.3

Source: Tables 24 and 25.

[a] Includes all employees other than those classified as Negro.

Officials and managers, which includes the important supervisory group, increased by 11 (68.8 percent). Most of these 11
Negro males either were promoted or hired into a foreman's
job. The field research revealed cases where a Negro male had
been hired or promoted to supervise all types of groups, ranging from an all-white female group to racially mixed departments where both males and females worked. Supervision is
one of the most sensitive areas in which to make changes. Most
employers, who were interviewed, think that when a Negro has
the demonstrated ability to supervise, there will be minor or no
difficulty in placing him in such a role. Since equal employment
opportunity is a relatively new thing in many plants, a large

reservoir of managerial talent has not developed and employers are faced with a difficult task of selecting qualified blacks from their existing work forces for supervisory positions. This situation will change as more Negroes enter skilled jobs and develop sensitivity to the work environment. While the fact that only 11 additional black males entered official and managerial positions in textiles between 1966 and 1968 may represent insignificant progress to some, it appears quite important to those who have an understanding of the locational and labor market aspects of the industry.

In the professional category, which includes those with highly specialized training, Negro males increased by 4 (200.0 percent). The male professional category increased by only 33 overall, with white males rising by 29. Given the fact that the professional jobs usually require a college education and particular knowledge in a specific field, such as chemistry or engineering, it is not surprising that Negro males increased by only 4. The Negro male who possesses the qualifications for the professional jobs has not been attracted to the textile industry. Other industries in the South, and companies located in other parts of the country, have had more appeal for the college-educated Negro. Even though some textile companies are located in or near progressive cities in the South close to predominantly Negro colleges, they have difficulty in competing with more prestigious industries and with northern companies who send recruiters into the area to seek Negro talent. One employer in a diversified southern city explained that his company had invested a considerable amount of money and time in trying to facilitate educational programs in a nearby all-Negro college, but the company had not been able to attract even one of the black graduates to its offices.

Negro male technicians increased by 8 (72.7 percent). Most of the discussion in regard to Negro professionals would apply when examining the employment record of Negro technicians. A Negro male with technical skill generally leaves the South as he is attracted to the higher wage-paying and more glamorous industries in the North. If he remains in the South, he seeks employment opportunities in the same kind of industries that may attract him to other parts of the country. Even though job opportunities in the industry appear to be relatively equal today, there is not likely to be much change in the number of Negroes represented in the professional and technical categories in the future. Several employers interviewed in this study discussed programs instituted to provide summer technical employment for Negro college students with the hopes of having them become permanent employees after graduation. Most were not encouraged at the prospect of keeping many of these students, since they understood the nature of their competition.

No Negro males were found in the sales category in either 1966 or 1968, and there was an actual decline of seventeen in white salesmen. Problems surrounding the employment of Negro males in sales jobs were discussed earlier. Just as in other industries, such as steel, Negroes face major obstacles in obtaining sales jobs in textiles. Some companies have attempted to employ Negro males in their New York sales offices, but even these efforts have been thwarted. It is likely that the industrial sales area will be the last to show progress in terms of Negro employment in this country since it is intimately tied in with factors somewhat external to the firm, such as housing, social attitudes, and community outlook.

Negro males made a more rapid advance in the office and clerical jobs in textiles than in any other white collar area between 1966 and 1968. While the total number of male office and clerical workers declined by 138, Negro males in the category increased by 59 (38.6 percent). It is significant that Negro males increased, while white males decreased by 197 (4.1 percent).

Negro females. The Negro female has been unrepresented in the textile industry's white collar job structure. Of the 56 Negro females added in white collar jobs during 1966-1968, 51 were hired in the office and clerical category, five in the technical group, and one in the officials and managers category. The one Negro female in sales disappeared by 1968, giving a net increase of 56 in the total Negro female employment.

The 51 Negro females added to the office and clerical category, which represented an increase of 196.2 percent between 1966 and 1968, were employed mainly as typists, payroll clerks, and general stenographers. Employers appear willing to hire qualified Negro females, but they are not well represented in the labor market. The public school facilities in black neighborhoods of the South have not developed adequate resources to train students in commercial courses, such as typing and shorthand. Also, there has been little motivation on the part of black students in the past to take advantage of such courses when available because of general discriminatory employment practices. While these practices have begun to disappear, it may require the passage of considerable time to change the image of the past.

The number of Negro female technicians increased by five (500.0 percent) in the two-year period, 1966-1968. This represents a positive change since there was only one Negro female employed as a technician in the companies studied in 1966. Negro females held only one position in the officials and managers category in 1968, which indicates that they were excluded from supervisory positions. This may reflect the fact that prior to recent years Negro women were not hired in large numbers, if at all, in the operative and craftsmen jobs, from which a foreman or supervisor would be promoted. It is to be expected that Negro women will be represented in the officials and managers category in the future since they have become an important part of the blue collar picture of the industry and upgrading will occur over time.

Blue Collar Occupations

The positive changes in Negro blue collar employment were dramatic between 1966 and 1968. Total employment increased by 4,424 (1.9 percent), while Negroes in blue collar jobs increased by 11,210 (45.1 percent). This reveals that employment of whites in blue collar jobs decreased by 6,786 (3.3 percent); white males declined by 6,636 (5.6 percent), while white females declined by 150 (0.2 percent) in blue collar jobs. Negro males and females shared the blue collar employment gains almost equally, but the relative position of Negro females improved more significantly.

In each of the craftsmen, operative, laborers, and service workers categories, the total number of white employees declined, while the number of Negroes increased. White employees declined as follows: craftsmen, 139 (0.4 percent), operatives, 5,248 (3.5 percent), laborers, 992 (5.2 percent), and service workers, 407 (10.1 percent). In marked contrast to the above, Negro employment rose as follows: craftsmen, 489 (85.2 percent), operatives, 8,769 (70.0 percent), laborers, 1,830 (19.5 percent), and service workers, 122 (5.1 percent). On the basis of race and sex, it is interesting to note that white male employment declined in all blue collar categories in contrast to increases in Negro male employment, except in the service worker classification. Negro and white female employment increased in all blue collar job categories, except that white female employees decreased in the operative area. Apparently, white males are entering new industries that have entered the South and employers in textiles have had to resort to the employment of females and, in particular, black women who have not been a part of the employment picture in the past.

It is important to note that Negro males made major advances in the skilled and semiskilled jobs. In the craftsmen category, they increased by 409 and whites declined by 475, yielding a decrease in the number of such jobs of 66. Also, in the operative category, Negro males increased by 4,396; whites decreased by 4,339, resulting in a positive increase in jobs of 57. In both cases, it will be seen that Negro male advancement was considerable when viewed against a downward trend in white male employment. The same general pattern held in the laborers category and in the service workers group where both white and Negro overall employment declined.

The Negro female situation is even more interesting than that of Negro males. Indeed, the most dramatic employment gains in the industry occurred in the Negro female group. For many years, Negro females were ignored as a source of labor in textile operations. The statistics reveal that they are now providing a major source of labor supply. Between 1966 and 1968, Negro female craftsmen increased by 80 (129.0 percent), while white females in this category increased by 336 (11.2 percent). In the operative group, Negro females increased by 4,373 (155.9 percent), but white females declined by 909 (1.1 percent). Negro females increased their numbers more significantly than white women in both the laborers and service workers categories.

The statistics in Table 27 reveal some interesting facts regarding Negro blue collar employment in the textile industry. Negroes have been making rapid gains, and the advances have been the most significant in the important craftsmen and operative categories. This indicates that there has been some upgrading of Negroes and that new opportunities are being made available. Negroes have replaced whites in many instances and in all types of jobs. The changes are impressive when compared to the past when Negroes were eliminated from the industry as a matter of policy.

The advance in the Negro's position in blue collar jobs is highlighted in Table 28, which presents a percentage distribution of Negroes in blue collar occupations. It can be seen that there was a heavier concentration of Negroes in the important craftsmen and operative positions in 1968 than in 1966. In 1966, 2.3 percent of all Negroes in blue collar jobs were in craftsmen positions, but in 1968 this had risen to 2.9 percent. The same trend occurred in the operative group where 50.0 percent of all Negroes were located in 1966, but by 1968 this had risen to 58.5 percent. The concentration of Negroes in unskilled and service worker occupations declined in the period covered.

TABLE 28. *Textile Mill Products Industry*
Percentage Distribution of Negroes in Blue Collar Jobs
South Region, 1966 and 1968

Occupational Group	All Employees		Male		Female	
	1966	1968	1966	1968	1966	1968
Craftsmen	2.3	2.9	2.4	3.4	1.5	1.5
Operatives	50.0	58.5	46.6	52.7	67.0	74.6
Laborers	37.4	30.8	41.1	36.0	18.9	16.1
Service workers	9.5	6.9	9.0	6.9	11.9	6.9
Total blue collar	99.2	99.1	99.1	99.0	99.3	99.1
Total	100.0	100.0	100.0	100.0	100.0	100.0

Source: Tables 24 and 25.

NEGRO EMPLOYMENT IN THE TEXTILE OPERATIONS OF RUBBER AND CHEMICAL COMPANIES

As indicated earlier, the man-made fiber part of the textile industry has grown substantially over the past decade. Diversified chemical and rubber companies have been active in this field. A study of employment in the traditional textile industry may overlook operations of chemical and rubber companies producing synthetics. In order to avoid this oversight, and to reflect minority employment patterns in a growing segment of the broader textile industry, five rubber companies representing 15 plants and four chemical companies representing 21 plants were selected for study. All of these plants produce products that are classified as textiles or man-made fibers. The data for these companies are summarized in Table 29, which shows the relative position of Negroes in comparison to the traditional textile industry, characterized by firms such as Dan River, Fieldcrest, and Bibb. It should be noted that data for 1966 and 1968 contain the same plants which are all located in the South and in areas confronted with the same general labor market characteristics as discussed in reference to other textile plants. In this regard, it may be assumed that any differences in the numbers may be explained in part by company equal employment policy and its implementation.

TABLE 29. *Textiles, Chemicals, and Rubber* [a]
Percent Negro Employment by Occupational Group
South Region, 1966 and 1968

Occupational Group	Textiles[b]		Chemicals[c]		Rubber[d]	
	1966	1968	1966	1968	1966	1968
Officials and managers	0.1	0.2	*	0.3	0.1	1.2
Professionals	0.1	0.3	0.1	0.4	—	0.4
Technicians	0.6	1.0	0.8	2.1	4.0	9.6
Sales workers	0.2	—	—	—	—	—
Office and clerical	1.2	1.9	0.9	2.1	2.5	3.1
Total white collar	0.6	1.0	0.4	0.9	1.4	3.3
Craftsmen	1.6	2.9	1.6	2.5	4.8	6.0
Operatives	7.8	12.9	6.2	11.9	12.1	18.3
Laborers	33.0	38.3	40.2	34.8	40.0	55.6
Service workers	37.1	40.8	48.1	50.7	56.3	63.9
Total blue collar	10.7	15.3	7.7	11.2	14.7	20.3
Total	9.5	13.4	5.7	8.5	12.8	17.5

Source: Tables 4, 25 and A-24 to A-27.

[a] Includes textile operations of rubber and chemical companies.
[b] 40 companies, 417 plants.
[c] 4 companies, 21 plants.
[d] 5 companies, 15 plants.
* Less than 0.05 percent.

A general hypothesis was made at the outset that the Negro's relative position in chemical and rubber plants manufacturing man-made fibers in the South would be better than that found in traditional textile firms. This hypothesis was based on the fact that all of the rubber and chemical plants were members of na-

tional corporations, who belonged to Plans for Progress, and who
had corporate headquarters outside of the South. It was expected
that these northern-based companies would have been involved
with equal employment matters earlier than the southern regional textile companies. The statistical record indicates that the
hypothesis can be only partially substantiated.

The relative position of Negroes in both rubber and chemical
plants increased between 1966 and 1968 in the same way as it
did in textiles; however, in the rubber firms studied, the Negro's
overall relative position in both 1966 and 1968 was much better
than that found in either chemicals or textiles. On the other
hand, the blacks overall position in chemicals was less than that
in textiles in both 1966 and 1968. A look at the aggregate data
may mask some important changes in the employment of Negroes
in the job categories.

White Collar Occupations

In the total white collar jobs, the Negro's relative position was
better in rubber but slightly lower in chemicals than in textiles
in 1968. The change in most of the white collar job categories
between 1966 and 1968 was more impressive in chemical and
rubber firms than in textiles. Since it is probably much more
difficult to integrate white collar jobs in terms of available talent
and to induce qualified blacks to remain in areas where the
plants are located, progress in Negro employment in these areas
may reflect vigorous employer policy. A northern-based firm
may find it more challenging to improve the Negro's position in
white collar areas and may invest in such programs rather than
in training in the blue collar fields. Much of the discussion with
employers in chemical and rubber firms centered on programs
for office and clerical and technical personnel, while textile firms
focused on the operative and craftsmen jobs.

As one examines the white collar jobs, the technical and office
and clerical classifications reflect almost all of the increase in
Negro employment. Several companies have led the way in opening up job opportunities for Negroes in white collar occupations
in the rubber and chemical industries. If Firestone and Uniroyal
were deleted from the rubber figures and Celanese and Du Pont
were omitted from chemicals, the Negro's relative position in
each industry would drop dramatically. Since chemical and rubber operations do not vary greatly within their respective indus-

tries in terms of the requirements in white collar jobs, and since the plants are located in similar labor markets, it can be assumed that company policy has played a major role in increasing the Negro's relative position in these companies and in the industries when taken in the aggregate. Within the textile industry, the Negro's relative overall position has increased in white collar jobs, but, in 1968, it was less than that found in rubber and slightly more than that in chemical plants.

Just as was true in the case of rubber and chemicals, the most rapid changes in Negro employment in textiles in the white collar jobs occurred in the technical and office and clerical fields. The Negro's relative position in the official and managers, professional, and sales categories did not change greatly in textiles, rubber, or chemicals between 1966 and 1968. In the rubber companies, Negro representation in the officials and managers category increased from 0.1 percent to 1.2 percent and in chemical plants it rose from less than 0.05 to 0.3 percent. The foregoing can be compared to the slight increase in Negroes from 0.1 to 0.2 percent in the textile plants. Negro professionals rose from 0.0 to 0.4 in the rubber plants between 1966 and 1968, but their number increased by the same small proportion as in textiles and chemicals. Negro salesmen did not appear in any of the plants studied for 1968.

On balance, the hypothesis as stated is partially substantiated by the data on white collar jobs. By 1968, Negroes had a better relative position in such jobs in rubber firms but slightly less in chemicals than that found in textiles. The differences noted can be explained in part by management policy, which places emphasis on the recruitment and placement of white collar personnel.

Blue Collar Occupations

An examination of the Negro's relative position in total blue collar jobs presents a similar picture to that shown above. Negroes were better represented in the total blue collar categories in textiles and rubber than in chemicals in both 1966 and 1968. In the particular job categories, some interesting patterns emerge, and the general hypothesis stated is only partially substantiated on the basis of blue collar jobs.

As noted in Table 29, Negro craftsmen and operatives fared better in rubber plants than in either chemicals or textiles where their relative position was basically the same. It should be indicated, however, that in both job categories Negroes were slightly better represented in textiles than in chemicals. While the Negroe's relative position in the laborer category was greater in chemicals than in either rubber or textiles in 1966, it was less in 1968. In the service worker category, the Negro's relative position was better in both chemicals and rubber than in textiles in 1966 and 1968.

Some of the rubber companies appear to have begun earlier and maintained more progress in hiring and upgrading Negroes than their counterparts in textiles and chemicals. A part of the difference in the utilization rate of Negroes in the chemical, textile, and rubber companies may be explained in terms of technology, but most employers in the three industrial groups indicated that the blue collar labor mix in man-made fiber and cotton textile plants would not vary a great deal. Slightly higher skill requirements may be present in some chemical operations, compared to traditional textiles and tire cord production, but it is probably not a major factor in explaining the Negro's position in chemicals compared to textiles and rubber. It is more likely that an aggressive equal employment program on a plant level, based on an imaginative corporate policy, would account for the differences in the Negro's relative blue collar position in the companies studied.

CHAPTER VI

Negro Employment in the Textile Industry in the South Region, 1966 and 1968

The previous chapter discussed the overall picture of Negro employment in the southern textile industry. It is not sufficient, however, to analyze the southern textile industry as though it represented a homogeneous mass of mills, managements, and working people. Differences in the nature of and approach to problems in textile operations exist within, as well as between, the various states of the South. Experiences in dealing with specific problems, such as minority employment, differ between states such as Alabama and North Carolina and also between areas within a state, such as Charleston and Greenville, South Carolina or Rome and Macon, Georgia. Much has been written about the Piedmont section of North and South Carolina, in particular, with the implicit understanding that the area is somewhat different from the Coastal Plains and Mountain sections of the respective states. The cultural, social, and economic background of the people residing in particular parts of the South has a great deal to do with the attitude and approach taken toward racial employment problems.

The data and discussion presented in the following sections attempt to highlight the trends in Negro employment between 1966 and 1968 in the major southern textile producing states and in some particular areas of these states. As indicated earlier, about 70 percent of all textile employment is in the South, with over 50 percent of all employees in the three states of North Carolina, South Carolina, and Georgia. Over 60 percent of all textile employees, compared to about 20 percent in all manufacturing, work in nonmetropolitan areas and the percentage is higher in some states: Georgia, 70 percent; North Carolina, 86 percent; and South Carolina, 77 percent. In some metropolitan areas, such as Greensboro-High Point and Winston-Salem in North Carolina; Greenville, South Carolina; and Columbus and

Macon in Georgia, textile employment accounts for 25 percent or more of all jobs in manufacturing.[103]

Table 30 shows the percent Negro employment by state and sex for 1966 and 1968. An overview of these data indicates the relative position of Negroes in textiles in 1966 and 1968 and the direction of change in the Negro's status. There was a definite increase in the Negro's position in southern textile plants between 1966 and 1968. Men and women shared the gains shown; however, the overall relative position of Negro females improved more than that of Negro males. The general pattern of improvement was found in each of the states studied, with the most rapid advances being made in Georgia, North Carolina, and South Carolina. This is not surprising since the largest concentration of employees in the industry is found in these states. Among the states, the Negro's total representation appears to be the highest in Georgia. In fact, if the Georgia data were eliminated, the relative position of Negroes in all southern states combined would decline by several percentage points. The records indicate that Negro employment, as a percentage of all employees, has been greater in Georgia textile plants for a longer period of time than in any other southern state. Negro employment as a percentage of all textile employment in Alabama,

TABLE 30. *Textile Mill Products Industry*
Percent Negro Employment by State and Sex
South Region, 1966 and 1968

State	All Employees		Male		Female	
	1966	1968	1966	1968	1966	1968
Alabama	8.9	12.3	12.8	16.5	3.4	6.7
Georgia	13.9	18.3	18.7	22.5	6.5	12.3
North Carolina	9.1	13.3	12.4	15.9	4.5	9.7
South Carolina	8.3	12.4	11.7	15.9	2.1	6.7
Tennessee	0.9	1.5	1.1	1.3	0.5	1.9
Virginia	10.1	13.7	13.5	17.3	4.3	8.1
Total	9.5	13.4	13.0	16.6	4.0	8.8

Source: Tables 24, 25, A-4 to A-9, and A-11 to A-16.

---

103. U.S. Bureau of Labor Statistics, *Labor in the Textile and Apparel Industries*, Bulletin No. 1635 (Washington: Government Printing Office, 1969), pp. 17-18.

TABLE 31. *Textile Mill Products Industry*
Percent Negro Employment by Occupational Group and State
South Region, 1966 and 1968

Occupational Group	South 1966	South 1968	Alabama 1966	Alabama 1968	Georgia 1966	Georgia 1968	North Carolina 1966	North Carolina 1968	South Carolina 1966	South Carolina 1968	Tennessee 1966	Tennessee 1968	Virginia 1966	Virginia 1968
Officials and managers	0.1	0.2	—	0.2	0.1	0.3	0.1	0.2	0.2	0.2	—	—	0.1	0.2
Professionals	0.1	0.3	1.1	1.0	—	—	0.1	0.4	—	0.2	0.6	—	—	0.3
Technicians	0.6	1.0	0.5	1.8	0.4	0.3	0.3	1.1	1.1	1.2	1.1	—	—	0.9
Sales workers	0.2	—	—	—	0.8	—	—	—	—	—	—	—	—	—
Office and clerical	1.2	1.9	1.4	1.6	1.2	2.1	1.2	1.9	1.4	2.1	0.9	0.6	0.7	1.3
Total white collar	0.6	1.0	0.8	1.0	0.6	1.1	0.6	1.0	0.8	1.1	0.5	0.2	0.3	0.8
Craftsmen	1.6	2.9	1.0	3.2	2.0	3.3	1.6	2.5	1.9	4.1	0.1	0.2	0.9	0.8
Operatives	7.8	12.9	7.0	11.7	12.1	18.3	7.8	13.1	6.6	11.9	0.9	1.7	6.3	10.5
Laborers	33.0	38.3	30.4	34.1	47.8	47.8	33.8	38.2	25.6	33.6	2.0	3.7	40.9	44.2
Service workers	37.1	40.8	23.5	30.8	57.4	53.5	33.5	37.5	48.3	48.4	5.0	7.2	18.2	28.0
Total blue collar	10.7	15.3	9.8	13.7	15.6	20.7	10.4	15.2	9.3	14.0	1.0	1.7	11.9	15.9
Total	9.5	13.4	8.9	12.3	13.9	18.3	9.1	13.3	8.3	12.4	0.9	1.5	10.1	13.7

Source: Tables 24, 25, A-4 to A-9, and A-11 to A-16.

North Carolina, South Carolina, and Virginia ranged from about 8 to 10 percent in 1966 to 12 to 13 percent in 1968; in Georgia, the range was from 13.9 to 18.3 percent. The low Negro representation in Tennessee (0.9 percent in 1966 and 1.5 percent in 1968) reflects in part the limited number of plants studied and the fact that Negroes constitute a very small proportion of the total population in the textile areas of the state.

On balance, the record of improvement in Negro employment in textiles in the South as a whole and in each southern state between 1966 and 1968 is impressive. Compared to several other industries, the textile experience is even more striking; for example, the percent Negro employment in 1966 and 1968, respectively, in paper was 6.6 and 7.3; in steel 12.8 and 13.3; and in rubber 8.1 and 8.3.[104] The following section discusses the Negro employment situation by occupational distribution.

OCCUPATIONAL DISTRIBUTION, 1966 AND 1968

A study of the occupational distribution of Negroes in the South Region of the industry gives a more specific picture of the kind of improvements that have occurred and is reflected in the aggregate statistics in the preceding section. Table 31 shows percent Negro employment by occupation and state for 1966 and 1968. The data portray the concentration of Negroes in blue collar categories and indicate areas where employers should give additional attention in their efforts to utilize blacks in the industry.

In examining the occupational data by state, it should be borne in mind that only 14.6 percent of all employees in the textile industry were classified in white collar jobs, compared to 30.7 percent in all manufacturing.[105] The textile industry does not employ a large number of people in any of the white collar categories. On the other hand, 85.3 percent of all employees were classified in blue collar jobs in 1968, and a majority of these employees were operatives.

---

104. See *The Negro in the Paper Industry* in this Series and Herbert R. Northrup, Richard L. Rowan, *et al.*, *Negro Employment in Basic Industry*, Studies of Negro Employment, Vol. I (Philadelphia: Industrial Research Unit, Wharton School of Finance and Commerce, University of Pennsylvania, 1970), Parts Four and Five.

105. U.S. Bureau of Labor Statistics, *Labor in the Textile and Apparel Industries*, p. 68.

White Collar

The Negro's relative position in the white collar areas is not a good one, but, interestingly enough, it is only 1.0 percentage points less than in some industries with plants in many parts of the country, such as paper, steel, and rubber. There was a small improvement in the Negro's overall white collar position in each state studied between 1966 and 1968, except in Tennessee. This must be balanced against the lack of progress made in particular occupations in various states.

There were no black sales people in the industry in the states studied in 1968. One Negro salesman was noted in a Georgia firm in 1966 but he had disappeared by 1968. The person was either misclassified in 1966 or left the industry by 1968. Discrimination against Negroes reveals itself more vividly in sales than in any other job category. Interviews with employers reflect a concern about this condition, and there is an indication that positive steps will be taken by some employers to correct it. The large firms with New York offices appear ready to experiment with Negro salesmen outside of the South. Until it is tried, there is no way to test the general thinking among employers that Negro salesmen may lead to fewer sales for their companies. The fears are probably exaggerated, and there is reason to believe that a qualified Negro sales person may be just as effective in the field as his white counterpart.

The most consistent gains for Negroes in white collar jobs appear to have occurred in the office and clerical category. In all of the states, except Tennessee, employers increased their hiring of Negroes in clerical jobs. Negroes constituted 2.1 percent of all office and clerical employees in Georgia and South Carolina textile plants in 1968, while in the other states the percentage ranged from 0.6 in Tennessee to 1.9 in North Carolina.

In the officials and managers category, which includes the important supervisory jobs in the plant, no significant changes occurred in any state in the Negro's relative standing between 1966 and 1968. Alabama plants appear to have placed Negroes in supervisory positions for the first time and minor advances were made by blacks in Georgia, North Carolina, and Virginia. There were no Negro officials and managers in the Tennessee plants studied, and the percentage remained the same in South Carolina. The data indicate small, but very important, changes. If the beginning efforts of employers in the southern textile industry are successful in introducing black supervision in the mills, much greater progress can be made in the future. It probably has been a wise decision on the part of employers to move slowly and with care in this job category, since a careless placement could wreck the progress for blacks for years to come.

The Negro professional is a relative newcomer to the textile industry and, even in 1968, he did not appear at all in the plants studied in Georgia and Tennessee; in the South Carolina and Virginia plants, he made his first appearance. In Alabama, Negro professionals held about one percent of the total jobs in the category, while in North Carolina firms, Negro representation was less, 0.4 percent. Professional workers make up a very small proportion of all employees in the textile industry, and there are particular problems, as discussed earlier, in attracting qualified Negroes into these jobs.

Negroes make up a small proportion of all workers classified as technicians in the textile industry, even though their representation is greater here than in most white collar jobs. The Negro's relative position in the technicians category improved slightly in Alabama, North Carolina, and South Carolina between 1966 and 1968, but declined in Tennessee and Georgia. In Virginia, Negroes entered the technicians category for the first time in the period studied.

Textile employers in the southern states have a tremendous challenge to improve the Negro's relative position in white collar jobs. Large firms, such as Burlington in North Carolina, J. P. Stevens in South Carolina, Dan River in Virginia, Bibb in Georgia, and West Point Pepperell in Alabama, can lead the way toward establishing effective equal employment programs to utilize qualified Negroes in prestigious white collar jobs. A combination of factors, including a tight labor market and government pressure, has caused an awakening on the part of the employers to the necessity of developing adequate methods of bringing blacks into all aspects of their employment picture.

Blue Collar

The overall relative position of Negroes in the South in blue collar jobs increased considerably between 1966 and 1968 (10.7 to 15.3), and in each state studied, the increases followed a definite pattern of improvement: Alabama, 9.8 to 13.7; Georgia,

15.6 to 20.7; North Carolina, 10.4 to 15.2; South Carolina, 9.3 to 14.0; Tennessee, 1.0 to 1.7; and Virginia, 11.9 to 15.9. The data show, in general terms, a rapid movement of blacks into the southern textile industry within a relatively short period of time.

In the important craftsmen category, which includes loom fixers, maintenance people, and other skilled employees, Negroes have improved their general position in each of the states, except in Virginia where their status remained basically unchanged. On a relative basis, the change in the employment of Negro craftsmen was substantial in Alabama and South Carolina plants; however, the improvements in North Carolina, Georgia, and Tennessee, although smaller, should be noted. Virginia is the only state where the ratio was less in 1968 than in 1966. Negroes have made a breakthrough in recent years in most southern textile areas into the top jobs in the blue collar hierarchy. The Negro craftsmen data indicate that some upgrading has been made by employers and also that Negroes have been hired, probably for the first time directly into skilled jobs in the plant. Positive signs of change have occurred also in the position of Negro operatives in the South and in each of the states studied. Over 10 percent of all employees in the operatives category were black in 1968 in Alabama, Georgia, North Carolina, South Carolina, and Virginia. The highest proportion was found in the Georgia plants, where they constituted 18.3 percent of all operatives. There is an interesting consistency in the 1968 percentage of Negro operatives in the states of Alabama, 11.7 percent, North Carolina, 13.1 percent, South Carolina, 11.9 percent, and Virginia, 10.5. These figures were arrived at from a rather low approximate 7 percent Negro representation in each state as late as 1966. Within a brief time period, Negroes have increased their position in the operatives category rather substantially.

Negroes continue to hold heavy proportions of all jobs in each of the important textile producing states in the laborers and service workers categories. The laborers group includes unskilled, low-paid employees, while the service workers classification includes janitors and outside helpers. By 1968, over 30 percent of all employees in these two categories were black in Alabama, Georgia, North Carolina, South Carolina, and Virginia. The largest representations occurred in Georgia where 53.5 percent of all service workers and 47.8 percent of all laborers were black;

also, in South Carolina, 48.4 percent of all service workers were black in the same year. Negroes have been hired in the past to perform the least desirable tasks in terms of working conditions and wages. The importance of the entrance of Negroes into the industry, even at the unskilled level, should not be discounted, however, since valuable work and work-related experience can be obtained, particularly among those who have never had an opportunity to work and to become accustomed to an industrial environment. Some have looked upon the utilization of Negroes at the basic unskilled level as an important link in the transition of blacks from agriculture to industry. The textile industry brought the untrained, poor white out of the cotton fields and into the mainstream of economic life in the South, and it appears that the same process is about to repeat itself with the unskilled, poor black person.

While one may not be too impressed with a heavy black representation at the lower levels of the blue collar ladder, it hopefully marks a beginning. If employers look upon the matter in this way and assure upgrading and promotional opportunities to blacks so situated, the future can be quite optimistic in terms of Negroes gaining access to operative, craftsmen, and supervisory positions. The jobs of selecting, training, and placing qualified Negroes from a relatively large body of unskilled employees will not be easy for textile management. It is essential that the personnel function be upgraded to cope with difficult problems ahead.

CHANGES IN EMPLOYMENT, 1966 TO 1968

The previous section presented a picture of the relative position of the Negro in the southern states by occupational distribution in the textile industry. While percentage changes are important in making comparisons of the Negro's relative employment status over time, they do not reveal the significant absolute changes that have occurred. Table 32 shows absolute changes in Negro employment by job category between 1966 and 1968. An examination of these data indicates the actual progress made by textile employers in utilizing Negroes. The data also suggest areas where further effort is needed to provide equal employment opportunities for blacks.

TABLE 32. Textile Mill Products Industry

Change in Employment by Race, Occupational Group, and State
Southern States, 1966 to 1968

Occupational Group	Alabama Number	Percent	Georgia Number	Percent	North Carolina Number	Percent	South Carolina Number	Percent	Tennessee Number	Percent	Virginia Number	Percent
Officials and managers	126	12.5	95	5.2	467	9.2	110	3.1	62	14.4	3	0.2
Negro	2	*	4	400.0	3	50.0	1	12.5	—	—	2	200.0
White	124	12.3	91	5.0	464	9.2	109	3.1	62	14.4	1	0.1
Professionals	9	9.9	5	1.5	140	16.9	—52	—9.4	—28	—17.5	18	5.6
Negro	—	—	—	—	3	300.0	1	*	—1	*	1	*
White	9	10.0	5	1.5	137	16.5	—53	—9.6	—27	—17.0	17	5.3
Technicians	31	16.0	107	37.5	136	20.0	69	11.2	21	22.1	30	10.3
Negro	3	300.0	—	—	7	350.0	1	14.3	—1	*	3	*
White	28	14.5	107	37.7	129	19.1	68	11.1	22	23.4	27	9.3
Sales workers	—15	—45.5	9	7.0	31	12.8	—2	—2.9	—68	—98.6	—1	—33.3
Negro	—	—	—1	*	—	—	—	—	—	—	—	—
White	—15	—45.5	10	7.8	31	12.8	—2	—2.9	—68	—98.6	—1	—33.3
Office and clerical	93	7.4	225	9.6	598	10.4	105	3.2	—256	—45.4	—62	—3.8
Negro	4	22.2	25	86.2	53	76.8	22	46.8	—3	—60.0	9	81.8
White	89	7.1	200	8.6	545	9.6	83	2.6	—253	—45.3	—71	—4.4
Total white collar	244	9.4	441	9.0	1,372	10.9	230	2.9	—269	—20.4	—12	—0.3
Negro	9	45.0	28	87.5	66	84.6	25	40.3	—5	—71.4	15	125.0
White	235	9.1	413	8.4	1,306	10.5	205	2.6	—264	—20.1	—27	—0.8

TABLE 32—Continued

Occupational Group	Alabama Number	Alabama Percent	Georgia Number	Georgia Percent	North Carolina Number	North Carolina Percent	South Carolina Number	South Carolina Percent	Tennessee Number	Tennessee Percent	Virginia Number	Virginia Percent
Craftsmen	224	7.9	255	5.0	—1,071	—7.8	981	9.9	337	33.7	—376	—11.9
Negro	71	263.0	78	78.8	91	40.4	254	132.3	2	200.0	—7	—23.3
White	153	5.5	177	3.6	—1,162	—8.6	727	7.5	335	33.5	—369	—11.8
Operatives	—246	—1.5	—361	—1.3	2,861	4.8	541	1.4	187	3.1	539	4.2
Negro	752	64.8	1,654	49.8	3,578	77.7	2,140	83.4	53	98.1	592	72.1
White	—998	—6.5	—2,015	—8.3	—717	—1.3	—1,599	—4.4	134	2.3	—53	—0.4
Laborers	—141	—5.0	707	19.6	667	7.0	—565	—6.9	—219	—33.6	389	10.9
Negro	56	6.5	336	19.4	678	21.1	469	22.3	3	23.1	288	19.8
White	—197	—10.1	371	19.7	—11	—0.2	—1,034	—16.9	—222	—34.7	101	4.8
Service workers	—380	—36.4	23	1.9	140	5.9	75	6.7	14	10.1	—157	—30.1
Negro	—41	—16.7	—35	—5.1	149	18.6	38	7.1	4	57.1	7	7.4
White	—339	—42.5	58	11.3	—9	—0.6	37	6.4	10	7.6	—164	—38.5
Total blue collar	—543	—2.3	624	1.7	2,597	3.1	1,032	1.8	319	4.1	395	2.0
Negro	838	36.6	2,033	34.8	4,496	50.8	2,901	53.7	62	82.7	880	36.7
White	—1,381	—6.6	—1,409	—4.5	—1,899	—2.5	—1,869	—3.5	257	3.3	—485	—2.7
Total	—299	—1.2	1,065	2.5	3,969	4.1	1,262	1.9	50	0.6	383	1.6
Negro	847	36.7	2,061	35.1	4,562	51.1	2,926	53.5	57	69.5	895	37.1
White	—1,146	—4.9	—996	—2.7	—593	—0.7	—1,664	—2.7	—7	—0.1	—512	—2.4

Source: Tables A-4 to A-9 and A-11 to A-16.

* Unable to compute percentage.

White Collar Occupations

Between 1966 and 1968 there was a net addition of only 138 Negroes made in white collar jobs by the southern textile companies studied. During the same period, 1,868 whites were added. The 138 Negroes who were added were distributed as follows: office and clerical, 110; technicians, 13; officials and managers, 12; professionals, 4; and sales, -1. About 80 percent of all Negroes added in these categories were classified as office and clerical personnel. These data show that Negroes are not making great strides in entering white collar jobs in the textile industry. While progress has been made, as indicated by the percentage changes discussed earlier and shown in the appendix tables, much remains to be done by employers to enhance the opportunities for blacks to enter white collar occupations.

On a state basis, the total of 138 Negroes added to white collar jobs was distributed as follows: North Carolina, 66; Georgia, 28; South Carolina, 25; Virginia, 15; Alabama, 9; and Tennessee, -5. The figures are not particularly surprising since a considerable number of the firms studied were located in North Carolina and only a few in Tennessee. It is interesting to note, however, the absolute lack of additional Negroes in some of the categories in some states. For example, in Alabama, no Negroes were brought into the professional group; in Georgia, none were added to the professional or technicians groups; in Tennessee, the number of Negro professionals, technicians, and office and clerical personnel actually declined; and in South Carolina, the number of Negro officials and managers, professionals, and technicians increased by only one person. The employment record of North Carolina firms was somewhat better than that in other states, but even there only 66 Negroes were added to the white collar occupations and 53 of those were office and clerical employees.

One of the most significant aspects of the white collar picture presented in an examination of the absolute figures is the general lack of Negro representation in the officials and managers category which contains supervisory personnel. Apparently, it remains a rare case where Negroes supervise other Negroes or whites, or racially mixed departments in the southern textile industry. In the increase of 863 official and managers jobs between 1966 and 1968, Negroes held only 12 of them: 2 in Alabama; 4 in Georgia; 3 in North Carolina; 1 in South Carolina; none in Tennessee; and 2 in Virginia. In North Carolina, where employers added 467 officials and managers between 1966 and 1968, only 3 were black. Employers appear to be concerned about this situation and have indicated in interviews that they will move as quickly as the circumstances permit. The employer's caution here is based on a fear that placing the "wrong" black in a supervisory position could lead to tension and strife within the plant. Also, since the opportunity for Negroes to perform in the operatives and craftsmen occupations is very recent, employers contend that time has not permitted the development of expertise and acceptability of many blacks for supervisory roles. While these factors represent real problems to employers, it remains significant that few Negroes have gained a place in the important officials and managers category.

Blue Collar Occupations

In marked contrast to the white collar occupations, Negroes have made rapid advancement into blue collar jobs in the textile industry (see Table 32). Indeed, the entire increase in the total number of blue collar workers between 1966 and 1968 can be accounted for by Negro employment. Blue collar employees increased in each state studied, except Alabama, where a decline of 543 workers occurred. In absolute terms, the total net increase in blue collar employment amounted to 4,424; 11,210 Negroes were added and 6,786 whites dropped out of the industry, giving a net addition of 4,424 blacks. It should be noted, again, that the same companies and plants were studied for 1966 and 1968, so that the changes are quite revealing in actual figures.

Additions of Negro blue collar employees by state appeared as follows: Alabama, 838; Georgia, 2,033; North Carolina, 4,496; South Carolina, 2,901; Tennessee, 62; and Virginia, 880. On the other hand, decreases in white blue collar employees were: Alabama, 1,381; Georgia, 1,409; North Carolina, 1,899; South Carolina, 1,869; and Virginia, 512. These statistics indicate the pattern of employment in southern textile plants. Negroes are being hired in relatively large numbers in blue collar jobs while whites are moving out of the industry. An examination of the data on the basis of sex, as shown in Table 33, reveals that Negro males and females have shared the blue collar employment gains in the industry in recent years. Apparently, the existence of new industrial activity in the South has lured whites away from textiles and, in their absence, textile employers have been forced to open employment opportunities to Negroes.

TABLE 33. Textile Mill Products Industry
Change in Blue Collar Employment by Race, Sex, and Occupational Group Southern States, 1966 to 1968

Occupational Group	Alabama		Georgia		North Carolina		South Carolina		Tennessee		Virginia	
	Number	Percent	Number	Percent	Number	Percent	Number	Percent	Number	Percent	Number	Percent
Male												
Craftsmen	—124	—4.5	29	0.6	—589	—4.8	754	8.4	162	16.6	—298	—9.7
Negro	30	111.1	66	69.5	75	36.1	241	157.5	2	200.0	—5	—17.9
White	—154	—5.7	—37	—0.8	—664	—5.5	513	5.8	160	16.5	—293	—9.7
Operatives	—269	—3.4	—445	—3.2	1,152	4.3	—244	—1.2	—106	—3.1	—31	—0.5
Negro	407	43.9	747	28.1	1,751	55.1	1,170	52.1	7	17.5	314	47.1
White	—676	—9.8	—1,192	—10.7	—599	—2.5	—1,414	—8.0	—113	—3.4	—345	—6.0
Laborers	—35	—1.7	192	6.3	—7	—0.1	—575	—8.4	—58	—13.7	194	7.0
Negro	51	6.4	188	12.3	307	10.4	337	16.6	—		185	14.8
White	—86	—6.6	4	0.3	—314	—7.0	—912	—18.9	—58	—14.2	9	0.6
Service workers	—313	—39.8	—8	—0.9	—82	—4.2	18	1.9	14	11.3	—139	—30.0
Negro	—29	—16.6	—59	—12.7	41	6.0	—10	—2.2	4	66.7	8	9.4
White	—284	—46.5	51	11.2	—123	—9.6	28	5.7	10	8.5	—147	—38.8
Total blue collar	—741	—5.5	—232	—1.0	474	1.0	—47	—0.1	12	0.2	—274	—2.2
Negro	459	23.8	942	19.8	2,174	30.9	1,738	35.5	13	21.7	502	24.7
White	—1,200	—10.4	—1,174	—6.7	—1,700	—4.1	—1,785	—5.6	—1	*	—776	—7.3
Total	—565	—3.7	—9	*	1,397	2.4	—120	—0.3	—205	—3.5	—313	—2.1
Negro	468	24.0	962	20.1	2,208	31.1	1,753	35.4	8	12.3	511	25.1
White	—1,033	—7.8	—971	—4.7	—811	—1.6	—1,873	—5.0	—213	—3.7	—824	—6.3

TABLE 33—Continued

Occupational Group	Alabama		Georgia		North Carolina		South Carolina		Tennessee		Virginia	
	Number	Percent	Number	Percent	Number	Percent	Number	Percent	Number	Percent	Number	Percent
Female												
Craftsmen	348	386.7	226	58.1	—482	—32.2	227	23.9	175	625.0	—78	—72.9
Negro	41	**	12	300.0	16	94.1	13	33.3	—	—	—2	**
White	307	341.1	214	55.6	—498	—33.7	214	23.5	175	625.0	—76	—72.4
Operatives	23	0.3	84	0.6	1,709	5.3	785	4.1	293	11.3	570	8.8
Negro	345	148.7	907	138.3	1,827	127.9	970	304.1	46	328.6	278	179.4
White	—322	—3.8	—823	—6.3	—118	—0.4	—185	—1.0	247	9.6	292	4.6
Laborers	—106	—14.9	515	93.1	674	32.5	10	0.7	—161	—70.0	195	25.0
Negro	5	8.6	148	74.0	371	143.2	132	185.9	3	**	103	50.7
White	—111	—16.9	367	104.0	303	16.7	—122	—9.4	—164	—71.3	92	15.9
Service workers	—67	—26.1	31	10.8	222	53.1	57	35.0	—	—	—18	—31.6
Negro	—12	—17.1	24	10.5	108	94.7	48	64.9	—	—	—1	—10.0
White	—55	—29.4	7	12.1	114	37.5	9	10.1	—	—	—17	—36.2
Total blue collar	198	2.0	856	5.7	2,123	5.8	1,079	5.0	307	10.7	669	9.0
Negro	379	105.3	1,091	100.2	2,322	127.7	1,163	231.2	49	326.7	378	102.2
White	—181	—1.9	—235	—1.7	—199	—0.6	—84	—0.4	258	9.1	291	4.1
Total	266	2.5	1,074	6.4	2,572	6.3	1,382	5.8	255	8.0	696	8.0
Negro	379	105.3	1,099	100.7	2,354	128.4	1,173	230.5	49	288.2	384	102.7
White	—113	—1.1	—25	—0.2	218	0.6	209	0.9	206	6.5	312	3.7

Source: Tables A-4 to A-9 and A-11 to A-16.

* Less than 0.05 percent.

** Unable to calculate percentage.

In the important craftsmen category, which contains the skilled employees, the net change between 1966 and 1968 amounted to 350; total black craftsmen increased by 489 (80 females and 409 males), and total white craftsmen declined by 139 (a decrease of 475 males and an increase of 336 females). Black males and white females made the net gains in the craftsmen category. This denotes a scarcity of white male labor in the textile industry, which can be accounted for in part by white males choosing alternative employment opportunities in many areas of the South. The data also suggest that employers are beginning to use women in skilled jobs where they have not been used in the past.

Negro male employment increased in the craftsmen category in the states as follows: Alabama, 30; Georgia, 66; North Carolina, 75; South Carolina, 241; Tennessee, 2. In Virginia, the number of Negro male craftsmen declined by 5. In Alabama, Georgia, North Carolina, and Virginia, the number of white male craftsmen declined significantly, compared to the smaller increases in the number of Negro males. For example, in North Carolina, white male craftsmen declined by 664, whereas black male craftsmen increased by 75; and, in Alabama, white males declined by 154, while Negro males increased by 30 in the skilled category. Negro female employment increased by 80, with over one-half of the increase occurring in Alabama plants. About a dozen black female craftsmen were added in each of the states of Georgia, North Carolina, and South Carolina. A decline of two black female craftsmen occurred in Virginia, and no change was registered in Tennessee.

The pattern of change provides room for optimism concerning the Negro's future role in the southern textile industry. Obviously, employers are allowing blacks to participate in more highly skilled jobs. If the change is a response only to a tight labor market situation, it still remains an important one. Over time, and assuming the gains can be held in a healthy economy, lessons will be learned by employers and black employees alike; employers will learn that discrimination in the past has been costly in terms of qualified manpower, and employees will develop valuable job skills and work habits.

The operatives category contains the largest number of employees in the textile industry. Between 1966 and 1968, the net change in the operatives group was 3,521, including 3,464 females and 57 males; total black operatives increased by 8,769, including 4,396 males and 4,373 females; and total white operatives decreased by 5,248, including 4,339 males and 909 females. The number of white operatives declined in each state studied, except Tennessee, where an increase of 134 appeared. On the other hand, the number of Negro operatives increased in every state studied. This demonstrates again the importance of blacks in the employment structure of the textile industry in the South. Many plants would have considerable difficulty in maintaining operations without the availability of Negro labor.

Negro male employment increased in the operatives category in the states as follows: Alabama, 407; Georgia, 747; North Carolina, 1,751; South Carolina, 1,170; Tennessee, 7; and Virginia, 314. The number of white male operatives declined significantly in each state. In South Carolina, for example, the number of white male operatives declined by 1,414, but the number of Negro male operatives increased by 1,170. The increases in Negro female employment in the operatives category followed the same pattern as that shown for Negro males. White female operatives declined in each of the states, except Virginia and Tennessee, where their numbers increased more than that of black females.

An examination of the data, on the basis of race and sex in the operatives category, reveals dramatic changes occurring in the southern textile industry. Negroes are entering the industry and whites are leaving.

The laborers category contains the unskilled jobs in the textile industry. Negroes have been hired as laborers in the past, more so than in any other job classification, but upward mobility has been a problem. Changes in promotional policies have occurred since 1960, and it appears that blacks hired as laborers today will have an opportunity to advance to semiskilled and skilled jobs as qualifications permit. If this projection is accurate, then it is significant to note any advances that Negroes are making in the laborers category.

Between 1966 and 1968, the total number of laborers increased by 838; females increased by 1,127 and males declined by 289; total black laborers increased by 1,830, including 1,068 males and 762 females. The number of black laborers, both male and female, increased in each state, except in Tennessee, where no change was registered in the number of black males. In contrast to the change in the Negro laborer's position, the number of white laborers declined by 992, including a decline of 1,357 white males and an increase of 365 white females. White male laborers decreased in Alabama, North Carolina, South Carolina, and Tennessee for a combined total of 1,370, while an addition of 4 white male laborers was made in Georgia and 9 in Virginia. White female laborers decreased in Alabama, South Carolina, and Tennessee by a total of 397, but in Georgia, North Carolina, and Virginia, their numbers increased by 762. On balance, blacks made significant gains over whites in the laborers category in southern textile plants.

Apparently, it was not possible for employers to recruit white male laborers except in minor instances noted. A few white females were added, but the major changes occurred in the increases of black males and females in all states except Tennessee. In North Carolina alone, 678 Negroes were added to the laborers group, whereas 11 whites were deleted; and, on the basis of sex, 307 black males were added, while 314 white males were deleted and 371 black females and 303 white females were added. This pattern reveals, again, what appears to be happening throughout the Piedmont section, with Negroes entering the industry in substantial numbers and white males, in particular, leaving to accept alternative job opportunities.

The service workers category includes the janitorial personnel, outside workmen, and plant guards and security people. As a rule, the service worker is not in a direct line of progression in a plant, and there is little expectancy on the part of those classified as service workers to move out of the job for which they were hired.

It is not surprising that the total number of employees in the service worker group declined by 285 between 1966 and 1968. Automatic cleaning devices have contributed to the decline in the number of jobs available in services. Some increase in the total number of black and white females occurred in this classification, but was offset by decreases in the total number of black and white males. The most significant changes in the job category occurred among black females with an increase of 167, all of which occurred in North Carolina, Georgia, and South Carolina plants, and white males with a decrease of 465, all occurring in plants in the states of Alabama, North Carolina, and Virginia. Most of the increase in black female service workers occurred in North Carolina plants, and most of the decrease in white male service worker employment took place in Alabama and Virginia plants.

TABLE 34. Textile Mill Products Industry
Change in Employment by Race and Sex
Southern States, 1966 to 1968

State	All Employees			Male		Female	
	Total	Negro	White	Negro	White	Negro	White
Alabama	—299	847	—1,146	468	—1,033	379	—113
Georgia	1,065	2,061	—996	962	—971	1,099	—25
North Carolina	3,969	4,562	—593	2,208	—811	2,354	218
South Carolina	1,262	2,926	—1,664	1,753	—1,873	1,173	209
Tennessee	50	57	—7	8	—213	49	206
Virginia	383	895	—512	511	—824	384	312
Total	6,430	11,348	—4,918	5,910	—5,725	5,438	807

Source: Tables 32 and 33.

Summary

Table 34 presents a summary of employment activities between 1966 and 1968 in the companies studied. An examination of the data leads to the following conclusions: (1) Total employment increased in all states but Alabama; total Negro employment *increased,* but total white employment *decreased* in all states. It appears that Negroes are making rapid gains in southern textile plants while whites are leaving or not entering the industry. (2) On the basis of sex, total black male employment *increased,* but total white male employment *decreased* in all states. Negro males are making gains as white males enter new job situations in other industries. (3) Total black females *increased* in all states and total white females *increased* in all states, except in Alabama and Georgia. Gains in employment among females have been substantial in the textile industry. Negro female employment advanced more than that for white females in all states except Tennessee. In North Carolina, for example, it should be noted that the total black female employment increased by 2,354, while total white female employment increased by only 218 between 1966 and 1968. (4) On balance, textile employers have hired black males and females, and to a lesser extent, white females, in the absence of white male labor.

A change of the magnitude noted in the racial employment structure of textiles has probably never occurred before in southern industry. The employment of blacks in southern textile plants in all job categories can have a significant economic and social impact. Discrimination, based on feelings of white superiority, may be constructively attacked and partially eliminated as whites and blacks begin to share equal job opportunities in the small, nonmetropolitan textile plants. A major learning experience for all parties—employers, employees, and community leaders—is in store for those residing in the areas of change.

CHAPTER VII

Management and Racial Employment Policy in the Textile Industry

The quantitative aspects of Negro employment in the textile industry are analyzed in the previous chapters. Statistical data are necessary to reflect the Negro's position in the industry, but they do not provide a complete picture of employment activity. An evaluation of employment policy can lead to a better understanding of the Negro's job position and future prospects for his utilization in the industry. This chapter discusses several aspects of racial employment policy, including manpower planning, recruiting, selection, training, and upgrading. Some of the problems associated with integrating the work force in a textile plant are also discussed. The analysis of qualitative factors is based on plant visits and personal interviews with representatives of the textile industry.

EMPLOYMENT POLICY

Employee relations, industrial relations, and personnel management are related terms for a functional area of business that deals with human resources. Within the corporate environment, this area generally competes with others such as production, marketing, and finance for recognition and budget. Human resource management has not been a well-developed, functional area of companies in the textile industry. In some respects this is surprising since labor costs constitute a significant part of the total cost structure in textiles. The general lack of formal organization to handle personnel problems complicates the task of achieving many goals in a company, including that of equal employment opportunity.

Sound policy must be developed in order for the firm to reach its objectives in an efficient manner. The formulation and implementation of policy determines, in large measure, the success of a company in pursuing its goals. A useful policy definition is stated below:

Policies are guides to future decisions and actions. Their purpose is to provide a point of departure for future decisions or to approve in advance appropriate action to be taken in recurring situations. Thus, the use of policies facilitates decentralization of responsibility. Policies may be issued as written statements, or they may be derived as unwritten understandings of past actions . . . The need for both major and minor policy guides exists at virtually all levels of the management structure.[106]

There is a need for a clear declaration of personnel policy at all levels of the firm in which racial employment becomes an integral part. Difficult problems associated with Negro utilization can be minimized if authority and responsibility are clearly delineated in company policy. In the absence of effective policy, which provides the basis for rules and procedures, the line foreman may be continuously frustrated by the entrance of blacks into the plant.

Organizational structures in the textile industry vary from highly decentralized companies with autonomous units, wherein each subsidiary theoretically sets its own policies, to centralized firms where the corporate staff establishes policy and attempts to coordinate its implementation. The complex human problems, growing out of difficult labor market situations and increasing demands to integrate all levels of the firms in the industry, have caused some serious thinking among management people about the organization and upgrading of the personnel function. One industrial relations director in a recently revamped personnel department made the following observation:

There was a time when Mr. X, who was plant superintendent, ran the plant and the town where it was located; he decided who had their back steps repaired, where the sewer lines went, etc.; but new technology came in and more detailed jobs were added; he could no longer spend time on so many things; he needed assistance; the personnel man has had a job to educate his own management as to his worth; he has had to show that personnel talent can save the company money. Personnel is a great challenge to the industry. Prior to two years ago, no planning of hiring was done.[107]

The foregoing indicates an awareness of the necessity to create and invest in a personnel program with capable management.

---

106. J. Thomas Cannon, *Business Strategy and Policy* (New York: Harcourt, Brace and World, 1968), p. 10.

107. Personal interviews.

In the context of racial employment problems, one newly appointed personnel director stated:

The employment policy of this company in regard to Negroes is based on the concept of involvement. If we can involve people in each other's lives, then, the matter of race can be forgotten. Plant supervision needs to know the families of our minority employees. One of the most difficult things for our foremen to do is to talk to Negroes about their families. As we have tried to implement this concept of involvement, we see some interesting things happening. Recently the white girls in the office got together and gave a shower for a Negro girl who was leaving because of pregnancy. These girls had become interested in the black girl's life and baby and this promoted good employee relations in the office. In another instance, Negroes participated in the local golf tournament and one of them won it. This provided a basis for much conversation and communication in the plant.[108]

The statement cited above demonstrates that there is some attention being given to racial employment matters.

There are examples, of course, of unenlightened attitudes concerning the management of human resources in textile plants. The president of a middle-sized company that maintains no personnel function as such said: "Our employment policy is that we hire anyone and treat them right." [109] Obviously, this is a nebulous policy, and one that could lead to chaos. It would not be very helpful to a superintendent who may be in a quandary as to what to do about training and upgrading or promoting blacks in the mill. In another case, the plant manager in an autonomous unit in a highly decentralized company, who was expected to handle most personnel and related matters, said: "I just can't get conditioned to the new people coming into the plant; people aren't responsible; they won't work; people will choose welfare over work." [110] A well-planned program to recruit, select, and train those coming into the plant could, no doubt, assist this manager in overcoming the problems leading to his general frustration.

Affirmative Action Programs

In the absence of effective corporate personnel organization and philosophy in regard to racial employment, it has been diffi-

108. *Ibid.*

109. *Ibid.*

110. *Ibid.*

cult for the textile industry to adjust to mandates of the federal government. President John F. Kennedy enunciated a concept of affirmative action in reference to equal employment opportunity in 1961 in Executive Order 10925. This concept was carried forth in President Johnson's Executive Order 11246. The idea of affirmative action made it explicit that the nation's contractors should practice nondiscrimination in employment in a vigorous manner. In addition to stating a policy concerning minority employment, employers were required to develop and implement a program that would lead to substantial improvement of the Negro's position in all occupational categories. The major federal agencies created by the executive orders and the Civil Rights Act of 1964 to supervise nondiscrimination in employment are the Equal Employment Opportunity Commission (EEOC) and the Office of Federal Contract Compliance (OFCC). The Department of Defense figures prominently in the picture through the Assistant Secretary of Defense (Manpower and Reserve Affairs), as the Department of Defense Contract Compliance Officer, and the Director of the Defense Supply Agency, who serves as the Deputy Contract Compliance Officer for Contract Compliance Operations. Companies in the textile industry that wish contracts with the federal government must have their equal employment programs reviewed and approved before the contract is awarded.

Subsequent to the EEOC hearings held in Charlotte, North Carolina in January 1967 and referred to in a previous chapter, the EEOC, OFCC, and Department of Defense compliance personnel met and agreed on a plan to review the equal employment programs in the textile industry of North Carolina and South Carolina. During the year 1967, interagency discussions were held and final plans to conduct the compliance reviews were completed in January 1968. It was agreed that the OFCC would review the ten largest companies in the industry and EEOC would investigate smaller firms with cooperation from the Department of Defense. The first review was made at Dan River Mills in January 1968 and the Defense Supply Agency was charged with the responsibility of working with the company in developing an affirmative action program. Reviews and discussions continued at Dan River, J. P. Stevens, and Burlington Industries throughout most of 1968 with no approval of an affirmative action program. The major deficiencies found by the Defense Supply Agency were:

1. The companies did not provide in detail "specific goals and time tables for the prompt achievement of full and equal employment opportunity" as required in Section 60-1.40 of the OFCC Rules and Regulations.

2. OFCC policy and recent court decisions require that contractors remedy the present effects of past discrimination. Acceptable contractor programs to meet this requirement had not been formulated.

3. The companies had not provided a meaningful plan to assure fairness and nondiscrimination in recruiting, selection, placement, promotion, and upgrading.

4. There still remains some company housing that is occupied on a segregated basis.

The Defense Supply Agency recomendations were indorsed to Deputy Secretary of Defense Packard.[111]

It appears that items 1 and 3 above were the most crucial ones for the industry. They indicate that there were no policies, plans, or programs to achieve equal employment opportunity.

During the difficult days of attempting to get a satisfactory nondiscriminatory program agreed upon by the three large companies, an award for the production of cloth was pending. Even though the areas of disagreement remained over equal employment opportunity, Assistant Secretary of Defense Packard awarded $9.4 million in contracts to Dan River, J. P. Stevens, and Burlington in February 1969. Secretary Packard indicated that he had reached a "gentlemen's agreement" that "the firms would cease racial discrimination in their hiring practices." [112] Secretary of Labor Shultz supported Secretary Packard's position in a speech at the National Press Club on March 27, 1969:

As you know, we had a little difficulty recently involving some textile manufacturers. We could have blocked their defense supply contracts, but David Packard, Deputy Secretary of Defense, himself a forward-looking man in West Coast civic affairs, believed we could get results from these contractors. He took the conciliatory approach but he did it by getting a personal commitment from chief executive officers. He well knew that if the spirit of compliance failed, he could move in at any time and cancel contracts or declare the companies ineligible for further contracts, which are awarded many times a year.

Dave Packard's strategy is paying off.[113]

---

111. Bureau of National Affairs, *Daily Labor Report*, March 27, 1969, p. AA-4.

112. *Atlanta Journal*, February 12, 1969.

113. Bureau of National Affairs, *Daily Labor Report*, March 27, 1969, p. AA-5.

Secretary Packard's decision to make an award to the textile companies, while the compliance agencies were still unsatisfied with their equal employment activities, provoked a Congressional hearing, induced the wrath of civil rights groups, and officials in federal agencies claimed that they had been completely ignored. Senator Walter Mondale "accused the Defense Department . . . of wrecking the civil rights compliance system for Federal contractors and called for cancellation of clothing contracts to three southern mills charged with racial discrimination." [114] Despite the criticism made against the Department of Defense action, written affirmative action programs emerged for the first time in the textile industry. Burlington, Dan River, and J. P. Stevens are now operating under an agreed upon nondiscriminatory employment program. These programs establish the firm's commitment to practice equal employment opportunity in recruitment, selection, training, placement, and upgrading of minority employees. One important feature of the textile programs that distinguishes them from those found in other industries is the requirement for quarterly EEO-1 type reports to be furnished to the federal compliance agencies. This is a built-in mechanism to force close attention to the implementation of the stated affirmative action programs.

Some of the other firms in the industry, in addition to the big three cited above, are beginning to develop written affirmative action programs, but such activity was not widespread in mid-1969. The majority of the smaller and middle-size textile firms, where most of the industry's employees are found, have not established written equal employment programs. Many of these firms have employed Negroes, but since they may not be government contractors, they have seen no necessity to write out a policy for minority employment. Significant advantages could accrue to most companies in following the guidelines established by affirmative action programs. In a labor market that is tight and heavily black, and where employers face the future possibility of using large numbers of Negroes in their operations, a positive minority employment program can serve as an effective means of communicating to line management and to the work force.

---

114. *The Washington Post*, February 27, 1969, p. A2.

Recruiting and Selection

In order to understand the recruiting and selection procedures used in the textile industry, one has to be aware of the environment in which these activities occur. The bulk of the industry is located in the South and most of the companies are relatively small and in nonmetropolitan areas. The industry is concentrated in the areas of the South where major industrial growth has occurred over the past decade. Many high-wage paying (higher than textile wages) companies have entered this labor market once dominated by the textile industry. Not too many years ago, textile firms in North Carolina and South Carolina could be assured of a steady influx of cheap white labor to keep the mills operating. This situation has changed drastically over a relatively short period. Today, textile mills are finding it exceedingly difficult to find qualified personnel, and have had to resort to the use of black labor.

Blue Collar. In the blue collar areas, most employers depend on walk-ins to furnish the great bulk of labor. Employee referrals, newspaper and radio spot ads, and employment services are used in particular instances. As whites have begun to accept alternative employment opportunities in many areas, employers have had to open their doors to blacks and, as a result, those who are walking through the plant gates seeking employment are Negroes. The black who presents himself to the mill today is similar to his white counterpart who was employed in the post-Civil War period. He may have little education, a poor work history, and no understanding of discipline in an industrial environment. If he is hired, and many times he will be out of desperation, the employer faces a problem of trying to develop skills so that he can be upgraded.

Employers report, however, in many cases that the Negro female is usually able to show some educational background, but this may not mean much in an area where a segregated school system has provided an inferior education. Also, the Negro female who is recruited into the plant may bring additional problems. While she may be a good employee, home responsibilities may cause her to be absent. Selection procedures are few and almost no standards are used: "We don't even check police records anymore." "We may hire a man who can't read or write if he has some experience on a job." [115] No tests are used to screen

---

115. Personal interviews.

applicants. Apparently, if a person is physically able to get to work, and has some manual dexterity, he is a likely candidate for employment.

White Collar. Recruitment programs for management and white collar personnel are somewhat different from those stated for blue collar employees. The general feeling among textile employers is that there is little use to expend energy in trying to recruit top-level managerial talent (officials and managers, professionals) among Negroes, particularly where a college education is needed. As a consequence, there is not much recruiting in the Negro colleges among textile employers. One personnel director in a large textile company said: "Negroes are anxious to leave areas where our facilities are located, and they do not want to return here once they have an education. We do not recruit in Negro colleges." [116] Other employers reflected the same thinking even though they may do some recruiting in the Negro schools. Several of the major companies in the industry indicated that they did recruit in the Negro colleges but have had no success. "Negroes will not go to small southern towns where the mills are located; they do not look upon the textile industry as a good source of employment anyway." [117]

These observations represent a real dilemma for southern textile managers. It is no doubt true that the industry is not glamorous or particularly appealing to blacks. A black college graduate is not likely to want to remain in an environment that may have been hostile and which furnishes him with little or no opportunity for housing, or cultural outlets. Employers have not been able to recruit black employees in the colleges that offer specific textile programs. Table 35 shows the number of students enrolled in textile curricula in 1969, and there was only one black person in the total enrollment.

In white collar areas outside of those requiring advanced training, such as office and clerical and technicians positions, companies have made some effort to recruit blacks. Employers claim, however, that Negro girls, who can type and do clerical operations, usually leave the rural areas for the cities of the South and North or Washington, D. C. Also, the Negro male, who is a high school graduate and capable of training as a technician, is generally not attracted to the mills if he can obtain employment in other industries.

---

116. *Ibid.*
117. *Ibid.*

TABLE 35. Enrollment in Textile Curricula, October 1969

Program	Auburn	Clemson	Ga. Tech	Lowell	N.C. State	P.C.T.&S.	S.E. Mass.	Texas Tech.	I.T.T.	M.I.T.	T.R.I.	Total
Freshman	52	31	24	—	134	145	26	4	—	—	—	416
Sophomore	47	29	43	6	169	131	41	2	—	—	—	468
Junior	57	26	48	11	141	134	43	5	—	—	—	465
Senior	57	34	59	30	197	152	42	2	—	—	—	573
Unclassified	—	—	—	40	2	—	—	—	—	—	—	42
TOTAL	213	120	174	87	643	562	152	13	—	—	—	1,964
B.S. Degrees 68-69	77	45	46	39	229	136	48	4	—	—	—	624
B.S. Degrees 69-70	—	35	49	30	199	150	39	2	—	—	—	504
Foreign	1	6	4	—	39	66	3	2	—	—	—	121
Female	7	3	5	120	22	107	19	1	—	—	—	284
Enrollment by Curricula												
Textile Eng.	25	—	27	43	—	83	—	4	—	—	—	182
Textile Chem.	19	20	11	1	105	76	12	—	—	—	—	244
Textile Science	—	37	136	—	—	—	—	—	—	—	—	173
Textile Tech.	—	—	—	3	536	—	116	9	—	—	—	664
Textile Design	—	—	—	—	—	135	24	—	—	—	—	159
Textile Mgt.	169	—	—	—	—	268	—	—	—	—	—	437
I.M. Textile Option	—	63	—	—	—	—	—	—	—	—	—	63
TOTAL	213	120	174	47	641	562	152	13	—	—	—	1,922
Graduate Programs in Textiles												
M.S. Programs	—	64	24	20	46	—	4	3	17	2	—	180
M.S. Degrees 68-69	—	19	14	—	17	—	4	—	6	—	—	60
M.S. Degrees 69-70	—	20	11	—	15	—	3	—	7	—	—	56
Ph.D. Programs	—	25	—	—	15	—	—	—	1	9	—	50
Ph.D. Degrees 68-69	—	4	—	—	—	—	—	—	—	—	—	4
Ph.D. Degrees 69-70	—	3	—	—	—	—	—	—	—	—	—	3
TOTAL	—	135	49	20	93	—	11	3	31	11	—	353

Source: National Council for Textile Education.

Training and Orientation

Once an employee is recruited and selected for employment, he enters the firm with some expectation of training. Beach observes that:

> In small companies (in manufacturing, a small company is generally considered to be one having under 500 employees) training is, to a great extent, of the on-the-job variety, and it is done by line supervision. Where personnel departments exist in these companies the planning and co-ordination of training activities is typically one of the many responsibilities of the personnel manager. It is rare to find specialization carried to the point of having a separate training section within the personnel department.[118]

This observation is borne out in the many small textile manufacturing firms in the South. If any training is done at all, it is usually conducted in the on-the-job fashion and by a plant foreman. Of course, in large textile companies, a separate training section is normally charged with the training function. A few of the textile fiber plants of chemical companies have elaborate training facilities.

Various types of training programs are conducted by companies in the textile industry. These are usually classified as management training, retraining for supervisors, and entry-level training for laborers and operatives. Even though training facilities have been opened to Negroes in the textile industry, they have not participated in them, except at the entry level, to a significant extent.

It is generally agreed that most laborers and operatives jobs in a textile mill can be learned quickly, and there is no necessity for major training programs. The typical procedure is for an employee to spend from three to six weeks in on-the-job training once he has been hired. Most of the employers interviewed thought that additional effort should be put into developing better training methods in light of high turnover rates. One industry spokesman said: "We are now even training our sweepers; there must be a better way of preparing every person to do his job more efficiently; if a man is well trained, he can see the value of his services to the firm." [119] The absence of well-defined training opportunities can deny an employer valu-

---

118. Dale S. Beach, *Personnel: The Management of People at Work* (New York: MacMillan Company, 1965), p. 318.

119. Personal interviews.

able sources of personnel talent. In a large tire cord plant, a personnel director described the manner in which a Negro scrubber had trained himself to be a doffer by observing others. A process of personnel review and training can provide many advantages to the firm.

Even though there is a general lack of extensive training in the textile industry, several programs initiated by particular companies are worthy of mention.

Company A is a large fiber producing firm with plants in North Carolina and South Carolina. In the past few years, it has experimented with a training program for clerical employees. The company states its position as follows:

> The need for capable office workers in business, government, the professions, and education is never satisfied. And qualified secretaries, vital to the success of almost any organization, are becoming harder and harder to find. But there is a large, barely-tapped reservoir of talented young people who can fill these needs. It exists among millions of persons from minority ethnic groups who may not have seriously considered the advantages and the availability of a career in office work. Company A . . . is deeply interested in training young people for office careers, and in broadening job opportunities for black Americans.

One of the most successful efforts of the company has been in training high school graduates to be "efficient and resourceful workers" at the company's plants and offices. The company selects a number of Negro girls each year to attend a clerical training program at a predominantly Negro college for eight weeks in the summer. The program concentrates on written communications, production typing, shorthand, office machines, and general secretarial duties. At the completion of the program, the company offers the graduates a job in one of their plants or offices. This same company operates a training program for technicians in connection with another predominantly Negro college. It also maintains a full-time training staff with excellent facilities for its newest fiber plant in North Carolina. In regard to the latter operation, the personnel director said, "We have jobs and we have people; we do not think in terms of female jobs, male jobs, Negro jobs, and white jobs. We must train all of our people." [120]

Company B is a small textile firm in Georgia. It was the only firm in the industry where an MA-5, National Alliance of Businessmen, training program was found to be in effect. The com-

---

120. Information obtained in personal interviews.

pany was given a grant to train 250 people, 50 in each group, for a ten-week period in ten job categories. Almost 100 percent of the enrollees were blacks, who attended four hours of class each day, and spent four hours in the plant on a job. The program was enjoying tremendous success with about 90 percent finishing the training program and between 80 and 90 percent remaining with the company. The personnel director in the company was very optimistic about the training under MA-5: "It was designed by businessmen who understand the realities of the situation; this was not true of government programs, which we found to be difficult to live with." [121] Most firms have not applied for grants under the NAB program, but, as this instance shows, it can be a very valuable training device.

In addition to the training aspects of a job, orientation for new employees should be carefully planned and implemented. This is particularly true for the large body of blacks who are now entering the textile plants, many of whom have never worked before or been inside of a large, noisy factory. In large measure, orientation procedures are very inadequate in textile mills. At best, a man or woman may be given a half day or maybe a full day of orientation which consists of an illustrated lecture given in a cramped space. It goes without saying that an employee who does not understand the importance of what he is doing in the production process is not likely to develop much interest in coming back after a few days or appearing at stated times. A person needs to understand how his work fits into that of another person's and what is likely to occur in his absence.

Promotion and Upgrading

The textile industry is characterized by a high percentage of its employees working in the semiskilled operatives job category. Long, narrow lines of progression are not found in textile plants and seniority is normally used only to move an employee from one shift to another. Within any department, such as spinning, knitting, and weaving, there are very few lines of promotion. A spinner, knitter, or weaver is likely to remain in his job for

---

121. *Ibid.* (Since this research was completed in 1969, textile participation in the NAB program has expanded. Total participation in Alabama, Georgia, North Carolina, and South Carolina in 1970 amounts to $5,705,510 in federal money and 3,505 jobs. See Release No. 07036, May 6, 1970, of the ATMI.)

many years unless he is promoted into a fixer's job. This means, of course, that opportunities for upgrading are rare once a person has been trained to an operator's job. Given the operating characteristics of the industry, there is not a great deal that the employer can do about the situation.

The problem of blacks in the past has been in gaining access to the operative positions in textile mills, and there remain some cases where most of the hard, unpleasant laboring jobs are held only by Negroes. Additional effort will have to be made by employers to train and upgrade those who have been denied opportunities. Employers recognize the advantages of moving qualified people into operative positions in the mills regardless of race.

NEGRO EMPLOYMENT PROBLEMS

Some of the specific problems associated with the entrance of large numbers of Negroes into the textile industry are discussed in this section.

Turnover

Employers in the textile industry consider turnover to be one of their major problems. Many companies report turnover rates in the area of 45 to 60 percent, but these figures may be misleading without closer study. Certainly there is a relatively high level of stability among employees in certain operative and craftsmen jobs. A high turnover rate may result from a bad experience in a limited number of jobs in the plant. For example, in the card room of one company, sixty employees were hired to perform fifteen jobs in one year. One employer estimated that 80 percent of the turnover in his company occurred in 20 percent of the jobs. Also, the greatest amount of turnover appears to occur within the first six months of employment.

While no one seems to be sure what accounts for high turnover in the industry, several factors appear to be pertinent: tight labor market conditions, which provide alternative employment opportunities; influx of people who have never worked before, and who have no established work habits; poor supervision; undesirable working conditions, including hot, dirty work, and second and third shifts with some weekend work in seven-day operations; young workers; and female employees with responsibilities at home. It is difficult to estimate the relationship, if any, between black employment and high turnover rates.

Rozelle, in regard to shift work, reports that "many Negroes have an aversion to the third shift." [122] A few employers in our study asserted that "young Negro males will not work on Saturday night," and "Negroes have a different life style; they receive their pay on Friday, get drunk on Saturday and report to work on Monday." On the other hand, in contrast to what Rozelle found and the assertions of the employers cited, most industry spokesmen interviewed indicated that the response of blacks and whites to shift work is about the same in textile plants. Except in highly unusual cases, no one desires to work on the night shifts for a long period of time.

Turnover among whites and blacks in the industry may be different in some respects. It is no doubt true that many whites have left textile plants to enter better-paying jobs in more attractive industries that have entered the South in recent years. The fact that whites are quitting the textile industry has opened up jobs to blacks for the first time. Employers have been forced to bring blacks into the mills in large numbers. Without adequate orientation and training, many blacks became discouraged and left their jobs to stay at home, or dropped out of the labor force, only to be replaced by those who may do the same thing. As more and more Negroes enter the mills, employers will find it necessary to improve supervision, general employment practices, including recruiting and orientation, and to become involved with helping to solve basic problems in the Negro family. Negro females, who provide a major source of textile employment today, must be able to take care of their responsibilities at home while they are working; otherwise, they will drop in and out of the work force.

Female Employees

One of the most significant things to happen in employment in the textile industry in the past few years has been the entrance of Negro females into production areas. In the past, if a Negro female were hired, she generally was used as a sweeper or as a laborer. The situation has changed drastically with Negro females becoming the major source of labor supply in many textile centers. Employers have been pleasantly surprised with the results of bringing Negro females into operative jobs in the mills. Rozelle quotes one employer as follows:

---

122. Walter N. Rozelle, "The Mill and the Negro," in *Textile Industries*, November 1968, Vol. 132, No. 11, p. 60.

If I were to segregate our employees into four groups—Negro men,
Negro women, white men, and white women—I would most likely rate our
female Negro employees first in (a) desire to work and (b) educational
level. I was astounded at the number of Negro women who filed applications with us, and were formerly employed as domestics, even though
they had at least a high school education. The telephone was kept hot for
awhile by irate housewives accusing us of "stealing their help." [123]

The findings of our study concur with this statement. All of the
employers interviewed stated that Negro females are good employees, better educated than Negro males, and very responsible
on the job. One employer stated: "Our best production employee is the Negro female, age 27 to 30, who has worked formerly as a domestic. She many times bears the major responsibility for her family at home and is therefore a responsible
person at work."

There are, of course, problems associated with the employment
of Negro females who have small children at home and who have
had work experience only as a low-paid domestic. There are
times when it is difficult for a working mother to leave her
children if there is no one at home to take care of them. Also,
a Negro female who has worked for $3.00 per day will be able
to make considerably more in a textile plant, and the economic
motivation for work may be stifled after a short period of time.
A Negro female may also be frightened by a noisy manufacturing plant and find it difficult to adjust. These problems suggest
several areas where additional efforts should be made by employers in order to insure continued success in employing Negro
females:

1. *Day care centers.* A full time day care center (twenty-
four hours a day) to assist working females with their family
problems and, in particular, the care of children would probably
result in a better work experience in the mills. A joint venture
undertaken by a company and a community, which could be operated in places such as Greensboro, Greenville, and Macon, would
offer enormous opportunities for employers to stabilize their
work force and for Negro females to become a regular part of
the employment structure.

2. *Orientation for Negro females.* Employers have begun to
take constructive steps in the direction of preparing entering
employees for the work environment but much remains to be

_____
123. *Ibid.*, p. 62.

done to prepare a woman for entrance into a situation that is often completely foreign. If a Negro female has never been near a piece of heavy equipment, inside a factory, or introduced to the discipline of a plant, going to work in a textile mill can be a frightening experience. The size of a spinning room, the noise of a weaving room, and the movement of people and materials in a production process may be confusing to one unaccustomed to such an environment.

3. *Economic motivation.* The Negro female, who has been making only a few dollars a day as a servant, may find it rather pointless to work more than a few days a week in a textile mill where she can triple her previous weekly earnings. This may be particularly true if she does not understand from her orientation and training program that her job is related to others in the plant and that she is a vital link in a total production operation. An employer who is able to relate the employee to the job situation in a scientific manner may overcome some of the temptation of an employee to withdraw from the job once a certain sum of money has been earned. Also, a trained guidance person, associated with the personnel department or day care center, may be valuable in assisting the Negro female in household management and in developing the concept of saving.

Facility Desegregation

The process of desegregation of rest rooms, lockers, water fountains, and break areas in the textile mills has followed the general pattern of desegregation of public accommodations in the South. By the time Negroes were being hired in textile plants in the mid-1960's, most of the bitter confrontation between blacks and whites over integrated facilities was over, or at least, it was not widespread. A few minor incidents occur as employers move to desegregate facilities, but no major problems have evolved. One employer reported that "while the rest room integration is the most uncomfortable thing, it is not likely to become a real problem." In several other cases, employers indicated that the major complaints over rest rooms have come from Negro females who react to the general uncleanliness of white female employees in the mill. In the newer plants, toilet facilities are built in such a way that only one person can enter at a time, which avoids the possibility of contact between whites and blacks. It also prevents people from congregating and wasting time.

One of the revealing aspects of this study was the appearance of cordial relations between Negroes and whites at break areas and in eating places in the plants. It was a usual situation to find blacks and whites talking, eating, and joking together during their lunch or break periods.

Company Housing

Until recent years, it had been a common practice for companies in the southern textile industry to own homes that they rented to production employees. This practice grew out of the need for housing on the part of the poor whites who moved into textile manufacturing villages with no place to live. Employers literally had to take care of all of the basic needs of the people who were employed in the early textile mills. While much criticism attended the rise of the southern mill village, it offered an opportunity for whites to enter the economic life of the area after being shunted off to the mountains and farms during the Civil War days. During more prosperous times, employees have elected to live outside of the mill village and own their homes in places of their choice. Since most of the company houses had become quite old by 1960, and it was uneconomical for employers to maintain them, they were sold to the employees or torn down. There has been a general demise of the mill village, and it is likely to disappear completely in the near future under government pressure to desegregate housing.

Even though there has been a general trend among textile employers to sell or tear down company houses, there are a few who hold on to past practices. Cannon Mills still owns approximately 2,000 houses, about 50 of which are occupied by Negroes, and there appears to be little or no enthusiasm for getting rid of them. "Cannon Mills executives . . . blanch at the thought of giving away 2,000 homes and say that selling them to employees might have drawbacks, too. One executive recalls that a nearby textile company sold its houses to employees but then had to close its mills, leaving the occupants jobless and stranded." [124] The Cannon Mills situation is the last strong throwback to the paternalistic past in the textile industry. "Cannon Mills rents many of its houses for less than $20 a month, and residents

---

124. Neil Maxwell, "Mr. Charlie's Town: Powerful C.A. Cannon Rules Kannapolis, N.C., but He Faces Challenge," *Wall Street Journal*, April 29, 1969.

don't have to fret about forgetting when the rent is due; it is deducted from their paychecks. So are their water bills, their light bills, and even their medical bills, if they go to the county hospital and leave with a balance due." [125] The federal government has recently brought suit to end segregated company housing at Cannon. If the suit is successful, it most likely will mean that the houses will be sold to the occupants, and segregated housing will replace segregated company housing. Of course, Cannon claims that the houses have never been segregated; "they say no Negroes have applied to move into houses vacated by whites." [126] It is somewhat surprising that some people in Kannapolis, where Cannon operates, think that a race riot would result from integrated housing. Certainly Mr. Cannon, who owns the houses and employs the residents, could control the situation; that is, if he wanted to.

A company in Georgia, which has decided to keep its company houses and integrate them, takes a different point of view from that expressed by Cannon. This employer indicates that "we are going to continue to keep our company houses and operate them on an integrated basis. So far, the homes have been integrated with no problems. Some threatened to move if Negroes moved in next door, but no one has done so as yet." [127] Officials in this company take the point of view that mill housing could help solve the ghetto problems by providing decent living arrangements for blacks and whites alike, who could learn to live together in an integrated community. While the idea is an interesting one, it is not likely to be followed in many textile communities. Attitudes based on a long history of rigid segregation in housing are not easy to overcome. An employer in another Georgia community took a firm conservative stand on the housing problem: "We're not going to integrate them. We have enough problems without getting into the housing mess." [128] His position will eventually yield under government pressure.

On balance, the company-owned house in the southern textile industry is becoming a thing of the past. In cases where the employer has not already discovered it to be uneconomical and

---

125. *Ibid.*

126. *Ibid.*

127. Personal interviews.

128. *Ibid.*

unfeasible to operate them, government pressure to desegregate will cause the remaining company-owned houses to be sold or torn down. In a very few isolated cases, integration of housing may occur, but it is not likely to be widespread. On a nationwide scale, the housing problem for blacks has not been solved, and it would be unrealistic to expect a different situation in the southern textile mill town.

External Influences

Trade unions and the federal government represent two external influences that concern textile employers. While the fight against trade union organization has been a part of the history of the industry, the Negro worker brings an added dimension to the problem in the mind of employers. The federal government also looms large as an instrument of change in areas where the status quo is preferred by many, and it is therefore considered to be an undesirable force.

Trade Unions. Previous discussions in the study have indicated that trade unions have not made major inroads into the southern textile employment picture. This does not mean that they have been insignificant to employers. Many bitter battles have been fought over organization and some companies have paid a high price to keep the union away from the employees. The situation continues in some areas as the recent confrontations between J. P. Stevens and the union signify.

Most of the employers interviewed in this study expressed a concern for the future in regard to organization. When the question is raised as to whether or not Negroes are more likely to join a union than whites, the response is generally couched in terms of, "We don't know; it is hard to tell; on balance, though, we suspect that Negroes are more prone to join unions than whites." This suspicion is not preventing employers from hiring Negroes in large numbers. It is probably true that Negroes would be more likely than whites to vote as a group in a union election, but this could result in either a victory or a defeat for the union. In at least one instance an employer reported that because Negroes voted as a bloc, the union had won the election, but in another case the bloc voting led to the union's defeat.

Since there is little experience on which to base a conclusion, it is difficult to predict what impact the presence of Negroes in textile plants will have on future organization. Tactics used by unions and reactions displayed by employers will probably continue to determine whether or not unions organize textile workers regardless of racial factors. At the present time, there appears to be little activity on the part of the textile unions in attempting to organize. They have not indicated publicly any particular concern about the Negro and, as far as it has been possible to determine, there are no plans to attempt to capitalize on the entrance of Negroes into the industry. In cases where the union does exist in the southern textile plants, there has not been any apparent effort to represent the Negro or guarantee his employment rights, and this could be a deterrent to further organization of blacks. On the other hand, employers continue to take an active interest in keeping their plants unorganized.

The Federal Government. Executive Orders 10925 and 11246, referred to earlier in the study, and the Civil Rights Act of 1964 created the federal agencies, EEOC and OFCC, that textile employers have been confronted with over the past few years. While most employers have felt harassed at various times by visits from representatives in these agencies, many admit that the changes in employment practices insisted upon under the law have been needed and are constructive. Indeed, it probably would not have been possible to have integrated mills in some instances without government orders. Since employers have had to rely on Negro employees to fill production and other jobs in recent years, government pressure has given them a prop to persuade white employees to cooperate.

Unlike the situation in other industries, such as paper, Negroes would have been hired in textile mills without government pressure in the 1960's. The labor market brought the major change. It is unlikely, however, that full equal employment opportunity will exist in the industry unless the government continues to exert pressure. Negroes will not share proportionately in white collar jobs and in many of the craft positions unless there is some outside inducement for the employer to offer the opportunity. This is just as true, of course, in other American industries, whether they are located in the South or in other parts of the country.

CHAPTER VIII

Concluding Remarks

The textile industry has been a part of the entire industrial development in the United States. From the late eighteenth century, when Samuel Slater opened the first cotton factory in Pawtucket, Rhode Island, to the mid-1920's, textile production was concentrated in New England, New York, and Pennsylvania. Except in a few locations in New York and Pennsylvania, the Negro population was practically nonexistent, and there was little likelihood of finding Negroes working in the mills. In about 1924, the South emerged as the major textile producing region of the country. Mills were located in many places where there was a large black population. These plants were established at a time when there was still an abundance of cheap, white labor in a segregated society, and a policy of not hiring blacks prevailed. Changes in the racial employment structure of the southern textile industry did not become generally effective until the mid-to-late 1960's when government pressure for equal employment opportunity coincided with a tight labor market situation.

As we move into the decade of the 1970's, a virtual revolution in employment is occurring in the southern textile industry. The basic element in this major change centers on the blacks entering blue collar, semiskilled, operative positions in the mills. Some have argued that an examination of the statistical record of Negro employment in textiles does not reveal much reason for optimism because most blacks are concentrated in semiskilled and unskilled job categories. But the same is true for whites. The large majority of jobs in the textile industry are classified in the lower-skill areas. It is an inherent characteristic of the industry.

One of the most significant aspects of the large number of Negroes entering operative jobs is the fact that this provides an introduction to an industrial environment for those who have never experienced factory life. Mr. Charles F. Myers, president of the American Textile Manufacturers Institute in 1969, has stated to the South Carolina Textile Manufacturers Association that:

The improving role of the Negro in the textile industry is reflected not only in initial employment but in opportunities for advancement. The industry serves as an excellent training ground for teaching skills to many who have previously engaged in only unmechanized agricultural production. In this way, the Negro can participate in an industrial society and advance to higher paying jobs as skills and abilities are developed.[129]

As Cleghorn has further indicated, the textile industry provides a stepping stone for blacks who wish to enter into a more productive work situation.[130]

Upward mobility in a textile plant is limited by the nature of its operations. An operative is likely to remain in his or her job for life by choice. A craftsman's position may be that of a loom fixer in a production unit or electrician in the maintenance area. Since there is considerable stability among employees in the limited number of skilled jobs in textiles, abundant opportunities for advancement do not exist. In regard to Negroes, of course, the important consideration is whether or not they will be provided equal opportunities for whatever openings do occur or whether or not they will be given a chance to enter training classes to improve their skills. This study has found that employers are now seeking to promote and upgrade the most capable person in the plant, regardless of race.

The relatively new world in which textile employers find themselves demands modifications in their attitude and behavior. The Negro female, who has been found to be so valuable as an employee, will necessitate some consideration as to economic motivation, child care, and family maintenance. At the same time, the Negro male who may have been looked upon as shiftless and undependable can become a productive element in the plant if adequate training, orientation, and supervision are provided. The problems attendant upon the entrance of the "new" employee—the Negro—into the textile mill suggests an urgent need for management to give critical attention to the development of personnel and/or industrial relations expertise. A beginning has been made in this direction, but a great deal remains to be accomplished.

---

129. Charles F. Myers, Jr., "The Communications Challenge of the Textile Industry," an address to the annual meeting of the SCTMA, Sea Island, Georgia, May 16, 1969, p. 9.

130. Reese Cleghorn, "The Mill: A Giant Step for the Southern Negro," *New York Times Magazine*, Nov. 9, 1969, pp. 34-35, 142-145, 147, 156.

As is true in most industries in the United States, the Negro does not participate in any significant way in white collar job categories. Among the officials and managers, professionals, technicians, sales workers, and office and clerical personnel, Negroes are conspicuously absent, with the exception of a few in technical and clerical jobs. The officials and managers category, of course, includes supervision in the plant. Social and psychological factors make it extremely difficult to place a black man or woman over a white person in a small town textile plant. But experiments are being conducted. In a South Carolina plant, the author found a black supervisor in an all-white female department, and, in another instance, a black female was supervising a racially mixed, male and female department. It is not impossible, obviously, for blacks to supervise whites, but it is an area that requires sensitive management. While many may not be satisfied with the numbers of blacks entering supervisory positions in the mills, the qualitative aspects of the employers' efforts should be examined carefully.

The problems of management associated with white collar employment are somewhat different from those related to blue collar jobs. Apparently, it is an extremely difficult task to attract qualified Negroes into professional, technical, and clerical jobs in the textile industry. Efforts made by employers to recruit in these areas have not been very successful. The usual complaint is that Negroes with a college education desire to leave the South or they prefer to enter industries with more attractive working conditions. This probably does not explain entirely the general lack of Negroes in white collar jobs. Discriminatory practices still exist, in some measure, and the most imaginative and creative methods of bringing blacks into such jobs have not been developed. Employers are still able to staff their white collar jobs with white employees, and there has not been the same pressure as found in blue collar occupations to recruit blacks. In a few instances, where the employer has conscientiously sought to develop ways to attract Negroes into technical and clerical positions, the results have been rewarding. The technicians training class and the special clerical program operated at a predominantly Negro school, referred to earlier, have been quite successful in attracting Negroes into at least one company. A Negro industrial relations staff member in one company suggested that it will be relatively easy to persuade talented Negroes to return to the South when employers are able to demonstrate that there are real opportunities in top jobs in the industry.

The racial employment problems discussed throughout the study indicate a real challenge to management. Unless it is simply to muddle through, management will find it increasingly more important to establish or upgrade the personnel function in order that effective utilization of human resources can be planned. A consideration of only the short-run costs of developing an equal employment opportunity program can be misleading in the decision-making process. It is useful to consider also the time and money spent on such programs as an investment that can have enormous long-run returns.

The social, political, and economic environment in which people live in the South can benefit from the positive racial employment changes that are now occurring in the textile industry. People who work together have an opportunity to learn and understand each other. One mill owner in Alabama said: "One of the major by-products of the Civil Rights Act, which forces us to integrate our plants, is that we have begun to understand people as human beings." [131] The prospects for the future are encouraging, but the final outcome will depend on the quality of the effort.

---

131. Personal interviews, March 1969.

Appendix A
STATISTICAL DATA

TABLE A-1. *Textile Mill Products Industry*
Employment by Race, Sex, and Occupational Group
2315 Establishments, United States, 1966

Occupational Group	All Employees			Male			Female		
	Total	Negro	Percent Negro	Total	Negro	Percent Negro	Total	Negro	Percent Negro
Officials and managers	39,729	132	0.3	37,910	106	0.3	1,819	26	1.4
Professionals	7,385	20	0.3	6,883	18	0.3	502	2	0.4
Technicians	7,541	92	1.2	5,795	82	1.4	1,746	10	0.6
Sales workers	6,362	16	0.3	5,710	9	0.2	652	7	1.1
Office and clerical	49,575	809	1.6	13,233	452	3.4	36,342	357	1.0
Total white collar	110,592	1,069	1.0	69,531	667	1.0	41,061	402	1.0
Craftsmen	112,253	2,938	2.6	86,637	1,937	2.2	25,616	1,001	3.9
Operatives	450,562	32,093	7.1	197,503	21,597	10.9	253,059	10,496	4.1
Laborers	89,459	20,513	22.9	66,955	17,824	26.6	22,504	2,689	11.9
Service workers	16,754	5,059	30.2	13,640	4,000	29.3	3,114	1,059	34.0
Total blue collar	669,028	60,603	9.1	364,735	45,358	12.4	304,293	15,245	5.0
Total	779,620	61,672	7.9	434,266	46,025	10.6	345,354	15,647	4.5

Source: U.S. Equal Employment Opportunity Commission, *Job Patterns for Minorities and Women in Private Industry, 1966*. Report No. 1 (Washington: The Commission, 1968), Part II.

TABLE A-2. *Textile Mill Products Industry*
Nonsalaried Employment by Race and Sex
South Carolina, 1918-1968

	All Employees			Male			Female		
Year	Total	Negro	Percent Negro	Total	Negro	Percent Negro	Total	Negro	Percent Negro
1918	48,169	4,438	9.2	30,935	3,439	11.1	17,234	999	5.8
1919	51,462	5,232	10.2	34,051	3,875	11.4	17,411	1,357	7.8
1920	54,529	5,625	10.3	36,579	4,166	11.4	17,950	1,459	8.1
1921	55,085	4,076	7.4	37,199	3,283	8.8	17,886	793	4.4
1922	61,382	4,505	7.3	41,276	3,693	8.9	20,106	812	4.0
1923	66,674	5,036	7.6	44,365	3,950	8.9	22,309	1,086	4.9
1924	64,780	4,564	7.0	43,158	3,643	8.4	21,622	921	4.3
1925	70,068	4,658	6.6	45,734	3,742	8.2	24,334	916	3.8
1926	73,969	4,824	6.5	47,545	3,734	7.9	26,424	1,090	4.1
1927	79,772	5,014	6.3	51,054	4,108	8.0	28,718	906	3.2
1928	79,170	4,681	5.9	50,704	3,886	7.7	28,466	795	2.8
1929	72,223	4,196	5.8	46,220	3,572	7.7	26,003	624	2.4
1930	67,036	3,868	5.8	43,599	3,191	7.3	23,437	677	2.9
1931	66,032	3,249	4.9	43,203	2,617	6.1	22,829	632	2.8
1932	67,004	3,123	4.7	44,972	2,570	5.7	22,032	553	2.5
1933	80,154	3,993	5.0	52,917	3,426	6.5	27,237	567	2.1
1934	86,666	4,207	4.9	57,640	3,526	6.1	29,026	681	2.3
1935	83,592	3,827	4.6	55,283	3,315	6.0	28,309	512	1.8
1936	85,350	3,578	4.2	56,198	3,190	5.7	29,152	388	1.3
1937	95,181	4,441	4.7	62,263	3,871	6.2	32,918	570	1.7
1938	90,122	3,880	4.3	58,208	3,362	5.8	31,914	518	1.6
1939	96,139	3,855	4.0	62,512	3,342	5.3	33,627	513	1.5
1940	92,725	3,724	4.0	61,072	3,555	5.8	31,653	169	0.5
1941	102,342	4,117	4.0	66,789	3,927	5.9	35,553	190	0.5
1942	110,992	4,625	4.2	71,236	4,430	6.2	39,756	195	0.5
1943	115,926	5,106	4.4	68,503	4,833	7.1	47,423	273	0.6
1944	113,716	5,366	4.7	65,031	4,936	7.6	48,685	430	0.9
1945	109,517	5,559	5.1	61,851	5,103	8.3	47,666	456	1.0
1946	111,950	5,933	5.3	67,228	5,509	8.2	44,722	424	0.9
1947	118,056	6,544	5.5	72,533	6,140	8.5	45,523	404	0.9
1948	126,143	6,552	5.2	77,577	6,206	8.0	48,566	346	0.7

TABLE A-2. (continued)

Year	All Employees			Male			Female		
	Total	Negro	Percent Negro	Total	Negro	Percent Negro	Total	Negro	Percent Negro
1949	124,379	6,298	5.1	77,052	5,987	7.8	47,327	311	0.7
1950	124,556	6,020	4.8	77,655	5,719	7.4	46,901	301	0.6
1951	130,838	6,345	4.8	81,155	6,057	7.5	49,683	288	0.6
1952	130,457	6,235	4.8	80,793	5,903	7.3	49,664	332	0.7
1953	133,555	6,257	4.7	82,028	5,933	7.2	51,527	324	0.6
1954	127,250	6,005	4.7	78,862	5,716	7.2	48,388	289	0.6
1955	127,186	5,928	4.7	79,484	5,687	7.2	47,702	241	0.5
1956	127,492	6,003	4.7	80,615	5,796	7.2	46,877	207	0.4
1957	125,824	5,982	4.8	79,997	5,754	7.2	45,827	228	0.5
1958	122,422	5,736	4.7	78,990	5,535	7.0	43,432	201	0.5
1959	120,665	5,640	4.7	77,570	5,448	7.0	43,095	192	0.4
1960	122,877	5,728	4.7	79,969	5,524	6.9	42,908	204	0.5
1961	122,028	5,550	4.5	79,432	5,303	6.7	42,596	247	0.6
1962	124,862	5,982	4.8	80,609	5,713	7.1	44,253	269	0.6
1963	127,526	6,257	4.9	81,871	5,919	7.2	45,655	338	0.7
1964	128,651	7,309	5.7	82,249	6,810	8.3	46,402	499	1.1
1965	133,294	8,220	6.2	85,319	7,323	8.6	47,975	897	1.9
1966	138,225	13,997	10.1	90,484	11,429	12.6	47,741	2,568	5.4
1967	140,700	20,068	14.3	87,884	15,365	17.5	52,816	4,703	8.9
1968	142,543	23,642	16.6	87,885	17,463	19.9	54,658	6,179	11.3

Source: Department of Labor of the State of South Carolina, *Annual Reports,* 1939 and 1968.

TABLE A-3. *Textile Mill Products Industry*
Employment by Race, Sex, and Occupational Group
17 Companies, 27 Plants
New York and New England, 1968

Occupational Group	All Employees			Male			Female		
	Total	Negro	Percent Negro	Total	Negro	Percent Negro	Total	Negro	Percent Negro
Officials and managers	998	4	0.4	967	4	0.4	31	—	—
Professionals	284	1	0.4	241	—	—	43	1	2.3
Technicians	193	—	—	147	—	—	46	—	—
Sales workers	990	3	0.3	973	3	0.3	17	—	—
Office and clerical	2,660	119	4.5	872	59	6.8	1,788	60	3.4
Total white collar	5,125	127	2.5	3,200	66	2.1	1,925	61	3.2
Craftsmen	1,773	7	0.4	1,548	5	0.3	225	2	0.9
Operatives	6,927	121	1.7	3,433	76	2.2	3,494	45	1.3
Laborers	2,610	10	0.4	1,746	6	0.3	864	4	0.5
Service workers	464	2	0.4	437	1	0.2	27	1	3.7
Total blue collar	11,774	140	1.2	7,164	88	1.2	4,610	52	1.1
Total	16,899	267	1.6	10,364	154	1.5	6,535	113	1.7

Source: Data in author's possession.

TABLE A-4. Textile Mill Products Industry
Employment by Race, Sex, and Occupational Group
13 Companies, 44 Plants
Alabama, 1968

Occupational Group	All Employees			Male			Female		
	Total	Negro	Percent Negro	Total	Negro	Percent Negro	Total	Negro	Percent Negro
Officials and managers	1,137	2	0.2	1,113	2	0.2	24	—	—
Professionals	100	1	1.0	88	1	1.1	12	—	—
Technicians	225	4	1.8	186	4	2.2	39	—	—
Sales workers	18	—	—	8	—	—	10	—	—
Office and clerical	1,357	22	1.6	520	22	4.2	837	—	—
Total white collar	2,837	29	1.0	1,915	29	1.5	922	—	—
Craftsmen	3,052	98	3.2	2,614	57	2.2	438	41	9.4
Operatives	16,379	1,912	11.7	7,558	1,335	17.7	8,821	577	6.5
Laborers	2,672	912	34.1	2,065	849	41.1	607	63	10.4
Service workers	663	204	30.8	473	146	30.9	190	58	30.5
Total blue collar	22,766	3,126	13.7	12,710	2,387	18.8	10,056	739	7.3
Total	25,603	3,155	12.3	14,625	2,416	16.5	10,978	739	6.7

Source: Data in author's possession.

TABLE A-5. *Textile Mill Products Industry*
Employment by Race, Sex, and Occupational Group
20 Companies, 62 Plants
Georgia, 1968

Occupational Group	All Employees			Male			Female		
	Total	Negro	Percent Negro	Total	Negro	Percent Negro	Total	Negro	Percent Negro
Officials and managers	1,923	5	0.3	1,902	5	0.3	21	—	—
Professionals	345	—	—	314	—	—	31	—	—
Technicians	392	1	0.3	285	1	0.4	107	—	—
Sales workers	138	—	—	126	—	—	12	—	—
Office and clerical	2,567	54	2.1	752	44	5.9	1,815	10	0.6
Total white collar	5,365	60	1.1	3,379	50	1.5	1,986	10	0.5
Craftsmen	5,307	177	3.3	4,692	161	3.4	615	16	2.6
Operatives	27,097	4,972	18.3	13,310	3,409	25.6	13,787	1,563	11.3
Laborers	4,322	2,065	47.8	3,254	1,717	52.8	1,068	348	32.6
Service workers	1,229	657	53.5	911	404	44.3	318	253	79.6
Total blue collar	37,955	7,871	20.7	22,167	5,691	25.7	15,788	2,180	13.8
Total	43,320	7,931	18.3	25,546	5,741	22.5	17,774	2,190	12.3

Source: Data in author's possession.

TABLE A-6. *Textile Mill Products Industry*
Employment by Race, Sex, and Occupational Group
21 Companies, 168 Plants
North Carolina, 1968

Occupational Group	All Employees			Male			Female		
	Total	Negro	Percent Negro	Total	Negro	Percent Negro	Total	Negro	Percent Negro
Officials and managers	5,535	9	0.2	5,473	9	0.2	62	—	—
Professionals	970	4	0.4	936	3	0.3	34	1	2.9
Technicians	815	9	1.1	608	7	1.2	207	2	1.0
Sales workers	273	—	—	246	—	—	27	—	—
Office and clerical	6,330	122	1.9	1,986	78	3.9	4,344	44	1.0
Total white collar	13,923	144	1.0	9,249	97	1.0	4,674	47	1.0
Craftsmen	12,668	316	2.5	11,655	283	2.4	1,013	33	3.3
Operatives	62,253	8,184	13.1	28,237	4,928	17.5	34,016	3,256	9.6
Laborers	10,195	3,896	38.2	7,445	3,266	43.9	2,750	630	22.9
Service workers	2,530	950	37.5	1,890	728	38.5	640	222	34.7
Total blue collar	87,646	13,346	15.2	49,227	9,205	18.7	38,419	4,141	10.8
Total	101,569	13,490	13.3	58,476	9,302	15.9	43,093	4,188	9.7

Source: Data in author's possession.

TABLE A-7. *Textile Mill Products Industry*
Employment by Race, Sex, and Occupational Group
19 Companies, 112 Plants
South Carolina, 1968

Occupational Group	All Employees			Male			Female		
	Total	Negro	Percent Negro	Total	Negro	Percent Negro	Total	Negro	Percent Negro
Officials and managers	3,656	9	0.2	3,577	8	0.2	79	1	1.3
Professionals	501	1	0.2	476	1	0.2	25	—	—
Technicians	687	8	1.2	490	4	0.8	197	4	2.0
Sales workers	68	—	—	58	—	—	10	—	—
Office and clerical	3,359	69	2.1	1,061	58	5.5	2,298	11	0.5
Total white collar	8,271	87	1.1	5,662	71	1.3	2,609	16	0.6
Craftsmen	10,903	446	4.1	9,728	394	4.1	1,175	52	4.4
Operatives	39,451	4,706	11.9	19,672	3,417	17.4	19,779	1,289	6.5
Laborers	7,656	2,576	33.6	6,281	2,373	37.8	1,375	203	14.8
Service workers	1,189	576	48.4	969	454	46.9	220	122	55.5
Total blue collar	59,199	8,304	14.0	36,650	6,638	18.1	22,549	1,666	7.4
Total	67,470	8,391	12.4	42,312	6,709	15.9	25,158	1,682	6.7

Source: Data in author's possession.

TABLE A-8.   Textile Mill Products Industry
Employment by Race, Sex, and Occupational Group
5 Companies, 11 Plants
Tennessee, 1968

Occupational Group	All Employees			Male			Female		
	Total	Negro	Percent Negro	Total	Negro	Percent Negro	Total	Negro	Percent Negro
Officials and managers	492	—	—	485	—	—	7	—	—
Professionals	132	—	—	123	—	—	9	—	—
Technicians	116	—	—	81	—	—	35	—	—
Sales workers	1	—	—	1	—	—	—	—	—
Office and clerical	308	2	0.6	84	—	—	224	2	0.9
Total white collar	1,049	2	0.2	774	—	—	275	2	0.7
Craftsmen	1,338	3	0.2	1,135	3	0.3	203	—	—
Operatives	6,159	107	1.7	3,278	47	1.4	2,881	60	2.1
Laborers	433	16	3.7	364	13	3.6	69	3	4.3
Service workers	153	11	7.2	138	10	7.2	15	1	6.7
Total blue collar	8,083	137	1.7	4,915	73	1.5	3,168	64	2.0
Total	9,132	139	1.5	5,689	73	1.3	3,443	66	1.9

Source: Data in author's possession.

TABLE A-9. *Textile Mill Products Industry*
Employment by Race, Sex, and Occupational Group
7 Companies, 20 Plants
Virginia, 1968

Occupational Group	All Employees			Male			Female		
	Total	Negro	Percent Negro	Total	Negro	Percent Negro	Total	Negro	Percent Negro
Officials and managers	1,356	3	0.2	1,330	3	0.2	26	—	—
Professionals	339	1	0.3	330	1	0.3	9	—	—
Technicians	321	3	0.9	242	3	1.2	79	—	—
Sales workers	2	—	—	2	—	—	—	—	—
Office and clerical	1,560	20	1.3	400	10	2.5	1,160	10	0.9
Total white collar	3,578	27	0.8	2,304	17	0.7	1,274	10	0.8
Craftsmen	2,794	23	0.8	2,765	23	0.8	29	—	—
Operatives	13,470	1,413	10.5	6,393	980	15.3	7,077	433	6.1
Laborers	3,945	1,742	44.2	2,970	1,436	48.4	975	306	31.4
Service workers	364	102	28.0	325	93	28.6	39	9	23.1
Total blue collar	20,573	3,280	15.9	12,453	2,532	20.3	8,120	748	9.2
Total	24,151	3,307	13.7	14,757	2,549	17.3	9,394	758	8.1

Source: Data in author's possession.

TABLE A-10. Textile Mill Products Industry
Employment by Race, Sex, and Occupational Group
17 Companies, 27 Plants
New York and New England, 1966

Occupational Group	All Employees			Male			Female		
	Total	Negro	Percent Negro	Total	Negro	Percent Negro	Total	Negro	Percent Negro
Officials and managers	989	3	0.3	960	3	0.3	29	—	—
Professionals	229	1	0.4	205	—	—	24	1	4.2
Technicians	135	—	—	86	—	—	49	—	—
Sales workers	856	2	0.2	833	2	0.2	23	—	—
Office and clerical	2,630	52	2.0	966	31	3.2	1,664	21	1.3
Total white collar	4,839	58	1.2	3,050	36	1.2	1,789	22	1.2
Craftsmen	1,435	9	0.6	1,352	9	0.7	83	—	—
Operatives	7,212	67	0.9	3,740	38	1.0	3,472	29	0.8
Laborers	2,906	3	0.1	2,055	3	0.1	851	—	—
Service workers	523	3	0.6	503	2	0.4	20	1	5.0
Total blue collar	12,076	82	0.7	7,650	52	0.7	4,426	30	0.7
Total	16,915	140	0.8	10,700	88	0.8	6,215	52	0.8

Source: Data in author's possession.

TABLE A-11. *Textile Mill Products Industry*
Employment by Race, Sex, and Occupational Group
13 Companies, 44 Plants
Alabama, 1966

Occupational Group	All Employees			Male			Female		
	Total	Negro	Percent Negro	Total	Negro	Percent Negro	Total	Negro	Percent Negro
Officials and managers	1,011	—	—	990	—	—	21	—	—
Professionals	91	1	1.1	81	1	1.2	10	—	—
Technicians	194	1	0.5	141	1	0.7	53	—	—
Sales workers	33	—	—	25	—	—	8	—	—
Office and clerical	1,264	18	1.4	502	18	3.6	762	—	—
Total white collar	2,593	20	0.8	1,739	20	1.2	854	—	—
Craftsmen	2,828	27	1.0	2,738	27	1.0	90	—	—
Operatives	16,625	1,160	7.0	7,827	928	11.9	8,798	232	2.6
Laborers	2,813	856	30.4	2,100	798	38.0	713	58	8.1
Service workers	1,043	245	23.5	786	175	22.3	257	70	27.2
Total blue collar	23,309	2,288	9.8	13,451	1,928	14.3	9,858	360	3.7
Total	25,902	2,308	8.9	15,190	1,948	12.8	10,712	360	3.4

Source: Data in author's possession.

TABLE A-12. *Textile Mill Products Industry*
Employment by Race, Sex, and Occupational Group
20 Companies, 62 Plants
Georgia, 1966

Occupational Group	All Employees			Male			Female		
	Total	Negro	Percent Negro	Total	Negro	Percent Negro	Total	Negro	Percent Negro
Officials and managers	1,828	1	0.1	1,813	1	0.1	15	—	—
Professionals	340	—	—	332	—	—	8	—	—
Technicians	285	1	0.4	191	—	—	94	1	1.1
Sales workers	129	1	0.8	119	—	—	10	1	10.0
Office and clerical	2,342	29	1.2	701	29	4.1	1,641	—	—
Total white collar	4,924	32	0.6	3,156	30	1.0	1,768	2	0.1
Craftsmen	5,052	99	2.0	4,663	95	2.0	389	4	1.0
Operatives	27,458	3,318	12.1	13,755	2,662	19.4	13,703	656	4.8
Laborers	3,615	1,729	47.8	3,062	1,529	49.9	553	200	36.2
Service workers	1,206	692	57.4	919	463	50.4	287	229	79.8
Total blue collar	37,331	5,838	15.6	22,399	4,749	21.2	14,932	1,089	7.3
Total	42,255	5,870	13.9	25,555	4,779	18.7	16,700	1,091	6.5

Source: Data in author's possession.

TABLE A-13. *Textile Mill Products Industry*
Employment by Race, Sex, and Occupational Group
21 Companies, 168 Plants
North Carolina, 1966

Occupational Group	All Employees			Male			Female		
	Total	Negro	Percent Negro	Total	Negro	Percent Negro	Total	Negro	Percent Negro
Officials and managers	5,068	6	0.1	5,009	6	0.1	59	—	—
Professionals	830	1	0.1	805	—	—	25	1	4.0
Technicians	679	2	0.3	525	2	0.4	154	—	—
Sales workers	242	—	—	202	—	—	40	—	—
Office and clerical	5,732	69	1.2	1,785	55	3.1	3,947	14	0.4
Total white collar	12,551	78	0.6	8,326	63	0.8	4,225	15	0.4
Craftsmen	13,739	225	1.6	12,244	208	1.7	1,495	17	1.1
Operatives	59,392	4,606	7.8	27,085	3,177	11.7	32,307	1,429	4.4
Laborers	9,528	3,218	33.8	7,452	2,959	39.7	2,076	259	12.5
Service workers	2,390	801	33.5	1,972	687	34.8	418	114	27.3
Total blue collar	85,049	8,850	10.4	48,753	7,031	14.4	36,296	1,819	5.0
Total	97,600	8,928	9.1	57,079	7,094	12.4	40,521	1,834	4.5

Source: Data in author's possession.

TABLE A-14. *Textile Mill Products Industry*
Employment by Race, Sex, and Occupational Group
19 Companies, 112 Plants
South Carolina, 1966

Occupational Group	All Employees			Male			Female		
	Total	Negro	Percent Negro	Total	Negro	Percent Negro	Total	Negro	Percent Negro
Officials and managers	3,546	8	0.2	3,484	8	0.2	62	—	—
Professionals	553	—	—	543	—	—	10	—	—
Technicians	618	7	1.1	461	7	1.5	157	—	—
Sales workers	70	—	—	62	—	—	8	—	—
Office and clerical	3,254	47	1.4	1,185	41	3.5	2,069	6	0.3
Total white collar	8,041	62	0.8	5,735	56	1.0	2,306	6	0.3
Craftsmen	9,922	192	1.9	8,974	153	1.7	948	39	4.1
Operatives	38,910	2,566	6.6	19,916	2,247	11.3	18,994	319	1.7
Laborers	8,221	2,107	25.6	6,856	2,036	29.7	1,365	71	5.2
Service workers	1,114	538	48.3	951	464	48.8	163	74	45.4
Total blue collar	58,167	5,403	9.3	36,697	4,900	13.4	21,470	503	2.3
Total	66,208	5,465	8.3	42,432	4,956	11.7	23,776	509	2.1

Source: Data in author's possession.

TABLE A-15. *Textile Mill Products Industry*
Employment by Race, Sex, and Occupational Group
5 Companies, 11 Plants
Tennessee, 1966

Occupational Group	All Employees			Male			Female		
	Total	Negro	Percent Negro	Total	Negro	Percent Negro	Total	Negro	Percent Negro
Officials and managers	430	—	—	426	—	—	4	—	—
Professionals	160	1	0.6	157	1	0.6	3	—	—
Technicians	95	1	1.1	88	1	1.1	7	—	—
Sales workers	69	—	—	47	—	—	22	—	—
Office and clerical	564	5	0.9	273	3	1.1	291	2	0.7
Total white collar	1,318	7	0.5	991	5	0.5	327	2	0.6
Craftsmen	1,001	1	0.1	973	1	0.1	28	—	—
Operatives	5,972	54	0.9	3,384	40	1.2	2,588	14	0.5
Laborers	652	13	2.0	422	13	3.1	230	—	—
Service workers	139	7	5.0	124	6	4.8	15	1	6.7
Total blue collar	7,764	75	1.0	4,903	60	1.2	2,861	15	0.5
Total	9,082	82	0.9	5,894	65	1.1	3,188	17	0.5

Source: Data in author's possession.

TABLE A-16. *Textile Mill Products Industry*
Employment by Race, Sex, and Occupational Group
7 Companies, 20 Plants
Virginia, 1966

Occupational Group	All Employees			Male			Female		
	Total	Negro	Percent Negro	Total	Negro	Percent Negro	Total	Negro	Percent Negro
Officials and managers	1,353	1	0.1	1,326	1	0.1	27	—	—
Professionals	321	—	—	316	—	—	5	—	—
Technicians	291	—	—	203	—	—	88	—	—
Sales workers	3	—	—	3	—	—	—	—	—
Office and clerical	1,622	11	0.7	495	7	1.4	1,127	4	0.4
Total white collar	3,590	12	0.3	2,343	8	0.3	1,247	4	0.3
Craftsmen	3,170	30	0.9	3,063	28	0.9	107	2	1.9
Operatives	12,931	821	6.3	6,424	666	10.4	6,507	155	2.4
Laborers	3,556	1,454	40.9	2,776	1,251	45.1	780	203	26.0
Service workers	521	95	18.2	464	85	18.3	57	10	17.5
Total blue collar	20,178	2,400	11.9	12,727	2,030	16.0	7,451	370	5.0
Total	23,768	2,412	10.1	15,070	2,038	13.5	8,698	374	4.3

Source: Data in author's possession.

TABLE A-17. Textile Mill Products Industry
Employment by Race, Sex, and Occupational Group
9 Companies, 11 Plants
New York and New England, 1964

Occupational Group	All Employees			Male			Female		
	Total	Negro	Percent Negro	Total	Negro	Percent Negro	Total	Negro	Percent Negro
Officials and managers	293	—	—	289	—	—	4	—	—
Professionals	33	—	—	31	—	—	2	—	—
Technicians	41	—	—	17	—	—	24	—	—
Sales workers	1	—	—	1	—	—	—	—	—
Office and clerical	362	—	—	88	—	—	274	—	—
Total white collar	730	—	—	426	—	—	304	—	—
Craftsmen	702	3	0.4	691	3	0.4	11	—	—
Operatives	3,434	19	0.6	1,945	10	0.5	1,489	9	0.6
Laborers	1,424	8	0.6	1,066	7	0.7	358	1	0.3
Service workers	223	4	1.8	220	4	1.8	3	—	—
Total blue collar	5,783	34	0.6	3,922	24	0.6	1,861	10	0.5
Total	6,513	34	0.5	4,348	24	0.6	2,165	10	0.5

Source: Data in author's possession.

TABLE A-18. Textile Mill Products Industry
Employment by Race, Sex, and Occupational Group
3 Companies, 4 Plants
Alabama, 1964

Occupational Group	All Employees			Male			Female		
	Total	Negro	Percent Negro	Total	Negro	Percent Negro	Total	Negro	Percent Negro
Officials and managers	32	—	—	32	—	—	—	—	—
Professionals	1	—	—	1	—	—	—	—	—
Technicians	51	—	—	51	—	—	—	—	—
Sales workers	—	—	—	—	—	—	—	—	—
Office and clerical	37	2	5.4	17	2	11.8	20	—	—
Total white collar	121	2	1.7	101	2	2.0	20	—	—
Craftsmen	136	—	—	135	—	—	1	—	—
Operatives	988	10	1.0	308	10	3.2	680	—	—
Laborers	161	5	3.1	96	4	4.2	65	1	1.5
Service workers	51	4	7.8	38	4	10.5	13	—	—
Total blue collar	1,336	19	1.4	577	18	3.1	759	1	0.1
Total	1,457	21	1.4	678	20	2.9	779	1	0.1

Source: Data in author's possession.

TABLE A-19. *Textile Mill Products Industry*
Employment by Race, Sex, and Occupational Group
7 Companies, 20 Plants
Georgia, 1964

Occupational Group	All Employees			Male			Female		
	Total	Negro	Percent Negro	Total	Negro	Percent Negro	Total	Negro	Percent Negro
Officials and managers	353	1	0.3	351	1	0.3	2	—	—
Professionals	114	—	—	112	—	—	2	—	—
Technicians	85	—	—	30	—	—	55	—	—
Sales workers	33	—	—	30	—	—	3	—	—
Office and clerical	703	7	1.0	209	7	3.3	494	—	—
Total white collar	1,288	8	0.6	732	8	1.1	556	—	—
Craftsmen	1,482	8	0.5	1,476	8	0.5	6	—	—
Operatives	7,876	931	11.8	4,262	831	19.5	3,614	100	2.8
Laborers	1,221	566	46.4	1,088	512	47.1	133	54	40.6
Service workers	537	305	56.8	418	209	50.0	119	96	80.7
Total blue collar	11,116	1,810	16.3	7,244	1,560	21.5	3,872	250	6.5
Total	12,404	1,818	14.7	7,976	1,568	19.7	4,428	250	5.6

Source: Data in author's possession.

TABLE A-20. Textile Mill Products Industry
Employment by Race, Sex, and Occupational Group
9 Companies, 66 Plants
North Carolina, 1964

Occupational Group	All Employees			Male			Female		
	Total	Negro	Percent Negro	Total	Negro	Percent Negro	Total	Negro	Percent Negro
Officials and managers	1,343	—	—	1,335	—	—	8	—	—
Professionals	325	—	—	321	—	—	4	—	—
Technicians	291	—	—	222	—	—	69	—	—
Sales workers	145	—	—	126	—	—	19	—	—
Office and clerical	1,982	14	0.7	681	12	1.8	1,301	2	0.2
Total white collar	4,086	14	0.3	2,685	12	0.4	1,401	2	0.1
Craftsmen	7,031	54	0.8	5,926	54	0.9	1,105	—	—
Operatives	19,291	868	4.5	9,491	790	8.3	9,800	78	0.8
Laborers	3,529	734	20.8	2,832	718	25.4	697	16	2.3
Service workers	344	210	61.0	322	202	62.7	22	8	36.4
Total blue collar	30,195	1,866	6.2	18,571	1,764	9.5	11,624	102	0.9
Total	34,281	1,880	5.5	21,256	1,776	8.4	13,025	104	0.8

Source: Data in author's possession.

TABLE A-21. Textile Mill Products Industry
Employment by Race, Sex, and Occupational Group
9 Companies, 32 Plants
South Carolina, 1964

Occupational Group	All Employees			Male			Female		
	Total	Negro	Percent Negro	Total	Negro	Percent Negro	Total	Negro	Percent Negro
Officials and managers	730	—	—	730	—	—	—	—	—
Professionals	169	1	0.6	169	1	0.6	—	—	—
Technicians	136	—	—	94	—	—	42	—	—
Sales workers	4	—	—	4	—	—	—	—	—
Office and clerical	941	23	2.4	425	23	5.4	516	—	—
Total white collar	1,980	24	1.2	1,422	24	1.7	558	—	—
Craftsmen	2,644	30	1.1	2,531	30	1.2	113	—	—
Operatives	11,000	424	3.9	6,184	423	6.8	4,816	1	*
Laborers	1,607	387	24.1	1,467	383	26.1	140	4	2.9
Service workers	170	89	52.4	161	81	50.3	9	8	88.9
Total blue collar	15,421	930	6.0	10,343	917	8.9	5,078	13	0.3
Total	17,401	954	5.5	11,765	941	8.0	5,636	13	0.2

Source: Data in author's possession.

* Less than 0.05 percent.

TABLE A-22. *Textile Mill Products Industry*
Employment by Race, Sex, and Occupational Group
1 Company, 4 Plants
Tennessee, 1964

Occupational Group	All Employees			Male			Female		
	Total	Negro	Percent Negro	Total	Negro	Percent Negro	Total	Negro	Percent Negro
Officials and managers	105	—	—	105	—	—	—	—	—
Professionals	21	—	—	20	—	—	1	—	—
Technicians	3	—	—	2	—	—	1	—	—
Sales workers	—	—	—	—	—	—	—	—	—
Office and clerical	80	—	—	15	—	—	65	—	—
Total white collar	209	—	—	142	—	—	67	—	—
Craftsmen	412	2	0.5	387	2	0.5	25	—	—
Operatives	2,214	13	0.6	746	11	1.5	1,468	2	0.1
Laborers	235	10	4.3	166	9	5.4	69	1	1.4
Service workers	40	4	10.0	26	4	15.4	14	—	—
Total blue collar	2,901	29	1.0	1,325	26	2.0	1,576	3	0.2
Total	3,110	29	0.9	1,467	26	1.8	1,643	3	0.2

Source: Data in author's possession.

TABLE A-23. *Textile Mill Products Industry*
Employment by Race, Sex, and Occupational Group
3 Companies, 13 Plants
Virginia, 1964

Occupational Group	All Employees			Male			Female		
	Total	Negro	Percent Negro	Total	Negro	Percent Negro	Total	Negro	Percent Negro
Officials and managers	310	—	—	310	—	—	—	—	—
Professionals	138	—	—	136	—	—	2	—	—
Technicians	118	—	—	106	—	—	12	—	—
Sales workers	—	—	—	—	—	—	—	—	—
Office and clerical	568	5	0.9	201	5	2.5	367	—	—
Total white collar	1,134	5	0.4	753	5	0.7	381	—	—
Craftsmen	1,938	7	0.4	1,797	7	0.4	141	—	—
Operatives	5,450	244	4.5	2,819	200	7.1	2,631	44	1.7
Laborers	810	249	30.7	695	197	28.3	115	52	45.2
Service workers	192	78	40.6	184	74	40.2	8	4	50.0
Total blue collar	8,390	578	6.9	5,495	478	8.7	2,895	100	3.5
Total	9,524	583	6.1	6,248	483	7.7	3,276	100	3.1

Source: Data in author's possession.

TABLE A-24. *Textile Mill Products Industry*
Employment by Race, Sex, and Occupational Group
Textile Plants Operated by Chemical Companies
4 Companies, 21 Plants
South Region, 1968

Occupational Group	All Employees			Male			Female		
	Total	Negro	Percent Negro	Total	Negro	Percent Negro	Total	Negro	Percent Negro
Officials and managers	5,916	15	0.3	5,772	15	0.3	144	—	—
Professionals	3,236	13	0.4	3,178	11	0.3	58	2	3.4
Technicians	2,520	53	2.1	1,783	18	1.0	737	35	4.7
Sales workers	1	—	—	1	—	—	—	—	—
Office and clerical	2,514	52	2.1	756	19	2.5	1,758	33	1.9
Total white collar	14,187	133	0.9	11,490	63	0.5	2,697	70	2.6
Craftsmen	10,082	249	2.5	9,924	244	2.5	158	5	3.2
Operatives	27,872	3,308	11.9	16,537	2,249	13.6	11,335	1,059	9.3
Laborers	1,455	506	34.8	1,051	452	43.0	404	54	13.4
Service workers	889	451	50.7	829	413	49.8	60	38	63.3
Total blue collar	40,298	4,514	11.2	28,341	3,358	11.8	11,957	1,156	9.7
Total	54,485	4,647	8.5	39,831	3,421	8.6	14,654	1,226	8.4

Source: Data in author's possession.

TABLE A-25. *Textile Mill Products Industry*
Employment by Race, Sex, and Occupational Group
Textile Plants Operated by Rubber Companies
5 Companies, 15 Plants
South Region, 1968

Occupational Group	All Employees			Male			Female		
	Total	Negro	Percent Negro	Total	Negro	Percent Negro	Total	Negro	Percent Negro
Officials and managers	728	9	1.2	719	9	1.3	9	—	—
Professionals	243	1	0.4	233	1	0.4	10	—	—
Technicians	376	36	9.6	223	17	7.6	153	19	12.4
Sales workers	24	—	—	19	—	—	5	—	—
Office and clerical	524	16	3.1	182	14	7.7	342	2	0.6
Total white collar	1,895	62	3.3	1,376	41	3.0	519	21	4.0
Craftsmen	2,215	133	6.0	1,708	118	6.9	507	15	3.0
Operatives	6,422	1,178	18.3	3,559	828	23.3	2,863	350	12.2
Laborers	630	350	55.6	598	343	57.4	32	7	21.9
Service workers	496	317	63.9	426	260	61.0	70	57	81.4
Total blue collar	9,763	1,978	20.3	6,291	1,549	24.6	3,472	429	12.4
Total	11,658	2,040	17.5	7,667	1,590	20.7	3,991	450	11.3

Source: Data in author's possession.

TABLE A-26. Textile Mill Products Industry
Employment by Race, Sex, and Occupational Group
Textile Plants Operated by Chemical Companies
4 Companies, 21 Plants
South Region, 1966

Occupational Group	All Employees			Male			Female		
	Total	Negro	Percent Negro	Total	Negro	Percent Negro	Total	Negro	Percent Negro
Officials and managers	5,411	2	*	5,276	2	*	135	—	—
Professionals	3,478	5	0.1	3,441	2	0.1	37	3	8.1
Technicians	2,407	20	0.8	1,824	7	0.4	583	13	2.2
Sales workers	26	—	—	22	—	—	4	—	—
Office and clerical	2,723	24	0.9	809	11	1.4	1,914	13	0.7
Total white collar	14,045	51	0.4	11,372	22	0.2	2,673	29	1.1
Craftsmen	10,314	167	1.6	10,203	166	1.6	111	1	0.9
Operatives	23,976	1,483	6.2	13,047	968	7.4	10,929	515	4.7
Laborers	1,848	743	40.2	1,530	707	46.2	318	36	11.3
Service workers	956	460	48.1	883	415	47.0	73	45	61.6
Total blue collar	37,094	2,853	7.7	25,663	2,256	8.8	11,431	597	5.2
Total	51,139	2,904	5.7	37,035	2,278	6.2	14,104	626	4.4

Source: Data in author's possession.

* Less than 0.05 percent.

TABLE A-27. *Textile Mill Products Industry*
Employment by Race, Sex, and Occupational Group
Textile Plants Operated by Rubber Companies
5 Companies, 15 Plants
South Region, 1966

Occupational Group	All Employees			Male			Female		
	Total	Negro	Percent Negro	Total	Negro	Percent Negro	Total	Negro	Percent Negro
Officials and managers	672	1	0.1	665	1	0.2	7	—	—
Professionals	208	—	—	199	—	—	9	—	—
Technicians	224	9	4.0	132	3	2.3	92	6	6.5
Sales workers	19	—	—	17	—	—	2	—	—
Office and clerical	476	12	2.5	185	10	5.4	291	2	0.7
Total white collar	1,599	22	1.4	1,198	14	1.2	401	8	2.0
Craftsmen	1,988	95	4.8	1,535	89	5.8	453	6	1.3
Operatives	6,573	794	12.1	3,676	659	17.9	2,897	135	4.7
Laborers	718	287	40.0	658	269	40.9	60	18	30.0
Service workers	449	253	56.3	390	207	53.1	59	46	78.0
Total blue collar	9,728	1,429	14.7	6,259	1,224	19.6	3,469	205	5.9
Total	11,327	1,451	12.8	7,457	1,238	16.6	3,870	213	5.5

Source: Data in author's possession.

Index

PART SIX

PART SIX

CONCLUDING ANALYSIS

by

RICHARD L. ROWAN

and

HERBERT R. NORTHRUP

TABLE OF CONTENTS

LIST OF TABLES

Concluding Analysis

The preceding studies in this volume describe and analyze the racial employment patterns in five of the South's major industries—paper, lumber, tobacco, bituminous coal mining, and textiles. These industries have had an interesting pattern of development in regard to human resource management. Out of the many varied and complex situations surrounding employment practices in southern industry emerges the common thread of the Negro struggling to achieve equal opportunity or a rightful place in the work environment. How far we have come in making this goal a reality and what problems are encountered in so doing are revealed in the studies in this volume.

Table 1 compares the racial-occupational breakdown of all southern manufacturing industries [1] reporting to the Equal Employment Opportunity Commission with four of the five southern manufacturing industries (paper, tobacco, textiles, and lumber) included in our studies. Bituminous coal mining is not included since the data were not available from EEOC. In addition, Table 1 shows a composite view of the occupational breakdown for three of the five industries (paper, tobacco, and textiles) for which we had a field sample in 1966.

A cursory examination of the data in Table 1 indicates that our four-industry sample is representative of Negro employment in southern industry. The four southern manufacturing industries in our study employed approximately 27 percent of all southern manufacturing industry then subject to EEOC regulation and employed Negroes in virtually the same ratio for each occupational group as did southern manufacturing in general. The three-industry field sample also indicates the same characteristics as in all southern manufacturing. The slightly smaller Negro blue collar ratio for the three industries reflects the absence of the lumber industry which has the highest proportion of Negroes in the group.

In Volume I of these Studies, we set forth a series of hypotheses which are examined in terms of six basic industries.[2] We be-

---

1. Standard Industrial Classifications 19-39.

2. Herbert R. Northrup, Richard L. Rowan, *et al.*, *Negro Employment in Basic Industry*, Studies of Negro Employment, Vol. I (Philadelphia: Industrial Research Unit, Wharton School of Finance and Commerce, University of Pennsylvania, 1970), Part One, Chapter I; Part Eight, Chapter I.

TABLE 1. Selected Southern Industries and All Southern Manufacturing Industries Employment by Race and Occupational Group South Region, 1966

Occupational Group	Southern Manufacturing Industries Reporting to EEOC (SIC 19-39)			Four Southern Manufacturing Industries Reporting to EEOC (SIC 21, 22, 24, 26)[a]			Three Industries Combined Field Sample[b]		
	Total	Negro	Percent Negro	Total	Negro	Percent Negro	Total	Negro	Percent Negro
Officials and managers	213,006	1,093	0.5	48,470	178	0.4	23,138	58	0.3
Professionals	133,131	484	0.4	10,781	27	0.3	6,776	13	0.2
Technicians	88,204	1,355	1.5	9,636	112	1.2	5,330	51	1.0
Sales workers	82,300	1,731	2.1	9,270	89	1.0	3,469	45	1.3
Office and clerical	258,140	4,721	1.8	52,408	934	1.8	25,259	469	1.9
Total white collar	774,781	9,384	1.2	130,565	1,340	1.0	63,972	636	1.0
Craftsmen	587,302	27,461	4.7	135,350	4,929	3.6	65,503	1,191	1.8
Operatives	1,456,988	182,625	12.5	470,181	48,596	10.3	215,383	20,117	9.3
Laborers	465,691	160,250	34.4	143,150	55,478	38.8	56,773	20,606	36.3
Service workers	66,574	25,240	37.9	19,689	7,822	39.7	10,138	4,492	44.3
Total blue collar	2,576,555	395,576	15.4	768,370	116,825	15.2	347,797	46,406	13.3
Total	3,351,336	404,960	12.1	898,935	118,165	13.1	411,769	47,042	11.4

Source: U.S. Equal Employment Opportunity Commission, *Job Patterns for Minorities and Women in Private Industry, 1966,* Report No. 1 (Washington: The Commission, 1968), Part II; and data in authors' possession.

[a] Paper, lumber, textiles, and tobacco.

[b] Paper, textiles, and tobacco.

lieve it is also useful to summarize our findings in regard to the five key southern industries studied in the light of thirteen of these fourteen hypotheses. (The fourteenth concerns service industries and is therefore inapplicable here.) In most of the following analysis, the paper industry is treated as two separate industries, paper mills and paper converting plants, as was done in Part One.

DEMAND FOR LABOR

All of the industries studied, except coal mining, showed an increase in the percentage of Negro employees between 1964 and 1698 (Table 2). During this period, total employment was increasing in the paper and textile industries but in the tobacco, lumber, and coal mining industries, it declined or remained relatively stable. Actually, however, the percentage of Negroes in the southern paper mills remained stable. The increase occurred entirely in the converting plants.

Negroes have had a varied employment experience in the southern paper mill industry. In the early days of industrial expansion in the South, they were used extensively in the many unskilled jobs. Existing mores adopted from the lumber industry permitted Negroes to be segregated into all-black departments

TABLE 2. *Selected Southern Industries*
Percent Negro Employment
1964 and 1968

Industry	1964	1968
Paper and allied products	12.6	13.2
Pulp, paper, and paperboard mills	12.6	12.2
Paper converting plants	12.6	17.1
Lumber	42.0	42.5
Tobacco	20.9	22.2
Textiles	6.8	13.4
Coal mining	a	a

Source: Parts One through Five, above.

[a] Comparable data for coal mining are not available. Barnum explains, however, that Negro employment relative to whites has declined consistently since the 1930's (see the Barnum study included in this volume).

and into work requiring heavy labor, particularly outdoor labor. As technology changed, Negroes were disproportionately affected. Since they were assigned to low skill areas, they were eliminated quite easily as automation proceeded. Stringent labor-management rules that governed work assignments did not allow Negroes to be placed in many jobs in the plants so they were systematically excluded with whites available in the labor market. Negroes find themselves at a great disadvantage in the industry's mills today as jobs begin to open up under federal government pressure. Shut out for so long and denied opportunities for education and training, many Negroes find it difficult to qualify for openings requiring skills and knowledge in an automated paper mill. Paper mill wages are high and qualified white labor remains available to the industry. Moreover, employment increases slowly and turnover is low. This, of course, further complicates the job problems of Negroes who must face severe competition.

The situation is dramatically different in converting plants where most jobs require little skill. Wages are much lower, demand for labor increases rapidly in times of industry expansion, and turnover is high. The dramatic increase in the percentage of Negroes in southern converting plants in the four-year period is a product of the expansion of the industry, its location in urban areas where Negroes are concentrated, and the disinterest of whites in taking jobs as other opportunities become greater.

The lumber industry, characterized by its low wages and skill requirements, has always employed a large number of Negroes especially in the operative and laborer categories. In both 1964 and 1968, nearly 50 percent of the operatives employed in this industry were Negro. Total employment in the industry has been relatively stable over much of the past decade and is likely to remain so in the future, with plywood production making up for any inroads of plastics or metals into the wood furniture business. In view of the history of Negro utilization, and other preferable opportunities for whites, one can expect no change in the lumber industry's racial-occupational pattern of employment.

The tobacco industry has never been a large employer, with technological progress and automation historically offsetting increases in product demand, and more recently, with declining product demand and continued automation reducing labor demand. Located almost entirely in the states of Kentucky, North Carolina, and Virginia, the industry, which once had an almost all black factory labor force, adopted a rigorous segregation policy that confined Negroes to particular departments. After minimum wage legislation was adopted, these departments were sharply affected by a changeover from hand to machine production. The demand for labor in "Negro jobs" in the industry declined steadily after 1933, but Negroes were largely denied opportunities in the better paying areas of production.

The adverse health impact attributed to cigarette smoking reduced the demand for the industry's product soon after the racial-occupational segregation pattern was broken by government intervention and civil rights legislation, and the job decline continues. American Tobacco has closed a plant in Louisville, Kentucky and Liggett & Myers has recently announced it will discontinue operations in Richmond, Virginia. Philip Morris in Richmond and Brown & Williamson in Petersburg, Virginia, are gaining an increasing share of a declining market. Their factories, which are located in tight labor markets where new industry is attracting white labor, are thus opening new opportunities to Negroes in the tobacco industry. Generally, however, the demand for labor is shrinking. The once nearly all black employee industry, in which the proportion of Negroes had fallen to about 25 percent in 1960, is not likely to see its black percentage rise above that figure in the foreseeable future.

The textile industry gives probably the clearest example of the effects of a tight labor market situation on the Negro's job position. Throughout most of its history from 1890 to 1960, Negroes were conscientiously avoided as potential manpower for the industry; the industry was reserved for whites. Such a policy could be implemented because an abundance of white labor was available in the South. Industrialization in the South in the period from 1950 to the present introduced new work opportunities in major proportions. Whites began to move into better paying positions in more attractive industries leaving vacancies for Negroes. This situation, combined with federal government pressure, dramatically changed the employment structure of the textile industry between 1964 and 1968. There is probably no other industry that has undergone such a fundamental change. Negroes have been hired in large numbers in the operative category, where they were seldom hired before 1964, and craftsman positions are also opening up. These changes are in direct response to a labor market phenomenon. Negroes are likely to find textiles a prime source of employment in the future. Of course, the decline in the Vietnam fighting and consequent decreased military procurement, together with increased imports, is having an adverse affect on employment in the industry. This could subsequently reduce Negro textile employment.

In the bituminous coal mining industry, Negroes achieved their greatest gains in the periods of expanding demand and nonunion operations of the Southern Appalachian fields. Decreasing demand and rapid mechanization since the late 1930's were accompanied by a steady reduction in the number and proportion of black miners. By 1960, the Negro miner had become a disappearing phenomenon. During the 1950's, 73 percent of the Negroes were eliminated from the industry while a 54 percent reduction in the number of whites also occurred. Meanwhile, Negroes left the coal mining areas at a faster rate than did whites.

During the last five years, a critical shortage of labor in the mines has developed as the demand for coal has increased and older miners have retired. But, interestingly enough, Negroes have not been attracted to fill these vacancies. Years of employment discrimination and lack of protection by a once equalitarian union have discouraged Negroes from remaining in coal producing areas, and from returning there by a promise of better treatment than in the past.

NATURE OF THE WORK

The extent of Negro employment is greatly affected by the nature of work in an industry. Occupational mix, attractiveness of the work, and the pattern of job progression are all significant factors in this regard. Although racial division of work is no longer deliberately carried out in southern industry, the possibility of finding Negroes in some jobs, and perhaps not in others, still remains as a concomitant of past practice based upon these factors.

Occupational Mix

Table 3 shows the heavy concentration of employees in blue collar occupations in 1968 in all of the industries studied. The percentage of blue collar to total employees in the industries ranged from 77.7 in paper converting plants to 87.1 in textiles, with bituminous coal mining probably having an even higher blue collar percentage. Within the specific blue collar job categories, over 50 percent of all employees were classified as operatives and laborers. This indicates that the preponderance of

TABLE 3. *Selected Southern Industries*
Percentage Distribution of Employees
by Race and Occupational Group, 1968

Occupational Group	Pulp, Paper, and Paperboard Mills		Paper Converting Plants		Lumber		Tobacco		Textiles	
	All Employees	Negro Employees	All Employees	Negro Employees	All Employees	Negro Employees	All Employees	Negro Employees	All Employees	Negro Employees
Officials and managers	7.5	0.1	7.8	0.1	7.3	0.3	6.7	0.6	5.2	0.1
Professionals	3.9	0.2	1.8	—	2.4	*	1.9	0.1	0.9	*
Technicians	2.2	0.3	0.9	0.1	1.7	0.2	2.3	0.3	0.9	0.1
Sales workers	0.2	—	2.9	0.1	0.8	—	2.6	0.3	0.2	—
Office and clerical	6.8	2.0	8.9	1.2	4.1	0.1	6.8	1.2	5.7	0.8
Total white collar	20.6	2.6	22.3	1.5	16.3	0.6	20.3	2.5	12.9	1.0
Craftsmen	27.2	4.7	16.5	6.6	13.8	6.5	9.7	1.0	13.3	2.9
Operatives	37.1	46.3	38.0	51.5	29.5	32.4	39.8	31.0	60.8	58.5
Laborers	13.3	39.9	22.2	37.6	39.4	59.4	26.3	55.7	10.8	30.8
Service workers	1.8	6.5	1.0	2.8	1.0	1.1	3.9	9.8	2.2	6.8
Total blue collar	79.4	97.4	77.7	98.5	83.7	99.4	79.7	97.5	87.1	99.0
Total	100.0	100.0	100.0	100.0	100.0	100.0	100.0	100.0	100.0	100.0

Source: Preceding industry studies.

Note: Comparable data are not available for bituminous coal mining, but the great bulk of employees in the industry —probably approximately 90 percent—are blue collar, and two-thirds of those are in semiskilled or unskilled categories.

* Less than 0.05 percent.

employees in the southern industries studied are working in semi-skilled or unskilled jobs requiring little education or training. Unless deliberately prohibited by discriminatory practices, Negroes should find easy access to these industries. Of course, data in Table 2 have already indicated that this has occurred.

Once Negroes gain entrance to an industry, however, it does not follow necessarily that they will move into better paying jobs. Discriminatory seniority systems, such as were in existence for many years in the paper and tobacco industries, have blocked progress. Moreover, the large percentage of craftsmen in the paper industry and the historic barriers to Negroes learning the trades, have played a significant role in reducing Negro representation in this category. And historically, they have been barred from white collar employment in the South.

Table 3 provides another way to look at the occupationally disadvantaged status of Negroes in southern industry by comparing the distribution of Negroes among occupational groups with that of all employees. In none of the industries was the percent of the black employees in white collar positions more than 2.6. Not even one percent of the black labor force was in any of the top white collar occupations, while only in the paper mills was 2 percent of the black employees in the office and clerical group.

These southern industries, as noted, are heavily blue collar oriented, in contrast to such industries as aerospace, chemicals, or petroleum. Table 3 shows that the white collar complement varies from 12.9 percent in textiles to 22.3 percent in paper converting. In no case, however, did the proportionate distribution of black employees in white collar jobs equal one-fifth that of the total, and for the most part, it was only about one-tenth or less. In the craftsman occupation, the situation was similar, with the proportion of Negroes one-half to one-ninth of the total. In the operative jobs, Negroes were close to parity or above, and in the bottom blue collar jobs, their concentration exceeded that of all employees.

The relative position of Negroes, by occupation, in the paper, lumber, tobacco, and textile industries is shown in Table 4. As one scans the data, it becomes immediately apparent that the Negro's position increases as the jobs become less attractive.

White collar occupations. In the officials and managers category, which contains the line and staff managerial personnel, Negroes are practically nonexistent. They appear occasionally in

TABLE 4. *Selected Southern Industries*
Percent Negro Employment by Occupational Group
1966 and 1968

Occupational Group	Pulp, Paper, and Paperboard Mills		Paper Converting Plants		Lumber		Tobacco[a]		Textiles	
	1966	1968	1966	1968	1966	1968	1966	1968	1966	1968
Officials and managers	0.1	0.2	0.1	0.3	1.2	1.5	1.2	1.9	0.1	0.2
Professionals	0.1	0.5	—	—	0.2	0.4	1.0	0.7	0.1	0.3
Technicians	0.4	1.8	2.9	1.2	3.2	4.7	2.2	3.0	0.6	1.0
Sales workers	—	—	—	0.3	0.8	—	2.2	3.1	0.2	—
Office and clerical	2.6	3.7	2.4	2.3	2.4	1.6	3.5	3.9	1.2	1.9
Total white collar	0.9	1.6	1.2	1.1	1.6	1.6	2.2	2.8	0.6	1.0
Craftsmen	1.6	2.1	4.2	6.9	17.0	20.0	1.9	2.2	1.6	2.9
Operatives	12.5	15.3	16.8	23.1	42.4	46.8	14.7	17.3	7.8	12.9
Laborers	37.6	36.8	24.2	28.9	61.3	64.1	47.2	47.0	33.0	38.3
Service workers	45.4	45.0	52.6	48.7	37.3	44.4	65.9	55.2	37.1	40.8
Total blue collar	13.9	15.0	16.5	21.7	47.8	50.5	26.9	27.1	10.7	15.3
Total	11.2	12.2	13.0	17.1	42.1	42.5	21.8	22.2	9.5	13.4

Source: Preceding industry studies.

Note: Comparable data unavailable for bituminous coal mining.

[a] These data reflect a downward bias because of the exclusion of the independent stemmeries which have virtually all-black labor forces.

line management positions where they may supervise an all-black department. Recently, a few have been employed in nonsupervisory jobs in racially mixed departments, but the number is as yet very small. It follows that the industry with the largest overall percentage of Negroes would be the one with the best opportunity for Negroes to advance to managerial positions. Actually, however, the tobacco industry, with its background of all-black departments, has a slightly better record than lumber which has almost twice the percentage of Negro employees.

One of the key problems faced by Negroes in their efforts to move into the prestigious top of the white collar world is that, with the abolishment of all-black departments, supervisors and foremen will be expected to direct the activities of integrated work forces. This represents a major change in the southern work environment and its implementation is not likely to be rapid. Second, given a history of discrimination in education and employment, Negroes generally have not been able to gain experience or background, such as professional work or training, or work in skilled occupations, that is essential for promotion to managerial positions.

There are few Negro professionals or technicians in any of the industries studied. These job categories usually require a high school certificate (for technicians) and perhaps an advanced degree (for professionals). A Negro with sufficient educational attainment to enter a professional or technical job generally avoids the industries studied, since employment opportunities in more glamorous industries are now available to them both inside and outside of the South. The job problems of qualified Negroes are not as great in categories which require independent research and laboratory analysis as they would be in sales or supervisory management where sensitive social and personal barriers exist. Employers find that a history of discrimination now deprives them of an opportunity to attract qualified professional and technical Negro employees in their southern operations.

Discrimination in white collar fields is more vividly demonstrated in sales than in any other employment area. Negroes, North or South, have made little significant progress in entering sales jobs. In 1968, there was a total of two in the paper companies studied, 41 in tobacco companies, and none in textiles or lumber firms. The figure for tobacco reflects an important consumer orientation aspect of the industry. A few black salesmen have traditionally been used to serve the black community and now several serve mixed clientele. In the other industries noted, the products are not easily identified by the consumer, and there has been no major pressure by black groups for the firms to hire Negro salesmen. The question of black salesmen conjures up a large number of imaginary (and some real) fears on the part of company management. Loss of contracts and white customers lurks in their minds as a possibility if blacks are used to sell to whites.

It should also be noted in all fairness that the southern data exclude company home offices in some cases and thus do not reflect changes or progress of recent years. This is especially the case for all tobacco companies except Reynolds, but applies also to the paper industry.

Some progress for Negroes has occurred at the bottom of the white collar ladder in the office and clerical jobs, but proportionally they still made up only 2 to 4 percent of total employment in that category in 1968. Further positive change can be expected in this job area as most employers conscientiously attempt to encourage qualified blacks to enter their organizations. The problems of integrating blacks into formerly all-white clerical departments have not been serious where management has taken constructive measures to assure its successful implementation.

On balance, Negroes in the southern industries studied have a long way to go before they achieve any proportionate representation in white collar jobs. Progress is being made, but it is slow. The statistics provide room for optimism but frustration for those involved is likely to remain unless the pace can be accelerated. Affirmative action policies are now a part of most companies' standard operating procedure, but their implementation will require a major investment in human resources before significant returns are witnessed.

Blue collar occupations. Negroes are disproportionately represented in the bottom blue collar jobs in all of the industries studied. Historically, Negroes have been hired for the hot, dirty, heavy work in southern industry and this is reflected in the data in Table 4.

Negro representation in the skilled craftsman occupational group in the paper mills, tobacco, and textile industries was almost the same (between 2 and 3 percent) in 1968 regardless of the fact that there are rather striking differences in the composition of a skilled job in those industries. Unquestionably, paper mills require higher skills and more complicated equipment than do the other industries studied. In the paper converting plants, Negro mechanics have made considerable progress and, in 1968, comprised nearly 7 percent of the craftsmen. The relatively low wages combined with the location of many of these plants adjacent to higher paying industries greatly reduce competition of whites for jobs.

Negroes have also made significant gains in the skilled jobs in textiles in recent years, but the percentage is still low. In the lumber industry, however, the figures for Negro craftsmen stand out in stark contrast to comparable data for other industries. A large 20 percent representation of blacks in 1968 in the craftsmen category in lumber results from the heavy preponderance of Negroes in the industry for many years. The craftsmen group in this industry includes a great deal of hot, dirty, unpleasant, and low wage work.

In the operatives group, Negroes have made rather important gains in the past few years. This indicates a positive change since it suggests some upgrading in the industries studied; more Negroes will gain experience and develop qualifications to move into skilled areas. The most dramatic increase in the operatives group in recent years has been in the textile industry where Negro representation increased from 7.8 to 12.9 percent in the period 1966 to 1968. Although textiles was late in admitting Negroes, even in semiskilled jobs, there is a possibility that the recent trend will continue and large numbers of Negroes will be shown in the operative group of the future. This is, of course, a reflection of industrial expansion in the South and a tight labor market, coupled with federal government pressure. Representation of blacks in operative jobs is about the same in the paper and tobacco industries, but higher in the paper converting plants. Once again the striking contrast to other southern (and northern) industries is the lumber industry with 46.8 percent of the operative jobs held by blacks in 1968 in the companies studied.

As would be expected from the nature of the work, Negroes hold large proportions of the laborers and service workers jobs in all of the industries. These jobs traditionally were reserved for blacks, and it has been only in the last few years that much upward mobility has occurred.

The Negro Female

Table 5 shows the extent of Negro female employment in the industries studied in 1966 and 1968. Several conclusions emerge from the data.

Negro females have participated only rarely in the white collar employment areas; less than one percent of all females employed in such jobs in the lumber and textile industries were Negro in 1968, while in tobacco Negro female representation was 3.6 percent and in paper 1.5 percent in 1968. By 1968, Negro females were beginning to be hired in office and clerical jobs and on occasion in professional and technician categories, but no major change had occurred. With the exception of a few in textiles, the studies did not find any Negro females working in the officials and managers classification which includes supervisory help. The

TABLE 5. *Selected Southern Industries*
Negro Percentage of Female Employment by Occupational Group 1966 and 1968

Occupational Group	Paper		Lumber		Tobacco		Textiles	
	1966	1968	1966	1968	1966	1968	1966	1968
Officials and managers	—	—	—	—	—	—	—	0.5
Professionals	—	—	—	—	4.3	2.4	1.6	0.8
Technicians	0.8	1.3	—	—	1.3	2.1	0.2	0.9
Sales workers	—	—	1.3	—	2.7	—	1.1	—
Office and clerical	0.6	1.6	0.5	0.3	2.8	4.0	0.3	0.7
Total white collar	0.6	1.5	0.5	0.3	2.6	3.6	0.3	0.7
Craftsmen	3.3	5.0	44.7	48.3	—	—	2.0	4.1
Operatives	3.1	8.8	32.4	44.0	7.5	9.8	3.4	8.3
Laborers	7.9	9.2	63.6	73.0	29.1	30.1	13.8	22.7
Service workers	59.4	64.3	84.7	80.0	73.5	66.9	41.6	46.8
Total blue collar	5.2	9.4	52.6	66.0	17.9	18.4	4.5	9.7
Total	3.2	6.0	37.0	44.8	15.7	16.0	4.0	8.8

Source: Preceding industry studies.

Note: Barnum notes that there are almost no females in the coal mining industry.

absence of Negro females reflects, in part, the general discriminatory practices against women in industry. Of course, black females have additional problems compounded by a history of lack of educational opportunities that would assist them in qualifying for white collar jobs. Social amenities involved with operating an office work force have also caused employers to move with caution in hiring black females.

In the blue collar occupations, Negro females have been employed in large numbers in plant services, such as cleaning and scrubbing. In fact, in 1968, Negro females constituted well over 50 percent of all females in the service worker classification in the paper, lumber, and tobacco industries and 46.8 percent in textiles. On the other hand, in the important craftsmen occupational group, at the top of the blue collar ladder, Negro females were not represented at all in the tobacco industry, and had slight representation in the paper and textile industries. An interesting contrast is in the lumber industry, where black females comprised 48.3 percent of the female craftsmen. It should be observed, however, that Negro females significantly improved their relative position in the skilled jobs in the industries studied between 1966 and 1968. Upgrading occurred for black women in the paper, lumber, and textile industries. Perhaps the most important change to be noted in Table 5 is the major advancement of Negro females in the operatives category. In the lumber, paper, and textile industries, particularly, Negro women appear to have made dramatic strides in expanding opportunities as operatives in recent years.

Character of the Work

Occupational mix is not the only aspect of work nature affecting the extent of Negro employment. The unpleasant, difficult, and dangerous nature of logging and sawmill work has always made those "Negro jobs," and the paper industry adopted the use of Negroes in such work. Tobacco stemmeries were historically humid, dusty, and generally unpleasant; indeed, working with tobacco before the advent of the cigarette machine was historically considered fit only for Negroes. Even in the coal mines, where no work can be considered pleasant, Negroes were given the worst jobs—loading the cars.

In textiles, Negroes were confined to outside jobs. The appropriateness of the work for women provided an ample labor supply and permitted the exclusion of Negroes until the labor market stresses of the 1960's. As so often has occurred, the elimination of labor by machinery has meant in coal mining also the elimination of Negro laborers in favor of white machine operators.

The unpleasantness of the work can be mitigated by the wages paid. Coal mining in 1969 paid hourly wages almost one-third above the average for all manufacturing, while the wages in paper mills are significantly higher than those in the other industries under discussion here. In both these industries, the work can be exceedingly unpleasant, but nevertheless white employees, except in the mill woodyards, have competed strongly for the work, although declining employment and the dangers inherent have greatly reduced the ability of the mines to attract labor in recent years. On the other hand, the low wage structure of the textile mills has reduced its attractiveness to white workers as other opportunities have become available, thus inducing the industry to turn to the black labor reservoir. The same situation typifies the paper converting plants.

Pattern of Occupational Progression

The manner in which employees move from one job to another is largely determined by an industry's structure. In the tobacco industry, for example, temperature, ventillation, and cleanliness requirements dictate that cigarette making be physically separated from processing operations. It was quite natural, therefore, to confine intraplant movement of employees to departments because departments were located in separate buildings. Moreover, prior to 1933, processing was hand work; manufacturing was machine work. The separation of the races, dictated by southern mores, fit well into the historical methods of production.

In lumber, physical separation is nonexistant. The mill is in the woods, close to the source of supply. Workers are comingled, jobs related, and separation or segregation impractical.

Paper manufacturing is a different situation. Long, narrow progression lines are required for the development of necessary skills, and proficiency in one sector of the work, such as the pulp mill, does not provide the training to handle skilled work in another sector, for example, the paper mill. By excluding Negroes from work on a progression line, they could be effectively and easily barred from a whole sector of the industry.

In paper converting plants, the situation is quite different. Skills are minor and jobs relatively easily learned. Unskilled Negroes have been in a position to take over the machine operations and have done so in large numbers as the demand for labor increased.

Textiles features unskilled operations in large part. The work is easily learned. Once barriers were let down, there were no long progressions to be overcome as in the paper industry.

The nature of the work has thus always been a significant determinant of the number of Negroes employed, and will continue to be so until the vestiges of past discrimination are eliminated, and the black man's disadvantaged educational attainment, training, and industrial experience have been overcome. It follows that the longer the intraplant progression and the higher the skill requirements of an industry, the more time will elapse before the impact of past discrimination is eliminated. To put it in comparative industry terms, Negro employment is likely to increase much more rapidly and to achieve equality faster in southern textile mills than in southern paper mills.

TIME AND NATURE OF INDUSTRY'S DEVELOPMENT AND COMMUNITY MORES

The industries discussed in this volume have been a part of the South's economic development for many years. Their roots were planted in a segregated society where jobs were expected to be divided on a racial basis just as were seats on a public bus or in a theater. In some cases, Negroes were assigned their place in society long before the arrival of the employer. Employers and unions followed the established practices in a community. Negroes were assigned to "Negro work" and the all-black departments in industry began to develop, or as in the case of textiles, the industry was treated as a virtual white preserve.

The result of a racial division of work is clearly depicted in Table 4 which shows Negro proportions of employment by industry and occupational group for 1966 and 1968. With only minor exceptions, Negroes have not participated in the white collar jobs in the paper, lumber, tobacco, textile, and coal mining industries. The history prior to 1964 was one of absolute exclusion based on a segregated society. Community mores strongly influenced employer decisions. Until quite recently, an employer would have found it quite difficult to place a Negro in an office or clerical job or in a professional or technical position in a southern community, and the placement of a Negro supervisor over a racially mixed work force remains a sensitive problem.

Interestingly enough, the long history of discrimination in society and in employment in the South led to a major participation of blacks in the industries studied, with the exception of textiles, in the lower rungs of the blue collar ladder. Many unskilled jobs have been present in industries such as paper, lumber, and tobacco, and Negroes were hired in large numbers. Of course, they were brought in to perform jobs that whites did not wish to hold. Since it was normally assumed that blacks were not capable of performing in high level jobs, not only was no provision made for their promotion or upgrading, but discriminatory rules were developed to maintain their place and the status quo. The discussion of the paper industry in Part One makes the above abundantly clear, where it is shown how blacks for years were locked into unskilled positions. This reflects, in large measure, the attitudes and mores of the small towns where paper plants have been located in the South. We shall return to this point in our discussion of union policies.

Looking at the time of an industry's origin more closely, one can understand better how the employment and segregation patterns developed. Tobacco and lumber, for example, date from colonial times and the utilization of slave labor. The outdoor, rural environment of lumber and the concomitant unpleasant working conditions, permitted it to remain a heavily black employee industry. Tobacco, on the other hand, saw the development of an indoor factory system in the latter part of the nineteenth century when the push for segregation and the demand to confine factory jobs to whites were in full bloom. Negro progress in the industry ceased for about 80 years while the better jobs were given to whites.

Textiles, on the other hand, had only a modest pre-Civil War history. The modern southern textile industry developed as almost a postwar crusade to aid in the reconstruction of the South. Given the times, it developed its nearly lily-white character as part of that crusade. Moreover, as the South's most important industry for many years, textiles' racial employment pattern set the pace for northern companies which established southern plants. A few industries in which certain departments required backbreaking or dirty, unpleasant work employed Negroes for that purpose. Most, however, reserved jobs for whites in southern facilities. Even Henry Ford, who prior to 1940 operated the most integrated facilities in the country, and probably the world, hired no Negroes for assembly or similar factory work in the South.[3]

The paper industry in the South, prior to the 1950's, was primarily a minor adjunct to lumber operations. It later developed as a separate industry, adopting the policies of lumber for its outdoor (yard and logging) labor, and of southern industry for indoor work. Thus, unlike textiles, it employed large numbers of Negroes, but in "Negro jobs"—heavy, outdoor work.

The coal mines utilized Negroes in large numbers as demand rose, but virtually eliminated them as wages and working conditions improved, mechanization progressed, and demand fell. The relation of this industry's racial policies to union policies is, however, a key factor and will be discussed below.

Comparison with "Basic" Industries

It is instructive at this juncture to compare the racial-occupational pattern of the southern oriented industries studied in this volume with the six "basic" industries examined in Volume I of our Studies of Negro Employment. Table 6 sets forth the percent Negro employment for southern facilities of the automobile, aerospace, steel, rubber tire, petroleum, and chemical industries for 1966 and 1968.

Comparing Tables 4 and 6, we find that in 1968 only the steel industry had a larger percentage of Negroes in its southern plants than did our southern oriented industries set forth in Table 4, although probably only aerospace had as small a percentage of Negroes in that year as did bituminous coal. The reasons for these results are clearly found in the structure and historical development of these industries. Thus in examining these data in Volume I, we noted the overwhelming steel lead in Negro utilization in the South, with a black percentage double that of rubber tires, which in turn was slightly ahead of automobiles and petroleum refining. Chemical and aerospace brought up the rear.

Looking at the occupational content, it becomes clear that all the industries have a large overconcentration in the bottom two categories, although automobiles less so than the others. The large number of Negro laborers and service employees accounts for the heavy Negro employment, and the relative insignificance of these classifications reduces the

----

3. *Ibid.*, Part Two, pp. 55-58.

TABLE 6. *Six Basic Industries*
Percent Negro Employment by Occupational Group
South Region, 1966 and 1968

Occupational Group	Automobiles		Aerospace		Steel		Rubber Tires		Petroleum Refining[a]		Chemicals[b]	
	1966	1968	1966	1968	1966	1968	1966	1968	1966	1968	1966	1968
Officials and managers	0.8	0.6	0.3	0.5	0.3	0.3	0.3	0.6	0.1	0.2	0.1	0.3
Professionals	0.6	0.7	0.6	0.7	0.3	1.3	—	—	0.2	0.2	0.2	0.4
Technicians	2.7	3.1	1.4	1.8	0.8	4.2	0.9	3.1	0.6	0.8	1.0	2.0
Sales workers	—	—	—	0.5	—	—	—	—	—	—	—	0.4
Office and clerical	2.9	3.3	3.0	3.8	1.2	2.5	1.1	1.6	0.3	1.1	1.1	2.3
Total white collar	1.9	1.9	1.4	1.8	0.7	1.8	0.6	1.1	0.3	0.5	0.5	1.0
Craftsmen	0.4	0.4	2.3	3.2	7.4	7.8	2.1	3.4	1.7	2.2	1.3	2.0
Operatives	12.4	13.6	8.3	10.0	31.9	35.8	12.6	12.9	21.0	27.0	8.5	11.0
Laborers	14.9	16.2	42.1	36.4	62.8	50.8	40.7	50.5	78.4	69.0	46.9	41.5
Service workers	24.4	25.4	35.5	38.0	28.2	26.5	66.9	60.7	45.3	45.0	33.4	32.4
Total blue collar	12.2	13.2	6.9	7.8	28.4	26.6	13.5	13.5	12.8	15.0	9.1	10.2
Total	9.7	10.3	3.7	4.4	22.5	21.3	11.4	11.5	9.3	10.7	6.3	7.3

Source: Herbert R. Northrup, Richard L. Rowan, *et al.*, *Negro Employment in Basic Industry*, Studies of Negro Employment, Vol. I (Philadelphia: Industrial Research Unit, Wharton School of Finance and Commerce, University of Pennsylvania, 1970), Part Eight, Table 5, p. 732.

[a] Author's estimates for 1968; regional breakdowns not available on comparative basis.

[b] Data may have 1-2 point downward bias because of omission of chemical plants with less than 500 employees.

Negro ratio for such industries as aerospace and chemicals, and to a lesser extent, automobiles.[4]

Like steel, the southern based industries studied in this volume are heavily blue collar oriented. Where that is not the case, such as aerospace, the proportion of Negroes employed will be much lower until all aspects of past discrimination are erased. Until then, the data in both our earlier volume and in this one reaffirm the significance of the nature of work and of the time and nature of the industry's development.

CONSUMER ORIENTATION AND IMAGE CONCERN

In Volume I of the Studies, it was pointed out that

Companies which sell to consumers usually align their marketing and racial policies very carefully. They are more likely to be on the lookout for means to avoid offending any group, and especially majority opinion. Thus, they desire to move slightly ahead, but not too far. It is not unusual for such companies to work assiduously behind the scenes in a community to work out problems. Racial unrest can alienate a group, alter buying habits, and is generally bad for business.[5]

The industries covered in the present volume are not heavily consumer oriented, but there are some important exceptions.

The tobacco industry deals directly with consumers even though brand names are not usually associated with a particular company. R. J. Reynolds has long been concerned with its image. The company has attempted to develop equal employment opportunities and it has been influential in maintaining racial harmony in the towns in which it manufactures its products. Moreover, unlike other tobacco companies, it operates nonunion and has therefore been free to change without union consent.

The paper industry is not consumer oriented to a large extent and Scott Paper Company is the only large one in the industry that markets its products under the company name. This may help to explain why Scott has moved ahead of other firms in the industry in developing equal employment programs. In contrast to this situation, the Crown Zellerbach Company in Bogalusa, Louisiana did not move to eliminate discriminatory practices until considerable federal government and court pressure was exerted. The company also has not participated broadly in resolving the difficult racial problems in Bogalusa. Apparently, Crown

---

4. *Ibid.*, Part Eight, p. 733.

5. *Ibid.*, p. 734.

Zellerbach has not felt vulnerable to outside pressures in deciding not to become as deeply involved in local racial issues as have many other companies. The situation might have been different if the company sold its product directly to consumers under its own name.

Consumer orientation in the textile industry is not strong, and similar to the paper industry, few companies market their products under company name. Even where this is done, it has not made very much difference in regard to eliminating discriminatory practices. Cannon Mills in Kannapolis, North Carolina markets its products under the Cannon name, and at the same time maintains a highly segregated company town. Civil rights groups have not participated in boycotts against the company and little change has come about under government pressure. On the other hand, Burlington Mills has developed a concern for its image and has begun to experiment with equal employment programs.

The coal and lumber industries have little or no consumer orientation and they have not expressed a great concern about racial matters. In this regard their attitude is similar despite far different employment patterns and racial employment trends.

MANAGEMENT ETHNIC ORIGIN

We found no evidence that ethnic origin had any particular influence over racial policies in the firms studied.

COMMUNITY CRISES

The overriding community crisis in the South since the mid-1950's has been that of educational integration. The impact has undoubtedly been significant. To some, it has exacerbated racial antagonisms and blocked progress. Thus a former paper union official who is now a management consultant has written:

The 1954 Supreme Court decision literally froze the friendly and cooperative spirit that was then in evidence between whites and Negroes. Things continued on much as before, but further progress, for a period at least, was no longer possible. There was, in fact, some retrogression. Caustic and bitter comment, from both white and Negro, was increasingly heard in [union] meetings and conferences. It is safe to say, even now in 1967, that the icy conditions created by the high court's decision have not thoroughly thawed.[6]

6. Homer L. Humble, *Unions are Forever, or Rat Race* (New York: Vantage Press, 1969), p. 55.

Actually, what the outlawing of school segregation did was to turn the attack of Negroes on other vestiges of the segregation, and to challenge the invidiously discriminatory seniority systems in the paper and tobacco industries and the discriminatory hiring policies which perpetuated them. Obviously, such an attack on the status quo was certain to sharpen tensions, but to those who were denied equal opportunity, that was scarcely too great a price to pay.

For the most part, management in these industries has moved forward cautiously on the civil rights front. In the desegregation movement, many undoubtedly worked assiduously behind the scenes to avoid trouble and to yield to the equal rights of Negroes. In numerous communities, desegregation was accomplished without incident because of these efforts. The activities of the Reynolds Tobacco management in Winston-Salem, North Carolina, were especially notable in this regard.

Commitment to public facility desegregation inevitably caused management to look more sharply at plant practices. Most change therein did not come until the 1960's. But the school crisis, the lunchcounter sit-ins, and the similar push for equal rights for citizens were a necessary prelude to employment desegregation as well as a certain augur that such desegregation would occur. To argue that education desegregation "blocked progress" is to ignore fact and reality.

IMPACT OF TECHNOLOGY

The concentration of Negroes in unskilled and service work makes them especially susceptible to technological displacement. Moreover, the inferior educational background of many southern Negroes, resulting from years of unequal opportunity and an unequal, segregated school system handicaps those who might otherwise qualify to operate complicated or automated equipment.

Among the industries studied in this volume, coal mining, paper mills, and tobacco have experienced the greatest amount of technological advancement, and the impact on employment has been the most immediately observable. In coal mining, employment has been most seriously affected by the substitution of machinery for hand operations and by the substitution of strip mining, basically a machine operation utilizing relatively few persons, for the much more labor-intensive underground mining. Rapidly changing mining technology, the prior concentration of Negroes in the hand loading jobs (the easiest to mechanize), and the failure both of the industry and of the United Mine Workers to provide even a semblance of equal opportunity in work operating mechanical equipment at a time when employment in the Southern Appalachian coal fields was declining rapidly, have led to a considerable elimination of Negroes from coal mining jobs and their migration away from coal mining areas.

In the pulp and paper mills, advancing technology came heavily in the 1950's and affected all aspects of production, but severely reduced potential Negro employment through the mechanization of woodyard operations where they have traditionally been concentrated. Mechanization also eliminated laboring jobs in and around the pulp mill, again jobs held largely by Negroes. As a result, combined with a continuation of the practice of limiting Negro employment to woodyards and to a few other labor and service jobs, mills built after 1950 employed a substantially smaller proportion of Negroes than did those built earlier. Thus between 1950 and 1960, the *number* of Negroes in the southern paper industry barely increased from 19,726 to 20,061, but the *proportion* declined from 20.8 percent to 13.9 percent.[7] It is quite likely that if paper converting plant employment could be separated from these data, one would find both an absolute decline in Negro employment in the mills and a greater percentage drop.

The paper converting industry, on the other hand, has experienced little technological advancement and still employs large numbers of persons in unskilled jobs, including a sizeable proportion of Negroes (17.1 percent of all employees in 1968 in our sample, see Table 4). With wages increasing in these plants, it is not difficult to foresee mechanization becoming more prevalent and black employment adversely affected.

The tobacco industry was always heavily mechanized insofar as cigarette production is concerned, but mechanization of the processing departments, especially the stemmeries, did not commence on a significant scale before 1933. Minimum wage legislation and higher wages as a result of unionization led to a rapid mechanization of these areas. With Negroes barred by a rigid racial-occupational segregation pattern from employment in manufacturing departments, such mechanization reduced the proportion of black tobacco workers in the three principal tobacco

---

7. See Part One above, Table 13, p. 34.

manufacturing states from more than 60 percent in 1930 to a maximum estimated 26.8 percent in 1960.[8]

The lumber industry in the South remains one that is not heavily mechanized. Featured by small mills, diverse ownership, and sharp competition, it continues to operate in small scale units with few economies of large scale and consequent investment in expensive equipment apparent. Thus mechanization is unlikely to be a strong factor affecting employment in the immediate future.

The textile industry has gone through many phases of improved methods and labor rationalization, and the impact of foreign competition could generate a movement toward consolidation because of the resultant price pressure on small concerns. Until now, however, there has been little impact on black employment because such employment is too new to have been affected by technological or other changes which occurred before 1960.

The costs of technological advancement since the late 1960's, and in the future, cannot so lightly be charged to Negro labor alone. This is being realized by southern industry. It requires not only the opening of once all-white departments to black employees, which has been largely accomplished, but also special efforts to train Negroes so that they can qualify for positions on progression lines that lead to skilled jobs. A beginning has already been made in the paper and tobacco industries, but the results will be slow because new opportunities in both are relatively sparse. Coal mining at a time of labor shortage has demonstrated no substantial changes in policies, a fact attributable in no small measure to the policies of the United Mine Workers, discussed in the following section.

NATURE OF UNION ORGANIZATION

Of the five industries examined in this volume, coal mining and paper are very highly unionized; tobacco is completely unionized except for the largest company; and textiles and lumber operate mostly nonunion. An examination of the union racial policies for these southern oriented industries, and a like examination of the effects of managerial racial policies where unions are absent, cannot avoid the conclusion that the net impact of

---

8. See Part Three above, Tables 10 and 11, pp. 29 and 31. The reasons for the estimates are given in Part Three.

unions on the employment opportunities of Negroes has been distinctly negative.

Nowhere is this sad fact better illustrated than in the case of the coal mining industry. The United Mine Workers set the pace for the racial policies of America's industrial unions, admitting Negroes without discrimination and affording them full rights within the organization. But no sooner had the Southern Appalachian coal fields been unionized than the percentage of Negroes therein commenced to decline. The wage policies of the UMW induced the coal operators to mechanize rapidly, and Negroes, being concentrated in the loading jobs, were disproportionately affected. The situation worsened during the two decades after World War II. Both the operators and the UMW ignored the plight of the black miners, and little change has occurred to date.

In 1944, one of the authors in concluding his analysis of union racial policies in the coal mines, wrote:

If, as predicted, employment in the bituminous coal industry declines when peace returns, and if past experience is any guide, Negroes will suffer disproportionately heavy losses in jobs. This is particularly likely to occur in instances where machines replace men. These postwar adjustments will put the equalitarian policies of the UMW to their severest tests. If Negroes continue to bear the brunt of technological unemployment, the UMW will no longer be able to claim that it adheres to a policy of racial equality as steadfastly as any other American labor union.[9]

The UMW not only failed the test; its completely indifferent attitude, still extant, toward the plight of its onetime black members forfeits any claim which it once had of interest in equality of opportunity or in the welfare of black miners.

Both the Tobacco Workers International Union and the unions of the paper industry quite naturally organized along the lines of industry practice and southern mores of the period when they unionized their industries beginning in the 1930's. The net effect was to institutionalize the status quo of the period and to lock Negroes into the segregated departments in which they were then employed. Unions in both industries stood by as mechanization displaced Negroes while expanding operations in other departments employed new white workers. As in the case of the United Mine Workers, the leaders of these unions were unwilling or un-

9. Herbert R. Northrup, *Organized Labor and the Negro* (New York: Harper and Brothers, 1944), pp. 170-171.

able to risk the wrath of their dominant white membership by any effective action in behalf of black members who paid the same union dues and theoretically had the same rights within the unions as did the whites.

In the 1960's, pressed by the government, these unions went along with policies designed to end segregation and discrimination, the Tobacco Workers International Union more willingly, the paper unions later. All the organizations grasped the government position that segregated locals should be abolished, and the TWIU accomplished this by June 1967. Recently the president of the Pulp, Sulphite and Paper Mill Workers has ordered the elimination of all separate local charters. As was noted in the paper and tobacco industry studies, segregated locals, even though organized as a device to serve and to perpetuate discrimination, also provide representation, power, and support to Negro trade unionists. Government insistence that they be abolished is simplistic; union officials' rush to do so is not necessarily motivated by a desire to eliminate discrimination.

In the tobacco and paper industries, the course of discriminatory events prior to 1960 might well have been no different if unions had been absent. Certainly nonunion Reynolds Tobacco maintained the racial-occupational segregation pattern of the tobacco industry as did the union firms. But Reynolds was able to move fastest and furthest in part because there were no union-institutionalized seniority districts with which to contend and no white worker opposition supported by the organized force of union labor. Moreover, at Reynolds there were no craft union barriers to overcome as is the case in the mechanical and maintenance departments of most other tobacco companies and in most southern paper mills as well.

In the lumber industry, unions are weak and have had no discernible impact on racial employment policies. In paper converting plants, there have been some discriminatory seniority systems and assignment to Negroes of a preponderant proportion of the most disagreeable jobs without union protest or interference. In general, however, unions have not been a significant factor in racial employment policy in such converting plants, and the demand for labor relative to supply has insured the widespread utilization of black labor.

The textile industry's reversal of its seventy-year racial exclusionist employment policy was accomplished with so little difficulty in part because of the absence of effective unionism. With no formal lines of progression or seniority, no "affected class" or problems of "rightful place," the industry was able to alter its employment policy once it overcame its own managerial blocks to change. In a real sense, its very exclusion of Negroes in the past, combined with the absence of unionism, has made its current integration job much easier than that of tobacco or paper manufacturing. The latter two industries pioneered in employing Negroes while the textile industry shut its doors to nonwhites. But because tobacco and paper allowed collective bargaining to institutionalize the status quo of bygone years, their problems of integration are the more severe today.

It may be argued that unions, which have contributed so much to the well being of the American worker, are internal political organizations and must therefore adhere to the wishes of their dominant white majorities. Certainly, as we have already noted, an espousal of a strong position against segregation would have meant the elimination of that leadership. Yet democracy involves also the protection of the minority against majority tyranny. We can explain why unions perhaps could not protect their black members. Unfortunately that does not alter the fact that they did not, but rather aided and abetted invidiously discriminatory practices against those, who like their white union brothers, were paying dues to the organizations.

When all this is said, it must also be emphasized that in all these five industries, employment is a management function. It was the companies which established the racial employment policies and practices. In the final analysis, prime responsibility rests with management for the bad, as well as for the good.

INDUSTRIAL LOCATION

All the industries discussed herein are located in areas that are readily accessible to Negroes. The only general exception is the coal mining industry, and the fact that there are few Negroes in many coal producing areas today is more the result of discrimination than the cause of low Negro utilization since Negroes have migrated away from these areas because of discrimination and underemployment.

A few tobacco plants—the newest facilities of Philip Morris, R. J. Reynolds, and Lorillard—are located on the outskirts of cities and are accessible only by automobile. This is typical of most pulp and paper mills. Insofar as Negroes are proportionately less likely to own automobiles, this is a handicap. Yet the impact does not appear to be a significant determinant of Negro employment. On the other hand, lumber mills in largely Negro rural areas and converting plants in center cities typically utilize Negro labor much more heavily than do those located away from the centers of Negro population. Indeed, we found that location was the principal determinant of the extent of Negro utilization in paper converting plants.

ROLE OF GOVERNMENT

We have noted before that governmental intervention was essential in order to insure progress toward equal employment.[10] There is no evidence in this volume to contradict that view; certainly in the paper industry, it does not seem likely that there would have been material progress without government intervention. One must also reach a similar conclusion for the tobacco industry.

Lumber has been largely unaffected by governmental civil rights activities, as have the paper converting plants. Labor market factors have been far more important. In textiles, government insistence gave the industry the rationale which it required to meet its labor force needs, but despite these needs hesitancy existed before government intervened.

But government policy is multifaceted and confusing. Government-imposed minimum wages led to mechanization of the tobacco stemmeries and the elimination of thousands of Negroes from that industry. Government support of unionism and collective bargaining helped to institutionalize discriminatory union practices in paper and tobacco. Government also bolstered the power of the United Mine Workers to increase wages and benefit costs, with resultant rapid mechanization but no government interference in the discriminatory displacement of Negroes from the mines. Government has compelled the elimination of separate black locals without realistically appraising the consequences; and government has harassed and antagonized unions and employers and wasted funds by duplication and interagency rivalry in civil rights inspections and compliance.

Yet for all its inconsistencies and waste, government action remains essential to a continuation of the fight against discrimina-

---

10. Northrup and Rowan, *et al.*, *op. cit.*, Part Eight, p. 741.

tion. There is need for leadership, understanding, and constructive analysis. There is also a need for the compliance agencies to concentrate their efforts where the jobs are. A declining industry such as tobacco is not a fruitful place for repeated compliance investigations that harrow old grounds. We repeat our point of an earlier volume.

By familiarizing themselves with the nature and structure of various industries, the compliance agencies could concentrate their efforts on the areas where the most potential for increased Negro employment exists. Thus, by examining the occupational breakdowns, employment trends, training needs, locational problems, and the other variables discussed herein, effective means of increasing Negro employment become clearer. No two industries are exactly alike. Approaching industries by understanding the needs of their production processes affords the greatest opportunities for effective utilization of government compulsion toward equal opportunity. It is hoped that the information contained in this volume and others in this series will aid in developing the most rational government-industry relationship toward the goal of equal opportunity.[11]

MANAGERIAL POLICIES

Management policy establishes the guidelines for action within a company. It is not created in a vacuum. Many factors, such as plant size and location, community mores, production processes, the labor market, and consumer orientation, play a part in determining an employer's personnel policy.

Since the 1960's, the southern companies studied herein have been challenged to develop equal employment policy and affirmative action programs for its implementation. In general, activity has been slow. Unless considerable pressure is exerted from the outside, most companies are reluctant to disturb collective bargaining arrangements (paper, coal mining, and tobacco) or prevailing community attitudes (textiles and lumber) through strong equal employment pronouncements and programs. Of course, exceptions do arise within an industry, when a company is concerned with its consumer orientation. Scott Paper Company and Reynolds Tobacco Company, for example, have attempted to move ahead in their respective industries to develop plans for the improvement of minority employment and utilization. Although these companies are aware of product identification and the significance of a strong equal employment posture as a market aid,

---

11. *Ibid.*, p. 742.

they are also fortunate in having on their staffs managers with a philosophical commitment to equal employment opportunity and strong top executive support to put that commitment into practice.

Racial employment policy is meaningless unless it is clearly disseminated in an organization with the expectation that action will follow. Crown Zellerbach was a member of Plans for Progress with an affirmative action program at corporate headquarters when discriminatory practices were being continued at the Bogalusa, Louisiana plant. Government action based on civil rights legislation prompted change at Bogalusa; discriminatory work rules prevailed regardless of company policy prior thereto.

As community institutions, ideas, and beliefs begin to change in the South, it can be expected that effective racial employment policy will be more widely developed. The authors of the studies in this volume found very little racial antagonism on the part of managers interviewed in their respective industries. Most managers have gone beyond the point of questioning the usefulness of employing Negroes. The major factors that are being addressed today are those of how to bring minorities into the firm and how to upgrade those who are presently a part of the employment structure, without seriously interrupting production or relations with employees in the industry.

CONCLUDING REMARKS

The industries discussed in this volume are the traditional ones of the South. Today the South is industrializing at a rapid rate. New industries uninhibited by practices of another era now dot the southern landscape. In the 1960's, for the first time in this century, the South gained more migrants than it lost to the North and West.

Industries such as aerospace and electrical manufacturing already employ a larger proportion of Negroes in white collar positions in their southern operations than do the industries examined in this volume. With new people and new industries, new racial policies will prevail. The rate of change, however, is likely to vary considerably, depending as does change, on the variety of industrial, institutional, and human factors discussed throughout this volume.